What people are saying about David Vance's
THE BUSINESS OF LEARNING

"Finally, the definitive business book for learning and development professionals and leaders! This is a much needed and extremely comprehensive resource that fills an important need in our profession. *The Business of Learning* is a "must read" as well as an invaluable, just-in-time resource from one of the most respected CLO's of the past decade."

Ed Betof Ed.D., Senior Fellow, The Conference Board and Executive Director, Leaders as Teachers Institute, Corporate University Exchange. Formerly Global VP of Talent Management and CLO BD (Becton, Dickinson and Company)

"Every learning professional should have a library of business books containing a primer on business fundamentals, a guide to strategic planning, a tome on economics, and a how-to manual on managing the learning function. David Vance has masterfully assembled the entire collection into a single volume. *The Business of Learning* should be on the bookshelf—and at the right hand—of every learning professional."

Mark Allen, Ph.D., editor and co-author of *The Corporate University Handbook* and *The Next Generation of Corporate Universities* and professor at Pepperdine University's Graziadio School of Business and Management

"I can think of no one better than Dave Vance to apply business and economic concepts to learning and development. As an economist and former president of one of the country's most respected corporate universities he is uniquely qualified."

Norm Kamikow, Former Editor in Chief, *Chief Learning Officer* magazine, and President, MediaTec Publishing Inc.

"One of the biggest challenges with the learning and development function is to be clearly connected to the business. Dave Vance shows a road map to connect learning to the business from the very beginning to evaluation. It is the most comprehensive treatment available on the topic of running the learning and development function like a business. This book is a must read for any person in a leadership role in the learning and development function."

Jack Phillips, Chairman, ROI Institute, Inc.

"A great resource guide for all learning leaders. *The Business of Learning* leverages David's economic background to provide breakthrough insights on managing the learning function for greater effectiveness and efficiency which will contribute to our industry's continued evolution."

Cedric T. Coco, Former SVP Learning & Organizational Effectiveness, Lowe's Companies, Inc.

SECOND EDITION

THE BUSINESS OF LEARNING

How to Manage Corporate Training to Improve Your Bottom Line

A Practical Guide to Applying Business and Economic Concepts to Learning

David L. Vance, Ph.D.

Poudre River Press
WINDSOR, COLORADO

ISBN (Printed Book): 978-0-9845853-0-4
ISBN (eBook): 978-0-9845853-1-1
LCCN 2017938476

First Edition: © 2010 David Vance
ISBN (Printed Book): 978-0-9845853-7-3 • ISBN (eBook): 978-0-9845853-8-0 • LCCN 2010929142

Dedication

THIS BOOK IS dedicated to my wife, Barb, to my son, Andy, and to my brother, Tom, for their unwavering support and love.

Contents

Part Two—**Strategic Alignment and the Business Plan for Learning**

Part Three—**Managing the Learning Function throughout the Year**

Part Four—**The Economics of Learning: Improving Your Efficiency and Making Better Choices**

Part Five—**Conclusion**

Appendices

List of Tables

List of Figures

About This Book

Why Is This Topic Important?

IN MOST ORGANIZATIONS learning is not strategically aligned to the most important goals of the organization, nor is it managed as effectively and efficiently as it could be. Consequently, the investment in learning and development (L&D) is not producing the return it should be, and L&D is often the first area to be cut in tough times. Even in good times, the mismanagement of the learning function contributes to the belief that learning is not a strategic contributor to an organization's success, leading to sub-optimal funding levels as management directs scarce resources to areas perceived to have greater returns. It doesn't have to be this way. Learning professionals need to adopt a business mentality and apply business and economic concepts to the learning function. The opportunity for improvement in outcomes, effectiveness and efficiency is huge and immediate. This is the only way to realize the full potential of an organization's learning expenditures and the only way for learning professionals to win a "seat at the table."

What Can You Achieve with This Book?

By learning the concepts and following the recommendations in this book, you can dramatically improve the impact, effectiveness and efficiency of your learning function. You will achieve much more for the same expenditure, and, better yet, it will be directed to the highest priority needs of your organization and aligned with the expectations of your senior leaders. Through the creation of a business plan for learning and disciplined execution throughout the year, you will manage the function more effectively, deliver enhanced value, and gain much needed credibility. Although this book includes some theory, it is a practical guide on how to manage a real learning function with all its day-to-day complexities. The goal is to provide you with enough concrete recommendations, checklists, examples, templates, and tips so that you can immediately begin successful implementation.

Who Can Benefit from This Book?

This book is written for three groups. First, it is for those managers in a learning function who want to learn how to run learning more like a business in order to improve its impact, effectiveness and efficiency. These managers may be experienced learning professionals who want to learn business and economic concepts so they can apply them to learning, or they may be experienced business professionals who now find themselves managing a learning function and want to know how to apply their knowledge to learning. Second, the book is written for those at a university who want to learn how to manage the learning and development function. Third, it is for executives who want to improve the bottom-line impact of their investment in learning.

How Is This Book Different?

This book provides the most comprehensive treatment available on the topics of running learning like a business. Not only does it provide significantly more detail than others on topics such as business fundamentals, calculation of the fully-burdened labor rate, strategic alignment, governance, and the business case for learning, but it also describes in detail how to create a business plan for learning, including a forty-page sample plan. It breaks new ground by applying economics to learning to answer questions about program selection, size, and duration, as well as the effects of scale on cost. The book contains more than 180 tables and figures to clearly illustrate the concepts, some of which are available online as templates. Lastly, you will find over 110 terms defined in the glossary. It also provides detailed checklists, timelines, reports, sample meeting agendas, and templates—everything needed to implement all the recommendations.

What is New in the Second Edition?

The second edition updates and expands the work of the first edition—including more explanation, cases, and tables—to better illustrate the concepts from the first edition. It also extends those concepts in response to feedback from the first edition and adds brand new material, particularly on the treatment of unaligned learning, reaching agreement on the planned impact of learning, Talent Development Reporting principles (TDRp), and measurement. The second edition contains an appendix dedicated to TDRp, created in 2010-2012 to provide standards for the profession in terms of measurement, reporting, and management, and both the measurement and execution chapters have been rewritten to incorporate TDRp.

How Is This Book Organized?

The book is organized into five parts. Part One provides all the business basics you need, a comprehensive discussion of learning costs, and the business case for individual learning programs. Part Two covers the strategic alignment process, the business case for the learning department, and the creation of a business plan for learning. Part Three addresses ongoing management of the function throughout the year, including governance and the use of measurement and scorecards in execution. Part Four focuses on improving efficiency and provides an economic framework for making decisions about the level of investment in learning. Part Five pulls it all together. The book is designed so you can access any chapter directly for reference.

Acknowledgements

THIS BOOK WOULD not have been possible without the help and encouragement of many people.

Family and friends provided encouragement throughout the process. My wife, Barb, and my son, Andy, were always supportive and encouraging, as was my brother, Tom. Family, of course, also includes our two Spinone Italianos, who were always more than happy to provide company for a writing break and would come get me when I had been working too long.

Since my background was not in the learning field, I had a lot to learn myself and could not have succeeded without the help of many at Caterpillar and in the learning profession. Very special recognition goes to my mentor, Fred Goh, at Caterpillar University, who patiently taught me about this wonderful field. Thanks also to those in Cat U's predecessor organization who worked patiently with me as I came aboard. I also appreciated very much the time seasoned leaders in other organizations were willing to spend sharing their experiences and their advice. Although there were many, I am particularly grateful for the learning professionals at GE, Motorola, IBM, and Nestle who spent time with me in 2000.

I was fortunate to have an absolutely outstanding team at Cat U, which allowed us to accomplish so much. Some of us had a business background and others brought the learning expertise. Together we constituted a very diverse group dedicated to learning about learning, improving, and making Cat U a valued, strategic business partner for the organization. The core senior leadership team stayed together for all of the first four years, which contributed greatly to our success. Deeply felt thanks to Chris Arvin, Sheryl Tipton, Ruud Kronenburg, Fred Goh, Ron Riekena, and Alice Barbour. Other key contributors include Alice Winget, Jayne Henneberg, Reed Stuedemann, and Elizabeth Shultz. I could not have asked for a better team, and I learned a lot from each of them.

Throughout my time as president of Caterpillar University, I was continually amazed at the open and sharing nature of the global learning community. Learning professionals were always willing to share their ideas and provide advice. I benefited tremendously from the conferences, meetings, publications, and networks of ATD and the ATD Benchmarking Forum, the Conference Board Learning and Development Roundtable, and *Chief Learning Officer* magazine. We also learned from each benchmarking visit (and there were a lot!), especially when we visited others but also when we hosted.

A number of other colleagues also provided critical support to Caterpillar University and contributed to our success. I am particularly grateful to Kent Barnett (former CEO of Knowledge Advisors) for his assistance in automating the collection and analysis of our measurement data, and to Gaj Kasbekar and the team of Tata Interactive Services for assistance as we embraced e-learning. I also want to give special thanks to Merrill Anderson of Cylient (previously MetrixGlobal), who served as a trusted advisor to us on many matters, conducted our higher-level evaluations, and taught me much about the measurement field. All three were true partners to Cat U and important contributors to our success.

I would like to recognize a few professional colleagues in particular who served as role models and thought leaders and who always asked good questions to make me think more deeply about the issues or possibilities: Frank Anderson and Chris Hardy, who led the truly innovative and groundbreaking Defense Acquisition University, and Michael Echols, Vice President for Strategic Initiatives at Bellevue University. I am also grateful to Don Kirkpatrick and Jack Phillips, who were always willing to provide guidance and advice, and to Josh Bersin and Bob Danna of Bersin & Associates for their encouragement and assistance in final review and marketing.

I also want to acknowledge organizations like ATD, Corporate University Xchange (CUX), and the International Quality & Productivity Center (IQPC) for hosting award competitions and recognizing the achievements of Cat U. We learned more about ourselves, industry best practices, and opportunities for improvement every time we entered these annual competitions. So, thank you for helping us to continually improve.

My learning journey continued after retiring from Caterpillar. I am grateful for the opportunity provided by Manoj Kutty and Tata Interactive Services to partner in the development of a computer-based simulation for learning professionals, which offered a testing ground for many of the concepts in the book.

I have also learned a tremendous amount since the first edition was published through my consulting and my work with Kent Barnett (former CEO of Knowledge Advisors), and the group of industry thought leaders he pulled together in 2010-2011 to develop the TDRp. My learning continued with the Center for Talent Reporting, home of TDRp, where we have been busy sharing and teaching TDRp to improve the state of the profession. In particular, I want to acknowledge and thank Peggy Parskey, the assistant director for the Center, for her help in figuring out how to best refine, explain, and apply the principles. I also have learned much from my students in the Ph.D. programs at the University of Southern Mississippi and Bellevue University where I have been teaching courses in human capital management since 2010 using this book.

I am very grateful for those brave souls who volunteered to review the manuscript. They provided excellent suggestions to improve the book, making it much easier to read and understand. My sincere appreciation goes out to Rick Heiken, Lilian Li, Bill Karr, Dan Chenoweth, Laurie Bassi, Tom Vance, and Andy Vance.

I also want to acknowledge Edward Trolley and David van Adelsberg, who wrote *Running Training Like a Business* in 1999. This was one of the first books I read after moving into the learning function, and the authors' concept of running training like a business made a lasting impression.

Last, I want to acknowledge the outstanding assistance provided by About Books, the publishing consulting company that helped me publish both editions of this book. It not only provided all the advice, direction, and assistance that I needed but helped make the journey efficient and enjoyable. Thanks to Deb Ellis, Cathy Bowman, Allan Burns, Carol White, Dick Hanna, and Debi and Scott Flora.

Special Recognition

THE OPPORTUNITY TO lead Caterpillar University would not have been possible without the strong support of the senior leadership at Caterpillar. In particular, I want to recognize Glen Barton, CEO when we launched Cat U, and Jim Owens, who succeeded Glen. Glen and Jim both believed in the potential of a well-run corporate university and were active champions for learning and for Cat U. We would not have survived the 2000–2001 recession without their strong support. Both provided leadership to our board of governors, demonstrating their commitment to learning and to Caterpillar University's success. They were always available for advice and guidance, and I was truly fortunate to have their confidence, trust, and support. We simply would not have succeeded without their personal commitment to learning and Cat U.

I also want to recognize the board of governors, which provided outstanding guidance and advice over the years. They were always willing to meet with me personally to discuss the issues of the day, and I valued their unique perspectives and their frankly expressed views. We did not always agree, but I always learned from them.

Last, I want to express appreciation for the officers and other senior leaders who championed learning and were willing to give this new concept, Caterpillar University, a chance to succeed.

Foreword

IN A TYPICAL year U.S. corporations, nonprofits, and government organizations spend more than $160 billion on learning and development (L&D).[1] Worldwide, this amount is over $300 billion—a sum that would make up the GDP of the thirty-fifth largest country in the world. And the actual investment in organizational learning is even greater because these numbers do not include the cost of time spent in classes, time spent reading and engaging with learning materials, and time invested by executives in the planning and resource allocation of training.

With this enormous investment comes tremendous potential for value. Some organizations (Accenture, for example, which spends more than $700 million per year on training) claim that employee development is among their top business strategies.[2] Caterpillar, Deloitte, GE, IBM, Procter & Gamble, and many other global brands continuously invest two to three times more on training per employee than their competitors do. These organizations understand that learning and development is not simply an employee benefit; it is a strategic imperative for long-term success.

We also know that the people who have chosen careers in training and development are often some of the most talented individuals in the company. Our research shows that people in the L&D profession have excellent educational backgrounds (more than 70% have college degrees and more than 18% have advanced degrees), they often have many years of business experience (typical training managers have ten or more years of tenure), and they come to this profession with a desire to teach, develop training programs, and enhance individual and business performance.[3] I find training professionals to be some of the hardest working, most professional people I have worked with in my career.

Yet despite this large investment and the tremendous passion and expertise in the training industry, many training organizations still struggle to gain acceptance, stay aligned with their business leaders, and avoid being viewed as a "cost center" that is the first thing to be cut during a downturn. This year we studied the perception of L&D by business leaders and found that the training department in most companies has a negative net-promoter rating, not something to be proud of. Quite frankly, the world of L&D has changed rapidly, and we need to be more technology savvy and better aligned than ever. Despite this problem, our research shows that learning and careers are now the #2 talent issue around the world.[4] With jobs being changed by technology and AI faster than ever, "digital learning" now makes up the lifeblood of a successful organization, enabling people to change jobs and learn new skills all the time. In fact, our research with Glassdoor now shows that among employees under the age of 35, "ability to learn and grow" is the single most important factor in people's perception of your company as a place to work.

Given these issues, our discussions with HR leaders still show that many training professionals struggle to align well with business leaders and get new budgets to re-engineer their operations.

Why is this?

Quite simply, many training professionals are not trained in or familiar with the basic principles and practices of running a business. They don't speak the language of business, they may not feel comfortable interacting with the CEO or other top leaders, and they often don't understand how to build a true "business plan" for their L&D team.

This valuable book, written carefully and meticulously by Dave Vance, helps solve this problem. Dave's background as the former Chief Economist for Caterpillar and the former President of Caterpillar University gives him a unique and powerful perspective on how to understand the real "business of corporate learning." He addresses some of the most important topics we all must understand: how business people think, what terms and concepts they use to make decisions, and how basic business functions are planned and measured.

Not only does Dave clearly explain these principles and practices in the book, but he also gives us specific examples, models, checklists, and a business plan to follow. And throughout the book Dave explains how difficult and important it is to build strong processes for alignment, governance, planning, and operational measurement.

In my experience as an analyst and consultant in this industry over the years, I have come to realize that despite all the wonderful people-related skills we apply (instructional design, content development, learning technology, collaboration and coaching, performance management, and more), none of this really matters if the programs we develop are not 100% aligned with the current and urgent needs of a business. And one cannot truly understand these complex needs without the rigor and discipline of a process for business planning and management, which is the focus of Dave's book.

If you are a training professional, a training manager, a training director, or even a learning executive, you will find this book a wealth of information on "how to manage" your training programs and your training organization like a business operation. You will learn to speak clearly about the financials of the learning function and see how top business executives think. These principles and skills will help you become a better-aligned, more powerful learning professional.

Let me make one final point. The principles of this book really do work. In our research on best practices in the operations and management of corporate learning (our High Impact Learning Organization® research program), we have studied more than five thousand organizations' different approaches to managing corporate training. We have looked at sixty-two different practices and processes that make up a typical L&D function and correlated these practices against various measures of impact. The one that most consistently predicts a high degree of business results is the existence of a "well-aligned, financially driven business plan for learning." This book will teach you how to build such a plan—and make it a powerful, ongoing process to manage, govern, and operate training with the highest levels of efficiency, effectiveness, and alignment.

Thank you, Dave, for continuing to update such an important book. I urge you, the reader, to take the time to read this book carefully—it will help you improve your organization, your programs, and your own career.

Josh Bersin
Founder and Principal, Bersin by Deloitte
May 16, 2017

---

1. For more information see *The Corporate Learning Factbook® 2015: Benchmarks, Trends and Analysis of the U.S. Corporate Training Market*, Bersin by Deloitte. Available to research members at www.bersin.com/library or for purchase at www.bersin.com/factbook.

2. For more information see *Learning Organizational Alignment Learning As a Core Business Strategy at Accenture*, Bersin & Associates / David Mallon, May 2010. Available to research members at www.bersin.com/library.

3. For more information see *The Career Factbook for HR and Learning Professionals*, Bersin & Associates / Josh Bersin, June 2009. Available to research members at www.bersin.com/library.

4. Deloitte Human Capital Trends 2017.

Preface to the Second Edition

IN THE SEVEN years since the first edition was published, good progress has been made in the field, creating the need for an expanded and updated second edition. Most significantly, a group of industry thought leaders and leading practitioners came together from 2010-2012 to create Talent Development Reporting principles (TDRp), which provide a framework and set of standards for the measurement, reporting, and management of human capital. The second edition thoroughly incorporates TDRp, and an introductory white paper on TDRp may be found in the appendix. Feedback from readers, students, and colleagues also highlighted the need to cover additional scenarios and circumstances so that the book's recommendations can be more easily adopted across a wider variety of organizations. Consequently, in the second edition you will find more examples as well as alternative approaches to creating a business case. The glossary has also been expanded and updated, providing a very comprehensive resource for learning practitioners.

My hope is that the movement to run learning with business-like discipline will continue to grow and will propel the profession to add even greater value to our organizations.

Introduction

CORPORATE LEARNING IS a $300+ billion per year business that must be managed as a business to deliver significant, bottom line results to an organization.[1]

In many organizations learning expenditures represent 3–4% or more of payroll and even more if the indirect costs of learning are included, such as the value of participants' time.[2] Managed well, the learning function can become an indispensable, strategic partner with a significant impact on an organization's goals. Managed poorly, learning will be viewed as a cost with questionable value and little connection to an organization's goals or success.

Running learning like a business is the only way to realize the full potential of learning and maximize its impact on an organization's results.

Fortunately, no new concepts are required for success. The application of standard business practices like strategic alignment, development of a business case, creation of a business plan, and disciplined execution will dramatically improve the effectiveness of the function. Likewise, the application of standard economic concepts and analysis can significantly improve efficiency and decision making.

Unfortunately, few in the profession have been trained in these methods, and fewer still have had an opportunity to practice them or learn from others who are using them. Consequently, many lack the knowledge, experience, and confidence to employ these management practices. So, a business-like approach to learning is not the norm, and when one exists, the leader often has come from outside of human resources (HR) and may have an MBA or experience managing a business.

This, then, is the challenge: First, improve the business acumen and management capability of learning professionals who do not have business background or experience. Second, help learning professionals, both from the field and from other disciplines, apply these concepts to the learning function. And third, provide sufficient detail, examples, and templates so that learning managers will have the knowledge, tools, and confidence to actually implement these concepts.

My goal in writing this book is to meet the above challenge and provide the reader with exactly what is needed to manage learning with much greater impact, effectiveness and efficiency. Greater impact on outcomes will come from aligning learning to the goals of the organization and planning learning's contribution more carefully with the goal owner. Greater effectiveness will come from planning and executing higher quality initiatives, and greater efficiency will come from ensuring the right people participate in the right learning at the right time at the right cost.

The bottom line is that learning must be run like a business. Many organizations already dedicate significant resources to learning. If so, they need to be managed well and deliver the greatest possible return. Other organizations currently under-invest in learning, and a convincing business case can be made for greater investment. In either case the key to success is to understand that learning can benefit from the application of proven business and economic concepts.

There are some today who already manage this way, and we all can continue to learn from them. This book, though, is for those who are not there yet but would like to be. It is for those who want to improve, especially those who want to transform the way they manage. It is also for those who want to improve just a particular aspect of their management or who just want to compare these recommendations to their existing practices.

Theory will be provided where it is important, but the focus will be primarily on the practical. For some topics such as needs analysis, measurement, and evaluation, a large body of literature already exists, so the emphasis will be less on technique per se and more on its role in the management of learning. For other topics like strategic alignment, the business plan for learning, use of net benefit dollars, use of estimates and forecasts, and the economics of learning, little or no literature exists, so the coverage of these subjects will be more expansive.

Every organization is unique, and any implementation has to be tailored to that organization. The primary focus will be on learning functions in for-profit corporations, but many of the recommendations will apply as well to nonprofit organizations, educational institutions, government bodies, and the military. It is also the case that some learning functions have a total of one person on staff whereas others have hundreds. Although the recommendations apply to organizations of all sizes, some are easier to implement if there is a staff. Strategies, examples, and templates will be provided for both small and large organizations.

The book is organized into five parts, which follow a logical sequence. Imagine you are a newly appointed chief learning officer (CLO) or VP of learning. In a nutshell, here is what you need to do:

1. Learn what your existing resources are (staff and budget), where they are deployed, and what they are producing. Know and understand your costs.
2. Align the organization's learning to its strategy and goals, focusing on the highest-priority goals. Also, ensure that all essential learning needs are met such as basic skills training and compliance-related learning.
3. Choose the right solutions to meet the identified needs. Develop a business case to show the benefits and costs clearly.
4. Create a business plan for learning with the right strategically aligned and essential learning solutions that have specific, measurable goals. Include measurement strategy.
5. Create a governing body (or bodies) to provide input for and approval of the business plan and use this governing body to help you manage learning throughout the year.
6. Execute the approved business plan with discipline, using standard reports which show year-to-date progress against plan.
7. Measure results to ensure value is being delivered and to make improvements.
8. Implement plans to improve operating efficiencies and reduce costs.
9. Promote, communicate, and improve.

Part One serves as the foundation, laying out basic business fundamentals (Chapter 1), the business case for learning at a program level (Chapter 2), and a discussion of learning expenditures and resources (Chapter 3). Part Two shows how to align learning strategically (Chapter 4), develop a business case for the entire learning function (Chapter 5), and create a business plan for learning (Chapter 6). Part Three deals with the day-to-day operations of the function once you have a business plan in place. It provides the concepts and tools to set up governing bodies (Chapter 7), manage the measurement process (Chapter 8), and execute the business plan with discipline (Chapter 9). Part Four employs some economic concepts like marginal analysis to improve your efficiency and decision making to ensure that the best programs, options (instructor-led, web-based, simulation, performance support, blended), and durations (for example, a one-day or five-day program) have been selected and that you can make the best decisions about pricing a course, canceling a class, or revising the plan (Chapters 10 and 11). Finally, Part Five concludes with guidance on organizational structure and funding for the learning function (Chapter 12) and recommendations about how to pull all of this together for a successful transformation (Chapter 13).

Another way to view the organization of the book is by the pyramid below. The bottom three rows represent the foundation necessary to create and support the business plan for learning (middle three rows), which then must be successfully executed (top two rows) to deliver the planned results. Since success requires combining a business approach to learning with L&D expertise, these two factors are placed beneath the pyramid in support of all the activities above them. This visual representation of the content will serve as a process map to be used throughout the book to remind the reader where we are.

FIGURE A

The Business of Learning Pyramid

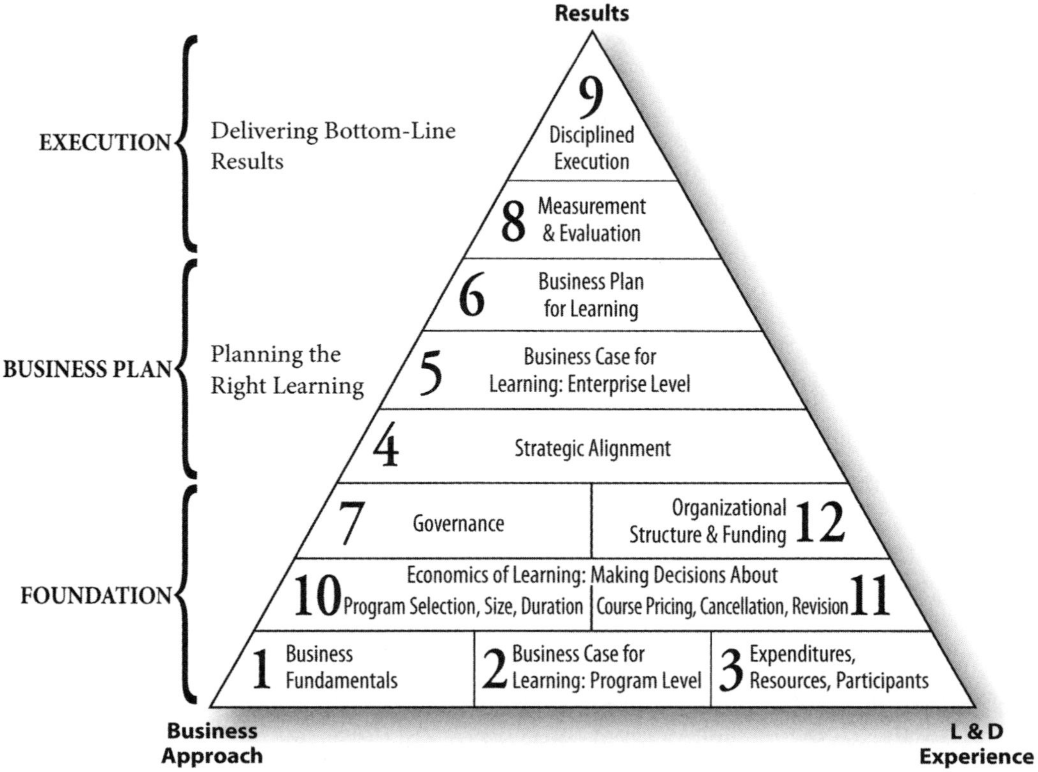

As a practitioner, I have wrestled with all the issues faced by those who manage learning. I didn't always start with the right answer. I made mistakes and learned a lot along the way. My goal is to share these lessons with you. Although every recommendation may not be right for you, all of the recommendations are practical, and I have personally implemented most of them. Since they have worked for me and for others, they may also work for you. The book is intended to be a practical guide, and you will find numerous real-world examples as well as advice, lessons learned, checklists, and templates. Examples from the Caterpillar University experience are also included.

Finally, a few words about terminology. When the word "we" is used throughout the book, it refers to the Caterpillar University staff in the context of practices at Caterpillar Inc. or to the learning profession more generally. The term "learning" will be favored over "training," so you will see "learning function" rather than "training function" and "VP for learning" rather than "VP for training." I will leave it to others to draw out the distinctions between learning and training but simply note that in practice they are often used interchangeably. The term "chief learning officer" (CLO) will be used as well as "VP for learning" to describe the head of the group responsible for learning. This book is about managing the function, whatever it is called and whatever the title of the person managing it. I will generally refer to it as a function, recognizing that there are many forms and many names, including the traditional learning or training department and the corporate university. The above nine steps are consistent with what a corporate university should do, but in fact some call themselves corporate universities without implementing the above steps, and others do implement these steps (and more) but prefer not to be called a corporate university.

---

1. Training Industry estimates that global spend on learning and development was $359 billion in 2016. Source: https://www.trainingindustry.com/wiki/entries/size-of-training-industry.aspx extracted on May 5, 2017.

2. ATD estimated that in 2015 the average organization in their annual survey spent 4.25% of payroll on training while the ATD BEST organizations spent 3.16%. Source: State of the Industry 2016 published by ATD (TD.org), page 19.

Reader's Guide

SINCE IT IS meant to be a practical and comprehensive guide, this book provides all the detail necessary to implement the recommend practices, even in complex organizations. That means more detail is provided than some will need. So, skim or skip the detail that does not apply to you. You can always come back to it later if you need it.

Likewise, Part Four provides a deep dive into economic theory and its application to learning, including lots of graphs and tables (and lots of numbers!). Consider this optional—the rest of the book does not depend on Part Four. If you would like to see how economics can be applied to learning and used to answer questions about program selection, size, and duration, and if you want to learn more about the impact program size has on cost, Part Four is for you. If you are a little bit curious, three-page executive summaries have been prepared for each chapter that do not contain any graphs or tables. Read the summaries and then you can decide whether to skim or read the chapters in more detail. If economics was one of the worst courses you ever had and tables full of numbers make your head hurt, just skip the detail for Part Four.

The book is written to be used as a reference, so feel free to pick the chapters you need. It is recommended, however, that you familiarize yourself with all the concepts in Chapter 1 on business fundamentals since they will be used throughout the book. If developing a business case for learning is of interest, it is recommended that you read Chapter 2 (business case at the program level) and Chapter 4 (alignment) before Chapter 5 (business case at the enterprise level). Likewise, if you want to learn how to create a business plan for learning, read Chapters 2 through 5 before Chapter 6 (business plan). If you are interested in governance, go straight to Chapter 7. Measurement is Chapter 8, execution is Chapter 9, and organizational structure and funding are the topics of Chapter 12.

More detailed guidance will be provided at the start of some chapters.

Glossary

Application Rate (level 3): This is a measure of the extent to which the new knowledge or skills have actually been applied on the job. Application may be measured by observation or through participant self-assessment. The measure is also known as *behavior* (Kirkpatrick) and is commonly referred to as level 3.

Accrual Basis: An accounting term denoting that financial statements reflect income when it is earned and expense when it is generated or used. For example, if a service or product is used or consumed in April but not paid for until June, it will be recorded as an April expense.

Aligned Learning: Learning aligned to the goals of an organization. These programs contribute directly to achieving an organization's goals.

Allocated Costs: Training costs that have been allocated or assigned to specific programs like leadership or sales, used to determine the amount and proportion of training dollars by program.

Attributable Costs: Labor and related and overhead costs that can be attributed or assigned to funded projects or otherwise recovered by billing clients or charging participants.

Attributable Hours: Hours the training staff can attribute or assign to funded projects or otherwise recover by billing clients or charging participants.

Average Cost: Average cost is the total cost divided by the number of units produced in manufacturing. In training, it is the total cost divided by number of participants.

Balance Sheet: One of three common financial statements that shows assets and liabilities at one point in time.

Bottom Line: Profit or net income. The last (bottom) line of the income statement.

Budget: A detailed document showing planned income and expense.

Budget Cost: Costs that are included in the budget and typically reported monthly in the departmental expense statement. Budget costs include items such as salaries, consultants, travel, and supplies. Budget costs do not include opportunity costs, which are an economic cost rather than an accounting cost.

Burden: The dollar amount of labor and related and overhead costs that are not allocated or assigned to any specific program.

Burden Rate: The burden divided by the attributable or assigned hours. It is expressed as dollars/hour and must be added to the labor and related rate to calculate the fully-burdened labor and related rate.

Business Acumen: An understanding of business concepts and their application to make better decisions.

Business Case: A document or presentation that describes the benefits and costs associated with a proposed investment.

Business-centric Learning: Learning that is offered in response to a business need and directly benefits the business or organization. Examples include sales training, leadership development, and compliance-related training.

Business Plan: A document or presentation that completely describes the goals and activities required to achieve the goals for a year. For learning this would include a discussion of strategic alignment, the business case, a detailed work plan, evaluation strategy, and budget.

Cash Basis: An accounting term denoting that financial statements reflect actual collection and expenditure of cash. For example, a payment made to a vendor in June will be reflected as a June expense regardless of when the service or product was consumed.

Chief Financial Officer (CFO): The person responsible for an organization's finances and financial systems. The position oversees accounting and treasury.

Cash Flow Statement: One of three common financial statements showing the sources and uses of cash for operating, investing, and financing activities for a period of time.

Chief Learning Officer (CLO): The person responsible for learning in an organization, typically used in larger organizations where the person has enterprise-wide responsibilities.

Class: A specific training delivery or event that may be instructor-led in the classroom, facilitated online, self-paced, or web based. An example is a two-hour instructor-led session for 23 participants on May 15.

Competency: A characteristic (like leadership) important to achieving the goals of an organization.

Competency Model: A collection of the competencies that are important to an organization. They may include the level of proficiency necessary for organizational success.

Course: A training topic that has classes available for it. For example, a course may include four closely related and integrated classes over a four week period.

Curriculum: A category or group of courses.

Depreciation: The decline in value of a physical asset through time.

Discretionary Learning: Learning that is not mandated by law, required for employees to meet the minimum competency level necessary for their position, or required to fulfill professional certification. Discretionary learning is often scaled back or eliminated during episodes of cost cutting.

Effectiveness Measure: One of the three types of TDRp measures recommended for all initiatives and departments. Effectiveness measures are about the quality of the initiative and are usually gathered through a survey, test, or focus group. Examples include participant satisfaction, amount learned, and application. (The other two types of TDRp measures are *efficiency* and *outcomes.*)

Efficiency Measure: One of the three types of TDRp measures recommended for all initiatives and departments. Efficiency measures are about counts, percentages, and rates, where a measure will be efficient or not in comparison to a plan, benchmark, trend, or history. Examples include number of participants, courses, hours, and costs; percentage of courses delivered on time or employees reached by learning; and utilization of courses, instructors, seats, or rooms. Also referred to as level 0, volume, or activity measures. (The other two types of TDRp measures are *effectiveness* and *outcomes.*)

Essential Unaligned Learning: Learning that is not directly aligned to the high-level goals of the organization but is nonetheless deemed so important that it must be provided. Compliance-related learning is an example since there is usually not a high-level goal regarding compliance but it is understood that it must be provided to minimize the risk of noncompliance. Another example is basic skills training required for employees new to a position to attain a minimum level of competency. Other examples include project management and change management.

Estimate: The goal owner or learning professional's reasoned guess based on partial information about the past or current value of a measure. For example, the actual impact of learning for the first quarter may not be known, but an estimate is made. Used when the actual value is not yet available.

Expense: Cost. The amount of money spent (cash basis) or the value of a product or service used (accrual basis).

EVP (Executive Vice President): Usually a direct report to the CEO.

Fixed Cost: A cost that does not vary or change in the period under consideration. In learning, the development cost of a course is considered fixed since it will not change regardless of the number of participants.

Forecast: The goal owner or learning professional's projection or reasoned guess for the future value of a measure once the year is already underway. The forecast will often differ from the plan (original goal) and may differ from the estimate. For example, the plan may have been a 10% increase in sales for the year, but by July it is evident the plan will not be achieved and the forecast is now for a 7% increase in sales. Forecasts are typically made for all measures that are actively managed.

Formal Learning: Learning that is organized or directed by someone else for the learner, such as an instructor-led class or web-based training.

FTE (Full-Time Equivalent): This is a way of measuring full-time (52 weeks x 40 hours/week) effort when some employees are part-time. For example, if two part-time employees each work half-time, the full-time equivalent of the two employees is 1.0.

Fully-Burdened Labor Rate: The labor rate expressed in dollars/hour, which includes the burden rate and fully reflects all costs. Used in calculating quotes for projects when the goal is to fully recover costs.

Goal: The desired organizational outcome or objective, such as increasing sales by 10% next year.

Goal Owner: The person responsible and accountable for achieving the planned outcome for a goal, such as the SVP of sales. Synonymous with sponsor.

Gross Benefit: The dollar benefit of a learning program before any costs are subtracted.

ILT (Instructor-Led Training): The traditional form of instruction, with a class meeting face to face with an instructor.

IM&E (Indirect Material and Expense): A common category of overhead expense found on departmental income statements, often including all external expenses (which would appear in a corporate income statement), such as travel, consultants, printing, telephone, leases, office supplies, and so on.

Income: Revenue. The amount of money collected (cash basis) or earned (accrual basis).

Income Statement: The most common financial statement, which shows income (revenue) and expense (cost) in some detail. The statement concludes with net income or profit, the difference between income and expense.

Informal Learning: Learning not organized or directed by someone else. The participant learns on his own through discovery, such as through social learning, networking, and knowledge sharing.

Initiative: Includes efforts not typically considered a program. Examples might include getting employees to complete a development plan or supervisors to spend at least one hour per week coaching. For purposes of simplification, however, the term programs will be understood to encompass initiatives.

Internal Charges: A common category of overhead expense found on departmental income statements, which includes internal charges within the company like IT, HR, legal, occupancy.

Isolated Impact: The impact of learning on achieving the goal. Typically, many factors are responsible for achieving a goal so an isolation methodology must be employed to separate or isolate the contribution of learning from all the other factors. Also known as *Phillips's level 4 Business Impact*, isolated impact serves as both an outcome measure and an effectiveness measure.

Labor Rate: The hourly cost of labor expressed as dollars/hour. For a group it is the total labor cost divided by the total hours.

Labor and Related Rate: The hourly cost of labor and related costs expressed as dollars/hour. Related costs include health care, vacation pay, incentive pay, profit sharing, employer-paid employee taxes (like Social Security and unemployment in the U.S.). Used to calculate opportunity costs.

Last Year's Results (or Actuals): The results for the last complete fiscal year.

Learning (level 2): Used as an effectiveness measure, learning is a measure of the amount learned or how well it was learned. Learning is typically measured through a test at the end of each module or course. It is also known as Kirkpatrick and Phillips' *level 2.*

Learner-centric Learning: Learning that is typically offered in response to requests from employees and which is not directly aligned to a high-level business or organizational goal.

Level 0: Refers to all efficiency measures. Also referred to as *volume* or *activity measures*. See *Efficiency Measures.*

Level 1 (Participant reaction or satisfaction): Refers to the first level of the Kirkpatrick/Phillips' effectiveness measures. See *Participant Reaction.*

Level 2 (Learning): Refers to the second level of the Kirkpatrick/Phillips' effectiveness measures. See *Learning.*

Level 3 (Application): Refers to third level of the Kirkpatrick/Phillips's effectiveness measures. See *Application Rate.*

Level 4 (Results): Refers to fourth level of Kirkpatrick's four effectiveness measures, which is the business result when training has been applied.

Level 4 (Impact): Refers to fourth level of the Phillips' five effectiveness measures and to the isolated impact of training on the business results.

Level 5 (ROI): Refers to fifth level of the Phillips' five effectiveness measures and to the return on investment of the training. See *Return on Investment* and *Isolated Impact.*

L&D (Learning and Development): A very common name for the learning field and for a learning function.

LMS (Learning Management System): A computer-based system to list classes, register for classes, take online classes, and record completions. May also offer online evaluation and online individual development plans.

Loss: Refers to net income, which is negative (expense exceeds income).

Mandatory Learning: Learning that is required by law or by the senior leadership of an organization. All employees in the target audience are expected to take mandatory learning and typically there are negative consequences for not complying.

Measures to Manage: The select few measures that will be actively managed throughout the year and consequently will be included in three TDRp reports. Each measure to manage will have a plan or target set before the year begins and, once the year is underway, year-to-date results will be reported each month. Ideally, the forecast for how the measure is likely to end the year should also be updated each month.

Measures to Monitor: These are all the measures that are not managed and represent most measures an organization collects. Measures to monitor do not require a plan, year-to-date results, nor a forecast, and the measures should not appear in regular monthly reports. These measures are important enough to collect but not important enough to manage on a monthly basis. The measures reside in a database until they are needed.

Marginal Cost: The cost of producing one more unit in manufacturing. In training, the cost of adding one more participant.

Needs Analysis: A structured and disciplined exploration of an organization's need and the ability of learning to at least partially meet that need.

Net Benefit: Gross benefit less the total cost of learning, including opportunity cost.

Net Income Profit: Calculated as income (revenue) less expense (cost). Often referred to as the bottom line.

Nonattributable Costs: Labor and related and overhead costs that cannot be attributed or assigned to funded projects or otherwise recovered by billing clients or charging participants. For labor and related it includes the value of all nonattributable hours. For overhead this will include non-project IM&E costs and probably all internal charges.

Nonattributable Hours: Hours the training staff cannot attribute or assign to funded projects or otherwise recover by billing clients or charging participants. These include vacation and sick time, time spent in staff meetings and personal development, and time spent marketing. For leaders they also include time spent managing others, budgeting, and ongoing financial and operational management.

Non-essential Unaligned Learning: The learning not directly aligned to the high-level goals of the organization, which may be deferred or eliminated without great harm to the organization. Examples would include most general studies courses. See *Essential Unaligned Learning* for examples of courses which are deemed essential.

Nonprofit: Usually refers to an organization or activity where the financial goal is to break even (net income equals $0).

Operations Report: One of the three standard TDRp reports, the operations report includes aggregate data on the key effectiveness and efficiency measures for all the programs or initiatives managed by the L&D department for which data are available.

Opportunity Cost: The value of what is given up. In learning it is at least the value of the participant's time in class and in transit calculated as hours x labor and related rate. In some cases like a program for sales people it will be the net income not generated because they were in class.

Outcome Measure: One of the three types of TDRp measures, the outcome measure is either the isolated impact of the learning initiative on the organizational goal or a proxy for isolated impact. The outcome measure may be expressed qualitatively or quantitatively. A qualitative outcome measure will be expressed as an adjective such as high, medium, low, essential, very important, or important. A quantitative outcome measure using isolated impact will always be expressed in the same unit as the goal. For example, a 1% increase in sales due to learning in support of a goal to increase sales by 5% is an outcome measure for a consultative selling initiative. The application rate of learning sometimes serves as a proxy for isolated impact and will appear as an outcome measure. Outcome may also refer to the business outcome or result itself, such as the 5% increase in sales. (The other two types of TDRp measures are *effectiveness* and *efficiency*.)

Overhead: A category of expense found on the income statement referring to costs not directly related to production. On many corporate income statements overhead costs will be called sales, general, and administrative (SG&A). On departmental income statements overhead costs may be called indirect material and expense (IM&E) and internal.

Participants: Those enrolled in, engaging in, or completing any type of learning, including formal or informal. Participants may be measured as unique (not allowing for duplication by name) or total (allowing for the same person taking more than one course to be counted more than once). The number of participants is an efficiency measure.

Participant Reaction or Satisfaction (level 1): The participants' reaction to or satisfaction with the training they just completed. The information is usually gathered in a post-event survey immediately following completion. Also known as Kirkpatrick and Phillips' *level 1*, participant satisfaction is an effectiveness measure.

Performance Support: A repository for information, processes, and perspectives that inform and guide planning and action. It may provide all the help and assistance needed to complete a task and may be preferred in some cases to formal learning.

Percent (%) of plan: A calculation of progress to date to achieve the plan for the measure being reported. By formula, % of plan (annual) = year-to-date results / plan (annual)

Plan: The qualitative or quantitative goal or target set for the measure being reported for the next year.

Planned Contribution from Learning: The qualitative or quantitative isolated contribution of learning toward the organization goal agreed to prior to the development of the learning by the goal owner or sponsor and the learning manager. Examples would include "High or Significant" contribution to a 5% increase in sales (qualitative) or a 20% contribution to a 5% increase in sales (quantitative) due to sales-related training.

Planned Impact of Learning: The qualitative or quantitative isolated impact of learning toward the organization goal agreed to prior to the development of the learning by the goal owner or sponsor and the learning manager. Examples would include "significant increase in sales due to learning" (qualitative) or "a 1% increase in sales due to training" (quantitative, found as planned contribution from learning x organization goal, or, 20% x 5% increase in sales = 1% increase in sales due just to training).

Program: Training initiative spanning days, weeks, or months often with multiple courses and potentially other learning components (e.g. informal learning, capstone projects, coaching, self-study) that is typically repeated for cohorts or learners. A program is defined to include initiatives as well. For example, a program may include one instructor-led course, plus performance support tools, plus two hours of self-paced online learning for the same 23 participants. A program may also be composed of courses for different target audiences. For example, a safety program may consist of courses for employees and different courses for supervisors.

Program Report: One of the three standard TDRp reports, the program report includes the outcome measure and key effectiveness and efficiency measures for the programs or initiatives in support of one organizational goal. Typically, there will be one program report for each important goal supported by learning.

Proxy: A next-best or stand-in measure when the desired measure is not available. In learning, the application rate is often used as a proxy for impact since it is both highly correlated with and predictive of impact.

Qualitative Impact: The isolated impact of learning on an organizational goal expressed as an adjective such as essential, low, medium, or high.

Quantitative Impact: The isolated impact of learning on an organizational goal expressed as a number or percentage such as a 1% increase in sales due just to learning.

Reach: The percentage of employees touched by formal or informal learning, calculated as total unique participants divided by total employees. Reach is an efficiency measure.

Return on Expectations (ROE): Created by Donald and James Kirkpatrick to describe their evaluation model, which begins with the expectations of the goal owner (stakeholders) and seeks to build a chain of evidence through levels 1-3 that the stakeholder's expectations were met through the training. Unlike Phillips's ROI, ROE is not a measure in itself and cannot be calculated. Rather, it is a process focused on identifying and meeting the expectations of the stakeholder.

Profit: Net income. Calculated as income (revenue) less expense. Often referred to as the bottom line.

P&L (Profit and Loss): A P&L statement is the same as an income statement.

Return on Investment (ROI): In business it is the net income from the project divided by the capital cost of the project. In training, it is the net benefit of the project divided by the total cost of the project, including opportunity cost. ROI is expressed as a percentage.

Scale: Size. In training it usually refers to the number of participants taking a class or course.

SG&A (Selling, General, and Administrative): This is a category of expense on the income statement representing overhead or costs not directly related to production.

Sponsor: The person responsible and accountable for achieving the planned outcome for a goal, such as the SVP of sales. Synonymous with *goal owner.*

Strategic Alignment: The process of proactively aligning or matching learning programs with organizational goals, ensuring that training addresses the highest priority goals.

SVP (Senior Vice President): Usually a direct report to the CEO.

Summary Report: One of three standard TDRp reports, the summary report includes the organization's key goals and outcome measures for learning in support of those goals as well as the most important effectiveness and efficiency measures aggregated at the enterprise level.

Talent Development Reporting principles (TDRp): Measurement, reporting, and management standards for L&D and HR, including a framework for measurement (three types of measures) and reporting (three standard reports). Developed in 2010-2012 by a group of industry thought leaders and leading practitioners.

Total Cost: Fixed plus variable cost. In terms of learning programs it also means all the costs associated with a program, including development, delivery, management, reinforcement, and opportunity costs.

Total Participants: One of the two measures for participants, total participants counts all instances of participation, allowing for duplication. For example, if a person takes five courses, there will be five total participants or five instances of participation. Total participants is correlated with the resources (staff, budget, rooms) required for learning. (The other measure of participants is *total unique participants.*)

Total Unique Participants: One of the two measures for participants, total unique participants is an unduplicated count of all participants. In other words, it is a by-name measure of participants. For example, if a person takes five courses, there will be five total participants but only one unique participant. The measure of total unique participants is used to calculate the reach of learning (total unique participants/total employees). (The other measure of participants is *total participants.*)

Unaligned Learning: Learning that is not directly aligned to any organizational goals.

Unallocated Costs: Costs that have not been allocated or assigned to any specific program, such as leadership and sales.

Variable Cost: A cost that varies or changes in the period under consideration. In learning, materials are a variable cost since they increase with scale and will increase throughout the year as the number of participants in a course increases.

WBT (Web-Based Training): Online instruction that may be synchronous (the instructor and students meet online at the same time) or asynchronous (the lesson is recorded, and the students can access it at any time).

YTD (Year to Date): The value of a measure from the start of the year to the present.

Year-to-Date Results (or Actuals): The results from the start of the fiscal year through the most recent month for which actuals are available.

PART ONE

Introduction to the Business of Learning

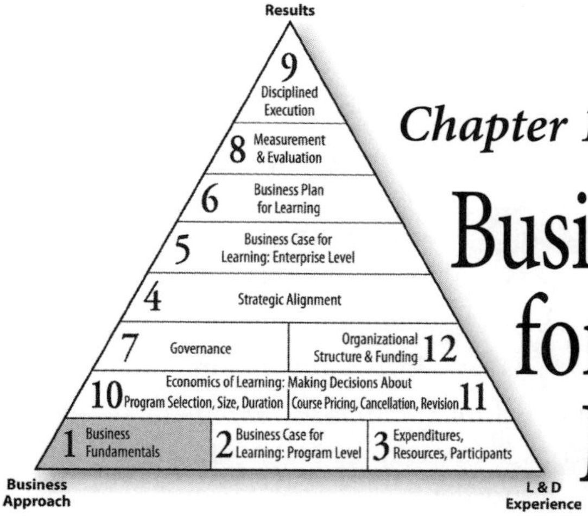

Chapter 1

Business Fundamentals for the Learning Manager

TO BE SUCCESSFUL, you must understand business basics and be able to make a compelling case for learning. The good news is you do *not* need a business degree or experience running a business to do this. This chapter will provide all the business fundamentals you need. We begin with the basics, which seem simple and straightforward, so much so that you may be tempted just to skim over them. That could be a mistake. Many learning professionals are very uncomfortable speaking the language of business. For most this reflects a lack of knowledge and experience and for some just a lack of confidence. Whatever the cause, this inability severely handicaps them as they try to have operating or strategic discussions with organizational leaders and later try to make the business case for investing in learning. So, be sure you are comfortable with the concepts that follow. They are the foundation of your business mentality.

Key Concepts for Chapter 1

1

1. A learning manager must speak the language of business to succeed.
2. Organizations exist to perform a mission.
3. Success is measured by comparing actual performance to goals.
4. A business plan will contain a vision, mission, and strategy along with specific, measurable goals.
5. Progress against these goals is measured daily, weekly, monthly, quarterly, and annually through scorecards and detailed reports.
6. The income statement is the most important financial statement for the learning manager.
7. A learning manager must understand depreciation and cash basis versus accrual basis accounting.
8. Knowing your labor costs, particularly fully-burdened labor costs, is essential for managing the function.
9. Understanding variable and fixed costs is also essential for managing the function successfully.

Reader's Guide

This is a long chapter, and you may not need to read it all. The first section on speaking the language of business should be read by all since it sets the tone for the rest of the book. The next four sections ("Why Do Organizations Exist?," "How Do Organizations Measure Their Success?," "How Do Organizations Track Their Progress and Keep Score?," and "How About Financial Reports?") will be most helpful for those who have not managed an organization before. If you have had profit and loss (P & L) responsibility before, you should already be familiar with these concepts. The last three sections ("The Income Statement for a Learning Function," "The Labor Rate and Fully-Burdened Labor Rate," and "Variable and Fixed Expenses") focus specifically on the learning function and should be meaningful even for those who have had business experience outside of learning. The last three sections contain a lot of detail (especially on calculating the labor rate). Skim the detail if you do not need it right now, but a learning manager should understand the basic concepts even if your business manager or accountant will make the actual calculations.

Speaking the Language of Business

Special thanks to Rick Heiken for the suggestion to include this section and for his assistance in writing it. Rick and I were colleagues at Caterpillar. After his retirement he taught business acumen for Caterpillar University and now has developed his own business acumen program.

To be a successful learning leader and run the learning function as a business, you must make "the language of business" an integral part of daily communication. Not everyone will have or need the same depth of knowledge or vocabulary, but if everyone has a basic understanding of the language of business, it will be easier to implement the guidance provided in this book, and your objectives will be reached much sooner.

Learning program managers, college deans, program directors, and most definitely the chief learning officer (CLO) or vice president of learning must be fluent in the language of business. Those who aspire to executive leadership positions in their organizations must become fluent. And a basic understanding is essential for everyone in the learning organization, regardless of their role, to better understand why running the organization "as a business" is important to its success.

The language of business is the language of finance and financial measurements. A basic fundamental of business is that every decision made in the process of running the business will eventually make its way to financial statements, which, as this book explains, are the key metrics by which performance will be evaluated and the future of the learning function will be determined. For simplicity we can say the language of business is the language of money. Nonprofit and for-profit businesses, and even the business of running a successful household, are all driven by the need to create revenue, control costs, and have funds available to finance growth.

Ultimately, money is the common denominator for measuring, evaluating, and managing the business. Decisions are made based on whether the issue in question will increase earnings, cover cost, and sustain future operations. There is no other denominator that can effectively track and objectively compare the diverse activities required to make a business work.

Consider the three levels of employees in Figure 1.1 below and their respective responsibilities. Think about where you are now and where you would like to be in the future. Think about the others in your organization. How rich does the financial vocabulary have to be at each level?

FIGURE 1.1
The Language of Business

	Supervisor, Staff	***Middle Management***	***Officers Upper Mgt.***
Focus	Tasks, Things Specific Sales, Costs Operational Details	⇄	Company Goals Profit Big Picture
Language	Departmental Activity	⇄	$

At the left are staff and supervisors. The business language they speak is a reflection of the immediate demands of departmental activity. This language is recognizable by a vocabulary that describes tasks, things, events, activities, and people (suppliers, colleagues, clients). Daily conversations at this level revolve around designing and delivering courses, selecting and managing vendors, determining who should participate in classes, managing classroom usage, setting prices for courses, gathering and analyzing participant feedback, and managing budgets. Metrics used for individual performance reviews at this level are characterized by this same vocabulary. Money is discussed in terms of the costs of learning, staying within budget, and pricing courses, but *relatively little* time is spent discussing learning activity in terms of impact on financial performance.

At this level many decisions are not based on financial considerations, and little attention is usually paid to corporate financial results. Efforts to explain quarterly or annual results often do not resonate with the people at this level. If revenue and profit are going up and the executives are happy, then everyone is happy. They just do not know exactly why revenue and profit are rising. If the revenue and profit are going down and the executives are unhappy, then everyone is concerned and maybe scared. They just don't understand exactly why. Add to this how difficult it is to explain the rationale for many top-level decisions impacting the allocation of resources to the learning community. Not clearly understood, these decisions are often received with skepticism, disbelief, or anger. Expanding the financial vocabulary of people at this level will result in higher levels of engagement and commitment as well as improve communication and shut down the all-too-often uninformed rumor mills.

Next, consider the officers and senior management to the right in the diagram. Most of this group's time is spent talking with a vocabulary that is recognizable by the focus on achievement of corporate goals, long-term strategies, optimum resource allocation, and financial performance. Money is truly the language of business at this level. Every decision eventually impacts a company's financial statements, and this level of management understands that truism better than any other. Financial performance is the lens through which these managers see the world and communicate among themselves and the company's stakeholders, shareholders, and analysts. To be effective, they must be able to understand the impact of any strategy, of any suggestion, or of any activity on the company's financial performance and goals. The only common denominator across the different goals and across a diverse organization is money.

Yes, their discussions will include consideration of tasks, things, people, and events, but this part of the discussion will quickly shift to the impact on the company's goals and ultimately the impact on earnings. Issues are quickly "monetized," and the questions become "How much will it cost?," "Where are we going to get the money to fund it?," "How much will it increase income or reduce expense?," and "What effect will it have on long-term earnings?" Without answers to these questions, they cannot make good decisions.

Finally, consider the group in the middle, which has to speak the language of both the other groups. They are the translators. They need to understand the language of departmental activity since they will set goals for the supervisors, manage and evaluate their performance, and resolve conflicts. On the other hand, this group reports to officers and upper management who have less time for or interest in these operational details. As discussed above, upper management wants to know the impact of any recommended activity on the company's goals and specifically its impact on revenue and expense.

So middle managers translate the language of daily detail and activity (which the people who work for them speak) into the language of money (which the people they work for speak). Getting the learning budget approved and requesting additional staff are typical examples. Likewise, middle management must translate the decisions and directives from upper management, usually presented in the language of money, into the language of departmental activity. Think of a directive to cut expenses 10% and its impact on people, things, and events. Middle managers are the only ones in a position to do this since supervisors and staff do not speak or understand the financial vocabulary spoken by top-level managers, and upper management is too far removed from the vocabulary of daily activity.

Middle management and upper management have to speak the language of money in order to succeed. Technical expertise in a field is no longer the key to success, and hard work alone will not get you promoted to middle or upper management. The key to your future success lies in speaking the language of business and delivering business results in the language of money. View this as the new requirement for success.

FIGURE 1.2
Career Success Requires Increasing Fluency in the Language of Business

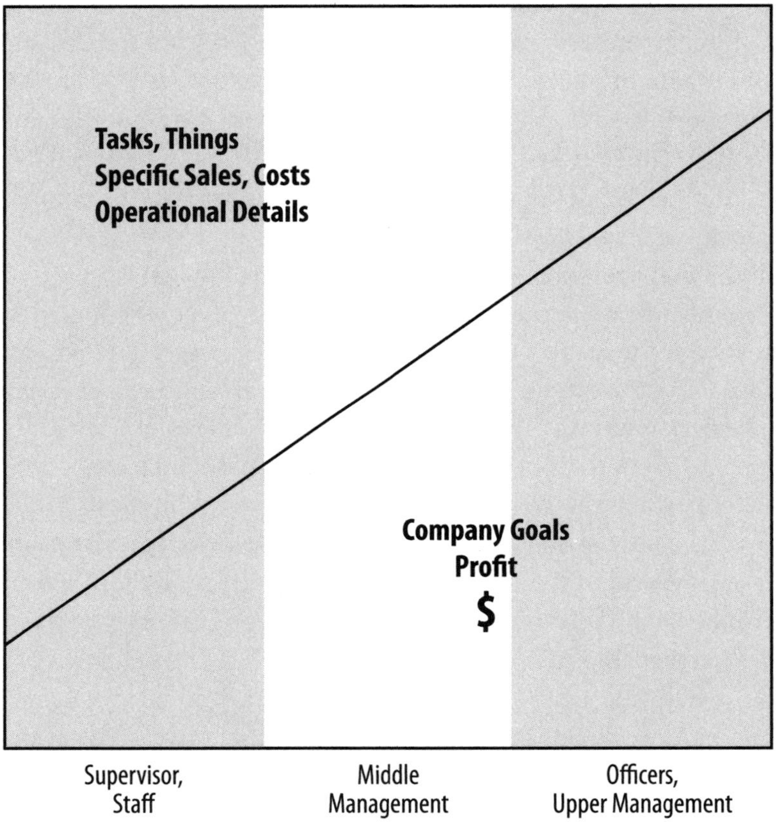

The above figure illustrates that career success requires a growing fluency in the language of money. Supervisors and staff will spend little of their time talking in terms of money. Officers and upper management, on the other hand, will spend most of their time talking about money and company goals. Successful middle managers will spend more and more of their time talking in terms of dollar impact on company goals and profit, and these are the ones most likely to be promoted.

The rest of this book is dedicated to teaching the language of business necessary for a manager to become a CLO or rise to the ranks of upper management.

Why Do Organizations Exist?

Organizations exist to perform a mission. A for-profit company wants to sell a product or service and make a profit. A nonprofit organization or government entity wants to deliver a service and not exceed its budget. The mission or purpose statement for each would describe what they want to provide, to whom they want to provide it, and perhaps how they intend to provide it. The better a for-profit company performs its mission, the more profit it will make. The better a nonprofit or government entity performs its mission, the more service it can provide, perhaps at a lower cost or higher value.

How Do Organizations Measure Their Success?

Organizations measure their success by comparing actual performance to goals. For-profit companies will have a profit goal. Many also will have goals for sales, market share, number of customers, new products or services launched, deals completed, cost reduction, quality, and efficiency. Nonprofits and government entities may have goals for the number of people served, quality of service, new programs, response time, efficiency, and cost reduction. They also will have a goal not to exceed their budget for costs.

Specific and Measurable Goals

Goals should be specific and measurable. For example, a cost reduction goal might call for a 10% reduction in product cost by June 30, 2017. It states exactly *what* is to be measured (product cost), *how much* it is to be reduced (10%), and *when* it must be accomplished (June 30). If there is any doubt about *who* is responsible or *where* it is be performed, that should be added as well: Manufacturing will deliver a 10% reduction in product cost for all North American plants by June 30, 2017. The goal needs to be stated specifically enough so there is no doubt whether it was met or not.

> ADVICE: While a specific, measurable goal may be stated as a level (like $12 million in sales), it will be helpful for our work if the goal is restated as the "delta" or change from last year. For example, if sales for 2016 were $10 million and the goal for 2017 is $12 million, the delta is $2 million or a 20% increase in sales. So, the goal would be "Increase

sales by 20%." If the goal itself is already expressed in percentages, the statement becomes a little trickier. For example, if customer satisfaction was 72% (the percent checking one of the top two boxes on a five-point scale indicating they were very satisfied or satisfied) in 2016 and the goal is to achieve customer satisfaction of 75% in 2017, the delta would be a 3 percentage point increase. If we were to simply say the goal is to increase customer satisfaction by 3% some might interpret that to mean 3% x 72% = a 2.16 percentage point increase to 74.16%. To avoid potential confusion, the goal would best be stated as "Increase customer satisfaction by 3 points to 75%."

Also, separate conjoined goals. Here is an example of a conjoined goal: "Increase sales by 10% while reducing operating costs by 5%." These are two separate thoughts and different action items will be required to accomplish each one. Consequently, each should stand alone as a goal: "Increase sales by 10%" and as the next goal "Reduce operating costs by 5%."

The Business Plan

In many organizations these goals will be collected into a business plan. Typically, the plan will be created each year prior to the organization's fiscal year, which is the 12-month period it chooses for purposes of measuring results and paying taxes. (Often the fiscal year is simply the calendar year, January 1st through December 31st, but it doesn't have to be.) The business plan will usually contain goals, strategies, and action items. A goal may encompass a number of strategies or critical success factors that must be accomplished if the goal is to be accomplished. These in turn will be executed through action items, which are very specific in nature.

For example, a company may have a goal to increase sales by 20% next year. This goal will be accomplished through two strategies: 1) increase market share by 10 points; 2) increase the price received on every sale by 10%. Both of these would have specific action items or plans to accomplish them, such as: a) increase learning for the sales force so they close 15% more sales; b) launch two new products by June 30; and c) increase advertising by 25%. The business plan may be a written document or a PowerPoint presentation. It may simply be a list of action items and goals, or it may provide a more comprehensive and exhaustive discussion, including context around the goals, such as the environmental and competitive challenges facing the company.

Mission and Vision Statements

An organization should also have a mission and vision statement. These may be contained in the annual business plan or not. The mission is the organization's purpose. It answers the question "What do you do day in and day out?" The vision is an aspirational statement about what the organization wants to achieve in the future, typically over the next five to ten years. It answers the question "What do you want to become or be?" Goals, strategies, and action items are how the organization plans to achieve the vision.

Example

Figure 1.3 provides an example of a mission and vision statement along with goals and strategies for a retail company that is currently (2017) number three in its industry. The company has three goals to support its mission and achieve its vision of becoming number one by 2025.

FIGURE 1.3

Example of Mission and Vision Statements, Strategies, and Goals

Mission: Provide our customers with quality products and service to meet their needs in a convenient and cost-effective manner.

Vision: Be the industry leader in sales, profitability, and customer satisfaction by 2025.

Goals and Strategies

- Increase sales by 20% in 2017.
    - Close 15% more sales in 2017.
    - Launch two new products by June 30 and four new products by December 31, 2017.
    - Increase advertising by 25% in 2017.
- Increase profitability by 10% in 2017.
    - Limit growth in operating costs to 10% in 2017.
    - Limit growth of overhead costs to 5% in 2017.
    - Reduce warranty costs by 4% in 2017.
- Increase customer satisfaction by 2 points in 2017.
    - Increase online help by five staff members in 2017.

Each of the above strategies or key performance indicators (KPIs) would have action items detailing what needs to take place to achieve it.

Accountability

So the business plan will be a collection of goals and actions that are specific and measurable. Success will be measured by how well the organization performs against these goals. If the goal was to increase profit by 20%, how close did the company come? The board of directors will hold the CEO responsible for delivering all the top-tier goals. The CEO will hold her direct reports responsible for delivering on these goals with each direct report responsible for one or more of the top-tier goals. This responsibility will then cascade down the leadership chain until every goal has an owner, someone ultimately responsible for achieving that particular goal. In most organizations the leaders' annual performance review and subsequent salary increase and/or bonus will depend on how well they met their goals.

How Do Organizations Track Their Progress and Keep Score?

Every organization needs to know how well it is doing. The board of directors, the organization's leaders, and its employees want to know how they are doing. After all, their future depends on it in terms of their employment, pay, and benefits. If it is a publicly traded company, the stockholders and bondholders will demand to know how it is doing, or they will not invest in it. Banks and financial institutions will not make loans and credit available without knowing that the organization is financially viable and capable of repaying the loan.

Annual, Quarterly, Monthly, and Year-to-Date Measures

So organizations must track their progress against the goals they have set for themselves. Generally, organizations will use a variety of reports and scorecards to track their progress on at least a monthly if not weekly or daily basis. The reports may be organized by strategy, by department, by region, by product, or any number of ways.

The Basics

However it is organized, a typical report will have at least the following for each goal (with a sales example in parentheses):

1. Last year's results or actuals (sales of $100 million)
2. The annual goal for this year (sales of $120 million)
3. Year-to-date (YTD) results or actuals for this year (sales of $50 million for the first six months)
4. YTD results as a % of plan (42%)

From these we can calculate that the sales goal for this year represents a 20% increase over last year ($120 - $100)/$100). We may not be doing so well this year since we are only 42% ($50/$120) of the way to our goal and the year is already half over.

More Is Better

Additional information would be helpful to determine if we are in trouble. Year-to-date results or actuals for this same time last year would be good to have:

1. Year-to-date (YTD) results for last year (sales of $30 million for first six months of last year)
2. YTD results for this year compared to YTD results for last year (up 67%)

Now we can calculate two things: Six months into last year we had achieved 30% ($30/$100) of our annual plan goal ($100 million). This year we are at 42%, so maybe we are okay. It could be that demand for our product is always stronger in the second half and we expect sales always to be higher in the second half. We can also calculate the increase in YTD sales at 67% ($50/$30), which tells us we are running 67% ahead of last year's pace. Our plan was only to beat last year by 20%. This year is looking better and better. If we keep this pace up, we will end the year at $167 million ((.67* $100) +$100) or ((1+.67)*$100). Bonus time! Many reports would include the 67%, the comparison of this year's year-to-date results with last year's year-to-date results.

Monthly Measures

Sometimes, a report will also include results for just the month, the same month last year, and a comparison to the same month last year:

1. Results or actuals for current month ($12 million)
2. Results or actuals for this month last year ($8 million)
3. Current month compared to same month last year (up 50%)

These two additional pieces of information confirm we are doing much better than last year. For this month we are up 50% ($12/$8) over last year, even more than the YTD comparison, so we have great momentum.

Monthly and YTD Plan Measures

Sometimes the annual goal is broken down into sub-goals for each month. This is especially useful when results are not spread out evenly though the year as in our example here. If you have enough historical information to deduce the seasonal pattern or if you have good information about the spread of sales in the coming year, you might plan or budget for each of the twelve months:

TABLE 1.1: **Use of Seasonal Patterns to Forecast Monthly and YTD Sales**

	Historical Percentage Annual Sales	*Monthly Sales Plan*	*Year-to-Date Sales Plan*
January	3%	$3.6	$3.6
February	4%	4.8	8.4
March	5%	6.0	14.4
April	6%	7.2	21.6
May	7%	8.4	30.0
June	8%	**9.6**	**39.6**
July	9%	10.8	50.4
August	10%	12.0	62.4
September	11%	13.2	75.6
October	12%	14.4	90.0
November	12%	14.4	104.4
December	13%	15.6	$120.0
TOTAL	100%	$120.0	

The pattern clearly shows stronger sales in the last six months of the year. In fact, 67% of sales have historically occurred in the July through December period. These monthly "seasonals" can be used to allocate this year's annual forecast by month. So, January sales are expected to be 3% of annual or $3.6 million (.03 x $ 120 = $3.6). Once the plan for each month is calculated this way, the cumulative or running total is the YTD plan for any given month.

When goals are provided for each month, the report will show plans for the month and YTD plan and include the percentage comparison to actual results:

1. Monthly plan ($9.6 million for June)
2. Monthly results compared to monthly plan (up 25%)
3. YTD plan ($39.6 million through June)
4. YTD results compared to YTD plan (up 26%)

With this we can calculate that results for the month are $2.4 million ($12 - $9.6) or 25% ahead of plan ($2.4/$9.6) and year-to-date results are $10.4 million ($50 - $39.6) or 26% ahead of plan ($10.4/$39.6). This is still good news because both the most recent month and the first six months are running considerably higher than up by 20%, which was the planned increase for the year. But the YTD comparison to plan of up 26% does indicate we may not end the year at $167 million (above from comparison to last year's YTD results) but more like $151 million ((1 + .26) * $120). There still will be a bonus, but not quite as big.

Monthly and YTD plan information may also be provided even when all months are assumed to be the same. In this case each month is simply the annual plan divided by 12.

Sample Report

Table 1.2 provides an example of what a report containing all of the above measures might look like.

The first row for total dollar sales contains all the numbers used in the examples above. In addition, data are provided for four other goals and for two regions. This format would be typical for a one-page operating report.

Summary

Okay, time for a breather. Although all this information can be very helpful, it can also become overwhelming and sometimes even appear to be conflicting.

TABLE 1.2: **Operating Report for a Company**

Operating Report for Vega Inc

Sales Department • Information through June 30, 2017

	June					June YTD					YTD Actual			
	2016 Actual	2017 Actual	% Change vs. 2016	2017 Plan	Actual vs. Plan	2016 Actual	2017 Actual	% Change vs. 2016	2017 YTD Plan	Actual vs. Plan	as a % of Annual Plan	2016 Actual	2017 Plan	% Change vs 2016
Total														
Dollar Sales (Mil $)	$8.0	$12.0	50.0%	$9.6	25.0%	$30.0	$50.0	66.7%	$39.6	26.3%	41.7%	$100.0	$120.0	20.0%
Number of new products	2	4	100.0%	3	33.3%	10	19	90.0%	16	18.8%	59.4%	21	32	52.4%
Number of new stores	2	2	0.0%	2	0.0%	6	9	50.0%	8	12.5%	50.0%	12	18	50.0%
Advertising (Mil $)	$0.4	$0.5	25.0%	$0.5	0.0%	$2.5	$3.0	20.0%	$3.0	0.0%	48.0%	$5.0	$6.3	25.0%
Market Share (%)	25.0	27.0	8.0%	26.0	3.8%	23.5	25.7	9.4%	25.0	2.8%	97.0%	24.0	26.5	10.4%
Eastern Region														
Dollar Sales (Mil $)	$5.0	$7.0	40.0%	$5.0	40.0%	$16.0	$27.0	68.8%	$21.0	28.6%	41.5%	$52.0	$65.0	25.0%
Number of new products	1	2	100.0%	2	0.0%	6	11	83.3%	9	22.2%	61.1%	11	18	63.6%
Number of new stores	1	1	0.0%	1	0.0%	2	5	150.0%	5	0.0%	50.0%	7	10	42.9%
Advertising (Mil $)	$0.2	$0.3	50.0%	$0.3	0.0%	$1.4	$1.6	14.3%	$1.6	0.0%	48.5%	$2.8	$3.3	17.9%
Market Share (%)	26.0	28.0	7.7%	27.0	3.7%	25.0	27.0	8.0%	26.0	3.8%	98.2%	25.5	27.5	7.8%
Western Region														
Dollar Sales (Mil $)	$3.0	$5.0	66.7%	$4.6	8.7%	$14.0	$23.0	64.3%	$18.6	23.7%	41.8%	$48.0	$55.0	14.6%
Number of new products	1	2	100.0%	1	100.0%	4	8	100.0%	7	14.3%	57.1%	10	14	40.0%
Number of new stores	1	1	0.0%	1	0.0%	4	4	0.0%	3	33.3%	50.0%	5	8	60.0%
Advertising (Mil $)	$0.2	$0.2	0.0%	$0.2	0.0%	$1.1	$1.4	27.3%	$1.4	0.0%	47.5%	$2.2	$3.0	34.1%
Market Share (%)	23.3	25.6	9.7%	24.9	2.8%	21.8	24.2	11.0%	23.9	1.3%	95.5%	22.4	25.3	13.2%

When this happens, step back and ask yourself, "What question am I trying to answer?" and "What am I going to do with the answer?" Be as specific as you can. Let the answer to those questions guide you. In our example above, questions and answers might be the following:

> "How did sales do in June?"
> **Answer:** Use monthly data to compare to last year and then compare to plan: "June was a very good month. Sales were up 50% over June last year and were 25% over plan for the month."
>
> "How are sales doing for the first six months?"
> **Answer:** Use year-to-date data to compare the first six months' sales to last year's and then to plan: "Very strong. Sales are $20 million or 67% ahead of last year's sales at this same time, and we are $10.4 million or 26% ahead of plan for the first half."
>
> "Are we going to make plan?"
> **Answer:** Use year-to-date comparisons and compare YTD results with the annual plan. Then project through the end of the year: "Very likely. In fact, it looks like we should exceed the business plan. We are running 26% ahead of plan so far, and if we keep up this pace, sales should total about $151 million for the year, exceeding the plan by $31 million. I know we have only booked 42% ($50/$120) of our annual plan, but you have to remember most of our sales always come in the second half, and this year should be no different."

Note that in this case we used the YTD plan comparison (26%) rather than last year's YTD comparison (67%) to extrapolate the $151 million total for the year (67% gave us the $167 million). In practice, if the YTD plan data are based on good history or solid information about what pattern to expect this year (like advance orders), then the YTD plan comparison is probably more accurate and you should use it. If you don't have good information on this year's sales pattern or you believe this year will unfold exactly like last year, then use the comparison to last year's results to estimate the total sales for this year. When in doubt, we would use the more conservative figure, $151 million in this case, since it is better not to raise expectations too high.

Scorecards

Scorecards are special purpose reports with selected data from much lengthier reports and are meant to focus attention on those few items that are most important. Just as there are many layers to report (for example, country, region, state, and district), there will be layers for scorecards. Except at the lowest reporting level, there is always more detail available at the next level down to answer questions. Scorecards are typically published monthly or weekly but may be compiled as often as daily or as infrequently as quarterly or semi-annually.

Example of a Simple Scorecard

The following example illustrates a high-level scorecard that could be used by senior management and the board of directors for Vega Inc. Key goals concerning sales, profit, market share, operating costs, and customer satisfaction have been selected for inclusion. Typically, a high-level scorecard like this would focus on no more than ten to fifteen key goals.

TABLE 1.3: **Sample Scorecard for a Company**

June YTD

	2016 Actual	*2017 Plan*	*% Increase*	*2017 YTD*	*% of Plan*	*Act. Vs. YTD Plan*	*2017 Forecast*	*vs. Plan*
Sales (Mil $)	100	**120**	**20%**	**50**	**42%**	**26%**	**140**	**17%**
Profit (Mil $)	10.0	13.0	30%	5.0	39%	18%	15	15%
Market Share (%)	24.0	26.5	10%	25.7	97%	3%	26.0	(2%)
Op. Costs (Mil $)	80	88	10%	37	42%	22%	103	17%
Cust. Sat. (points)	60	62	+2	61	50%	100%	62	100%

The scorecard in the first three columns reminds readers of the goals for the year and how they compare to last year. Then it presents year-to-date results and compares them to the annual and YTD plans. The last two columns introduce a forecast for the year, which was unlikely to be found on the detailed report since the forecast is a matter of judgment. The board of directors will want to know how management believes the year will end. For sales, we had earlier calculated that they would be $151 million if the pace of the first six months continued through the end of the year. Of course, it may not. Leaders will usually be somewhat conservative and allow for some slow down or unexpected event. In this example the forecast was set at $140 million, a 17% increase over plan instead of 26%.

The Balanced Scorecard

Kaplan and Norton popularized the notion of a balanced scorecard in a *Harvard Business Review* article in 1992, building on earlier work by Art Schneiderman at Analog Devices. They argued that traditional financial reports (covered in the next section) omitted key measures of performance, especially measures that would be more predictive of success in the future. In addition to financial measures, they recommended including measures in the areas of learning and growth, internal processes, and the customer. Taken together, measures in these four areas would provide a more balanced view of performance. Further, they recommended that some measures be leading rather than lagging indicators so the scorecards would be more predictive. For example, one could easily argue that investing more in employee learning and growth should lead to improved internal processes, which would lead to better customer service, which in turn would lead to higher profit (the financial measure). So, investment now in learning and growth or in internal process improvement should lead to improved financials later in the year or in coming years.

We will examine scorecards for learning in great detail in Chapter 9.

How About Financial Reports?

Financial reports are a very important source of information, especially to those outside the company like investors and bankers who do not have access to the detailed operating reports and scorecards discussed above. There are three main financial reports used by organizations:

1. Income statement or profit and loss statement
2. Balance sheet
3. Cash flow statement

The income statement is the most important in managing the learning function, but we'll provide an overview of all three so you are familiar with them. Then we'll focus on the income statement for the learning function. The good news is that you do not have to create them (accountants in your organization will take care of that), and you don't need to be a financial analyst to use them.

Income Statement

The income statement shows sales or revenue, expenses or costs, and the difference, which is net income or profit (loss) for a period of time, usually a month or year. Costs are usually broken into several main categories like operating costs, overhead costs (like sales, general and administrative, and research and development), interest, and taxes. General and administrative is the big bucket for all overhead costs not detailed elsewhere and is often combined with selling costs into sales, general, and administrative (SG&A).

TABLE 1.4: **Simplified Income Statement**
Millions of Dollars

January 1, 2016 to December 31, 2016

Revenue	$100	
Operating Costs		
Cost of good sold	$76	
Sales, general & adminstrative (S,G&A) expense	$11	Also called Overhead
Research and development expense	$3	
Other operating expenses	$1	
Total operating expenses	$91	
Operating profit	$9	
Interest expense	$4	
Profit before taxes	$5	
Provision for income taxes	$2	
Profit	$3	

The income statement answers questions like the following (answers from Table 1.4)

> "Is this company making any money?"
> **Answer:** Yes, $3 million.

> "How much did this organization spend and on what?
> **Answer:** $76 million to procure the goods, $11 million on overhead, $3 million on R&D, $1 million on other overhead expense, $4 million on interest expense, and $2 million for taxes.

As you have already surmised, there seem to be multiple names for the same item (income or revenue, expenses or costs, net income or profit). The same is true for the above, where gross profit may be called gross margin and operating profit may be called income from operations. Not to worry. It is the concept of the income statement that is important to understand here, and your version of this for the learning function will have simpler terms! We will focus on the income statement for the learning function in depth below.

Balance Sheet

The balance sheet shows assets, liabilities, and owners' equity for a point in time like the end of the month or year. Assets are things you own or others owe to you. Your buildings, computers, and inventory are assets if you own them. If you have receivables, which are what clients owe you but have not yet paid you, these are assets. Liabilities are the opposite. They are claims on you by others. They may be what you owe someone else (like loans you have not paid off) or a payment someone has made to you that you have not earned yet (like an advance payment). You are on the hook for liabilities. In for-profit companies retained earnings are the accumulation through the years of the net income you have earned. It appears in the balance sheet along with liabilities because retained earnings are a claim on the company by the owners. For nonprofits and government entities, there would be a surplus in place of retained earnings, which represents the annual surpluses accumulated through time.

The balance sheet is divided into two main parts, which have to be in balance or equal each other: 1) assets and 2) liabilities and owner's equity. Assets will be divided between current and long-term assets, with long-term meaning lasting longer than one year. Likewise, liabilities are divided between short- and long-term, with debt being split depending on when the payments are due. Finally, owners' equity is split between the capital stock, which is the original amount of money invested in the stock of the company, and the accumulated retained earnings, which is all the net income earned in the past.

The balance sheet answers questions like the following (answers from Table 1.5):

"What is the value of our assets?"
Answer: Total assets are $48 million

"How much do others owe us?"
Answer: Receivables are $18 million

TABLE 1.5 : **Simplified Balance Sheet**
Millions of Dollars

	December 31, 2016
Assets	
Current Assets	
Cash	$ 4
Receivables	18
Inventories	14
Total current assets	36
Long-Term Assets	
Property, plant, and equipment	
(Net of accumulated depreciation)	10
Investments and other long-term assets	2
Total long-term assets	12
Total Assets	$ 48
Liabilities and Owners' Equity	
Current Liabilities	
Payables	$ 6
Accrued expenses	4
Current portion of debt	3
Total current liabilities	13
Long-term Debt	5
Total Liabilities	$ 18
Owners' Equity	
Capital stock	20
Retained earnings	10
Total owners' equity	30
Total Liabilities and Owners' Equity	$ 48

"How much cash do we have on hand?'
Answer: $4 million

"How much do we owe others?"
Answer: Total liabilities are $18 million

"What are we worth?"
Answer: Owners' equity is $30 million

Cash Flow Statement

The cash flow statement (or statement of cash flows) shows where the cash came from and where it went for a period of time like a month or a year. It is organized differently than the income statement since it is not intended to clarify where the profit came from but instead the sources and uses of cash. It may be divided into three parts: cash flows from operating activities, cash flows from investing activities, and cash flows from financing activities. A positive number is a source of cash whereas a negative number is a use of cash.

Aren't you glad there are accountants to prepare these? It may look like a bewildering mess of positive and negative numbers, and the complicated statements certainly would be. But we are just trying to understand where the money comes from and where it goes, and conceptually anyway, it is not that hard.

It starts with operations and picks up the net income from the income statement. This is the first source of cash for your company. Then it adds back in expenses that did not actually require cash outlays (like depreciation: see below). This is another source of cash, so it is positive. Some other operational items, however, did not show as an expense in the income statement but did use cash (like increasing inventory), so these appear with a negative sign. They are using cash. In our example above net income provided the starting $3 million, but the operations used a net $1 million in cash, so we are only up $2 million at this point.

Next, we see what cash was provided from the sale of non-financial assets. In our example, we didn't sell any buildings or businesses, so there is no extra cash coming in. Since we are expanding, however, we did buy a new building and more equipment, which cost us $4 million. This is a use of cash, so it appears as a negative. Where did we get the $4 million? Read on.

TABLE 1.6: **Simplified Cash Flow Statement**
Millions of Dollars

January to December 2016

Cash Flows from Operating Activities	
Net Income	$ 3
Adjustments to reconcile net income to net cash from operating activities	
Depreciation	2
(Increase) decrease in receivables	(2)
(Increase) decrease in inventories	(2)
Increase (decrease) in payables	1
Total adjustments	(1)
Net Cash Provided by Operating Activities	2
Cash Flows from Investing Activities	
Proceeds from sale of assets	0
Proceeds from sale of discontinued businesses	0
Purchase of additional property, plant, equipment	(4)
Net Cash Provided from Investing Activities	(4)
Cash Flows from Financing Activities	
Proceeds from borrowing	3
Repayment of borrowings	(2)
Sale (repurchase) of stock	1
Dividends paid	(1)
Net Cash Provided from Financing Activities	1
Change in Cash	(1)
Cash at Beginning of Year	5
Cash at End of Year	$ 4

The last focus area is financing. Here we'll collect all our proceeds from borrowing and all our repayments. We'll also capture the cash generated from selling company stock and what it costs us to pay dividends to the shareholders. In our example, first note that we have to pay $2 million back this year to banks and bondholders. Plus, we need $1 million for the dividend payment. If you are keeping track, we needed $4 million for the new building and $3 million for repayments and dividends, for a total of $7 million. Operations will provide $2 million, so we are still $5 million short. We did start the year with $5 million, but we can't spend all of our cash (we always need some cash on hand). Assume we are comfortable going down to a $4 million cash balance at year end, which provides $1 million for us to use. We still need $4 million. We get that by borrowing $3 million in new money and selling $1 million of stock. We end the year with a $4 million cash balance. All those positive and negative cash flow items totaled just $1 million.

By the way, if you are in a large organization, this is what your treasury colleagues do for a living. They manage corporate cash throughout the year so that you do not have to spend time each month worrying about whether enough cash is available to make payroll. If you are in a small company, however, cash flow is a very real concern every single month. You will have to manage your cash to ensure there is enough for payroll, tax payments, the utility bill, and all other critical expenses.

The cash flow statement answers questions like the following (answers from Table 1.6):

"Where does our cash come from?"
Answer: Borrowing, operations, and sale of stock

"Where is it going?"
Answer: Primarily growth-related activities like purchase of plant and higher receivables and inventory

"How much did we pay in dividends?"
Answer: $1 million

"How did our cash balance change during the year?"
Answer: Down $1 million

The three statements are obviously related. Net income or profit from the income statement adds to retained earnings on the balance sheet and is the first item on the cash flow statement. Ending cash is the same on both the balance sheet and cash flow statement. Depreciation is an expense (usually) on the income statement, and this reduces the value of plant, property, and equipment on the balance sheet. It is also a key adjustment to net income on the cash flow statement.

There are two more concepts with regard to financial statements you should know. We have mentioned one above: depreciation. The other concerns the way books are kept, and this gives rise to many items on the balance sheet and many of the adjustments on the cash flow statement. You are likely to encounter both managing the learning function, even if you never see a balance sheet or cash flow statement. We'll start with the second one first.

QUESTION: Where does learning and development (L&D) in particular or HR in general appear in the three statements? Interestingly, L&D or HR appears only as an expense in the income statement and as a liability in the balance sheet. In the income statement L&D or HR will be part of Sales, General & Administrative Expense. In other words, it will appear as overhead. In the balance sheet, the unpaid portions of regular and vacation pay for L&D or HR staff will be included under Accrued Expenses along with any other labor-related obligations where benefits have been earned but not yet paid.

Unfortunately, accountants and CFOs are trained to look for ways to reduce overhead expense and accrued expense so this automatically puts L&D and HR in a defensive position when it comes to budgeting and cost reduction. This why it is so important for learning professionals to be able to speak the language of business and have a rudimentary understanding of financial statements. With this, learning professionals can point out that learning initiatives, when properly conceived, designed, delivered and reinforced, can increase sales and reduce other overhead expenses, more than offsetting the cost of the initiatives. In other words, the bottom line (profit) will increase—not decrease—from investing more in learning. This in turn will improve the balance sheet by increasing retained earnings and will positively impact cash flow by increasing net income from operating activities.

Cash Basis versus Accrual Basis Accounting

Some organizations keep their books and report on a cash basis whereas others use an accrual basis. So, the income statement and balance sheet for an organization may be on the cash basis or accrual basis. (Whichever it is, the same basis will be used for both.)

Cash Basis Accounting

Reporting on a cash basis is just like it sounds. The full amount of the cash transaction is reported when it occurs. If you receive $100 on March 20 for consulting work, the $100 will be income for March. If you pay $70 for materials on March 25, the $70 will be an expense for March. On a cash basis, your income statement for March shows income of $100, expenses of $70, and net income of $30.

Accrual Basis Accounting

Most large organizations, however, use the accrual basis, which means income is going to be placed (accrued) in the month it was earned. (Generally accepted accounting principles [GAAP] require accrual basis accounting for large organizations.) Say that you did $80 worth of work for a client in March but did not receive payment until April 28. Since you did the work in March, you count the

TABLE 1.7: **Comparison of Income Statements on Cash and Accrual Bases**

Cash Basis

	January	*February*	*March*	*April*
Income	$95	$90	**$100**	**$80**
Expense	55	65	**70**	**60**
Net Income	$40	$25	$30	$20

Accrual Basis

	January	*February*	*March*	*April*
Income	**$100**	$110	**$80**	$120
Expense	85	**70**	**60**	80
Net Income	$15	$35	$20	$40

$80 as income in March. You do *not* count the $100 received in March as income for March. (Perhaps it was accrued as income for January, so it has already been counted.) The accrual basis for expenses means that the expense is counted when it is incurred or used, not when it is paid. So if you used $60 worth of materials in March to generate the $80 in income, then your expense would be $60 even if you did not write a check to pay for it until April. You do *not* count the $70 paid out in March as an expense for March (perhaps it was accrued back in February). On an accrual basis, your income statement for March shows income of $80, expenses of $60, and net income of $20.

Cash Basis versus Accrual Basis

The important point here is to understand there are two versions of the income statement (same goes for the balance sheet). Both are correct, even though one shows net income for March of $30 and the other net income of $20. They are simply different ways of looking at the *same facts*.

Many would say that the accrual method gives a truer picture of an organization's health since it is reporting income when actually earned and expenses when actually incurred. This is why GAAP demands its use for large organizations. Imagine a situation in which a company receives a very large payment in January for work performed in September of the previous year. Assume also that the expenses for that work were all paid in the previous year. Under the cash basis, the net income for the previous year will have the expense but not the income for that work while just the opposite will be the case for the current year. Under the accrual basis, the income and expense for the same work will be reflected in the same month and same year.

Many small organizations and sole proprietorships, however, use the cash basis for its simplicity. The cash basis also avoids the potential problem of having to pay income tax on net income that has not yet been realized on a cash basis. For example, suppose your net income on a cash basis is $10,000 and your income tax is $2,000. The $2,000 tax can easily be paid from the $10,000. Now, suppose that you used the accrual basis and your net income is $30,000 due to a large amount of very profitable work done in November and December (will not be reflected until February or March on the cash basis). At the same tax rate, your income tax payment is $6,000, which is 60% of your cash net income.

ADVICE: You should know whether your organization, and particularly your function, reports on a cash or accrual basis.

Depreciation

Physical assets lose value through time or depreciate just like your car. There are schedules for depreciation, which tell you that your new computer will depreciate in value to zero in three years (useful life equals three years) whereas your office building has a useful life of forty years. To make life interesting, these schedules might be different for financial reporting purposes and for calculating your income taxes, and to make life more interesting, there are different ways to depreciate. The straight line method figures the same amount each year: 33.3% for our computer and 2.5% for the office building. The accelerated method speeds it up with bigger amounts in the early years and smaller amounts in the later years, which lets you have a bigger expense right away and which, in turn, means less net income right now and less tax right now. (When it comes to taxes, the general rule is to reduce your taxes *now* so you can keep more of your money *now* so you can invest it *now*).

The income statement (accrual basis) will show depreciation expense, which usually is *not* the entire cost of the asset. For example, say you purchased a computer for $3,000. Further, assume it has a useful life of three years and you are going to depreciate it on a straight-line basis (same amount each year or $1,000 per year). In the year of purchase, your income statement will include an expense of $1,000 for the computer. The cash flow statement for that same year will show that you spent $3,000 on equipment.

The Income Statement for a Learning Function

Anyone managing a learning function in an organization should have some form of an income statement for his department. Unless it is a stand-alone entity, the manager is unlikely to have a balance sheet or cash flow statement. So, our focus will be on the income statement, which is usually provided on a monthly basis to all departments, divisions, and business units within an organization. In some cases income statements may even be generated for subunits inside the learning function, perhaps by college or program (leadership, sales, manufacturing, etc.) or by function (development, delivery, technology, etc.).

Note: In many departments this will be called the departmental expense statement, rather than an income statement, and it will contain only expense items. If this is the case in your department, you can focus on just the expense discussion and your "bottom line" will be total expense rather than net income.

Your Income Statement

It may not be an "official" income statement since the learning function does not report results to the public or pay taxes on its profit, but it should contain the same essential elements, namely revenue, expenses, and net income or surplus. Since you are not producing or procuring "goods," it will not have cost of goods sold or gross profit, and it is unlikely to have taxes or interest expense. It will have more detail about all your costs, and so it will look different than an "official" income statement. The expense groupings typically will focus on several major expense categories like labor and overhead. The good news is that you have only one statement, and it is much simpler than the three we just described.

> ADVICE: Find out who your accountant is. There should be one assigned to cover the HR area, or your HR or learning group may be large enough to have your own full-time accountant. Get to know the person. Visit with her on a regular basis. Take your accountant to lunch. You need this person, and you want a strong relationship in place before an emergency occurs or budget time rolls around.

Probably on a Cash Basis

Your department income statement is likely to be on a cash basis even if you work for an organization that uses the accrual method. In most cases it is not worth the trouble and effort to treat all transactions on an accrual basis, which means that receivables and payables have to be created, tracked, and retired. Typically, organizations using the accrual method will have a dollar threshold to determine whether a department-level item requires the accrual treatment. For example, the threshold may be $50,000. If your learning group has an expense greater than $50,000, it would then be booked in the month incurred (used), and a payable would be created. Likewise, if you perform work for a party outside your company that is worth more than $50,000, it would be booked as income the month it is done, and a receivable would be created. If the work was for internal customers, it probably would not be booked until it was charged since there are likely a number of internal transactions each month that cancel each other out. The larger your company, the higher the threshold is likely to be.

We will assume your department is on a cash basis for the following discussion.

Income

Let's start with income. In an "official" income statement, this line would be called sales or revenue, and yours may use these "correct" terms. But it may also just label the sales or revenue "income," which is understood to be your revenue. Your income statement should show the sources of your income. In most cases, the statement will be a combination of income from other business units (your internal clients like marketing) and from corporate. Some statements will include income from companies other than your own (external clients), which purchase services from your learning group and actually write a check to your company (real sales!).

The proportion of these three sources to the total will depend on your business model. If you operate as a fully funded or subsidized cost center, then 100% of your revenue may come from corporate. If that is the case, there may not even be an income portion to your income statement; you might just have the expenses. On the other hand, if you are structured as an internal profit center, then the income statement will show how much each business unit has paid you that month for your services. There may still be a corporate component, but typically it would be less than the revenue from your internal clients. Finally, you may be structured as an external profit center, in which case you are expected to generate net income for the organization by selling your services to other entities. You will have significant revenue from external clients in addition to internal revenue and corporate support.

Expenses

Expenses come next. Typically, labor and related come first and may be the largest or second largest expense. Labor will include all the direct costs of employment, such as regular salary and overtime for both permanent and part-time employees. (Detail may be provided for these breakouts.) Related includes all the indirect costs of employment like employer-paid taxes (FICA or Social Security

TABLE 1.8: **Income Statement for a Learning Function**

Vega Inc

Vega Corporate University

June YTD Income Statement

(Thousands of Dollars)

	June					June YTD								
	2016 Actual	*2017 Actual*	*% Change vs. 2016*	*2017 Plan*	*Actual vs. Plan*	*2016 Actual*	*2017 Actual*	*% Change vs. 2016*	*2017 YTD Plan*	*Actual vs. Plan*	*YTD Actual as a % of Annual Plan*	*2016 Actual*	*2017 Plan*	*% Change vs. 2016*
Income														
CORPORATE	54.2	41.7	-23.1%	41.7	0.0%	325.0	250.0	-23.1%	250.0	0.0%	50.0%	650.0	500.0	-23.1%
BUSINESS UNITS	132.4	145.2	9.7%	137.5	5.6%	705.4	885.4	25.5%	850.0	4.2%	53.7%	1,400.0	1,650.0	17.9%
EXTERNAL	14.2	11.2	-21.1%	20.8	-46.2%	64.8	111.5	72.1%	115.0	-3.0%	44.6%	150.0	250.0	66.7%
TOTAL	200.8	198.1	-1.3%	200.0	-1.0%	1095.2	1246.9	13.9%	1215.0	2.6%	52.0%	2,200.0	2,400.0	9.1%
Expenses														
LABOR & RELATED														
Labor for full-time employees	78.5	82.5	5.1%	84.0	-1.8%	435.5	450.1	3.4%	475.0	-5.2%	45.0%	950.0	1,000.0	5.3%
Related for full-time employees	19.6	20.6	5.1%	21.0	-1.8%	108.9	112.5	3.4%	118.8	-5.2%	45.0%	237.5	250.0	5.3%
Total for full-time employees	98.1	103.1	5.1%	105.0	-1.8%	544.4	562.6	3.4%	593.8	-5.2%	45.0%	1,187.5	1,250.0	5.3%
Labor for part-time employees	21.5	24.8	15.3%	22.0	12.7%	100.3	135.4	35.0%	125.0	8.3%	54.2%	200.0	250.0	25.0%
Related for part-time employees	2.2	2.5	15.3%	2.2	12.7%	10.0	13.5	35.0%	12.5	8.3%	54.2%	20.0	25.0	25.0%
Total for part-time employees	23.7	27.3	15.3%	24.2	12.7%	110.3	148.9	35.0%	137.5	8.3%	54.2%	220.0	275.0	25.0%
Total Labor & related	121.8	130.4	7.1%	129.2	0.9%	654.7	711.6	8.7%	731.3	-2.7%	46.7%	1,407.5	1,525.0	8.3%

	June					June YTD								
	2016 Actual	2017 Actual	% Change vs. 2016	2017 Plan	Actual vs. Plan	2016 Actual	2017 Actual	% Change vs. 2016	2017 YTD Plan	Actual vs. Plan	YTD Actual as a % of Annual Plan	2016 Actual	2017 Plan	% Change vs. 2016
INDIRECT MATERIAL AND EXPENSES (IME)														
Dues and subscriptions	1.6	1.0	-38.8%	2.1	-52.9%	12.0	11.7	-2.5%	12.5	-6.4%	46.8%	23.5	25.0	6.4%
Office supplies	3.4	3.7	8.8%	2.5	48.0%	14.1	14.5	2.8%	15.0	-3.3%	48.3%	28.9	30.0	3.8%
Materials	1.9	2.1	10.5%	3.5	-40.0%	17.0	18.4	8.2%	18.0	2.2%	46.0%	37.6	40.0	6.4%
Printing	1.8	2.1	16.7%	1.8	16.7%	8.2	10.7	30.5%	9.0	18.9%	53.5%	21.2	20.0	-5.7%
Mailing/shipping	1.2	1.1	-8.3%	0.8	32.5%	4.6	5.2	13.0%	5.0	4.0%	52.0%	9.8	10.0	2.0%
Telephone	2.7	2.7	1.9%	2.5	8.0%	14.1	14.9	5.7%	15.0	-0.7%	49.7%	29.4	30.0	2.0%
Lease for copiers, printers	15.0	1.3	-91.7%	1.3	0.0%	7.2	7.6	5.6%	7.5	1.3%	50.7%	14.5	15.0	3.4%
Travel & entertainment	6.5	9.1	40.0%	5.0	82.0%	32.8	35.6	8.5%	30.0	18.7%	59.3%	56.8	60.0	5.6%
Consultants	35.4	43.2	22.0%	37.5	15.2%	165.0	194.5	17.9%	175.0	11.1%	48.6%	350.0	400.0	14.3%
Total IME	69.5	66.2	-4.6%	57.0	16.3%	275.0	313.1	13.9%	287.0	9.1%	49.7%	571.7	630.0	10.2%
INTERNAL CHARGES														
Occupancy	12.1	12.5	3.3%	12.5	0.0%	72.5	75.0	3.4%	75.0	0.0%	50.0%	145.0	150.0	3.4%
HR	1.3	1.3	0.0%	1.3	0.0%	7.5	7.5	0.0%	7.5	0.0%	50.0%	15.0	15.0	0.0%
IT	4.6	5.0	8.7%	5.0	0.0%	27.5	30.0	9.1%	30.0	0.0%	50.0%	55.0	60.0	9.1%
Accounting	1.3	1.3	0.0%	1.3	0.0%	7.5	7.5	0.0%	7.5	0.0%	50.0%	15.0	15.0	0.0%
Legal	0.4	1.4	250.0%	0.4	233.3%	2.5	3.5	40.0%	2.5	40.0%	70.0%	5.0	5.0	0.0%
Total internal charges	19.6	21.4	9.2%	20.4	4.8%	117.5	123.5	5.1%	122.5	0.8%	50.4%	235.0	245.0	4.3%
TOTAL EXPENSES	210.8	218.0	3.4%	206.6	5.5%	1047.2	1148.2	9.6%	1140.8	0.7%	47.8%	2,214.2	2,400.0	8.4%
Net income	(10.1)	(20.0)	98.5%	(6.6)	203.4%	48.0	98.7	105.7%	74.3	33.0%		(14.2)	0.0	-100.0%

and disability, and state unemployment), health care insurance, and pension contributions. Related may also include an accrual for unused vacation time. In all, related expenses may easily amount to 25% or more of the labor costs.

> ADVICE: Know the percentage of your related costs to labor costs, and know the percentage of labor and related to total costs.

Overhead expenses are the other big category. They may be called overhead or indirect material and expenses (IM&E). In either case it means all the other expenses required to support the function. These may be divided between external and internal costs. External costs are those paid to another entity outside your company. Examples would be office supplies, leases for computers, copiers and printers, and telephone as well as consultants and vendors you have hired. Internal costs are those "paid" to others inside your company through intra-company accounting transfers. Examples here might be charges for the office space your group occupies and for internal IT, HR, and accounting support.

The bottom line will be net income, profit, or surplus, depending on your structure. If your business model is to operate as a fully funded cost center, your goal will be to break even if income is shown. If there is no income shown since you are automatically and fully funded by corporate, then your job is to hold expenses below budget. If you are an internal or external profit center, then your goal is to break even or achieve (exceed) the budgeted profit.

Sample Income Statement for a Learning Function

A typical income statement for a learning function is provided in Table 1.8. This income statement contains results through June as well as last year's actuals and the plan for this year. Detail is provided for income and for labor and related expenses, indirect material and expenses, and internal charges.

Answering a Specific Question

The statement contains a wealth of information. If you are looking for something specific, such as total labor and related costs for June, you can go directly to the item ($130,400) and then compare it with the plan for the month ($129,200) and to last year's June expenditure ($121,800). You would conclude that you are just about on plan for the month (.9% above). You might also note that although the total L&R is near the plan for the month, L&R for part-time employees is running 12.7% over plan, while L&R for full-time employees is 1.8% below plan. Do you know why part-time labor is over plan? You would also see that part-time labor is running 8.3% over plan for the first six months of the year, so June was not an aberration. Full-time labor is running 5.2% below plan YTD, so perhaps you have had trouble filling full-time positions and are substituting part-time labor. In total and for the first six months, L&R is 8.7% higher than last year but 2.7% below plan, so you are okay.

Providing an Overall Analysis

Suppose, instead of looking for a particular item, you were interested in the big picture. What does this statement tell us about how you are doing overall? Where are the areas of concern?

The best approach is to start with the plan for the big picture, then look at YTD results for trend, and finally look at the most recent month's results to see whether the trend looks sustainable. Always focus first on the groupings (such as income or IM&E) and then look at the significant (large dollar) individual line items.

Start with the plan. Look at the plan for 2017. Notice that the goal is to break even, which you came very close to accomplishing last year. Income is budgeted to increase 9.1%, which will offset an 8.4% increase in costs. On the income side a $250,000 (17.9%) increase is planned for business unit revenue, which combined with a $100,000 (66.7%) increase in external revenue should more than offset a $150,000 (23.1%) planned decrease in corporate funding. So, you really need the large increases in business unit and external revenue to offset the drop in corporate funding.

On the expense side the largest increase is budgeted for L&R, which will rise $117,500 or 8.3% from last year. This increase exceeds inflation or a typical merit increase, so it looks like you are adding part-time employees (part-time labor is up 25%), and perhaps you added a full-time employee partway through last year and this year you have her expense for the entire year. IM&E is budgeted to be up about $58,000 or 10.2%, driven primarily by consultant expenses rising $50,000 or 14.3%. Perhaps you have decided to use more consultants instead of adding another full-time employee to provide greater flexibility to meet fluctuating demand. No other IM&E line item is exceptional. Internal charges are budgeted to increase only $10,000 or 4.3%, which is a little higher than inflation. On closer examination, the $5,000 (9.1%) increase in IT explains half of the total increase for internal charges, so you would want to understand this one in particular, especially since three other internal providers are not increasing their charges at all.

Look at YTD performance next. For the six months through June, you have a net income of $98,700, which is $24,400 or 33% better than the plan of $74,300. That is great! If the second half is as good as the first half, you could finish the year almost $50,000 over plan!

What explains the great first half? Total expenses are actually $7,400 or .7% over plan, so it must be income that is exceeding the plan. Sure enough, total income of $1,246,900 is almost $32,000 or 2.6% over budget. Corporate funding is right on budget, which is no surprise because you know exactly what you will get for the year. Business unit demand, however, is up even more than you planned. At $885,400 it is running 25.5% ahead of last year and $35,400 or 4.2% ahead of plan. This more than offsets lagging external sales. So the income side looks good. If these trends hold for the rest of the year, you could end the year 2%+ or $50,000 over plan (.02 x $2,400,000 = $48,000).

On the expense side you are running .7% over budget. Even if you end the year 1% over budget on total expenses, that would be $24,000 (.01 x $2,400,000 = $24,000) and would still leave you with net income of $24,000 versus the plan of breaking even. (If income exceeds plan by $48,000 and expenses exceed plan by $24,000, the net will exceed plan by the difference.)

Are there any worrisome expense trends? Labor and related expense is running at $19,700 or 2.7% under plan as lower full-time labor costs more than offset higher part-time labor costs. So L&R should be okay unless full-time hiring picks up *and* part-time employment continues to exceed plan.

IM&E, however, is running significantly (9.1%) over plan. Actual spending is $26,100 ($313,100 - $287,000) over budget and can be explained almost entirely by just two line items. Consultant spending is $19,500 or 11.1% over budget, and T&E (travel and entertainment) spending is $5,600 or 18.7% over plan. We need to understand why these are over budget. If you are using consultants to handle the unexpected demand from the business units, then this might make perfect sense. After all, total income is running almost $32,000 over plan, and you have to get the work done somehow, especially if you have had some unplanned openings in full-time positions. If the higher T&E spending is related to the higher workload, this may be appropriate as well. If it is for non-client, non-project specific work, then you would want to explore further.

Internal charges are basically on plan (.8% over), with legal being the only item over budget.

So, the year-to-date results are very encouraging! It looks like you are on track to exceed plan for net income by at least $24,000 (conservative estimate with income 2% over plan and expenses 1% over plan) because of stronger than expected business unit demand. Since the plan was to break even, this means you would end the year with a net income of $24,000 instead of $0. Your net income is running $50,000 ($98,700 - $48,000) higher than this time last year, so that provides further confidence that you will end the year better than last year.

Last, look at monthly performance. Here we want to see whether the last month's performance is in line with the year-to-date results or whether it looks like a new trend might be emerging, which would cause us to reconsider our rosy forecast about ending the year above plan. Unfortunately, monthly data tends to be very volatile and may provide false signals, especially if you are on a cash basis. Still, if a number seems out of line or troubling, you would want to research it.

In our example, June had a loss of $20,000, which seems out of line with our forecast of beating the plan for the year. Note, though, that the plan was for a loss of $6,600, and last June there was a loss of $10,100. So, the seasonal pattern is at work here, and a loss is the norm for June. Either income always is off in June or expenses always run high or both. Still, the loss is $13,400 higher than plan, so we need to understand why.

The primary culprit is expenses, which are $11,400 or 5.5% over plan. Within expenses, the problem is IM&E, specifically consultants and T&E. Consultant expenses were $5,700 or 15.2% over budget, and T&E was $4,100 or 82% over plan. Just like in the YTD analysis above, we need to understand why these two items are over plan. June income is actually under plan by $1,900, so the extra costs were not for work booked in June. There could be a timing issue, however, especially if you are on a cash basis. Perhaps the higher consultant and T&E spending were for work done earlier in the year, but the bills were just paid in June.

Labor and related expenses were just about on plan for the month (+.9%). L&R, though, was *under* budget versus the YTD results and is over for the month of June, so the trend of below plan L&R may be reversing. Full-time L&R costs for the month were only 1.8% below plan versus YTD of 5.2% below plan, and part-time L&R costs were 12.7% over plan versus 8.3% for YTD. If this trend continues, the YTD lower spending for L&R could be reversed by year end.

The Labor Rate and Fully-Burdened Labor Rate

The labor and related rate and the fully-burdened labor and related rate are two of the most important rates or costs for a learning manager to know. The first plays a major role in understanding the cost structure of the department, and the second is essential to quote project costs and allocate total costs.

The Labor Rate

Since labor costs will likely be the single largest cost in the department, understanding these costs is critical to managing the function well.

Hourly Rate for Labor

The labor rate is simply the hourly rate of pay. For a single employee it is the person's hourly pay or, if the employee is on a salary, the annual pay divided by the number of hours in a year for which he is paid, usually 2,080 (52 weeks x 40 hours per week = 2,080 hours in a year).

TABLE 1.9: **Calculation of Hourly Labor Rate Where All Employees Are Full-Time**

	Hourly Rate	*Annual Hours*	*Annual Salary*
Employee 1	$8.00	2,080	$16,640
Employee 2	$8.00	2,080	$16,640
Employee 3	$15.00	2,080	$31,200
Employee 4	$10.50	2,080	$21,840
Employee 5	$25.00	2,080	$52,000
Employee 6	$12.00	2,080	$24,960
Employee 7	$22.00	2,080	$45,760
Employee 8	$28.00	2,080	$58,240
Employee 9	$18.00	2,080	$37,440
Employee 10	$40.00	2,080	$83,200
Total		20,800	$387,920
Simple Average	$18.65	2,080	$38,792
Weighted Average	$18.65		

For a group of people with different salaries or hourly rates, it represents the weighted average of their pay (weighted by hours). It is calculated by dividing the total labor costs by the total hours. For example, if a department spends $387,920 per year on labor for its ten employees, all of whom work standard weeks and are paid for 2,080 hours per year (vacation, holidays, and sick days are paid), then the labor rate for the department is $18.65 per hour ($387,920/20,800 hours). Table 1.9 illustrates this simple case, in which $18.65 per hour is both the simple and weighted average. (Simple average is just the sum of the ten hourly rates divided by ten.)

In this simple case the average hours are just 2,080 (since everyone together worked 2,080 hours), and the average salary is $38,792. Notice that the range in salary, however, is quite large, from a low of $16,640 to a high of $83,200.

When some employees are part-time (or some full-time employees work fewer than forty hours per week), the weighted average labor rate diverges from the simple average rate. In Table 1.10 the labor rate equals $20.75 ($345,280/16,640 hours) and is no longer the simple average of the ten rates. The $20.75 rate is

TABLE 1.10: **Calculation of Hourly Labor Rate Where Some Employees Are Part-Time**

	Hourly Rate	*Annual Hours*	*Annual Salary*
Employee 1	$8.00	1,040	$8,320
Employee 2	$8.00	520	$4,160
Employee 3	$15.00	2,080	$31,200
Employee 4	$10.50	2,080	$21,840
Employee 5	$25.00	2,080	$52,000
Employee 6	$12.00	1,040	$12,480
Employee 7	$22.00	2,080	$45,760
Employee 8	$28.00	2,080	$58,240
Employee 9	$18.00	1,560	$28,080
Employee 10	$40.00	2,080	$83,200
Total		**16,640**	**$345,280**
Simple Average	**$18.65**	**1,664**	**$34,528**
Weighted Average	**$20.75**		

the one to use and the one that will be printed in corporate reports. The rate is "weighted" by the hours worked for each employee. Since employees with the higher hourly rates worked more hours (they are all full-time), the weighted average labor rate is higher than the simple average. With some employees now working part-time, the average hours worked per year has decreased to 1,664, and the average salary has also decreased to $34,528.

Since the focus is on the weighted average, from now on the weighted average will be shown as the total. Just remember that the total hourly rate is a weighted average and will be sensitive to changes in both the rates and hours for individual employees.

In larger learning functions, there will be several subgroups. One may focus on design and development while another focuses on delivery. There may be a separate technical support group or a customer relations group. Or the learning department may be organized into colleges with one for sales, one for business, and so forth. These subgroups are likely to have different labor rates. Table 1.11 illustrates a department with two subgroups, each with five employees. Notice the

TABLE 1.11: **Calculation of Hourly Labor Rates with Subgroups**

		Hourly Rate	*Annual Hours*	*Annual Salary*
Group 1	Employee 1	$8.00	1,040	$8,320
	Employee 2	$8.00	520	$4,160
	Employee 3	$15.00	2,080	$31,200
	Employee 4	$10.50	2,080	$21,840
	Employee 5	$25.00	2,080	$52,000
	Subtotal	**$15.07**	**7,800**	**$117,520**
Group 2	Employee 6	$12.00	1,040	$12,480
	Employee 7	$22.00	2,080	$45,760
	Employee 8	$28.00	2,080	$58,240
	Employee 9	$18.00	1,560	$28,080
	Employee 10	$40.00	2,080	$83,200
	Subtotal	**$25.76**	**8,840**	**$227,760**
	Total	**$20.75**	**16,640**	**$345,280**

tremendous difference between the two subgroups. Group 2 has an hourly labor rate of $25.76, more than $10 an hour greater than group 1. Consequently, group 2 will have to recover a lot more revenue than group 1 to break even.

The total hourly rate for the department is unchanged at $20.75.

Hourly Rate for Labor and Related

Since related expenses can be 25–50% or more of base salary (labor expense), most analyses of labor costs are made using the labor and related expense. Recall that related includes all the other costs directly associated with employment, such as employer-paid taxes on employees, health care, pension accrual or employer match, vacation and sick day pay, and perhaps bonuses. These costs can quickly add up, and they vary directly with the number of employees and/or their salaries or hours worked.

TABLE 1.12: **Calculation of Hourly Labor & Related Rates with Subgroups**

		Labor Costs			*Related Costs*		*Total Labor & Related*	
		Hourly Rate	*Annual Hours*	*Annual Salary*	*$*	*% of Salary*	*Costs*	*Hourly Rate*
Group 1	Employee 1	$8.00	1,040	$8,320	$1,248	15.0%	$9,568	$9.20
	Employee 2	$8.00	520	$4,160	$416	10.0%	$4,576	$8.80
	Employee 3	$15.00	2,080	$31,200	$7,176	23.0%	$38,376	$18.45
	Employee 4	$10.50	2,080	$21,840	$4,586	21.0%	$26,426	$12.71
	Employee 5	$25.00	2,080	$52,000	$13,520	26.0%	$65,520	$31.50
	Subtotal	**$15.07**	**7,800**	**$117,520**	**$26,946**	**22.9%**	**$144,466**	**$18.52**
Group 2	Employee 6	$12.00	1,040	$12,480	$1,872	15.0%	$14,352	$13.80
	Employee 7	$22.00	2,080	$45,760	$10,982	24.0%	$56,742	$27.28
	Employee 8	$28.00	2,080	$58,240	$16,307	28.0%	$74,547	$35.84
	Employee 9	$18.00	1,560	$28,080	$5,616	20.0%	$33,696	$21.60
	Employee 10	$40.00	2,080	$83,200	$33,280	40.0%	$116,480	$56.00
	Subtotal	**$25.76**	**8,840**	**$227,760**	**$68,058**	**29.9%**	**$295,818**	**$33.46**
	Total	**$20.75**	**16,640**	**$345,280**	**$95,004**	**27.5%**	**$440,284**	**$26.46**
	Average	**$18.65**	**1,664**	**$34,528**	**$9,500**		**$44,028**	**$23.52**

Organizations typically produce monthly reports showing labor and related expenses along with number of employees, hours worked, and the labor rates. Table 1.12 is an example that extends Table 1.11 by adding the related labor costs. In this case related costs represent 27.5% of direct labor costs (salaries) for an additional expense of $95,004. Total labor and related costs are $440,284 for an hourly rate of $26.46. (Average shows the simple average for comparison.)

This is what your labor is truly costing. Group 2 has an hourly labor and related rate of $33.46, almost twice the rate of group 1. As a manager you will need to be sure that group 2 is worth the additional $15 an hour. If you charge for services, be sure you can recover the higher costs for group 2.

The Fully-Burdened Labor Rate

As a learning manager, you will often have to estimate the expense of a learning program or allocate costs among different programs. In both cases, your goal is to identify all the relevant costs and allocate them correctly. Some are relatively simple, such as the cost to hire a consultant or rent a classroom. It is easy to estimate the actual cost and to attribute that cost to a particular program, project, or client. Generally speaking, labor costs and the rest of your overhead costs are much trickier.

The fully-burdened labor rate is the key to success here. "Fully-burdened" simply means that all non-project specific overhead costs have been added in. In other words, the labor and related rate has been "burdened" by overhead costs to provide a more complete picture of your costs. It is meant to answer the following questions:

> "How much do we have to charge per hour to recover all of our costs?" ("What is our billable rate?")
>
> or
>
> "What hourly rate should we use to allocate all of our expenses to programs?'

So, if you are quoting a project or estimating its expense, these are the steps to take:

1. Forecast the number of hours of staff time required.

2. Multiply by the fully-burdened labor rate.
3. Add project specific costs like use of a vendor for development or delivery, materials, and classroom rental.

If you are trying to allocate all of your costs by program, the steps are similar:

1. Allocate hours by program.
2. Multiply by the fully-burdened labor rate.
3. Add project-specific costs like the use of a vendor for development or delivery, materials, and classroom rental.

We will start with the labor and related costs and then add in the overhead costs.

Calculation of Billable or Attributable Hours

It is unlikely that the labor and related rate calculated in the last section ($26.46) will allow you to recover (or attribute) all of your labor and related costs. This is because all of your employees will not be able to bill or attribute all of their hours to client or project work. Even those employees in "production" (design, development, and delivery) will not be able to work on a client's project forty hours per week, every week. From time to time they will take vacation or call in sick. Every country has a number of national holidays, and many regions celebrate other holidays as well. Employees have to attend staff meetings, write goals, and have regular performance evaluations—all of which take time. Ideally, they will participate in learning themselves, and this could be another forty hours per year or more.

Leaders may spend only a part of their time involved with specific projects. The rest may be spent setting goals, coaching, providing feedback and taking part in higher level staff meetings. Employees in support functions such as accounting, marketing, HR, and LMS are not working directly on specific learning programs, and none of their time may be billable.

So, the first step in setting a rate to recover labor and related costs is to determine your billable or attributable hours. How many hours can the learning staff dedicate to actual project work for your internal or external clients? Allow for all the factors described above. Table 1.13 shows how the hours might be calculated.

TABLE 1.13: **Calculation of Attributable Hours**

		Annual	*Not Attributable to Client or Project Work*								*Attributable Time*	
		Hours	***Holidays***	***Vacation***	***Sick***	***Meetings***	***Training***	***Perf Mgt***	***Support***	***Total***	***Hours***	***%***
Group 1	Employee 1	1,040	0	0	0	80	30	24	0	134	906	87%
	Employee 2	520	0	0	0	40	20	24	0	84	436	84%
	Employee 3	2,080	88	120	24	100	40	24	200	496	1,584	76%
	Employee 4	2,080	88	80	24	200	40	24	0	356	1,724	83%
	Employee 5	2,080	88	120	24	150	40	108	300	830	1,250	60%
	Subtotal	**7,800**	**264**	**320**	**72**	**470**	**170**	**204**	**400**	**1,900**	**5,900**	76%
Group 2	Employee 6	1,040	0	0	0	80	30	24	50	184	856	82%
	Employee 7	2,080	88	160	24	120	40	24	200	656	1,424	68%
	Employee 8	2,080	88	120	24	150	60	24	500	966	1,114	54%
	Employee 9	1,560	88	80	24	100	30	24	0	346	1,214	78%
	Employee 10	2,080	88	160	24	200	30	120	750	1,372	708	34%
	Subtotal	**8,840**	**352**	**520**	**96**	**650**	**190**	**216**	**1,500**	**3,524**	**5,316**	60%
Total		**16,640**	**616**	**840**	**168**	**1,120**	**360**	**420**	**1,900**	**5,424**	**11,216**	**67%**
Average		**1,664**	**62**	**84**	**17**	**112**	**36**	**42**	**190**	**542**	**1,122**	**71%**

Notice that the non-billable or nonattributable hours differ by employee. Part-time employees may not be eligible for vacation, holiday, or sick pay and will probably spend less time in meetings. In this example several employees provide general support. Since it is a small group, there is not a full-time accountant or marketing or HR person. The leader of group 1 is employee 5, and the leader of both group 2 and the whole department is employee 10. Both must dedicate more time to performance management and to overall support activities such as marketing, budgeting, financial review, and coordination with other departments.

For the department in total, 67% or two-thirds of their time is attributable to specific clients or projects. Conversely, 5,424 hours or 33% of the total hours are not attributable. If you need to recover your costs, that means you can only bill for the 11,216 hours that are attributable, *and* you will have to increase your rate on those 11,216 hours enough to cover the cost of labor and related for the other 5,424 hours you cannot bill.

A range of 60–80% for attributable or billable hours would be reasonable for a learning function. It becomes very difficult to push the ratio above 80% because of all the factors we have considered. A ratio below 60% may force your hourly rate to be quite high and may invite questions about nonproductive time.

Calculation of Attributable and Nonattributable Labor and Related Costs

Once the attributable time has been calculated, the total labor and related costs can be divided between those that are attributable to specific clients or projects and those that are not. Table 1.14 applies the percentage of attributable time from Table 1.13 to the labor and related cost by employee to calculate the total that is and is not attributable. For example, employee 1 is expected to spend 87% of his time on project work. His total salary ($9,568) is multiplied by the 87% attributable ratio to calculate the salary attributable to projects ($8,335). The hourly rate is found as the attributable salary ($8,335) divided by the attributable hours (906) and equals $9.20, the same as in Table 1.12. The nonattributable salary is just the total salary ($9,568) less the attributable salary ($8,335) or $1,233. The hourly rate for nonattributable time is the same. (Salary [$1233] divided by the nonattributable hours [1040 - 906 = 134] equals $9.20, the same as above and in Table 1.12.)

Notice that the group rates and the department rate are *not* the same as Table 1.12 and *not* the same for the attributable and nonattributable. The rates in Table 1.14 are different than in Table 1.12 because the hours are different. (Remember that the group and total rates will change when the hours for each employee

TABLE 1.14: **Calculation of Attributable and Nonattributable L & R Costs**

		Annual	Total	Attributable Time		Labor & Related Costs: Attributable			Labor & Related Costs: Nonattributable		
		Hours	L&R Costs	Hours	%	$	%	Rate	$	%	Rate
Group 1	Employee 1	1,040	$9,568	906	87%	$8,335	87%	$9.20	$1,233	13%	$9.20
	Employee 2	520	$4,576	436	84%	$3,837	84%	$8.80	$739	16%	$8.80
	Employee 3	2,080	$38,376	2,584	76%	$29,225	76%	$18.45	$9,151	24%	$18.45
	Employee 4	2,080	$26,426	1,724	83%	$21,903	83%	$12.71	$4,523	17%	$12.71
	Employee 5	2,080	$65,520	1,250	60%	$39,375	60%	$31.50	$26,145	40%	$31.50
	Subtotal	**7,800**	**$144,466**	**5,900**	**76%**	**$102,675**	**71%**	**$17.40**	**$41,791**	**29%**	**$22.00**
Group 2	Employee 6	1,040	$14,352	856	82%	$11,813	82%	$13.80	$2,539	18%	$13.80
	Employee 7	2,080	$56,742	1,424	68%	$38,847	68%	$27.28	$17,896	32%	$27.28
	Employee 8	2,080	$74,547	1,114	54%	$39,926	54%	$35.84	$34,621	46%	$35.84
	Employee 9	1,560	$33,696	1,214	78%	$26,222	78%	$21.60	$7,474	22%	$21.60
	Employee 10	2,080	$116,480	708	34%	$39,648	34%	$56.00	$76,832	66%	$56.00
	Subtotal	**8,840**	**$295,818**	**5,316**	**60%**	**$156,456**	**53%**	**$29.43**	**$139,362**	**47%**	**$39.55**
Total		**16,640**	**$440,284**	**11,216**	**67%**	**$259,131**	**59%**	**$23.10**	**$181,153**	**41%**	**$33.40**
Average		**1,664**	**$44,028**	**1,122**	**71%**	**$25,913**	**59%**		**$18,115**	**41%**	

change because they are weighted averages.) For group 1 the rate for attributable labor and related is $17.40 versus $18.52 in Table 1.12 and versus $22.00 for nonattributable in Table 1.14. For the department as a whole, the rate is $23.10 for attributable labor and related costs and $33.40 for nonattributable labor and related costs.

In this example $259,131 or 59% is attributable and $181,153 or 41% is not. The $181,153 is important because we have to find a way to recover this expense since it is not directly charged to a client or project. (Notice that the 59% attributable by dollars is not the same as the 67% attributable by hours. The 59% is calculated or weighted based on dollars and not hours, so the 59% reflects the fact that the employees with the higher salaries had fewer attributable hours.)

Calculation of Attributable and Nonattributable Overhead Costs

The next step is to determine which overhead costs are directly attributable to client or project work and which are not. Most consultant or vendor expenses should be attributable to specific projects, and you should be able to assign these expenses to a client or program. Most printing and materials may be for client-related projects. Table 1.15 shows how you might calculate these.

Internal charges generally will not be attributable to any specific project. Some IM&E items like dues, leases, and telephone also will not be attributable. Other IM&E items like printing, office supplies, and travel will likely be partially attributable. And consultants, vendors, or university partners may be entirely attributable to specific projects. In our example $172,000 or 40% is attributable and $253,000 is not. So, the $172,000 can be charged (or attributed) directly to a client, but we have to find a way to recover the $253,000, which is not charged directly to a client.

TABLE 1.15: **Calculation of Attributable and Nonattributable Overhead Costs**

		Attributable		*Nonattributable*	
	Total	*$*	*%*	*$*	*%*
Indirect Material and Expense (IME)					
Dues and subscriptions	$25,000	$0	0%	$35,000	100%
Office supplies	$30,000	$5,000	17%	$25,000	83%
Materials	$40,000	$40,000	100%	$0	0%
Printing	$20,000	$15,000	75%	$5,000	25%
Mailing/shipping	$10,000	$2,000	20%	$8,000	80%
Telephone	$30,000	$0	0%	$30,000	100%
Lease for copiers, printers	$15,000	$0	0%	$15,000	100%
Travel & entertainment	$60,000	$30,000	50%	$30,000	50%
Consultants	$80,000	$80,000	100%	$0	0%
Total IME	$310,000	$172,000	55%	$138,000	45%
Internal Charges					
Occupancy	$60,000	$0	0%	$60,000	100%
HR	$10,000	$0	0%	$10,000	100%
IT	$30,000	$0	0%	$30,000	100%
Accounting	$10,000	$0	0%	$10,000	100%
Legal	$5,000	$0	0%	$5,000	100%
Total internal charges	$115,000	$0	0%	$115,000	100%
Total Overhead Expenses	$425,000	$172,000	40%	$253,000	60%

Calculation of the Burden Rate

The $181,153 in nonattributable L&R costs and the $253,000 in nonattributable overhead costs constitute the "burden" that must somehow be recovered. The good news is that we now have all the information needed to calculate the burden rate for the department. The burden rate is simply the nonattributable costs or "burden" divided by the attributable hours. It is the burden or extra cost that must be recovered for each hour billed or attributed to recover or allocate all of your costs.

TABLE 1.16: **Calculation of Burden Rate**

Nonattributable L & R Costs	$181,153
Nonattributable Overhead Costs	$253,000
Total Burden	$434,153
Attributable Hours	11,216
Burden Rate	$38.71

For every hour charged to a client or dedicated to a project you must add $38.71 ($434,153/11,216) to the labor and related hourly rate to fully account for your non-project specific costs of $434,153.

Calculation of the Fully-Burdened Labor Rate

The fully-burdened labor rate is the labor and related rate plus the burden rate. A rate can be calculated for the entire department, for subgroups, or for individual employees. For purposes of estimating program costs and quoting projects, you will probably want to use subgroup or individual rates. For simplicity, we will start with a rate for one employee.

Rate for One Employee. Say employee 4 is going to be working on a program for a client. You estimate it will require forty hours of her time and you want to know how much to quote the client. The fully-burdened labor rate is the employee's labor and related rate of $12.71 per hour (from Table 1.12) plus the departmental burden rate of $38.71 for a total of $51.42 per hour.

Fully-burdened labor rate = L&R rate plus burden rate
= \$12.71 + \$38.71
= \$51.42 per hour

Notice that the burden rate is three times the L&R rate. If you charge less than \$51.42 per hour, you will not recover all your costs.

To finish the quote, multiply the estimated hours (forty) by the fully-burdened labor rate (\$51.42 per hour) and then add in the project-specific costs like vendors, materials, and travel. If the project-specific costs were \$7,500, the total quote would be:

Project quote = hours attributable to project x fully-burdened labor rate + project- specific costs
= 40 hours x \$51.42 per hour + \$7,500
= \$2,056.80 + \$7,500
= \$9,557

Rate for Several Employees. If several employees will work on the project, just repeat these steps for each employee and sum. Suppose employee 1 was going to put in one hundred hours, employee 3 sixty hours, and employee 5 (the leader) twenty hours. Assume specific project costs remain \$7,500.

Fully-burdened labor rate for employee 1	=	\$9.20 +\$38.71	=	\$47.91
Fully-burdened labor rate for employee 3	=	\$18.45 +\$38.71	=	\$57.16
Fully-burdened labor rate for employee 5	=	\$31.50 +\$38.71	=	\$70.21

Fully-burdened costs for employee 1	=	\$47.91 x 100 hours	=	\$4,791.00
Fully-burdened costs for employee 3	=	\$57.16 x 60 hours	=	\$3,429.60
Fully-burdened costs for employee 5	=	\$70.21 x 20 hours	=	\$1,404.20
Total fully-burdened labor costs	=			\$9,624.80
Project quote	=	\$9,625 + \$7,500	=	\$17,125

You could also calculate the weighted average rate for the team of three employees. It would be the total (\$9,624.80) divided by the total hours (180) for a team rate of \$53.47. This would answer the project sponsor's question about the labor rate she is being charged. You have quoted an average rate of \$53.47 for 180 hours of work. Remember, though, this rate is dependent on the number of hours each team member works. If it turns out the leader needs to work more hours on the project, the average (weighted) rate will rise.

Rate for a Group or Department. It is often helpful to know the rate for a group or subgroup. In the early stages of estimating costs, you may not know which employees will work on the project. You could use the rate for the whole department or for a subgroup and then refine it later if need be. Administratively, some groups prefer to have just one or a few rates. Many will have a rate for each college or each function (design and development, delivery).

In this case calculate the fully-burdened labor rate just as we did above but use the attributable group labor and related rates from Table 1.14.

Fully-burdened labor rate	=	attributable L&R rate plus burden rate
Total Department Rate	=	\$23.10 + \$38.71 = \$61.81
Group 1 Rate	=	\$17.40 + \$38.71 = \$56.11
Group 2 Rate	=	\$29.43 + \$38.71 = \$68.14

So, when you are asked what your labor rate is, here are the answers:

- The average labor rate for the department is \$20.75 (Table 1.10).
- The average labor & related rate for the department is \$26.46 (Table 1.12).
- The average fully-burdened labor rate for the department is \$61.81.

Use the first result to answer questions about salary levels along with the average salary of \$34,528. Use the second to answer questions about your total labor and related costs along with the average labor and related cost of \$44,028. Use the third to answer questions about your average billing or recovery rate.

Final Check

As a final check, make sure all the costs have been included. For the year as a whole, the costs calculated using the fully-burdened rate should equal total costs.

First, review the budget for the year:

TABLE 1.17: **Annual Budget Showing Attributable and Nonattributable Expenses**

		From Your Worksheet	
	Budget	*Attributable*	*Nonattributable*
Expenses			
Labor			
Full-time employees	$292,240		
Part-time employees	$53,040		
Total	$345,280		
Related			
Full-time employees	$85,851		
Part-time employees	$9,152		
Total	$95,003		
Total L&R			
Full-time employees	$378,091		
Part-time employees	$62,192		
Total	$440,283	$259,131	$181,153
Indirect Material Expense			
Dues and subscriptions	$25,000		
Office supplies	$30,000		
Materials	$40,000		
Printing	$20,000		
Mailing	$10,000		
Telephone	$30,000		
Leases	$15,000		
Travel & entertainment	$60,000		
Consultants	$80,000		
Total IME	$310,000	$172,000	$138,000
Internal Charges			
Occupancy	$60,000		
HR	$10,000		
IT	$3,000		
Accounting	$10,000		
Legal	$5,000		
Total internal charges	$115,000	$0	$115,000
Total Overhead Expenses	$425,000	$172,000	$253,000
Total Expenses	$865,283	$431,131	$434,153

Note that project-specific or attributable overhead costs are $172,000. You will recover these directly from the client or allocate them to direct project expenses. These project-specific costs should not be built into the fully-burdened labor rate and spread over all the team's work since you know exactly what client they are for. That leaves the rest of the expenses ($865,283 - $172,100 = $693,283) to be recovered or allocated through the use of the fully-burdened labor rate.

Now, we can check our work. We had earlier projected a total of 16,640 hours, and we estimated that 67% or 11,216 hours would be attributed to projects for clients in which we need to recover our expenses or at least account for our expenses. So, use the fully-burdened labor rate to calculate the attributable costs and then compare to budget:

Recovery from fully-burdened labor rate = attributable hours x fully-burdened labor rate = 11,216 hours x $61.81 = $693,261

The $693,261 matches the $693,283 with a rounding error of $22. If we charge the clients for the project-related overhead costs and charge out our 11,216 work hours at a weighted average rate of $61.81, we will recover all our costs. In practice, of course, you might use the rates for each individual or the rates for the two groups, but the answer will be the same. You have fully recovered or allocated all your costs.

> CATERPILLAR EXPERIENCE: We used a department-wide fully-burdened rate most often although we did calculate rates by college or subgroup on specific occasions.

Variable and Fixed Expenses

In business it is very important to distinguish variable expenses from fixed expenses. Typically, these will not be identified as such in the income statement, but the difference is critical for managing the business.

Variable Costs

A variable expense is one that changes or varies when the amount of service or product you provide changes. In manufacturing, all the inputs like steel and electricity needed to produce one additional product are variable expenses. If you decide to stop production, there are no more inputs required and thus no more variable costs. These variable costs scale up and down in response to production. In the learning arena, handout materials for a class would be an example of a variable cost. You need one set per student. If you do not schedule the class, you don't have to buy the material. If you double the number of students, you will need to double the sets. So, the cost of handout materials is proportional to the number of students. Likewise, the use of consultants or vendors to develop courses and deliver them could constitute a variable expense. As demand increases, you ask them to develop and deliver more courses. If demand drops, you scale their effort back. If demand really falls, you stop using them completely.

Fixed Costs

A fixed cost is one that does not change within the relevant time period. Thus, it is fixed or constant, and you can't get rid of it even if you want to. In manufacturing an example of a fixed cost could be a building or machinery you own and cannot or do not want to sell. Suppose demand drops unexpectedly for your product and you shut down the assembly line. You plan to restart it when demand picks up so you don't want to sell the building or the machinery in it. These are fixed costs for you—there is no way to avoid them right now (the actual costs might appear as depreciation or a lease payment). Contrast these fixed costs with your variable costs, the inputs like steel and electricity, which you do not have to incur if you stop production.

For a learning function, fixed costs could include the rent, lease, or charge for your office space, including the building, furniture, copiers, and printers if you have committed to them for a year or more. In contrast, the paper and ink for a copier is a variable cost and will reflect your usage of the copier. You may have an annual contract with a learning management system (LMS) provider, which includes a base charge and a variable rate, depending on the number of users. Then, the base charge is a fixed cost for the year, and the per-head charge is a variable cost.

Fixed and Variable Costs in Practice

Some items found on the income statement will have both fixed and variable components, so you can't tell just by looking at the name of the item. Labor and related costs are the most important here. If your staff are all full-time, permanent employees, and if you do not intend to lay anyone off involuntarily, then your labor and related costs are 100% fixed. If you have some part-time employees whose hours can be scaled up and down, then your part-time labor and related costs are variable whereas your full-time employment costs are still fixed. If you are prepared to shed (or add) full-time as well as part-time employees depending on the amount of work you get, then your labor and related costs are truly variable. You have eliminated the fixed-cost component.

Impact on Profitability

Your company, especially if it is subject to cyclical movements in the economy or rapid shifts in market share, will try to maintain a significant amount of variable expense to respond to changing market conditions, even if it costs a little more to do so in the short run. This is the only way to ensure that profit goals (cost goals for a nonprofit) can still be realized if demand suddenly declines. The following example makes this clear where variable expenses vary with income.

TABLE 1.18: **Importance of a High Variable-Cost Structure**

	Low Variable Cost Structure	*High Variable Cost Structure*
Base case: Sales of $100		
Income	$100	$100
Expense		
Variable	$30 (30%)	$70 (70%)
Fixed	$60	$20
Total	$90	$90
Profit	$10	$10
20% Drop in Demand: Sales of $80		
Income	$80	$80
Expense		
Variable	$24 (30%)	$56 (70%)
Fixed	$60	$20
Total	$84	$76
Profit	($4)	$4

With a high variable-cost structure the company in this example could sustain a 20% drop in demand and still make a profit. With a low variable-cost structure, this company would have a loss of $4. This illustrates why business managers are so concerned with fixed and variable costs.

Planning for a Drop in Demand

As the manager of the learning function, you also need to manage your variable costs strategically so that you are prepared for a sudden drop in demand. In fact, your company's leaders should demand this of you. First, you need to understand how much demand for your services may fluctuate during the year and over several years. Second, you need to understand your cost structure and know how much of your current expenses are variable in the short term (a month or two), medium term (six to twelve months), and longer term (several years). Third, you need to adjust your expense structure so that you have enough variable costs to cut expenses when necessary and to ramp up when necessary.

ADVICE: Increase your variable cost structure by:

1. Using part-time employees whose hours you can change.
2. Using consultants, vendors, or university partners to develop some or all of your content.
3. Using consultants, vendors, or university partners to deliver some or all of your instructor-led training (ILT).
4. Building a usage component into your contract with an LMS provider so your costs are not entirely fixed for the year.

Do not enter into multi-year agreements with vendors or, if you do, negotiate an escape clause that allows you to break the agreement with only one or two months' notice.

CATERPILLAR EXPERIENCE: At Caterpillar, each service center business unit like HR and learning was responsible for ensuring its variable cost structure would allow for total expenses to be reduced 25% within twelve months. At Caterpillar University we accomplished this by having a significant number of flexible employees (about 25%) who were part-time and could scale their hours up or down by using consultants and vendors to both develop and deliver learning under the supervision of Cat U program managers and by agreeing only to flexible contracts with escape provisions and a duration no longer than twelve months. The flexible employee base sacrifices some efficiency in that desks are not utilized 100% of the time, and two part-time employees do require more time to manage than one full-time employee. Likewise, we paid more to vendors for a flexible one-year contract than a binding three-year contract. Nonetheless, we gladly accepted this slight loss of short-term efficiency in order to have maximum flexibility in the event of a downturn.

Conclusion

Congratulations! You have survived the longest chapter in the book. The good news is that you now have an excellent foundation to understand and apply the concepts and recommendations in the rest of the book.

To review, here are the key points from this chapter:

1. You must speak the language of business to be successful.
2. Organizations exist to perform a mission. They will have specific goals.
3. Success is measured by comparing actual performance to goals.
4. A business plan will contain a vision, mission, and strategy along with specific, measurable goals.
5. Progress against these goals is measured daily, weekly, monthly, quarterly, and annually through scorecards and detailed reports.
6. The income statement is the most important financial statement for the learning manager. It will contain critical income and cost information, and it will compare results to budget.

7. A learning manager must understand depreciation and cash basis versus accrual basis accounting.
8. Knowing your labor costs, particularly fully-burdened labor costs, is essential for quoting projects and managing the function.
9. Understanding variable and fixed costs is also essential for managing the function successfully through downturns.
10. Remember, you do not need to be an accountant or have a degree in business to be a successful learning manager. Just understand and apply the concepts in this chapter.

Chapter 1 to Do List

1. Find out whether your organization has a business plan and a longer-term strategic plan. If so, get a copy and read it.
2. Know your organization's vision, mission, strategy, and key goals.
3. Get a copy of your organization's annual report. Read it.
4. Review your learning function's monthly reports and income statement in light of the discussion in this chapter. You should understand virtually everything on them.
5. Get to know your accountant well. Meet with her regularly.
6. Find out whether your organization is on a cash or accrual basis.
7. Find out whether your learning function's reports are on a cash or accrual basis.
8. Analyze your labor and related costs. What percentage are the related costs?
9. Calculate your fully-burdened labor costs.
10. Analyze your fixed and variable expenses. What percentage are variable expenses?
11. Create a scenario for a significant drop in demand. Are your costs flexible enough?

Further Reading

Gargiulo, Terrence with Anjay Pangarkar, et al. *Building Business Acumen for Trainers: Skills to Empower the Learning Function*. San Francisco: Pfeiffer, 2006.

Haskins, Mark. *The Secret Language of Financial Reports*. New York: McGraw Hill, 2008.

Ittelson, Thomas. *Financial Statements*. Franklin Lakes, New Jersey: Career Press, 1998.

Kaplan, Robert and David Norton. "The Balanced Scorecard—Measures That Drive Performance," *Harvard Business Review*. February 1992.

——. *The Balanced Scorecard: Translating Strategy into Action*. Boston: Harvard Business School Press, 1996.

Pangarkar, Ajay and Teresa Kirkwood. *The Trainer's Balanced Scorecard*. San Francisco: Pfeiffer, 2009. (See Chapters 1 and 2.)

Schneiderman, Arthur. *The First Balanced Scorecard*. E-book available at www.scheiderman.com, last updated August 13, 2006.

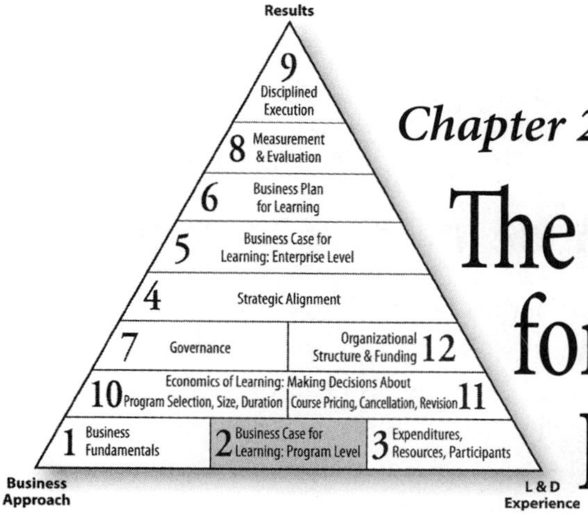

Chapter 2

The Business Case for Learning: Program Level

IN CHAPTER 1 WE focused on the fundamentals of business. An organization exists to perform a mission, and its success will be measured by how well it performs that mission. In Chapter 2 we will focus on how learning improves performance and contributes to that success. This is the business case for learning. In for-profit companies it often translates into higher net income by either increasing revenue or reducing expense. In nonprofits it may mean an increase in surplus or simply the ability to provide more services and/or to lower costs. Our goal in this chapter is to provide a framework to discuss these impacts by identifying the ways in which learning can improve performance, and then for some common learning programs, discuss the impact in greater depth. For some, we will suggest ways these might be quantified so that the mental model of learning's impact is clear, whether or not these are actually quantified in reality. (Chapter 8 will provide much more detail on the real-world quantification of benefits.) The bottom line here is that without a convincing business case for individual learning programs and for the learning function

Key Concepts for Chapter 2

2

1. An organization invests in learning to achieve goals and improve performance.
2. Learning has both direct and indirect impacts on performance.
3. Learning can impact results indirectly through higher employee engagement.
4. Learning programs may increase revenue, decrease expense, or both.
5. The business case for learning must ensure that learning will improve performance and that the benefits exceed the costs.
6. The business plan for learning is a comprehensive plan for the entire organization, including strategic alignment, the business case for all programs, detailed work plans, a discussion of resources and costs, and a budget.

as a whole, learning will never attain a "seat at the table" and never realize its strategic potential to enable and accelerate an organization's success.

Why Does an Organization Invest in Learning?

Organizations invest in learning for a variety of reasons. In some, learning is viewed as a benefit like health insurance or vacation. In these companies leaders seek to provide a "competitive" level of learning and tuition reimbursement to attract and keep desirable employees. Others may take a more philosophical approach and argue that it is just the right thing to do since people are their greatest asset. Still others seek to use learning as a way to increase employee engagement and loyalty.

Although all these reasons are valid, they should be secondary to the most important reason of all: *An organization should invest in learning to achieve its goals and improve its performance.* This means both accelerating the speed to accomplish the organization's goals and reducing the cost in money and time required to achieve them. In this way learning will contribute directly to an organization's success and will be viewed as a valued, strategic partner. As a secondary benefit, investing in human capital will also increase engagement and loyalty and, if properly designed and executed, will be seen as an important benefit by employees. It will be the right thing to do for all the right reasons.

Some organizations can certainly exist without investing in learning and, in some cases, may even be able to achieve their goals. After all, informal learning will occur spontaneously in any workplace where employees learn from each other and learn from their own mistakes. It may take a long time, but if the task is not too complicated, employees will probably figure it out eventually. Most of us have moved into new jobs without formal orientation or training, and we did figure it out. The point is that even in this case, in which formal learning or performance support is not an absolute requirement for success, an investment in learning, properly directed and managed, may enable an organization to achieve its goals faster and at lower cost. In other words, learning will improve performance.

Most organizations, however, cannot achieve their goals without some formal learning or performance support for their employees. Unlike companies in the above paragraph, these organizations may have more aggressive goals and more complicated jobs. They need skilled employees as soon as possible. Waiting for employees to acquire the required skills on their own is simply not feasible and in many cases would be prohibitively expensive. For most, there is competition, and usually a lot of it, meaning each company is looking for every advantage to get ahead and stay ahead. Speed, productivity, and cost are all important. For these organizations, the investment in learning is absolutely required for their success, and how that investment is managed can have a significant impact on their success.

> Note on Terminology: We will define learning or training programs to include formal learning, informal learning, and performance support. By formal learning we mean learning that is organized or directed by the L&D department, such as an instructor-led class or online classes or modules where there are specific learning objectives and a structured curriculum. Informal learning occurs when participants learn on their own through discovery, such as through discussions, coaching, reading, social media, networking, and knowledge sharing. The L&D department may organize or facilitate these processes by making a knowledge sharing platform available or by connecting participants with coaches. Performance support is information or guidance to help participants successfully perform a task at the time of need. It may be a simple job aid like a list of tasks with instructions or something more complicated. Performance support is sometimes the preferred solution over formal learning. Best practice would be to use whichever approach (formal, informal or performance support) best addresses the need, and often two or all three will be combined in a blended approach for maximum impact.

The Impact of Learning

In this chapter we will explore the impact learning can have on an organization's success at a conceptual level. Our goal is to establish the framework to make the business case for learning so that the learning manager can clearly articulate how learning will help the organization achieve its goals and improve performance. In some organizations this may be enough to "make the case" for learning. In other organizations some quantification of expected benefits may be required. The quantification may be at an impact level like reduction in injuries or an increase in sales, or it may be expressed as time and costs saved to accomplish the goal. In some cases, the impact may be translated directly into an expected return on investment. This chapter will focus more on the conceptual, but we will indicate how some of the benefits could be quantified and the return calculated just so we are all clear about the impact learning can have. Chapters Five and Eight will provide more detail on the actual quantification for planning and reporting.

Impact of Learning on Performance

Let us take a closer look at how the investment in learning helps a company to accomplish its goals and improve performance. Learning and development (L&D) has the potential to improve performance both directly and indirectly. Both paths are important.

FIGURE 2.1

How Learning Impacts Performance

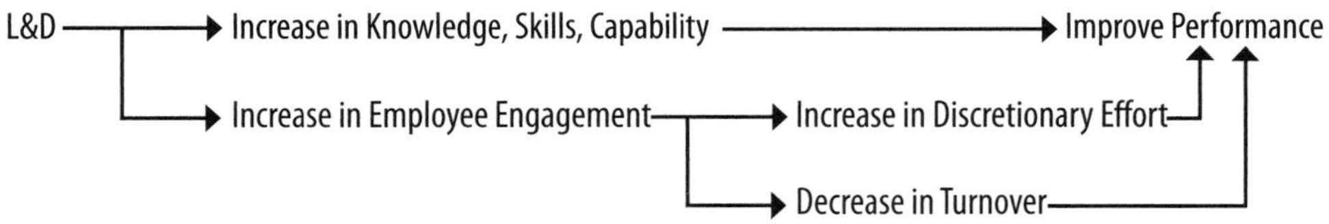

The direct path increases knowledge, skills, or capability, which leads directly to improved performance. Examples are sales learning, which leads to higher sales, safety learning, which leads to fewer injuries and less downtime, and technical training, which leads to faster and higher-quality manufacturing.

The indirect path reflects the fact that an investment in people, your employees, will improve their engagement with your organization. They will appreciate your confidence in them and feel valued, and, in turn, will identify more closely with your organization and its mission. Consequently, they are likely to work harder, provide more discretionary effort, and contribute more ideas and suggestions for improvements. This translates directly into higher production and/or lower labor costs, which means improved performance. Higher employee engagement also leads to greater loyalty and lower turnover, which means lower recruitment costs and less time lost training new hires. Once again, we have improved performance.

In this book, we will focus primarily on performance-driven, or business-centric, learning, which is aligned to the business goals of the organization and is explicitly designed to improve business performance. Talent-driven learning refers to learning which is focused solely on improving the knowledge, skills and capability of the employees, but is not directly tied or aligned with business goals. For example, in professional service companies like consultancies, law firms and auditors, both types of learning are likely to be present. Learning for the sales development staff to increase sales would be performance driven since the firm has a goal to increase sales. There will be even more learning, however, that is talent driven and aimed at increasing their overall capability. This learning is necessary to provide employees with the knowledge of how to do their work. These companies are unlikely to have an annual goal to increase the knowledge of their employees but they cannot survive without a highly skilled workforce. Of course, the more capable the employees become the more sales they are likely to generate, but this is an indirect link rather than a direct link like in the case of a sales program for the sales staff. (See Bersin for a good discussion of "performance-driven" versus "talent-driven" training, which provides additional insight into the impact of learning on organizational performance.)

Both types of learning are important and both are likely to lead to improved performance and increased employee engagement. Recently, there has been increased interest in learner-centric or self-directed learning where employees are deemed to know best what they need. The implication is that L&D should simply respond to their needs and ensure that they can find whatever they want as easily as possible within or outside the organization. This approach, however, only makes sense in support of a goal to increase employee engagement and as a supplement to formal or informal learning or performance support in support of a business goal.

Overview of Learning Programs

Now, let's look at a number of common learning programs in greater detail and be more specific about the benefit from learning. (In Chapter 5 we will discuss how to have this benefit discussion with the owner for the goal.) If learning is going to have an impact on the ultimate measure of performance in a for-profit company, namely net income or profit, then it has to increase revenue or reduce expenses. Since learning itself is a cost, it must increase income or reduce other expenses by more than its own cost to have a positive net impact on the organization. (To be more precise, the learning must actually increase income by enough to cover the cost of achieving that additional income—like the cost of goods sold—as well as the cost of the learning itself. In other words, the net income from the additional sales due to training must exceed the cost of the training in order for the training to be worth undertaking.) This is simply how leaders and good managers think. As a learning manager you need to be able to make the case in terms your leaders will understand, and that means in their terms! The same disciplined approach can be applied to nonprofits and governmental organizations, with the focus on reducing costs and accomplishing mission objectives.

(Note: In this chapter we focus on developing the business case for particular programs. For an excellent discussion of the business case for investment in learning on a national level, see the three books by Michael Echols under "Further Reading.")

The framework to make a business case for a learning program should include the following elements:

- Learning program
- Corporate goal supported by the learning program
- Primary impact of the learning on income or expense
- Planned results
- Potential for calculation of dollar impact
- Other important benefits like increasing employee engagement

All of these elements are required to think critically about the value of a learning program and to make the business case for investment in that program. Figure 2.2 provides an example for the programs, which are described in the four sections below. In practice, the direct or indirect impact on performance, the primary impact on income or expense, expected results, and the potential and difficulty of calculating impact on net income will depend on each particular situation.

Learning Programs with a Primary Impact on Income

We will start by exploring several examples of learning's primary impact on income.

Sales Training

Let's examine first how learning can increase sales or revenue, which is very often a high-priority goal. Sales or marketing related training is the obvious candidate here. A good program for your sales associates can increase their knowledge of a product and increase their ability to engage customers successfully,

FIGURE 2.2

Framework for Making the Business Case for Learning

Learning Program	*Corporate Goal*	*Primary Impact on*	*Potential To Calculate Impact on Net Income?*	*Likely to Increase Engagement?*
Sales Training	Increase sales	Income	Yes	Yes
Innovation Learning	Increase patents	Income	Yes, but more subjective	Yes
Safety Training	Reduce injuries	Expense	Yes	Yes
Technical and Professional Training	Increase effectiveness and productivity of current employees	Expense	Yes	Yes
	Reduce time to proficiency for employees new to the job	Expense	Yes	Yes
Compliance-related Training and Performance Support	Reduce probability of violations	Expense	Very subjective	No
New Hire Orientation	Reduce time to proficiency and increase engagement for new employees	Expense	Yes, but more subjective	Yes
Leadership Programs	Improve leadership	Income & Expense	Subjective, may use impact on productivity	Yes
Performance Management Programs	Increase employee performance and engagement	Income & Expense	Subjective, may use impact on productivity	Yes
Tuition Reimbursement	Increase employee competency and engagement	Income & Expense	Difficult, may use reduction in turnover	Yes
General Studies	Increase employee competency and engagement	Income & Expense	No	Yes

understand their needs, and suggest a solution to meet those needs. This, in turn, should lead to higher close rates and higher transaction prices as your sales associates do a better job of selling the value in your product or service. Your customers will be happier with the whole process and more likely to become repeat customers who recommend you to others. All of these lead to higher dollar sales.

The bottom line impact on profit will depend on the costs of those additional sales. For example, suppose sales have increased $100,000 because of your learning program. (We'll discuss how to arrive at the $100,000 in Chapter 8.) Your accountant, who is now one of your best friends, can tell you the cost of those sales. Let's say it cost $70,000 (not including the cost of the training program) to produce and sell the product that was sold for $100,000. Then, the margin on the additional sales resulting from your great learning program is $30,000 or 30%. This is how much goes to the bottom line in the form of higher profit or net income before considering the cost of the learning itself.

Now, if it cost $10,000 to train the salespeople who generated the incremental $30,000 in profit, you have a great business case for learning! For an investment (cost) of $10,000, the company can realize an increase in net income of $20,000. The net gain or improvement in profit is $20,000 or a 200% ($20,000/$10,000) return on your investment.

Innovation Learning

Another learning program targeted at increasing income is innovation. More companies are focusing on ways to help their engineers and other professionals become more innovative. These programs are meant to challenge their mental models and perhaps the existing organizational paradigms to encourage thinking outside the box. The goal, of course, is to make a discovery or create a design or come up with an idea that will give your company a competitive advantage. The business case here depends on the likelihood and potential value of the innovation. The leaders in charge of the effort should be able to help quantify both the probability and value of the innovations expected from the learning program. Then, the business case is made (or not) by comparing those values with the expected cost of the learning program. For example, suppose the learning costs $60,000 and the probability of an innovation worth $500,000 to the bottom line is 20%, making the expected value equal to $100,000 (20% x $500,000). The expected net profit from this investment is $40,000 ($100,000 - $60,000) or 67% ($40,000/$60,000) return.

Learning Programs with a Primary Impact on Expense Reduction

Next, we'll look at ways learning can reduce costs. Most learning programs fall in this category.

Safety Training

Safety training is one example and can find application to almost all organizations. Safety training teaches employees about safety in the workplace. Employees learn how to identify and avoid risks. Successful safety training will contribute directly to fewer injuries. This, in turn, will reduce the costs of health care for injured workers and reduce labor costs since a replacement will not have to be hired or paid overtime to make up for the injured employee. In some cases a serious injury may shut down an assembly line or other place of work, causing a loss in production. Your safety managers will be able to provide an estimate of the current cost of injuries, and once you agree on the reduction due to your safety training, you will have the cost reduction for your business case. Unlike an increase in sales, all of this cost reduction flows directly to the bottom line and increases profit. So, the net benefit of your safety training is simply the cost reduction attributable to training (say $100,000) less the cost of the training (say $60,000) or $40,000. The return is 67% ($40,000/$60,000).

Technical and Professional Training for Current Employees

Another example of a learning program designed to reduce costs is technical and professional training. Think of training for factory workers, trades people (electricians, plumbers, etc.), service professionals (call centers, logistics, shipping, receiving, etc.) and other professionals (engineers, etc.) where knowledge, skill, and ability are applied every day to produce and service products or provide services. Errors here lead to higher warranty costs, replacements, discounts in pricing, missed deadlines, lost customers, lost sales, and potentially to lawsuits. Errors may also lead to downstream losses if the production line has to be stopped or a product has to be recalled. Each of these entails a cost, and managers in charge of these functions are likely to have an estimate for what the errors are costing. A well-conceived and implemented training program can increase employee's skills, knowledge, and abilities and directly reduce these errors and associated costs. Once you agree on the impact learning may have, you can calculate the cost reduction attributable to learning.

Technical and Professional Training for Employees New to the Job

An important extension of technical and professional training involves employees new to a position. Here the goal is to provide them with the training they need to learn their new job and become fully effective as quickly as possible. The business case is made by comparing the "informal learning only" scenario with the "formal plus informal learning plus performance support" scenario. The benefit is the shorter time to become fully effective (meaning fewer other employees are required to cover for the new person) and fewer mistakes made until becoming fully effective. For example, it might take twelve months for an engineer to be fully effective if he has no formal learning available. The engineering supervisor can tell you that formal learning and/or performance support will cut the time to become fully effective by half, saving $20,000 in overtime costs and avoiding $30,000 in mistakes and rework. So, your training will reduce costs by $50,000 per engineer at a cost of, say, $30,000. Bottom line impact to profit will be $20,000 ($50,000 - $30,000) or a 67% ($20,000/$30,000) return.

Compliance-Related Training

A final example of a direct reduction in expense is compliance-related training. Most organizations want to protect themselves and their employees from predictable and costly mistakes. These generally include violations of law resulting from not knowing or following government or company procedures and processes. Examples here might include violations relating to discrimination, sexual harassment, affirmative action, hiring, firing and promotion practices, fraud, and insider trading. Each of these could result in severe civil penalties for the company, and some could also lead to civil or criminal complaints against the employee.

An effective compliance training program can increase the knowledge of employees about the risks and reinforce the correct procedures and processes. Some courses will also improve an employee's skill and ability in handling these situations. Performance support may also be very effective in providing guidance on the correct procedures and processes, especially when the procedures and processes are used infrequently. Thus, training and performance support will reduce the likelihood of a violation and improve an employee's skill in following the procedures and processes. A risk management officer will be able to help quantify the risk if that is not already done. Unlike injuries or errors, these violations and subsequent fines are rare. In fact, they may not have occurred yet in your company. Still, the potential cost of even a single violation is so large, it is worth quantifying it. Then the business case is straightforward. For an investment of, say, $50,000 in training and performance support you can dramatically reduce (agree on the percentage, say 90%) the chance of a violation that could cost your organization $1,000,000 in fines and legal costs plus an undetermined loss in reputation and brand value. Most CEOs would consider this $50,000 investment a bargain!

New Hire Orientation

New hire orientation is another example that applies to all organizations. A formal orientation program for employees new to the company will accelerate their acclimatization to the company and begin to build employee engagement. New hire programs typically cover the history and culture of the company; current vision, mission and goals; organization of the company; its products and services; benefits and resources; and career management and growth opportunities. Many programs include product demonstrations, plant tours, customer visits, meetings with company leaders, and plenty of socialization opportunities.

The benefits of a new hire program are large. First, it accelerates the acclimatization of the new employee and can dramatically reduce the time required for the employee to be fully effective, which represents an increase in productivity that avoids further labor and related costs. Second, the impact on employee engagement is huge. A new hire program is your opportunity to make a lasting first impression about what a wonderful place your company is to work at. And you want employees to feel good from day one about deciding to join your team. Although engagement began with the image your company portrays and continued with the application and recruiting process, a good orientation program conducted in the first month or two can create a bond between your company and new employees that can last for their entire careers. As noted before, this increased engagement will reduce costs through greater discretionary effort and through lower turnover. So, the business case for a new hire program should include the value of increased productivity and lower turnover for the new hires.

Learning Programs with Significant Impact on Both Income and Expense

Last, we will examine some important learning programs that have significant impact on both income and expense.

Leadership Training

Some programs lead to an increase in revenue and a reduction in expense. Leadership programs typically would fall into this category. Most large organizations have programs for first-time supervisors, and some have leadership programs for leaders who supervise leaders. The supervisor programs teach the fundamentals of leadership as well as company procedures, especially how to manage the performance process, including setting goals, providing feedback, evaluating performance, and determining salaries. Leaders would also learn how to conduct efficient meetings, how to form and use teams, and how to delegate effectively. Higher-level leadership programs would focus more on organizational strategy, company challenges, and leading multi-function organizations. Good leadership programs will contribute to better leaders, and even if you believe leadership talent is largely innate, most people would agree that any leader has room for improvement. A good leadership development program will accelerate a leader's development and enable her to be a more effective leader more quickly than relying solely on informal learning.

What are the benefits of a good leadership program? First, a leader should provide more effective leadership for his team. By setting better, more clearly defined goals, by managing performance better throughout the year, by delegating more effectively, by better matching employee strengths to tasks, by using teams more effectively, by communicating more clearly, and by building trust, a leader will create a more productive workplace. More will be accomplished for the same number of employees as distractions, wasted time and confusion are decreased. So, labor and related costs will be lower than they otherwise would have to be to accomplish the same amount of work. Second, in some cases, this increased productivity will translate directly into higher sales, leading to an increase in revenue. Third, good leadership is the most important driver of employee engagement. So, formal training for leaders will improve their performance as leaders, which in turn will lead to higher levels of employee engagement, which in turn will result in lower costs and perhaps higher revenue.

Some leaders will appreciate the value articulated above without further quantification. They will compare the unquantified benefit with the known cost and make a decision, whether the investment is likely to produce high enough benefits to justify proceeding. If quantification is desired, an estimate of increased productivity resulting from leadership training may be used. Since there are many other benefits, this is a very conservative approach. Reach a consensus on the productivity improvement likely from the leadership training not just for the leader but also for the leader's team. Good leadership is likely to be reflected in better and shorter goal-setting sessions, performance reviews, and staff meetings. Improvement in the range of 3–7% would be reasonable for a two to five day course. (Would you really want to conduct a leadership program if the improvement is less?) Apply the percentage to the labor and related costs for the leader and the team, which gives you the cost reduction or return from the leadership program very conservatively calculated.

Performance Management Training

Another program with similar benefits is performance management for employees. We discussed performance management above from the leader's point of view, but employees benefit from the learning as well. Although the benefit will be greater if the leader has taken it as well, there is still benefit to employees understanding better the goal-setting process, performance reviews, the feedback process, and salary determination. This type of program will increase their productivity and increase their engagement, especially if a large number of employees don't understand the current process. As with leadership, we would recommend agreeing on a conservative figure for the percentage increase in productivity and applying that to the labor and related costs of the employees expected to take the training.

Tuition Reimbursement

Tuition reimbursement, although not a single focused program like the above, can have significant impact on both income enhancement and expense reduction. Well-structured and managed tuition reimbursement programs will help ensure that an organization has the talent it needs to succeed. By making it possible for employees to get technical training or an undergraduate or graduate degree, an organization is investing in its human capital to increase productivity and its ability to identify and take advantage of emerging market opportunities. The knowledge and skills acquired through additional education should also enhance employees' ability to identify and implement cost-reduction opportunities. Moreover, investing in employees is likely to lead to greater engagement and loyalty, providing indirect benefits as well.

Although not covered further in this work, several institutions focusing on the tuition reimbursement segment have made a convincing business case for investment in learning through tuition reimbursement. Bellevue University (located in Bellevue, Nebraska) is a leader in this field. Michael Echols, Director of the Human Capital Lab and Vice President of Strategic Initiatives for Bellevue University, estimates that the ROI to a company that provides tuition reimbursement to its employees and has average employee turnover is well over 50%. (The ROI is very sensitive to the company's turnover, and if the turnover rate exceeds 35%, it may be impossible to have a positive ROI since the company cannot capture the value for those employees who are leaving.) On average, Echols believes that the ROI for tuition reimbursement is positive and attractive based on the average incremental value of a bachelor's degree in the U.S. and tuition costs similar to Bellevue's. (Source: Private correspondence with Michael Echols, February 12, 2010.) Tuition reimbursement targeted at specific courses for specific individuals should have an even higher return than open enrollment bachelors programs.

General Studies

General studies is a category of offerings often not targeted to a particular corporate objective or target audience. Many learning functions offer a number of courses, especially soft skill courses, which are of general interest. There may also be a number of technical or professional courses that are not offered in direct response to a specific corporate objective but that many employees will willingly take. A number of vendors offer suites or libraries of online courses, which the company "rents" for a quarter or a year, often with the ability to change the course offerings on a quarterly basis in response to demand.

General studies courses normally would be selected to improve employee competency and would have relevance to the audience and to the company's industry or market. In addition to building competency, general studies courses should improve employee engagement since the participants will appreciate the company's interest in them and the ability to increase their own skills.

The Impact on Employee Engagement

All of the learning programs discussed above (with the exception of compliance-related training) are expected to increase employee engagement as well as directly contribute to higher income or lower expense. In addition, learner-centric or self-directed learning utilizing resources outside the L&D department (and the company) will likely increase employee engagement. Higher engagement should lead to greater discretionary effort by employees and less turnover. Greater discretionary effort may result in higher production and increased innovation, which could lead to higher sales, but we will focus on the potential for cost reduction, which is usually a stronger case.

Higher employee engagement, everything else being equal, will lead to fewer turnovers. Engaged employees are less likely to be looking for other job opportunities and less likely to accept an offer if one is made. The costs of turnover have been well documented, and your HR professionals can help you quantify them for your organization. For many companies the cost of replacing an employee can equal a year's salary when all the costs are considered, including searching and recruiting, overtime, temporary help to perform the job until the position is filled (or lost production if the work is not performed), training for the replacement, and lost productivity until the replacement becomes fully effective, which may take several months to more than a year.

Higher employee engagement will also lead to greater discretionary efforts by your employees, which means they will work harder, longer, and more efficiently than they otherwise would. They are committed to the success of your company, and even when no one is watching, they will put more into their jobs. They have tied their own success and satisfaction to the success of the company, and they will go out of their way to help a company succeed. This means that fewer employees and less overtime are required than if engagement was lower. Your labor and related costs will be lower, perhaps significantly lower, because your employees are such hard and productive workers. Obviously, it is hard to quantify but nonetheless very real. What CEO would not want this kind of engagement? It cannot be bought, but it can be earned by, among other things, investing in training for your employees and creating an environment where learning is valued.

Since these indirect impacts are harder to value, one strategy in making the business case for learning is to add these at the end of the analysis, after you have already summarized and totaled up the value of the more direct impacts. The impact from higher employee engagement is just one final reason to invest in learning.

How About Nonprofits?

The business case for nonprofits is similar to that of for-profit companies, but there are some differences. Some nonprofits will be able to substitute "surplus" for "profit" in the above discussion to make it relevant for them. The programs described above to reduce costs in for-profit companies will reduce costs the same way in nonprofit organizations. Some nonprofits have sales and would benefit from sales training programs just like a for-profit company. Others may not have sales, but they may have fundraising. Fundraisers will respond to good training in just the same way sales people do and with similar results. There will be a higher close rate, and the transaction value (gift) will be higher, leading to more funds raised. This, in turn, is higher income and will lead to a higher surplus.

Some organizations, though, are not measured through an income statement. Government and the military are perfect examples. They have a clearly defined mission and have resource constraints, just like the private sector, but their goal is not higher profit. Government bodies strive to provide quality services in a responsive and cost-effective manner. The military strives to meet its mission objectives in the most effective and efficient manner possible. Learning, properly planned and managed, can help these organizations achieve their goals as well. Success may be measured in terms of cost reduction, higher proficiency levels, shorter time to proficiency, lower turnover, customer satisfaction, and more people served.

The Business Case for Learning

Making the Decision to Provide Learning

You should be ready now to make the business case for learning, at least at the conceptual level. Your business case will depend on the circumstances, but you will need to answer the following general questions about the proposed learning (which may include formal or informal learning and/or performance support):

1. Is it in support of an important goal, or is it required for compliance purposes?
2. Will it make a difference in achieving the goal or improving performance?
3. Is the expected benefit worth the cost?

More specifically, you need to go through the decision tree illustrated in Figure 2.3 in deciding whether to proceed. If you decide to proceed, then the business case will follow the logic you just went through.

The goal is to have you approach this as a business decision. You need to determine first what the learning is meant to address. Is it an important organization goal or not? If not, you may not want to dedicate resources to it unless it is required. If it is directed toward an important goal, can that goal be achieved

FIGURE 2.3
Decision Tree to Provide Learning

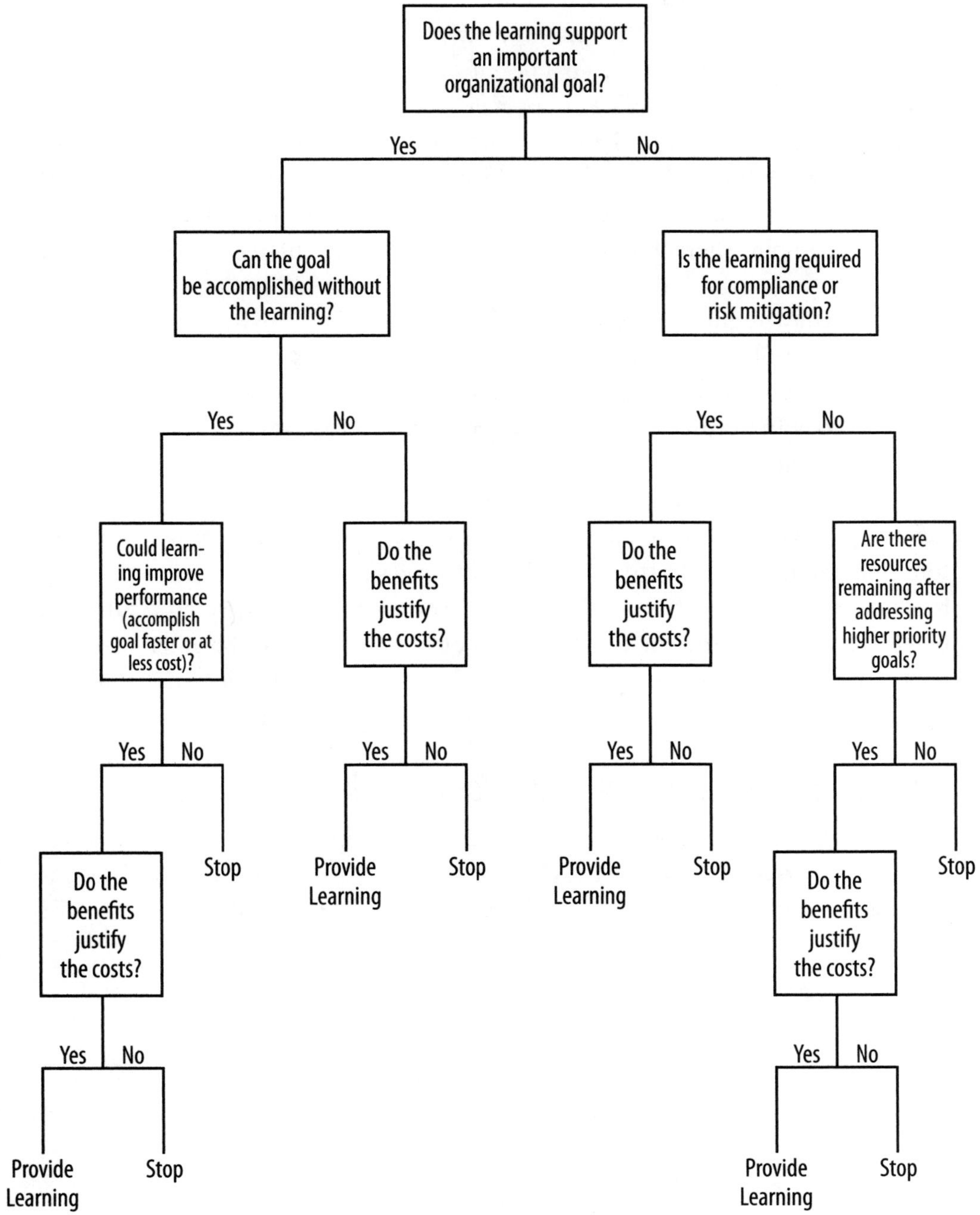

without it? If it cannot be, your business case for the learning comes down to a comparison of expected benefits and costs. You still have to determine how much learning to provide and the most effective and efficient form, but you should provide the learning as long as the benefits justify the costs. The only other alternative is for leadership to remove the goal or alter it so it can be accomplished with no formal learning or performance support.

In most cases, though, the case is not so clear-cut. There may be genuine differences of opinion about whether formal learning or performance support is really necessary and whether it would be worth the investment. Take a sales goal, for example. There will probably be some, perhaps many, in the marketing community who believe they can accomplish their goal without another learning program. They might be arguing for more sales people or higher incentives or a reorganization of regional and district offices. There will be others in marketing who believe a consultative sales program would be very beneficial and may be the only way to achieve the aggressive sales goal. In this case more work is required to make the business case. You will have to get more specific about the impact a learning program will have in terms of higher sales or market share, and you will have to project the costs for the program. You may also have to project the bottom line impact on profit from the additional sales and compare that to the costs to determine whether it is worth doing. In some cases the expected return will be very compelling and the decision will be made to proceed. In other cases the expected return may not be so favorable and the funds would be better spent on other learning with a higher expected return or perhaps not on learning at all.

An Example of a Business Case for an Individual Program

Now would be a good time to provide an example of a complete business case for one program. Assume the above process has been followed and the decision has been made to provide sales training. The following example employs the framework for making a business case presented earlier in the chapter.

Example of the Business Case for Sales Training

Learning program: A one-day instructor-led course to improve consultative selling skills and four one-hour online learning modules to increase product knowledge for our one hundred-person sales force to be implemented by February 28 and completed by April 30. The one-day course will be conducted at headquarters in Atlanta, and performance support tools will be available following the training.

Alignment to organizational goals and priority: Increasing sales by 10% is one of the top three company goals for next year.

Background: The sales organization has struggled over the past two years to attain the annual sales goals. The incentive structure was changed two years ago but did not lead to higher sales. Last year, the districts and regions reorganized to provide better coverage and be more responsive to customers. Sales did improve, but the goal was not achieved. Several new products are being introduced next year, and one-half of existing products are being updated. After meeting with all the sales leaders, the VP of marketing believes the skills, knowledge, and capability of the sales force need to be increased in order to achieve next year's goal. The learning team also talked with sales leaders, conducted a focus group of sales associates, and talked with the top ten and bottom ten performers to confirm the need for learning. In particular they need to learn consultative selling skills, and they need greater product knowledge so they can sell value more effectively.

Planned Cost: Development and delivery are projected to cost $300,000. Since the learning will be conducted in conjunction with the already planned February sales meeting, there will be no additional travel costs. Additional accommodation costs will be $550 per person for a total of $55,000. In addition to these out-of-pocket expenses, an allowance is made for the margin on the sales lost while the sales force is in learning. This is estimated to be $100,000 for a total cost of $455,000.

Planned Impact: As a result of this learning, the sales force is expected to increase the close rate for prospective customers from 30% this year to 35% next year. Also, discounts are projected to decrease from an average

7% this year to 5% next year. As a result of these performance improvements and a generally improving economy, sales volume should increase by 8% and market share should increase by 4 points. Price realization should increase 2%, and resulting dollar sales should increase 10%, thus making plan. Marketing and learning agree that all improvement in close rates will reflect the impact of learning while one-half of the improvement in price realization will be attributed to learning. Overall, about 60% of the improvement in dollar sales should reflect the impact of learning. The impact of learning on their selling skills and product knowledge is expected to last for several years, but to be conservative, the benefit will only be calculated for the first year.

***Planned Benefit and Return on Investment*:** A 10% increase in dollar sales should lead to a $1.2 million increase in net income. Learning is expected to produce 60% or $720,000 of that. The net benefit is $265,000 ($720,000 - $455,000) for a return on investment of 58% ($265,000/$455,000).

The Business Plan for Learning

So far, we have talked in terms of making the case for a single learning program. The request may have come from the goal's owner like the VP for marketing. The learning department is responding to the request for a program, and many departments find themselves in this reactive mode most of the time. In fact, many judge their success by how quickly and completely they can respond to this stream of requests that comes in throughout the year. Some departments are more proactive, and someone in the learning department suggests that learning should be undertaken to support a corporate objective. This is certainly preferable to being reactive but is still not strategic. There is no guarantee that learning resources are being directed toward the highest-priority goals of the organization.

The preferred approach is both proactive and strategic, namely the creation of an annual business plan for learning. A good organization will have a business plan for the year with strategies and goals, and so should a learning function. Just like at the organizational level, the process to create it is as valuable as the resulting document or PowerPoint presentation. The process involves the following steps:

FIGURE 2.4

Steps in the Creation of the Business Plan for Learning

1. Know your current costs, where your resources are deployed, and what they are producing.
2. Read your organization's business plan and long-term strategy. (If they do not exist or if they are not shared, you will have to get this information by asking.) Then meet with your organization's leaders, goal owners, and your governing bodies to understand the strategy, goals, and challenges for next year.
3. Within the learning function, decide which of these goals learning can support and the type of learning you would recommend. Strategically align the new, revised, or existing learning to the organization's goals.
4. Meet with the goals' owners and key stakeholders to share your thoughts on how learning can help them achieve their goals. Refine and agree on the planned learning, planned impact, benefits, and costs with them and your internal staff. This is the business case at the enterprise level.
5. Compile all of this (description of current spending, programs, target audiences, results; description of the planning process, including a list of those who have provided input; the organization's goals and the strategic alignment of learning to those goals; the business case for learning, including your recommended learning programs for next year along with planned impact, benefits, and costs; and an evaluation strategy) into a draft business plan for learning (written or PowerPoint document).
6. Share this draft plan with your governing board, senior leaders, and key stakeholders. Solicit their feedback.
7. Revise based on their feedback and any revisions to your organization's business plan for next year.
8. Get formal approval of the business plan for learning from your governing body or CEO.
9. Share the approved plan with your staff and with others in the organization.

(These steps will be covered in detail in the following chapters. Chapter 3 will cover all aspects of step 1, and Chapter 4 will discuss the strategic alignment process in detail [steps 2 and 3]. Chapter 5 will describe how to refine the expected benefits and costs to make the business case for learning [step 4], and Chapter 6 will describe the creation of the business plan itself [steps 5-9].)

The business plan for learning includes the business case and detailed work plan for each important program, but more importantly it demonstrates that learning is aligned to the organization's key goals and is dedicated to improving organizational performance. *Strategic alignment and the creation of a business plan are the most important processes of the year for the learning function.*

Unfortunately, very few learning functions go through this process and fewer yet put the results in writing. This process is mandatory if you want to be considered a strategic partner and if learning is going to have the maximum impact on your organization's success. Without such a process, the learning manager has not earned and does not deserve a "seat at the table." Period.

Now at this point, some will complain that it is too complicated, takes too much time, and requires too many meetings. For the VP of learning or the CLO, this is one of the most important aspects of your job. You must make the time for this, which may require reprioritizing your time or delegating more of your current activities. You may already be spending a lot of time throughout the year meeting with people and discussing the impact learning can have, but you may be in a reactive mode. That is not an efficient approach, and it will never be strategic. You may be able to adopt the approach we outline, actually spend less time in meetings, and produce a business plan for learning.

The strategic business planning process addresses many of the primary criticisms leveled against learning, and thus strengthens the business case for learning:

- Training is not a strategic partner. The training staff are not helping us achieve our most important goals.
- Training is not aligned to the organization's goals.
- Training has different priorities (some would say training has its own priorities).
- The training staff don't listen to us.
- No one knows where the money spent on training goes or what the goals were.
- There is no accountability. Money is not well spent.
- The return on training is nonexistent or unknown.

Without a disciplined strategic alignment and business planning process in place, is it any wonder that training is continually under fire? Your detractors are not against learning per se. They would readily admit that their formal education was beneficial and that the pursuit of knowledge and enhancement of skills is a good thing. They are not so sure about corporate or organizational training for the reasons listed above. They suspect the money is not being well spent. Very often, they would be right. Some are even openly hostile and would eliminate or significantly reduce learning budgets if they could. This is terribly unfortunate because learning can make such a positive impact on an organization.

The process described in this book, combined with disciplined, business-like execution and evaluation, will address all these complaints. In fact, learning has the opportunity to be one of the most strategically aligned, well-planned, and well-executed functions in an organization. Learning, broadly defined and properly conceived and executed, has a role to play in achieving almost any organizational objective. How many other functions can make the same claim? The potential for learning's impact on the organization is tremendous. It is time to realize that potential.

Conclusion

This chapter has established a framework for thinking about the different types of learning and the different ways learning can improve performance. Most learning programs will have a direct impact on performance by increasing income or reducing expense. Some will have an indirect impact as well by improving employee engagement. In some cases a learning program will have a quantifiable impact on the bottom line. In other cases it will not, or it will be impractical or unwise to measure it. Either way, a compelling business case should be made for the learning, clearly articulating the benefits and costs of the learning in terms that resonate with senior executives. Sometimes learning will not have a role to play in improving performance, or the cost may exceed the benefit. In other words, learning is not always the answer.

After exploring costs and strategic alignment, Chapter 5 will revisit the business case at the enterprise level.

Chapter 2 to Do List

1. How is learning viewed today in your organization? Is it seen as an employee benefit or as a way to increase employee engagement rather than a strategic contributor to the organization's success?
2. Review your learning programs and determine which have direct, indirect, or both direct and indirect impacts on organizational goals or performance.
3. How many of these impacts can be quantified? How many can be expressed in dollars?
4. Review the business case for learning logic. Do you go through a similar process currently? If not, would this work for you or can you adapt it to your needs?

Further Reading

Bersin, Josh. *The Training Measurement Book. Best Practices, Proven Methodologies, and Practical Approaches.* San Francisco: Pfeiffer, 2008.

Echols, Michael. *ROI on Human Capital Investment,* second edition. Arlington, Texas: Tapestry Press, 2005.

——. *Competitive Advantage from Human Capital Investment.* Arlington, Texas: Tapestry Press, 2006.

——. *Creating Value with Human Capital Investment.* Wyomissing, Pennsylvania: Tapestry Press, 2008.

Elkeles, Tamar and Jack Phillips. *The Chief Learning Officer: Driving Value within a Changing Organization through Learning and Development.* Burlington, Massachusetts: Butterworth-Heinemann, 2007. (See Chapters 1 and 2.)

Pollock, Roy, Andrew McK. Jefferson, and Calhoun Wick. *The Six Disciplines of Breakthrough Learning.* Hoboken: John Witey, 2015. (See Chapter 1.)

Rossett, Allison and Lisa Schafer. *Job Aids & Performance Support.* San Francisco: Pfeiffer, 2007. (See Chapters 1 and 2.)

Rothwell, William, John Linholm, and William Wallick. *What CEOs Expect from Corporate Training: Building Workplace Learning and Performance Initiatives That Advance Organizational Goals.* New York: Amacom, 2003.

Van Adelsberg, David and Edward Trolley. *Running Training Like a Business: Delivering Unmistakable Value.* San Francisco: Berrett-Koehler, 1999. (See Chapters 1–3.)

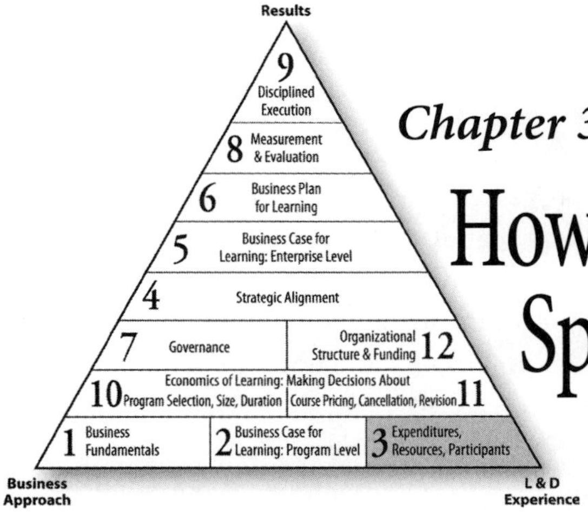

Chapter 3

How Much Are We Spending, and Where Is It Going?

THIS IS ONE of the first questions any new VP for learning should ask. It certainly will be the first question the company's chief financial officer will ask. You will not even have the opportunity to talk about the benefits of learning, let alone make a business case for learning, until you have demonstrated that you have a firm grasp on your company's current expenditures for learning. Why would anyone give you additional funds if you do not know how your existing funds are being used? The answer, of course, is that they will not. So, this must be the starting point in building the business case for learning and will be an important chapter in your business plan for learning. You need to know how much is currently being spent and what it is being spent on. You need to know how many resources are dedicated to learning, where they are, and what they are doing. And you need to know how many employees, customers, dealers, or suppliers are being served (whether or not they are benefiting from this learning is a question for Chapter 8). Finally, it would be good to have an idea about how much time participants are investing in learning.

Key Concepts for Chapter 3

3

1. Credibility depends on a thorough understanding of costs and resource allocation.
2. You will need a process to gather, organize, and present cost and resource data.
3. You will also need a process to gather, organize, and present participant data.
4. Opportunity costs are a critical but often overlooked cost of learning and should always be used in decision making.

Reader's Guide

This chapter provides considerable detail on how to gather, analyze, and present information even for complex organizations. If your application is not as complex, you can skim or skip the parts that do not apply to you. Just be sure you can generate the types of tables shown to present the information. Last, the section on opportunity costs is very important for all readers. Every learning manager needs to understand the concept thoroughly and how opportunity costs are calculated.

How Much Is the Organization Currently Spending on Learning?

Of all the questions raised above, this is the most basic. It also is likely to be the most difficult to answer. The difficulty will depend on the scope of your inquiry, the complexity of the organization, the extent of your authority, and your organization's accounting systems and practices. If you are responsible for only a portion of your organization's learning, and if that portion reports directly to you, then you should be able to answer the question about total learning costs for your own group without too much difficulty. The challenge is much greater if you are trying to answer the question for the entire organization, where there are multiple learning functions, especially when many do not report to you. We will first explore what it takes to get these costs and then how you might present them.

Getting the Costs

The easiest case will be a very small organization with one location, a centralized learning department, which provides all the learning for the organization and an accounting system (and culture) that drives all learning-related expenditures through the central learning group. As long as we are only interested in accounting-type costs (we will discuss opportunity costs below), the answer can be found by looking at the total expense line in the income statement for the learning function. The expense line items will tell you how much is spent for labor and related and how much for overhead like consultants, materials, travel, and occupancy.

Even in this simplest of all cases, though, there are still issues. Take travel costs, for example. If employees travel to attend a course, shouldn't those expenses be counted as a learning expense? Some organizations have an accounting system that allows for separate tracking of learning-related travel and entertainment (T&E), almost like a separate line item. In this case it may already be included in your total learning expenses as a line item. Or you may need to locate it on a separate report and add it in manually to your total. Most companies, however, have only one line item for travel and entertainment expenses, and this will include all of the non-learning related T&E for sales calls, supplier visits, etc. So, the accounting system will not give a complete picture of learning costs, and you may need to track the T&E for learning manually so you can add that, by hand, to the learning costs generated by the accounting system. Although this may be feasible in a small organization with one location, imagine the practical difficulties in a large, complex organization.

Most organizations, however, are more complicated than our simple case above. Even a relatively small company may have multiple locations, and even if there is a centralized learning function, it is possible that some training will occur in the remote locations that the central learning group is not aware of. Depending on how the books are kept, these learning expenditures at the other locations may not appear as expenses in the centralized learning group's income statement. They may appear in the income statement for the remote location under a line item for learning, and it may be possible to access this information directly if all locations use the same accounting system and accounting codes and if central accounting lets you have this access. If the locations do not use the same accounting system or different codes or you cannot access the system, then you will have to get the information from accounting the old-fashioned way. You will have to ask.

The next level of complexity would be a medium to large company with multiple business units in multiple locations with multiple learning functions. There is likely to be a corporate learning function at the headquarters location, but there are also numerous other learning groups around the company. Each large business unit or location probably has its own learning department, even if it is just one or two people. If authority is centralized in the corporate learning function (all other learning groups report directly to corporate learning and not their own HR department), and if all units and locations are using the same accounting system and codes, then the entire corporation's learning expenditures should roll up automatically into corporate learning's reports. In this case the income statement for corporate learning will have all the entire corporation's learning costs, including the line item detail for labor and related and overhead such as consultants, travel and entertainment, printing, etc.

Often, though, the other learning groups do not report directly to corporate learning. Instead, they report to HR, operations, or some other department within their own business unit. In this case the learning costs of each business unit or location will not be reflected in the income statement for corporate learning. And it is highly unlikely costs will be consolidated at the corporate level at the necessary functional level of detail (like for learning functions). As VP for learning you may be able to access the income statement for the learning function for each business unit, especially if all units are using the same accounting system. If that is not possible or will not work, then you will have to ask. You may also face resistance from the learning managers in those groups and possibly the head of the business unit as well. They may be reluctant to give you *their* costs and will ask why you want them and what you intend to do with them. So there could very well be some organizational issues that make gathering the data difficult.

At the far end of the spectrum are the large, complex organizations with multiple legal entities and multiple business units in multiple locations, each with its own learning function, using numerous accounting systems that are not integrated and are themselves in numerous languages. In this case there is little hope of finding the answer on one report. Instead, there will be an income statement for the entire corporation and for each legal entity, which will include a line for selling, general, and administrative (SG&A) expenses. Learning costs will be buried in this number. There will be no aggregation of learning expenses for the enterprise. You will have to create a process to gather the learning costs from all the different groups, and it will likely involve a template that they can fill in so that you get consistent information from all the different groups. A sample template is included as Appendix A, which can be used to gather information on costs, programs, resources, and participants.

> CATERPILLAR EXPERIENCE: We used a template similar to appendix A to gather information from our twenty-eight business units, each of which had its own learning budget and staff. We found that each submission had to be checked carefully, and we had to go back to many units with questions, which led to revisions. In other words, it was an iterative process that took four to six weeks.

Organizing the Costs

It will be easiest to place all the costs in a worksheet with cost items as the rows and the different learning groups as columns. The right-hand column will be the enterprise total for any given line item, and the bottom row will be the total costs for each group. This will be your data source for further analysis, comparison among groups, and for presentation.

TABLE 3.1 **Worksheet for Enterprise Cost Data**
Thousands of Dollars

		Manufacturing									
	Corporate	*BU1*	*BU2*	*BU3*	*Total*	*Marketing*	*R&D*	*IT*	*Financial*	*Other*	*Total*
Labor & related											
Full-time employees	2,600	280	210	210	700	140	140	140	70	0	3,790
Part-time employees	225	25	25	25	75	0	0	25	25	25	375
Total	2,825	305	235	235	775	140	140	165	95	25	4,165
Overhead											
Dues, fees, subscriptions	30	2	1	2	5	4	5	3	3	1	51
Materials, printing	105	18	39	17	74	26	24	7	7	3	246
Equipment leases	18	3	2	2	7	1	1	1	1	0	29
Travel	105	11	13	5	29	42	20	9	0	0	205
Consultants and vendors	720	58	63	32	153	95	22	58	11	27	1,086
Occupancy	350	30	24	24	78	20	20	30	20	10	528
Internal charges	70	10	8	8	26	4	4	6	4	2	116
Miscellaneous	15	6	8	3	17	3	2	4	1	1	43
Total	1,413	138	158	93	389	195	98	118	47	44	2,304
Total Expenses	**4,238**	**443**	**393**	**328**	**1,164**	**335**	**238**	**283**	**142**	**69**	**6,469**

This example assumes that each of the following units has a learning professional on staff and/or spends money on training outside of the corporate group: three manufacturing business units (BU) or plants, one central marketing function, a research and development (R&D) group, an IT group, and a financial group. If there is no learning provided by anyone outside your own group and if all spending for learning comes through your group, you do not need this worksheet. Your income statement should have all the data you need.

Presenting the Costs

You finally have gathered all the costs. Now you are ready to present them. You may want to start with a slide describing the process to get the cost information, which will help establish its credibility. Then you have several options for presenting the costs, depending on the amount of detail you wish to present.

How Much Is Currently Being Spent?

The first slide would be a high-level summary of enterprise-wide expenses suitable for sharing with your CEO or governing board. It might be as simple as this:

TABLE 3.2

Enterprise Learning Expenditures for 2016 (Summary)

Millions of Dollars

Labor & related	$4.2
Overhead	$2.3
Total	$6.5

This answers the question of what the organization is currently spending on learning ($6.5 million). Typically, though, you would probably want to provide a little more information to highlight some of the larger or more critical expenditures.

TABLE 3.3

Enterprise Training Expenditures for 2016 (Some detail)

Millions of Dollars

Labor & related	
Full-time employees	$3.8
Part-time employees	.4
Total	$4.2
Overhead	
Consultants and vendors	$1.1
Occupancy	.5
Materials, printing	.2
Travel	.2
Other	.2
Total	$2.3
Total Expenses	**$6.5**

This report provides significantly more detail yet does not overwhelm the reader with information. Essentially, you are providing detail on expenses over $200,000 and you have listed them in descending order so the largest expenses appear at the top of each category. (Leaders like information arranged this way—with an order to it.) Of course, the threshold will be different in every case, but try not to exceed seven or eight line items for a high-level summary. Your audience will not remember more detail anyway. The item "Other" in this example includes dues, leases, internal charges, and miscellaneous, which individually are less than $200,000.

Note: The rounding of numbers may sometimes lead to what appears to be a mistake in addition. For example, the overhead costs used in Tables 3.1–3.3 sum to $2.304 million (see Table 3.1) and are shown in Tables 3.2–3.3 as $2.3 million. However, if you add up the rounded components in Table 3.3, the sum is $2.2 million. This frequently occurs when you add numbers that have been rounded. Always use the actual total. If you worry the reader may think you have made a mistake in addition, you can add a note saying that the numbers may not add up to the sum shown because of rounding.

ADVICE: For presentation purposes, know what is standard in your corporate culture in terms of presenting numbers. For example, it may be standard practice to round the numbers and not show more than three digits. It may also be standard not to show more than one digit to the right of the decimal point. In the above example, two digits (4.6 for labor and related) are enough to convey the message. Going to three (4.58) would not have added much, and using only one (5) would lose information for the smaller expense line items like travel, which would round to zero. If we were dealing with expenses in the tens of millions (or thousands), then you might use three digits as in 46.5 with one digit to the right of the decimal point, especially if some of the line items were not in the tens like 1.7. If all your numbers are in the hundreds (but with some in the tens), then you may not need to go to the right of the decimal point at all. You would simply round to whole numbers like 245 and 57. In any case, find out what your CEO, CFO, and others like to see.

Where Is It Being Spent?

For your next slide, you may want to show a breakdown of costs by business unit or location. A report by business unit (BU) might look like Table 3.4, where the majority of spending occurs at the corporate learning function ($4.2 million), but a sizable amount still occurs out in the business units ($2.3 million).

TABLE 3.4

Enterprise Learning Expenditures for 2016 by Business Unit

Millions of Dollars

Corporate University	$4.2	66%
Manufacturing BUs		
Business Unit 1	.4	
Business Unit 2	.4	
Business Unit 3	.3	
Total Manufacturing	$1.2	18%
Marketing	$ .3	5%
IT	$ .3	4%
R&D, Finance, Others	$.4	7%
Total	$6.5	100%

In this example the percentage of the total is also shown. (Use the original data in Table 3.1 to calculate percentages, not the rounded data in this table.) This is always an option; just be careful not to put too much information on one slide. This last example could just as easily have shown regions of the world or of your country. The data in Table 3.4 could also be displayed as a pie chart.

What Is It Being Spent On?

Your chief financial officer (CFO) will be glad you now know your costs. The next question is likely to be: "What is the money being spent on?" If he asks for something specific, you can certainly try to provide that. More often, though, he will not know exactly what he wants. It is your job to present information in a meaningful way and that will either answer the CFO's question or help him be more specific. A good place to start is by providing information by program. For example, how much is being spent on leadership programs, safety programs, and sales programs? Since some of the costs (like for a learning management system or LMS) support all programs, you may want to show these separately. You also may need a general studies category to collect the program or course costs, which are not included in the selected programs. (It is like the "other" or miscellaneous category.)

Getting the Program Costs

The challenge here may be more difficult than getting the accounting data above. It will be easier if you have organized the corporate function into colleges focused on the critical program areas. For example, many corporate universities have a leadership college and a sales or marketing college. Some have engineering, IT, technical and manufacturing colleges. (See Figure 3.1 for an example.) Even if they are not called colleges, many learning functions are organized around programs. If these colleges or program focus areas have been assigned distinct accounting codes, then the accounting system should generate income statements for each college, and you will at least know the program breakdown for your central learning function. You may still have one or two categories not attributed to a program area, such as costs of the LMS or the costs of the CLO's office (call this administrative). Just make sure these are not large compared to the program costs.

FIGURE 3.1

Typical Organizational Structure for a Programs-Based Corporate University

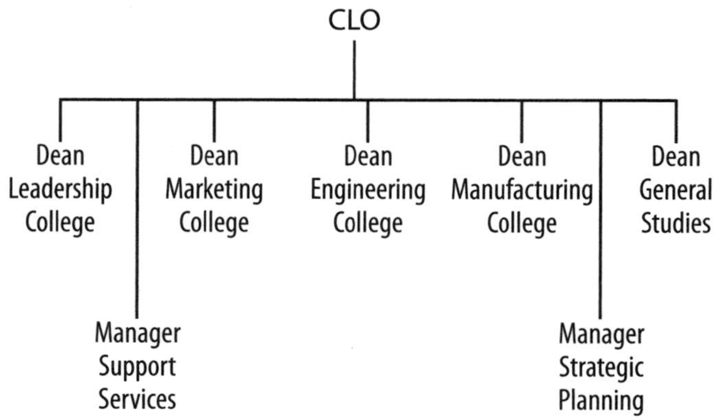

Note: *Dean may also be called Director or Program Manager*

FIGURE 3.2

Typical Organizational Structure for a Functional-Based Corporate University

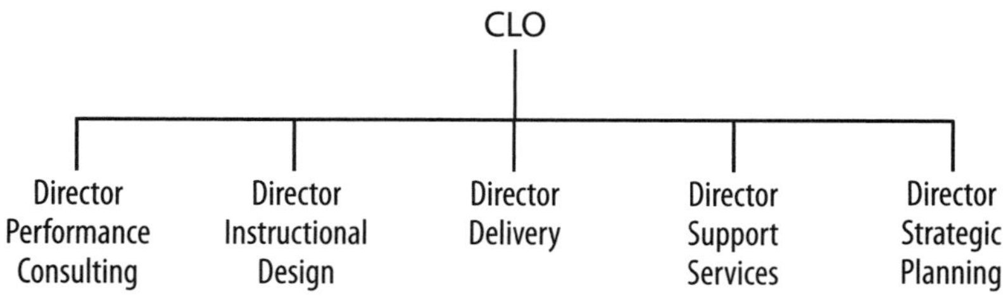

If you are not organized by program area but by function (like performance consulting, design, and delivery in Figure 3.2), then you will have to estimate the costs dedicated to the different programs. Start with the total costs for your group. Subtract the general support costs that cannot be attributed to any program like the LMS or office of the CLO (CLO, administrative assistant, and their expenses).

TABLE 3.5
Determination of Corporate Costs to Be Allocated
Thousands of Dollars

Total Costs	$4,238
Less Administrative	
LMS	100
Office of CLO	300
Total Administrative	$400
Costs to Be Allocated	$3,838

Apportion the remainder among the program areas based on the number of employees assigned to those programs or some other readily available indicator of costs. In the following example the percentage of staff time dedicated to each program (like 2.7/28.5 = 9.5% for leadership) is multiplied by the total cost to be allocated ($3,838) to find the program cost ($364 for leadership):

TABLE 3.6
Allocation of Corporate Program Costs

Programs	*Staff*	*Percent of Total*	*Allocated Cost (Thousands of $)*
Leadership	2.7	9.5	$364
Marketing	3.7	13.0	498
Engineering	2.3	8.1	310
Safety	2.8	9.8	377
Technical Skills	7.9	27.7	1,064
Compliance	1.6	5.6	215
General Studies	7.5	26.3	1,010
Total	28.5	100.0	$3,838

In this example the staff count included part-time employees and allows for a person's time to be split among programs. The CLO and her administrative assistant were not included since their costs are not included in the $3,838,000. Also note that Tables 3.5 and 3.6 are examples of your internal worksheets, not slides for presentation.

If vendor costs are substantial, and since you probably know exactly which programs they worked on, you could improve the accuracy of program cost allocation by subtracting the total vendor expenses out to calculate costs to be allocated and then add them back in program by program:

TABLE 3.7
Determination of Corporate Costs to Be Allocated
(with significant vendor costs)
Thousands of Dollars

Total Costs	$4,238
Less Administrative	
LMS (a vendor)	100
Office of CLO	300
Total Administrative	$400
Less Other Vendor Costs	$620
Costs to Be Allocated	$3,218

TABLE 3.8
Allocation of Corporate Program Costs
(with significant vendor costs)

Programs	*Staff*	*Percent of Total*	*Allocated Cost (1,000$)*	*Vendor Cost (1,000$)*	*Total Cost (1,000$)*
Leadership	2.7	9.5	$306	$58	$364
Marketing	3.7	13.0	418	74	492
Engineering	2.3	8.1	261	53	314
Safety	2.8	9.8	315	63	378
Technical Skills	7.9	27.7	891	179	1,070
Compliance	1.6	5.6	180	32	212
General Studies	7.5	26.3	846	162	1,008
Total	28.5	100.0	$3,218	$620	$3,838

Now you have costs by program for your own learning function. If there are no other learning groups in the organization and all learning dollars are controlled by your group, you are done. If there are other learning groups whose costs are not reflected in your own income statement, then you will have to collect the program information from them. You can collect this information in the same template you used to collect the cost data. (See Appendix A.) You will need to decide which program areas to ask about. Do not ask for more than ten because it becomes too difficult and the data will be less meaningful. For example, you might choose leadership, safety, technical skills, sales, engineering, IT, business acumen (understanding business fundamentals and how to apply them in your organization to make better decisions), soft skills (team building, writing), and all other. You will have to define each of the program areas carefully so the learning professionals in the field know what to include. Provide examples of programs you know are being conducted. In particular, define something like soft skills carefully so they know what goes in it and what goes in "all other."

To help them allocate their total costs, you might suggest they allocate staff time as in Table 3.6 or 3.8 or look at attendance records for the classes. They also may need an administrative category, but be sure to define what they can include in it. Their job is to apportion their total expenditures into these ten or eleven program or administrative areas, just like you did at the corporate level. You may also want to provide them a worksheet to save time and improve consistency.

> ADVICE: Consistency is critical when other groups are filling out the template. Be sure to provide clear guidelines and definitions. Also, provide them with a list of all known learning initiatives and the program or category you want them placed in. Share your draft template with the other learning groups and ask for their feedback before finalizing. They will suggest improvements. The extra time spent setting up and communicating the template will save considerable rework later and vastly improve the quality of the data.

Once the learning groups send you their program costs, you will have to review them for reasonableness and to make sure the components add to the total. You may have to go back to them for clarification and additional information. You will also learn what improvements to make so next year's cost-gathering exercise goes more smoothly.

Organizing the Program Costs

The final step is adding up all the costs by program from the learning groups and then adding them to your own corporate university costs. Here you might have a worksheet with the programs as rows and the learning groups as columns. The right-hand column will be the enterprise total by program, and the bottom row will be the total spending by each learning group.

TABLE 3.9: **Worksheet for Program Costs**

Thousands of Dollars

		Manufacturing									
	Corporate	*BU1*	*BU2*	*BU3*	*Total*	*Marketing*	*R&D*	*IT*	*Financial*	*Other*	*Total*
Program											
Leadership	364	40	30	35	105	40	15	32	41	13	610
Marketing	492	0	0	0	0	184	0	0	0	0	676
Engineering	314	18	15	15	48	0	93	0	0	0	455
Safety	378	96	99	69	264	0	17	0	0	9	668
Technical Skills	1,070	134	105	103	342	0	18	166	33	18	1,647
Compliance	212	33	38	25	96	30	25	25	32	10	430
General Studies	1,008	62	51	36	149	59	50	35	36	19	1,356
Total Program	3,838	383	338	283	1,004	313	218	258	142	69	5,842
Administrative	400	60	55	45	160	22	20	25	0	0	627
Total	4,238	443	393	328	1,164	335	238	283	142	69	6,469

Presenting the Program Costs

You are ready to present learning expenditures by program. Typically, this would be done with pie charts showing the program, dollar amount, and percentage of total. One pie chart might be sufficient to show costs for the entire organization.

FIGURE 3.3

Enterprise Program Costs (pie chart)

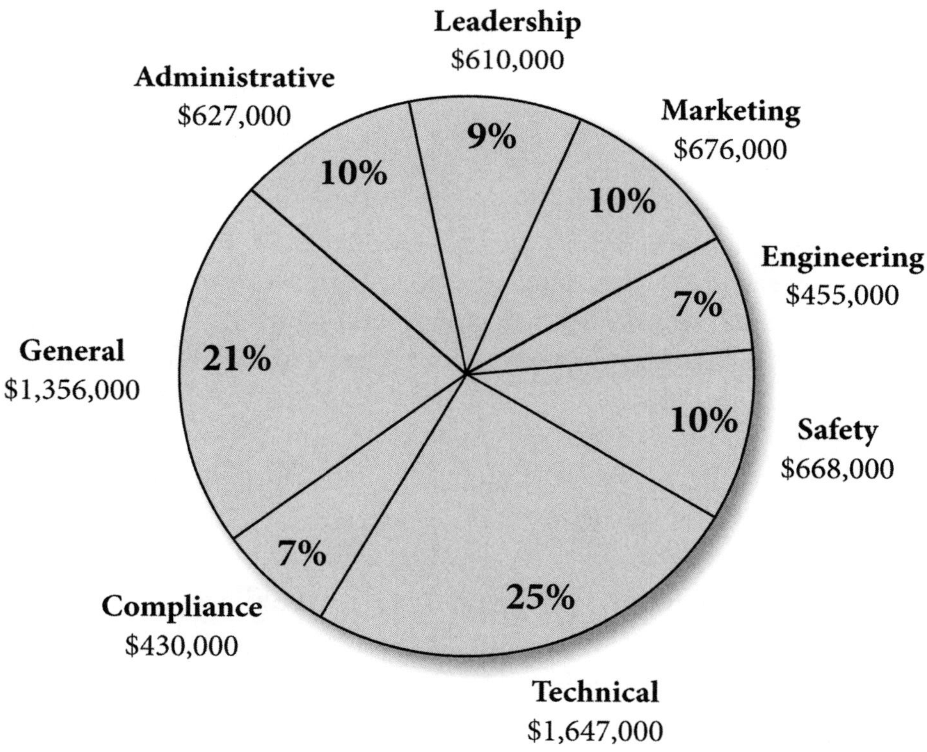

If it is too complex for a pie chart, then a simple table with percentages will work as well.

TABLE 3.10
Enterprise Program Costs (table)

Programs	*Thousands of $*	*Percentage*
Leadership	$610	9%
Marketing	676	10
Engineering	455	7
Safety	668	10
Technical	1,647	25
Compliance	430	7
General	1356	21
Administrative	627	10
Total	$6,469	100%

You might also want to show program spending in a stacked bar chart with the bottom of each bar representing the corporate university expenditure and the top part the sum of the other learning groups (see Figure 3.4). This is an easy way to show both the total spending for each program and the proportion between corporate and the business units.

If you had only two or three business units, you might show each individually on the stacked bar chart. Avoid showing more than three or four contributors on the bar chart because it will become too busy.

How Many Resources Are Dedicated to Learning?

This is likely to be the third question from the CFO. And it probably was the second question you asked when you became CLO, right after asking how much the organization is currently spending on learning. All organizations manage their headcount carefully, so it is critical to know how many employees are engaged in learning. Like costs, it is not as simple as it first appears. In addition to full-time employees there may be part-time employees who will provide much greater flexibility for you (and increase your variable rather than fixed costs). So, it will be important to distinguish between the two. You also may want to break out consultants and partners who are performing work that otherwise would be

FIGURE 3.4

Enterprise Program Costs (stacked bar chart)

(Thousands of Dollars)

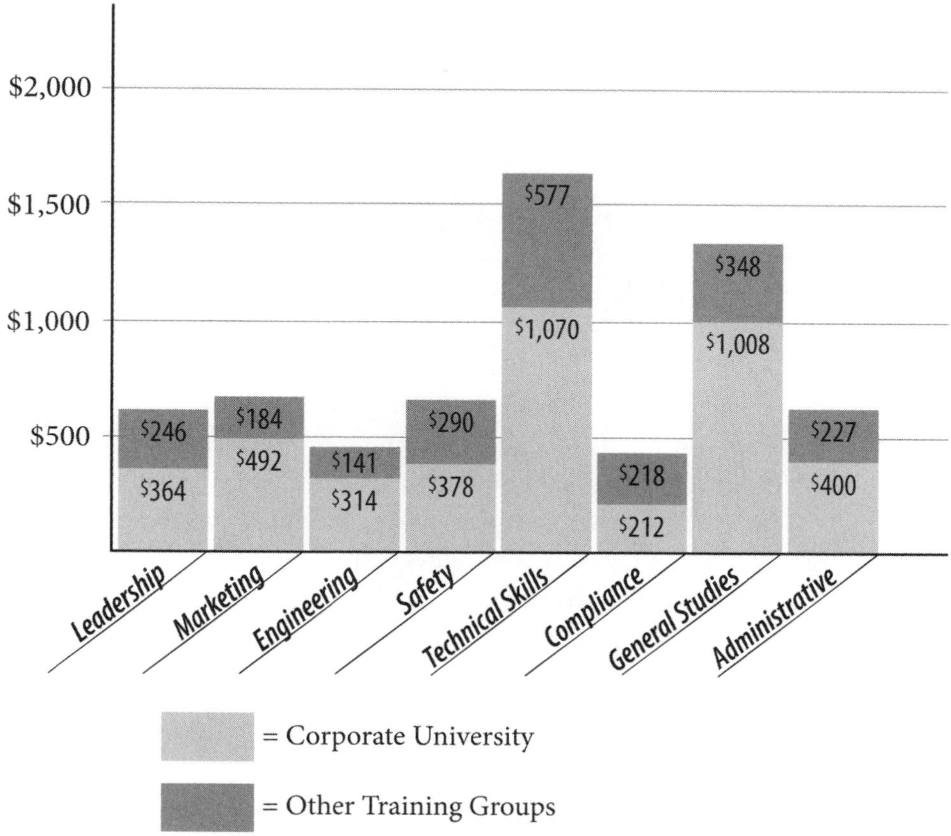

performed by full- or part-time employees. This is especially true if you are working to increase your variable cost structure and want to highlight that.

Getting the Resource Data

Most organizations have a system (or systems) for tracking and reporting employment. It may be integrated with the financial reporting or be a separate system. In any case, employment reports should be available at least on a monthly if not real-time basis. So, you will have employment information for your own learning group. You may not have access to the same data for the other learning groups in your organization. In this case you will need to collect this information on the same template used above for costs.

Information on consultants and partners most likely will have to be collected manually for your own function and other learning groups in the organization. Some companies do have sophisticated purchasing systems that require purchase orders over a certain threshold and require (or allow) for tracking by type of purchase. If this is the case in your organization, you could ask purchasing to provide a report showing all contractors used for learning. If that is not available, purchasing or accounting may be able to provide a report showing all consultants paid by learning functions in the organization. This approach probably will not be complete and may include some consultants who provided services other than development and delivery of learning. So, you still will need to compile the data manually.

You will know the consultants and partners used by your own group, and you will have records of your expenditures with them. You can use the template to gather similar information from other learning groups. Key information to gather includes the name of the partner or consultant, expenditures on them, what type of service they provided (development, delivery, measurement, other), and perhaps whether the work was performed under a master contract. (If you have not gathered this kind of data before, it will provide a good base for beginning to identify opportunities to better manage your consultant/partner spending.)

Organizing the Resource Data

Add this information to that for your own function to get a complete picture of the numbers and amount of external resources being used in place of employees. The worksheet might be organized with rows as the types of resources and columns as the learning groups from the business units (see Table 3.11). In your worksheet, you would have a column for each unit like manufacturing BU1, manufacturing BU2, and so forth, and you would have row for each external resource. If there is no learning provided by others outside your group, the worksheet is just the corporate column. Remember, this worksheet is not showing where the learning is delivered but where the resources are located.

TABLE 3.11: **Worksheet for Resource Data**

External Resources Are in Thousands of Dollars

			Manufacturing									
	Type	*Corporate*	*BU1*	*BU2*	*BU3*	*Total*	*Marketing*	*R&D*	*IT*	*Financial*	*Other*	*Total*
Employees												
Full-time		26	4	3	3	10	2	2	2	1	0	43
Part-time		9	1	1	1	3	0	0	1	1	1	15
Total		35	5	4	4	13	2	2	3	2	1	58
External Resources												
Vendor 1	1	$45				$0						$45
Vendor 2	1	$92				$0	$28					$120
Vendor 3	2	$115	$16			$16						$131
Vendor 4	3	$245	$42	$63	$32	$137						$382
Vendor 5	3	$223				$0						$223
Vendor 6	3					$0	$67				$14	$81
Vendor 7	2					$0		$22				$22
Vendor 8	2					$0			$34			$34
Vendor 9	1					$0			$24			$24
Vendor 10	3					$0				$11	$13	$24
Total		$720	$58	$63	$32	$153	$95	$22	$58	$11	$27	$1,086

Note: Vendor Type 1 = Delivery ($189), 2 = Development ($187), 3 = Both ($710)

Presenting the Resource Data

How Many Resources Are Dedicated to Learning?

Start with a high-level summary showing the number of employees and external resources. This answers the basic question about how many resources are dedicated to learning (forty-three full-time employees, fifteen part-time employees, and ten consultants and partners).

TABLE 3.12

Summary of Enterprise Learning Resources (high level)

Employees	
Full-time	43
Part-time	15
Total	58
External Resources	10

You might want to add more detail, including expenses, so that the spending on external resources can be compared to labor and related costs for employees. Depending on the number and type of external resources, you also might provide more detail.

TABLE 3.13

Summary of Enterprise Learning Resources (with some detail)

Expenses Are in Thousands of Dollars

	Number	*Expense*
Employees		
Full-time	43	$3,790
Part-time	15	375
Total	58	$4,165
External Resources		
For development of learning	3	$187
For delivery of learning	3	189
For both development & delivery	4	710
Total	10	$1,086
Total Resources	68	$5,251

It also may be helpful to show the breakdown between corporate and the business unit learning functions.

TABLE 3.14
Summary of Enterprise Learning Resources
(for Corporate and Business Units)

	Corporate	*Business Units*	*Total*
Employees			
Full-time	26	17	43
Part-time	9	6	15
Total	35	23	58
External Resources	5	5	10

You could also combine Tables 3.13 and 3.14 into a six-column table showing dollar amounts as well as number of employees and external resources.

Where Are They Located?

Location of the resources is also important. You might show location by business unit or by geographic area like district, country, or region. (You would have to gather additional data.)

TABLE 3.15
Enterprise Learning Resources by Location

	North America	*South America*	*Europe*	*Asia*	*Total*
Employees					
Full-time	26	3	8	6	43
Part-time	5	2	4	4	15
Total	31	5	12	10	58
External Resources	5	1	2	2	10

How Many Are Served by Learning?

This is the last central question. As a manager of the learning function, you certainly want to know how many you are reaching with your current programs. Your leaders will want to know as well and will likely want to track this on a monthly or quarterly basis. There are two ways to answer this question.

The first is by the number of unique participants, and this is probably what your leaders have in mind when they ask the question. The count of unique participants removes duplication from participants taking multiple courses. The second is by total participants, which counts every course for every participant. In other words, it allows for duplication, and the total participant count may be greater than the number of employees. For example, if an employee takes two courses, she counts as one unique participant with two instances of participation. Both counts are important, and employees typically take more than one course per year, so total participation likely will be much higher than unique participation. The number of unique participants indicates how many employees are being touched by learning while the total participant count is a better answer as to how much learning is being provided. Your L&D budget will be driven more by the count of total participants than unique participants since the number of instructors, classrooms and other variable expenses all will increase in proportion to the rise in total participants.

Warning: Be careful when adding up unique participants. A sum of unique participants should not contain any double counting of individuals. If there are no common participants in the groups being summed, then you can simply add up all the unique participants in each group. However, if there are some participants who are in more than one group, you cannot add up the participants in all the groups. In this case you would have to rely on your learning management system (LMS) or registration lists to give you an unduplicated count.

Let's look at some examples to make the computations clear. We will start with the case when each program consists of just one course and then examine the case for programs with multiple courses.

When each program consists of just one course

Suppose two learning programs or initiatives are recommended in support of a goal to increase sales by 10%. One program consists of a consultative selling skills course and another program consists of product features training. Each program consists of just one course. Both are for the same audience of 100 salespeople.

Program	*Courses*	*Target Audience*	*Unique Participants*	*Total Participants*
Consultative selling skills	1	All western region reps	100	100
Product features	1	All western region reps	100	100
Total for two programs	2		100	200

Since the same 100 salespeople took both courses, the program total for unique participants counts them only once.

Now suppose that we have the same two courses but the salespeople taking the product features training are different than those taking the consultative selling skills course.

Program	*Courses*	*Target Audience*	*Unique Participants*	*Total Participants*
Consultative selling skills	1	All western region reps	100	100
Product features	1	All eastern region reps	110	110
Total for two programs	2		210	210

In this case the number of unique participants for the two programs is 210. There are 210 unique (distinct and unduplicated) salespeople in these programs.

Next, suppose the 100 western region salespeople participate in both programs, the 110 eastern region reps take just the selling skills program, and 50 central region salespeople take just the product features training.

Program	*Courses*	*Target Audience*	*Unique Participants*	*Total Participants*
Consultative selling skills	1	100 western reps, 110 eastern reps	210	210
Product features	1	100 western reps, 50 central reps	150	150
Total for two programs	2		260	360

In this case the total number of unique participants in the two programs is 260 not 360 (100 from the western region, 110 from the eastern region, and 50 from the central region). Note that you cannot sum the count from each program because the 100 western region reps are in both programs.

When a program consists of more than one course

Last, consider the case where a program consists of multiple courses. In this case, the number of total participants equals the number of unique participants x number of courses.

Suppose the consultative selling skills program now consists of two courses (one two-day ILT and one 30-minute WBT) and the product features training consists of four 60-minute WBTs.

Program	*Courses*	*Target Audience*	*Unique Participants*	*Total Participants*
Consultative selling skills	2	100 western reps, 110 eastern reps	210	420
Product features	4	100 western reps, 50 central reps	150	600
Total for two programs	6		260	1020

Notice that the total number of unique participants remains unchanged at 260, but the number of total participants is now much higher at 1020 reflecting that each of the 210 took two courses and each of the 150 took four courses.

The total number of unique participants can never exceed the total number of employees. (If there is turnover during the year, then the total of unique employees may exceed the headcount on December 31 if every employee took a course.)

It is natural to break this down by target audience or affiliation. In addition to providing learning for employees of your organization, do you provide any learning for independent dealers or distributors of your product, suppliers to your company, or customers or purchasers of your product or service?

Getting the Participant Data

Many organizations have a learning management system (LMS) that tracks who has taken a course. Typically the LMS is also used to host the electronic catalogue of available courses, handle registration and notification, and maintain a transcript or record for every user showing what they have taken, when they completed it, and the grade or score for (if applicable) the course. If you are fortunate enough to have such a system and if it includes all your users, you should be able to run a report very easily to generate both the number of unique and total participants.

In many cases, though, a single LMS will not be used by all business units and will not cover all users, especially users who are not employees. Marketing may have a different system for dealers and customers. Purchasing may use something else to track learning they are providing to suppliers. In this case, you will need to collect the information on learning participants from the business units. You can add questions to the template to get this data, but first you will need to establish the categories you want to ask about like supplier, customer, and dealer. Perhaps there are other types of categories that are more meaningful for your organization.

If there is no LMS at all, then you will have to collect data from the paper records or electronic worksheets used to register learners manually. In this case it may be too difficult to collect unique participants. If you know the ratio of unique to total participants for a subgroup or sample, you could apply it to the total to get an estimate of the unique participants for the enterprise.

Organizing the Participant Data

Once you have the data, organize it by unit and category of participant. Remember, the purpose of this worksheet is to add up data from different sources. It is not to show how much learning was provided to marketing or IT (that comes later). These business units are included because they have their own learning staff or spend their own funds, and their participants are not captured in the corporate LMS. If a marketing employee took a course listed in the corporate LMS, then she is counted under corporate. The marketing column is capturing the participants who took courses *not* in the corporate LMS (like a course provided to dealers or customers).

TABLE 3.16: **Worksheet for Participant Data by Source**

		Manufacturing									
Participants	***Corporate***	***BU1***	***BU2***	***BU3***	***Total***	***Marketing***	***R&D***	***IT***	***Financial***	***Other***	***Total***
Total											
Employees	40,000	4,500	3,250	3,600	11,350	480	293	900	155	126	53,304
Dealers	66				0	696					762
Suppliers	42	138	234	319	690						732
Customers	25				0	150					175
Total	40,133	4,638	3,484	3,919	12,040	1,326	293	900	155	126	54,973
Unique											
Employees	16,000	1,500	1,300	1,200	4,000	320	195	450	155	105	17,152
Dealers	55				0	580					595
Suppliers	35	125	195	245	565						572
Customers	25				0	150					155
Total	16,115	1,625	1,495	1,445	4,565	1,050	195	450	155	105	18,474

It may be possible with your LMS to generate a report that would categorize participants by business unit or function (like manufacturing and marketing). The report might look like the following:

TABLE 3.17: **Worksheet for Participant Data by Participant's Business Unit**

	Manufacturing									
Participants	*BU1*	*BU2*	*BU3*	*Total*	*Marketing*	*R&D*	*IT*	*Financial*	*Other*	*Total*
Total										
Employees	8,500	7,250	7,600	23,350	8,480	2,293	8,900	6,155	4,126	53,304
Dealers				0	762					762
Suppliers	150	247	335	732						732
Customers				0	175					175
Total	8,650	7,497	7,935	24,082	9,417	2,293	8,900	6,155	4,126	54,973
Unique										
Employees	2,693	2,493	2,393	7,578	2,705	791	2,835	1,944	1,298	17,152
Dealers				0	595					595
Suppliers	127	197	248	572						572
Customers				0	155					155
Total	2,820	2,690	2,641	8,150	3,455	791	2,835	1,944	1,298	18,474

Notice in this report that only the business units are listed, not the corporate learning function. Learning taken by employees of the corporate learning function would appear under "Other," which would include HR.

Presenting the Participant Data

A simple slide to answer the question would show totals for the enterprise (see Table 3.18). The answer is 18,474 unique participants and 54,973 total participants for the year, which means that participants took an average of almost three (2.98) courses per person.

TABLE 3.18

Enterprise Participation in Learning for 2016 (summary)

	Unique Participants	*Total Participants*
Employees	17,152	53,304
Dealers	595	762
Suppliers	572	732
Customers	155	175
Total	18,474	54,973

A more detailed slide could show some, but not all, of the information from Table 3.17. Perhaps the focus is just on employees and the three manufacturing units have been consolidated.

TABLE 3.19

Employee Participation in Learning for 2016 (detail)

	Unique Participants	*Total Participants*
Manufacturing	7,578	23,350
IT	2,835	8,900
Marketing	2,705	8,480
Financial	1,944	6,155
Other	2,089	6,419
Total	17,152	53,304

Note: It is not possible to generate Table 3.19 from 3.16 without data from the corporate LMS indicating the business unit of each employee.

CATERPILLAR EXPERIENCE: At Caterpillar our CEO, CFO, and Board of Governors were interested in all the information presented above: costs by location and program, staffing, and participants. We included this information in our annual business plan for learning and briefed them at the December Board of Governors meeting. I met with group presidents not on the board individually once per year and reviewed the plan with them, including this basic information. This was absolutely essential to our gaining credibility in a culture that demanded accountability.

Opportunity Costs: The Value of Participants' Time

In the first section of this chapter we examined the costs of learning. We limited ourselves to accounting-type costs like those you would find in the income statement. There is another important cost that never appears in the financial statements but is typically one of your largest costs. It is opportunity cost. This is an economic concept rather than a financial concept and can seldom be measured with precision. Nonetheless, it is very real and should play an important role in how you manage the learning function.

Opportunity cost is basically the value of what was given up in order to do something. For example, suppose you are in sales and add value by closing deals that result in additional profit for the company. You have an opportunity to attend a three-day instructor-led sales learning program to make you more effective in closing deals. You believe that you will be able to close more deals and at higher prices if you attend the course. What will you give up by attending? Well, you give up three days of your time closing deals. And what is that worth? At a minimum it is worth what the company pays you—that is, your salary and benefits (labor and related from Chapter 1). If you are not worth that, the company should pay you less or replace you. So, at a minimum, opportunity cost is the value of your time. (If you make $60,000 per year and receive benefits valued at 25% of that [$15,000], then three days of your time is worth at least 3/260 * $75,000 = $865 [52 weeks per year x 5 days = 260 days]).

Sometimes, opportunity cost may be more. In this case, if you are in class, then you are *not* closing deals, which means you are *not* increasing your company's profits. If you close $1,000,000 worth of sales each year and the profit margin is 10% on those sales, then you generate $100,000 worth of profit per year through your work, and you are more than covering your salary and benefits. It also means, though, that the company's opportunity cost to send you to the three-day class may be higher than $865. Unless you can somehow make up for the lost three days of sales, your attending that class cost your company 3/260 * $100,000 = $1154. This is the opportunity cost or value of your time to the company. And it can easily exceed the cost of the course itself, especially for highly paid employees or employees with a high impact on the bottom line. This opportunity cost, however, never appears on the income statement as an expense. It is a hidden or invisible cost of learning.

> WARNING: Use only one of the two methods to calculate opportunity cost. Do not calculate both and add them together. If you can make a direct calculation of the impact on net income, as we did in the sales training example, then use this methodology since it is more accurate. If you do not have the information to make this calculation, then default to using hours in training x labor & related rate. The default methodology will provide a conservative estimate of opportunity cost.
>
> Also, if replacement workers are hired to fill in for the employees in training, then do not calculate the opportunity cost of the participants' time away from work. You will add the replacement workers' labor & related cost to your total cost of learning instead. Likewise, if you pay overtime to workers to take learning outside of regular working hours, you do not need to calculate their opportunity cost. Instead, you will add their labor & related cost for overtime into the total cost of learning. In these cases we will use an actual budget cost instead of the opportunity cost.

Calculating Opportunity Costs for the Enterprise

You certainly want to take opportunity costs into consideration when designing a course, but you also might want to have an idea about how large they are for your organization. You may be able to generate a report from your LMS to get the total number of class hours (after all, it already contains the length of each course and the total participants). You could multiply by the average labor and related for the enterprise to calculate a minimum for opportunity cost for classes. (If you don't have total classroom hours, make an estimate of average class duration and multiply by the number of classes offered.) You will still need to add an estimate for the opportunity costs of travel time back and forth to class. So, take an estimate of the average travel time round trip (say, 60 minutes) and multiply by the labor and related amount. Finally, you need an estimate of time spent for online learning (you might use 45 minutes per course) and multiply by the average labor and related rate. Add these three components together for an estimate of total opportunity costs for the participants of your learning (see Figure 3.5).

FIGURE 3.5

Work Sheet for Calculating Opportunity Costs

Inputs

Average labor & related per hour = $36

($75,000 / (260 days x 8 hrs = 2080 hours)

Number of total (not unique) participants for instructor-led classes = 500

Average instructor-led class duration = 4 hours

Round trip travel time = 1 hour

Number of total (not unique) online participants = 800

Average online class duration = 45 minutes (.75 hour)

Calculation of opportunity cost for time spent in class	
500 total participants x 4 hours per class x $36 per hour =	$72,000
Calculation of opportunity costs for travel time	
500 total participants x 1 hour per class x $36 per hour =	$18,000
Calculation of opportunity cost for time spent online	
800 total participants x .75 hour per class x $36 per hour =	$21,600
Total opportunity costs =	$111,600

You may also want to calculate the total number of hours, which was 3,100 (also $111,600/$36).

Presenting Opportunity Costs

The recommendation is to include opportunity costs as a note at the bottom of a summary expenditure slide. This way, the magnitude of the opportunity cost can be better compared to the other costs. Since it is not a financial cost and since it will always be an estimate, it should not be included as a line item expense in an income statement.

TABLE 3.20
Including Opportunity Costs As a Note on the Learning Expenses Slide

Enterprise Learning Expenditures
Thousands of Dollars

Labor & related	$335
Overhead	$456
Total accounting expenses	$791
Note: Opportunity costs based on 3,100 hours at $36 /hr	$112

ADVICE: Showing a total including the opportunity costs ($791 + $112 = $903) is not recommended because leaders often remember bottom line figures especially well, even if they don't remember exactly what was included. So, if you show a total of $903,000, they are likely to remember that accounting-type learning costs are $903,000, forgetting that opportunity costs were included. Next time they see an income statement, they will say, "I thought we spent $903,000 last year. Where did the $791,000 come from?" This happened the second year in Cat U after we had added opportunity costs to the accounting costs the previous year. Never underestimate the memory of your senior leaders, but recognize that it will not be perfect!

Conclusion

The importance of knowing and communicating learning costs and resources cannot be overstated. A learning manager simply cannot expect to have credibility if she does not know these and share them with senior leaders. In all but the simplest cases, this will involve gathering data not readily available in published reports. The data often will be estimated and subject to a margin of error. This approach is okay, and you won't be alone in your organization if you do it this way. Use your professional judgment, question data that does not look right, and look for ways to improve the process next year. The fact remains that no one else in your organization can do a better job of pulling this information together.

Chapter 3 also introduced the concept of opportunity cost. This is one of the most important concepts in economics and a key component in total learning cost. In fact, opportunity cost will often be the single greatest cost in a multi-day instructor-led course.

Chapter 3 to Do List

1. Set up a process to collect learning cost and resource and participant data.
2. Gather the data, organize it, and present it.
3. Let others know that you know what the learning costs are and that you have a process in place to update the information annually.
4. Calculate labor and related rates and opportunity costs for your target audiences.
5. Calculate opportunity costs for key programs.
6. Calculate opportunity costs for the enterprise or organization.

Further Reading

Case, Karl, Ray Fair, and Sharon Oster. *Principles of Economics*, ninth edition. Upper Saddle River, New Jersey: Pearson Prentice Hall, 2009. (See Chapter 1 for a discussion of opportunity costs.)

Gargiulo, Terrence, Ajay Pangarkar, Teresa Kirkwood, and Tom Bunzel. *Building Business Acumen for Trainers*. San Francisco: Pfeiffer, 2006. (See page 92 for a discussion of opportunity cost.)

PART TWO

Strategic Alignment and the Business Plan for Learning

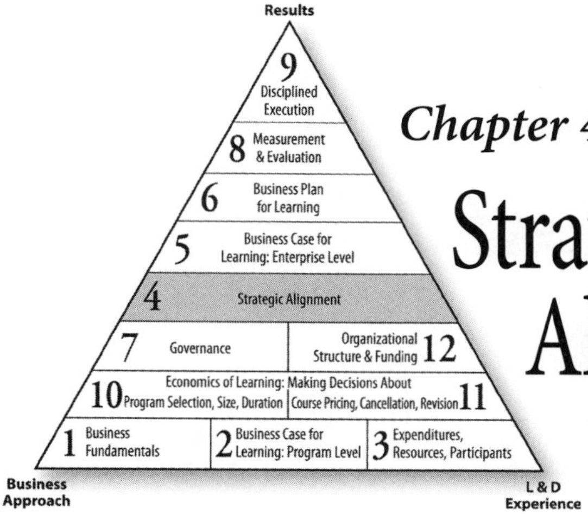

Chapter 4

Strategic Alignment

STRATEGIC ALIGNMENT OF learning to an organization's highest priority goals is the single most important action a learning manager can take to improve effectiveness, contribute to an organization's success, and earn a seat at the table. Understanding the cost structure, making the business case for individual programs, disciplined execution, and measurement are all important, but all come in a distant second to strategic alignment. This chapter will provide the rationale, process, and tools to get strategic alignment right, and will focus primarily on the process. The next chapter will provide more detail on needs analysis and learning programs, and Chapter 6 will focus on the entire business planning process, which starts with strategic alignment.

ADVICE: The next several chapters describe some key recommended processes like strategic alignment in great detail. Do not be discouraged if you cannot implement all these steps next year or in the next several years. If you agree with the process in theory, make as much progress as you can each year toward

Key Concepts for Chapter 4

4

1. Strategic Alignment is proactive and completed before the year begins.
2. It ensures resources are focused on the highest priority organization goals.
3. It requires discussions with the CEO, executives, sponsors, and governing board members.
4. It is an iterative process of discovery, priority setting, and consensus building.

whatever your goal may be. If you cannot get a meeting with the CEO this year, start with the SVPs. If you cannot get agreement on planned impact for all major initiatives, start with two or three. The key is to have a vision in mind of where you would like to be in a few years and then make progress each year toward it.

Definition of Strategic Alignment

Strategic alignment is the proactive process of ensuring that learning is carefully planned and directed to help meet the highest priority goals of an organization. "Proactive" and "highest priority" are the key words here. Proactive means that the vast majority of learning for the coming year is planned *before* the year even begins, typically as part of the overall business planning process for the next fiscal year. Highest priority means that planning and budgeting process for learning focus first on ensuring that the most important goals of the organization are supported by the appropriate learning. If higher sales is the number one goal for next year and if learning can contribute to achieving that goal, then learning to support higher sales better be the learning department's highest priority. Learning may also support lower-priority goals, and some learning may not be aligned at all, but your budget and staff must first be allocated to ensure that the highest-priority goals are supported. Last, strategically aligned learning should not only be linked to the highest-priority goals but should contribute meaningfully to their achievement. Learning's impact on the goal should be measurable and the dollar value of that impact should exceed the cost of the learning.

Recall from Chapter 1 that an organization exists to perform a mission, and there will be a strategy with specific, measurable goals to accomplish that mission. The highest performing organizations invest in learning to meet these goals, so learning must be directly linked to these strategic goals if it is to have its greatest impact. The failure to strategically align learning to organization goals is the single biggest failure in learning today and is the primary reason learning is not considered a strategic partner.

The result of the strategic alignment process will be a prioritized list of organizational goals with learning programs clearly aligned to those goals, including learning's planned contribution or impact on the goals. (Chapter 4 will focus on the alignment and planned impact while chapter 5 will focus on the business case for each program.) The process is also likely to uncover "unaligned learning" or learning that does not directly support your organization's goals (covered in Chapter 5).

Note: Most authors agree that you must start by 1) understanding the needs of the business, 2) ensuring that your proposed programs will help meet those needs, and 3) agreeing on measures of success. Some make the additional important point that you must agree on roles and responsibilities for all involved to deliver the agreed-upon measures of success. Others also define alignment to include the business case for the learning (Phillips), which we will address in detail in the next chapter. Last, yet others (Smith) define alignment to include the involvement of senior leaders in teaching, which we will not address.

Strategic Alignment Is Proactive

The first requirement to achieve strategic alignment is that the planning process for next year's learning must be completed before the year begins. Of course, there will always be some unexpected or unplanned learning that comes up, but the vast majority is planned in advance. As long as an organization's mission and strategy don't change during the year, you should be able to plan 70–90% of next year's learning before the year even starts. And with good business planning process coupled with strong governance, you will not need to change priorities during the year.

This is not the case in most organizations today. Instead, organizations are in a reactive mode and respond to requests for learning programs as they come in throughout the year. In fact, it has been common to measure efficiency by how quickly a learning department can respond to this "surprise" request for learning. And this request is often *urgent*. The message may be, "We have just launched a new product and the sales force is having trouble selling its value. We need a one-day course right away!" Traditionally, the learning department would jump into action, do a quick needs analysis to understand the issue, confirm that learning is a solution, and then develop and deliver that solution.

It is very hard to manage commitments and resources in this type of reactive mode. What do you do when multiple requests come at the same time and require the same resources? How do you say yes to one and no to another or tell one they will have to wait for three months? How do you plan for next year's staffing when you don't know how many requests will come in and what they will entail?

There is a better way.

Focus on the Highest-Priority Goals

Not only is the reactive approach difficult to manage, but there is no guarantee that over the course of the year your resources will be focused on the highest-priority learning. You may have been overwhelmed and had to turn away or delay requests. How did you decide what to turn away or which to delay? What if your staff and budget were already committed for the next three months when a high-priority request came in? Do you halt work on the existing projects (those customers won't be happy) or delay the higher priority request? Even if your staff was able to meet all the requests that came in, was that the best use of your staff and budget? Are you sure? Could they have been working on some learning that would have had a larger payoff for the organization?

The alternative is to create a process that identifies the highest-priority organizational needs upfront and then plans for the appropriate learning to support them. The learning should be prioritized in the same order as the organization's goals. This proactive approach will ensure that you focus on the most important learning from the organization's viewpoint. In other words, you are taking a business point of view.

> ADVICE: Be a business person first and a learning professional second. That means clearly understanding your organization's vision, mission, strategy, and goals. Remember why your job exists. It is to help the organization achieve its goals. The best way to do that is to strategically align learning to your organization's goals, making sure that the highest-priority goals become your highest-priority learning. You will only succeed in this endeavor if you do the strategic alignment proactively, before the year begins, as part of an agreed-upon business planning process.

What Strategic Alignment Is Not

Just to be clear, strategic alignment cannot be accomplished after the year is over, nor is it "proven" to have existed if all the evaluation scores for a program are high, including the return on investment (ROI). In other words, it won't work to justify your initiatives after the fact.

Some organizations claim to be strategically aligned without following the process described above. They engage in what we call "backward mapping" where they draw a line or connect each of their existing programs to some organizational goal. It is certainly possible that by chance the learning initiatives for a particular year will align with the organization's objectives. After all, you would hope that the business units requesting the learning are aligned with the organization's overall goals, and thus the requests from the units should reflect the organization's goals. In this case, if you look at a list of ten to twenty learning initiatives deployed over the past year, it is possible that each could be connected back to an organizational goal. If so, your learning is aligned, right?

Not necessarily. The question still remains whether you did the right learning. Were those the right ten to twenty projects to do? Perhaps some other initiatives should have been deployed instead of those on the list. Furthermore, did the highest-priority goals receive the highest-priority treatment from the learning department? Is that reflected in your staff and budget allocations? Did your priorities reflect the organization's priorities?

The only way to know that you allocated your learning resources to the highest-priority goals—that you did the *right* learning—is to go through the strategic alignment process. There is no shortcut to the proactive process of planning your learning before the year begins so that you are sure to address the highest-priority organizations goals.

Some skip this upfront process and seek to justify their programs after the fact based on measurement of results. They may have very high satisfaction scores showing the participants enjoyed the learning and intend to apply it. They may have tested for acquisition of knowledge or skills and found successful transfer. They may have even followed up three to six months later and found the participants had applied their learning and changed their behavior. Some might have conducted an in-depth impact and ROI analysis that shows beyond any doubt that the learning had a significant positive impact with bottom-line results. All of this indicates that the learning was good and impactful, but none of it tells us that it was the right learning to be conducting in the first place! Even a learning initiative with an ROI above 100% may be the *wrong* initiative to undertake. The only way to know is to go through the strategic alignment process.

The Strategic Alignment Process

The process is straightforward in theory but may require some time to implement depending on your organization and scope of responsibility. At its simplest the process starts with an understanding of your organization's mission, strategy, and goals, including its priorities. Then, beginning with the highest priorities, you need to decide whether learning can contribute to achieving the goals. If so, what would that learning look like and what might it accomplish? The process concludes with a review of the planned learning, planned impacts, and budget allocation to ensure that the highest-priority goals have received the appropriate allocation of resources. All of this takes place in the business planning period before the fiscal year begins. (Long-term organizational goals, like improved leadership, will likely require a multiple-year approach, but the discussion can still begin in the business planning period.)

The process can best be described in five steps:

FIGURE 4.1

The Five Steps of Strategic Alignment

Step 1A: Meet with the CEO

- Read business and strategic plans first if available
- What are the organization's goals? Priorities?
- Which will be the most challenging?
- Who is the owner for each?
- Prioritize goals (if not already done)

Step 1B: Meet with Senior Executives, Governing Board Members

- What are priorities?
- Which are most challenging?
- What has worked well? Not so well?

Step 2: Meet with the Goal Owners

- Start with the owners of the highest priority goals
- Learn more about their goals, challenges
- How quickly must they show results?
- What has worked well before? Not so well?

Step 3: The Learning Function Makes an Initial Determination Whether Learning Is Required to Achieve a Goal or Can Accelerate Progress

- If yes,
  - Who is the target audience?
  - What type of learning would be best (formal, informal, performance support)?
  - Duration?
  - How can opportunity costs be minimized?
  - What impact is expected on goal from the learning? High or low?
  - Complete preliminary prioritization
  - Schedule second meeting with the owner to present your recommendations
- If no,
  - Schedule a second meeting with an owner, if necessary, to share thinking that learning is not part of the solution. (The owner may convince you otherwise.)

Step 4: Meet with Owners of Goals Where Learning Has Likely Impact (Second Meeting)

- Share recommendations for learning programs
- Discuss duration, opportunity costs
- Discuss target audience: who, how many, where?
- Will it be required or voluntary? Who enforces?
- What impact is planned?
- What is your role in success? Owner's role?

Step 5: Finalize Strategic Alignment

- Meet with owners for a third time (if necessary) to reach agreement on
  - Target audience
  - Timing of development and deployment
  - Reinforcement plans
  - Planned impact
  - Roles and responsibilities
- Finalize strategic alignment document
  - Secure CEO approval if you are not including a business case

Each step will be described in turn. In reality, the process is usually not as long and complicated as the above steps imply. Often the agreements of step 5 can be reached sooner and in fewer meetings, especially if the goal owner is already employing learning. The first year of strategic alignment will be the hardest, but subsequent years should become much easier. Typically, there will be "carry over" goals from the year before, and the learning program may be spread out over several years, so some discussions will simply be updates.

Step 1A: Meet with the CEO

To be successful, the strategic alignment process must start at the top. If your learning function has responsibility for the entire enterprise, then the top is the CEO. If you have responsibility for just one division, then the top is the head of that division. You, as CLO or VP for Learning, will need to talk with many officers and stakeholders to complete the process, but the first strategic alignment meeting should be at the top. Since the organization invests in learning to achieve its goals, and since the CEO (or division president) is the only person who can speak for the *entire* organization in terms of priorities, it is very difficult to align learning to the highest-priority goals of the company without the input, counsel, and approval of the CEO or division president.

(Note: In the following discussion on strategic alignment, it will be assumed for simplicity that the learning function has enterprise responsibility and thus that the top person is the CEO. If you have responsibility for a division or business unit, then just substitute the title of your head person for CEO. If you are in a service center arrangement in which you support all the units but have not been given explicit responsibility for enterprise learning, then your top person is the CEO.)

Preparation

Before you schedule the meeting with the CEO, you will need to prepare. First, you want to make sure your boss is on board with the strategic alignment planning process. If this is new to your organization, you need to articulate the benefits of this approach clearly and make sure your boss is comfortable with it. You may also need to work some change management with your own staff so they know why you will be meeting with the CEO, other officers, and key stakeholders.

Second, find out whether your organization has a written business plan and a written long-term or strategic plan. Many will have both. If possible, get a copy and read it. Your boss may have one, or it may be available online. Some organizations have one or both, but they are restricted to just the top people. In this case, your boss may at least be able to share the goals and metrics even if he cannot give you a copy. If copies do not exist or are not available to you, that is okay. But you need to have done your homework and pursued them. If they do exist and are available to you, your CEO will have assumed you have read them before your meeting. Be prepared.

Third, be prepared to explain the strategic alignment process and the business planning process you are proposing, including the benefits of this approach, a timeline, a list of the others you plan to meet, and the outcome of this process. You might mention other organizations that have used this approach and how it benefited them.

Fourth, have your list of questions (discussed below) ready.

Okay, you are ready to set up the appointment. In some cultures (like Caterpillar) the CLO or VP for learning could simply make the request directly to the CEO and/or assistant by phone or email, sharing the reason for the meeting and the time desired (30–60 minutes). In other cultures you might have to work it up the chain. Your boss will know and can give you guidance. Needless to say, this is not a meeting that the CLO or VP for learning delegates.

The Rationale

You will need to explain what you are attempting to accomplish to the CEO. This is where you need to know your organization's vision, mission, and strategy as well as its culture and put the rationale in terms that are right for your CEO and culture. Your business acumen is critical here, and, remember, this is a business discussion, not a learning discussion.

The following is a rationale that will work for some (but may need to be modified to fit your culture), especially in for-profit business organizations:

"Thank you for agreeing to meet with me today. I believe we have an opportunity to get a lot more out of the money we spend on learning by doing a better job of aligning learning to our company's highest-priority goals. Currently, we have lot of unaligned learning, which gets good reviews from our employees but isn't helping us accomplish our most important company goals. Even where it appears to be in alignment, we don't have a process to prioritize our spending and make good decisions about tradeoffs.

"With your help, our current investment in learning can have a much bigger impact on our corporate goals and results. We need your help in understanding what our most important company goals are and how you would prioritize them...."

(Note: This discussion is easier if you are new to the CLO position. If you have been in the position for a while, the CEO may ask why we have had all this unaligned learning, and you should be prepared with an answer. You might answer in this way: "In our efforts to continuously improve, we have been benchmarking best-in-class learning organizations and believe the practice of strategic alignment used by others will work for our company as well and be a real improvement over the traditional approach.")

If you replace "corporate" and "company" with "organization," this approach should work for many nonprofit and government organizations as well.

If the issue is not so much unaligned learning as difficulty in meeting conflicting requests, then make the rationale in those terms:

"Thank you for agreeing to meet with me today. We have really struggled over the past few years to meet all the units' requests for learning. We are happy they come to us and pleased that demand for our services is growing, but I believe we have an opportunity to get a lot more out of the money we already spend on learning by doing a better job of aligning learning to our company's highest-priority goals. Today, we don't have a process to prioritize our spending and make good decisions about which requests to accept and which to turn away. My worry is that we are not supporting the company's highest-priority goals to the extent we should.

"With your help, our current investment in learning can have a much bigger impact on our corporate goals and results. We need your help in understanding what our most important company goals are and how you would prioritize them...."

Notice that in both examples, the discussion is about getting more from the *existing level of investment in learning*. This is not the time to ask for more funding. In fact, depending on your company's finances, you might even suggest that as a result of this process, you will be able to reduce the spending on learning and still have a greater impact on the company's goals (especially if there is a lot of unaligned learning).

At this point, your CEO will be pleased to hear you want to help the company achieve its goals and even happier to hear that you have a plan to increase the impact of the current investment in learning or to spend less on learning and still increase learning's impact. She will now be ready for your questions.

The Questions

The questions will depend on whether a business or strategic plan exists and whether you have access to it.

If no plan exists or you do not have access to it, then the following are recommended questions (assuming you are conducting the interview several months before the end of the current fiscal year):

1. "What are the corporate goals for this year?"
   "How is success measured?"
   "How are we doing?"
   "What is the hardest one?"
2. "What are the goals for next year?" Or "What do you think the goals will be for next year?" (Any new ones?)
   "How will success be measured?"
   "Which is likely to be the most difficult?"
3. "Can you prioritize next year's goals for me?"
4. "Who is the owner for each one so I can follow up with them to learn more and discuss how learning can help them achieve their goals?"

If plans exist and you have read them, then you might start this way:

1. "I read this year's business plan. We certainly have a number of challenging goals."
   "How are we doing?"
   "What is proving the most difficult?"
2. "Have the plans (goals) changed for next year?" (Any new goals? Any removed?)
   "Have the targets or metrics changed?"
   "Which is likely to be the most difficult?"

   Questions 3 and 4 would be the same as above.

In either case your objective is the same. You need to understand the strategy, and you need to know what the highest priority goals are. You could ask, "What is our strategy for next year?" before asking about objectives, but it will usually come out in the discussion. What you really need are the specific, measurable goals (for example, increase unit sales in Europe by 10% by September 30) for next year and a sense of their priority.

The Discussion

The CEO should have little trouble talking strategy and goals. He may have to look up the specifics (for example, 10% by a certain date), but this discussion will flow easily. After all, this is what they do, and they will be happy you asked. The danger is that you run out of time, especially if there are a lot of goals. You want to spend some of your time understanding the big picture, but most of it should be spent getting a sense for priority and how difficult the highest-priority goals will be to achieve. You are listening for context, background, lessons learned, and points of sensitivity.

If the goals are not prioritized in advance, this may be a little harder. If there are many, do not worry about ranking them all. Ask for the top three. The CEO will generally say something like, "They are all important, but the most important for next year are...." Or you may classify them by high and low or high/medium/low. If the CEO is still having trouble prioritizing, ask about what the board of directors is holding him responsible for this year. It will not be a list of twenty goals. It will almost certainly be less than ten, and that may provide a clue for next year's priority.

Your CEO will know what officer has been assigned responsibility for each goal. (It will generally be a direct report to the CEO or the next level down.) You need to know that because you are going to talk with these officers next.

Notice that this conversation has been a strategic business discussion. You have not talked about learning or funding or how many staff you have. This has not been a discussion about you or the learning function although the CEO may have indicated that she expects learning to play a critical role in achieving many of the objectives. It has been primarily a discussion about your organization's strategy and goals. Ideally, by the end of the discussion, you will have answers to your questions and hopefully the support of the CEO for this new strategic alignment and business planning process. (You may need to reference this discussion with the CEO and her support in the following discussions with sponsors.)

This is your first step in becoming a strategic partner, in earning a seat at the table. And for the most part, you have been just a very active listener.

> CATERPILLAR EXPERIENCE: At Caterpillar we started the strategic alignment process each year in August with the CEO. It was a 30–60 minute meeting in which we (CLO and director of strategic learning) asked the questions listed above. The meeting was fast-paced,

and the CEO always provided the needed direction and counsel. We both took notes and compared results after the meeting.

ADVICE: There may be cases in which an organization has not prioritized its goals and the CEO is reluctant to do so. (For example, the CEO may say they are all of equal priority.) In this case you may try several other approaches. If you have a governing board, put it on the agenda and see if you can at least assign a high, medium, or low rating to each goal. If that is not an option, have the learning community help determine the priorities. Or simply assign a priority ranking yourself and then share it and your thinking with the CEO or governing board for review. Sometimes this will get them engaged. In any case, do not give up! Always do the best you can given your circumstances and then try to improve the process next year.

Step 1B: Meet with Senior Executives, Governing Board Members

Executives

Senior executives would include all the direct reports to the CEO who are not goal owners. In large organizations there may be group presidents or senior vice presidents (SVPs) who are not goal owners themselves. Instead, their direct reports (VPs) are the goal owners. Of course, they are indirectly responsible since the VP reports to them. Start with the rationale, your meeting with the CEO, and the fact she is onboard.

For this group use the CEO questions. If they have enterprise-wide responsibility, then ask them to answer from an enterprise-wide perspective. The strategy and goals should be the same, but do not be surprised to find the priorities and perhaps even how success is measured are different. In organizations without a centralized strategy or without enterprise-wide responsibility, ask them to answer from their own division's or region's perspective. Proceed just as if they were the CEOs of their own companies. Do not mention that their strategy, goals, and priorities are different than the CEOs or may conflict. You need to know this, but it is not your place to resolve any internal differences.

Governing Board Members

If you have a governing body (an internal board of directors), you should interview them as well. (Chapter 7 will discuss governing bodies in detail.) Since they provide you with direction and will help determine priorities, you need their input at the start of the strategic planning process. You may already have interviewed some if they are executives or goal owners. Others may be department or business unit heads. In any case you want them to represent the entire enterprise when they answer. This is not a discussion about next year's learning needs for a particular department or unit.

For this group ask about progress on this year's goals and why they feel progress is or is not being made. Tell them what you have heard (but not from whom) about goals for next year. Ask them what they think about priorities for next year and what will be difficult.

> CATERPILLAR EXPERIENCE: We scheduled meetings with the board of governors to follow immediately after the meeting with the CEO. Meetings with the goal owners followed. These meetings were scheduled for an hour. Initial meetings were concluded by the end of September.

Step 2: Meet with Goal Owners

Your next series of meetings will be with the owners of the goals. Like the meeting with the CEO, these are meetings that the CLO or VP for learning needs to attend. They should not be delegated to someone on your staff, but you can certainly have a senior member of your team accompany you. If you have too many goals for you to meet personally with all owners, you may want to focus on the highest-priority seven to ten and have one of your direct reports talk with the others.

After your meeting with the CEO, set up your meetings with the goal owners. Do not let them delegate this meeting to one of their direct reports. You must meet with them. If necessary, you might mention you were talking with the CEO about their goal and that you need to follow up with them personally. This is another reason for starting at the top. It gives you credibility and some leverage as you work your way down. Let them know you want to learn more about their goals in this first meeting and then in later meetings explore how learning can help them achieve their goals. Their performance evaluation and subsequent merit increase (and bonus/profit sharing if applicable) will directly depend on whether a specific, measurable goal is achieved. Consequently, they should be interested in how you can help them succeed.

Since you already know the goals, you can start by asking for more detail about them, how they contribute to the overall strategy, how they will be measured, and how the owners plan to achieve them. In particular, you will want to get a deeper understanding about what makes each goal difficult, what has been tried before, what seems to be working, how quickly they have to show results. The owners will be able to provide much more detail than the CEO, and you will learn what worries them about delivering on their goals. Ask them all who has responsibility for meeting the goal within their own organizations. It may well be several people with at least one reporting directly to the owner. Ideally, a representative from the college that covers the goal under discussion or a representative from your internal relationship management team who is assigned to this business unit will be able to accompany you for the interview.

> ADVICE: Throughout the process of strategic alignment, business case development, and actual course development, delivery, and evaluation, it will be helpful to have well-defined and consistent instructional design processes that all learning professionals follow. This is especially true in larger, more complex organizations. Many learning functions have adopted HPI (human performance improvement), ADDIE (analyze, design, develop, implement, evaluate), or SAM (successive approximation model) as guiding models or processes for needs assessment, development, and follow through. Since Caterpillar had adopted Six Sigma as our overall approach to problem-solving, we integrated Six Sigma methodology with HPI to come up with a blended model, which our Six Sigma course development teams could use. The model identified the steps to be followed in analyzing a business need and determining whether learning had a role to play, developing the learning and piloting it, and evaluating its impact and making recommendations for improvement. The model also identified the roles and responsibilities for all those involved. The key is to have a model and follow it.

Step 3: The Learning Function Makes an Initial Determination Whether Learning Is Required to Achieve a Goal or Can Accelerate Progress.

Review of Meeting with the Goal Owner

After each interview, meet with the appropriate people in your learning function, share and discuss what you learned about this particular corporate goal, and begin to determine whether learning can support achieving this goal. If it can, what form might it take (formal learning, informal learning, or performance support)? Who would be the target audience?

Assuming that the program is well-designed, executed, and reinforced, what impact could it have on the corporate goal? High impact means that learning will be the single biggest contributor to achieving the organization's goal. Medium impact means that learning will be an important contributor but not the most important single factor. Other action items will also be important contributors. Low impact means that learning has a small role to play in achieving the goal, and other action items will be far more important to results. For example, if the goal is to reduce injuries and learning alone could deliver 50% or more of the reduction, then it has high impact. If learning, by itself, could deliver 20–50% of the reduction, then it has a medium impact. Low impact would be less than a 20% contribution. In some cases the learning may simply be deemed Essential, meaning that the training must be conducted by law (compliance-related training), accepted practice, or necessity. Think of the training required of new employees before they are put in front of customers or on an assembly line. If training is deemed essential, then withholding it would result in clear harm to the organization.

Preliminary Findings

At this point you have probably talked with at least ten to fifteen very senior people in your organization. This is time-consuming but very worthwhile. Their input will be the basis for your understanding of next year's strategy and prioritization of corporate goals. You have taken notes (even better if someone accompanied you to each interview and took notes as well), reviewed them, and discussed them with your staff. At this stage, you have probably not done a detailed needs analysis. Consider this more as a "macro" needs analysis, in which the goal is to determine whether learning has a role to play in achieving the various organizational objectives. It is time to summarize your preliminary findings.

- First, list the corporate goals for next year, showing the CEO's priorities. Make a mental note whether some of the goal owners, executives, or board members had different priorities. Add any goals not on the CEO's list at the bottom (lowest priority).
- Second, place the owner's name by the goal.
- Third, indicate whether learning has a role to play in achieving the goal for next year. If it does, add the potential impact: high, medium, low, or essential.

Table 4.1 shows what strategic alignment might look like at this preliminary stage.

TABLE 4.1
Preliminary Findings on Organizational Goals, Priorities, and Learning Impact

Priority	*Corporate Goal*	*Sponsor*	*Could Learning Support?*	*Potential Impact of Learning*
1 High	Increase sales by 10%	Ortega	Yes	Medium
2 High	Reduce defects by 20%	D'Agote	Yes	High
3 High	Reduce injuries by 25%	Swilthe	Yes	High
4 Med	Improve leadership score by 5 points on survey	Wang	Yes	Medium
5 Med	Increase employee retention by 5 points	Dreise	Yes	Medium
6 Med	Increase innovation by 20% (patent applications)	Chan	Yes	Medium
7 Med	Reduce purchasing costs by 5%	Murphy	Yes	High
8 Low	Increase internal bench-strength for officers	Dreise	Yes	Low
9 Low	Open office in Beijing	Li	No	None
10 Low	Reduce technical support complaints by 30%	Salvatore	Yes	High
11 Low	Reduce exposure to fraud and insider trading	Omwetti	Yes	Essential

This summary of preliminary findings has several benefits. First, it represents your understanding of the corporate goals and their priority. In the absence of a written business plan for next year, this is information the learning function would not have had.

Second, if there were significantly different opinions expressed in the interviews about the corporate goals or priorities, it gives you an opportunity to follow up on this before you make any final recommendations about alignment. You may need to schedule a second meeting with the CEO.

Third, it captures the results of the "macro" needs analysis to provide early warning on any gaps or omissions. Have you missed any key owners? Are there any goals or areas of concern raised by the CEO, senior executives, or governing board members not covered?

You have successfully discovered your organization's strategic goals, their owners, and their priorities. You have also made a preliminary assessment of the type of impact learning might have on achieving these goals. You are well on your way to achieving strategic alignment!

Preliminary Prioritization of Learning

Now you are ready to make some initial decisions about the prioritization of learning. Your effort here will depend on your preliminary findings and on your resources (staff and budget). If you anticipate sufficient resources to address all the learning identified to support all the goals, then prioritization is not an issue at this stage. Continue to work on the detailed needs analyses for all the learning programs identified above with the owners and their staff.

In many organizations, however, it may not be feasible to address all the possible learning for all the goals. In some cases, resources may not even be sufficient to address all the possible learning for the highest-priority goals. You may need to make some preliminary decisions so you can direct your staff on where to continue to pursue the more detailed needs analyses. You also need to be able to manage expectations when you and your staff talk with owners or their staff. If you may not have sufficient resources to address their learning needs, then you do not want to mislead them into thinking you are committed to meeting their needs.

Your initial prioritization of next year's investment in learning should reflect both the priority of the organization's goal and the potential impact learning might have on it:

TABLE 4.2
Preliminary Prioritization of Learning for Next Year: Include or Not?

		Potential Impact of Learning	
		High	**Low**
Organizational Priority	High	Definitely Yes	Perhaps
	Low	Perhaps	Definitely No

The upper left-hand combination is easy: You should allocate resources first to the high priority and high impact learning. Dedicate all your resources to this learning if staff or budget is severely limited. Likewise, the lower right-hand combination is straightforward: Do not dedicate any resources here even if you have budget available. It is a waste of money and your staff's time. It would be better to redeploy your staff and not spend your budget. Applying this prioritization to the goals in Table 4.1, we might decide not to dedicate resources to the goal of increasing bench strength since it is low priority and the potential impact of learning is low.

The other two combinations are less clear. In the real world, the answer is "It depends." There may be a case where the priority is high and the owner believes learning will have a major impact. You and your staff are not so sure about the potential impact of learning in this case. It may be politically wise to proceed in this case *as long as you have fully funded the learning for the high/high combination*. Likewise, there may be times when you would support a lower priority when the impact of learning will be particularly high, especially if it is more of a medium priority or on the line between high and low. Again, be sure to fund the high/high opportunities first.

You might add a column to the preliminary findings table to indicate whether investing in learning next year will be a priority and will be included in the plan (see Table 4.3). Notice that no learning is recommended for two of the goals.

At this stage you definitely plan to support all the high-priority goals, all of the medium-priority goals, and two of the low-priority goals, in which learning would have a high impact on results or is deemed essential. Of course, resources for next year will determine how much you can actually accomplish.

You have now completed your preliminary strategic alignment. It is a work in progress, and the process is iterative. It serves to provide you with direction and focus as you refine your needs analyses and move toward final strategic alignment.

There may be some learning requested by the owner but which you are not planning to include in the business plan because you believe learning will not help achieve the goal. You need to meet with these owners and share your thinking. They may convince you otherwise. No need to follow up with the owners when you both agree in the first meeting that learning does not have a role to play.

TABLE 4.3
Preliminary Strategic Alignment

Priority	*Goal*	*Owner*	*Could Learning Support?*	*Potential Impact of Learning*	*Include in Plan?*
1 High	Increase sales by 10%	Ortega	Yes	Medium	Yes
2 High	Reduce defects by 20%	D'Agoto	Yes	High	Yes
3 High	Reduce injuries by 25%	Swilthe	Yes	High	Yes
4 Med	Improve leadership score by 5 points on survey	Wang	Yes	Medium	Yes
5 Med	Increase employee retention by 5 points	Dreise	Yes	Medium	Yes
6 Med	Increase innovation by 20% (patent applications)	Chan	Yes	Medium	Yes
7 Med	Reduce purchasing costs by 5%	Murphy	Yes	High	Yes
8 Low	Increase internal bench-strength for officers	Dreise	Yes	Low	No
9 Low	Open office in Beijing	Li	No	None	No
10 Low	Reduce technical support complaints by 30%	Salvatore	Yes	High	Yes
11 Low	Reduce exposure to fraud and insider trading	Omwetti	Yes	Essential	Yes

Step 4: Meet with Owners of Goals Where Learning Has Likely Impact (Second Meeting)

Your preliminary strategic alignment shows you where to focus your follow-up discussions and efforts. Most of your time (and your staff's time) should be spent on the high/medium-priority and high/medium-impact learning, so schedule meetings with these owners first. As time and resources permit, schedule meetings with other owners in which learning can have an impact. You may be able to delegate some of the follow-up meetings for the lower-priority goals.

Owners Where Learning Is Recommended for Inclusion in the Plan

The purpose of the second meeting is for you to share your understanding of the owner's goal and measure of success and then share your suggestions for how learning can help them achieve their goal. You want them to confirm your understanding of the goal, what makes it hard to achieve, and what has been tried before and succeeded or failed. You also want their reaction to your suggestions, and you want to confirm your thoughts on the likely impact of learning. In scheduling the meeting, allow enough time for your staff to have met with their staff so that you have their input and perhaps a tentative agreement on the role learning might play in achieving the objective. This may have entailed a detailed needs analysis.

Even though your team discussed potential learning programs with his staff, present them as yours. If the owner does not like them, do not mention his staff liked them. Understand whether the owner believes other types of learning might be better or whether the owner believes learning will not be needed this year to achieve the objective. If the owner likes the suggestions, you can share the credit with his staff.

If there is general agreement that learning can play a role, tell the goal owner that you would like to see if the two of you can reach agreement on the importance or impact of learning so that each of you will know how much effort to expend (the higher the planned impact, the more effort will be required from both the owner and learning department) and so that you and the owner are on the same page with what can be expected from learning. Of course, you also want to make sure that the proposed learning will make a meaningful contribution to achieving the goal. Last, you would also like to agree on some roles and responsibilities to which you can hold yourselves accountable.

There are two ways to do this. Both approaches begin by reaching agreement on the relative importance of learning with regard to achieving the goal. The first approach ends by characterizing the relative importance of the learning initiative as high, medium, low or essential and will be referred to as the qualitative approach. The second, or quantitative approach, ends with the percentage contribution learning might have on achieving the corporate goal (like a 20% contribution toward achieving the goal of a 10% increase in sales) and the resulting impact on the goal (like a 2% increase in sales due just to training (20% contribution x 10% increase in sales = 2% increase in sales due just to training)). Readers familiar with Phillips will recognize the second approach as level 4 impact. Recognize, though, that we are talking about *planned* impact rather than actual impact.

The first step in the process, common to both approaches, is to ask the owner to identify all the drivers or factors that are likely to contribute to achieving the goal. The second step, also common to both approaches, is to ask the owner to prioritize them. The third step is where the two approaches diverge. For the first or qualitative approach, use the prioritized list to elicit a high, medium or low impact for each factor. The adjective next to the learning initiative is the relative contribution we are looking for. For the second approach, ask the owner to assign percentages to each contribution so that the percentages sum to 100%. The percentage next to the learning initiative is the percentage contribution of learning to achieving the goal.

Let's look at an example for learning in support of the goal to increase sales by 10%. Here are the factors listed by the SVP of Sales when we asked about the drivers of sales for next year:

Drivers

- Hiring five new salespeople
- Economic growth
- New salesperson incentive system
- New advertising campaign
- New products
- Consultative selling skills and product features training

Next, ask the SVP to prioritize them. Ties are okay—this is just a planning exercise.

Prioritized Drivers

1. Economic growth
2. Consultative selling skills and product features training
3. New products
4. New salesperson incentive system
5. Hiring five new salespeople
6. New advertising campaign

For the first approach, go through the list from top to bottom asking about the relative importance of each driver. If the owner says the first driver is more important than all the others or is the dominant or key driver, designate its relative contribution as High. If there is no dominant driver, but the owner says it is very important, designate it Medium. In this case we will assume the SVP of Sales described economic growth as the dominant driver so it is designated High. Then ask about the next driver. If the first driver is Medium, ask whether the second driver is just about as important as the first. If it is, then it too will be Medium. In our example, since the first driver was High, the second has to be Medium or Low. In our case the SVP of Sales explains that both the training and new products will play very important roles in achieving the 10% increase in sales, not as important as the economy but certainly more important than the last three factors. So, we have one High, two Mediums, and thee Lows. It would be possible to have one High and the rest Low, or one Medium and the rest Low. (Note: For this methodology to work there does need to be a forced ranking. There should be at most one High. If there is a High, then you should have at most two Mediums. If there is no High, then you should have at most three or four Mediums. If there are more than five drivers, there should be one or more Lows.)

Prioritized Drivers	***Relative Contribution***
1. Economic growth	High
2. Consultative selling skills and product features training	Medium
3. New products	Medium
4. New salesperson incentive system	Low
5. Hiring five new salespeople	Low
6. New advertising campaign	Low

In this example, the owner believes (and you concur) that learning can play a very important role, not quite as important as the economy but just as important as new products and more important than the three other factors. (This is the definition of medium impact.) Especially if you and the owner have agreed upon a High or Medium impact, you need to thoroughly discuss your mutual roles and responsibilities so that each of you is clear on what you must do to deliver the planned impact.

For the second, or quantitative approach, ask the owner to assign percentages to each so that the percentages total 100%. It may take several iterations to adjust the percentages in order for the total to be 100%. The percentage next to the learning programs is what we are looking for. There is no guarantee it will be achieved, but by talking it through and then coming up with concrete action items, roles and responsibilities you will both have a better idea of what will be required to achieve it. Ties are fine and since this is only a planning exercise and our goal is to be roughly right, increments of 5%–10% make sense. Remember, this is a planning exercise about an uncertain future. We simply want to get on the same page about what can be expected from learning and what it will take to deliver it. (From a strategic alignment view point, we also want to make sure it will make a meaningful contribution to achieving the goal.)

Prioritized Drivers	***Relative Contribution***
1. Economic growth	50%
2. Consultative selling skills and product features training	20%
3. New products	15%
4. New salesperson incentive system	5%
5. Hiring five new salespeople	5%
6. New advertising campaign	5%
	100%

At this point you might check for understanding by asking just a few questions. "So, just to review, you believe economic growth will be two to three times more important than training or new products? And both training and new products are about three to four times as important as the new incentive system, new hires, and the advertising campaign? This seems reasonable to me and I am comfortable that our two learning programs might contribute about 20% towards your goal of increasing sales by 10%. This means that training by itself should lead to 2% higher sales (20% x 10% increase in sales). Now let's agree on what it is going to take to help you get these additional sales from learning."

Next, you want to start asking questions about what will be required for learning to achieve the planned impact on the goal. Remember, this is an iterative process. All the answers will not come from this meeting. But it is important to put the questions on the table in front of the owner even if his staff and your staff will work out the details. Important questions include:

1. Who is the target audience? By when must the learning be fully deployed?
2. Will the training be voluntary or mandatory? How receptive are they likely to be?
3. Who will be responsible for ensuring the target number of participants is achieved?
4. What positive reinforcement is planned for taking the training and applying the learning (and negative consequences for not doing so)?
5. How much will the planned impact depend on the owner's role as champion and change agent?

Answers to these questions directly affect the impact of the learning. Just asking these questions is likely to make the owner reconsider the potential impact (usually down). For example, if a program is not delivered until the second half of the year, there will be less than six months to impact sales. Or, if there are two hundred sales people and all need the learning to achieve the 2% sales increase but only half take the course, then the maximum planned impact is just a 1% increase in sales.

Answers to these questions are critical not only for your final strategic alignment but for you to run your function like a business. You must have clarity on what the learning function is responsible for (for example: needs analysis, design, delivery, measurement) and what the owner is responsible for (for example: identifying the appropriate target audience, making subject matter experts available to design the learning, ensuring the target audience takes the learning by agreed-upon dates, and effective sponsorship and change management). It is absolutely critical to have these discussions *before* the plan for learning is completed and before the year begins.

The college dean or representative from relationship management probably will want a follow-up meeting with people in the owner's area who have responsibility for the goal. This is now both a discussion about business results and a discussion about the impact learning might have on those business results. A series of meetings may be required to come to some consensus on a final recommendation to take to the owner.

If the goal owner will not engage or if you are not comfortable having this discussion yet, then make a conservative plan for the impact of learning based on what you do know. If you are comfortable you might share this with the goal owner who might now understand what you are trying to do. In fact, she might say that she doesn't agree with your planned impact and thinks that it is too high or too low. Now they are engaged and you can ask them what they think it should be. You can also use a governing body if you have one for advice on coming up with a reasonable and conservative planning impact. Last, you can always put your assumptions and planned impact in writing and share with your CFO and CEO. Typically these leaders are not shy and will give you feedback which you can use to adjust the planned impact up or down. Remember, this is just a planning exercise, albeit an important one. Go as far as you are comfortable going and think of this as a multiyear journey. Perhaps in year one you come up with the planned impacts internally within your own department and then in year two you engage the goal owners. This won't have the legitimacy or build the strategic partnership like direct engagement with the owners, but it is a start that you can improve upon in years two and three.

Owners Where Learning Is Not Recommended for Inclusion in the Plan

There may be cases in which you believe learning would have some impact on achieving a goal but you have chosen not to include it in the plan. You may have excluded it because your resources are insufficient to fund all learning programs, so the goal it supports has low priority and/or the impact of learning on that goal is projected to be low. In any case you need to share your reasoning with the owner. She may convince you that learning will have a higher impact on the goal or she may be able to secure additional funding.

In terms of the goals in Table 4.3 above, you would need to have this type of discussion with VP Dreise.

Step 5: Finalize Strategic Alignment

Meet with Owners for Third Time (if necessary)

Schedule the third meeting with the owner when the final recommendation is ready. The goal of this meeting is to agree on the learning program, target audience, deployment schedule, planned impact, costs, and the roles and responsibilities of both the owner and the learning function. Details like specific locations for training can be worked out once the year has begun, but you and the owner need to agree on the major issues. The CLO and the owner need to be at all three meetings, at least for the highest priority goals. Neither one can delegate. If the owner is not willing to meet and come to agreement on these items, it may be better to direct your efforts elsewhere, where learning is likely to have a greater impact.

Finalize Strategic Alignment

You have completed the second and third meetings with all the owners of high-priority goals where learning can have a high impact. Also, you have had a second or third meeting with some other owners of lower priority goals, where the impact of learning is high, and some owners with higher priority goals, where the impact of learning is medium or perhaps even low.

Now you can refine the preliminary strategic alignment document to reflect what you have learned in the second and third meetings. More detailed needs analyses have now been completed, and agreement has been reached with the owners on specific learning programs, planned impact, roles, and responsibilities. You can now include specific learning programs with anticipated target audiences.

Although the organization's priorities did not change, it is likely some of your preliminary estimates of impact and prioritization of learning programs have changed. In some cases after digging deeper and completing a more detailed needs analysis, the impact of learning will turn out to be less than you previously thought, and you will no longer even recommend it. Suppose for example that the planned impact of innovation learning is revised down to low and you decide to drop it. In other cases, you discovered learning can play a more important role than originally anticipated and is now on your recommended list.

Approval of the Final Strategic Alignment

If you are not proceeding to develop a business case or business plan for learning, then the last step is to secure approval from the CEO and your governing body. You have already solicited their input and you have prioritized the organization's goals according to the CEO's input, so there should not be any major surprises or pushback in terms of the goals and their priority. It is always possible, though, that something has changed since you met with them, and you may need to update the strategic alignment based on their comments. The discussion is more likely to be about your assessment of learning's potential impact and your chosen target areas for learning investment. They may want to invest in learning in some areas that are low priority or where learning has lower impact. It should be a good discussion!

Share draft versions of the documents described below, starting with a recap of the process described in Figure 4.1. Next, you might share the matrix of Table 4.6 and then the detail of Table 4.4 (if you used the first approach) or Table 4.5 (if you used the second approach). Incorporate their guidance and direction. You are done!

If you do plan to create a business case, your next step will be to build the business case on the foundation of strategic alignment. Hold off on seeking approval until the draft business case or plan is finished.

> CATERPILLAR EXPERIENCE: At Caterpillar we included the strategic alignment process and results in the Enterprise Learning Plan, which was our business plan for learning. Drafts were provided to the CEO and board of governors for their review and comment. The strategic alignment was approved as part of the overall approval of the Enterprise Learning Plan during the December board of governors meeting in preparation for the commencement of the next fiscal year on January 1st.

Strategic Alignment Results

It has taken time and effort, but you have now completed your strategic alignment, which will ensure that learning investment is focused on the highest priority goals where learning can have a high impact.

Benefits for the Learning Function and Goal Owners

The effort will save you considerable time through the year since much of the planning work is already done. And the majority of decisions about which learning to undertake have already been made so that you have a very good idea about your resource needs for next year. Creating a business plan for learning (Chapter 6) and a board of governors (Chapter 7) will ensure the process goes smoothly through the business planning cycle and through the year, but the hardest part is done.

The owners of the goals are also in an excellent position. They know how much of an impact they can plan on from learning and thus how much they will have to get elsewhere to achieve their goal. They know what is expected of them in terms of sponsorship and change management. And they have an idea about the costs of the program, even if the costs are not yet finalized.

Final Strategic Alignment

Results of the final strategic alignment can be shown in several ways. One is a table showing all the organization's goals in priority order along with the owners, planned learning programs, and the planned impact of learning. For large organizations, this table can easily be several pages long, depending on how much program detail is included. It would be used as an internal working document for the learning function and a summary version should also be included in the written business plan for learning. Tables 4.4 (using the first approach) and 4.5 (using the second approach) on the following pages provide two-page samples of these documents.

Note: In Table 4.4 planned impact is always calculated as goal x contribution from learning. For example, the planned impact of learning on sales is found as 10% increase in sales x 20% contribution from learning = 2% increase in sales due just to learning. The planned impact of learning on defects is calculated as a 20% reduction in defects x 70% contribution from learning = 14% reduction in defects due just to learning.

TABLE 4.4

Strategic Alignment of Learning to Organization Goals (A)

Priority	*Corporate Goal*	*Key Learning Programs*	*Target Audience*	*Unique Participants*	*Planned Impact of Learning*	*Owner*	*Include In Plan?*
1 High	Increase sales by 10%	Consultative selling skills (new)	Marketing employees	100	Medium	Ortega	Yes
		New product information (revised)	Marketing employees	100			
		Total key programs		100			
2 High	Reduce defects by 20%	Four Design courses (3 new)	New, other engineers	200	High	D'Agoto	Yes
3 High	Reduce Injuries by 25%	Five Safety courses (3 new)	Manufact. associates	2,500	High	Swilthe	Yes
		One Safety course (revised)	Factory supervisors	100			
		Two Safety courses (1 new)	Office employees	500			
				3,100			
4 Medium	Improve leadership score by 5 points on employee survey	Intro to supervision (revised)	New, other supervisors	100	Medium	Wang	Yes
		Leadership for managers (new)	Division managers	65			
		Advanced leadership (existing)	Department heads	15			
				180			
5 Medium	Increase employee retention by 10 points	Individual development plans	All employees	5,000	Medium	Dreise	Yes
		Performance management(new)	Mgt employees	2,500			
				5,000			

6	Medium	Increase innovation by 20% (patent applications)	Establish communities of practice Innovation workshop(new)	Design engineers Design engineers	100 100 100	Medium	Chan	No
7	Medium	Reduce cost of purchased materials by 5%	Five Purchasing courses (5 new)	Purchasing employees and managers	200	High	Murphy	Yes
8	Medium	Increase internal bench-strength for officers	None			NA	Dreise	No
9	Low	Open office in Beijing	Orientation	New employees	25	NA	Li	No
10	Low	Reduce technical support complaints by 30%	Product training (new) Customer relations skills (revised)	Call center employees Call center employees	50 25 50	High	Salvatore	Yes
11	Low	Reduce exposure to fraud and insider trading	One online fraud course (new) One online insider trading (existing)	Select employees Select employees	1,700 1,500 1,700	Essential	Omwetti	Yes

TABLE 4.5

Strategic Alignment of Learning to Organization Goals (B)

Priority	*Corporate Goal*	*Key Learning Programs*	*Target Audience*	*Unique Partici-pants*	*Planned Contribution from Learning*	*Planned Impact of Learning*	*Owner*	*Include In Plan ?*
1 High	Increase sales by 10%	Consultative selling skills (new)	Marketing employees	100			Ortega	Yes
		New product information (revised)	Marketing employees	100				
		Total key programs		100	20%	2% higher sales		
2 High	Reduce defects by 20%	Four Design courses (3 new)	New, other engineers	200	70%	14% reduction in defects	D'Agoto	Yes
3 High	Reduce Injuries by 25%	Five Safety courses (3 new)	Manufact. associates	2,500			Swilthe	Yes
		One Safety course (revised)	Factory supervisors	100				
		Two Safety courses (1 new)	Office employees	500				
				3,100	60%	15% reduction in injuries		
4 Medium	Improve leadership score by 5 points on employee survey	Intro to supervision (revised)	New, other	100			Wang	Yes
		Leadership for managers (new)	Division managers	65				
		Advanced leadership (existing)	Department heads	15				
				180	40%	2 point increase in leadership score		
5 Medium	Increase employee retention by 10 points	Individual development plans	All employees	5,000			Dreise	Yes
		Performance management(new)	Mgt employees	2,500				
				5,000	30%	3 point increase in retention		

6	Medium	Increase innovation by 20% (patent applications)	Establish communities of practice Innovation workshop(new)	Design engineers Design engineers	100 100 100	20%	4% increase in innovation	Chan	No
7	Medium	Reduce cost of purchased materials by 5%	Five Purchasing courses (5 new)	Purchasing employees	200	60%	3% reduction in costs	Murphy	Yes
8	Medium	Increase internal bench-strength for officers	None				NA	Dreise	No
9	Low	Open office in Beijing	Orientation	New employees	25	Low	Not essential	Li	No
10	Low	Reduce technical support complaints by 30%	Product training (new) Customer relations skills (revised)	Call center employees Call center employees	50 25 50	50%	15% reduction in complaints	Salvatore	Yes
11	Low	Reduce exposure to fraud and insider trading	One online fraud course (new) One online insider trading (existing)	Select employees Select employees	1,700 1,500 1,700	High	Essential	Omwetti	Yes

Notice that in the example, after the second or third meeting and after further needs analysis, the CLO decided not to recommend investing to support innovation this year (perhaps the underlying problem was the incentive structure). Of course, your CEO and governing body will have an opinion as well!

For general presentation purposes, at least three slides are recommended. The first would describe the process, including those who should be interviewed, like Figure 4.2.

FIGURE 4.2

Description of the Strategic Alignment Process

- Interviewed CEO, Group Presidents, Board of Governors with regard to goals and priorities
- Discussed goals in detail with each goal owner and explored whether learning could contribute to achieving the goal
- Compiled preliminary findings on goals, priorities, and the appropriateness & potential impact of learning. Identified target areas for learning.
- Held detailed discussions with targeted owners on potential learning programs, planned impact of learning, requirements, and costs. Refined impact and cost plans.
- Finalized strategic alignment and shared with CEO and Board of Governors for review. Revised as necessary
- Final version published

The second slide would be a matrix showing alignment of learning to the organization's goals, as in Table 4.6. The learning might be organized by program, area, or college.

TABLE 4.6
Strategic Alignment of Learning to the Organization's Goals

Summary Matrix

	Learning programs for								
Corporate Objectives	*Sales*	*Design*	*Safety*	*Leadership*	*Perf Mgt*	*Product*	*Purch.*	*Customer Skills*	*Compliance*
High Priority									
Increase sales	X					X		X	
Reduce defects		X							
Reduce injuries			X						
Medium Priority									
Improve leadership				X					
Increase ee retention					X				
Increase innovation									
Reduce purch. costs							X		
Increase bench strength									
Low Priority									
Open Beijing office									
Reduce tech sup complaints						X		X	
Reduce fraud & insider trading exposure									X

NOTE: Objectives in *italics* not addressed by training for next year.

This matrix clearly shows that learning is planned in support of eight of the eleven corporate objectives.

The third slide would be either Table 4.4 or Table 4.5 in their entirety or a condensed version. You might eliminate the rows containing goals not supported by learning and the columns for target audience, participants, and planned contribution of learning. Tables 4.7 and 4.8 provide examples.

TABLE 4.7
Summary of Strategic Alignment of Learning to Organization Goals (A)

Priority	*Corporate Goal* Medium	*Key Learning Programs*	*Planned Impact of Learning*	*Owner*
1 High	Increase sales by 10%	Consultative selling skills (new) New product information (revised)	Medium	Ortega
2 High	Reduce defects by 20%	Four Design courses (3 new)	High	D'Agoto
3 High	Reduce Injuries by 25%	Five Safety courses (3 new) One Safety course (revised) Two Safety courses (1 new)	High	Swilthe
4 Medium	Improve leadership score by 5 points on employee survey	Intro to supervision (revised) Leadership for managers (new) Advanced leadership (existing)	Medium	Wang
5 Medium	Increase employee retention by 10 points	Individual development plans Performance management (new)	Medium	Dreise
7 Medium	Reduce costs of purchased materials by 5%	Five Purchasing courses (5 new)	High	Murhpy
10 Low	Reduce technical support complaints by 30%	Product training (new) Customer relations skills (revised)	High	Salvatore
11 Low	Reduce exposure to fraud and insider trading	One online fraud course (new) One online insider trading (existing)	Essential	Omwetti

TABLE 4.8
Summary of Strategic Alignment of Learning to Organization Goals (B)

Priority	*Corporate Goal*	*Key Learning Programs*	*Planned Impact of Learning*	*Owner*
1 High	Increase sales by 10%	Consultative selling skills (new) New product information (revised)	2% higher sales	Ortega
2 High	Reduce defects by 20%	Four Design courses (3 new)	14% reduction in defects	D'Agoto
3 High	Reduce Injuries by 25%	Five Safety courses (3 new) One Safety course (revised) Two Safety courses (1 new)	15% reduction in injuries	Swilthe
4 Medium	Improve leadership score by 5 points on employee survey	Intro to supervision (revised) Leadership for managers (new) Advanced leadership (existing)	2 point increase in leadership score	Wang
5 Medium	Increase employee retention by 10 points	Individual development plans Performance management (new)	3 point increase in retention	Dreise
7 Medium	Reduce costs of purchased materials by 5%	Five Purchasing courses (5 new)	3% reduction in costs	Murhpy
10 Low	Reduce technical support complaints by 30%	Product training (new) Customer relations skills (revised)	15% reduction in complaints	Salvatore
11 Low	Reduce exposure to fraud and insider trading	One online fraud course (new) One online insider trading (existing) Performance support	Essential	Omwetti

Business Goals versus HR Goals

Some organizations may prefer to separate business goals and HR goals in their reports. In this case business goals may represent just the top goals of the CEO, which focus directly on the business like increasing sales, reducing costs, and improving productivity or quality. It is understood that HR goals like increasing employee engagement, improving leadership and boosting retention will indirectly support all the business goals. The process of strategic alignment is the same in either case with the difference being in how the results are displayed. Table 4.9 provides an example where the key business goals from the CEO are shown on top and the supporting HR goals are shown at the bottom.

TABLE 4.9
Summary Strategic Alignment of Learning to Business and HR Goals

Priority	*Business Goal*	*Key Learning Programs*	*Planned Impact of Learning*	*Owner*
1 High	Increase sales by 10%	Consultative selling skills (new) New product information (revised)	Medium	Ortega
2 High	Reduce defects by 20%	Four Design courses (3 new)	High	D'Agoto
3 High	Reduce Injuries by 25%	Five Safety courses (3 new) One Safety course (revised) Two Safety courses (1 new)	High	Swilthe
4 Medium	Reduce costs of purchased materials by 5%	Five Purchasing courses (5 new)	High	Murhpy
5 Low	Reduce technical support complaints by 30%	Product training (new) Customer relations skills (revised)	High	Salvatore
6 Low	Reduce exposure to fraud and insider trading	One online fraud course (new) One online insider trading (existing)	Essential	Omwetti

TABLE 4.9 *(continued)*

Priority		***HR Goal***	***Key Learning Programs***	***Planned Impact of Learning***	***Owner***
A	Low	Improve employee engagement score by 3 points on employee survey	Individual development plans More general learning opportunities Increased tuition assistance	Medium	Wang
B	Medium	Improve leadership score by 5 points on employee survey	Intro to supervision (revised) Leadership for managers (new) Advanced leadership (existing)	Medium	Wang
C	Medium	Increase employee retention by 10 points	Individual development plans Performance management (new)	Medium	Dreise

ADVICE AND CATERPILLAR EXPERIENCE: Contrast Table 4.9 where business and HR goals are separated with Tables 4.7 and 4.8 where the HR goals like improving leadership and retention are integrated with the business goals. Increasingly, organizations are coming to view some key HR goals as business goals, and HR goals like retention, leadership and engagement are included in the CEOs top five to seven goals. If your CEO includes some HR goals in her list of the top five to seven goals, then use the integrated approach shown in Tables 4.7 and 4.8. If your CEO lists just traditional business goals in his list but you can also support key HR goals, then use the approach shown in Table 4.9 to include the HR goals beneath the business goals. While I was at Caterpillar University, the CEO included goals to increase employee engagement and leadership in his top seven so we used the integrated approach.

The Seven Myths of Strategic Alignment

Rounding out our discussion of the strategic alignment process, here are seven common myths about strategic alignment. Expect to hear some of these as you suggest implementing your own strategic alignment process.

We are aligned because:

1. *We only do what senior leaders ask us.* This assumes that all of your senior leaders' requests are closely aligned to the company's goals, which is often not the case. Responding to all requests for training also means that you are not prioritizing the learning nor are you ensuring that it is likely to make a meaningful contribution to a high-priority company goal.
2. *We are aligned to HR goals.* This assumes that HR goals are closely aligned to company goals which is rarely the case. Instead, HR is more likely to have its own set of goals which may focus on employee engagement, leadership, compensation and benefits, and performance management. These goals may support the company's goals indirectly but not directly. In other words, HR is unlikely to have explicit goals, which mirror company goals like increase sales, reduce injuries or defects, etc. Consequently, while L&D should certainly support HR goals, it must also directly support the company's highest priority goals.
3. *We can connect everything we do to some company goal.* Any good L&D professional can look at a list of learning initiatives and make some connection back to a company goal even if it is very indirect. This is why surveys always report a high level of alignment. If they did not use a proactive, strategic process like the one described in this chapter, they cannot achieve true strategic alignment and will not know what portion of their learning spend is actually unaligned to company goals.
4. *My CEO, CFO, SVPHR are happy with what we are doing.* The presumption here is that these senior leaders know what they should expect from L&D and hold L&D to as high a standard as they hold other departments. Sadly, this is seldom the case. Many senior leaders have been conditioned to believe that L&D cannot be run with business discipline and thus their goal is to minimize the amount spent on it and hope for the best. If you asked them if they would like you to align your learning resources to their most important goals and then work closely in partnership with other

senior leaders to make a meaningful contribution to achieving those goals, what do you think they would say? So, your senior leaders may be happy with what you are doing today because they don't know any better.

5. *Everyone is happy with what we are doing.* This is an extension of the last myth. Ignorance of learning's potential to impact company goals is no reason not to do better. Employees and mid-level managers may indeed be happy with L&D today, but what if you told them that the company could develop them in a way that would not only increase their personal capability but would also contribute significantly to helping the company succeed? Don't you think they would be interested? Don't you think they would appreciate that their learning is aligned with the most important company goals and, as a result of applying that learning, they could make a meaningful contribution to the company?
6. *We win awards.* It is sad but true that many organizations do not have very high standards for their awards. And the judges themselves may not be familiar with what true strategic alignment looks like and it is often difficult when judging an award to know what process an applicant used to align their learning. Every applicant will say that their learning is strategically aligned, but as discussed above, most actually mean that they can connect their learning to some company goal after the fact. They did not follow a process upfront designed to guarantee strategic alignment.
7. *We develop people, and people are responsible for accomplishing our company's goals.* Therefore, we are aligned. You might assume that I am making this up but I have heard this from more than one organization. By this line of reasoning, everything L&D has ever done or will ever do in the future meets the alignment test. Clearly, there are many L&D initiatives which are not directly aligned to the company's goals, and that is fine. Let's just be honest about this and thoughtfully manage the mix of aligned and unaligned learning.

How Do Competencies Fit In?

About now many of you may be wondering how competencies fit in. A competency is simply a characteristic like leadership that is important to achieving the goals of an organization. Although we have not talked about them, competencies and competency models can certainly be used to address identified needs and improve performance. But we do need to be clear about their role. They are a means to the end and not an end in themselves. The end is determined through the strategic alignment process: achieving the highest priority organization goals. To the extent competency models can help achieve these goals, great—use them appropriately. But if your competency models do not serve your highest priority goals, you need to reexamine your continued investment in them.

For many of your highest priority goals, a competency-based approach will make sense. Through your discussions with the project sponsor and your needs analysis, you will have confirmed that learning can play an important role in achieving the objective. You will have identified the key competencies required and the proficiency levels that must be attained to produce the desired results. You can create instruments to discover the target audience's current level of proficiency and then design learning to bring the participants' competencies to the desired level. Just remember: your goal as learning manager is to help achieve the organization's goal (higher sales, for example). By raising the participants' competency level to proficiency or beyond, the participants should move the organization closer to its goal. It will not be enough to demonstrate that competency levels have been increased or proficiency attained. Bottom line performance must improve.

> ADVICE: The danger in practice is that some competency approaches and models become very complex, resource intensive, and expensive. Some take years to develop and implement. And once a lot of effort or resource has been invested, it becomes increasingly difficult to walk away from it or scale it back, even as organizational priorities change. So, be careful in opting for a complex competency model as part of your recommended learning. It may be exactly the right approach for you to take, especially if the goal is likely to remain a high priority

for years to come (like leadership or sales, perhaps). Too many organizations, however, have chosen competency approaches that are so complex that the program is never fully implemented and the anticipated benefits are never realized.

Conclusion

Congratulations! You now know how to complete the single most important process a learning manager can perform. You are prepared to align learning strategically to the highest priority objectives of your organization, and you can do so in a very professional and disciplined way, which will allow you to be proactive and take a strategic focus. You no longer need to be reactive, juggling priorities on a daily basis in response to urgent requests for learning. You will be on your way to becoming a valued, strategic business partner.

Chapter 4 to Do List

1. If you have not already done so, read your organization's business and strategic plans. If they are not available, talk with your boss about the organization's vision, mission, strategy, and key goals for the current year.
2. Resolve to become more strategic next year. Create a plan, including a timetable, to implement a strategic planning process. (It may be multi-year.) Include a change management plan.
3. Share the plan and its benefits with your boss and with your own employees. Answer their questions and address their concerns. Secure their approval and support.
4. With the appropriate lead time, schedule the first interviews with your leaders.

Further Reading

Allen, Mark, ed. *The Corporate University Handbook: Designing, Managing and Growing a Successful Program*. New York: Amacom, 2002. (See Chapter 4.)

Elkeles, Tamar and Jack Phillips. *The Chief Learning Officer: Driving Value within a Changing Organization through Learning and Development.* Burlington, Massachusetts: Butterworth-Heinemann, 2007. (See Chapters 1, 2, and 4.)

Israelite, Larry, ed. *Lies About Learning: Leading Executives Separate Truth from Fiction in a $100 Billion Industry*. Alexandria, Virginia: ASTD Press, 2006. (See Chapter 7.)

Kirkpatrick, James, and Wendy Kirkpatrick. *Training on Trial: How Workplace Learning Must Reinvent Itself to Remain Relevant*. New York, New York: AMACOM, 2010.

Mantyla, Karen, ed. *The Learning Advantage: Blending Technology, Strategy and learning to Create Lasting Results.* East Peoria, Illinois: ASTD Press, 2009. (See Chapter 6.)

Pangarkar, Ajay and Teresa Kirkwood. *The Trainer's Balanced Scorecard*. San Francisco: Pfeiffer, 2009. (See Chapters 2–5.)

Phillips, Jack and Patty Phillips. *Beyond Learning Objectives: Develop Measurable Objectives That Link to the Bottom Line.* Alexandria, Virginia: ASTD Press, 2008.

Phillips, Patricia, and Jack Phillips. *10 Steps to Successful Business Alignment*. Alexandria, Virginia: ASTD Press, 2012.

Smith, Rita. *Strategic Learning Alignment*. Alexandria, Virginia: ASTD Press, 2011.

Van Adelsberg, David and Edward Trolley. *Running Training Like a Business: Delivering Unmistakable Value*. San Francisco: Berrett-Koehler, 1999. (See Chapter 3.)

Vanthournout, Donald, et al. *Return on Learning: Training for High Performance at Accenture*. Chicago: Agate, 2006. (See Chapter 4.)

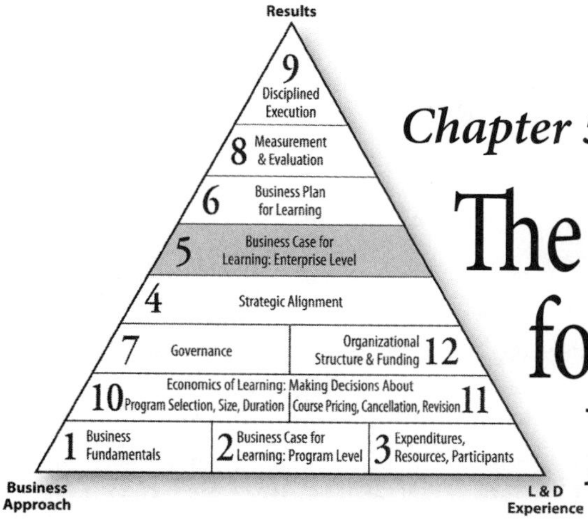

Chapter 5

The Business Case for Learning: Enterprise Level

THE BUSINESS CASE for learning starts with results of the strategic alignment (Chapter 4), ensures that all the benefits and costs have been included, and adds in the unaligned learning and unallocated costs to present a complete picture of benefits and costs. There is not a clear dividing line between the end of strategic alignment and the start of the business case at the enterprise level. Strategic alignment must come first to ensure that your learning is aligned to the highest priority goals of the organization. Discussions with each owner about the planned impact and costs of learning are part of the overall strategic alignment process and constitute the foundation for the business case. Now, these planned impacts and costs for the strategically aligned learning must be refined and agreed upon and then combined with the benefits and costs of unaligned learning and any other unaccounted-for costs to create the business case for learning.

Key Concepts for Chapter 5

5

1. The business case for learning starts with the results of the strategic alignment process.
2. Final, refined benefits (impact) and budget costs must be agreed upon for each strategically aligned program. Opportunity costs must be added.
3. Costs and benefits must be determined for unaligned programs.
4. Costs not included elsewhere, if any, must be included to present a complete business case.
5. Benefits (impact) must be compared to total costs for each program and for the entire learning function to make the business case for learning.
6. The right level of investment in learning depends on the needs of the organization to achieve its goals, the impact learning can have on meeting those needs, and the projected return of the investment in learning.

In its most elementary form, a business case simply brings together the benefits and costs of a proposed project or investment so an informed decision can be made on whether to proceed. While this seems very logical, it is often the case that decisions are made without a comparison of the benefits to the costs. Very often, the costs will be known but the benefits are never quantified. In other cases the benefits may be quantified but the costs are not compiled. Regrettably, there are many instances where L&D proceeds to invest in learning without having examined either the benefits or the costs.

Benefits and Costs for Strategically Aligned Learning

If benefits and costs were not refined in the strategic alignment process or new information has become available, now is the time to complete the refinement. Your goal is to know the total costs for each recommended program, which includes the budget cost (development and delivery by both staff and vendors) and the opportunity cost for the participants. For benefits, you will want to confirm the planned impact of learning on each corporate goal that came out of the strategic alignment process (like a 5% increase in sales), and you may want to calculate the dollar value of that impact as well as its impact on net income.

At a minimum the output of strategic alignment will be tables such as 4.7 or 4.8 and Table 4.6 with the recommended programs and some estimate of planned impact. The learning staff likely will have been working to complete more detailed needs analyses to confirm the efficacy of the proposed learning and to refine the impact and cost plans. Both need to be refined to the point where the owner and learning managers are comfortable and ready to include them in the business case. The budget costs will be included in the owner's and/or learning function's budget, while the impact of the learning will be embedded in the business plan of the sponsor as well as the learning organization.

Refinement of both benefits and costs will occur simultaneously as the business case comes together. Benefits will be addressed first.

Making the Benefits Explicit

In the second or third discussion with the goal's sponsor or owner in the strategic alignment process, the CLO would have asked about the planned impact of the learning program being discussed. At first, the discussion may just try to identify whether the planned impact is likely to be high, medium, or low. Later in the second or third meeting, it may be possible to be more precise. For example, can both parties agree that this program, if well-designed, implemented, and reinforced, could lead to a 5% increase in sales with a bottom line impact of $1.5 million on net income? Can you at least agree on the 5% planned impact of learning? If not, you will still be able to use the results of the qualitative approach where the goal owner characterized the impact with an adjective rather than a number.

Note: We will assume first that you and the goal owner have reached agreement on a percentage contribution of learning (the quantitative approach) because this will allow us to best illustrate the development of a powerful and compelling business case. Later in the chapter we will explore how to create a less compelling but still very worthwhile business case using the qualitative approach to learning's planned impact.

This process was discussed in the previous chapter. The following two sections reinforce and expand on that discussion since results of that discussion are absolutely critical to make the business case.

Discussions with the Goal Owner on Planned Impact

If the owner has not had this type of discussion before, it is best to approach it in stages. In the first meeting with the owner, do not ask about the impact of learning at all. Instead, ask about all the factors that will influence achieving the goal. Next, you might ask which of those the owner believes will be most important for this next year. What are the top three? The first meeting should be a business discussion with the owner doing virtually all of the talking. Your role is to ask questions, listen and learn.

In your next meeting you share your initial thoughts about how learning can help achieve the 10% increase in sales. You explain that consultative selling skills combined with modules on product knowledge (especially the new features) could improve your sales force's ability to sell the value of the new product and realize higher pricing (lower discounting). Now you are ready to facilitate the discussion covered in Chapter 4 about a reasonable plan for the impact of learning. At the end of this facilitated discussion the owner will have indicated that she thinks the learning will have a high, medium or low impact on achieving her goal or perhaps she will have provided a percentage contribution (like 20%) toward achieving the goal. If she offers a range, you can be conservative and accept the lower end or suggest a compromise in the middle. Your mission here is to come up with an impact the goal's owner is totally comfortable with and will readily volunteer to others when asked. (The test is this: Suppose the CEO were to ask the owner at lunch whether she was going to use learning to achieve her goal next year and, if so, what impact she expected from the learning. How would the sponsor answer? She needs to give the CEO the same answer she just gave you.) You have already discussed this internally within the learning function. Does the owner say what you expected? If not, ask more clarifying questions to understand why the owner believes the impact will be higher or lower than you and your staff were thinking. Do not press for consensus yet. Let the owner reflect on it while you and your team do the same.

If necessary, meet one last time to reach agreement on the program specifics and planned impact. By now you may have refined your program recommendations and have preliminary agreement with the owner's staff on the target audience and deployment & completion deadlines. Remember, both you and the owner need to be comfortable with all aspects of the plan. The "right" answer for planned impact is not a "high" impact or a 70% (or greater) contribution to the goal. It is what you both believe is a reasonable and achievable impact that is good enough for *planning purposes.*

If achieving the goal will have a bottom line impact on net income (most will), in the first or second meeting you should also ask what that dollar impact will be. In most cases the CEO and owner (and perhaps the board of directors) will have thought this through and have a number in mind. In our sales example, the answer might be: "Assuming a 30% margin on incremental sales, a 10% or $25,000,000 increase in sales should contribute an additional $7.5 million in net income." In fact, they may have started with a desired increase in profit ($7.5 million) and worked backward to calculate the required increase in sales ($7.5/30% = $25). Current sales are $250 million, so we need a $25/$250 or 10% increase in sales. This figure tells you how much is at stake and will be useful in computing the planned dollar impact of learning.

If the goal's expected impact on net income (like $7.5 million) does not exist, not to worry. You can derive a dollar impact from learning without it.

Summary of First Two or Three Meetings

After two or three meetings with the owner of the goal, you should have agreement on the following:

1. Whether learning has a role to play in achieving the goal
2. Specific learning programs with target audience identified
3. Start and completion dates for development and deployment
4. Role of the owner in making subject matter experts available, championing the learning, leading the necessary change management, and providing reinforcement (or negative consequences) for the desired change in behavior
5. Learning objectives and agreed measures of success
6. Planned contribution of learning on the corporate goal (20% of the 10% increase in sales)
7. Planned impact of learning (2% increase in sales)
8. Planned impact of achieving goal on net income ($7.5 million) if possible
9. Planned costs for learning, both budget and opportunity

What to Do if the Goal Owner Doesn't Cooperate

There will be instances where the goal owner simply will not engage in the process we have described. They may not perceive any value in the discussion or they may say something like, "You are the experts in learning so you tell me what the impact will be." In yet other cases, there may not be a single owner of the goal. Instead the goal may be "shared" among all top leaders (everyone is supposed to do their part in helping to achieve it but no single leader is accountable) or there may be a committee of three or four leaders jointly responsible. In these cases it may be difficult or impossible to facilitate the discussion outlined above, and you will need to come up with your own planned impact. Advice here is to be very conservative and humble. You can work with your staff and perhaps staff in the goal owner's organization to come up with some conservative planning assumptions. Then share these with the goal owner who may now better appreciate what you were trying to do and provide guidance. If not, share them with a governing board or the CEO and ask for their feedback. Better yet, if you have a governing board for learning, engage them in the process to help come up with reasonable plans for impact.

Calculating the Planned Impact of Learning on Net Income

If you have used the quantitative approach, you are now ready to calculate the expected impact of learning on net income, if appropriate. There may be programs where it is not feasible or desirable to try to assign a dollar value to the impact of learning. For some organizations leadership learning and courses on performance management, personal growth, and other "softer" programs may fall into this category. (These are examples of talent-driven learning and unlike performance-driven learning they may not align directly to corporate goals. In some cases there will be a high-level goal for employee engagement or leadership and you will be able to reach agreement on the planned impact. Converting this to dollars can be more challenging but many use the value of improved productivity, which is relatively easy to measure, as a very conservative proxy for all the benefits of the program.) In some nonprofit organizations the focus may be more on cost reduction than net income or surplus, and the calculations could be modified accordingly.

Where it is appropriate, however, the calculation is easy if items 6 and 8 from above are available. The planned dollar impact of learning is simply: planned contribution from learning on the corporate goal multiplied by planned impact on net income of achieving goal. For example,

$$20\% \times \$7.5 \text{ million} = \$1.5 \text{ million.}$$

In our example the two learning programs for the sales force, properly designed, delivered, and reinforced, should contribute $1.5 million to the bottom line before expenses. Since learning expenses have not yet been subtracted, the $1.5 million will be referred to as the gross benefit of learning going forward. (Note: Jack and Patti Phillips refer to gross benefit as the program benefit.)

The 20% impact figure is good to share because it provides a way for others to assess the reasonableness of the $1.5 million. The mental check will be, "Is it reasonable to assume that these learning programs for these sales people delivered early in the year could contribute 20% of our planned increase in sales?"

If the planned impact on net income from achieving the goal (the $7.5 million in our example) is not available, then work with the sponsor to determine the gross benefit of the learning directly. What would a 2% increase in sales be worth? The marketing organization should know or be able to find out, perhaps with the help of accounting. For these high-priority goals it will not be as difficult as you might think to arrive at a plan for gross benefit. Many people have already been thinking about the impact of achieving the goal even if it has not been formally communicated.

If you have some programs where it is not possible or does not seem appropriate to calculate the planned impact in dollar terms (gross benefit), then you can pass on them. In this case your summary table will contain some "NA" or "Not Available" or "Not Appropriate" entries instead of numbers.

Making the Costs Explicit

At a minimum the business case will need to include costs for all the recommended programs aligned to the organization's goals. Ideally, it also will include costs for the unaligned learning and learning-related costs not accounted for elsewhere so that a complete picture of benefits and costs for the entire learning function may be presented.

Costs for the Strategically Aligned Learning

Since the strategically aligned learning is the most important learning, complete costs for this learning must be included in the business case.

Once there is initial agreement on the recommended learning programs (for example, a consultative sales program for 100 sales employees at headquarters in the first quarter), it is time for the learning staff to begin costing out the program. This may occur before the second meeting with the owner where the program recommendation is made (if you are confident the owner will agree with the recommendation) or after the meeting (if you wish to wait for the owner's feedback or clarification). In any case it is an iterative process and will continue as you and the owner refine the program, target audience, and timing and make decisions about insourcing, outsourcing, and the use of internal subject matter experts.

Budget or accounting costs as well as opportunity costs must be calculated and shared with the sponsor and his staff. Budget costs are the development and delivery costs, including program-related purchases, the value of the internal learning staff's time, and the cost of outsourcing to vendors, consultants, or university partners. For costing internal staff, you will need to forecast the amount of time and multiply by their fully-burdened labor and related rate. (Fully-burdened means that you apportioned all of your nonprogram-related overhead to your staff. This hourly rate allows you to recover all of your nonprogram related costs. Your accountant can help. See Chapter 1 for a detailed explanation.)

For outsourced course development and delivery, use a forecast of their cost based on past experience or procure some informal estimates (much easier to do if you have some preferred partners who work closely with you). Since it is just the beginning of the process, do not start by sending out an RFP (request for proposal). You can do this later once you have completed a more detailed needs analysis, refined the requirements, and reached agreement with the owner.

For opportunity costs, find out the labor and related rate for the target audience from the owner or someone on his staff and then multiply by the number of hours the participants will be engaged in learning, including the travel time. This gives you a minimum opportunity cost. For some target audiences, the opportunity cost may be greater. For example, in our sales example, the owner may be able to provide an estimate of the sales likely to be lost when the sales people are in class. You would then multiply the lost sales by the profit margin expected on those sales to calculate the true opportunity cost. (It should be greater than the value of their time.) See Chapter 3 for more detail.

It is important to share both the budget costs and the opportunity costs with the owner in the second or third meeting for two reasons. First, the owner needs to know what the total costs will be, even if the budget costs do not fall in his budget. The opportunity costs in particular may be an eye opener and surprise the owner, which may lead to a good discussion about ways to reduce both budget and opportunity costs, just the type of discussion that should be occurring in the second and third meetings as you refine the programs. Second, total costs must be compared to the planned impact and benefits of the program to make a decision about whether to proceed. It may be that total costs exceed the benefits or are simply too high compared to the planned impact or benefit. In this case you will have to find a way to reduce the costs or increase the benefits or else scrap the program. (Do not include it in the business case as a recommended program.)

If there are many strategically aligned programs, focus most of your effort on the programs supporting the highest priority goals, the programs with the highest planned impact, and the programs with the highest planned costs.

The Net Benefit of Aligned Learning

Now that costs have been planned, the net benefit of learning can be estimated for each recommended program where it is appropriate (and for all strategically aligned learning if dollar net benefits are forecast for all or most programs). This may not be of interest to the owner but will certainly be of interest to the learning manager, CLO, and governing board.

Calculation of Net Benefit and ROI

The net benefit of learning for a particular program is simply the gross benefit of learning less the total cost of the learning. In our sales example, assume the budget cost (development and delivery) for the two courses is $490,000 and assume the opportunity cost is $117,000 for a total cost of $607,000. The net benefit of learning is then $1.5 million minus $607,000 or $893,000. By formula, net benefit = gross benefit - total cost = $1.5 million - $607,000 = $893,000.

For those who would like to compute an expected ROI for the learning, it is simply the net benefit ($893,000) divided by the total cost ($607,000) or 147%. By formula, ROI = net benefit/total cost = $893,000/$607,000 = 147%.

Presenting the Data

The net benefits of all the strategically aligned learning programs now can be summed and presented. Start with the "ideal" case where dollar benefits are appropriate for all programs and where each goal's impact on net income is available. (We will relax this assumption shortly.) An example is provided in Table 5.1.

Notice that learning for the top five priorities has been presented in detail while learning for the remainder of the strategically aligned learning is presented as a summary. Decision makers often like to focus on the vital few, in this case the top five. Of course, the detail for each program included in "Subtotal for Other Programs" would be available and could be shared. (Note: Tables 5.2–5.4 build on this first table, but you would share only your final table with senior leadership. Furthermore, you might want to share a more concise version first and keep the more detailed table in reserve. See Table 5.5 for an example of a summary version.)

In Table 5.1 the gross benefit of learning is $7.8 million for the top five priorities and another $3.05 million for the rest of the aligned learning for a total gross benefit of $10.85 million. After subtracting both budget and opportunity costs, the net benefit of the aligned learning is $3.979 million for an ROI of 58%. Notice that the net benefit of the top five priorities was $2.952 million (ROI of 61%) versus the net benefit of the rest of the aligned learning at $1.028 million (ROI of 51%). As expected, learning for the top priorities has much more impact than the learning for lower priorities.

TABLE 5.1

2017 Business Case for Strategically Aligned Learning (with Impact of Corporate Goals on Net Income)

Priority	Corporate Goal	Impact on Net Income (thous $)	Key Learning Programs	Target Audience	Unique Partici-pants	Total Partici pants	Planned Contribution from Learning	Planned Impact of Learning	Thousands of Dollars: Gross Benefit	Budget Cost	Budget Impact	Opport-unity Cost	Net Benefit	ROI
1	Increase sales by 10%	$7,500	Consultative selling skills (new)	Marketing employees	100	100								
			Ten NPI modules (10 new)	Marketing employees	100	1,000								
			Total key programs		100	1,100	20%	2% higher sales	$1,500	$490	$1,010	$117	$893	147%
2	Reduce defects by 20%	$3,000	Four Design courses (3 new)	New, other engineers	200	800	70%	14% reduct. in defects	$2,100	$570	$1,530	$512	$1,018	94%
3	Reduce Injuries by 25%	$2,000	Five Safety courses (3 new)	Manufact. associates	2,500	12,500								
			One Safety course (revised)	Factory supervisors	100	100								
			Two Safety courses (1 new)	Office employees	500	1,000								
			Total key programs		3,100	13,600	60%	15% reduct. in injuries	$1,200	$410	$790	$376	$415	53%
4	Improve leadership score by 5 points on employee survey	$3,000	Intro to supervision (revised)	New, other supervisors	100	100								
			Leadership for managers (new)	Division managers	65	65								
			Advanced leadership (existing)	Department heads	15	15								
			Total key programs		180	180	40%	2 point increase	$1,200	$582	$618	$302	$316	36%
5	Increase retention by 5 points	$6,000	Individual development plans	All employees	5,000	5,000								
			Performance mgt (new)	Mgt employees	2,500	2,500								
			Total key programs		5,000	7,500	30%	1.5 point increase	$1,800	$340	$1,460	$1,150	$310	21%
Total for Top Five Priorities		**$21,500**	**Learning for Top Five Goals** Courses: 20 New , 2 Revised		**5,000**	**23,180**	**46%**	**Range = 20%-70%**	**$7,800**	**$2,392**	**$5,408**	**$2,457**	**$2,952**	**61%**
Total for All Other Goals		**$5,000**	**Learning for All Other Goals** Courses: 16 New , 2 Revised		**1,950**	**4,725**	**61%**	**Range = 50%-70%**	**$3,050**	**$1,245**	**$1,805**	**$778**	**$1,028**	**51%**
Grand Total for All Goals		**$26,500**	**Total for All Aligned Learning** **Courses: 36 New , 4 Revised**		**5,000**	**27,905**	**49%**	**Range = 20%-70%**	**$10,850**	**$3,637**	**$7,213**	**$3,234**	**$3,979**	**58%**

Also note that Table 5.1 shows the budget impact of the learning, which is simply the gross benefit less the budget costs. The budget impact is the bottom line (net income) impact of the learning. In this example the budget impact is $7.213 million, meaning that net income should increase by $7.2 million because of this learning. It is considerably higher than the $4 million net benefit of learning, which includes $3.2 million of opportunity costs. (Recall that opportunity costs do not appear as a visible expense and are not included in the income statement.)

The highest priority strategically aligned learning is the most critical part of the business case and should be the first area of focus. If resources do not allow for a complete business case, start with this. You can always add the case for unaligned learning and the unallocated costs at a later date.

Before concluding this section, we need to relax our assumption of complete data availability. Table 5.1 includes a column for the impact of the corporate goal on net income. When this information is available, it allows the reader to easily calculate the dollar impact of learning on net income. For example, if a 10% increase in sales will generate $7.5 million in net income and if the learning programs designed to increase sales are expected to contribute half or 20% to the 10% increase in sales, then the dollar impact of learning will be $7.5 million x 20% or $1.5 million.

Often, however, the impact of the corporate goal on net income will not be available. In this case, simply eliminate the column as in Table 5.2. Without the impact on net income, the expected percentage impact on corporate objectives at a summary level (46%, 61%, and 49% in Table 5.1) cannot be calculated, but the range of impact still provides good information. For the rest of this chapter, we will assume that the impact of the corporate goal on net income is not available and therefore will not include that column in the tables that follow.

Benefits and Costs for Unaligned Learning

It is common for a learning function to offer courses not aligned to any of an organization's goals or at least not aligned directly to those goals. Examples include courses to improve writing, reading, listening, communicating, and teaming skills, all of which contribute to an employee's effectiveness and personal growth but usually do not contribute directly to achieving an organization's goals. Typically, there is not a specific (by name) target audience identified in advance to

TABLE 5.2

2017 Business Case for Stragically Aligned Learning

Priority	Corporate Goal	Key Learning Programs	Target Audience	Unique Partici-pants	Total Partici-pants	Planned Contribution from Learning	Planned Impact of Learning	Gross Benefit (Thousands of Dollars)	Budget Cost (Thousands of Dollars)	Budget Impact (Thousands of Dollars)	Opport-unity Cost (Thousands of Dollars)	Net Benefit (Thousands of Dollars)	ROI
1	Increase sales by 10%	Consultative selling skills (new)	Marketing employees	100	100								
		Ten NPI modules (10 new)	Marketing employees	100	1,000								
		Total key programs		100	1,100	20%	2% higher sales	$1,500	$490	$1,010	$117	$893	147%
2	Reduce defects by 20%	Four Design courses (3 new)	New, other engineers	200	800	70%	14% reduct. in defects	$2,100	$570	$1,530	$512	$1,018	94%
3	Reduce Injuries by 25%	Five Safety courses (3 new)	Manufact. associates	2,500	12,500								
		One Safety course (revised)	Factory supervisors	100	100								
		Two Safety courses (1 new)	Office employees	500	1,000								
		Total key programs		3,100	13,600	60%	15% reduct. in injuries	$1,200	$410	$790	$376	$415	53%
4	Improve leadership score by 5 points on employee survey	Intro to supervision (revised)	New, other supervisors	100	100								
		Leadership for managers (new)	Division managers	65	65								
		Advanced leadership (existing)	Department heads	15	15								
		Total key programs		180	180	40%	2 point increase	$1,200	$582	$618	$302	$316	36%
5	Increase retention by 5 points	Individual development plans	All employees	5,000	5,000								
		Performance mgt (new)	Mgt employees	2,500	2,500								
		Total key programs		5,000	7,500	30%	1.5 point increase	$1,800	$340	$1,460	$1,150	$310	21%
Total for Top Five Priorities		**Learning for Top Five Goals** Courses: 20 New , 2 Revised		**5,000**	**23,180**	**Range = 20%-70%**		**$7,800**	**$2,392**	**$5,408**	**$2,457**	**$2,952**	**61%**
Total for All Other Goals		**Learning for All Other Goals** Courses: 16 New , 2 Revised		**1,950**	**4,725**	**Range = 50%-70%**		**$3,050**	**$1,245**	**$1,805**	**$778**	**$1,028**	**51%**
Grand Total for All Goals		**Total for All Aligned Learning** **Courses: 36 New , 4 Revised**		**5,000**	**27,905**	**Range = 20%-70%**		**$10,850**	**$3,637**	**$7,213**	**$3,234**	**$3,979**	**58%**

take these courses, and they are offered on open enrollment. Many organizations buy access to a suite of courses from online providers, which may make several hundred courses available to employees.

Since these courses are not aligned with an organization's goals and since there are often hundreds of them, it does not make sense to evaluate each one to the same level of detail as the strategically aligned courses. This is not to say the unaligned courses are without value. The learning function should only make courses available that are believed to have value and, more specifically, to have value that exceeds their total cost. Operationally, however, these decisions may have been made on a suite of courses and with a much more cursory review.

For business case purposes, the unaligned learning will be considered as a bundle and not as individual courses. Furthermore, assumptions will be made about the gross and net benefits of this bundle of unaligned learning. In practice, you may be able to group your unaligned learning into several discrete bundles to refine both the forecasting of costs and benefits.

For unaligned learning, the best starting point is with costs.

Costs for Unaligned Learning

Budget costs for these courses include both development and delivery, just as with the aligned courses. Since you are not making course-by-course decisions here, you may be able to group these to forecast their costs more easily. One group might be the courses your staff will have to develop. Estimate their time and calculate the resulting cost using their fully-burdened labor and related hourly rate. Another group might be the courses you purchase from vendors. Forecast next year's cost based on current year costs adjusted for any change in volume and content or get an estimate from your vendor. A third group might be the courses your staff will be teaching. Here again use their fully-burdened labor and related hourly rate multiplied by the number of hours to forecast the cost. Then forecast what you will pay vendors or partners to deliver courses based on experience or quotes.

Opportunity costs are also important for the unaligned learning. Since there is not a specific target audience, it will be easiest to estimate the total number of hours of unaligned learning (from your learning management system) and multiply by an average hourly labor and related rate. You may be able to segment those taking the unaligned learning into several groups and use a more refined labor and related rate for each group.

Your goal for unaligned learning is to be "in the ball park," meaning close (+/- 20%). It is probably not worth the time to try to be more precise.

The Gross and Net Benefits of Unaligned Learning

An assumption will have to be made about the gross benefit of unaligned learning. You can forecast the budget and opportunity cost for the unaligned learning, but it is probably not worth your time to try to forecast the planned impact or gross benefit from each course. So, make an assumption and share the assumption explicitly so others may comment on it. There are three approaches.

Setting the Gross and Net Benefit

The first approach is ultra-conservative and may be politically unwise. Assume the unaligned learning has *no* impact and *no* value. In this case the gross benefit from this learning is zero, and the net benefit is simply the negative of the costs. For example, if budget costs are $300,000 and opportunity costs are $400,000, the total cost for unaligned learning is expected to be $700,000. Since there is no gross benefit or value, the net benefit is ($700,000). By formula,

net benefit = gross benefit - total cost = 0 - $700,000 = -$700,000.

The problem with this approach is that you are telling your leaders the unaligned learning is worthless. They may, quite logically, respond, "Why are you recommending we spend $300,000 on this learning if *you* believe it has no value. Let's just eliminate it." Of course, you would explain that it does have value, but you just wanted to be very conservative.

The second approach is conservative but more balanced. Assume that the unaligned learning is worth at least its total cost. In other words assume a net benefit of zero. After all, you would not be recommending that $300,000 be spent on these programs if you did not believe it had value *and* that this value was at least equal to the budget cost and opportunity cost. By formula,

net benefit = gross benefit - total cost = $700,000 - $700,000 = $0.

Operationally, just set the gross benefit equal to the total cost.

The third approach is to assume unaligned learning is worth more than its total cost. There are two problems here. First, you will have to select a gross benefit arbitrarily. Second, a high net benefit will increase your total net benefit for all

TABLE 5.3

2017 Business Case for Aligned and Unaligned Learning

								Thousands of Dollars					
Priority	*Corporate Goal*	*Key Learning Programs*	*Target Audience*	*Unique Partici-pants*	*Total Partici-pants*	*Planned Contribution from Learning*	*Planned Impact of Learning*	*Gross Benefit*	*Budget Cost*	*Budget Impact*	*Opport-unity Cost*	*Net Benefit*	*ROI*
1	Increase sales by 10%	Consultative selling skills (new)	Marketing employees	100	100								
		Ten NPI modules (10 new)	Marketing employees	100	1,000								
		Total key programs		100	1,100	20%	2% higher sales	$1,500	$490	$1,010	$117	$893	147%
2	Reduce defects by 20%	Four Design courses (3 new)	New, other engineers	200	800	70%	14% reduct. in defects	$2,100	$570	$1,530	$512	$1,018	94%
3	Reduce Injuries by 25%	Five Safety courses (3 new)	Manufact. associates	2,500	12,500								
		One Safety course (revised)	Factory supervisors	100	100								
		Two Safety courses (1 new)	Office employees	500	1,000								
		Total key programs		3,100	13,600	60%	15% reduct. in injuries	$1,200	$410	$790	$376	$415	53%
4	Improve leadership score by 5 points on employee survey	Intro to supervision (revised)	New, other supervisors	100	100								
		Leadership for managers (new)	Division managers	65	65								
		Advanced leadership (existing)	Department heads	15	15								
		Total key programs		180	180	40%	2 point increase	$1,200	$582	$618	$302	$316	36%
5	Increase retention by 5 points	Individual development plans	All employees	5,000	5,000								
		Performance mgt (new)	Mgt employees	2,500	2,500								
		Total key programs		5,000	7,500	30%	1.5 point increase	$1,800	$340	$1,460	$1,150	$310	21%
Total for Top Five Priorities		**Learning for Top Five Goals** Courses: 20 New , 2 Revised		**5,000**	**23,180**	**Range = 20%-70%**		**$7,800**	**$2,392**	**$5,408**	**$2,457**	**$2,952**	**61%**
Total for All Other Goals		**Learning for All Other Goals** Courses: 16 New , 2 Revised		**1,950**	**4,725**	**Range = 50%-70%**		**$3,050**	**$1,245**	**$1,805**	**$778**	**$1,028**	**51%**
		Total for All Aligned Learning Courses: 36 New , 4 Revised		**5,000**	**27,905**	**Range = 20%-70%**		**$10,850**	**$3,637**	**$7,213**	**$3,234**	**$3,980**	**58%**
		Unaligned Learning Courses: 2 New , 1 Revised		**4,000**	**4,000**	**Assume Net Ben = 0**		**$700**	**$300**	**$400**	**$400**	**$0**	**0%**
Grand Total		**Total for All Learning** **Courses: 38 New , 5 Revised**		**10,950**	**31,905**	**Range = 20%-70%**		**$11,550**	**$3,937**	**$7,613**	**$3,634**	**$3,980**	**53%**

learning and may raise suspicion since it was arbitrarily selected to improve your overall performance.

The second approach is recommended since the first approach is too conservative and the third approach too arbitrary. If you choose the third approach, be sure to select a gross benefit that will produce an ROI *less* than that for the aligned learning. It is highly unlikely that unaligned learning, in total, would ever have a higher ROI than aligned learning, in total.

Presenting the Data

Data for the unaligned learning now can be added to that for the aligned learning (see Table 5.3).

Notice that unaligned learning was assumed to have a net benefit of zero and thus including it did not increase the total net benefits for all programs. The ROI did decrease from 58% for aligned learning to 53% for all learning because costs went up for the unaligned learning with no increase in net benefits. Nonetheless, a 53% return and $4 million in net benefits is still very impressive.

Some Special Cases

There are a few special cases that may not fall neatly into the above categories of aligned or unaligned learning.

One is new hire orientation. In some companies the new hire orientation will be part of a strategic, aligned goal related to reducing turnover or increasing employee engagement. In companies without such a goal, the new hire program may be considered part of the unaligned learning. In contrast to the above examples of unaligned learning, however, there will be a by-name target audience, and it will not be offered in open enrollment. In this case it probably makes sense to break it out from the rest of the unaligned learning. Costs for the new hire orientation can definitely be isolated from other costs, and an assumption can be made about gross benefit (perhaps in terms of increased engagement and reduced turnover).

Another special case would be technical or professional learning (or any other compulsory learning) employees must take to keep current in their jobs. Here there is a specific target audience although the courses may be offered in open enrollment. If these courses are not part of a plan to address a specific strategic goal, then they should probably be shown separately in the unaligned learning category. Unlike the first type of unaligned learning, these courses are not discretionary. Costs for these programs can easily be isolated and an estimate made of the gross benefit of these courses.

Finally, there is the special case of tuition reimbursement. Many organizations reimburse their employees for university or technical school courses at approved institutions. Since this is unlikely to serve just one strategic goal, it may also need to be shown separately in the unaligned category. Costs are easily segregated from other learning expenses. Work by Michael Echols at Bellevue University and others can be used to establish a reasonable range for ROI, depending on the goal of the tuition reimbursement program. (See Echols's *ROI on Human Capital Investment.*)

Any "special cases" representing a large investment should be listed separately as a subcategory of aligned or unaligned learning or as a third category, in addition to aligned and unaligned learning.

Other Costs

There may be some other learning costs that have not yet been allocated or included. Most learning functions have support functions whose staff supports those who work directly with your internal customers. Support groups might include those who maintain the learning management system, who conduct measurements, who compile the business plan, or who perform HR or accounting for the group. The CLO, senior staff, and administrative assistants may fall into this category as well. It may also be the case that there are some staff who work directly with internal customers but whose time has not been fully committed to the aligned or unaligned programs. Ideally, these costs have already been identified and included in the nonattributable costs used to determine the fully-burdened labor rate (see Chapter 1). If these costs have not been included in the burden rate and thus in the costs for all the learning discussed above, you need to capture them now.

The goal is to make sure you have captured all of your costs. When all three types of budget costs (aligned, unaligned, and other) are added together, the total should equal the total budget costs for learning. In an organization where all the spending for learning is done by the learning function, the sum should equal the learning budget for the function. If your sum does not at least equal your budget, there are some costs missing.

TABLE 5.4

2017 Business Case for Learning

Priority	Corporate Goal	Key Learning Programs	Target Audience	Unique Partici-pants	Total Partici-pants	Planned Contribution from Learning	Planned Impact of Learning	Gross Benefit (Thousands of Dollars)	Budget Cost (Thousands of Dollars)	Budget Impact (Thousands of Dollars)	Opport-unity Cost (Thousands of Dollars)	Net Benefit (Thousands of Dollars)	ROI
1	Increase sales by 10%	Consultative selling skills (new)	Marketing employees	100	100								
		Ten NPI modules (10 new)	Marketing employees	100	1,000								
		Total key programs		100	1,100	20%	2% higher sales	$1,500	$490	$1,010	$117	$893	147%
2	Reduce defects by 20%	Four Design courses (3 new)	New, other engineers	200	800	70%	14% reduct. in defects	$2,100	$570	$1,530	$512	$1,018	94%
3	Reduce Injuries by 25%	Five Safety courses (3 new)	Manufact. associates	2,500	12,500								
		One Safety course (revised)	Factory supervisors	100	100								
		Two Safety courses (1 new)	Office employees	500	1,000								
		Total key programs		3,100	13,600	60%	15% reduct. in injuries	$1,200	$410	$790	$376	$415	53%
4	Improve leadership score by 5 points on employee survey	Intro to supervision (revised)	New, other supervisors	100	100								
		Leadership for managers (new)	Division managers	65	65								
		Advanced leadership (existing)	Department heads	15	15								
		Total key programs		180	180	40%	2 point increase	$1,200	$582	$618	$302	$316	36%
5	Increase retention by 5 points	Individual development plans	All employees	5,000	5,000								
		Performance mgt (new)	Mgt employees	2,500	2,500								
		Total key programs		5,000	7,500	30%	1.5 point increase	$1,800	$340	$1,460	$1,150	$310	21%
Total for Top Five Priorities		**Learning for Top Five Goals** Courses: 20 New , 2 Revised		**5,000**	**23,180**	**Range = 20%-70%**		**$7,800**	**$2,392**	**$5,408**	**$2,457**	**$2,952**	**61%**
Total for All Other Goals		**Learning for All Other Goals** Courses: 16 New , 2 Revised		**1,950**	**4,725**	**Range = 50%-70%**		**$3,050**	**$1,245**	**$1,805**	**$778**	**$1,028**	**51%**
		Total for All Aligned Learning Courses: 36 New , 4 Revised		**5,000**	**27,905**	**Range = 20%-70%**		**$10,850**	**$3,637**	**$7,213**	**$3,234**	**$3,980**	**58%**
		Unaligned Learning Courses: 2 New , 1 Revised		**4,000**	**4,000**	**Assume Net Ben = 0**		**$700**	**$300**	**$400**	**$400**	**$0**	**0%**
		Other Costs (not included elsewhere)		NA	NA			NA	$600	($600)	$0	($600)	NA
Grand Total		**Grand Total for All Learning** **Courses: 38 New , 5 Revised**		**5,000**	**31,905**	**Range = 20%-70%**		**$11,550**	**$4,537**	**$7,013**	**$3,634**	**$3,380**	**41%**

The only costs here will be budget costs. There are no opportunity costs since there are no program participants associated with these costs.

Generally, there will not be benefits associated with these costs. View them as overhead, which is necessary to achieve the overall benefits of learning but does not make sense to allocate to individual programs. The cost should be small anyway. If the number becomes large and makes sense, you might assign gross benefits to equal the cost so that the net benefit is zero.

The Business Case for Learning at the Enterprise Level

With the addition of other costs, the business case for learning is complete. It brings together benefits and costs for all of the recommended programs, as well as any unallocated costs to show the total value of the investment in learning. The approach, however, is flexible enough to allow for a scaled-down version that still adds significant value even when net benefits are not appropriate or available.

The Complete Business Case

For the function or enterprise as a whole, the net benefit of learning is the sum of the net benefits for aligned learning plus the net benefit from the unaligned learning less the other costs. The complete business case for learning is shown in Table 5.4.

Notice that the inclusion of the other costs reduces the total net benefits by $600,000 to $3.38 million and the ROI from 53% to 41%. Total budget costs to produce these net benefits will be $4.537 million and will result in a bottom line budget impact of $7.013 million.

Since Table 5.4 contains a lot of detail, you may want to present a summary table instead, especially in a PowerPoint presentation where the numbers of Table 5.4 become hard to read. Table 5.5 below is an example of how you might summarize the key information from Table 5.4.

TABLE 5.5

2017 Summary Business Case for Learning

2017 Priority	*Corporate Goal*	*Target*	*Planned Impact of Learning*	*Unique Partici pants*	*Total Partici pants*	*Gross Benefits*	*Budget Costs*	*Opportunity Costs*	*Total Net Benefits (thous.)*
1	Increase Sales	10%	2%	100	1,100	$1,500	$490	$117	$893
2	Reduce Defects	20%	14%	200	800	$2,100	$570	$512	$1,018
3	Reduce Injuries	25%	15%	3,100	13,600	$1,200	$410	$376	$415
4	Improve Leadership	+5 pts	+2 pts	180	180	$1,200	$582	$302	$316
5	Increase Retention	+5 pts	+1.5 pts	5,000	7,500	$1,800	$340	$1,150	$310
Subtotal Top Five Prioities				**5,000**	**23,180**	**$7,800**	**$2,392**	**$2,457**	**$2,952**
Subtotal Other Goals				1,950	4,725	$3,050	$1,245	$778	$1,028
Total All Goals				**5,000**	**27,905**	**$10,850**	**$3,637**	**$3,234**	**$3,980**
Unaligned Learning				4,000	4,000	$700	$300	$400	$0
Other Costs (not incl elsewhere)						NA	$600	$0	($600)
Grand Total for All Learning				**5,000**	**31,905**	**$11,550**	**$4,537**	**$3,634**	**$3,380**

(Notice that the subtotal for unique participants for the top five priorities is *not* the sum of the five programs and that the grand total is *not* the sum of the three subtotals. Since some employees have participated in more than one program, a simple sum cannot be used. The maximum number of unique employees is the total number of employees, namely 5,000. See Chapter 3 for more on calculating unique and total participation.)

Table 5.5 highlights the corporate goal and target, planned impact of learning, number of participants, benefits, costs, and net benefits. After presenting this once you may find that senior leaders don't need to see opportunity costs or that they would like to see the budget impact or ROI, and you can modify them accordingly.

The enterprise-level business case for learning clearly makes the following points:

1. Learning is strategically aligned to the highest priorities of the organization.
2. Learning can contribute significantly to achieving the top five goals of the organization with a planned bottom line (budget) impact exceeding $5 million.

3. Learning also has an important role to play in achieving the remaining goals with a planned bottom line impact of almost $2 million.
4. Including all the costs and offerings of the learning function as well as the opportunity costs of the participants' time, the net benefits of learning should exceed $3.3 million for an ROI, conservatively estimated, of about 40%.

This is the essence of your business case for learning. Strategic alignment, the results of in-depth discussion of benefits and costs with the owner of each goal, and a careful accounting of costs, including opportunity costs, are all evident in the business case.

> CATERPILLAR EXPERIENCE: In Cat U's second year (2002) we created our first business case for learning titled *The Business of Learning*. It provided each college within Cat U the opportunity to clearly articulate the alignment of its programs to the company's critical success factors, its detailed work plans, and a five-year projection of costs, impact, and benefits. Since this was the first time a detailed plan for learning had been created and since the learning field was new to most of us, this provided a tremendous opportunity to learn more about the potential impact of our programs and to develop a shared vision for the potential of learning at Caterpillar. It forced us to think more critically about both the costs and expected benefits of learning and gave us the opportunity to refine our procedures for calculating costs and benefits. *The Business of Learning* helped establish our credibility as business-minded learning professionals and became the basis for the more complete business plan for learning the following year.

Flexibility in Creating the Business Case

In the real world it may not be possible or desirable to create the business case described above. The approach is very flexible and allows the practitioner to adjust for her own circumstances.

Lack of Planning Resources

It may be that all the data for a complete business model theoretically could be gathered, but constraints of staff or time make it impossible. No problem. Start with the basics: learning for the top priorities. Complete the strategic alignment and business case just for those top three to five priorities identified by your CEO. Do not worry about the rest of the learning. It will not be a complete picture of learning investment and results, but it will make the case for learning to support the highest priority goals of the organization. Next year, you might try to address all the aligned learning.

Goals and Learning Programs without Dollar Impact

It may be that there are a number of organizational goals and learning programs that do not lend themselves to the type of bottom line dollar impact described above. Again, this is not a problem.

In our example only one of the top five (leadership) would fall in this category. The first three goals are readily quantifiable, and most organizations are able to quantify at least the direct cost of losing employees for the fifth goal. In this case, you can do one of two things: assign a rather arbitrary net income impact value to the goal (like $3 million for leadership in Table 5.1) or leave it undefined (N/A). If you assign a value, be very conservative—so conservative that people will comment on how conservative your estimate is. Given that is an important organizational goal, it may be easier than you think to reach agreement on a very conservative "placeholder."

Naturally, when you talk about it and later when you make the overall business case, you should be very humble and transparent. You should tell colleagues that it is not really possible to put a value on it, but it is too important to be ignored, so you have assigned a very conservative value to it. You will be happy to change it if they would like. If you choose to assign a value to the net income expected from achieving the goal (like $3 million), then you can apply the planned contribution from learning (like 40%) to calculate the gross benefit of learning ($1.2 million).

In some cases you may be able to agree on a gross benefit for learning even when the dollar impact of the goal is not available. For instance, you might have been able to agree that the planned leadership programs would have a gross dollar benefit of $1.2 million without ever knowing or discussing the impact on net income of better leadership in general (the $3 million in Table 5.1). In this case simply put an "N/A" in place of the $3 million.

TABLE 5.6

2017 Business Case for Learning without Dollar Impact for Leadership (Alternative A)

								Thousands of Dollars					
Priority	*Corporate Goal*	*Key Learning Programs*	*Target Audience*	*Unique Partici-pants*	*Total Partici-pants*	*Planned Contribution from Learning*	*Planned Impact of Learning*	*Gross Benefit*	*Budget Cost*	*Budget Impact*	*Opport-unity Cost*	*Net Benefit*	*ROI*
1	Increase sales by 10%	Consultative selling skills (new)	Marketing employees	100	100								
		Ten NPI modules (10 new)	Marketing employees	100	1,000								
		Total key programs		100	1,100	20%	2% higher sales	$1,500	$490	$1,010	$117	$893	147%
2	Reduce defects by 20%	Four Design courses (3 new)	New, other engineers	200	800	70%	14% reduct. in defects	$2,100	$570	$1,530	$512	$1,018	94%
3	Reduce Injuries by 25%	Five Safety courses (3 new)	Manufact. associates	2,500	12,500								
		One Safety course (revised)	Factory supervisors	100	100								
		Two Safety courses (1 new)	Office employees	500	1,000								
		Total key programs		3,100	13,600	60%	15% reduct. in injuries	$1,200	$410	$790	$376	$415	53%
4	Improve leadership score by 5 points on employee survey	Intro to supervision (revised)	New, other supervisors	100	100								
		Leadership for managers (new)	Division managers	65	65								
		Advanced leadership (existing)	Department heads	15	15								
		Total key programs		180	180	40%	2 point increase	NA	$582	-$582	$302	-$884	NA
5	Increase retention by 5 points	Individual development plans	All employees	5,000	5,000								
		Performance mgt (new)	Mgt employees	2,500	2,500								
		Total key programs		5,000	7,500	30%	1.5 point increase	$1,800	$340	$1,460	$1,150	$310	21%
Total for Top Five Priorities *		**Learning for Top Five Goals** Courses: 20 New , 2 Revised		**5,000**	**23,180**	**Range = 20%-70%**		**$6,60**	**$2,392**	**$4,208**	**$2,457**	**$1,752**	**36%**
Total for All Other Goals		**Learning for All Other Goals** Courses: 16 New , 2 Revised		**1,950**	**4,725**	**Range = 50%-70%**		**$3,05**	**$1,245**	**$1,805**	**$778**	**$1,028**	**51%**
Grand Total for All Goals *		**Total for All Aligned Learning** **Courses: 36 New , 4 Revised**		**5,000**	**27,905**	**Range = 20%-70%**		**$9,650**	**$3,637**	**$6,013**	**$3,234**	**$2,779**	**40%**

* Note: Dollar Impact totals DO NOT INCLUDE impact of leadership programs
Budget and Opportunity costs DO INCLUDE leadership programs

Sometimes, though, it will not be possible or practical to derive even the direct dollar impact (gross benefit) of a program (like the $1.2 million for learning). Let's look at two scenarios with different degrees of "soft" goals.

First Scenario: *The goals without dollar impact represent a small percentage of the total.* If you decide not to assign a value for gross benefit, put "N/A" in its place. Sum the gross benefits for the rest of the goals and put an asterisk by the sum with a note below telling the reader that the sum does not include the gross benefits for the goals with "N/A." You can probably still make an estimate of the impact learning can have on it (like increasing the leadership score by 2 points) but will not be able calculate the gross benefit, budget impact, net benefit, or ROI for this goal.

Now, you have to decide whether to include the budget and opportunity costs in the total. To be conservative, go ahead and include them. Explain to the reader or listener that costs are included for all programs even though no benefits have been included for the one program. This will bias net budget impact, net benefits, and ROI down. If the resulting business case is still strong, great! You made the case for the overall investment in learning *and* were very conservative.

If the learning costs for the goal without dollar benefits are high compared to the total costs for all programs, it will be misleading (and may be politically unwise) to include the costs without the benefits. In this case you may want to exclude the costs in the highlighted totals and instead include them as an addendum.

Table 5.6 shows the business case without a dollar impact for leadership with the costs included.

Notice that gross benefit, budget impact, and net benefit declined by $1.2 million (the dollar impact of leadership) from the comparable Table 5.1. (For simplicity we will focus just on the aligned learning.) ROI fell from 58% to 41%, which is still a healthy return on investment.

If it had been a large drop (for example, 58% to 10%), then you would need to consider removing the costs. A large drop would occur if the costs for the program are significant compared to the other programs and to the total, in which case leaving the costs for leadership learning in would seriously distort the comparison of costs to benefits. In this case it would be better to remove the costs from the heart of the table and include them as an addendum. That way, the total costs, including those for the leadership program, are still shown, and the net

TABLE 5.7

2017 Business Case for Learning without Dollar Impact for Leadership (Alternative B)

Priority	Corporate Goal	Key Learning Programs	Target Audience	Unique Partici-pants	Total Partici-pants	Planned Contribution from Learning	Planned Impact of Learning	Gross Benefit (Thousands of Dollars)	Budget Cost (Thousands of Dollars)	Budget Impact (Thousands of Dollars)	Opport-unity Cost (Thousands of Dollars)	Net Benefit (Thousands of Dollars)	ROI
1	Increase sales by 10%	Consultative selling skills (new)	Marketing employees	100	100								
		Ten NPI modules (10 new)	Marketing employees	100	1,000								
		Total key programs		100	1,100	20%	2% higher sales	$1,500	$490	$1,010	$117	$893	147%
2	Reduce defects by 20%	Four Design courses (3 new)	New, other engineers	200	800	70%	14% reduct. in defects	$2,100	$570	$1,530	$512	$1,018	94%
3	Reduce Injuries by 25%	Five Safety courses (3 new)	Manufact. associates	2,500	12,500								
		One Safety course (revised)	Factory supervisors	100	100								
		Two Safety courses (1 new)	Office employees	500	1,000								
		Total key programs		3,100	13,600	60%	15% reduct. in injuries	$1,200	$410	$790	$376	$415	53%
4	Improve leadership score by 5 points on employee survey	Intro to supervision (revised)	New, other supervisors	100	100								
		Leadership for managers (new)	Division managers	65	65								
		Advanced leadership (existing)	Department heads	15	15								
		Total key programs		180	180	40%	2 point increase	NA	Not incl	NA	Not Incl	NA	NA
5	Increase retention by 5 points	Individual development plans	All employees	5,000	5,000								
		Performance mgt (new)	Mgt employees	2,500	2,500								
		Total key programs		5,000	7,500	30%	1.5 point increase	$1,800	$340	$1,460	$1,150	$310	21%
Total for Top Five Priorities *		**Learning for Top Five Goals**		**5,000**	**23,180**	**Range = 20%-70%**		**$6,600**	**$1,810**	**$4,790**	**$2,155**	**$2,636**	**66%**
		Courses: 20 New , 2 Revised											
Total for All Other Goals		**Learning for All Other Goals**		**1,950**	**4,725**	**Range = 50%-70%**		**$3,050**	**$1,245**	**$1,805**	**$778**	**$1,028**	**51%**
		Courses: 16 New , 2 Revised											
Grand Total for All Goals *		**Total for All Aligned Learning**		**5,000**	**27,905**	**Range = 20%-70%**		**$9,650**	**$3,055**	**$6,595**	**$2,932**	**$3,663**	**61%**
		Courses: 36 New , 4 Revised											

* Note: Dollar benefits and costs of leadership programs NOT INCLUDED

Addendum	Costs for Leadership Training	$582		$302
	Total for All Aligned Learning	$3,637		$3,234

TABLE 5.8

2017 Business Case for Learning without Any Dollar Impacts

Priority	Organization Goal	Key Learning Programs	Target Audience	Unique Participants	Total Participants	Planned Contribution from Learning	Planned Impact of Learning	Budget Cost	Opport-unity Cost	Total Cost
1	Increase customer satisfaction score by 10%	Customer service skills (new)	Call center employees	20	20					
		New services information (revised)	Call center employees	20	20					
		Total key programs		20	40	20%	2% higher customer satisfaction	$25	$19	$44
2	Reduce complaints by 20%	Billing course (new)	Accounting employees	10	10					
		Service Sched. & Mgt course (new)	Logistics employees	15	15					
		Total key programs		25	25	70%	14% reduction in complaints	$35	$14	$49
3	Reduce Injuries by 25%	Five Safety courses (3 new)	Transportation ee's	100	500					
		One Safety course (revised)	Division managers	15	15					
		Two Safety courses (1 new)	Office employees	250	500					
		Total key programs		365	1,015	60%	15% reduction in injuries	$65	$45	$110
4	Improve leadership score by 5 points on employee survey	Intro to supervision (revised)	New supervisors	10	10					
		Leadership for managers (new)	Division managers	15	15					
		Advanced leadership (existing)	Department heads	5	5					
		Total key programs		30	30	40%	2 point increase	$35	$40	$75
5	Increase retention by 10 points	Individual development plans	All employees	1550	1550					
		Performance mgt (new)	Mgt employees	285	285					
		Total key programs		1550	1835	30%	3 point increase	$18	$32	$50
Total for Top Five Priorities		**Learning for Top Five Goals** Courses: 9 New , 3 Revised		**1,550**	**2,945**	**Range = 20%-70%**		**$143**	**$110**	**$253**
Total for All Other Goals		**Learning for All Other Goals** Courses: 3 New , 4 Revised		**650**	**650**	**Range = 20%-45%**		**$40**	**$48**	**$88**
Grand Total for All Goals		**Total for All Aligned Learning** **Courses: 12 New , 7 Revised**		**1,550**	**3,595**	**Range = 20%-70%**		**$183**	**$158**	**$341**

benefit/budget impact/ROI calculations are not biased. Table 5.7 illustrates the impact of moving leadership costs to the addendum.

With leadership costs removed, net benefits are now $3.663 million and the ROI increases to 61%, presenting a more accurate business case for learning. The addendum does show the total budget and opportunity costs, so that information has not been lost.

Second Scenario: ***The goals without dollar impact represent a large percentage of the total.*** For government organizations and the military this is likely to be the case. It may also be the case when a large amount of learning is for essential programs that are hard to quantify, such as professional or technical training for new hires to prepare them to be effective on the job. In these cases the learning is viewed as essential and nonnegotiable. Although there may be ways to deliver it more efficiently, everyone agrees it has to be provided.

To be clear, the goals are still specific and measurable but difficult or impossible to dollarize. In this case it will be better not to sum the impact on net income, budget impact, and net benefits, and there will be no ROI calculation. In fact, if most or all the goals fall into this category, just eliminate these columns entirely. Table 5.8 provides an example for a government agency without the dollar-related columns.

The business case retains its most important features. The organization's objectives are listed in priority order, and the learning programs are strategically aligned to those objectives, including the target audience and the number of participants. Discussions with the goals' sponsors have resulted in the expected impact of learning on those goals. Last, both budget and opportunity costs have been provided so leaders can make an informed decision about which programs to fund.

> ADVICE: Converting impact to dollars is helpful when it makes sense and has the added benefit that it allows for impacts to be added up for the programs. When it does not make sense, do not force it. You can make a convincing business case without dollarizing the benefits. Do the strategic alignment, make all the benefits (impact) and costs explicit, and then bring it all together in a table like 5.8. This approach may seem obvious, but remember that most learning professionals never get this far.

Creating a Business Case with Qualitative Impacts

Tables 5.1-5.8 reflect quantitative impacts of learning like a 2% reduction in sales due just to learning. In Chapter 4 we also described a qualitative approach which yielded a high, medium or low impact. This approach will still facilitate a good discussion with the goal owner to ensure that both of you agree on the relative importance of learning as well as the amount of effort that will be required and specific roles and responsibilities. The qualitative approach, however, will not allow you to calculate the gross benefit, net benefit, or ROI of the learning. Nonetheless, we can still create a business case although it will not be as compelling.

Remember that a business case requires that the benefits and costs of an initiative be compared in order to make the case for investment. That test can still be met using qualitative impacts, which will now appear in the Planned Impact of Learning column rather than quantitative impacts. There is no change in the display of budget, opportunity or total costs. Table 5.9 is an example of a business case using qualitative impacts.

Without a net benefit or ROI, the decision maker will have to make subjective judgment whether the learning for each goal is worth the cost, but at least she knows the cost and the goal owner's belief of the importance of the learning. The CLO would interpret the qualitative impacts for the decision maker to ensure understanding. For example, the CLO would explain that Medium impact implies that learning will be a very important factor in accomplishing the goal. In fact, without it, there is little chance the goal will be reached. Consequently, the SVP of Sales is fully supportive of this initiative and he believes that the $607,000 total cost is well worth it and will certainly bring far more than $607,000 to the bottom line. The CLO would talk the CEO through the planned learning for each goal and sum up by pointing out that learning is planned to support all five top-priority goals and a number of other important goals, and that in the goal owners' opinion learning will play a very important role in achieving each goal.

TABLE 5.9

2017 Business Case for Learning Using Qualitative Impacts

							Thousands of Dollars		
Priority	*Organization Goal*	*Key Learning Programs*	*Target Audience*	*Unique Participants*	*Total Participants*	*Planned Impact of Learning*	*Budget Cost*	*Opportunity Cost*	*Total Cost*
1	Increase sales by 10%	Consultative selling skills (new)	Marketing employees	100	100				
		Ten NPI modules (10 new)	Marketing employees	100	1,000				
		Total key programs		100	1,100	Medium	$490	$117	$607
2	Reduce defects by 20%	Four Design courses (3 new)	New, other engineers	200	800	High	$570	$512	$1,082
3	Reduce Injuries by 25%	Five Safety courses (3 new)	Manufact. assiciates	2,500	12,500				
		One Safety course (revised)	Factory supervisors	100	100				
		Two Safety courses (1 new)	Office employees	500	1,000				
		Total key programs		3,100	13,600	High	$410	$376	$786
4	Improve leadership score by 5 points on employee survey	Intro to supervision (revised)	New, other supervisors	100	100				
		Leadership for managers (new)	Division managers	65	65				
		Advanced leadership (existing)	Department heads	15	15				
		Total key programs		180	180	Medium	$582	$302	$884
5	Increase retention by 5 points	Individual development plans	All employees	5,000	5,000				
		Performance mgt (new)	Mgt employees	2,500	2,500				
		Total key programs		5,000	7,500	Medium	$340	$1,150	$1,490
Total for Top Five Priorities		**Learning for Top Five Goals** Courses: 20 New , 2 Revised		**5,000**	**23,180**	**Range = Med - High**	**$2,392**	**$2,457**	**$4,849**
Total for All Other Goals		**Learning for All Other Goals** Courses: 16 New , 2 Revised		**1,950**	**4,725**	**Range = Med - High**	**$1,245**	**$778**	**$2,023**
Grand Total for All Goals		**Total for All Aligned Learning** **Courses: 36 New , 4 Revised**		**5,000**	**27,905**	**Range = Med - High**	**$3,637**	**$3,235**	**$6,872**

You Have a Significant Amount of Unaligned Learning

The approach we have outlined so far in the last two chapters will work well for an organization where the majority of learning is directly aligned to company goals. In this case, the focus is on the strategically aligned learning, which occupies the top of each table, and the unaligned learning, which is grouped under the single row entitled "unaligned learning" near the bottom. If unaligned learning is a much more significant part of your offerings, you will likely want to expand its coverage in the business case table and in your accompanying analysis.

This may be the case where the L&D department is responsible for providing basic training to a large number of employees before they can start their job. Examples include the fast food restaurant industry, banks, call centers, and the military. The learning is important and absolutely essential to the success of the organization, but is not directly aligned to any particular goal. This may also be the case for more advanced training, such as when it is important to maintain credentials or keep up with ever expanding professional knowledge. Legal, accounting, engineering, and consulting firms are examples here. Last, the L&D department may be responsible for compliance-related training where there is no formal goal to be 100% compliant. In all these cases it should be readily agreed that the learning is essential, and consequently there will be no need to expend any effort to make a convincing business case. The training must be done and it should be done as efficiently as possible.

There may also be unaligned learning that is not essential but is provided to help employees develop and improve their performance. This could include various types of business skills such as writing, project management, and teamwork, and may include more general knowledge. Learning to support leadership development and improve employee engagement will also fall in the unaligned learning category if the company does not have explicit, high-level goals to improve leadership and engagement. For this non-essential unaligned learning, you may or may not choose to make a business case for it. If the investment is substantial, you may want to make a case based on planned benefits at least for the most significant programs.

Now we will share two ways for you to include this very important unaligned learning in your business case table. Many variations are possible, but hopefully these two scenarios will illustrate how significant amounts of unaligned learning may be included in your business case. The first scenario provides guidance when the aligned learning is more significant than the unaligned learning, while the second scenario offers an alternative to use when the unaligned learning is more significant than the aligned learning.

First Scenario: ***You have a significant amount of unaligned learning but your aligned learning is more important.*** The recommendation is to expand the unaligned learning section at the bottom of the table to include 1) the important individual unaligned learning programs, 2) a single line for all the other unaligned learning programs, and 3) a subtotal for all the unaligned learning. See Table 5.10 for an example. In this scenario, the aligned learning in support of the company's top five goals is still at the top of the table, since it has a significant impact on the company's success and represents a significant effort by the L&D group. The bottom half of the table, however, has been expanded to include detail on four significant learning initiatives that are not directly aligned to the company's top goals but are nonetheless essential for the organization. In this example, the four learning programs are basic skills for manufacturing, basic skills for engineering, advanced skills for engineering, and compliance–related training. Notice that the planned contribution of learning for each is "Essential" and consequently there is no need for gross benefit, budget impact, net benefit, or ROI. Since everyone has already agreed that these programs are absolutely essential, there is no need for a business case comparing benefits and costs to decide if the training should be provided. Instead, the goal is to provide the programs at the least cost consistent with delivering the planned learning objectives efficiently and effectively. A subtotal should be provided for your key unaligned learning programs followed by a single line for all other unaligned learning. Last, provide the total for all unaligned learning. You may also wish to add a line for the grand total of both the aligned and unaligned learning, which would show totals for number of courses, participants, and costs. (It would be misleading to show the grand total for gross benefit, budget impact, net benefit, and ROI since these were not calculated for the unaligned learning.)

The top half of Table 5.10 provides the same type of quantitative business case as we developed in the first part of Chapter 5, culminating in Table 5.4. The reader can easily see that the learning has been identified to support all top five goals as well as the other four goals (not shown in detail). Learning is expected to reach all 5,000 employees and contribute at least 20% to each goal and as much as 70% for the quality goal. The ROI is expected to be 58%. The alignment, impact and ROI together make a convincing business case for the proposed $6.9 million investment (budget cost + opportunity cost).

TABLE 5.10

2017 Business Case for Learning with Significant Unaligned Learning (Scenario 1)

Important Learning Directly Aligned to This Year's Corporate Goals

								Thousands of Dollars					
Priority	*Corporate Goal*	*Key Learning Programs*	*Target Audience*	*Unique Partici-pants*	*Total Partici-pants*	*Planned Contribution from Learning*	*Planned Impact of Learning*	*Gross Benefit*	*Budget Cost*	*Budget Impact*	*Opport-unity Cost*	*Net Benefit*	*ROI*
1	Increase sales by 10%	Consultative selling skills (new)	Marketing employees	100	100								
		Ten NPI modules (10 new)	Marketing employees	100	1,000								
		Total key programs		100	1,100	20%	2% higher sales	$1,500	$490	$1,010	$117	$893	147%
2	Reduce defects by 20%	Four Design courses (3 new)	New, other engineers	200	800	70%	14% reduct. in defects	$2,100	$570	$1,530	$512	$1,018	94%
3	Reduce Injuries by 25%	Five Safety courses (3 new)	Manufact. associates	2,500	12,500								
		One Safety course (revised)	Factory supervisors	100	100								
		Two Safety courses (1 new)	Office employees	500	1,000								
		Total key programs		3,100	13,600	60%	15% reduct. in injuries	$1,200	$410	$790	$376	$415	53%
4	Improve leadership score by 5 points on employee survey	Intro to supervision (revised)	New, other supervisors	100	100								
		Leadership for managers (new)	Division managers	65	65								
		Advanced leadership (existing)	Department heads	15	15								
		Total key programs		180	180	40%	2 point increase	$1,200	$582	$618	$302	$316	36%
5	Increase retention by 5 points	Individual development plans	All employees	5,000	5,000								
		Performance mgt (new)	Mgt employees	2,500	2,500								
		Total key programs		5,000	7,500	30%	1.5 point increase	$1,800	$340	$1,460	$1,150	$310	21%
Total for Top Five Priorities		**Learning for Top Five Goals** Courses: 20 New , 2 Revised, 5 Existing		**5,000**	**23,180**	**Range = 20%-70%**		**$7,800**	**$2,392**	**$5,408**	**$2,457**	**$2,952**	**61%**
		Learning for All Other Goals Courses: 16 New , 2 Revised, 4 Existing		**1,950**	**4,725**	**Range = 50%-70%**		**$3,050**	**$1,245**	**$1,805**	**$778**	**$1,028**	**51%**
Total for All Aligned Learning		**Learning for All Nine Goals** Courses: 36 New , 4 Revised, 9 Existing		**5,000**	**27,905**	**Range = 20%-70%**		**$10,850**	**$3,637**	**$7,213**	**$3,235**	**$3,980**	**58%**

Important Learning Not Directly Aligned to This Year's Corporate Goals

Corporate Need	Key Learning Programs	Target Audience	Unique Partici-pants	Total Partici-pants	Planned Contribution from Learning	Planned Impact of Learning	Gross Benefit (Thousands of Dollars)	Budget Cost (Thousands of Dollars)	Budget Impact (Thousands of Dollars)	Opport-unity Cost (Thousands of Dollars)	Net Benefit (Thousands of Dollars)	ROI
Best-in-class manufacturing	Basic skills for manufacturing Courses: 4 New, 2 Revised, 6 Existing	New manufacturing hires	300	1,200	Essential	Manufact. associates have required skills		$1,200		$1,550		
Best-in-class engineering	Basic skills for engineers Courses: 1 New, 1 Revised, 2 Existing	New engineers	30	120	Essential	New engineers have required skills		$200		$320		
Best-in-class engineering	Advanced skills for engineers Courses: 1 New, 2 Revised, 4 Existing	Experienced engineers	100	400	Essential	Experienced engineers keep current		$350		$500		
100% compliance with laws and regulations	Compliance-related training Courses: 2 New, 8 Existing	All employees	5,000	25,000	Essential	100% Compliance		$400		$1,200		
	Subtotal for key unaligned learning Courses: 8 New , 5 Revised, 20 Existing		**5,000**	**26,720**	**Essential**	**Corporate needs met**		**$2,150**		**$3,570**		
Other basic skills and general knowledge	All other unaligned learning Courses: 2 New, 1 Revised, 52 Existing	Various	5,000	8,000				$300		$400		
Total unaligned learning	**Total for all unaligned learning** Courses: 10 New , 6 Revised 72 Existing		**5,000**	**34,720**				**$2,450**		**$3,970**		
Grand Total	**Grand Total for All Learning** **Courses: 46 New, 10 Revised, 81 Existing**		**Grand Total** **5,000**	**62,625**				**$6,087**		**$7,205**		

In the bottom half of the table, we see that a significant amount of learning is also planned that is not directly aligned to the top goals of the company but nonetheless is essential for the ongoing success of the company. Although the CEO did not have an explicit goal to have best-in-class manufacturing and engineering, the L&D department is expected to ensure that employees in these areas can do their jobs well. Likewise, while the CEO did not have a goal to be compliant with all laws and regulations, the L&D department is expected to work with HR to make sure the proper training is provided. These four programs are all considered essential by the CEO and other senior leaders so the full costs are provided without listing net benefits or ROI. A subtotal is provided for the essential unaligned learning. Next, the non-essential unaligned learning is summed up in the line titled "Other basic skills and general knowledge" followed by the total for all unaligned learning. Notice that unaligned learning is planned for all 5,000 employees and that the number of total participants is expected to be higher than for aligned learning. The total cost of unaligned learning is expected to be $6.4 million, and the reader is reminded that the essential unaligned learning is required to meet company and employee needs.

Table 5.10 also includes a grand total at the bottom for participants and costs. These are the only measures for which we can sum both the aligned and unaligned learning.

Second Scenario: ***Your unaligned learning is more significant than your aligned learning.*** In some organizations the L&D department focuses most of its resources on important, but unaligned, learning of the nature described above. In the extreme case, the department has no learning aligned to the goals of the company, which may be the case as the L&D group begins its transition to become a strategic business partner. When the unaligned learning is more significant than the aligned learning, it may make more sense to reverse the order of Table 5.10 above and put the unaligned learning at the top of the table. Leading with unaligned learning, however, would only be appropriate if the focus is on individually identifiable, significant learning programs deemed essential, such as those in Table 5.11. If there is only general unaligned learning, for example team building and communication skills, then these would not be considered significant. In this case, the unaligned learning should be aggregated into a single line to be included below the aligned learning, as in Table 5.4.

Table 5.11 provides a scenario where there is significantly more unaligned learning than aligned and where the impact of the unaligned learning is likely to be greater than the impact of the aligned learning. This might be representative of a fast food company where the L&D function has historically been tasked with the tactical training for new hires rather than strategic learning in support of high-level company goals. Both types of training are very important but need to be considered differently. Since the unaligned learning is more significant—in terms of importance to the company, number of programs, number of employees reached, total participants, and total cost—Table 5.11 is constructed with unaligned learning at the top and aligned learning at the bottom. Given turnover rates in the industry, it should not be surprising that the number of new hires to be trained is very large and represents a massive training effort. In addition, a large number of new store managers need to be trained, and all 10,000 management employees must receive compliance-related training. And, unlike the case in Tables 5.1 - 5.10, here we assume that the company does not have a high-level leadership goal, which means that leadership training is, by definition, not aligned to the top goals of the organization. Consequently, it now appears under the unaligned learning section. (Remember that unaligned does not mean unimportant. It simply means the program is not in direct support of the CEO's top, named goals.) In all, unaligned learning is planned to meet five important company needs as well as to provide basic skills and knowledge. Unaligned learning programs are expected to touch 145,000 employees, representing an investment of $7.3 million.

The bottom of Table 5.11 focuses on the aligned learning, which in this case represents a much smaller effort than the unaligned learning. Learning has been identified to support three of the top five priorities, reaching 320 employees. Learning has also been identified to support a few more of the top nine goals and reach 1,000 employees. In all, aligned learning is planned to touch 1,200 unique employees (accounting for the overlap between the 320 and the 1000). This learning is expected to contribute 20% towards the sales goal, 70% towards the defect reduction goal, 60% towards the purchase cost reduction goal, and at least 50% towards the achievement of several other goals. In total, the aligned learning programs are expected to deliver an ROI of 88% at a total cost of just over $4 million.

Table 5.11 does not include a grand total for participants but one could be added. Total costs could also be shown, although the columns for costs would not line up so it might be confusing to the reader.

TABLE 5.11

2017 Business Case for Learning with Significant Unaligned Learning (Scenario 2)

Important Learning Not Directly Aligned to This Year's Corporate Goals

Corporate Need	*Key Learning Programs*	*Target Audience*	*Unique Partici-pants*	*Total Partici-pants*	*Planned Contribution from Learning*	*Planned Impact of Learning*	*Thousands of Dollars* Budget Cost	*Thousands of Dollars* Opport-unity Cost	*Thousands of Dollars* Total Cost
Best-in-class kitchen skills	Basic skills for food preparation Courses: 2 Revised, 4 Existing	New kitchen hires	100,000	600,000	Essential	New hires have required skills	$1,000	$16,000	$17,000
Best-in-class counter skills	Basic skills for counter associates Courses: 1 Existing	New counter hires	30,000	30,000	Essential	New hires have required skills	$300	$2,000	$2,300
Best-in-class store manager skills	Basic skills for new store managers Courses: 1 New, 3 Existing	New store managers	2,000	8,000	Essential	New store managers have required skills	$600	$1,200	$1,800
100% compliance with laws and regulations	Compliance-related training Courses: 2 New, 8 Existing	All management employees who need it	4,000	20,000	Essential	100% Compliance	$400	$1,200	$1,600
Improve leadership score by 5 points on employee opinion survey	Intro to supervision (revised Leadership for managers (new) Advanced leadership (existing) Total key programs	New, other supervisors Division managers Department heads	500 65 15 580	500 65 15 580	Essential	2 point increase	$582	$302	$618
Subtotal key unaligned learning	**Subtotal for key unaligned learning**		**136,580**	**658,580**	**Essential**	**Corporate needs met**	**$2,882**	**$20,702**	**$23,318**
Other basic skills and general knowledge	All other unaligned learning Courses: 2 New, 1 Revised, 52 Existing	Various	5,000	8,000	Significant	Corporate and employee needs met	$300	$400	$700
Total unaligned learning	**Total for all unaligned learning** Courses: 10 New , 6 Revised 72 Existing		**140,000**	**666,580**		**Corporate and employee needs met**	**$3,182**	**$21,102**	**$24,018**

Important Learning Directly Aligned to This Year's Corporate Goals

Priority	Corporate Goal	Key Learning Programs	Target Audience	Unique Partici-pants	Total Partici-pants	Planned Contribution from Learning	Planned Impact of Learning	Gross Benefit	Budget Cost	Budget Impact	Opport-unity Cost	Net Benefit	ROI
								Thousands of Dollars					
1	Increase sales by 10%	Consultative selling skills (new)	Marketing employees	100	100								
		Ten NPI modules (10 new)	Marketing employees	100	1,000								
		Total key programs		100	1,100	20%	2% higher sales	$1,500	$490	$1,010	$117	$893	147%
2	Reduce defects by 20%	Four Design courses (3 new)	New, other engineers	200	800	70%	14% reduct. in defects	$2,100	$570	$1,530	$512	$1,018	94%
3	Increase retention by 5 points	Individual development plans	Mgt, select empl	10,000	5,000								
		Performance mgt (new)	Mgt employees	5,000	2,500								
		Total key programs		10,000	7,500	30%	1.5 point increase	$1,800	$340	$1,460	$1,150	$310	21%
4	Reduce cost of purchased materials by 5%	Two purchasing courses (1 new)	Purchasing agents	20	40	60%	3% reduction in purchased cost	$900	$225	$675	$86	$589	189%
Total for Top Four Priorities		**Learning for Top Four Goals** Courses: 16 New , 1 Existing		**10,000**	**9,440**	**Range = 20%-70%**		**$6,300**	**$1,625**	**$4,675**	**$1,865**	**$2,810**	**81%**
		Learning for All Other Goals Courses: 16 New, 2 Revised, 4 Existing		**1,950**	**4,725**	**Range = 50%-70%**		**$3,050**	**$1,245**	**$1,805**	**$778**	**$1,027**	**51%**
Total for All Aligned Learning		**Learning for All Goals** Courses: 32 New , 2 Revised, 5 Existing		**10,000**	**14,165**	**Range = 20%-70%**		**$9,350**	**$2,870**	**$6,480**	**$2,643**	**$3,837**	**70%**

Note on formatting for both tables: Notice that the formatting is different for the unaligned learning between the two tables. In Table 5.10 the columns for gross benefit, budget cost, net benefit, and ROI are retained but left empty. In Table 5.11 these columns are deleted for the unaligned learning. The formatting in Table 5.11 is cleaner but you may wish to retain the format in Table 5.10 for consistency between the upper and lower halves of the table. You will also need to use the formatting of Table 5.10 if you wish to make a business case for the non-essential unaligned learning. In this case, you would need to assign a gross benefit to it, which would allow you to then calculate budget cost, net benefit, and ROI.

Review of the Combined Strategic Alignment and Business Case Process

Chapters 4 and 5 have described the processes of strategic alignment and business case development in great detail. Although the recommendation is to create a business plan that will incorporate both the strategic alignment and the business case, some will choose to stop at this point and present the results outside the context of a written business plan. In either case, a review of these two critical processes may be helpful. Chapters 4 and 5 can be summarized in the following seven-step process, including a step-by-step buildup of Table 5.4.

FIGURE 5.1

The Seven-Step Process to Create a Business Case

Step 1A: Meet with CEO

- Read business and strategic plans first if available.
- What are the organization's goals? Priorities?
- Which will be the most challenging?
- Who is the owner for each?
- Prioritize goals (if not already done).

Step 1B: Meet with Senior Executives, Governing Board Members

- What are priorities?
- Which are most challenging?
- What has worked well? Not so well?

Step 2: Meet with the Goal Owners

- Start with owners of highest priority goals.
- Learn more about their goals, challenges.
- How quickly must they show results?
- What has worked well before? Not so well?

Step 3: The Learning Function Makes an Initial Determination If Learning Is Required to Achieve a Goal or Can Accelerate Progress

- If yes,
  - Who is the target audience?
  - What type of learning would be best (formal, informal, performance support, a blend)?
  - Duration?
  - How can opportunity costs be minimized?
  - What is the potential impact on a goal from the learning? High, medium, or low?
  - Complete the preliminary strategic alignment.
  - Schedule a second meeting with the owner to present your recommendations.
- If no,
  - Schedule a second meeting with the owner, if necessary, to share the opinion that learning is not part of the solution. (The owner may convince you otherwise.)

Step 4: Meet with Owners of Goals Where Learning Has a Likely Impact (Second Meeting)

- Share recommendations for learning programs.
- Discuss duration, opportunity costs.
- Discuss target audience: who, how many, where?
- Will it be required or voluntary? Who enforces it?
- What impact is planned?
- What is your role in success? The sponsor's role?

Step 5: Complete Draft Business Case for Strategically Aligned Learning

- Meet with owners for a third time (if necessary) to reach agreement on:
  - Learning program
  - Target audience

        - Timing of development and deployment
        - Reinforcement plans
        - Roles and responsibilities
        - Planned impact, including dollar benefit if possible
        - Costs
    - Finalize strategic alignment document.
    - Complete a draft business case for strategically aligned learning (like Table 5.1 or 5.2).

Step 6: Forecast Unaligned Learning and Administrative Costs Not Accounted for Elsewhere

- Complete a draft business case for all learning (like Table 5.4).

Step 7: Meet with CEO and/or Governing Body

- Share process of alignment and business case development with them.
- Then share draft business case with the strategic alignment embedded.
- Incorporate their feedback and recommendations.
- Reconnect with owners if there were changes.
- The business case for learning is *done*.

Notice that step 5 changed from Figure 4.1, now that strategic alignment will be incorporated into a business case. Step 5 now includes a more detailed discussion with the owner on explicit benefits and costs, which are necessary for the business case. Step 5 concludes with the business case for the strategically aligned learning (Table 5.1 or 5.2).

Tables 5.12–5.15 below show the step-by-step buildup of Table 5.4, along with a subjective estimate of the cumulative value of the process.

TABLE 5.12

2017 Business Case for Learning

Step 1: CEO, Senior Executive, Governing Board Input

Priority	*Corporate Goal*	*Owner*
1	Increase sales by 10%	Ortega
2	Reduce defects by 20%	D'Agoto
3	Rdeuce injuries by 25%	Swilthe
4	Improve leadership score by 5 points	Wang
5	Increase retention by 5 points	Dreise
6	Increase innovation by 20%	Chan
7	Reduce cost of purchased materials by 5%	Murphy
8	Increase benchstrength for officers	Dreise
9	Open office in Beijing	Li
10	Reduce technical support claims by 30%	Salvatore
11	Reduce exposure to fraud and insider trading	Omwetti

TABLE 5.13

2017 Business Case for Learning

Steps 2,3: Owner Input and Your Initial Recommendations

60% of Value

Priority	*Corporate Goal*	*Key Learning Programs*	*Target Audience*	*Unique Partici-pants*	*Total Participants*	*Potential Impact on Corp Goal*
1	Increase sales by 10% for Product A	Consultative selling skills (new)	Marketing employees	100	100	
		Ten NPI modules (10 new)	Marketing employees	100	1,000	
		Total key programs		100	1,100	Medium
2	Reduce defects by 20%	Four Design courses (3 new)	New, other engineers	200	800	High
3	Reduce Injuries by 25%	Five Safety courses (3 new)	Manufact. associates	2,500	12,500	
		One Safety course (revised)	Factory supervisors	100	100	
		Two Safety courses (1 new)	Office employees	500	1,000	
		Total key programs		3,100	13,600	High
4	Improve leadership score by 5 points on employee survey	Intro to supervision (revised)	New, other supervisors	100	100	
		Leadership for managers (new)	Division managers	65	65	
		Advanced leadership (existing)	Department heads	15	15	
		Total key programs		180	180	Medium
5	Increase retention by 5 points	Individual development plans	All employees	5,000	5,000	
		Performance mgt (new)	Mgt employees	2,500	2,500	
		Total key programs		5,000	7,500	Medium
Total for Top Five Priorities		**Learning for Top Five Goals** **Courses: 20 New , 2 Revised**		**5,000**	**23,180**	
Total for All Other Goals		**Learning for All Other Goals** **Courses: 16 New , 2 Revised**		**1,950**	**4,725**	
Grand Total for All Goals		**Total for All Aligned Learning** **Courses: 36 New , 4 Revised**		**5,000**	**27,905**	

TABLE 5.14

2017 Business Case for Learning

Steps 4,5: Owner Agreement and Draft Business Case for Strategically Aligned Learning
80% of Value

Priority	Corporate Goal	Key Learning Programs	Target Audience	Unique Partici-pants	Total Partici-pants	Planned Contribution from Learning	Planned Impact of Learning	Thousands of Dollars: Gross Benefit	Budget Cost	Budget Impact	Opport-unity Cost	Net Benefit	ROI
1	Increase sales by 10%	Consultative selling skills (new)	Marketing employees	100	100								
		Ten NPI modules (10 new)	Marketing employees	100	1,000								
		Total key programs		100	1,100	20%	2% higher sales	$1,500	$490	$1,010	$117	$893	147%
2	Reduce defects by 20%	Four Design courses (3 new)	New, other engineers	200	800	70%	14% reduct. in defects	$2,100	$570	$1,530	$512	$1,018	94%
3	Reduce Injuries by 25%	Five Safety courses (3 new)	Manufact. associates	2,500	12,500								
		One Safety course (revised)	Factory supervisors	100	100								
		Two Safety courses (1 new)	Office employees	500	1,000								
		Total key programs		3,100	13,600	60%	15% reduct. in injuries	$1,200	$410	$790	$376	$415	53%
4	Improve leadership score by 5 points on employee survey	Intro to supervision (revised)	New, other supervisors	100	100								
		Leadership for managers (new)	Division managers	65	65								
		Advanced leadership (existing)	Department heads	15	15								
		Total key programs		180	180	40%	2 point increase	$1,200	$582	$618	$302	$316	36%
5	Increase retention by 5 points	Individual development plans	All employees	5,000	5,000								
		Performance mgt (new)	Mgt employees	2,500	2,500								
		Total key programs		5,000	7,500	30%	1.5 point increase	$1,800	$340	$1,460	$1,150	$310	21%
Total for Top Five Priorities		**Learning for Top Five Goals** Courses: 20 New , 2 Revised		**5,000**	**23,180**	**Range = 20%-70%**		**$7,800**	**$2,392**	**$5,408**	**$2,457**	**$2,952**	**61%**
Total for All Other Goals		**Learning for All Other Goals** Courses: 16 New , 2 Revised		**1,950**	**4,725**	**Range = 50%-70%**		**$3,050**	**$1,245**	**$1,805**	**$778**	**$1,028**	**51%**
Grand Total for All Goals		**Total for All Aligned Learning Courses: 36 New , 4 Revised**		**5,000**	**27,905**	**Range = 20%-70%**		**$10,850**	**$3,637**	**$7,213**	**$3,234**	**$3,979**	**58%**

TABLE 5.15

2017 Business Case for Learning

Steps 6,7: Add Unaligned Learning and Other Costs. Obtain Final Approval for Complete Business Case

100% of Value

								Thousands of Dollars					
Priority	Corporate Goal	Key Learning Programs	Target Audience	Unique Partici-pants	Total Partici-pants	Planned Contribution fron Learning	Planned Impact of Learning	Gross Benefit	Budget Cost	Budget Impact	Opport-unity Cost	Net Benefit	ROI
1	Increase sales by 10%	Consultative selling skills (new)	Marketing employees	100	100								
		Ten NPI modules (10 new)	Marketing employees	100	1,000								
		Total key programs		100	1,100	20%	2% higher sales	$1,500	$490	$1,010	$117	$893	147%
2	Reduce defects by 20%	Four Design courses (3 new)	"New, other engineers	200	800	70%	14% reduct. in defects	$2,100	$570	$1,530	$512	$1,018	94%
3	Reduce Injuries by 25%	Five Safety courses (3 new)	Manufact. associates	2,500	12,500								
		One Safety course (revised)	Factory supervisors	100	100								
		Two Safety courses (1 new)	Office employees	500	1,000								
		Total key programs		3,100	13,600	60%	15% reduct. in injuries	$1,200	$410	$790	$376	$415	53%
4	Improve leadership score by 5 points on employee survey	Intro to supervision (revised)	New, other supervisors	100	100								
		Leadership for managers (new)	Division managers	65	65								
		Advanced leadership (existing)	Department heads	15	15								
		Total key programs		180	180	40%	2 point increase	$1,200	$582	$618	$302	$316	36%
5	Increase retention by 5 points	Individual development plans	All employees	5,000	5,000								
		Performance mgt (new)	Mgt employees	2,500	2,500								
		Total key programs		5,000	7,500	30%	1.5 point increase	$1,800	$340	$1,460	$1,150	$310	21%
Total for Top Five Priorities		**Learning for Top Five Goals** Courses: 20 New , 2 Revised		**5,000**	**23,180**	**Range = 20%-70%**		**$7,800**	**$2,392**	**$5,408**	**$2,457**	**$2,952"**	**61%**
Total for All Other Goals		**Learning for All Other Goals** Courses: 16 New , 2 Revised		**1,950**	**4,725**	**Range = 50%-70%**		**$3,050**	**$1,245**	**$1,805**	**$778**	**$1,028**	**51%**
		Total for All Aligned Learning Courses: 36 New , 4 Revised		**5,000**	**27,905**	**Range = 20%-70%**		**$10,850**	**$3,637**	**$7,213**	**$3,234**	**$3,980**	**58%**
		Unaligned Learning Courses: 2 New , 1 Revised		**4,000**	**4,000**	**Assume Net Ben = 0**		**$700**	**$300**	**$400**	**$400**	**$0**	**0%**
		Other Costs (not included elsewhere)		**NA**	**NA**			**NA**	**$600**	**($600)**	**$0**	**($600)**	**NA**
Grand Total		**Grand Total for All Learning** Courses: 38 New , 5 Revis[illegible]		**5,000**	**31,905**	**Range = 20%-70%**		**$11,550**	**$4,537**	**$7,013**	**$3,634**	**$3,380**	**41%**

Remember that this is an iterative, evolutionary process. It starts with strategic alignment and ends with an approved business case. Be proactive. Begin at least two to four months before your fiscal year commences. Always tailor the approach to your situation and culture, and always approach it from a business perspective.

What Is the Right Level of Investment?

Now you know how to create a business case for learning. You may still be waiting, however, to learn exactly how much should be invested. For example, how do we know that $4,537,000 in Table 5.4 (or 5.12) is the "right" amount and not some amount higher or lower? That is a good question.

Some Common Approaches

Elkeles and Phillips address this issue very nicely in Chapter 3 of *The Chief Learning Officer*, which is titled "Setting the Investment Level." They list five strategies and suggest most companies use one or more of the five:

- Let others do it.
- Invest the minimum.
- Invest with the rest.
- Invest until it hurts.
- Invest as long as there is payoff.

A very brief summary follows. The reader is encouraged to see their work for a very interesting, detailed discussion.

Let Others Do It

In this approach a company lets other organizations make the investment in human capital for them. The strategy here is to hire people who already have the talent you require and/or outsource your labor needs. This approach allows a company to avoid investment in learning and development entirely. There would be no business case, and the answer to the question would be $0 or as close to $0 as possible.

Invest the Minimum

The next step up the ladder is to invest as little as possible. Perhaps an organization invests just enough for an employee to do his or her current job at a minimum level of proficiency. There might be no willingness or budget to build skills beyond that level or to prepare for a future position. This may be necessary in times of severe austerity or may be prudent when turnover is high regardless of investment. This approach, however, will not contribute to a long-lasting, high-achieving organization. Employee engagement is likely to be low, and involuntary turnover is likely to be very high.

In terms of the business case in Table 5.4, an organization following this strategy would likely not have a leadership program or programs to enhance retention. Sales, quality, and safety may be scaled back, and there would likely be no unaligned learning. The investment level in this case might be $1.5 to 2.25 million or less than half the $4.5 million in Table 5.4.

Invest with the Rest

This is a very common strategy, which relies on benchmarking studies to know what the rest are investing. The implicit assumption is that the rest know what they are doing, the rest are investing the right amount, and their right amount is right for us. In other words our challenges, our needs, and our level of human capital are exactly like the rest. In the absence of any alignment of learning to the organization's goals, any needs analyses, and any consideration of a business case, this is an understandable fallback strategy. Of course, it would be coincidental if the average investment for the rest were also the right investment for your organization. Chances are that your goals, challenges, and needs are unique.

Benchmark data are usually available for spending per employee and spending as a percentage of payroll (or sales). In our example this strategy would likely involve a higher level of spending than the minimum.

Invest Until It Hurts

This is essentially a strategy of over-investing. Elkeles and Phillips provide a number of examples of how this can occur. One is investing in the latest fads, which can lead to offering programs that really are not needed. Another is mandating a minimum number of training hours for employees (such as forty or eighty per year), regardless of whether the learning is needed to meet an organizational or individual need. They also suggest some employers do it simply because they can afford it. These employers are not worried about spending too much, so it is not an issue for them.

In terms of the business case in Table 5.4, over-investing would be investing more than the recommended amount of $4.5 million.

Invest As Long As There Is Payoff

This strategy employs an ROI methodology or mindset to select those learning programs that have historically shown an attractive return or are likely to show an attractive return in the future. Since Elkeles and Phillips believe in the importance of aligning learning to business goals, this strategy would apply the ROI methodology to the aligned programs and select all those likely to generate a sufficient return (at least greater than zero). In other words, to the extent allowed by the budget, fund all the programs with an attractive ROI aligned to the business goals.

This approach is consistent with the business case developed in Table 5.4. All included learning programs have a positive ROI, and all ROIs are above 20%, which is a reasonable threshold for selecting investment projects.

Recommended Approach

The recommended approach is "Invest as Long as There is Payoff," in which payoff may be defined as some threshold or minimum level of ROI, such as 20%, and where the projects have been strategically aligned. This approach ensures that only programs with a reasonable expectation of generating net benefits are chosen. When funds run out or when there are no more projects expected to deliver an attractive return, stop investing.

The Contribution of Strategic Alignment and Business Case

The strategic alignment process described in Chapter 4 and the development of a business case described in this chapter are simply extensions of the "Invest as Long as There Is Payoff" strategy to ensure that the investment decisions are proactive and strategic. Although this strategy can be applied to each learning program when it is requested (anytime during the year), the recommended approach is to review *all* of the strategically aligned learning programs at one time when the business case for learning is created. (Of course, in practice there may be a few new needs that surface during the year, giving rise to a few unplanned but strategically aligned programs, which will need to be considered outside the business plan process.)

The strategic alignment process will ensure that the highest priority corporate goals have been identified and that learning is first directed to these highest priority goals. The creation of the business case will ensure that all of the planned programs are evaluated and that the most important, impactful programs are funded. Without this proactive, strategic, and holistic approach, there is a very real possibility that investment funds will be exhausted before some high-priority programs are funded, simply because the high-priority programs were not requested until later in the year. So, while the "Invest as Long as There Is Payoff" strategy ensures only worthwhile programs are funded, it does not ensure that all the "right" programs are funded. The only way to ensure the right programs (highest priority, strategically aligned) are funded is to complete the strategic alignment and business case processes.

The Right Level of Investment

Now, we are finally ready to answer the question about the right level of investment.

The right level of investment in learning depends on the needs of the organization to achieve its goals, the impact learning can have on meeting those needs, and the projected return of the investment in learning. Learning programs should be funded as long as the payoff is attractive, starting with the highest priority strategically aligned learning.

Since the business case in Table 5.4 reflects the results of the strategic alignment process and all the recommended programs have an attractive return, the "right" answer is the $4.5 million budget cost on the bottom line of the worksheet. This is the amount the company should invest in learning. If $4.5 million in funding is not available, then the company should consider reducing the investment in unaligned learning (lowest priority) and learning for lower priority goals (6–11) in order to preserve funding for the higher priority goals (1–5).

Since this approach starts with organizational goals, the right amount of learning will always depend on an organization's own circumstances. Thus, "Invest with the Rest" makes no sense as a strategy since it assumes every organization has the same goals, challenges, and needs. It also assumes that the impact and return (payoff) of learning programs are identical for all organizations, which is most certainly not true. "Invest the Minimum" also makes little sense unless the minimum is defined as supporting all the strategically aligned goals. Investing less than the $4.5 million in Table 5.4 means that learning critical to the organization's performance will not be delivered, and the organization's goals should be lowered accordingly.

Last, "Invest Until It Hurts" implies that programs with insignificant payoff or negative ROI are being funded. This also does not make sense and is a waste of resources, not to mention the opportunity costs for all those involved. The money should be directed elsewhere in the organization to programs with higher expected payoff or returns to shareholders (contributors).

CATERPILLAR EXPERIENCE: In the second year of Caterpillar University we created a document entitled *The Business of Learning*. This was our first disciplined attempt to explicitly identify and quantify the costs and benefits from our learning programs. It started with strategic alignment (see Chapter 4) and then addressed each recommended program in detail. Costs and benefits were projected for five years. This was primarily a learning exercise for us in the learning function—a disciplined approach to carefully thinking about all the costs of each program as well as the impact and benefits that we expected. (Most of us were new to the learning field. We did not know what we could reasonably expect from learning programs or what the total costs were.) We had rich discussions about these likely costs and benefits, and we all learned a tremendous amount. Moreover, the process ensured that all the senior leaders in Cat U were approaching costs and benefits in the same manner—that we had a common, consistent approach. In other words, this helped us reach a common mental model for establishing the business case for learning.

The document was shared with senior corporate leadership and used to reinforce the potential impact of learning on corporate results. It also clearly demonstrated that we had done our homework. All the costs, including opportunity costs, had been clearly identified. The potential impact of learning on results had been carefully considered with all assumptions made transparent for review. And final estimates of dollar benefits, where appropriate, had been calculated very conservatively. It showed conclusively that we were bringing business discipline to learning and that funds invested in learning would be managed well.

In the end, the benefit of creating *The Business of Learning* was not so much in the identification of precise dollar costs and benefits, although these proved helpful in making our case. The greater benefit was in the process itself, including all the discovery and shared learning that occurred, and in the credibility the effort gave us.

Conclusion

The business case for learning is the natural extension of the strategic alignment process. Once it is complete, you are ready to make the business case for investing in learning at the organization or enterprise level. Impact, dollar benefits (in some cases), and costs are clearly articulated for the highest priority goals and in summary for the organization as a whole. The business case can stand alone and be presented to senior leadership for approval or be included in the written business plan and presented for approval. The latter approach is recommended because it is more comprehensive, more professional, and more likely to result in approval of the learning investment. The next chapter describes the other elements of a good business plan and recaps the entire process from strategic alignment to finished business plan.

Chapter 5 to Do List

1. If you are not creating a formal business case for learning today, resolve to create your first next year. You might choose to do it as part of an overall business plan for learning. Begin the planning now. Start with a change management plan. Get your staff and senior leadership on board.
2. Decide how much to accomplish your first year: just the highest priority strategically aligned learning, all strategically aligned learning, or aligned and unaligned learning and other costs.
3. Create a plan with a timetable to complete the strategic alignment and the business case.
4. Think about which programs have impacts that lend themselves to an estimate of dollar benefit.
5. Create the formal business case for learning. Do not let lack of data deter you. Just start. Do what is reasonable for you and your organization at this point in time. Improve as you go.
6. If you are not planning to incorporate the business case into a business plan for learning, have the business case approved by your CEO and governing board.

Further Reading

Echols, Michael. *ROI on Human Capital Investment*, second edition. Arlington, Texas: Tapestry Press, 2005.

Elkeles, Tamar and Jack Phillips. *The Chief Learning Officer: Driving Value within a Changing Organization through Learning and Development.* Burlington, Massachusetts: Butterworth-Heinemann, 2007. (See Chapter 3.)

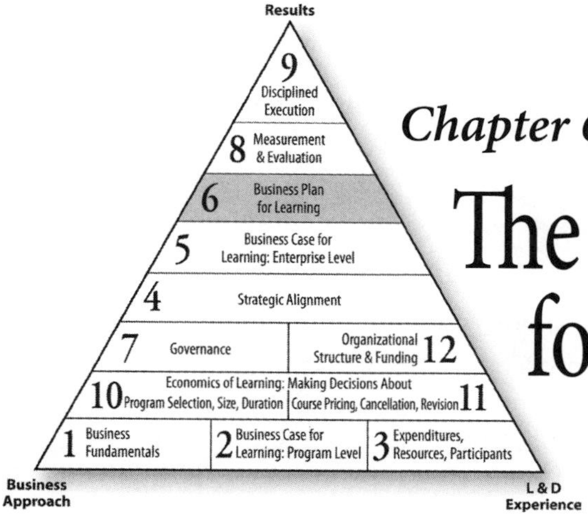

Chapter 6

The Business Plan for Learning

THE BUSINESS PLAN for learning is the natural culmination of the strategic alignment process and the business case for learning. It is both strategic and tactical, and it is proactive since it is completed and approved before the new fiscal year begins. The process of creating it and the final document are both key determinants of your success in securing resources and earning your place as a strategic partner. Like strategic alignment itself, the concept is simple and straightforward but seldom practiced with any rigor and discipline. Consequently, after strategic alignment and the process of creating the business case for learning, this approach represents the greatest improvement opportunity for the learning profession. This chapter describes the rationale and process for creating a written business plan for learning, including a suggested table of contents for both small and large organizations.

Key Concepts for Chapter 6

1. Both process and document are important.
2. It should be a written document.
3. Key elements are an executive summary, strategic alignment, the business case for learning, budget, and a detailed work plan.
4. Start modestly. You can add chapters and expand coverage in the following years.
5. Business plan goals must be specific and measurable.
6. Estimates and forecasts play an important role in the business plan.

What Is It, and Why Is It Important?

The business plan for learning is both a process and a document. Each is valuable in its own right, and each contributes to the other. The process is necessary to create the document, and the document summarizes and reinforces the results of the process. The process and resulting document represent the only way to ensure that the right learning is provided and that the investment in learning will deliver maximum value to the organization.

The Document

The business plan for learning is the single most important document a CLO will create each year. Just as a well-run organization will have a business plan (Chapter 1), every learning function should have one as well. Like the organization's plan, a business plan for learning should include the learning function's vision and mission, a business case for proposed investment, including specific, measurable goals for the coming year and resource requirements to accomplish those goals, and projected financials for the year. A business plan for learning should also include chapters on costs, deployment of resources, evaluation strategy, and other topics more specific to learning. In sum, the plan should pull everything that is important to the successful management of the learning function together in one document.

Ideally, a business plan for learning will be a written document rather than a PowerPoint presentation. Although a PowerPoint presentation would be better than nothing, the process of creating and reviewing a written plan will add more value and provide more opportunities for organizational learning. For most of us, the act of committing thoughts to paper in sentence form demands more discipline, more rigor, and clearer thinking than creating a slide. Many of us also read and reflect on the text in a page more carefully than on bullet points in a slide, and much of the value of forming a shared vision for next year's learning will come from others reading the work and providing feedback. Complicated topics are also easier to describe in sentences than in bullet points. Finally, if the CEO or other senior officers will be reading the plan, the writers are likely to spend more time making sure they have it right and that it is consistent. And CEOs generally are more likely to read and review a written business plan than a stack of slides. Ultimately, of course, the content is more important than the form, so if your culture will accept only PowerPoint, then use that.

The Process

A good business planning process ensures that all the right questions are asked of the right people at the right time. Then it ensures that the best answers are found to those questions. View it from a learning perspective (which should be easy for learning professionals!). You want to discover the best way to accomplish next year's goals, and the answers lie within the organization. You need to create a process for discussion, reflection, dialogue, and revision that ultimately produces a shared vision on the best way to accomplish next year's goals.

Now, it is true that many organizational planning processes fall short of this goal, especially from the learning point of view. The VP of learning, however, given her knowledge about learning theory, is in a particularly good position to craft and execute a robust planning process for next year's learning. The goal is to discover how the learning function can best support the objectives of the organization, particularly the highest priority objectives. This will maximize the impact of learning on the organization's success and consequently maximize the return on the learning investment.

The business planning process for learning is designed to do just this. The key components of this process have already been described: determination of costs, strategic alignment, and creation of a business case for learning. The end product is a business plan for learning that, if funded and properly executed, ensures the investment in learning delivers the highest possible value to an organization. In the absence of a well-designed and executed planning process, there is little chance that the right learning will be done.

Contents of the Business Plan for Learning

The business plan for learning will vary in complexity and length depending on the scope and complexity of the learning function and the overall organization. The plan is also likely to grow through the years as the learning function adds more chapters and shares more information. It may be as short as ten to twenty pages or considerably longer. Let's start with a simple one.

Your First Business Plan for Learning

The key to success is to keep the process manageable with an emphasis on progress over perfection. Start with the basics. You can always add more next year. The chief reason learning functions don't create business plans today is that the task seems overwhelming. Most would agree the concept makes sense, but they never start it because they believe that they do not have the time or resources. It does take time, but like change management, a little more time invested upfront (in this case before the year starts) will save a lot of time during the year and make it much easier to manage the function.

Here are the essential chapters to include in your first year:

FIGURE 6.1

Essential Chapters in Your First Business Plan for Learning

1. Executive Summary
2. Last Year's Accomplishments
3. Strategic Alignment
4. Business Case for Learning
5. Learning Resources, Expenditures, and Budget
6. Detailed Work Plans
7. Evaluation Strategy

These are the basics. A CLO can write this business plan up in eight to twelve hours once the strategic alignment and business case have been completed and all the information has been gathered on resources, expenditures, and budget. The detailed work plans should be delegated to those responsible for them, such as the college deans or senior program managers.

A thirty-six-page sample business plan for learning can be found in Appendix B, which contains all the chapters described above (and three more). It was created in about twelve hours and will give you an excellent idea of what a plan might look like.

Note on terminology: Next year's plan will be prepared in the closing months of the current fiscal year. So the 2017 business plan for learning will be prepared in late 2016. The chapter on last year's accomplishments refers to 2016, which will be "last year" once the New Year arrives. Also, final actuals for the current year (2016) will not be available when the plan is being prepared, so you will have to use estimates for the current year based on 10 or 11 months of data.

A brief description of each chapter follows.

Executive Summary

The executive summary provides the key take-aways from the document. It is especially important in a longer document, where few will read it in its entirety. Write it assuming someone will read *only* the executive summary. What must they know? In a ten-page plan, it should be condensed into one page or less.

Focus on the highlights from chapters two to five. In particular, be sure to discuss how many of the top goals will be supported by learning, the impact learning is planned to have on them, and the resulting net benefit or ROI. In other words, make the business case in brief for your proposed level of investment. By definition the detailed work plans of Chapter 6 are too detailed to summarize for the executive summary; you should have captured their essence in the summary for the business case. Consider a summary table comparing this year's performance against plan (see Appendix B, Table 1) and one comparing next year's plan with this year's estimated results (see Appendix B, Table 2).

Appendix B contains a three-page executive summary with two tables as an example.

> ADVICE: Tables do not speak for themselves! It is imperative that you refer to the table in the text and then tell the reader what you want them to take away from the table. In other words, write your text assuming the reader will not look at the table. Even when readers do look at the table, without your guidance, they may not focus on the same data or draw the same conclusions. So, don't leave their interpretation to chance. You have already spent time creating the table. Now be sure it conveys the intended message.

Last Year's Accomplishments

Use this chapter to take credit for your accomplishments this past year. Instead of waiting for others to give you credit for all your good work, take the credit by reminding everyone how much you've accomplished. Not only is this an opportunity to praise all the learning professionals in your organization, but it also helps establish credibility for what you want to accomplish this year. It is always easier to approve funds and additional staff for a successful function, so remind them how well you managed the resources they provided you with last year. Provide a table comparing estimated results to plan (see Appendix B, Table 3).

Focus on how this year's learning was aligned to the goals of the organization, how resources were focused on the highest priority needs, the impact learning had on achieving those goals, how happy the sponsors were with your help, how many people were served by learning, and any awards you received. You might also want to include a table showing financial performance versus plan.

In a ten-page plan this chapter may be one page or less. Appendix B contains a three-page example with two tables.

Strategic Alignment

This is a very important chapter but does not have to be lengthy. You simply need to describe the process in detail for your readers and share the results. You need to answer this question for the reader clearly: How did you decide which learning programs to recommend for next year? Share the timeline, names of individuals with whom you spoke, and prioritization criteria. Transparency is essential to establish credibility.

Once the process has been explained, share the results. A table like 4.5 is highly recommended to show visually the alignment of learning with organizational goals. You should also show a table like 4.4, which includes every goal for the organization, or 4.6, which focuses only on those goals for which learning is recommended. Be sure to talk the reader through the tables and highlight the key points. Simply including the table does not get the job done!

Appendix B contains a three-page example with figures and tables.

Business Case for Learning

This chapter is where you make the business case for learning by laying out the benefits and costs of the strategically aligned programs recommended in the previous chapter and by bringing in the unaligned learning and unallocated costs for completeness. Your strategic alignment work has ensured that the recommended learning is aligned with the organization's goals and that learning will have an important impact on achieving those goals. Now the reader needs to know how much it will cost and, depending on your culture and inclination, what the bottom line dollar benefit will be from the learning (impact on net profit in a for-profit company). The reader also needs to know how much unaligned learning there is and what it costs. Be sure to differentiate between the essential and non-essential unaligned learning. Only then can a final, well-informed decision be made about which of the programs to fund and, more broadly, what the budget for the learning function should be.

Start with summary comments about the benefits and costs of the learning targeted at the three to five highest priority goals. This is typically where learning's impact will be greatest, and it will be the area of greatest interest to your CEO and senior leaders. It is also where you have spent most of your time refining the programs, benefits, and costs. Talk the reader through the planned impact on each of the top three to five goals individually. Then work your way down to the lower priority programs in support of organizational goals and the nature and cost of the unaligned learning. Conclude with comments on the total benefits and costs and the net benefits of learning. A table such as 5.4 or 5.5, showing the alignment, programs, benefits, and costs, would be appropriate here. Remember that tables do not speak for themselves. This is especially important in making the business case, so walk the reader through the key measures in the table. Tell them how each measure is defined (like gross and net benefits, opportunity cost, and ROI). Take them through the calculations step-by-step for one of the goals. You have put a lot of effort into creating this table so be sure the reader is equipped to fully understand it.

If you have a significant amount of essential unaligned learning, walk the reader through the top programs, reminding them that the company's top leaders have deemed this learning essential and that your plan is to meet these needs in the most effective and efficient ways possible. If your essential unaligned learning is more significant than your aligned learning, you might choose to lead with unaligned rather than aligned learning.

This chapter may be one to two pages in a ten-page plan. Appendix B contains a three-page example with a table.

Learning Resources, Expenditures, and Budgets

This is the place to share information about current resources and expenditures and to present the budget for next year. For credibility you show that you know and understand the current resource structure for learning, including staffing and spending, and how these are allocated to programs. Decision makers are not likely to give you additional funds or staff if you cannot account for what you already have. Plus, it is important to know how resources are currently allocated so the reader has a baseline to judge your recommendations for next year. Are you suggesting a major shift in allocation or an increase in staff?

Your write-up should include answers to the following questions, with at least one table or figure for each answer:

- How much is the organization spending on learning?
  - See Enterprise Learning Expenditures (Tables 3.2, 3.3).
  - See Enterprise Learning Expenditures by Business Unit or Region (Table 3.4).
- What is it being spent on?
  - See Enterprise Program Costs (Table 3.10 and Figures 3.3 and 3.4).
- How many resources are dedicated to learning?
  - See Enterprise Learning Resources (Tables 3.12–3.15).
- How many employees, dealers, suppliers, and customers are being served by learning?
  - See Enterprise Participation in Learning (Tables 3.18 and 3.19).

This is also a good place to discuss the budget for next year (and how you did against this year's budget if that was not done in "last year's accomplishments"). All the necessary preparation has been done. You have described this year's accomplishments and what you spent to achieve them. You have described the strategic alignment process and laid out the business case for the upcoming year, including the expected impact of learning on the organization's goals. You have included a detailed work plan, including costs. It is time to pull it together in budget format and present the total costs and required staffing level to achieve the impact described above.

At a minimum you should present the following three tables and describe the key points. You may want to show more detail for income (corporate, business unit, external) and for expense (labor and related, indirect material and expenses, internal charges). Alternatively, the comparison of current year financial performance, like Table 6.1, could be included in the "last year's accomplishments" chapter.

This chapter may be one to two pages in a ten-page plan. Appendix B contains a five-page example with six tables.

TABLE 6.1: **Vega Corporate University**
2016 Financial Performance
Thousands of Dollars

	2015 Actual	2016 Plan	2016 Estimate	Variance $	Variance %
Income	$1,847	$2,250	$2,175	($75)	3.3%
Expense	$1,839	$2,250	$2,198	($52)	2.3%
Net Income	$8	$0	($23)	($23)	

TABLE 6.2: **Vega Corporate University**
2017 Budget for Learning
Thousands of Dollars

	2015 Actual	2016 Estimate	% Change	2017 Plan	% Change
Income	$1,847	$2,175	17.8%	$2,252	3.5%
Expense	$1,839	$2,198	19.5%	$2,252	2.5%
Net Income	$8	($23)		$0	

TABLE 6.3: **Vega Corporate University**
2017 Staffing Plan

	2016 Plan	Proj. Dec 31	2017 Plan
Part-Time Associates	7	11	10
[Full-time equivalents]	[4]	[6]	[5]
Total	29	30	30
[Full-time equivalents]	[26]	[25]	[25]

Detailed Work Plan

This chapter includes a short description of your programs (or at least the most important ones) including the following:

- Organizational goal it supports (for example, "10% increase in sales") and owner
- Brief description of the program itself (for example, "Two-day instructor-led course to improve consultative selling skills")
- Target audience by group and size (for example, "All forty-two district sales representatives")
- Beginning and ending deployment dates (for example, "Deployment to begin February 15 and be completed by March 31")
- Planned impact of learning on the goal (for example, "5% increase in sales")
- Targets or plans for the effectiveness measures which must be attained if the programs are to deliver the planned impact. For example, participant feedback must be at least 80% favorable, test scores must be at least 85%, and the actual application rate must be at least 80%.
- Who in the learning function is responsible for it (optional)

In a smaller organization you may be able to provide the detailed work plan for all of your programs. In a larger organization you may focus on the most important. In any case, this is information you already should have on each program. The question is whether to write it up and include it in the plan for every program or just the higher priority programs.

This chapter may be two to three pages in a ten-page plan. Appendix B contains a seven-page example.

Measurement and Evaluation Strategy

This chapter describes your measurement and evaluation strategy for the year. It might begin with a quick review of the different types of measures followed by the specific, measurable goals for evaluation. It should address the following questions:

- What types of measurement and evaluation are planned?
- For which programs? When?

- Who will perform the evaluations?
- How will the data be collected, organized, and presented?
- How will the results be used?

For example, your strategy might include the following in addition to the points above:

Efficiency Measures

- Use the learning management system (LMS) to collect data on unique and total participants for all courses, as well as number and type of courses and hours on instruction. Also, collect data on the use of communities of practice, including number of communities, unique and total participants, and time used. Share summary data in monthly reports (with detail available) to determine if the initiatives are on plan.
- Collect data on internal cycle time, including the start and completion dates for performance consulting (needs analysis), design and development, and delivery for all courses. Share summary data in monthly reports (with detail available) to determine if the initiatives are on plan.
- Collect data on planned and actual completion dates for each course and report as percentage meeting plan. Share summary data in monthly reports (with detail available) to establish a baseline.
- Calculate percentage of employees reached by learning and number with development plans. Report monthly and compare to plan.
- Calculate the utilization rate for our large suite of online courses and include in monthly reports to establish a baseline for improvement.

Effectiveness Measures

- Use an email survey to gather participant feedback electronically for all courses from a sample of participants within fourteen days of completing a course. Manage the feedback internally and in an ongoing basis throughout the year with real-time reporting. The results should be used to identify course content that needs to be reworked and instructors who need to be coached or replaced. Summary results should be captured in monthly reports, with detail available online.

- Gather data on comprehension at completion of the course (online test for online courses) for all compliance-related learning and certain other learning where a knowledge check is appropriate. (You could list the programs.) Manage the data internally and in an ongoing basis throughout the year with real-time reporting. Summary results should be captured in monthly reports (detail available online) and compared to plan.
- Gather level 3 data on intent to apply as part of the post-event survey described above. Use a follow-up survey after 90 days to gather actual application rate for key courses (specify). Report summary results in monthly reports and compare to plan to determine if management action needs to be taken.

Outcome Measures

- Engage a consultant to conduct Impact and Return Investment evaluations on the two highest-priority programs (consultative selling skills and design for engineers), using randomly selected samples and/or control groups. The study should be conducted in the third quarter, with results available by October 31st to determine if the programs are having the planned impact. Results also will be incorporated in your next year's business plan.

The evaluation strategy may be one page in a ten-page plan. Appendix B contains a three-page example.

Mature Business Plans for Learning

Your business plan for learning is likely to evolve through time as you modify it to fit your needs. It is also likely to expand as you add more detail and chapters. A mature plan might add chapters on evaluation, communication, continuous improvement, and history.

FIGURE 6.2

Chapters in a Mature Business Plan for Learning

1. Executive Summary
2. Last Year's Accomplishments
3. Strategic Alignment
4. Business Case for Learning
5. Learning Resources, Expenditures, and Budget

6. Detailed Work Plans
7. Evaluation Strategy
8. Communication Strategy
9. Continuous Improvement Strategy
10. History

A brief description of these three additional chapters follows.

Communication Strategy

This chapter describes your communication strategy for the year. How will the learning function communicate with the rest of the organization? The chapter might address the following types of questions and issues:

- Is there a communication strategy? What is it? Who is responsible for it?
- How often does the CLO communicate with the employees of the learning function? How?
- How often does the CLO communicate with senior leaders of the organization? With key stakeholders? With employees? With partners and vendors?
- How does the CLO communicate with other learning leaders in the organization?
- Are there regular newsletters to internal clients, employees?
- Are there internal press releases? External press releases?
- Is there a website for the learning function? What does it contain? How often is it updated? Does the organization's website have a link to it?
- Is there a brand for the learning function? How is it used?
- Is there an annual report for learning highlighting the accomplishments of the past year?
- How is the business plan for learning shared with the learning community in the organization? With others in the organization?

This chapter may be one to two pages in a fifteen-page report (a mature function likely will have a plan longer than ten pages). Appendix B contains a three-page example.

Continuous Improvement Strategy

The best learning functions are always striving to improve. This chapter would describe your strategy for improvement, including benchmarking other organizations, hosting benchmarking visits, inviting guest speakers, applying for industry awards, and attending conferences. Share what you believe to be successful or best practices (others may want to benchmark you), and share areas where you believe you can improve (looking for other organizations to benchmark). Include lessons learned and ideas gained from last year's benchmarking and conferences.

This chapter may be one page in a twenty-page plan. Appendix B contains a one-page example.

History

This chapter provides an opportunity to collect and preserve the history of the corporate university or learning department. Usually, startups or resets are so intense and people so busy that important milestones and accomplishments will go unrecorded. Before you know it, two or three years will have passed and some of the key contributors will have moved on. Soon the details of the first years will be forgotten. That is unfortunate because current and future learning leaders can learn a lot from those earlier challenges, setbacks, successes, and failures. Moreover, in many organizations a sense of history is an important part of the culture, and people take pride in the past.

So, this chapter might start small and grow through time, recording the significant events of each year. It will be a written record of your progress and will have more meaning in the future than you can imagine now. It can also become an important part of an orientation for employees new to the learning function and will give them a sense of their new organization's history.

This chapter may be one page in a twenty-page document. Appendix B contains a three-page example.

> CATERPILLAR EXPERIENCE: In 2006 we completed the last business plan for learning before my retirement. The company that year had sales of $41.5 billion and approximately 90,000 full-time employees. The independent dealer network had more than 117,000 employees. Since Cat U had enterprise responsibility for learning, and since Caterpillar spent more than $100 million on learning, our Enterprise Learning Plan ran to more than one hundred pages to

cover all the major enterprise-wide initiatives. The chapters were similar to those recommended above, and each dean wrote his or her own detailed work plans. Our process started in August with interviews of the CEO and board of governors. It concluded with approval by the CEO and board of governors in December or January (if there were revisions coming out of the December board of governors review). The process and resulting plan were absolutely key to our success, including our strategic focus, ability to execute, increased funding, and overall support.

For more on the Caterpillar process, see Chapter 6 by Fred Goh (former Director of Strategic Learning for Cat U) in Karen Mantyla's *The Learning Advantage.*

Creating the Business Plan for Learning

The process starts with the strategic alignment process and an understanding of your current resources and concludes with approval of the plan by the CEO and/or governing body. In both process and documentation it should be comprehensive and pull together all the essential elements of a successful learning function.

The Steps

Creating the business plan for learning is a nine-step process. These steps were first introduced in Chapter 2 and are now presented organized by major activity. (Steps 2–5 are simply a condensed version of the seven-step process in the last chapter to create the business case.)

FIGURE 6.3

Steps in the Creation of the Business Plan for Learning

Current Costs, Resource Deployment, and Participants

1. Know your current costs, where your resources are being deployed, and how many people you are serving.

Strategic Alignment

2. Read your organization's business plan and long-term strategy. (If they do not exist or if they are not shared, you will have to get this information by asking.)

Then meet with your organization's leaders, governing bodies, and goal owners to understand the strategy, goals, and challenges for next year.

3. Within the learning function, decide which of these goals learning can support and the type of learning you would recommend.
4. Meet again with the goals' owners and key stakeholders to share your thoughts on how learning can help them achieve their goals. Reach agreement on the planned learning, planned impact, benefits, and costs. Share with your internal staff.

The Business Case for Learning

5. Complete the refinement of costs and benefits for recommended programs with the goals' owners and secure their agreement. Add in unaligned learning and other costs.

The Business Plan for Learning

6. Compile all of this (description of current spending, programs, target audiences, results; description of the planning process, including a list of those who have provided input; the organization's goals and the strategic alignment of learning to those goals; your recommended learning programs for next year along with planned impact, benefits, and costs; and a measurement and evaluation strategy) into a draft business plan for learning (written or PowerPoint document).
7. Share this draft plan with your governing board and senior leaders. Solicit their feedback.
8. Revise it based on their feedback and any revisions to your organization's business plan for next year.
9. Get formal approval of the business plan for learning from your governing body or CEO. Share the approved plan with your staff and with others in the organization.

Current Costs, Resource Deployment, and Participants

Step 1: Know your current costs, where your resources are being deployed, and how many people you are serving. This is your foundation. Without this knowledge you will have no credibility.

This is listed first simply because the CLO needs to know these before he meets with the CEO, CFO, and other senior executives and governing board members as part of the strategic alignment process. It is highly likely that, in the course of the conversation, some of them will ask what is currently being spent on learning, where it is being spent, and how many people are being reached. They may ask about current or past results. So, a well-prepared CLO will have actuals for last year and perhaps estimates for the current year. If these data have never been collected before, then the CLO will have a plan to collect them for the current year and will schedule another meeting to present them.

Chapter 3 explained in detail how to gather, organize, and present data on costs, staff, programs, and participants. The focus here is on current-year costs. If the plan for next year is being created in the last three months of the current year, then the process described in Chapter 3 is aimed at getting the current-year data. It will likely be a two-step process since actuals are not known yet for the current year. In step one ask for estimates for the current year (actuals will be available for the first eight or nine months; the last three to four months will be estimates). Use these estimates in creating the business plan for learning. After the year ends and actuals are available for the previous year, then repeat the process and collect the actuals. You can either update the business plan with these actuals or save them for use in next year's plan.

Strategic Alignment

Steps 2–4. This is the strategic alignment process that ensures your proposed learning is the right learning for next year. This is where the right questions (about alignment and impact) are asked of the right people (CEO, senior executives, governing board members, and goal owners/stakeholders) at the right time (before the new year begins). The result will be a clear understanding of the organization's goals and priorities and a clear understanding of the role learning can play in achieving those goals, including its likely impact. Chapter 4 describes this process in detail.

Chapter 6 integrates the strategic alignment process into the business planning process. The process as described in steps 2–5 could serve as a standalone process and never be included as part of a formal business plan for learning. It would still have tremendous value but may be harder to execute successfully if not formalized as part of the business plan for next year.

The strategic alignment process described in steps 2–4 generates specific program recommendations, planned impact, and includes an initial decision on what to include in the plan for next year. The output of this process will be a Table like 4.4 or 4.6. The process will also have generated initial cost estimates for the recommended programs, and these will be integrated into the plan in step 5.

The Business Case for Learning

***Step 5*:** Complete the refinement of costs and benefits for strategically aligned learning. Add in the costs and benefits of unaligned learning and the unallocated costs. This step is where all the benefits and costs come together to make the case for investing in learning. Chapter 5 describes the process in detail and will result in a table like 5.4 (5.5, 5.14 or 5.15), showing the benefits and costs of the aligned and unaligned learning as well as the unallocated costs for a complete picture of benefits and costs.

Like strategic alignment, the business case can stand on its own and does not have to be part of a business plan for learning. It will, though, be more persuasive as part of an overall written business plan.

The Business Plan for Learning

***Step 6*:** Compile all of this information into a draft of your business plan for learning. Almost all of the essential pieces have now been created. See earlier sections of this chapter for a suggested table of contents for a first-time plan and for a mature plan.

Someone in the learning function will need to serve as the manager for this process to lay out the timeline and then ensure that deadlines are met. The easiest way to compile all the necessary information is to assign chapters or parts of chapters to different individuals. The CLO may want to incorporate a progress check in her monthly staff meetings and may want to include it as part of her direct report's goals to ensure that this process receives the necessary attention.

An editor will also be needed to achieve consistency among the different authors. The CLO will want to read each chapter as it comes in as well, especially in the first year, to make sure the author has focused on the right content and at the right level of detail.

Once the plan is complete, the CLO should have her own staff review it. Discuss suggested changes and incorporate those that make sense.

The first business plan for learning is the hardest. Everyone is learning about the process and what the CLO expects. So, allow for lots of discussion and redrafts. Invariably, in the first year you will also discover a lot of information you wish you had but cannot get in time to include. That is okay. Make a note and plan to get it next year. Remember that you are starting with the basics, and both the process and the document will improve each year.

The second year is much easier than the first, and by the third year it is easy. The format has been established and templates exist for many things. Everyone knows exactly what is expected, and they actually gather information (and may even write some sections) through the year, which makes the crunch time even easier. By the fourth year it will be a finely-tuned institutionalized process.

> ADVICE: The first year will be hard, so be ready for it. The CLO needs to practice good change management, first with her own direct reports, then with the rest of the learning managers, and finally with all the staff. Explain the benefits of this approach and how it will make their lives easier during the year. Some, maybe many, will initially resist. They will complain it is bureaucratic, busywork, and a waste of their valuable time. The CLO needs to stand firm. Make the process as efficient as possible but stick to it. This is not the time for consensus decision making. It is the time for leadership, even if unpopular. The complaints will decrease in the second year and should disappear in the third year.

Step 7: You are now ready to share the draft with those who gave you the initial input and whose approval you will need. This may be done in person, or you can send it to them. In either case prepare a cover memo to attach to the plan that includes:

- A review of the process and where you currently are in that process
- Where they should focus their attention if their time is limited (executive summary, strategic alignment, business case, and budget). You might even call their attention to a few tables like Appendix B, Tables 2 and 6.
- What you want from them (questions, suggestions, changes, and ultimately approval)
- When you need to hear back from them

The memo should be no more than one page.

This is an opportunity to close the loop with them, and they should see their original input on goals and priorities captured in the plan. You now need them to tell you:

- Whether you got the organization goals or priorities wrong
- Whether they disagree with any of your program recommendations
  - Have you omitted some that they think are more important?
  - Have you included some they don't believe should be in the plan?
- Whether they disagree with any of the planned costs or benefits
- Whether they disagree with your budget for next year, including staffing

You do not need to ask these questions specifically in the cover memo, but this is what you are listening for in their reply. If they raise any of these issues, then you will need to follow up with them. After considering their points, you will need either to modify the plan to incorporate their feedback, convince them that a change is not necessary, or choose to live with some disagreement. It may be that some of the senior executives, all of whom report to the CEO, disagree, and you will never be able to please all of them anyway. If a suggestion or objection comes from your CEO, then you would be well-advised to address it.

Step 8: Make revisions based on their feedback and any revisions to your organization's business plan for next year. In addition to incorporating their feedback, new information may have become available for next year. Perhaps the economic outlook has changed and along with it the sales forecast and the earlier forecast for profit and cash flow. This change may affect your funding and staffing, and you may want to make a final adjustment before completing the plan.

Step 9: Now you are ready to get final approval of the business plan for learning. If you have a governing body like a board of governors, getting approval should be on the agenda for the meeting the month before the New Year begins so that the plan will be approved by the start of the year. All the board members will have given you input initially, reviewed the draft, and given you feedback. If they made substantive suggestions, you should follow up with them so they will not be surprised at the board meeting. If you do not have a governing board, then the CEO should approve it.

In either case, share the final changes with them before asking for approval. The actual approval should come easily since you have incorporated their input and feedback and since the work plan reflects the results of the close collaboration between the learning staff and the owner of each goal. If you have a governing board the approval will be captured in the minutes, and these can be shared with anyone over the course of the year who questions the priorities and focus of the plan. If approved by the CEO, have her sign it on the title page, which will serve to confirm that the plan has been officially approved. It will discourage others from "appealing" the plan during the year.

CATERPILLAR EXPERIENCE: At Cat U we added an additional step to the above process. Since Caterpillar had twenty-eight divisions (including North American marketing, European manufacturing, and financial products) and each division had its own learning function (not included in Cat U's budget), and since Cat U had overall responsibility for all enterprise learning (whether developed and deployed by Cat U or others), we required each of the twenty-eight divisions to submit an annual division-level business plan for learning to us as part of the planning process.

We provided a template for the divisions to use, specifying the required content and recommended optional content. The division learning plan included an estimate of cost and staffing for the current year by major program and a plan for the same for next year. The division learning plan also included plans to deploy Cat U-developed courses and other needs for the coming year (such as a leadership course for senior leaders, advanced courses for engineers, or business acumen).

The draft division learning plans were due to us in late October, so we had time to factor in the needs of the twenty-eight business units along with the input from the CEO, board of governors, and sponsors. In particular, their input helped us prioritize the learning initiatives for inclusion in the enterprise learning plan, especially when there was not a well-defined or active sponsor for an initiative. We focused on the highest-priority strategically-aligned learning that was common and global in nature. In other words, not only was it the right learning, but it was needed by a majority of divisions throughout the enterprise. If a program applied to only one or two divisions, it would have lower priority than a program to be used by twenty.

> We updated the division learning managers monthly through the fall on the programs Cat U was considering for the next year so they would know which programs we would provide and which they would have to provide. After the enterprise learning plan was approved by the board of governors in December, we updated the divisions on the final programs for next year. Then they would finalize their division learning plan, have their vice president approve it, and send it to us.

The Timetable

The time required for completion will vary depending on the scope of the learning function and the size and complexity of the organization. It will take at least two months and perhaps as long as four months. Remember, the goal is not to minimize the duration or time spent. It is to have a robust discovery and learning process that will produce a comprehensive and credible plan.

Learning Function with Limited Scope or a Smaller Organization

Assume in this case the organization is small or that the plan will be created for just one division or business unit of a larger organization. The example will assume a small organization led by a CEO. If it is instead for a division of a larger organization, just substitute the appropriate titles. The business plan for learning will be twenty to thirty pages in length. Calendar months are in parentheses for those organizations with a calendar year as their fiscal year.

FIGURE 6.4

Timetable for Creation of a Business Plan for Learning in a Smaller Organization

Month	Task
1 (Jan.)	CLO and direct reports agree on timetable for business planning process
	CLO appoints a manager for the business planning process.
	Agree on a table of contents. Make assignments for writing the document with deadlines
	Build responsibilities into performance goals for the year

8 (Aug.)	Review timetable. Confirm roles and responsibilities for learning staff.
	Schedule Month 10 (October) appointments with CEO, direct reports to CEO and governing board members
10 (Oct.)	Interview CEO first, then direct reports to CEO and governing board.
	Schedule appointments with owners of goals, other key stakeholders suggested by CEO
	First meeting with owner of each goal and other key stakeholders
	Learning staff begins work on program recommendations, potential impact of learning on achieving goals
11 (Nov.)	Second meeting with owners of goals. Recommend programs, discuss target audience, potential impact, costs
	Staff work to further refine.
	Compile cost, resource data.
	Write draft Chapters 2, 3, 4, 5, 6, and 7.
	Third meeting with owners. Reach final agreement on programs, target audience, impact, benefits, costs
12 (Dec.)	Revise Chapters 2, 3, 4, 5, 6, and 7.
	Write Chapter 1
	Complete draft and deliver to CEO and governing board
	Revise plan based on feedback from CEO and governing board
	Deliver final plan to CEO and governing body
	Obtain approval from CEO and governing board

In this example almost all of the work is completed in three months. The relatively short duration reflects the ease of scheduling appointments and an ability to reach decisions quickly. The goal, of course, is to put a good plan together, which may take more than three months.

Learning Function with Enterprise Scope and/or a Larger Organization

Assume in this case the learning function has an enterprise scope that may be global. The organization is large and complex with many goals. The business plan for learning may be more than fifty pages in length. Calendar months are in parentheses for those organizations with a calendar year as their fiscal year.

Figure 6.5

Timetable for Creation of a Business Plan for a Larger Organization

Month	Task
1 (Jan.)	CLO and direct reports agree on timetable for business planning process
	CLO appoints a manager for the business planning process.
	An editor is selected.
	Agree on a table of contents. Make assignments for writing the document with deadlines
	Build responsibilities into performance goals for the year
	Collect actual cost, resource and participant data from last year
6 (Jun.)	Review timetable. Confirm roles and responsibilities for learning staff.
	Schedule Month 8 (August) appointments with CEO, direct reports to CEO and governing board members
8 (Aug.)	Interview CEO first, then direct reports to CEO and governing board.
	Schedule appointments with goal owners, other key stakeholders suggested by CEO
	Create surveys to gather cost, resource, and participant data for current year
9 (Sep.)	First meeting with the owner of each goal and other key stakeholders
	Learning staff begins work on program recommendations, potential impact of learning on achieving goals
	Send out surveys to gather cost, resource, and participant data for current year from business units
10 (Oct.)	Second meeting with owners of goals. Recommend programs, discuss target audience, potential impact, costs
	Staff work to further refine.
	Compile cost, resource, and participant data.
	Write draft Chapters 2, 3, 4, 5, 6, and 7.
11 (Nov.)	Third meeting with owners of goals. Reach final agreement on programs, target audience, impact, benefits, and costs
	Revise Chapters 2, 3, 4, 5, 6, and 7.
	Write Chapter 1
	Complete draft and deliver to CEO and governing board

12 (Dec.) Revise plan based on feedback from CEO and governing board
Deliver final plan to CEO and governing body
Obtain approval from CEO and governing board

In this case the duration is five months, reflecting longer lead times for appointments, more goals, and lengthier decision making, which may result from owners involving more of their staff or simply more complex issues to be resolved.

The Importance of Specific, Measurable Goals

The creation of a business plan is a particularly good time to discuss the importance of specific, measurable goals. Recall from Chapter 1 that organizations exist to perform a mission and that their strategy is executed through establishing specific, measurable goals. The goals must be specific enough to provide absolute clarity about what is intended. The goal must be measurable so that progress can be reported and so that there will be no disagreement at the end of the period on whether the goal was met.

Setting Specific, Measurable Goals

It is essential that the business plan for learning contain specific, measurable goals. The strategic alignment and business case processes are iterative in nature, but before the business case and plan are finished, there must be final agreement on the specific, measurable goals. Without these, the plan will have little credibility and uncertain execution. Staff will not know what is expected of them, and senior leadership will not know what they can expect from learning. Everyone is likely to be disappointed.

In learning, the following questions should always be answered in the goal statement:

- What learning?
- How much or how many (number of days, hours, modules, courses)?
- For whom?
- By when?
- With what results?

An example of a specific, measurable goal for inclusion in the business plan for learning would be: Develop and deploy a two-day, instructor-led consultative selling skills course to the twenty-five sales representatives in the western district office by June 30 of next year and achieve a level 1 score of at least 80%, a level 2 score of at least 90%, an application rate of at least 80%, and a 3% increase in sales. This goal states exactly *what* is to be measured and *how much* or *how many* are expected: courses developed (one), courses deployed (one), participants (twenty-five), level 1 (80%), level 2 (90%), and an increase in sales (3%). The goal provides the date *when* it must be accomplished (June 30) and *who* the target audience is (sales reps in the western district office).

If there is any doubt about *who* is responsible for a goal or *where* it is be performed, that should be added as well: e.g., "The College of Marketing in the Corporate University will develop a two-day instructor-led consultative selling skills course and deploy it in Gotham by June 30 of next year to the twenty-five sales representatives of the western district office." The goal needs to be stated specifically enough so there is no doubt whether it was met or not.

In the business plan for learning the detailed work plan should contain goals that meet these criteria.

Use in Scorecards and Reports

Once specific, measurable goals have been created, they can be used in reports to manage progress through the year to ensure planned results are delivered. Scorecards can capture the most important information for review on a weekly or monthly basis. For the goal above, a report to evaluate progress in the college of marketing might include the number of courses completed on time, the number of participants, level 1 and level 2 scores, level 3 application rates, and the impact on sales—all compared to plan. Chapter 9 provides more detail.

Common Objections

At this point, some are likely to raise a number of objections to the use of specific, measurable goals in learning. Common objections include the following:

Objection: Specific, measurable goals like number of participants or level 1 are not appropriate for learning because we work with people who are inherently unpredictable and there are simply too many factors outside our control to hold us responsible.

Reply: Welcome to the real world! Your colleagues in other parts of the business also work with people, market to people, and sell to people. Yes, there are many factors beyond your control in learning, likewise for your colleagues. Your colleagues in sales have to commit to a market share goal and a sales goal in units or dollars. They have much less control over the outcome than you do. Their goals will be impacted by the state of the economy and by competitors' reactions, neither of which they can influence. In learning, we usually deploy within our own companies, where we at least have some influence. So, your colleagues will have little sympathy for you.

Objection: I may not be able to achieve the goal. I may get a bad performance review.

Reply: True. Sometimes you will not achieve the goal. This may be because the goal was set too high or contained too many restrictions and nobody could have achieved it. If you have regular performance updates with your manager, he should have a good idea of what you are doing and what your challenges and frustrations are. Your manager will take that into account in your performance review and in setting a more realistic goal for next year. On the other hand, the goal may be realistic, and you may fail to achieve it because your performance was not as good as it could have been. Perhaps you are in the wrong position. In any case, everyone else in your organization has the same worry. No exceptions will be granted for learning.

Objection: We do not have enough hard data to set specific, measurable goals.

Reply: Wrong. You should have data on the number of courses created and deployed, and you should be keeping track of whether the deadlines were met. You should have data on the number of participants and on their reaction to the course and, where appropriate, how much they learned. For important and expensive programs you should an evaluation strategy to measure application, impact, and perhaps net dollar benefits (see Chapter 8), so goals can be set for these as well.

The Role of Plans, Estimates, and Forecasts

Plans, estimates and forecasts play an important role in all the preceding chapters and will continue to be used very often throughout the rest of the book. In addition, later chapters will introduce the term "forecast" so all three terms need to be clearly understood and consistently employed.

Definitions

We have been using the terms "plan" and "planning" for the last several chapters, and hopefully by now you are comfortable with them. In the context of these three terms, a plan is a reasonable and achievable value for a goal we have. In other words, it is our educated, best-guess about what we can accomplish in the future. Examples include a 10% increase in sales at the company level or a 2% increase in sales due just to learning for the coming year. At the program level, we might plan for 300 unique participants and a 70% application rate, while at the department level we might plan to reach 90% of all company employees and receive an average satisfaction rating of 80% on all of our learning. These values are all plans, meaning there is no guarantee we will achieve them in the coming year.

Like a plan, a forecast is also about the future. Unlike a plan, however, a forecast may be made after the year has begun and consequently may contain some actual results. (The plan, once made, is fixed for the year. Some say it is set in concrete.) A forecast is a best guess about how the period (like the month, quarter, or year) is likely to end. Typically, after the year is underway, a forecast will be made and then it will be updated every month through the year as more information becomes available. For example, suppose a plan is approved to provide a program to 300 participants over the course of the year. By May only 70 have participated and it is clear that 300 are not going to attend for the year. You now believe that 200 is a better guess. 200 would be considered a forecast, since it is mostly about the future (the coming seven months). Moreover, the forecast would be compared with the plan (which is set at 300) and people would comment that the forecast shows demand falling short of plan.

In contrast to the plan and forecast, which are both about the future, an estimate is a value for the past, present, or near future which is not yet known with certainty but for which some actual data are available. For example, suppose it is April and you want to make a statement about the first quarter. Unfortunately, you only have actual results for January and February. You would use the January and February results to make a forecast for March, then add the values for the three months. Since you are talking about the past, your sum would be called an estimate. Now suppose your fiscal is the same as the calendar year and sometime in November you get year-to-date (YTD) data on the number of participants through October. You can use this information to make an estimate for the number of participants you expect in November (present) and a forecast for the number expected in December. Then you would add the November estimate and the December forecast to the October YTD actuals to get an estimate for the whole year. The 12-month figure is truly an estimate since it is not yet known with certainty, and it is also better characterized as an estimate than as forecast because actual results are available for 10 of the 12 months. On the other hand, if you were doing this exercise in April with only three months of actual results, then the 12-month figure would be better described as a forecast, since it contains nine months of forecasted data (April through December) and only three months of actuals.

The Use of Plans, Estimates and Forecasts

Since plans, estimates and forecasts will be used extensively in the business planning process, the learning manager needs to be comfortable with them. All three are used routinely in business, nonprofits, government, and the military. There is simply no way around employing them. You must be able to characterize performance in the time period just ending, and the only way to do that is by making an estimate that will also be the foundation for the plan you are about to make for the next period. Once the year is underway, you will begin to make forecasts of how the year is likely to end, which may reflect some planned action, some additional action you plan to take, or may simply reflect the lack of any special action.

So, you need to embrace all three. But you also need to be smart. Before making an estimate, look at all the data available. Chapter 1 illustrated the use of month-to-date and year-to-date data to draw conclusions and make an estimate. Likewise, for a forecast gather all the appropriate data and solicit help from experts and those with experience. In the strategic alignment and business case chapters, the CLO and learning managers had multiple meetings with owners of goals to reach agreement on the plan for learning's impact for the coming year. The CLO did not simply make this number up!

In addition to soliciting advice from the right people, it is critical that the process and assumptions be transparent. Readers of the business plan for learning need to know where the plans came from and what assumptions were made. Share these openly and ask for feedback. You may not get much feedback, but you will gain credibility.

Common Objections

Here are some common objections to the use of plans, estimates and forecasts in learning.

Objection: Plans are always wrong. I cannot use numbers that are wrong.

Reply: True, plans are usually wrong. If the plan was for 2,450 participants to take part in your learning next year, it is highly unlikely that exactly 2,450 will take part. You will have more or less. Having a plan, though, forced an explicit discussion of what you could expect, which is always a learning opportunity for all involved. It also allowed you to plan to make it happen. You had an idea about the number of instructors needed, classrooms, material, and so forth.

And what is the alternative, anyway? You have to plan based on some number. Without an explicit plan you might assume you will have the same number of participants next year as you had this year. That is fine if the numbers are not changing, but what if this year you had 1,200 and next year you are likely to have 2,450? Without a process to discover that you are likely to have 2,450, you will be planning on 1,200 and will be unprepared for the demand. Even if your plan is off by 10% (say 2,200), it is closer than the assumption next year will always be like this year.

Objection: Plans, estimates and forecasts are too subjective. They will have no credibility.

Reply: There is certainly an element of subjectivity in all three, and that is not necessarily bad. It reflects your professional judgment, which is the wisdom you have accumulated through your experience. Often, you are in the best position to make the plan, estimate or forecast—no one else knows as much about it or has the experience you do. In other cases you will need to seek out the professional judgment of others who have more knowledge and experience or who have a stake in setting the plan, like the goal owners.

Credibility will depend not just on the accuracy of the plan or forecast but on the process to make them. Involve others and be transparent about the process and the numbers it generates. It also pays to be humble because both plans and forecasts are seldom perfect.

Conclusion

You now have the knowledge to create a very comprehensive and professional business plan. The process is just as important as the resulting document since it is a process of discovery, learning, and continuous improvement. After the first year you will have many ideas for improving the process and the document for year two. Even your first plan, however, will make a convincing case for investing in learning and provide senior leadership with everything they need to decide on the level of investment in learning for next year. The contribution of learning to achieving the organization's goals will be clear. Creation of the business plan will increase your credibility significantly, and you will be on your way to becoming a strategic business partner and earning a seat at the table.

To review, key components of the business plan are

1. Executive Summary
2. Last Year's Accomplishments
3. Strategic Alignment
4. Business Case for Learning
5. Learning Resources, Expenditures, and Budget
6. Detailed Work Plans
7. Evaluation Strategy
8. Communication Strategy
9. Continuous Improvement Strategy
10. History

The first seven are the most important. Appendix B contains a sample business plan for learning. The plan should be approved by your CEO and governing body. Although some unanticipated needs will always arise, as long as the corporate goals do not change, the business plan for learning should represent 80% or more of the work you end up doing during the year.

Chapter 6 to Do List

1. Resolve to create a written business plan for learning next year. Begin the planning now.
2. Create a plan, including timetable and change management. Decide which chapters to include.
3. Make assignments for the different chapters. Assign someone to be editor.
4. Gather the cost, resource, and participant data, both estimates for the current year and plans for next year. Question the data. Refine it. Write the chapter on costs and resources.
5. Complete the strategic alignment.
6. Complete the business case.
7. Write the detailed work plans.
8. Finalize your estimated actuals for this year and your budget for next year.
9. Write the remaining chapters. Write the executive summary last.
10. Have the business plan reviewed. Make changes. Secure final approval.
11. Keep notes on improvements for next year.

Further Reading

Mantyla, Karen, ed. *The Learning Advantage: Blending Technology, Strategy, and Learning to Create Lasting Results*. East Peoria, Illinois: ASTD Press, 2009. (See Chapter 6.)

PART THREE

Managing the Learning Function throughout the Year

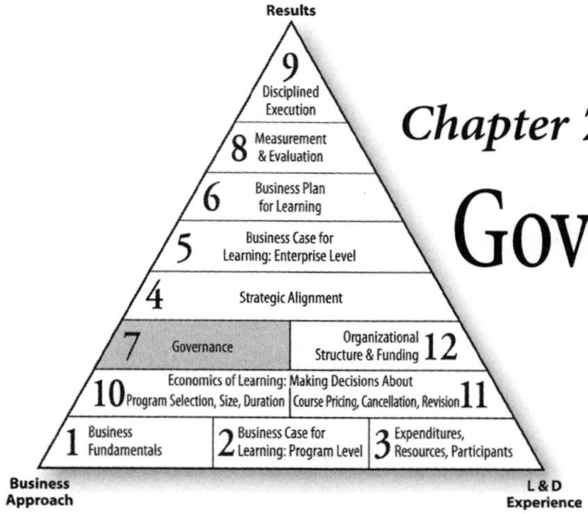

Chapter 7

Governance

GOOD GOVERNANCE IS essential for both the creation of an effective business plan and the successful execution of that plan through the year. Good governance ensures that you have the right input to make the best decisions and that you have support to implement them. Governing bodies play key roles in achieving strategic alignment and creating both the business case and business plan, and they play equally important roles in executing the plan, so it is time to examine them in detail. Like many of our other topics, governance is not difficult in concept but is often not implemented well in practice, especially at the enterprise level. So, like strategic alignment and the creation of the business plan, good governance represents an area of tremendous potential improvement for many organizations.

Key Concepts for Chapter 7

7

1. Every organization needs governance for the learning function.
2. The benefits of good governance far, far outweigh the additional work and complexity.
3. Most organizations would benefit from a layered approach to governance.
4. Governing boards should be run professionally, like boards of other organizations.

Why Have Governing Bodies?

There are at least six important reasons to have governing bodies like a board of governors, a learning council, or an advisory board. Each is important by itself, and together they make a very compelling case to invest the time and effort to create and maintain governing bodies.

Make Better Decisions

The first and most important reason is to help you make better decisions. By having a governing board composed of people from outside your department, you can take advantage of their experience, expertise, and point of view as you make decisions about strategy and priorities and about curricula and course content, design, length, and pricing.

If the board is diverse, you may have members representing a host of disciplines, such as marketing, engineering, finance, IT, and manufacturing, and they will definitely have different points of view than HR or learning does on many topics. You may have some members who have been with the company for twenty or thirty years and some who are new and bring perspective from other organizations. They will ask good questions, including questions you never thought to ask. They will challenge your assumptions, strategies, and proposed policies and programs in a constructive fashion, allowing you to make better decisions.

They can also help you avoid damaging mistakes. For example, suppose you are designing a course to meet a need for better leadership. Your instructional design team, after conducting the needs analysis, recommends a five-day, instructor-led course. It would be wise to share your plans with a governing body, perhaps a program advisory board, and solicit its feedback before proceeding. The board might tell you that five days is too long and that they would not let their own leaders be gone for five days to take the course, no matter how good it is. Or, if you are charging for the course, they may tell you that the price is far too high. These are both key decision variables that you care very much about and need to get right before developing the course. Without input from the advisory board, you might have invested in the five-day course only to find that very few would enroll.

Connections and Resources

A second important reason is to ensure that you are connected with the right people in the organization and that you have access to the resources you need. Especially in large, complex organizations, it is almost impossible for a CLO to know all the leaders in the company. From time to time, issues will arise for which it is important to work with others whom you do not know (and may not even know about). A diverse governing body will provide you with the lead and introduction you need, or a member will at least know how to find the person.

The same is true with organizational resources. It may be that someone else in the organization is already working on the same issue or has done so in the past. You may not be aware of that work, but a member of your governing body may be. Likewise, when funding or staffing is tight, someone on the governing body may know where additional resources may be found or suggest partners for collaboration.

Honest Feedback

A third important reason to have governing bodies is that they will give you honest feedback. Since they have a vested interest in your success, they will tell you what you need to hear even if it is not always pleasant. And then they will help you address it. This is much better than never finding out what others in the organization are saying behind your back or finding out too late to address the issues.

Board members may be customers of the learning department. Almost certainly they will be users, and they will give voice to many other users who can provide feedback through them.

Credibility and Legitimacy

A fourth reason to have governing bodies is to increase your credibility and legitimacy, which is especially important if you are launching a new learning group or reinventing an existing one. By definition, high-level governing boards will be composed of high-level leaders, and this sends an important message to an organization about the importance of learning. After all, if it is important enough for senior leaders to dedicate their time and attention to it, then the corporate university or learning department must be important. This message is particularly strong if the CEO sits on the board and if the CEO appoints SVPs or EVPs to sit on the board with him, which gives tremendous credibility and legitimacy to the learning group.

Advocates for Learning and the L&D Group

A fifth reason is that every member of a governing board is a potential advocate for learning and for the corporate university. This is especially important in startup or recovery mode or when you want to change the perception of the learning group. You need advocates throughout the organization in all business units and in all disciplines. Ideally, every governing board member will become an advocate.

Of course, they may not be advocates at the time of their appointment. Once on board, however, they have a vested interest in your success since it is now also their success. They will have a say and a vote in running learning, so it becomes more difficult to complain. You might even go out of your way to select some members who are outspoken detractors. Your challenge then is to work closely with them to understand their complaints, be responsive to their concerns where appropriate, and through time convert them to being advocates. This approach guarantees you will know the major complaints about learning firsthand and will force you to work closely with the detractors, which ideally will be a learning experience for both of you and the detractors. If you are successful in working with them and they become advocates, they are likely to be some of your most ardent and outspoken advocates.

Protection

The last reason may seem very self-serving, and it is. However, it is also true that in any organization you need protection from time to time. You may need to enact an unpopular policy like charging business units for services, which previously were "free," or raising course prices or enforcing prerequisites. You may need to eliminate some popular programs or turn off some unit's learning management systems as you move the organization to more centralized services. In any of these cases it is likely someone will complain to a business unit leader, who will complain to you and then to senior leaders, including the CEO. At this point the complaint is about *you*, and the aim is to reverse *your* policy or action. The question may be who approved this "stupid policy" in the first place and whether anybody even knows what the CLO is doing.

In these situations a board of governors, including the CEO, is absolutely invaluable. Assuming you had brought the issue before the board and gotten its input and counsel, made any necessary revisions it recommended, and then had it approved, you are now in a very strong position. When the aggrieved VP calls to complain, you can explain that the policy was reviewed, perhaps modified, and then approved by the board, including the CEO. At this point the discussion usually ends. If the VP had gone directly to the CEO to complain about you, the CEO would explain that the board reviewed and approved the policy. Unless there is new information or some consequences not foreseen by the board, this will be the end of it. In these cases the VP still does not like your policy, but you and the policy have been protected by the board. Without a board to first ensure that the proposed policy was thoroughly vetted and to provide political cover, your decision would have been appealed and possibly overturned. Whatever time you spent moving the proposed policy through the board was well worth it!

Effective Use of Governing Bodies

A CLO must make a number of decisions in forming governing bodies to ensure their operational effectiveness. Successful use of governing bodies also requires a very professional approach to planning and running the meetings and a commitment of sufficient resources to ensure success.

Decisions in Advance of Formation

Very important decisions must be made before governing boards are formed. These decisions provide the information necessary to secure approval for the boards and to solicit the first members. You will need to answer at least the following six questions.

1. How Much Authority Will the Governing Body Have?

First, you will have to decide whether it is to be a decision-making or advisory board. You may very well have both types, but any given board must be one or the other. A decision-making board will make decisions that are binding on you and the learning function. Analogies here would be a corporate board of directors or a city council. Typical decisions by a learning-related governing body include approval of next year's business plan, budget, staffing, funding model, course pricing, curricula, and vendors. The governing body might also approve the courses deemed to be mandatory and the consequences for not participating in mandatory offerings.

The alternative is an advisory body in which members provide non-binding advice. Under this model, issues will be discussed, and members will provide their thoughts, counsel, and feedback. A straw vote may even be taken, but it will be understood that the learning function is not bound by the consensus or vote of the advisory board.

Naturally, there are tradeoffs between the two approaches. A decision-making body limits the flexibility of the learning function. After all, they may not agree with your proposal, or they may direct you to do something you would prefer not to do. If there is initial resistance to your proposal, it may take several meetings to win them over, and you may have to modify the proposal to win their support. On the other hand, they probably have good ideas, and your final proposal is likely to be better for their input.

Also, members of a decision-making body are likely to be more engaged because their say and vote counts. This means they will spend more time preparing for the meeting and will be more likely to attend. At the meeting they will be more engaged in the discussion, and afterward they will be stronger advocates.

2. How Will Decisions Be Made?

Will decisions be made by consensus or by vote? If by vote, will it be a simple majority of those present, or will it require a majority of all members (present and absent)? Will there be a quorum requirement for decision making?

Your approach here may depend on your organization's culture. In some organizations nearly all decisions are made by consensus, whereas other organizations take a more formal approach with voting. In practice, many use a combination reserving votes for the more important matters, where a written record of the vote will be important. For example, formal votes where a motion is made, seconded, and then voted up or down may be used for approving the minutes, business plan, budget, pricing, and mandatory learning. Consensus may be used in approval of curricula, courses, and vendors.

You may want to link decision making to the type of governing body. Use a consensus approach for advisory bodies, which by definition are less formal, and use a voting approach for decision-making bodies.

3. What Will Be the Responsibilities and Scope?

You will need to articulate the responsibilities and scope for the governing body clearly. What types of input and counsel do you seek? What kinds of decisions will they be asked to make?

What is the body's purview in terms of organizational reach, discipline, and geography? The purview of the governing body may simply be purview of the learning function itself for a high-level governing board. For example, if the learning function has enterprise-wide responsibility, the high-level governing body likely will have enterprise-wide scope. Its decisions will apply to the whole enterprise. On the other hand, an advisory board for marketing would focus just on marketing-related learning issues, and a European advisory board would focus exclusively on learning matters in Europe.

4. How Often Will the Body Meet and for How Long? Where?

These very practical questions will determine how much you can bring before the body and will likely influence who can serve on the body. This question is typically the first one a prospective member will ask after you solicit their membership.

High-level governing bodies may meet quarterly for two to four hours. If a board includes the CEO and other senior leaders, it is unlikely they will have time to meet more frequently. If you are meeting quarterly, you will need at least two hours to conduct a reasonable amount of business. Three to four hours would be ideal. Lower level governing bodies may be able to meet every other month for several hours. Program advisory bodies may need to meet monthly as programs are being formulated.

In planning how often to meet and for how long, you want to be sure the members' valuable time is always put to good use. When a meeting is over, you will want to hear them say it was a great meeting, much was accomplished, and that they could have used a little more time. In other words, you want their satisfaction level to be extremely high. Nothing will kill a governing body faster than the perception that you are wasting the members' time. Consequently, it is advisable to start with shorter meetings and let them ask for the meeting frequency or length to be increased.

Location is also important and will need to be convenient for physical participants. You may also have virtual participants, so be sure the time is convenient for members who span multiple time zones.

5. How Many Will Be on the Body?

Size is an important consideration. You want enough members so that key divisions, geographies, and disciplines are represented. This is critical to establish legitimacy and credibility and to establish a broad network of advocates. On the other hand, you want the number to be small enough so that each member has adequate time to ask questions and contribute, or else they will lose interest and may stop attending.

For decision-making bodies, a good size would be six to seven if they can all attend regularly. If several will not be able to attend any given meeting, then you might increase the number to eight to ten so that you end up with six to seven in attendance. For advisory bodies, the number might go higher, especially if it is not critical for everyone to contribute at each meeting. In this case you might target ten to fifteen in attendance and a total of fifteen to twenty if 25% regularly cannot attend. (Remember, attendance will typically be lower for advisory groups.)

6. Who Will Serve and for How Long?

Finally, there is the issue of who will serve and for how long. The method of selection is very important and can easily determine their engagement and your ultimate success. Ideally, senior leaders in the organization will appoint members to serve on the governing bodies, and the appointees will feel honored by the appointment. It will be a mark of recognition and trust, and the appointees often will be highly promotable leaders.

In the ideal situation the CEO will sit on the high-level governing body like a board of governors and will appoint SVPs and VPs to join the board. In this case appointees are unlikely to decline and are very likely to attend every meeting. For lower level bodies the VPs might make the appointments of department heads, directors, and senior subject matter experts. For instance, you might ask the VP for marketing to appoint seven individuals to a marketing advisory board.

The key to success is appointment by a leader with position, credibility, and legitimacy within the scope of the governing body. This is always preferable to the CLO asking for members.

A term of two to three years is common for governing bodies. It may take a year for a new member to really come up to speed and be a very productive member of the group, especially if you are meeting just quarterly. On the other hand, some members may begin to become bored after three years, and you may want some new blood on the board. In many organizations people will rotate off their assignments in two to three years anyway, and a replacement will have to be selected. For a new governing body consider starting some members with one-, two-, and three-year terms to avoid a complete change of members at the end of the standard two- or three-year term.

You will also need a policy on substitutes for meetings. Will substitutes be allowed or not? If they are allowed, how often may they substitute? How many meetings can a member miss before being asked to resign?

Create a Charter

Once decisions have been made on the above questions, create a written charter with the following information:

- Name of governing body
- Purpose
- Roles and responsibilities
    - o Decision making or advisory
    - o Voting or consensus
- Scope
- Frequency and duration of meetings
    - o Is attendance mandatory?
    - o Is virtual attendance allowed?
- Selection of members, number, term length

At the first meeting of the governing body, the charter should be reviewed, modified as necessary, and approved by the group. The charter may be two to three pages in length.

As soon as a member is considered or appointed, send him the charter along with your cover letter, including the date, time, and location of the upcoming meeting. If the board is already functioning, you can also include a roster of current board members, minutes from the last meeting, and an agenda for the upcoming meeting.

Run the Boards Professionally

The charter is in place, and the initial members have been selected. It is now incumbent upon you to run the boards professionally. The effectiveness and efficiency with which you run the boards will directly reflect on you. Remember that the senior leaders on your boards will also sit on other boards, including for-profit companies and nonprofit organizations. They will be experienced in board service and will expect effective and efficient meetings. They will have no time to waste, and if you disappoint them, they will be quick to conclude that serving on your board is not a good use of their time. This will be bad for you and the learning function.

So, here is what you must do to succeed.

Allocate Sufficient Resources

First, make sure you have allocated sufficient resources to the boards. Make sure you have the time set aside for the boards you personally sit on. Then make sure your staff has sufficient time to lead their boards and to support all the boards. Make it a part of the performance goals.

Typically, the corporate university member on the board will chair it, and L&D staff will take notes and attend to audiovisual and computer matters. L&D staff will handle all the logistics. For example, the CLO would chair the high-level board of governors meeting. A person reporting directly to the CLO (direct report) might take minutes. Many of the direct reports (college deans and directors) might attend each meeting to make presentations and answer questions in their area. (The CLO would be an official, voting member of the board whereas direct reports would not be official members.) Support staff would be in attendance to operate the computer, ensure phone lines are working, and address other logistical issues.

A program-level advisory board might be chaired by the dean of that particular college or the most senior program person in that area. Someone from that person's staff would take minutes, and others would provide additional support. Additional time is required to prepare for each meeting and to follow up afterward. So, staff, time, and effort are required for each board. If you cannot commit this level of resource, do not create the governing body in the first place.

Use Agendas

The last item on the agenda of a meeting should be a preliminary agenda for the next meeting. The agenda provides an opportunity to solicit input from board members well in advance of the next meeting and increases their sense of ownership of the agenda. Ask about topics and duration.

At the start of a meeting, review the agenda and ask for any additional items. Follow this agenda and manage the discussion as best as possible to stay on topic and within the allocated time. If it looks like a topic is going to require more time, ask the board for guidance. The topic could be deferred to the next meeting, or an agenda item for this meeting might be shortened or deferred. The point is to manage the meeting proactively and make conscious, explicit decisions about time.

A typical agenda for a board meeting would have the following components:

FIGURE 7.1

Sample Agenda for a Board Meeting

1. Call to order
2. Approval of minutes from last meeting
3. Review of agenda
4. Follow-up items from last meeting
5. Review and update of developments since last meeting
   a. Review scorecard if available
6. Issues requiring a decision at this meeting
   a. Presentation (if needed), discussion
   b. Vote or consensus, or plan to follow up before decision is made
7. Presentation or other matters for their information
8. Review of preliminary agenda for next meeting including date, time, location
9. Adjourn

Plan on at least one substantive issue each meeting requiring input, discussion, and approval by the board. Members need to know and feel that they are making a difference by serving.

> ADVICE: Plan the meeting so that half of the total time is allocated for discussion and decision making. Do not present to them for the entire meeting or they will quickly lose interest and stop attending.

Advance Material

Send out advance material one to two weeks before the meeting. This should include the agenda, dashboard, financials, and abbreviated versions or summaries of the presentations along with any proposals requiring a vote. Do not send out presentations with forty slides. Remember, your board members' time is limited. They might spend fifteen to thirty minutes reviewing this material. What is really important for them to read? Ask for any additional agenda items.

Follow-up items from the previous meeting should be sent in the week following the previous board meeting.

All professionally run boards send advance material and follow-up material. Make sure you allocate the time and resources to do this.

Minutes

Minutes are the official record of the meeting. They are incredibly important since they represent the safe source for decisions taken at a meeting. It is human nature that we each remember events a little differently even immediately after a meeting, let alone six months later. To be effective, there must be one written record, approved by the board, of what transpired in the meeting. There will be differences of opinion that surface after the meeting about what was decided or who was given responsibility. The only way to resolve them is to refer back to the minutes.

For a board of governors meeting, one of your staff should take the minutes. If several staff are present, several should take notes. After the meeting compare notes, reach agreement, and have the person taking the minutes write them up. You need to review them and make sure they accurately reflect what transpired. If there are questions, check with your staff. Likewise, for other governing bodies, L&D staff will take the minutes, and the senior L&D leader chairing the board will make sure the minutes are accurate.

Minutes should be sent out within one week of the meeting. Ask for corrections. They need to be sent for review before the participants forget what transpired, which can occur quickly. Make any corrections and send them out again with the advance material.

In particular, the minutes must be very clear about proposals and policy issues. These will get the most attention and are likely to be the most discussed and debated. The minutes need to describe the original proposal or policy clearly, any revisions to it, the final version, and implementation plans. The minutes also need to include the vote or note that consensus was reached.

Four Levels of Governing Bodies

There are at least four levels of governing bodies. The highest has enterprise-wide responsibility and is primarily strategic. The lowest has business unit scope and is primarily tactical.

1. Highest level: enterprise board of governors, regents, or directors
2. Second level: enterprise learning council

3. Third level: enterprise college or program board (for example, marketing or leadership)
4. Fourth level: business unit, discipline, or geographic learning council

These may be decision making or advisory and may be called boards or councils. A learning function may have responsibility for a division instead of the enterprise, in which case the first three would be divisional instead of enterprise. Or the function may have responsibility for learning in a geographic area such as Asia, in which case there would be a board of governors for Asia, an enterprise learning council for Asia, or a leadership board for Asia. Number four allows for a governing board at a level lower than the first three.

We will examine each in turn.

Enterprise Board of Governors, Regents, Directors

This is the highest level governing body with responsibility for the oversight of learning at the enterprise level. It may be called a board of governors, board of regents, or board of directors for the corporate university. Ideally, the CEO will sit on this board and appoint its members. The CLO also will sit on this board as a voting member.

Suggested roles, membership, and meeting schedule follow.

FIGURE 7.2

Board of Governors

Role

- Provide enterprise leadership and direction to learning and to the L&D function
- Provide strategic guidance on all learning issues
- Set policy, approve budgets and staff levels
- Resolve disputes among divisions, business units, and vice presidents with regard to learning issues
- Provide input to the business plan for learning, help prioritize learning initiatives, review the draft plan and suggest changes, approve the final plan
- Approve dashboard goals
- Approve enterprise required learning

Membership

- o CEO
- o 4–5 EVPS, SVPs, or group presidents (direct reports to the CEO) or 2–3 from this group, plus 2–3 senior VPs (direct reports to group above)
- o Above officers are selected by the CEO to represent diverse business units, regions
- o CLO
- o Most senior corporate university staff (4–5) attend as non-voting members to present, answer questions, learn, get exposure to the CEO and senior corporate leaders

Meetings

- o Quarterly
- o 2–3 hours
- o Substitutes not allowed

Adapt the above for your particular situation. The key is CEO involvement. Even if the CEO does not have time to be a member, it is important that she appoints the others and makes expectations clear to them. The CEO should be at the first meeting to kick it off and should attend subsequent meetings at least annually.

If you have division or regional responsibility instead of enterprise or global, modify the roles to focus on your division or region. In place of the CEO, you want the head of the division or region and her direct reports as members.

A typical agenda for a board of governors meeting might look like this:

FIGURE 7.3

Sample Agenda for Board of Governors Meeting

1. Call to order
2. Approval of minutes from last meeting
3. Review of agenda
4. Follow-up items from last meeting
5. Review of dashboard
6. Financial review
7. Proposal for enterprise-wide curricula, program, pricing, mandatory learning, or other important issues

8. Vote on same
9. Program presentation
10. Review of preliminary agenda for next meeting including date, time, location
11. Adjourn

It is especially important at this level to have substantive issues on the agenda. Ideally, several matters will require input from the board, and one or two key decisions will be taken after good and perhaps spirited discussion. Members need to know they have made a contribution and that the level of discussion and decision making was worthy of their valuable time.

CATERPILLAR EXPERIENCE: We started the Board of Governors in our second year. It had seven members, including the CEO, two of the five group presidents (direct reports to the CEO), three vice presidents (one of whom was the VP for human services and my boss), and myself. We met quarterly for two hours. In the following year the CEO asked for the meetings to be extended to three hours.

The Board of Governors was a decision-making body, and we had formal votes on policy issues, budgets, and the annual business plan for learning. Discussion was often spirited—members were not shy about sharing their opinions, and the six of them often had different viewpoints. In these cases, after thirty to sixty minutes of good discussion and debate (during which members would often change their initial thinking), the CEO would generally try to bring the issue to resolution. Sometimes an issue would be held over until the next meeting. Since it was a decision-making body, the members did not always agree with my proposals. On several occasions we were told to move in a different direction or take a different approach. Their counsel almost always proved to be right, and we were better for having them not approve our initial plan.

Without question, the Board of Governors was one of the keys to our success. We always benefited from the members' counsel, and we always learned something at each meeting. Once the CEO placed a "non-supporter" of Cat U on the board, which I thought was a mistake since it would make my life more difficult. It did, but it also forced the two of us to have many long discussions about learning and Cat U. I came to appreciate his perspective and counsel. Eventually, he became one of our most outspoken advocates. Once again the CEO was right!

My only regret is not having initiated the Board of Governors sooner, as soon as Cat U was formed. I think the members could have been very helpful in the first year as we launched.

Enterprise Learning Council

In contrast to the board of governors, the enterprise learning council will focus more on tactical matters, such as when and how to deploy enterprise-wide learning. After the board of governors has approved these enterprise-wide learning initiatives, the learning council can provide advice on implementation. When multiple enterprise-wide initiatives have been approved for the year, the council can also help prioritize the roll out and formulate the change management plan. These meetings provide an excellent opportunity for the CLO to connect with business unit HR and learning professionals on a regular basis and also provide a forum to get feedback from the units and address issues common to them all.

These councils might be called boards or groups and will often be advisory in nature. In many organizations they will communicate through teleconferences.

FIGURE 7.4

Enterprise Learning Council

Role

- Provide enterprise leadership and direction to learning and your L&D function at a more tactical level than the board of governors
- Help manage the amount, timing, and sequencing of learning deployed to the enterprise
- Provide input to the annual business plan for learning, specifically on goals and measures that relate to enterprise deployments (how many participants can be reached in a year, what are acceptable course durations)
- Provide feedback on enterprise programs, systems, and processes

Membership

- o Division or Business Unit HR managers and senior learning professionals appointed or recommended by the head of their division or unit
- o CLO
- o About 15 members (10–20)
- o Broad representation. If not every division, then at least enough to represent the different types of divisions in the organization like manufacturing, marketing, engineering, and support and the different geographic areas
- o Senior corporate university staff attend as non-voting members to learn, answer questions, take notes, follow up

Meetings

- o Monthly (every other month at a minimum since the role is tactical and implementation plans may change on a monthly basis)
- o About two hours
- o Substitutes allowed

For a board like this, attendance is likely to be lower than for the board of governors. So, to have ten to fifteen members at a meeting, you may want fifteen to twenty people on the council. You might also allow for some substitution (an HR manager could send his or her learning manager), but you may want to set limits so the HR manager does not delegate this responsibility on a regular basis.

A typical agenda might include the following items:

FIGURE 7.5

Sample Agenda for an Enterprise Learning Council Meeting

1. Call to order
2. Introductions
3. Approval of minutes of last meeting
4. Review of agenda
5. Follow-up items from last meeting
6. Update from CLO on enterprise-wide learning initiatives
   a. Review of scorecard
   b. Review of development and deployment status
   c. Impact of corporate initiatives, strategies on learning

7. Discussion on development and deployment schedules
   a. Problems and issues. What is not working?
   b. Possible solutions
   c. Agreement to modify as necessary
8. Presentation by corporate learning staff on a key program for enterprise-wide deployment
9. Presentation by business unit learning leader on best practices or topic of interest
10. Review preliminary agenda for next meeting
11. Adjourn

CATERPILLAR EXPERIENCE: We started with the Board of Governors and college advisory boards. After several years, as we began to deploy more and more enterprise-wide programs, the HR managers of the business units began to complain that corporate HR (Cat U, compensation and benefits, organizational effectiveness, workforce planning, diversity, succession planning, and recruiting) was overwhelming the business units with initiatives. We (corporate HR) were launching more initiatives than the business units could deploy. They asked us to slow down and prioritize with their input. So we agreed. Learning, C&B, and a few others formed enterprise councils, consisting primarily of HR managers, to prioritize the initiatives and do a better job of change management.

At least for Cat U, this was a much needed improvement to give voice to the HR managers and learning professionals in the units who had to implement all that we developed. We met every one to two months for one and a half to two hours in person and by teleconference. Attendance was usually fifteen to twenty members, with representatives from units in North and South America and Europe and senior Cat U staff. We should have started meeting sooner.

Enterprise College or Program Board

These boards have an enterprise scope but focus on a particular program area like marketing or leadership. The boards will provide both strategic and tactical advice and direction for the enterprise-wide initiatives in that particular program.

They are especially important when the corporate university is started or when a major new program is planned. Most often these are advisory bodies.

This body, consisting of department heads, directors, and senior leaders in the targeted program area (not HR managers or learning professionals), can provide critical direction in planning, developing, and deploying programs. It can provide guidance to the team doing needs analysis and help secure subject matter experts. It can review the findings and recommendations of the needs analysis team and the college, providing input on how realistic the recommendations are (for example, "The recommended five-day, instructor-led course on consultative selling skills is too long and the anticipated price is too high"). It can also help with the overall change management of the initiatives. In short, these program-specific boards can really help you succeed as you plan, develop, and deploy learning.

In most cases, they will be chaired by the most senior corporate L&D leader for that program area (such as the dean in a corporate university with colleges).

FIGURE 7.6

Enterprise Program Board

Role

- Provide leadership and guidance to learning in a specific program or field
- Advise and provide direction on corporate goals for this field, alignment to those goals, prioritization, learning needs, and learning initiatives
- Provide specific guidance on
  - Plans to address corporate needs
  - Curricula, including the number of programs, sequencing, duration, format
  - Target audience and how best to reach them
  - Price for the learning (if using an internal charge-back model)

Membership

- Department heads, directors, senior leaders in the field recommended or appointed by the VP or head of the division or field (for example, the SVP of marketing)
- Dean or corporate university program manager providing leadership to this area

- About eight to twelve members with an expected attendance of six to nine
- Broad representation across subgroups and geographies so everyone feels represented

Meetings

- Quarterly (perhaps monthly or bimonthly in the early stages of planning and development going to quarterly as initial development is completed and the programs mature)
- About two hours
- Substitutes not allowed

A typical agenda might include the following items for a marketing-related board.

FIGURE 7.7

Sample Agenda for an Enterprise Program (Marketing) Board Meeting

1. Call to order
2. Approval of minutes of last meeting
3. Review of agenda
4. Follow-up items from last meeting
5. Update from the dean on enterprise-wide learning initiatives for marketing
    a. Review of development and deployment status
    b. Review of issues, problems, and opportunities
    c. Plans to address known issues
6. Discussion on programs and development and deployment schedules
    a. Problems and issues. What is not working? What can we do better?
    b. Possible solutions
    c. Agreement to modify as necessary
7. Presentation by corporate learning staff on a key marketing program for enterprise-wide deployment
8. Review preliminary agenda for next meeting
9. Adjourn

CATERPILLAR EXPERIENCE: Cat U established advisory boards for each of the initial colleges (marketing, leadership, engineering, and business) immediately upon organization. They were instrumental in our early success by ensuring that we closely coordinated with the leaders in each area, and they provided very practical advice on curricula, development, and deployment. (They were established two years before we began the annual business plan for learning process and thus were critical to ensure alignment in those first two years.) They also became early advocates for the corporate university and helped spread the word on our mission.

Some met monthly in the beginning, when all the initiatives were being planned while others met semi-monthly. After several years, meeting frequency had become quarterly.

Business Unit Learning Councils

The last governing body to be discussed is the division or business unit level governing council or board. Unlike the first three governing bodies described above, which all had an enterprise focus, the business unit learning council focuses just on learning for that particular unit. It is especially important for large divisions or units which themselves may contain several smaller organizations, facilities, or locations. In these cases the division or business unit level learning council can ensure consistency in learning across the unit and may be able to achieve synergies or cost reduction. It also provides an opportunity for multiple learning leaders in the same division but in different locations to come together regularly to plan and review learning for the entire division, including the preparation of an annual business plan for learning for that division.

The council might be led by the head of the division or unit (preferable) or delegated to the HR manager or other director or department head. Members would include senior learning staff and other directors and department heads and perhaps some senior managers.

FIGURE 7.8

Business Unit or Division Learning Council

Role

- Provide leadership and guidance to learning within the business unit or division
- Provide input to the business unit annual learning plan
- Prioritize learning initiatives
- Recommend the budget for learning
- Manage amount and timing of learning
- Manage the change management process for learning initiatives
- Regularly review progress against plan for learning initiatives
- Act as advocates for learning within the unit

Membership

- Head of the unit (if possible)
- Department heads, directors, senior managers
- HR Manager, learning manager
- Other learning professionals
- Members selected by the head of the unit
- About eight to twelve members
- Broad representation across the unit

Meetings

- Monthly to quarterly
- About two hours
- Substitutes not allowed

A typical agenda might include the following items:

FIGURE 7.9

Sample Agenda for a Business Unit Learning Council Meeting

1. Call to order
2. Approval of minutes of last meeting
3. Review of agenda
4. Follow-up items from last meeting
5. Update from learning manager on learning initiatives for unit (from corporate and from the unit itself)

   a. Review of development and deployment status
   b. Review of issues, problems, and opportunities
   c. Plans to address known issues
   d. Identification of issues to take up with corporate
6. Discussion of coordination of programs within the unit, opportunities for synergy and sharing
7. Presentation by learning manager or staff on upcoming programs for the unit
8. Review preliminary agenda for next meeting
9. Adjourn

CATERPILLAR EXPERIENCE: Several of the twenty-eight divisions at Caterpillar had division or unit-level learning councils that met monthly or semi-monthly. A few of these were very large divisions with more than five thousand employees in multiple sub-business units and locations. For these the learning council was a way to ensure a consistent and organized approach to learning across the division. Several other divisions had only three to four hundred employees but wanted to provide special focus on their learning. In one of these, the council created a strategic plan to improve the learning environment and provide more opportunities for their employees to learn and develop.

Conclusion

By now I hope you are convinced of the benefits of governing bodies and agree that it is worth the time and resources to create and use them. The four levels I have described should serve as a starting point for you to consider how they might best be structured for your situation. Since most organizations would benefit from multiple bodies, consider layering them in a way that makes sense for you.

If you were only to have one, make it the board of governors, which is crucial to your overall, continued success. Consider program boards at least during times when new programs are developed since they can help you get it right. And if your organization is large, especially if functions are decentralized, consider a learning council to get input and advice from business units and to help prioritize initiatives and manage the change.

Last, whatever you do with governing bodies, do it professionally. If you cannot do it professionally, do not do it at all because you will end up doing more harm than good.

Chapter 7 to Do List

1. If you do not have any governing boards, resolve to implement at least one.
   a. Consider a board of governors at the enterprise or division level.
   b. Also consider a program advisory board to advise on an important program in development.
   c. Write up the benefits and share with your boss.
   d. Create a draft charter that you can share with the CEO or division president.
2. If you have a governing body:
   a. Evaluate how successful it is. Solicit feedback from the members.
   b. Is there an opportunity to run it more professionally?
   c. Evaluate whether additional ones make sense.
3. Ask colleagues in other organizations about their governing bodies.

Further Reading

Wheeler, Kevin. *The Corporate University Workbook: Launching the 21st Century Learning Organization.* San Francisco: Pfeiffer, 2005. (See Chapter 4.)

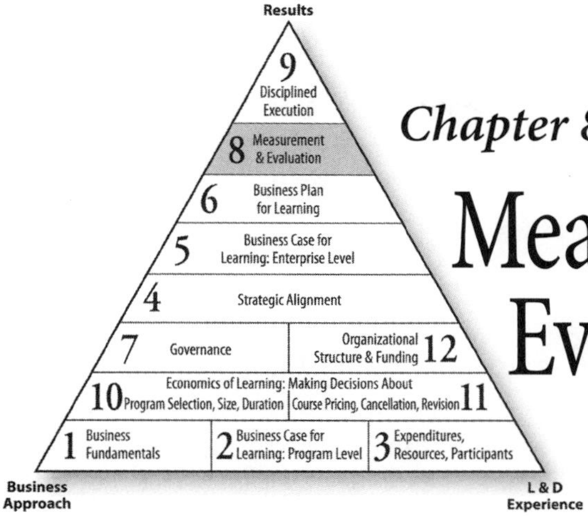

Chapter 8

Measurement and Evaluation

LIKE GOOD GOVERNANCE, good measurement and evaluation are required throughout the year to manage the learning function successfully. If learning is to be run like a business, metrics are required to tell us how we are doing and where we can improve. This chapter will examine measurement and evaluation in detail from a management point of view. It is not intended to be an in-depth exploration of the individual methods of measurement since there are already many published works dedicated just to this topic. (For example, see the numerous works by Jack and Patti Phillips on measurement and ROI.) Instead, it is meant to be a management discussion about the different measures and a guide about how to use them to run learning like a business.

Key Concepts for Chapter 8

8

1. There are many reasons to measure.
2. Objections to measurement can be overcome.
3. There are numerous ways to measure. Find those that are right for you.
4. Create a measurement strategy.
5. Use surveys, sampling, focus groups, and control groups to make the process manageable.
6. Net benefit dollars and ROI can be helpful. Don't get lost in the "ROI Controversy."
7. Do not worry about perfection or absolute certainty. They are myths and not helpful.

Why Measure?

Especially in this chapter, where there is so much misunderstanding and controversy, we need to start at the very beginning. Before talking about the pros and cons of different measures, we need to ask why we bother to measure anything at all. And then later, in the heat of the measurement battle, we need to remember what we are trying to accomplish with our metrics.

So, what are the reasons for measurement? There are many. Some will not apply to particular organizations or at a particular time. Some will apply to one program and not to another. With that in mind, here are some reasons to measure:

Show Results

Recall that organizations exist to perform a mission. The business case for learning established the contribution that learning would make to performing that mission and achieving the organization's goals. So the most important reason to measure is to show results, to show that the investment in learning is having the intended impact.

Metrics here might start with the high-level organizational goals like increased sales but would also include operational measures at the implementation level, such as number of courses developed and delivered, number of participants, their satisfaction with the learning, acquisition of knowledge, and application on the job. All of these are meant to show results against the top-level and detailed work plan goals in the business plan for learning.

Remember that at this point you have already completed your strategic alignment, developed the business case, created the business plan, and had it approved by your CEO and board of governors. Therefore, the learning you are about to measure is the *right* learning to meet your organization's highest priority goals.

Manage Better

Measurement is essential to managing the function on a daily basis. The next chapter will focus on disciplined execution of the business plan, but suffice it to say for now that without measurements you cannot possibly know where you have been, where you are now, and what changes you need to make to achieve the goals of your business plan.

The alternative to measurement is to manage without monthly, weekly, or daily reports. In this case a manager relies on the staff to "work hard" and accomplish as much as they can. If there are annual measures but no monthly numbers, then the group finds out at the end of the year how they did. There is no opportunity for mid-year corrections or reallocation of resources or to ask for help. The goal is either achieved or not—with no active management to ensure that it is.

The other case is even worse: no annual goal and no annual reporting. In this case the group never had a specific goal and never knows how it did. People (one hopes) work hard, and whatever they accomplish, that is it. Imagine a learning function that did not track courses delivered, participants, participant reaction, or any other measures, including impact on the organization's goals.

Improve

Continuous improvement is crucial to higher organization productivity and to long-term success. Measurement, combined with a comparison of performance against this year's goal, last year's performance, and the performance of others, is the best way to discover opportunities for improvement. Without measurement and comparison you might never know that your learning program is not as effective as it might be or that you are not reaching the target audience. Without data from benchmarking other organizations, you would not discover that it is possible to reduce time to delivery by 50% or reduce your system expenses by $50 per employee.

So, measurement is essential for continuous improvement. You should aspire to greater effectiveness and efficiency for the learning function. No matter how good a program you have, there is probably a way to make it better. If your organization is in a competitive environment, be assured that your competitors are searching for ways to improve and to gain advantage. Everyone in your organization needs to be engaged in continuous improvement, including everyone in the learning function, and measurement is the key.

Prove Your Worth

For some a desire to prove their worth may be the first reason that comes to mind for measurement. That is unfortunate because this is often done in a reactive and very defensive mode. The learning function has skipped the steps of strategic alignment, business case, and business plan and is now told to prove its worth or suffer major cuts in funding or, possibly, be eliminated all together. At this point measurement is unlikely to be of much help since the learning was not aligned to the most important goals of the organization to start with and since the function never got the buy-in of top leaders. If the function survives this round of cuts, it needs to start running like a business, beginning with strategic alignment.

If the learning function is being run like a business, then it may be valid to measure its contribution to the organization's success. The CLO or senior leaders may be curious about the value added from learning. In fact, they may be willing to invest even more in learning if the business case is solid. Measures of impact, dollar benefits, and ROI would all be possible measures here and may have been included in the business case as part of the annual business plan for learning.

Increase Funding

This is another common reason to measure and is basically the same as proving your worth. The hope is that measurement will prove your worth and increase the likelihood of additional funding or at least prevent a reduction in funding. The same caveats apply as above.

Increase Credibility

Like the above two reasons, this may or may not be a valid reason to measure. If the learning function is not being run like a business, then that is probably the reason for a lack of credibility. Measurement of unaligned, low-priority learning is not likely to improve the credibility of the group. In fact, it may have the opposite effect and convince even more people that the learning function is poorly managed since it is now wasting money measuring learning that should not have been done in the first place!

If the function is being run like a business, then this may be a valid, although not important, reason to measure. Credibility is important, and it may be that employees of the organization are not aware of the learning function's accomplishments. It is hard, though, to imagine very many measures that would be instituted for the sole purpose of enhancing credibility. Instead, it would make sense to share the results of measures already in place as part of a communication strategy to increase employees' awareness of the learning department's accomplishments.

Told To

This is not an elegant reason, but it happens. Usually it is not a good sign and may indicate the displeasure of your boss or senior leaders with the performance and management of the learning function. In the best case, the CLO is already running learning like a business and already measuring, but the boss would like even more measurement. Perhaps she has come back from a conference where leading organizations were sharing their measurement strategies and wants you to do more or try some different measures. In the worst case, the CLO is measuring very little, and senior leaders are questioning their return on the learning investment. The problems likely run much deeper than the measurement strategy and may reflect a lack of strategic alignment, business case and plan, and good governance.

Summary of Reasons to Measure

Seven reasons to measure have been discussed; you might think of others to add. The point is that there are many reasons to measure, and some are much stronger than others. The most important reasons to measure are to show results, manage better, and improve. These should apply to virtually all organizations although the application will differ. High-performing organizations, in which learning is run like a business, will proactively measure for these reasons. Lower performing organizations, in which learning is not run like a business, may measure for the same reasons although more from a defensive or reactive posture.

The next four reasons (prove your worth, increase funding, increase credibility, and told to) are less universal and more likely to be associated with learning departments that are not run like a business. Still, some well-run learning functions may measure for the first three of these reasons in addition to three primary reasons listed above.

> ADVICE: From an internal political point of view, if you are asked why you measure, answer with the first three even if you also want to prove your worth or increase funding and credibility. The first three should be the most important reasons for you, and the last three are really very self-serving. If you do the first three well, then there will not be a question about your worth, and your credibility (and perhaps funding) should be rising anyway.

The Levels and Types of Measurement

Just as there are many reasons to measure, there are also many ways to measure. While various measurements have been around for some time, Don Kirkpatrick introduced the four levels (called "steps" then) in his seminal dissertation published in 1954, titled *Evaluating a Human Relations Training Program for Supervisors to Measure Learning Behavior and Results*. He recommended that the effectiveness of training can and should be measured at four steps: reaction, learning, behavior, and results. In 1959 he was asked to share these steps with the learning profession in the *Journal of the American Society for Training Directors*. He described one step each month in the *Journal* from November 1959 to February 1960. Following this, the steps became known as the four levels of the Kirkpatrick model, and learning professionals began to apply them. Although Don published books on other topics in the interim, his first book on measurement came out in 1994, titled *Evaluating Training Programs*, which described his model in detail.

One of those who applied the four levels in practice in the 1970s was Jack Phillips. In 1983 he introduced ROI to training, which over time came to be considered the fifth level (level 5) of measurement. He formalized his five-level framework in 1992, with his first three levels being essentially the same as Kirkpatrick's. The interpretation and measurement of level 4, however, differs considerably between the two.

FIGURE 8.1

The Five Measurement Levels of Kirkpatrick and Phillips

	Kirkpatrick	*Phillips*
Level 1	Reaction	Reaction
Level 2	Learning	Learning
Level 3	Behavior	Application and Implementation
Level 4	Results	Business Impact
Level 5	—	Return on Investment (ROI)

Gene Pease, former CEO of Capital Analytics and Vestrics, introduced optimization as level 6. He makes a compelling case for going beyond ROI to discover how and where the learning may be adjusted or extended to provide even greater impact and ROI. Since optimization is a process rather than a measure, we will not include it as a recommended measure, but we certainly do recommend it as a best practice for any larger scale deployments where adjustments can be made after a pilot is completed. See *Optimize Your Greatest Asset – People* (2015) to learn more.

In 2008 Bersin & Associates introduced the Impact Measurement Model®, which added measures for alignment, utility, and efficiency. These areas are vitally important to the operational measurements of learning and, when combined with his other measures, provide a very comprehensive, practical, and actionable measurement strategy. There are endless possible measures, with more being suggested all the time, but we will focus on the original three from Kirkpatrick (levels 1–3) and Business Impact and ROI from Phillips (levels 4–5) as well as on the most basic level of all, level 0, which is where we will start. (The reader is encouraged to read Kirkpatrick and Phillips for a thorough description. What follows is just a high level summary of levels 0–5, with the emphasis on management application.)

In addition to classifying measures by the six levels, we will employ the framework of the Talent Development Reporting Principles (TDRp) to provide a higher level organization. TDRp is a set of industry standards developed by thought leaders and leading practitioners in 2010-2011 to provide guidance to the learning profession regarding measures and reports. Just as the Generally Accepted Accounting Principles (International Financial Reporting Standards outside the United States) provide guidance to accountants to classify their measures into four types (revenue, expense, assets and liabilities) and to create three standard statements with those measures (income, balance sheet and cash flow), TDRp calls for three types of measures for learning (efficiency, effectiveness, and outcome) organized into three standard reports (summary, operations and program). Efficiency measures are simply all the level 0 measures of activity and cost. Effectiveness measures are levels 1-5. Outcome measures are generally the level 4 impact measure which does double duty as both an effectiveness and outcome measure. The reasons for this classification and for the special treatment of outcome measures will become more apparent in the next chapter when we create the three reports. In this chapter we will discuss impact under the effectiveness measures. Appendix C provides an introduction to TDRp with examples.

Efficiency Measures (also called Level 0 or Volume Measures)

Efficiency measures provide information about the activity (volume, scope, timing, and utilization) and cost of training. These include such basic measures as number of participants and number of courses developed or delivered. They have been around so long that it they are taken for granted, which is unfortunate because they are the foundation for good management of the learning function.

If learning is to be run like a business, then learning managers have to know the basics, just like a businessperson needs to know sales, number of customers, and number of products.

As their name indicates, efficiency measures are often used to determine the efficiency of development and delivery, and a comparison is often made to industry benchmarks, previous performance, or current year plan. Figure 8.2 provides a list of the most commonly used efficiency measures.

FIGURE 8.2

Efficiency Measures for Learning and Development

Number of courses
Number of unique participants
Number of total participants
Available hours of training
Hours consumed in training
Utilization rate of courses, instructors, or classrooms
Percentage of employees reached by training
Cycle time (performance consulting, design and development, delivery, total)
Percentage of courses developed or delivered on time
Direct cost of learning (development, delivery, reinforcement, and management)
Opportunity cost (value of participants' time spent in training)
Tuition cost
Number of L&D staff (count and full-time equivalents)
Employees per L&D staff member
L&D cost per employee
L&D cost per learner (unique participant)

While efficiency measures are basic, some are more complicated than they first appear. Take participants, for example. It is likely you will want to measure both unique participants (how many took one or more courses) and total participants (one employee taking two courses counts as one unique participant but two total participants). From a management point of view both measures are important. The measure of total participants indicates the overall activity level, which will drive a number of variable costs like number of instructors, classrooms, or seats in the learning management system. Unique participants can tell you what percentage of a population has been reached by learning. Your CEO will likely want to know both. Are your systems set up to produce both measures accurately? Can you provide a breakdown by geographic area, business unit, and type of course taken?

Costs are an often-overlooked efficiency measure. Chapter 3 was dedicated to a discussion of costs and resources as well as participants. Your CFO may not care about levels 1–5 below, but she will definitely care about costs. How accurate are your cost measures? Most organizations struggle to produce cost measures down to the program level, but these are absolutely critical in order to make decisions about resource allocation.

Another overlooked efficiency measure is completion date. Running learning like a business means meeting a specific goal by a specific date. So, are you tracking whether the goals are completed by the date contained in the business plan? You need to be if you are going to manage the function effectively.

A good learning manager must start with efficiency measures and make sure the organization is capturing all the necessary efficiency measures at the detail necessary to make good management decisions. Efficiency measures may not be "sexy" or sophisticated like levels 4 or 5 are, but they are the foundation for successful management. Make sure your measurement strategy includes the appropriate efficiency measures.

Effectiveness Measures

Effectiveness measures provide information about the quality of the training. In the TDRp framework, effectiveness measures are the Kirkpatrick/Phillips five levels plus a few other less commonly used quality measures. Figure 8.3 provides a list of the most commonly used effectiveness measures.

FIGURE 8.3

Effectiveness Measures for Learning and Development

Measure	Survey Instrument
Level 1: Reaction or Satisfaction	
Participant	Post-event participant survey
Goal owner or sponsor	Post-event sponsor survey
Level 2: Learning	
Level 3: Behavior or Application	
Intent to Apply	Post-event participant survey
Actual Application	Follow-up survey

Level 4: Results or Impact	
Initial Estimate	Post-event participant survey
Actual Impact	Follow-up survey
Level 5: Return on Investment (ROI)	

As you can see from Figure 8.3, level 1 can be measured by both participant and goal owner reaction, while it is common to measure levels 3 and 4 both at the time of the learning and again at a later date when the actual can be better determined. We will explore each level in turn starting with level 1.

Level 1: Reaction or Satisfaction

Participant

This is the first of Kirkpatrick's four levels of measurement. Level 1 measures the participants' reaction to or satisfaction with the training they just received. Like level 0 it does not receive the respect it deserves. It seeks the most basic information from participants about the training they just received. Typically, a survey is administered at the end of class or sent by email within a few days. This is called a post-event survey, meaning that it is administered right after the conclusion of the training. The post-event survey may also be embedded in an online course where participants complete it before logging off. (The post-event survey may contain some predictive level 3 and 4 questions as well as level 1 questions. See levels 3 and 4 below.) Questions are formulated to elicit their immediate reaction to the learning and might include the following:

FIGURE 8.4

Sample Level 1 Questions

- Was the learning relevant to your work?
- Would you recommend this course to others?
- How would you rate the instructor?
- Were the materials helpful?
- Was the length of the class appropriate?
- How would you rate your overall satisfaction with the course?

A five-point Likert scale is recommended, although some prefer a seven-point scale. Often there is an opportunity to provide open-ended feedback. There may be ten to fifteen questions, and it may take two to five minutes to complete the survey. Since the survey is soliciting overall satisfaction with the course, the surveys are often referred to as "smile sheets."

One goal of these level 1 questions is to provide immediate feedback, especially for a new course or new instructor. There is always a possibility that a course has not been designed properly or not delivered effectively. If participants tell you the course is not relevant and cannot be applied and would not recommend it, you need to understand why immediately. Was the needs analysis flawed, or is this the wrong target audience? Were expectations for the course incorrectly communicated or is the course description inaccurate? Perhaps the content is fine, but the instructor needs to be coached or replaced. As a good learning manager, you need to resolve these issues as soon as possible and before more people take the course. Until it is fixed, you are producing "scrap," and it has a negative return on investment.

Another purpose of these level 1 measures is to track reactions through time. One of the reasons for measurement is to aim for improvement, and for that you need history to determine whether scores are trending up or down. If scores are trending down, you need to understand why, and you may want to put a plan in place to address it. Level 1 data will also reveal who the best instructors are and perhaps who the best course designers are. Then you can arrange for others to learn from them and improve your overall scores.

Level 1, like level 0, is foundational. If the learning is not relevant, if they cannot apply it, and if they are not learning because of a poor instructor, then it is scrap learning. It serves no purpose and will not accomplish an organization's goals. Worse, it has taken time and money to develop, and the opportunity cost of the participants' time might be significant. So with no benefit and a very definite cost, the return is certain to be negative.

Sponsor or Goal Owner

A level 1 measure of satisfaction may also be collected from the goal owner or sponsor of an initiative to discover how satisfied they are with your work and your relationship with them. Typical questions are whether you met the agreed-upon deadlines, whether the project came in on budget, how you were to work with, and whether they would recommend you to a colleague. (A five-point Likert scale is recommended.) The short survey might conclude with an open-ended question asking for comments or suggestions for improvement.

Level 2: Learning or Acquisition and Transfer of Knowledge

The second of Kirkpatrick's four levels measures how much participants have learned. This is accomplished through a test at the end of class or through questions embedded throughout the course. Online learning is especially conducive to surveys since the entire process can be automated. Typically, a "passing" score has been established, at perhaps 90%, meaning the participants have to answer 90% of the questions correctly to pass.

Level 2 is appropriate whenever the participant is expected to learn specific information such as in an engineering, safety, or product features course. It is also very commonly used in compliance-related courses like fraud detection, harassment, and discrimination, in which not only is it important for specific knowledge to be acquired, but it is important to have a record of successful completion by name in the company's database. This approach affords the organization some legal protection in case of a lawsuit since the company can argue that the employee had been instructed in the proper conduct and understood it well enough to pass the test.

The subject matter expert will generally supply the questions and determine the passing grade. If a surprising number of people are failing to pass, then the learning staff and the subject matter expert need to understand why. Perhaps the requisite knowledge is being acquired but the questions are not being worded correctly or are confusing. Or perhaps the content is confusing and not adequately preparing the participants for the questions. In the first case, the knowledge transfer is being underestimated and employees are being asked to repeat the course unnecessarily. In the second case, the course is scrap and needs to be fixed immediately.

Level 3: Application or Behavior

Level 3 measures the application of the new knowledge, skills or behaviors by the participants when they return to their job. They may have enjoyed the learning (high level 1) and learned a lot (high level 2), but the question now is whether their behavior has changed as a result of the learning. Are they actually applying what they learned to do something differently? Level 3 application is typically measured at two points in time. The first is intent to apply, which is measured in the post-event survey at the end of the course. The second is actual application measured several months after the course in a follow-up survey.

Intent to Apply

It is a best practice to measure the intent to apply the learning at the end of the course. This is done by including a question on intent to apply in the post-event survey. The intent to apply measure is a leading indicator of actual application and of impact and ROI. After all, if the participants do not intend to apply it or believe they will not be allowed to apply it, then it is highly unlikely they will actually apply it, resulting in scrap learning. Another post-event survey question that serves as a leading indicator of application includes the participant's assessment of supervisor support to apply the learning back on the job. If participants believe their supervisors are unlikely to provide the time or resources needed to apply the learning, or if the supervisors are simply not supportive of the training, then the actual application rate is likely to be low.

Actual Application

This is typically measured in a follow-up survey conducted about three months after the training. Participants will be asked if they have applied the knowledge or skills from their training, or alternatively, what percentage of their new knowledge and skills they have applied. Typically, an online survey is used, but the actual application may also be obtained from a phone survey, focus group, or observation.

In a survey or focus group, participants may be asked to describe at least one thing they are doing differently today because of the learning six months ago. If they cannot describe anything concrete, then the conclusion must be that they are not applying it. In some cases observation may be used. For example, it may be possible to watch workers who have taken a safety class to observe whether they are practicing the specific safety procedures they were taught. Either they are or they are not.

Many participants who indicated in the post-event survey that they intended to apply the learning will not in practice apply it or continue to apply it three to six months after the course. Despite the best intentions, other priorities may have arisen, or perhaps their boss did not have time to reinforce the learning. Perhaps there were no other positive incentives for them to apply the learning or negative consequences for not applying it. In any case, even many who intend to apply it do not. If they are not applying it, then regardless of level 1 and 2 scores, it is scrap. It took time to develop and deploy, but the organization is not receiving any benefit from it. The learning manager will need to understand why and develop an action plan to increase application.

Level 4: Results or Impact

In level 4 we are finally ready to measure the impact of learning on an organization's goals. Did the learning produce measurable results? Typically, the metric is already reported regularly. Examples include sales and market share for a consultative selling skills program, number of injuries for a safety program, leadership score on the employee opinion survey (EOS) for a leadership program, and design defects for an engineering program. Although an overall metric like sales will be reported regularly, what you really want to know is the isolated contribution of learning toward that goal. For example, if sales increased 10%, how much of that was attributable to learning and how much to all the other factors that influence sales? Like level 3 application, level 4 impact can be measured at two points in time. The first is an initial estimate provided at the end of the course in the post-event survey. The second is actual impact gleaned three months after the course in a follow-up survey or through other methods. We will address the actual impact first.

Actual Impact

NOTE: While Kirkpatrick and Phillips use similar terms for level 4 (results for Kirkpatrick and business impact for Phillips), they measure level 4 very differently. For Kirkpatrick, level 4 is measured by the business results themselves. For example, if training was designed to improve sales and if sales increased 10% following the training, then training resulted in increased sales as long as there is a strong chain of evidence supporting that training was effective (high levels 1-3). The Kirkpatrick level 4 results would simply be the increase in sales (10%). In contrast, Phillips measures level 4 impact as solely the increase in sales that resulted from the training—not the total increase in sales. In other words, Phillips focuses just on the isolated impact of training on the goal. In the example above, if sales rose 10% following the training, Phillips would ask how much of the 10% increase was due to the training and how much was due to other factors (like the economy, introduction of new products, etc.). If the answer is 40% due just to training, then the level 4 measure for impact would be 10% x 40% = 4% increase in sales due to training. Kirkpatrick fundamentally disagrees with both the need and the methodology to isolate the impact of training, arguing that such efforts are not productive due to

> the subjectivity involved—isolation efforts may be viewed by the goal owner as L&D seeking to claim credit for the increase in sales when it was a team effort. We will use the Phillip's approach for level 4 in this book, but we very much agree with Kirkpatrick that learning professionals must partner closely with the business to deliver impact from training since only business leaders can assure that the right employees take the training and actually apply it.

There are several ways to isolate the actual impact or contribution of learning. One is to use control groups. Sometimes this happens naturally as a learning program is deployed over several years to a large population. There may be similarly situated groups in which one group gets the learning now and another does not. If all the other factors are the same for both groups and the only difference is the learning, then you have a situation that can provide a controlled experiment. The difference in sales must be attributed to learning. Another method to isolate the impact of learning is to use regression analysis to establish a trend line in the absence of the learning. This answers the question of what performance would have been in the absence of training. The difference between the trend (without training) and the actual (with training) is then attributed to the training. (See Phillips for a full discussion of all methods to isolate impact.)

Frequently, though, such opportunities are not available, and the researcher will need to isolate the impact of learning another way. This is typically accomplished about three months after the learning by asking randomly selected participants a series of questions, leading to conservative estimates of impact. Here is how it might work:

- Start with level 3. Was the participant able to apply the learning?
  - If no, score 0 impact. Discuss why not.
- If the participant did apply the learning, what was the impact? (Sample answer: Sales went up 10%.)
- Were there other factors besides learning that may have produced the 10% increase?
  - If yes, what were they? (Answer: Improving economy, product price reduction, an increases in sales incentives, and the competitor's product had problems.)

  - o When you consider all these other factors, how much of the 10% increase do you think was due just to the learning? (Answer: 40% of the 10% or 4%.)
- How confident are you about the 4%? (Answer: 80% confident that it is at least 4%.)
  - o If the impact measure is not a reported number but is estimated, the researcher could ask for a confidence level for that as well.

So, the three steps are to: 1) confirm application and identify total impact, then 2) isolate the impact of learning, and finally 3) adjust for the confidence level of the estimate(s). In this example, say the salesperson did apply the learning and his or her sales increased by 10%. The salesperson estimates that 40% of the 10% increase is attributable to learning, so that means learning contributed to a 4% increase in sales (40% x 10% = 4%). Since the salesperson is only 80% confident about the 40% impact, scale down the impact accordingly (80% x 4% = 3.2%). So, learning is responsible for a 3.2% increase in her sales (32% of the 10% increase in sales). Thus, the isolation factor, adjusted for confidence, is 32%. Note that if a participant does not apply it, then learning has no impact on the goal (the isolation factor is 0, meaning no impact on sales).

Responses would be averaged over all those who were interviewed, including those who did not apply it. Say that the average isolation factor (adjusted for confidence) turned out to 28%. In other words, learning was responsible for about 28% of the sales increase. Other factors were responsible for about 72% of the sales increase. Further, assume that total sales went up 10%. Then, in percentage points, that means learning was responsible for 28% x 10% or 2.8% higher sales. This is meant to be a conservative estimate and should be shared with the sponsor of the goal to check on its reasonableness. If the goal owner thinks the isolation factor for learning should be lower, then lower it. (Remember, you had this discussion with the goal owner before the year started, when you were developing your business case. What did both of you think it would be then? Is it different now? Do you understand why it is different than you thought it would be?)

It is also possible to obtain the isolated impact in a follow-up survey of all participants rather than from a randomly selected sample. Simply add two questions to the follow-up survey where participants were asked about application. First, ask what percentage contribution the training had on their performance (such as increased sales). Second, ask how confident they are in their answer. For each question provide 11 boxes ranging from 0% to 100% in 10% increments. You will need to multiply the two answers to get the confidence-adjusted isolated impact which some survey programs can do for you. Alternatively, you could simply ask about percentage contribution and then scale it down by a range of 30% to 50% to make the confidence adjustment. You could also use the confidence factor obtained from a random sample of participants to apply to the all the survey respondents.

It is also now possible to isolate the impact of learning on an organization's goal statistically. A significant amount of data and effort is required, but statistical programs are available to isolate the impact of learning programs with a high level of confidence. So, when it is vital to isolate the impact of learning statistically and worth the effort to do so, there is now a proven option.

Initial Estimate of Impact

Just as with application, it is a best practice to measure the initial estimate of impact, which will be a leading indicator of actual impact and ROI. This is typically done as part of the post-event survey by adding the two standard questions discussed above to elicit an estimate of the isolated impact of the learning and the participant's confidence in that estimate. The two answers are then multiplied together for the confidence-adjusted isolated impact and then averaged over all the respondents.

Level 5: Return on Investment (ROI)

Jack Phillips introduced the concept of return on investment (ROI) from learning in his 1983 book *Handbook of Training Evaluation and Measurement Methods*. This was the first learning evaluation book published in the U.S. (Kirkpatrick's book was published in 1994.) Phillips' five-level framework was first published in 1992 in the *William and Mary Business Review* and later in the 1994 book *In Action: Measuring Return on Investment.*

ROI measures the value of the learning in relation to its cost. Even if learning is applied and produces impact, it generally will not be worth doing if the cost exceeds the value of the learning. In other words, not all impactful learning is worth doing. ROI is calculated as the net benefit in dollars divided by the total cost and is expressed as a percentage.

Here is the approach:

- Start with level 4 impact. For example, learning was responsible for a 30% reduction in injuries.
- Next find the monetary value or gross dollar benefit of the 30% reduction in injuries. In this case you would talk with your safety people, who probably already know what injuries are costing the company. (Remember, you had this discussion before the year started, when you developed the business case for learning. You and the goal's owner had agreed on the planned impact and the bottom line dollar value of that impact. Now you just need to apply the same reasoning to the actual impact.) Say the gross benefit from learning is $250,000.
- Now subtract the total cost of the learning (development + delivery + opportunity costs) from the gross benefit to find the net benefit. Say the total cost of learning was $150,000.
- Then net benefit = $250,000 - $150,000 = $100,000.
- Last, divide the net benefit by total cost to find ROI.
- ROI = $100,000 / $150,000 = 67%.

This learning generated a 67% return on the $150,000 invested in it. (For a detailed treatment see Phillips and Phillips, *The Value of Learning: How Organizations Capture Value and ROI and Translate Them into Support, Improvement, and Funds.*)

In many organizations investments are required to meet a minimum "hurdle rate" before they will even be considered by senior leaders or the board of directors. Companies typically rank order potential investments above the hurdle rate by the expected ROI and then make a decision about which ones to fund, considering, among many other factors, the expected return. If you are in an organization that considers learning an investment and includes it with other investments for consideration, then Phillips' ROI provides you with the measure you need to compete with the other investments. It is just one more way to run learning like a business and to convey results in a standard business format.

If ROI makes sense in your organization, you have probably already included ROIs in your business case for learning along with the planned impact learning would have on achieving your organization's goals. Three to six months after deployment you can now find out what the actual ROI was. It will never be exactly what you forecast, so there will always be a learning opportunity. If it turned out lower than you expected, why? What could you do differently next time to achieve higher impact and greater ROI? If it turned out higher than you expected, why? Are there lessons to be applied in developing and deploying future programs?

ROI measures also allow an interesting comparison among programs. Some will have high ROI, some low. Just like above, there are lessons to be learned by reflecting on the variances. To be clear, a program with a lower ROI is not necessarily inferior to one with a higher ROI. All of your key learning initiatives should be a result of your strategic alignment, business case, and business plan process. So they are all the *right* learning for the right reasons and have the support of senior leadership. With that said, what can you learn by comparing the different ROIs? Could the programs with lower ROIs have been developed, deployed, or reinforced any differently for higher impact and ROI?

We will revisit the concept of net benefit later in the chapter for a more detailed discussion.

Obstacles to Measurement

A number of obstacles and objections have been raised about measurement in general and the above six levels in particular. Before proceeding to the evaluation strategy, we need to address those. This section will address common obstacles to using the first five levels, and the next section will address the controversy surrounding the use of ROI in learning.

Seven obstacles and objections will be explored along with suggestions to overcome them. (These seven are the most common from my experience. See Phillips and Phillips, *The Value of Learning*, Chapter 1, for more on objections to measurement and evaluation and how to overcome them.)

Don't Know What to Measure

This is a common first obstacle that learning managers face. In light of the many ways to measure and perhaps numerous initiatives, it can seem overwhelming.

Start with level 0. You must gather data on the number of courses developed and delivered, completion dates, the number of participants, and costs. These are the basics of your business, just as sales and costs are the basics in a for-profit company. Employ a learning management system (LMS) to track participants, course offerings, and completions. Keep track of costs. Chapter 3 provides suggestions for gathering, analyzing, and presenting this information.

Next, you need an evaluation strategy for the higher levels of measurement. Start with level 1 for all courses but not all participants (use sampling). Do level 2 where appropriate and especially on compliance-related courses so your LMS will retain a record of those who took it and their score. If resources permit, focus levels 3 and 4 on your most important, highest-priority programs. Do one or two this year and then another one or two next year. Lastly, if appropriate, complete the ROI for those where level 4 impact has been established.

Include your measurement plans in the evaluation chapter of the annual business plan for learning and get senior leader input and buy-in before you start.

Don't Know How to Measure

This is an issue of technique. Many learning professionals do not know how to perform the measurements. This might include writing levels 1 and 2 surveys, conducting interviews or focus groups to ascertain application and impact, and isolating the impact of learning from other factors.

The good news is that there is a lot of help out there for you! Start by asking colleagues in your organization or others who have experience doing these things. Read a book or two on the subject. There are scores of books from which to choose. (Jack Phillips alone has written more than twenty!) And take advantage of the many workshops offered at conferences and as standalone programs. You will find sessions that range from one hour to five days. Start at the introductory level and go as deep as you like.

And, if you do not want to do it yourself, there are many excellent consultants who can help with any aspect of the measurement process. Even if you know how to do it, there are advantages to bringing in someone from the outside who is independent and a recognized expert. You can learn a lot from such a person.

There are also services like Knowledge Advisors (see KnowledgeAdvisors.com for more information) that offer automated data gathering systems. They have level 1 and 2 surveys with standardized questions (which allow you to compare your results with hundreds of other companies), or they will help you customize the survey. Surveys go out automatically after the class is over, and the provider aggregates all the data and generates reports for you.

So, this is not an obstacle that should stand in your way.

ADVICE: Just start. If you are new to measurement, you will not feel comfortable with measuring until you actually do it. If you wait until all the questions have been answered and you are completely comfortable, you will never start. You will make mistakes along the way, especially in the beginning. It is okay. You will learn and improve. Soon you will wonder why you did not start sooner.

It Cannot Be Measured

This may be the most common objection among learning professionals. Sometimes the statement is made just about levels 4 and 5, which admittedly are more challenging. Other times it is a broader comment about learning, meant to distinguish learning (viewed as difficult or inappropriate to quantify) from engineering, marketing, and other disciplines (viewed as easily and highly quantifiable).

Ideally, everyone would agree that levels 0 and 1 can be applied to any learning. There may be budget or staff constraints, but that is a different matter. All learning can be measured at these two basic levels. For the higher levels, it depends. Level 2 is not appropriate for all learning and measuring. Levels 3–5 can be resource intensive, so you may choose not to measure. Where it is appropriate, though, levels 2–5 can be applied to virtually any learning.

For levels 4 and 5, though, concern remains about the ability to isolate the impact of learning. Techniques exist to do just this, however, so that leaves only the concern about how well the techniques work. The objection is that the techniques are not perfect; we can never *really know* learning's impact, and therefore levels 4 and 5 should not be attempted. This argument reflects a lack of business experience on the part of the learning professional making it since there are few perfect techniques and absolute truths in the business world. A lot of data that at first blush appears to be completely objective (like market share and impact of advertising or research and development) actually contain estimates, and almost all decisions are based to some extent on estimates, forecasts, and sometimes just instinct. So, to those who are hesitant to isolate the impact of learning, we would say, "Welcome to the real world. Your estimates will not be perfect, but they can be good enough to be useful. Your colleagues in the business world live with and are judged by less than perfect data every day, so you can too."

So, here is how you might proceed. Establish the methodology beforehand as part of the business plan for learning and/or in conjunction with the sponsor.

Also, you and the sponsor have already agreed on a forecast of learning's impact as part of the business case. You might decide just to keep using the forecast and not actually measure level 4 impact this year. In any case, do not be afraid of uncertainty or estimates and do not wait for perfection or absolute certainty.

> CATERPILLAR EXPERIENCE: We measured a variety of programs at all six levels, including sales, safety, technical skills, leadership, and performance management. It is definitely possible, it was not painful, and we learned something in each case to help us improve.

Insufficient Staff, Budget, Time

Here the obstacle is insufficient resources, which can be a very real issue, especially in smaller functions. If you have few staff but a budget for consultants, consider using outside help. In some cases, though, the resources to undertake all the measurements you would like simply are not available.

Start with what you have and focus on level 0 for all and level 1 for the most important. Get input from senior leaders on your evaluation strategy so they have a sense of ownership and are more likely to fund it. Report regularly on your progress. Be transparent and honest and share what you do not know because of the lack of good measurements. Tell the leaders how you would manage better with a more complete measurement strategy.

No Support from the Top

Support from the top is critical for good measurement. Senior leaders need to provide input to your evaluation strategy, buy into it, and fund you appropriately.

To increase top-level support, get their input for your evaluation strategy. Make sure you are measuring what is important to them. Tell them the benefits of greater measurement. Share results regularly with them. That means the good and the bad. You are winning their trust. They already know that you are not perfect, and they will feel more comfortable (and supportive) when you admit to imperfection. So, be honest about results and about the lack of perfect measures. If you remain positive and professional, then you should slowly win their support.

No One Believes the Measurements Anyway

This is often the final objection and may be followed by the conclusion, "So why bother?"

If you find yourself in this type of environment, it may take a while to work your way out, but you need to start. First, be sure to get leaders' and sponsors' buy-in for your evaluation strategy *before* the programs are launched. Their support is key. If you get their buy-in upfront, there is a much greater chance they will believe the results. Second, be modest and humble, which is always good advice in the measurement space. Proactively tell them that the measures are not perfect and some estimation may be required. They will understand. Third, go slow. Start with levels 0 and 1. Then introduce a level 3 measure and perhaps in the second or third year introduce level 4. Do not rush it! You need to gain their confidence, and this may take one or two years. Be honest and transparent, openly disclosing when estimates have been used and data is incomplete.

> ADVICE: There may be some who never believe in corporate learning, regardless of what you do. Some, by virtue of their personal experiences, will be convinced that the impact of learning cannot be measured, and you will not be able to convince them otherwise. After several years as CLO I learned to stop worrying about them. Focus your energy on those in the middle who are skeptical but open minded. You can make a lot of progress with them.

Lack of Confidence

Lack of confidence is a serious obstacle holding the learning profession back. Many in the field will readily admit they lack confidence in measurement, statistics, and using numbers in general. In fact, some would say they were attracted to learning because they wanted to avoid numbers.

The lack of confidence is understandable. L&D professionals may not have been exposed to a lot of statistics at university, and measurement may not have been included in many of their courses. They may not have been asked to do much with measurement in their previous positions. Without formal preparation or practice, it is little wonder many in the profession are not comfortable with measurement.

The fact remains, however, that measurement is an integral part of running learning like a business. The learning function simply cannot be run effectively or efficiently without measurement. So, learning professionals must overcome this obstacle by:

- Learning the techniques
- Sharing concerns, issues, and solutions with colleagues
- Getting help if you can afford it
- Starting small and growing your measurement effort

Remember, all these measurements are only numbers. And many of these numbers are imperfect, incomplete, or estimates. Your colleagues in sales, R&D, manufacturing, and advertising already know this. They do not lose sleep over it. They do not apologize for it. And they do not hesitate to use their measurements to judge performance, make decisions, or justify raises. Learning professionals need to do the same.

The ROI Controversy

Now it is time to consider one of the more spirited controversies in learning.

Many experienced learning professionals are absolutely opposed to the idea of calculating an ROI. (For example, I was once in a room with fifteen other VPs of learning and discovered that not one of them would use ROI!) Many who feel this way feel *very strongly* about it. In fact, some will avoid even the topic. So, you might ask, what is going on?

Two things, I think. First, the isolation issue is an insurmountable hurdle for many. The isolation issue is simply the need to isolate the impact of learning from other factors to calculate the level 4 impact and the gross benefit for ROI. Conceptually, they don't believe there is any credible methodology to isolate impact. They would say that participant estimation is too subjective, control groups are impractical, and statistical techniques are too difficult or unproven. They may have personal experience presenting a ROI study that was not well received by senior leaders, and I can sympathize with their concerns. Nonetheless, we do have industry standard approaches for isolation, which have been refined by Jack and Patti Phillips and used for over 30 years by thousands of organizations. Are any of the methodologies absolutely bullet proof? Of course not. But they are good enough to produce estimates that will allow us to make the right decisions about learning. And, if senior leaders really want a high level of precision and certainty, we can now use the same type of statistical modeling that is used by pharmaceutical companies for their drug trials. So, the key here is to work closely with the goal owner from the start to agree on planned impact and other measures of success and then be very humble when you present impact and ROI. Tell them the goal of your measurement at this level is to be roughly right, see how close to plan you came, and be close enough to make the necessary decisions, such as whether to proceed from pilot to full-scale implementation or to repeat this kind of training next year. Remind them that you also want to identify opportunities for continual improvement, about which the ROI study will provide valuable insight.

Second, I believe that ROI has been used inappropriately by some in the learning field and has consequently acquired a bad reputation in the minds of many. I would guess that it was adopted by many learning functions seeking to prove their worth or prevent funding and staffing cuts. Many of these functions were already under fire and on the defensive, with senior leadership questioning their value. These functions had not strategically and proactively aligned their learning to their organization's highest priority goals. They had not developed a business case for learning or created a business plan and had not gotten the support and buy-in from senior leaders or a governing body. Now, having skipped all these important steps, they try to justify the programs that they have developed and deployed with a (hopefully) high ROI.

This approach is doomed to failure even if the ROI turns out to be high. First, you cannot skip all the upfront steps required for alignment, for creation of the business case and plan, and for approval. These steps are essential to build support, credibility, and legitimacy and must be done before the year starts or at least before program development begins. Credibility and legitimacy depend as much on the process as on the results, so learning managers must not short circuit the process.

Second, a high ROI does not justify the investment or guarantee that it was the right investment. Imagine a corporate university that is not run like a business. Without proper planning, it chooses to invest in a learning initiative that has been shown to help other companies. It develops and deploys the courses. Measurements show the following:

- Level 1 scores are high: the participants really like it and intend to apply it.
- Level 2 scores are high: they learned a lot.
- Level 3 scores are high: they are applying it on the job.
- Level 4 scores are high: the program is making an impact
- Level 5 score is high: ROI is very high, maybe the highest for any program this year

The above measurements confirm that the learning was good, well-received, applied, and impactful. None of these high scores, though, including the high ROI, proves that it was the right learning to do.

The only way to know if it is the right learning is to follow the steps in chapters four through six. Since in our example this was not done, it would only be the right learning by chance. Perhaps the strategic alignment, business case, and business plan processes would have resulted in this being a high-priority learning initiative, but perhaps not.

To be absolutely clear, let's make this example more concrete. The learning program in the example above is an innovation initiative for engineers with an ROI of 110%. All of the other initiatives had ROIs between 30% and 50%. One initiative for sales had a projected ROI of 25% but was not funded. If the learning manager had followed the recommended steps, he would have discovered that innovation is *not* a priority for next year and is not even a corporate goal. Increased sales, on the other hand, is a priority goal, but no learning was provided because the ROI was forecast to be low.

The learning manager should have invested in the sales initiative instead of the innovation initiative, even though the ROI for innovation was more than four times that of sales. Why? Because sales is a high-priority goal, and innovation is not a goal at all. As long as the ROI for sales learning is above the hurdle rate, the learning manager should consider funding it. Only after all the high priority goals have been addressed should the learning manager consider investing in unaligned learning.

At this point someone might point out that profit would be maximized by investing in innovation rather than sales since it has a higher ROI. In the short term that would be true, but a learning manager must trust the goals set by senior leaders. It is not the CLO's job to reprioritize the organization's goals. Trust the CEO and board of directors. For instance, it may be the case that the organization is getting ready to outsource its engineering and that is why innovation is not a goal for the next year. Of course, it would be fine in the planning process to raise the issue.

So, ROI cannot substitute for the planning process. It cannot take the place of strategic alignment, development of the business case, or creation and approval of the business plan. It cannot be used after the fact to justify learning, nor can it be used prospectively to rank learning projects.

ROI can, however, be used to measure results, manage better, and improve, but it must be used in conjunction with the processes described above. It must be applied only to the right learning. In this context it can be used to help evaluate funding levels and might serve as a tiebreaker among projects of equal priority. It might also be required from the learning function so that its investment requests can be compared to requests from other departments.

The real benefit of ROI analysis is to bring costs into the equation and to force a calculation of gross dollar benefits, which in turn will lead to a much deeper consideration of costs and benefits, and should lead to much richer internal discussions. This deeper reflection and richer dialogue will make everyone involved a better manager and will lead to ideas for improvement. Without question, it will force you to ask questions about how to reduce costs or increase benefits that you otherwise would never have done. It may even help prove your worth and increase your funding, but only if it is done in conjunction with the overall planning process.

Measurement Strategy

Having overcome the obstacles to measurement, we are ready to consider a measurement strategy. Every learning function should have one, ideally as part of the business plan for learning, but each will be different, reflecting the goals, size, complexity, funding, and maturity of the function.

The measurement strategy should include all the key measurement plans. It should reflect input from the senior leaders, governing bodies, sponsors, and, of course, the L&D professionals. The strategy should be reflected in the specific, measurable goals of the senior L&D staff, whether it is centralized in one measurement group or decentralized with program managers responsible for evaluation of their own initiatives.

A Suggested Measurement Strategy

The evaluation strategy for an organization will depend on a number of factors, including budget, staffing, maturity, previous evaluation work, senior leader input, and systems, as well as on the goals of the learning function and on the culture and business practices of the organization.

Below are suggestions to consider in creating a measurement strategy:

- Efficiency Measures
  - Level 0 or volume measures
    - For all courses and participants (unique and total)

    - All relevant costs down to the program level
    - Completion dates

- Effectiveness Measures
  - Level 1 or satisfaction
    - For all courses
    - At a minimum ask about relevance, quality of the instructor and content, overall satisfaction, and whether you would recommend the course to others
    - Consider automating, making it completely electronic
  - Level 2 or acquisition of knowledge
    - All compliance-related learning
    - Other learning where it makes sense
    - Easiest to implement for online courses
    - May be 20–50% of courses
  - Level 3 or application
    - For key courses aligned to key goals—may need to prioritize
    - Consider a multi-year strategy so that over a three- to five-year period, you have tested application on a variety of types of courses
    - Measure close to 100% of key courses aligned to the most important goals and there is no need to measure application for general, unaligned learning. Depending on your mix of courses, 10% to 30% of all the courses may be measured for application.
  - Level 4 or impact
    - For key courses
    - Consider using a third party for expertise and independence
  - Level 5 or ROI
    - For key courses
    - Consider doing for the same key courses as in level 4 since impact is required
    - Consider using same third party as in level 4
    - Perform only on those programs that are strategically aligned and approved by senior leadership
    - Perform only for the right reasons!

The actual measurement strategy would specify programs for levels 0–5 and perhaps the person responsible for the evaluation. See Appendix B for an example. It may also be helpful to summarize your measurement strategy in a matrix like Table 8.1, showing the planned measurements for each course or program.

TABLE 8.1

Measurement Strategy Matrix for Course-Specific Measures

	Effectiveness Measures				Efficiency Measures				
Program	Level 1	Level 2	Level 3	Levels 4 & 5	Number of Participants	Costs	Cycle Time	Development Completed on Time	Delivery Completed on Time
Consultative Selling Skills	P,S	X	I,A	IE,AI,R	U	X	X	X	X
NPI	P,S	X	I,A	IE,AI,R	U,T	X	X	X	X
Design for Manufacturing	P,S	X	I,A	IE,AI,R	U,T	X	X	X	X
Safety	P,S	X	I,A	IE,AI,R	U,T	X	X	X	X
Introduction to Supervision	P,S		I,A	AI,R	U	X	X	X	X
Leadership for Managers	P,S		I,A	AI,R	U	X	X	X	X
Advanced Leadership	P,S		I,A		U	X			X
Performance Management	P,S		I,A	AI,R	U	X	X	X	X
Purchasing	P,S		I,A	IE,AI,R	U,T	X	X	X	X
Product Training	P,S	X	I,A		U,T	X	X	X	X
Customer Relations Skills	P,S	X	I,A		U	X	X	X	X
Fraud Detection	P,S	X	I,A		U	X	X	X	X
Insider Trading	P,S	X	I,A		U	X	X		X
General (unaligned)					U	X			

Legend:
P = Participant
S = Sponsor or goal owner
I = Intent to apply
A = Actual application
IE = Initial estimate of impact
AI = Actual impact
R = ROI
U = Unique participants
T = Total participants (used when there is more than one course in the program)

Use of Sampling

Statistical sampling is an important concept for the learning manager and makes the task of measurement much easier. It means you do not need to gather data from every participant to evaluate performance and make decisions. For example, you do not need to survey every class participant to calculate the level 1 measure. Likewise, you do not need to interview everyone who took a course to calculate level 3 and 4 measures. A few will do.

The Concept of Statistical Sampling

It is the magic of statistics at work. You may recall fondly from your statistics course that a sample is a subset of the population where population is everyone in the group. As long as the sample is representative of the whole group (the population) and of sufficient size, and as long as the population is normally distributed (for small samples), data gathered from the sample will provide virtually the same results as data from the population. This is why pollsters only need to survey four or five thousand voters to make a prediction about how fifty million voters are likely to cast their ballots and why most polls quoted in a newspaper mention a sample size of only one thousand.

Let us examine the three conditions. First, the sample needs to be representative of the population. This is generally accomplished by choosing participants at random to be included in the sample (thus, the term "random sample"). Done properly, random sampling will ensure that the sample is representative of the whole group, meaning that it has the same characteristics (such as age, gender, education, political preference, and so on).

The second and third conditions go together and we will start with the third. Ideally, the population under discussion will be distributed normally with regard to the characteristic being examined, which means that most of the population will be centered around the average and that there will be fewer and fewer people the further away you get from the average. This is represented by the classic "bell"-shaped curve. Suppose you were interested in people's heights. If you made a graph of everyone's height in a group and it looked like the one below, the group would be normally distributed.

FIGURE 8.5

Example of a Normal Distribution
Adult Heights

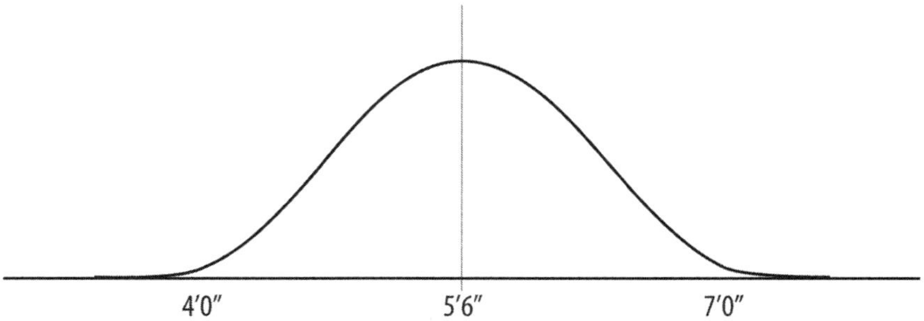

The average height is 5 feet 6 inches, and the average is in the middle of the distribution. About half are taller than average, and the other half are shorter. There are not many extremely tall or short individuals. The picture is balanced. A random sample of sufficient size drawn from this normally distributed population will produce about the same average as if you had measured everyone in the whole group. If you have a large enough sample, the underlying distribution does not even have to be normal in order for you to use the sample average to represent the population average.

Finally, the sample needs to be large enough to do its job—that is, ensure that conclusions drawn from the sample will be almost the same as conclusions drawn from the population. Pollsters could not ask just five people how they were going to vote and then extrapolate that to how fifty million will vote. Surprisingly enough, though, the magic number can be as low as *thirty*, although a higher number is required if there is a lot of variability in the answers. (A larger sample is also required to draw conclusions about subgroups.) If the population is normally distributed, the magic number can be even less than thirty.

Now, more is always better, and a larger sample size will allow you to be more confident about your results. Remember that pollsters always give their margin of error and perhaps the confidence level. They will say something like, "Our poll shows that 70% will vote for candidate A. The poll has an error margin of +/- 3%." The fine print may have included reference to a 95% confidence level and a sample size of 4,500. So, they are saying that they are 95% certain that 67% to 73% will vote for candidate A. If they had increased their sample to 7,000, the margin of error would be less, perhaps +/- 2% at 95% confidence. Or they might be 99% confident that it was 70% +/- 3%. In any case, a larger sample will make you more confident of the results, either by reducing the margin of error or increasing the confidence level.

Sampling in Practice

Now we are ready to apply the concepts to learning.

***Level 0*:** Do not use sampling here. You want complete information, meaning data on the whole population of participants and courses. This should be automated anyway so the cost is not that much greater for all the data than for some of it.

***Level 1*:** Instead of passing out hard copy surveys at the end of class, send an electronic survey a day or two after class. The response rate will likely be 30–40%, and that is all right as long as there is not a response bias (e.g., just those who liked it returned the survey or just those who did not like it returned the survey). If you are worried about response bias, follow up with thirty or so participants who did not return the survey and get them to complete it. See whether their answers are in line with those who returned it earlier.

Also, if you are surveying by paper, consider saving some money by not surveying every class when there are multiple classes in the same course taught by the same instructor. Remember the concept of the sample. Pick a few.

In general, you will want at least thirty responses for a valid measure. If you have less than thirty, be careful about drawing a conclusion. For example, if you have fifteen respondents out of one hundred and only eight reply that they can apply the course to their job, do not be too alarmed (yet). True, it is not a good sign, and it is certainly a warning signal, requiring you to pay close attention as more data come in. But it may just be how the data are coming in. If you get fifteen more responses and the results are the same, you have a problem. Let's say you have thirty responses out of one hundred, and only sixteen have reported they can apply the learning to their job. Your goal may have been 80–90%, and the data show about 50%—not even close. Statistics indicate that even if you contacted all one hundred, the answer would be the same: only half can apply it (plus or minus some margin for error). Now it is time to take the data seriously and look into it.

What if there are only fifteen people in the class and you get responses from all of them? Can you trust that? Yes, because that is the whole population. As long as you are only making conclusions about that one class, you have all the data you need.

How about if you get responses from ten out of fifteen or seventeen out of thirty? Now, you do not have responses from the whole population, and the sample size is less than thirty. Statistically speaking, you cannot be as confident about the conclusions you might draw. Practically speaking, if the percentage who cannot apply it seems high and worries you, take it seriously and look into it. Better to be safe and address any potential problem early.

This is especially true as the sample size approaches the population even when it remains below thirty. For example, suppose you get twenty-seven out of thirty. That is nearly the whole population, so you should take the data very seriously.

Finally, there is always the chance that for a small sample the underlying population is not normal, meaning we have to be very careful about how confident we are about any conclusions. You might become suspicious if the sample responses seem to fall into two or three subgroups. Suppose you send out one hundred surveys and get twenty responses. The question has a five-point scale. If eight answer 1, one answers 2, one answers 3, one answers 4, and nine answer 5, you may have a bimodal distribution (two peaks instead of one at the average). If you get a distribution of answers with multiple peaks or with no peaks at all, you might want to look into it further. Get more data and see if it persists. If it does, you may want to use focus groups or other means to understand what is going on.

***Level 2*:** Tests are often compulsory, so sampling is not an issue. If a student cannot pass the course without completing the test, you should have population data on all students. In this case the scores are exactly whatever they turn out to be, regardless of how many took the test. There is no margin of error and no confidence level. You can be 100% certain that the average score was the average score for that population.

***Level 3–4*:** Measurement at these levels is almost always performed on a random sample. So, first make sure that the selection process is random. Second, you need more than thirty respondents, which may require approaching many more depending on the response rate or willingness to participate.

Sometimes, for budget or other reasons, you cannot get thirty respondents. In this case some feedback is still better than none, but you cannot be entirely confident of your results. The key here will be the variability in the answers to your questions. If everyone or nearly everyone gives the same answers (for example, they all apply the learning, the impact isolation factor is 40–50%, and they are 70–80% confident in their estimate), then you would have high confidence in the results even if the sample size were 20. On the other hand, if the answers range from 0–80% and they seem to be spread evenly over the sample, then you probably should not trust the answers, even if the sample size were thirty or forty. In this case the variability (or variance in statistical terms) is high, which means a larger sample will be needed to be confident of the results.

Sampling Summary

The important point here is that sampling should play an important role in the measurement of learning. It will be used primarily for level 1 and levels 3 and 4. Often it simply is not practical to gather and process data on the whole population. Even when it is possible, sampling provides a way to get the same answers at a much lower cost. If a learning function has not used sampling before, change management may be required to overcome resistance and win the staff over.

CATERPILLAR EXPERIENCE: We introduced sampling for level 1 when we moved away from collecting surveys physically at the end of each class and began sending out electronic surveys in their place. The greatest resistance came from the experienced instructors, who were used to getting feedback the same day from all their students. They felt that the sample data could not be trusted since the response rate was about 35% and they were used to 100%. The concept of sampling was a hard sell.

We did compromise in one area, though. For a new class, especially if the new classes were scheduled on consecutive days (a repeat of the same class for different students), there was a real need to obtain immediate feedback so the instructor could make changes that evening before teaching it again the next day. Since the e-survey could not be done in one day, we agreed to make an exception to the e-surveys for new classes or new instructors, when immediate feedback was important.

Calculation and Use of Net Benefits

Net benefit is a very powerful and practical concept that is underused in the learning field. Most people think of it only as the numerator in the ROI calculation, but it has tremendous utility in its own right, and it avoids the stigma associated by some with ROI. Before leaving this chapter, we need to take a closer look at net benefit both as a measure and as a forecast. It was first introduced in Chapter 5 as a forecast and as a potential part of the business case, and we will return to its very important role in planning after a closer look at its role as a measure of performance.

Net Benefit As a Measure of Actual Results

Although it is a part of the ROI calculation, net benefit has great value as a standalone measure of dollar impact.

Calculation Overview

The general process for calculating net benefit was described earlier in the chapter. Briefly, start with a determination of gross benefit, which is the dollar value of the level 4 impact. Then find net benefit by subtracting the total cost. For many programs this is not as hard as it sounds. Remember, the goal of this exercise is to calculate a net benefit that is reasonable, useful, and credible. It most definitely is not to discover absolute truth or to establish absolute certainty. Therefore, we need to agree upfront that the number will not be perfect. Hopefully, though, it will be good enough to judge performance and to make decisions. That is all we ask.

We will explore the calculations for both "hard" and "soft" skills training. In each, however, the same basic principles apply:

1. Be conservative.
2. Be transparent.
3. Be humble. Do not oversell the concept.
4. Seek and take advice from others, particularly sponsors and subject matter experts.
5. Get their buy-in on the approach before development begins.
6. Get their buy-in on the results.
7. Be open to learning. Remember, this is as much a learning opportunity as a performance measure.

The following discussion assumes that all the gross benefits and costs for the programs occur in the plan year. In reality, some programs take more than one year to develop and deploy, and the improved performance accruing to the organization may well extend one or two years beyond deployment. So, you may need to make a multi-year calculation of net benefit and apportion it over several years.

For "Hard" Skills Training

The task is easier for courses like sales, safety, and technical skills, in which the corporate goal has already been quantified and the cost may have been estimated as well. In these cases reporting processes are probably already in place to track the company's success in achieving the goal.

Recall the business case from Chapter 5, in which the corporate goal was to increase sales by 10%, which was expected to contribute $7.5 million to the bottom line. At the end of the year, the company will know exactly how much sales increased and will have an estimate of the contribution to net income. Suppose that sales actually increased 12% and were responsible for a $8 million increase to the bottom line (accounting has this data). Further, assume that a level 4 evaluation was completed that showed learning was responsible for 30% (after applying both the isolation and confidence factors) of the 12% increase in sales. Now, it is easy and straightforward to find the gross and net benefit of the learning.

The estimated gross benefit would be 30% x $8.0 million or $2.4 million. Net benefit is found by subtracting total costs (all budget costs plus opportunity costs, which are now known with certainty) from gross benefit. If budget costs were $600,000 and opportunity costs were $120,000, then total costs were $720,000. Net benefit would be $2.4 million - $720,000 or $1.68 million. (Note that actual impact, gross benefit, and costs are all different than what was planned. Results and costs rarely come in exactly on plan. Learn from the variance.)

For "Soft" Skills Training

Determining the gross benefit for soft skills like leadership and performance management is not more difficult but is considerably more subjective. As we discussed in Chapter 5, you may decide that it is inappropriate, unwise, or unnecessary even to calculate the dollar benefit for a course like leadership, and that is fine. In the spirit of continual learning and improvement, however, you may wish to find the net benefit of a "soft" skills course like leadership, performance management, or innovation. The added benefit of this approach is that you will be able to sum the net benefits from your key programs to present a total net benefit to the organization, which may be helpful in many ways. Our standard caveats apply: the soft skills courses in this section are the result of a strategic alignment process, culminating in an approved business plan for learning; thus, this is not an exercise to justify investment in them.

Since most goals involving soft skills do not have a planned impact or reporting systems to track their progress and impact on the bottom line, the approach used above to calculate gross benefit for goals involving hard skills will not work. (For example, your friends in accounting will not have an estimate of the impact of improved leadership on net income.) Instead, it generally makes more sense to calculate the gross benefit of learning directly. One approach is to take a very conservative approach and identify just one or two of the many benefits from the learning, specifically one or two that are readily quantifiable. Productivity works in many cases. Obviously, there are many, many other reasons to improve leadership or performance management, and some of these other reasons have greater value than increased productivity. If a sponsor or senior leaders are willing to put a dollar value on those other reasons, great! Then you can proceed to isolate the impact of learning to find the gross benefit. If not, work with what you can quantify (like productivity) and remind people that this is a very conservative approach since many important benefits have been omitted.

Productivity would typically be measured in hours saved, and it is a good measure because it translates directly into labor and related costs, which are always a major expense. For example, a good leadership program should make the leader more efficient (saving time) and should also make interaction with her direct reports more efficient (saving time). The sum of time saved for the leader and her direct reports (and maybe others as well) is an increase in productivity. The leader and direct reports can now spend the new-found time on other important work, which they may not have been able to address before. Or, the organization may not need to hire as many new employees since the existing ones will now be more productive. In either case, this time saved through increased productivity attributable to better leadership can be conservatively valued at the labor and related cost for those involved.

The methodology works the same way as before. Focus groups or surveys are used to identify the benefits of the learning. All reported benefits are captured, but only one or two like productivity are converted to dollars. Now the impact of learning on the time saved is isolated from any other factors that may have played a role, and the impact is reduced further by a confidence factor. The result is a *very* conservative estimate of gross benefit along with a qualitative summary of the other benefits. The last step is to subtract total costs to derive net benefit.

Calculations are shown in Table 8.2 to determine the actual gross and net benefits of the three leadership courses contained in the business case in Table 5.1. Assume that an evaluation was conducted three months after the leadership courses were deployed. Among other benefits, it was found that productivity of the leaders and their direct reports increased 1.6% through more efficient meetings, goal setting, and performance evaluation (versus 1.5% in the plan). The labor and related rates for each group can be used to calculate the dollar value of the increased productivity.

TABLE 8.2

Calculation of Actual Gross and Net Benefits for Leadership Courses

	Annual Labor & Related $	
	Average	*Total*
Supervisor Course		
105 Supervisors	$100,000	$10,500,000
684 Direct Reports	$50,000	$34,200,000
Total		$44,700,000
Division Manager Course		
62 Division Managers	$155,000	$9,600,000
105 Direct Reports	$100,000	$10,500,000
Total		$20,100,000
Department Head Course		
13 Department Heads	$300,000	$3,900,000
62 Direct Reports	$155,000	$9,600,000
Total		$13,500,000
Total Labor & Related Expense		**$78,300,000**
Increase in productivity due to learning		1.6%
Gross Benefit = Value of 1.6% increase in productivity		$1,253,000
Total Cost		$832,000
Net Benefit		**$421,000**

In this example, estimated net benefit was $421,000 versus the planned amount of $316,000.

Net Benefit as a Forecast of Planned Results

Net benefit can be used not only as a measure of actual impact but as the planned impact for the initiative. Net benefits were used in this way in Chapter 5 to establish the business case for learning, which would be included in the overall business plan for learning to be submitted to the CEO and board of governors for approval (Chapter 6). Net benefit per person is an especially useful concept for planning and discussion.

Calculation for "Hard Skills" Training

The planned or expected net benefit of a program can be established through discussion with the goal owner as outlined in chapters four and five. Typically, for the high priority hard skills training, organizations will have already set specific measurable goals like a 10% increase in sales. These are very likely to be included in the organization's business plan. The recommended approach is to start at the corporate level with the goal (like a 10% increase in sales) and with the planned impact on net income of achieving that goal (for example, a $7.5 million impact to the bottom line). Then agree on the planned contribution from the learning on that goal (a best guess of the isolation factor). If it is agreed that learning, properly developed, delivered, and reinforced, should contribute 20% of the 10% increase in sales, then the gross benefit of learning should be $1.5 million. If total costs are projected by the learning department to be $607,000, then the net benefit of the sales learning program is forecast to be $893,000.

If the goal has not been quantified (for example, if the goal were just to increase sales), it should not be hard for the goal owner or sponsor of that goal to do so. As discussed in Chapter 5, it is also likely that the CEO and the goal owner have a plan of the impact that goal will have on net income (at least for the high-priority goals), even if it is not included in the plan document.

Calculation for "Soft Skills" Training

In contrast to the hard skills, many organizations will not even have specific measurable goals established for leadership, performance improvement, or innovation. Some do, and an example is provided in Table 5.1, where the goal is a five-point increase in the leadership score in the annual employee opinion survey. Even when organizations do have a measurable goal, it is unlikely that anyone will have calculated the impact on net income of achieving that goal (like the $3 million shown in Table 5.1). There also may not be agreement on the impact of learning on achieving the goal (like the 20% used in Table 5.1). Without the impact on net income ($7.5 million) and the impact of learning on the goal (40%), the dollar impact or gross benefit of learning ($7.5 million x 20% = $1.5 million) cannot be calculated. So, there is likely to be considerably less work already done around these goals than was the case with the hard skills.

TABLE 8.3

Calculation of Planned Gross and Net Benefits for Leadership Courses

	Annual Labor & Related $	
	Average	*Total*
Supervisor Course		
100 Supervisors	$100,000	$10,000,000
700 Direct Reports	$50,000	$35,000,000
Total		$45,000,000
Division Manager Course		
65 Division Managers	$157,000	$10,205,000
100 Direct Reports	$100,000	$10,000,000
Total		$20,205,000
Department Head Course		
15 Department Heads	$300,000	$4,500,000
65 Direct Reports	$157,000	$10,205,000
Total		$14,705,000
Total Labor & Related Expense		**$79,910,000**
Increase in productivity due to learning		1.5%
Gross Benefit = Value of 1.5% increase in productivity		$1,200,000
Total Cost = Budget + Opportunity = $582,000 + $302,000		$884,000
Net Benefit		**$316,000**

In this case it will generally be easier to calculate the net benefit directly, which requires deciding on a benefit like productivity and then agreeing on a conservative plan for its improvement due to the learning. This is simply your best thinking of the Level 4 measure of impact. For example, a leadership program might be conservatively planned to improve productivity for the leader and his direct reports by 1.5% for one year. Once you have agreed on the level 4 measure (1.5% increase in productivity), it is easy to calculate the dollar value or gross benefit of that increase using labor and related costs. Then subtract the total costs of learning to get the net benefit. Table 8.3 shows the calculation of the $316,000 net benefit for the three leadership courses in Table 5.1. (In contrast to Table 8.2, this table represents the plan for the number of participants and increased productivity.)

In either case, it is very important to be transparent with others and share the methodology and assumptions. In a footnote or on a page of explanation, lay out explicitly how you planned the net benefits and be clear about the factors that went into them. Tell the reader how gross benefit was calculated (for example, a 50% contribution to the sales goal from the sales course or a 1.5% increase in productivity for leaders and direct reports from a leadership course) and what costs were included. After reviewing your explanation, the reader should understand what you did and have an opinion about whether it was conservative, optimistic, or about right.

Net Benefit per Person

Net benefit per person is a particularly useful figure and one that others can relate to very easily. Find the net benefit per person by dividing total net benefits by the number of participants. In Table 5.1 the net benefit per person for sales learning is the total net benefit of $893,000 divided by the 100 expected participants, or $8,930 per person. If you calculate the net benefits directly, you may arrive first at the net benefit per person figure and then multiply by the number of participants to find the total net benefits.

Net benefit per person is intuitively appealing because it is easy to grasp, making it good for general communication. No knowledge of ROI is required to give it meaning, and no comparison to a benchmark is required to evaluate it. If people are told that the sales training program will yield a net benefit of $8,930 for every salesperson who takes it, and if they are told that the impact on profit has been very conservatively planned and that all the costs have been included, they can form an opinion about it. It will seem like an investment worth making or not. They may ask how that compares to net benefits of other programs, but the concept is straightforward, and they will engage in the discussion.

It also has the advantage of facilitating calculations. Within a reasonable range, your business plan forecast can be used to tally progress throughout the year. For example, as long as the forecast for participants remains in the neighborhood of 100 (say 90–110), you can use the $8,930 per person to keep track of net benefits. If the first 50 have gone through the course, the estimated benefit is 50 x $8,930 per person or $446,500, which makes monthly reporting much easier. Note, though, that if the forecast of course participants changes significantly (say, to 75 instead of 100), you will have to re-forecast the impact, budget cost, and net benefit. Even if the dollar impact or gross benefit per person has not changed, the cost per person may have increased, reducing your net benefit per person. (Chapter 11 will explore the impact of changing scale on cost in detail.)

Presenting Net Benefits

Planned net benefits were shown in Tables 5.1–5.5 as part of the business case for learning but could easily be pulled out as in Table 8.4, which highlights the impact of learning, the number of unique participants, and the net benefits for the top five programs.

TABLE 8.4

Planned Net Benefits for the 2017 Highest Priority Programs

Training Programs to	*Unique Participants*	*Total Net Benefit (thousands)*
Increase sales by 2%	100	$893
Reduce Defects by 14%	200	$1,018
Reduce Injuries by 15%	3,100	$415
Improve leadership by 2 pts	180	$3166
Increase retention by 1.5 pts	5,000	$3102
Total	5,000	$2,952

For business planning purposes, it is recommended that you 1) compare the current year's estimated results with this year's plan and 2) compare next year's plan with this year's estimated results. The first shows your performance against plan for the current year, and the second shows how next year's plan compares to this year's results.

The comparison of actual to plan for the current year is shown in Table 8.5:

TABLE 8.5

2016 Performance Against Plan for Impact, Participants, and Net Benefits

		2016 Plan					2016 Estimated Actual				
Priority	*Corporate Goal*	*Target*	*Planned Impact of Learning*	*Unique Partici pants*	*Total Partici pants*	*Total Net Benefits (thous.)*	*Result*	*Estimated Impact of Learning*	*Unique Partici pants*	*Total Partici pants*	*Total Net Benefits (thous.)*
1	Reduce Injuries	10%	5%	1,200	4,800	$240	8%	5%	1,167	4,698	$233
2	Reduce Defects	10%	5%	100	300	$400	11%	5%	103	276	$412
3	Increase Sales	5%	3%	120	120	$720	3%	2%	105	105	$420
4	Reduce Mfg Costs	6%	2%	1,400	7,200	$640	5%	3%	1,578	7,256	$900
5	Increase Innovation	4%	1%	200	200	$400	2%	1%	188	188	$383
	Subtotal Top Five Goals			**2,260**	**12,620**	**$2,400**			**2,189**	**12,523**	**$2,348**
	Subtotal Other Goals			1,430	2,996	$912			1,657	2,987	$910
	Total All Goals			2,874	15,616	$3,312			2,997	15,510	$3,258
	Unaligned Learning			3,500	3,500	$0			3,651	3,859	$0
	Other Costs (not included elsewhere)					-$600					-$600
	Grand Total for All Learning			**4,300**	**19,116**	**$2,712**			**4,552**	**19,369**	**$2,658**

This table provides the key information for senior leadership to assess the performance of the learning function by answering the following questions:

1. Did learning have the intended impact on achieving corporate goals?
2. Did learning reach the intended target audience?
3. Did learning deliver the planned net benefits?

In answer to the first question, learning had the expected impact on injuries (5% reduction), defects (5% reduction), and innovation (1% increase), even though corporate results for each were different than plan. Learning had slightly less impact than planned on sales (2% increase versus 3%) but slightly higher impact than expected on manufacturing costs (3% reduction versus 2%).

With regard to the second question, learning reached slightly more unique and total participants than planned (4,552 versus 4,300, and 19,369 versus 19,116, respectively).

Last, learning came close to delivering planned net benefits, falling just $54,000 or 2% short of $2.712 million.

The comparison of next year's plan to this year's estimated actual is shown in Table 8.6. Notice that the 2017 Plan numbers are exactly the same as in Table 5.4, and the 2016 estimated actuals are the same as in Table 8.5 above.

Since the focus here is on the 2017 plan, the top five priorities are the 2017 priorities, not the 2016 priorities. Notice that leadership and retention were not priorities in 2016 although they deteriorated so much that they became priorities for 2017. Data for the other two top five 2016 priorities is included in subtotal other goals. (Remember that Table 8.5 shows the top five for 2016.)

Although it does not make sense to compare the two subtotal lines for 2016 and 2017, it does make sense to look at the grand total and at the three programs that are priorities both years. The grand total line indicates a significant increase in total participants (65%) and net benefits ($722,000 or 27%) for 2017. This is driven by large increases in learning to increase sales and reduce defects and injuries.

TABLE 8.6

2017 Plan versus 2016 Estimated Actuals for Impact, Participants, and Net Benefits

		2016 Estimated Actual					*2017 Plan*				
2017 Priority	***Corporate Goal***	***Results***	***Estimated Impact of Learning***	***Unique Partici pants***	***Total Partici pants***	***Total Net Benefits (thous.)***	***Target***	***Planned Impact of Learning***	***Unique Partici pants***	***Total Partici pants***	***Total Net Benefits (thous.)***
1	Increase Sales	3%	2%	105	105	$420	10%	2%	100	1,100	$893
2	Reduce Defects	11%	5%	103	276	$412	20%	14%	200	800	$1,018
3	Reduce Injuries	8%	5%	1,167	4,698	$233	25%	15%	3,100	13,600	$415
4	Improve Leadership	-2 pts	NA	50	50	NA	+5 pts	+2 pts	180	180	$316
5	Increase Retention	-4 pts	NA	NA	NA	NA	+5 pts	+1.5 pts	5,000	7,500	$310
	Subtotal Top Five Goals			**1,425**	**5,129**	**$1,065**			**5,000**	**23,180**	**$2,952**
	Subtotal Other Goals			2,421	10,381	$2,193			1,950	4,725	$1,028
	Total All Goals			2,997	15,510	$3,258			5,000	27,905	$3,980
	Unaligned Learning			3,651	3,859	0			4,000	4,000	$0
	Other Costs (not included elsewhere)					-$600					-$600
	Grand Total for All Learning			**4,552**	**19,369**	**$2,658**			**5,000**	**31,905**	**$3,380**

Conclusion

Measurement and evaluation are very important but complex topics, which explains why entire books are dedicated to their more complete coverage. The goal of Chapter 8 has been to provide insight into the measures and explore them from a management point of view but not to make you an expert in the methodology. You are encouraged to dig deeper to learn more, and there are many, many resources to help you do that. Even more importantly, you are encouraged to raise the bar in your organization by exploring new measures and enhancing your evaluation strategy. Do not worry about the lack of certainty or the use or forecasts and estimates. Just do it.

Measurement is absolutely essential to ensure that planned results are delivered. Without a robust measurement and evaluation plan in place, you cannot know how you are doing, whether you are likely to make your plan, or where management attention should be directed. It is also the only disciplined way to learn from your experiences so that you can improve.

Chapter 8 to Do List

1. Reflect on the reasons for measurement. Why do you measure today? Should you measure for different reasons in the future?
2. Create a list of your efficiency measures and a list of your effectiveness measures.
3. If you do not have a measurement strategy, create one. Get buy-in from senior leaders.
4. If you are not comfortable with measurement, create an individual learning plan to improve your knowledge and confidence.
5. Consider getting an outside expert to help with your measurement and evaluation.
6. If you are not using sampling today, consider sampling for levels 1, 3, and 4.
7. Consider the use of net benefits for some key programs for which impact can be expressed in dollars.

Further Reading

Allen, Mark, ed. *The Corporate University Handbook: Designing, Managing, and Growing a Successful Program*. New York: Amacom, 2002. (See Chapters 9 and 10.)

Barnett, Kent and Jeffrey Berk. *Human Capital Analytics, Measuring and Improving Talent Development*, second edition. Tarentum, Pennsylvania: Word Association Publishers, 2011.

Bersin, Josh. *The Training Measurement Book: Best Practices, Proven Methodologies, and Practical Approaches*. San Francisco: Pfeiffer, an imprint of Wiley, 2008.

Boslaugh, Sarah and Paul Watters. *Statistics in a Nutshell.* Sebastopol, California: O'Reilly Media, 2008. (See Chapters 7 and 10.)

Capital Analytics and Bellevue University's Human Capital Lab. *Improving the Measurement of Sales Readiness Initiatives.* 2009.

Donnelly, Robert. *Statistics*, second edition. New York: Penguin Group, 2007. (See Chapters 12–14.)

Elkeles, Tamar and Jack Phillips. *The Chief Learning Officer: Driving Value within a Changing Organization through Learning and Development.* Burlington, Massachusetts: Butterworth-Heinemann, 2007. (See Chapter 8.)

Fitz-enz, Jac. *The ROI of Human Capital, Measuring the Economic Value of Employee Performance*, second edition. New York: AMACON, 2009. (Application of measurement and ROI outside the learning field.)

Fitz-enz, Jac and John Mattox II. *Predictive Analytics for Human Resources*. Hoboken, New Jersey: Wiley, 2014. (See Chapters 4 and 5 for use of the TDRp framework for efficiency, effectiveness, and outcome measures.)

Israelite, Larry (Editor). *More Lies About Learning*. Alexandria, Virginia: ATD Press, 2015. (See Chapter 7.)

Kirkpatrick, Donald and James Kirkpatrick. *Evaluating Training Programs: The Four Levels*, third edition. San Francisco: Berrrett-Koehler, 2006.

Kirkpatrick, James and Kirkpatrick, Wendy. *The Kirkpatrick Four Levels: A Fresh Look After 50 Years, 1959–2009.* Whitepaper, April 2009.

——. *Kirkpatrick Then and Now: A Strong Foundation for the Future.* St. Louis: Kirkpatrick Publishing, 2009.

Mattox II, John, Mark Van Buren and Jean Martin. *Learning Analytics*. Philadelphia: Kogan Page, 2016.

McCain, Donald. *Evaluation Basics*. Alexandria, Virginia: ASTD Press, 2005.

Pease, Gene, Boyce Byerly, and Jac Fitz-enz. *Human Capital Analytics*. Hoboken, New Jersey: Wiley, 2013. (See Chapter 7 on Optimization.)

Phillips, Jack. *Handbook of Training Evaluation and Measurement Methods*, third edition. Oxford, United Kingdom: Butterworth-Heinemann, 1997.

———. *Return on Investment in Training and Performance Improvement Programs*, second edition. Oxford, United Kingdom: Butterworth-Heinemann, 2003.

Phillips, Patricia and Jack Phillips. *The Value of Learning: How Organizations Capture Value and ROI and Translate Them into Support, Improvement, and Funds*. San Francisco: Pfeiffer, 2007.

———. *Measuring for Success: What CEOs Really Think about Learning Investments*. Alexandria, Virginia: ASTD Press, 2010.

———. *Measuring ROI in Learning & Development, Case Studies from Global Organizations*. Alexandria, Virginia: ASTD Press, 2012.

———. *Return on (ROI) Investment Basics*. Alexandria, Virginia: ASTD Press, 2005.

Pollock, Roy, Andrew Mck. Jefferson, and Calhoun Wick. *The Six Disciplines of Breakthrough Learning*. Hoboken: John Wiley, 2015. (See Chapter D6.)

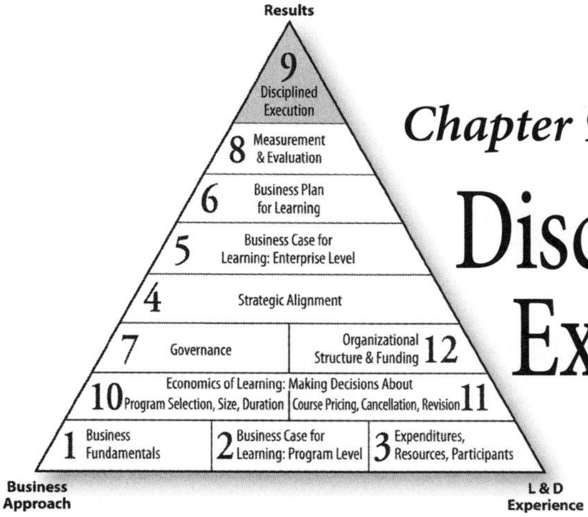

Chapter 9

Disciplined Execution

THE BUSINESS PLAN is complete, and your measurement and evaluation strategy is in place. Now it is time to execute the plan with the discipline to ensure that your goals are realized. Learning is no more difficult to manage in this respect than other aspects of business like sales, but successful execution requires disciplined weekly or monthly processes to review progress and take timely actions. Detailed reporting and scorecards along with clear accountability for specific, measurable goals are the key.

Key Concepts for Chapter 9

1. Specific, measurable goals are required and should come directly from the business plan.
2. Roles and responsibilities must be clear.
3. Processes and accountability are essential to successful execution.
4. Measures must be reviewed on at least a monthly basis, consistently.
5. Reports are the best way to review performance.
6. Reports should contain the measures that are most important and relevant for you this year.
7. Learning is no more difficult to manage than other aspects of business.

Specific, Measurable Goals

Successful execution begins with specific, measurable goals (or plans) and clear accountability for delivering those goals. The importance of specific, measurable goals in executing business strategy was first discussed in Chapter 1, and the process of setting these goals in conjunction with goal owners and senior leaders was explored in chapters four through six. The addition of very specific learning-related measures and the creation of an measurement strategy were explored in Chapter 8. Now, the challenge is to manage the function to meet these goals and deliver the planned results.

Specific, measurable goals or plans will be needed for the outcome, efficiency, and effectiveness measures included in the business plan. The VP of Training may also have additional efficiency and effectiveness goals that were not strategic in nature and thus not included in the business plan but which nonetheless are very important. If a business plan was not created, then the business case should provide goals for the outcome measures and the measurement strategy should provide direction for the efficiency and effectiveness measures. Figure 9.1 provides examples of specific, measurable goals for all three types of measures.

FIGURE 9.1

Examples of Specific, Measurable Goals (Plans)

Organization Goals

- Increase sales by 10%
- Reduce defects by 20%
- Reduce injuries by 25%
- Improve leadership by 5 points
- Improve retention by 5 points

Outcome Measures for Learning

- Increase sales by 2%
- Reduce defects by 14%
- Reduce injuries by 15%
- Improve leadership by 2 points
- Improve retention by 1.5 points

Efficiency Measures for the L&D Department

- Reach 5,000 unique participants
- Reach 31,905 total participants
- Meet 90% of promised development completion dates
- Meet 90% of promised delivery completion dates
- Reduce total cycle time by 10 days
- Reduce number of LMS complaints by 50%
- Increase LMS uptime to 99%
- Reduce LMS support ticket resolution time by 25%
- Limit budget costs to \$4.537 million
- Limit opportunity costs to \$3.674 million

Effectiveness Measures for the L&D Department

- Achieve a level 1 average score of 80% for participants
- Achieve a level 1 average score of 90% for sponsors
- Achieve a level 2 average initial pass rate of 90%
- Achieve a level 3 average intent to apply score of 90%
- Achieve a level 3 average actual application score of 70%
- Achieve a level 4 average initial estimate of impact of 70%
- Achieve a level 4 average final impact of 50%
- Achieve a level 5 average ROI of 41%

Notice that each goal is specific (clearly defines the measure) and measurable (can be measured and compared to the numeric target set for each). There should be no ambiguity at the end of the year over whether the goal was accomplished. (There are some who would say that outcomes are not measurable, but, as we discussed in the last chapter, there are a number of options to measure the isolated impact of learning, including the use of control groups, statistics, and participant estimation.) Also note that the outcome measure goals for learning are simply the planned impact of learning from the business case (Table 5.4). The organization goals, unique participants and total participants may also be found in the business case. The detailed work plans in the sample business plan (Appendix B) also contain the organization goals and outcome measures as well as the plans for the efficiency and effectiveness measures.

Clear Roles and Responsibilities

The next step to disciplined execution is to ensure that everyone clearly understands their roles and responsibilities with respect to achieving the goals.

Goal Owner

The sponsor or owner of a high-level goal will be accountable to the CEO or SVP/EVP for achieving the goal. Progress against the goal will be reviewed regularly and will be an important part of the goal owner's overall performance evaluation. Typically, the owner's merit pay and bonus will depend on their success and, longer term, their likelihood of promotion will depend on how well they execute important organization objectives. Suffice it to say, they have a lot riding on the success of this initiative.

Usually there are many factors that must be managed to achieve a single organizational goal. Learning may be one of several or one of many that contributes to successful execution. With regard to learning, a goal owner has an important role to play to ensure this component is successful. At a minimum, responsibilities would include:

- Meet with the CLO to discuss and agree on the strategic alignment, potential impact of learning, planned impact of learning, target audience, programs and completion dates, cost, and perhaps the gross benefit. Also, agree on the plans for level 1-3 effectiveness measures that will be required to achieve the planned impact.
- In addition, the two need to agree on mutual roles and responsibilities, which clearly identify what each must do to jointly achieve the planned impact (outcome). Neither one can deliver the planned impact from learning by acting alone. The goal owner lacks the learning expertise and since the target audience reports to the goal owner and not L&D, only the goal owner can ensure that the target audience actually takes and applies the training. If both parties are not fully engaged in a partnership, the learning will not be successful and the ROI will be negative.
- Designate a direct report to be responsible for the learning who will be the primary contact or liaison for the learning manager
- Provide subject matter experts and other resources as required, including funding
- Provide input to the learning programs and review and approve them in a timely manner
- Provide input for the measurement strategy
- Own change management, communication, and reinforcement for the target audience
- Determine and enforce positive rewards or negative consequences of not applying the learning
- Ensure the target audience takes the learning if it is mandatory
- Remove roadblocks and act as an advocate for the learning
- Review progress against plan on a monthly basis with the CLO or program manager using reports provided by L&D

CLO or VP for Learning

In addition to general responsibilities for the function as a whole, the CLO has very specific responsibilities to ensure the success of each major learning program in support of organization goals. These responsibilities include:

- Meet with the goal's owner to:
    - Ensure that the learning program is strategically aligned and will contribute to achieving the goal
    - Agree on the target audience, courses, and number of participants
    - Agree on completion dates
    - Agree on planned impact of learning, cost, and perhaps gross benefit
    - Agree on the plans for level 1-3 effectiveness measures that will be required to achieve the planned impact.
    - Discuss and agree on mutual roles and responsibilities required for success (see above)
    - Review progress as the initiative progresses
    - Close out project, review measures, agree on final impact (gross benefit if applicable), and capture lessons learned
- Assign a direct report to be the program manager responsible for the learning initiative
    - Include as a formal performance goal for the program manager
- Meet with the program manager to
    - Agree on targets or plans for the efficiency and effectiveness measures required for success
    - Agree on planned gross and net benefit if applicable
    - Discuss and agree on what help the CLO will provide
    - Discuss and agree on resources required for success
    - Remove roadblocks
- Meet with the goal owner and program manager throughout the year to ensure the program is on track to meet established goals. When the impact of learning is falling short of plan, or it appears it will fall short of plan by year end, work with the goal owner and program manager to take appropriate corrective actions.

The CLO also is responsible for deciding which efficiency and effectiveness improvements to make in the coming year for the department. Examples are in Figure 9.1 and might include reduced cycle times, improvements in meeting deadlines, increased uptime for learning systems, and higher level 1-5 effectiveness scores. Once measures are chosen for improvement, the CLO must:

- Work with her team to set specific, measurable goals or plans for each measure
- Ensure sufficient resources are provided to accomplish each goal
- Assign responsibility for each goal
    - o Incorporate goal into the responsible person's formal performance goals
- Ensure a reporting system exists to manage performance against goal on a monthly basis
- Use reports to actively manage performance against plan on a monthly basis to ensure that the goals for the effectiveness and efficiency measures are reached

Program Manager or College Dean

The program manager, or person with direct responsibility for the program, will have the most specific, measurable goals associated with the learning initiative. While the CLO was involved in discussions with the goal owner during the alignment and planning phase, the program manager will be responsible for developing the detailed work plan and then successfully executing the learning on a daily basis. Responsibilities would include:

- Attend the planning meetings with the CLO and goal owner
- In conjunction with the goal owner's learning liaison and the CLO, create and revise the planned learning program, target audience, start and completion dates, required resources, planned impact, costs, and gross and net benefit (if applicable). Also, recommend plans for level 1-3 effectiveness measures that will be required to achieve the planned impact.
- Review the goal owner's change management, communication and reinforcement plans, and suggest changes if needed
- Recommend measurement strategy to the CLO (and perhaps to the goal owner if interested)

- Create monthly reports to show progress against plan for the outcome measure (planned impact on the organization goal) and the efficiency and effectiveness measures required to achieve the desired outcome. Share with the liaison and the CLO.
- Meet at least monthly with the CLO to review progress against plan (may be in a staff meeting where all key programs are reviewed).
- Meet with the goal owner's liaison for learning on a regular basis to review progress

Summary

It is critical that the goal owner, CLO, and program manager all understand their roles and the roles of the other two as well if the planned impact on an organization goal is to be achieved. These three figures in particular must understand and agree on their roles before the learning program can begin. If they don't, then the program runs a high risk of not achieving all its goals, and the blame (rightly or wrongly) almost always goes to the learning function. Clarity is so important that it is worth first discussing the different roles and then committing them to paper. Some learning organizations ask the goal owner to sign a project document with roles and responsibilities as well as goals clearly defined. See Appendix D for an example of roles and responsibilities for each party.

Disciplined, Data-Driven Process

Once specific, measurable goals have been established and roles and responsibilities have been clearly defined, the key to successful execution of a business plan is a disciplined, data-driven process.

Disciplined

"Disciplined" means that there is a regular, predictable process with clear rules and expectations. For example, the CLO might review progress against goals with her direct reports the second Tuesday of every month from 8 A.M. to 10 A.M. Each program manager would report on progress against their program goals. Whenever a program was not meeting a goal, the program manager would explain why and what he was doing about it. The group would offer other suggestions. Each program manager would also share lessons learned and other insights. Others would report on the initiatives to achieve the efficiency and effectiveness goals.

The above process would be disciplined if the results meeting always occurred on the second Tuesday from 8–10 A.M. There may be other staff meetings, but this meeting should always be dedicated to a review of results, which means that the meetings can be scheduled years in advance—no excuses for conflicts! The agenda is always the same, and the participants know exactly what to expect. They know they will have to explain under-performing programs or initiatives and offer solutions. Consequently, they and their staff will be prepared for these meeting, which will make them very productive. It also makes it easy for a substitute to be productive because they know exactly what they will have to do.

This sounds simple and obvious. For many it is, and they would not think of managing any other way. Still, there are others who have not yet established a disciplined process. The alternative is an ad hoc process with meetings that may be scheduled with little notice and perhaps in response to an issue that sends staff scrambling. In other cases the results review may be combined with a regular staff meeting, which eliminates the special focus on results and may shortchange their review, depending on other agenda items.

Successful execution requires a disciplined process. The CLO must establish that process, nurture it, and reinforce it. Although the actual process will differ by organization, results should be compared to plan at least monthly. And in most organizations there is tremendous benefit in the CLO conducting this review with her senior learning managers as a group. They will learn from each other, and it reinforces the accountability.

> CATERPILLAR EXPERIENCE: The senior learning leaders met regularly every Tuesday from 8–10 A.M. The second Tuesday of each month was dedicated to a review of progress against goals. No other agenda items were considered. These meetings were scheduled for the whole year in advance.

Data Driven

The other key factor for success is that the process be data driven. By definition the specific, measurable goals are quantifiable, and progress against those goals needs to be quantified. The only way to do that is with data.

A learning management system should be able to collect virtually all the efficiency (level 0) measures you need to manage the function. These include the number of participants (unique and total), courses, completions, and participant demographics (location, business unit, and so on) as well as data on when courses have been put into use and retired. Most LMSs can also gather the level 2 results for online courses. With automated surveying levels 1, 2, and 3 should be available electronically even if the LMS did not offer that feature.

Of course, the challenge is greater if an LMS is not available for some or all of the participants. In this case more manual data gathering and analysis will have to be performed, which may limit how much is done and how timely it will be. If you are not able to collect level 1-3 data for all participants, focus first on the highest-priority aligned learning courses and second on the remainder of the aligned learning.

In any case, the available data will be presented on at least a monthly basis to determine progress toward goals. Some may be estimated or incomplete, which is okay. Just be sure the data is appropriately labeled, and update it when new information becomes available. (Note: We will use the terms report and scorecard interchangeably. A distinction will be made, however, between reports and dashboards. Dashboards typically are more visual in their presentation, often including dials with needles showing results. The name, of course, comes from the dashboard in a car where the driver gleans important information about the speed of the car from the speedometer in the dashboard. While dashboards satisfy the desire for a more visually pleasing presentation of the data, few can clearly show plan, YTD results, and forecast. Consequently, we will focus on reports.)

Use of Reports

A data-driven process requires data and the best way to manage all of this data is through the use of reports or scorecards which are focused on the most important information. An analogy can be made with the first paragraph in a newspaper article, wherein a journalist tries to convey the essence of a story in case a reader doesn't have time to read more. Likewise, a report or scorecard should provide the essential information about progress toward goals.

(Note: We will use the terms report and scorecard interchangeably. A distinction will be made, however, between reports and dashboards. Dashboards typically are more visual in their presentation, often including dials with needles showing results. The name, of course, comes from the dashboard in a car where the driver gleans important information about the speed of the car from the speedometer in the dashboard. While dashboards satisfy the desire for a more visually pleasing presentation of the data, few can clearly show plan, YTD results, and forecast. Consequently, we will focus on reports.)

Reporting Basics

Reports typically will be one or two pages in length and may contain ten to twenty measures. They may be on paper or in PowerPoint. They may also be layered with lower level reports providing more detailed information.

Reports should be constructed to focus on what is important for the current year and should include measures that tie back to the goals in a business plan for learning. Since space is so limited, a learning manager has to make a very conscious decision what to include that will reflect his own priorities for the year. Consequently, an organization's reports will be unique since no other organization has exactly the same goals or priorities. Be wary of adopting a generic report or a recommended "balanced" scorecard. Make the report fit your own needs for this year. If that does not include some of the recommended categories or line items, so be it.

Reports for the active management of a program or department should be designed to answer two primary questions:

1. How are we doing year-to-date compared to plan?
2. How is the year likely to end? Or: What is the forecast?

The answer to the first question tells us whether we are on track so far. If not, the discussion will turn to why and what can be done to get back on track. The second answer takes into account the first answer and projects results through the end of the year. If the forecast is still below plan, it may trigger more discussion about what else can be done and whether it is worth doing.

To answer these two questions, reports need to include at least the annual plan (goal or target) and year-to-date (YTD) results. Typically, last year's results will also be included, and the YTD results will be expressed as a percentage of plan. Some reports show YTD plan and compare YTD results against YTD plan instead of annual plan. The report should also contain a forecast for the year, and some will express the forecast as a percentage of plan. (See Chapter 1 for more information on scorecards in general.)

There are two levels and at least three types of reports required for learning. The first level is an executive report to be used by program managers, CLOs, and senior company leaders to actively manage the learning in order to deliver planned results. This executive report will include the key measures to be managed and will typically be generated monthly. It will include last year's results when available, this year's plan, year-to-date results, a comparison of YTD results to plan, and ideally a forecast of how the year is expected to end if no special action is taken. (Special action means staff, budget, or effort not included in the business plan or not previously approved.) The second level is a detailed report, which may be generated only on as-needed basis or it may be a report that is not regularly used by the program manager or CLO. This detailed report would not typically include a plan or forecast since the measures in it are not as important as those in the executive report and are not being managed on a monthly basis.

The three types reflect the different audiences for the reports and the different types of measures. The first type is a program report used by program managers, the CLO, and the goal owner, which focuses on efficiency, effectiveness, and outcome measures at an individual program level. The second type is an operations report used by the CLO, which focuses on efficiency and effectiveness measures aggregated across all programs or initiatives. The third type is a summary report showing alignment of learning programs to the organization's goals, impact on those goals (outcome measures), and the most important efficiency and effectiveness measures aggregated across all programs. The audience for the summary report might include the CEO, CFO, board of governors, CLO, L&D employees, and others interested in learning.

We will focus on the executive level reports and employ the Talent Development Reporting Principles (TDRp) framework. See Appendix C for an introduction to TDRp.

TDRp Reports

Following the schema above, TDRp calls for three executive reports: Program, Operations, and Summary. This is similar to accounting which has three statements: Income (or Profit & Loss), Balance Sheet, and Cash Flow. The TDRp reports organize the three types of measures (outcome, efficiency, and effectiveness) by target audience and purpose. The executive-level program report is designed to be used by the program manager and CLO on at least a monthly basis to manage the programs and initiatives in support of an individual organization goal such as increasing sales by 10%. A typical L&D department may have 3-10 program reports, depending on how many organization goals learning supports. The executive-level operations report is designed to be used by the CLO on at least a monthly basis to manage the department initiatives to increase efficiency and effectiveness. The summary report is designed to be shared with senior company leaders to show the alignment of learning to company goals, the impact of learning on company goals, and the most important efficiency and effectiveness measures at an aggregate level. The characteristics of the three reports are summarized in Figure 9.2.

Figure 9.2

The Three Executive-level TDRp Reports

	Program	***Operations***	***Summary***
Measures	Outcome Efficiency Effectiveness	Efficiency Effectiveness	Outcome Efficiency Effectiveness
Level of Data Aggregation	Learning specific to programs in support of one organization goal	All learning	All learning
Target Audience	Program Managers CLO Goal Owner	CLO	CEO, CFO SVP of HR Governing Board CLO L&D Employees
Purpose	Manage the efficiency and effectiveness measures to deliver the planned outcome	Manage the efficiency and effectiveness measures to deliver planned improvements	Demonstrate alignment and impact of learning Share improvements in efficiency and effectiveness

We will examine each executive-level report in detail starting with the program report.

Program Report

The program report is be used to manage the programs or initiatives in support of a particular organization goal, such as reducing injuries by 25%. It includes the programs, the organization goal, the goal owner's name, impact of the programs on the goal (the outcome measure), and the efficiency and effectiveness measures, which must be successfully managed to deliver the planned impact. The program report is designed to be used by the program manager and CLO on a monthly basis to manage programs. Goal owners and their staff will also be interested in it.

A simple program report is presented in Table 9.1. It contains one outcome measure (impact of learning), four efficiency measures (development completion date, unique participants, total participants, and delivery completion date), and three effectiveness measures (levels 1-3). As an executive-level report, it contains last year's actuals (2016 results), this year's plan (2017 plan), year-to-date results (YTD), a comparison of YTD results to plan, forecast, and a comparison of forecast to plan.

The report includes two courses in support of the goal to reduce injuries by 25%. Let's examine the report in detail working our way down the rows. We will focus first on construction of the report and the plan column, and then examine the year-to-date results and forecast. (Note: This program report does not employ all the data in the sample business plan or from chapters 4 and 5. Figure 9.2 will provide an example that is consistent with the all data from the book.)

It is important to start the program report with the organization goal and the outcome measure (impact of learning on the goal). This reminds the reader why this course was funded; namely, the course is expected to help reduce injuries. The top line provides the sponsor or goal owner's name: Swilthe, who is the VP of manufacturing. The course will not have the planned impact without Swilthe's very active involvement. The second line provides the organization goal: reduce injuries by 25%. The CEO and board of directors expect Swilthe to deliver the planned 25% reduction in injuries. The third line, importantly located right below the second, provides the outcome measure, which is the planned impact of the learning on the goal of reducing injuries. In this example, the learning is planned to have a high impact on the goal, meaning that learning is expected to be the dominant driver behind the reduction in injuries. (Recall that this is an example of a qualitative outcome measure. Alternatively, a quantitative outcome measure may be used such as a 15% reduction in injuries due to learning.) The outcome measure should always appear adjacent to the organization goal.

TABLE 9.1

Simple Program Report for Reducing Injuries

Results through June

Goal Owner: Swilthe, VP of manufacturing	Metric	2016 Actual	2017 Plan	YTD Results	YTD Compared to Plan	Forecast	Forecast Compared to Plan	Notes
Enterprise Goal: Reduce Injuries	%	8%	25%	10%	Below Plan	22%	88%	
Impact of Learning: High contribution for 2017	%	High	High		Below Plan		Near Plan	YTD and FC contribution based on level 1 and 3 results and ongoing discussions with sponsor

Programs to Reduce Injuries	Metric	2016 Actual	2017 Plan	YTD Results	YTD Compared to Plan	Forecast	Forecast Compared to Plan	Notes
Develop Two Courses								
Efficiency measure: Complete by 1/31	Number	NA	2	2	100%	2	100%	Both completed on January 29
Deliver Two Courses								
Efficiency measures								
Unique Participants	Number	452	3,000	2,800	93%	3,200	107%	Manufacturing leaders reponsible for attendance
Total Participants	Number	858	6,000	5,542	92%	6,300	105%	
Percentage complete by 3/31	%	NA	95%	92%	3% below	92%	3% below	100% completion achieved on April 22
Effectiveness measures								
Level 1: Participants	%	70%	80%	85%	5% above	82%	2% above	YTD sample size = 1872
Level 2: Test score	%	86%	90%	95%	5% above	92%	2% above	YTD sample size = 3848
Level 3: Application rate	%	53%	95%	75%	20% below	90%	5% below	YTD sample size = 270. Reinforcement plan in place

The next section shows the programs planned to achieve the high reduction in injuries. In this example, the program consists of just two courses. However, the courses must first be developed so "Develop Courses" appears as the first program activity. The chosen efficiency measure is the completion date and the specific, measurable goal is to have both courses developed by January 31. The second activity is to deliver the courses. In order to have a high impact on reducing injuries, Swilthe, the CLO, and the program manager all agree that the courses must be taken by 3000 employees. Since each employee must take both courses, total participants is 6000 (3000 x 2). Further, to have high impact, 95% must complete the courses by March 31, which is early enough in the year to significantly reduce injuries over the final nine months. Last, to have a high impact the effectiveness scores must be high. Specifically, level 1 must be 80% (they have to like it and believe it is relevant), level 2 must be 90% (high scores on the knowledge test), and level 3 must be 95% (nearly everyone must actually apply this impactful learning). The efficiency and effectiveness measures are integrally related to the outcome measure. If the learning is not delivered by March 31, or the right 3000 employees don't take both courses, or if they don't like it, learn it, and apply it, then the learning will not have the planned high impact on the goal, and company injuries will not be reduced by 25%.

That is the plan. Now, what is actually happening? In July, with six months of data for January through June, it appears that the reduction in injuries is below plan and that learning is having a below plan impact. Why? Both courses were developed on time so that is not the issue. Nearly all (92%) planned participants were reached by March 31 (100% completion achieved April 22) so that is not the issue. Participants like the learning (85% for level 1, 5 points above plan) and are testing above plan (95% versus 90%) so these are not the issue. Application is the problem. Nearly everyone must apply the new safe behaviors if injuries are going to be reduced significantly. Unfortunately, only 75% are applying their newly learned safe behaviors. This is why the year-to-date outcome measure is characterized as "Below Plan". The good news is that Swilthe, the CLO, and the program manager believe that the new reinforcement plans will dramatically boost application in the last six months allowing for a 90% overall application rate, just 5% below plan. Combined with deploying the training to more participants than plan (107%), the three leaders forecast that learning's impact will end the year "Near Plan" contributing to a 22% reduction in injuries, just shy of the planned 25% reduction.

TABLE 9.2

Program Report for Increasing Sales
(Consistent with the Sample Business Plan in Appendix B)

Results through June

Goal Owner: Ortega, VP of sales	*Metric*	*2016 Actual*	*2017 Plan*	*YTD Results*	*YTD Compared to Plan*	*Forecast*	*Forecast Compared to Plan*	*Notes*
Enterprise Goal: Increase Sales	%	3%	10%	4%	On Plan	10%	On Plan	
Impact of Learning: 20% contribution for 2017	%	2%	2%		On Plan		On Plan	YTD and FC impacts based on level 1 and 3 results and ongoing discussions with sponsor

Programs to Increase Sales	*Metric*	*2016 Actual*	*2017 Plan*	*YTD Results*	*YTD Compared to Plan*	*Forecast*	*Forecast Compared to Plan*	*Notes*
Develop Consultative Selling Skills Course								
Efficiency measure: Complete by 3/31	Number	NA	1	1	100%	1	100%	Completed on February 27
Deliver Consultative Selling Skills								
Efficiency measures								
Unique Participants	Number	0	100	102	102%	105	105%	Sales leaders reponsible for attendance
Total Participants	Number	0	100	102	102%	105	105%	
Percentage complete by 4/30	%	NA	100%	102%	2% below	102%	2% above	
Effectiveness measures								
Level 1: Participants	%	NA	80%	85%	5% above	85%	5% above	YTD sample size = 43
Sponsor	%	NA	90%	90%	On Plan	90%	On Plan	
Level 2: Test score	%	NA	90%	85%	5% below	85%	5% below	YTD sample size = 102
Level 3: Application rate	%	NA	85%	80%	5% below	83%	2% below	YTD sample size = 67. Reinforcement plan in place

	Metric	2016 Actual	2017 Plan	YTD Results	YTD Compared to Plan	Forecast	Forecast Compared to Plan	Notes
Develop 10 New Product Introduction Modules								
Efficiency measure: Complete by 4/30	Number	NA	10	10	100%	10	100%	Completed on April 15
Deliver 10 New Product Introduction Modules								
Efficiency measures								
Unique Participants	Number	120	100	102	102%	105	105%	Sales leaders reponsible for attendance
Total Participants	Number	120	1,000	945	95%	1,050	105%	
Percentage complete by 5/31	%	NA	100%	95%	5% below	95%	5% below	
Effectiveness measures								
Level 1: Participants	%	120	80%	79%	1% below	79%	1% below	YTD sample size = 47
Sponsor	%	120	90%	80%	10% below	88%	2% below	
Level 2: Test score	%	NA	90%	92%	2% above	92%	2% above	YTD sample size = 945
Level 3: Application rate	%	NA	85%	75%	10% below	80%	5% below	YTD sample size = 43. Reinforcement plan in place
Summary								
Total								
Courses/modules Developed	Number	NA	11	11	100%	11	100%	
Unique Participants	Number	120	100	102	102%	105	105%	
Total Participants	Number	120	1,100	1,047	95%	1,155	105%	
Cost (including opportunity cost)	Thousand $	$78	$607	$547	90%	$547	90%	
Level 4: Impact	%	NA	20%	19%	1% below	20%	On Plan	YTD sample size = 43
Net Benefit	Thousand $	NA	$893	$953	107%	$953	107%	
ROI	%	NA	147%	174%	Above Plan	174%	Above Plan	

A more complex program report is presented in Table 9.2. The report is constructed just like the simpler version in Table 9.1, but this report includes four activities in support of the goal. Consequently, while there is still just one outcome measure (impact of learning), there are now twelve efficiency measures and eleven effectiveness measures. (Actually, there are only five unique efficiency measures and seven unique effectiveness measures, but the measures are used for multiple programs.) Measures and data for this table are pulled from the business case in Table 5.4 and the sample business plan for learning in Appendix B.

The organization goal in this case is to increase sales by 10%. A quantitative outcome measure is employed here and the plan is to have learning contribute 20% towards the achievement of the goal, resulting in a 2% increase in sales just due to learning. Two programs will be developed and delivered to achieve this 2% increase in sales. The first is a consultative selling skills course, which is described in the Detailed Work Plan in the sample business plan. One efficiency measure (completion date) will be used for development to ensure it is developed on time. Three efficiency measures will be used to manage delivery including unique and total participants and completion. All 100 sales representatives must complete the course by April 30 if it is to have the planned impact. Four effectiveness measures will also be used to ensure the course delivers its planned impact on sales, including participant and sponsor satisfaction, test scores, and application rate. Bottom line, 85% of the 100 reps need to successfully apply the learning to make the 20% contribution toward the goal.

The second program consists of 10 new product introduction (NPI) modules to enable the reps to sell the value of the features in the new products being introduced. The 10 modules need to be developed by April 30 and then delivered to all 100 reps by May 31. Since each rep will take all 10 modules, total participants will be 100 x 10 = 1000. These will be the four efficiency measures for the second program. The four effectiveness measures will be levels 1-3 with level 1 for both participants and the goal owner, Ortega. Just as with the first program, the participants and owner need to be highly satisfied with the program, and the participants need to master the key learning objectives and then successfully apply the learning.

Since there are multiple programs, Table 9.2 includes a summary at the bottom which contains four efficiency measures (total number of courses/modules developed, total unique participants, total participants, and cost). It also includes three effectiveness measures (impact, net benefit, and ROI). Level 4 impact is the participant's estimate of the contribution toward higher sales due to the two courses and is best reported for both programs combined rather than each individually. If these two programs are not developed and delivered on time, or if the 100 reps do not take them, or if the quality is low and there is little application, then this $607,000 investment is unlikely to have the 20% planned impact resulting in a 2% increase in sales, and it is unlikely to deliver a 147% return.

The report shows that the two programs are on plan to deliver the planned 2% increase in sales. How do we know that? First, look at the chain of evidence provided by the efficiency and effectiveness measures. All 11 courses/modules were developed on time. Second, we achieved plan to have all 100 participants through the first course on time (actually, we had 102), and we were near plan for the 100 to each take 10 NPI modules (95% complete by May 31 and 100% complete by June 15) with the forecast showing 1050 by year end. The year-to-date application rates are just slightly below plan (5% below for the first program and 10% below for the second), but the forecast shows that these rates will improve in the second half due to new reinforcement plans which should result in achieving an 83% application rate for the first program and an 80% rate for the second, both very close to plan. So, these "leading indicators" of impact show that we are accomplishing what Ortega, the CLO, and the program manager all believed would be required to deliver a 2% increase in sales. Last, supplement the chain of evidence provided by the level 0-3 measures with the level 4 participant-reported isolated contribution to sales gathered from the reps two to three months after completing the second course. They are reporting that what they learned in both programs is responsible for 19% of their increased sales which is close to the planned 20% contribution. Combining all these measures, we have a very strong case that learning is indeed leading to a 2% increase in sales.

ADVICE: There will be times when progress is not being made on the corporate goal and when learning is still delivering value. Suppose sales were down 2% instead of up 6%. That may reflect a poor design and delivery of the learning, or it may reflect a host of other factors. It may be that without the learning sales would be down 8%, so learning is still contributing to increased sales, but other factors are proving to be even more powerful. Given the unknowns, the natural inclination may be to ignore the issue (after all, who knows what is really happening?), but that would be a mistake. It is better to use the scorecard to force a discussion on the issue and then try to identify what is driving the unforeseen decline in sales. Without this discussion, some people may just assume it was poor learning or that that learning does not impact sales. Better to get the issues on the table and reach consensus that the cause is not poor learning but rather some external driver like an unforeseen drop in industry demand due to a financial crisis.

Operations Report

The operations report is used to manage improvements in efficiency and effectiveness measures or to reach planned levels for each. In contrast to the program report, which focuses just on specific programs to achieve business goals, the operations report contains efficiency and effectiveness measures aggregated across all the courses for which data are available. For most efficiency measures the aggregate values will be counts or sums such as the number of unique participants reached by learning across the company or the total number of courses offered. For most effectiveness measures the aggregate values will be the simple average such as the average level of participant reaction, the average application rate, or the average ROI across all courses for which data have been collected. (In a simple average each course has the same weight. Just add up the effectiveness scores for all the courses and divide by the number of courses. In contrast, a weighted average weights the courses scores by the number of participants in each course. So a simple average would value the feedback from a course with 10 participants the same as that from a course with 500 participants. A weighted average would value the feedback from 500 participants as 50 times more important than the feedback from 10 participants.) The operations report is designed to be run monthly and used by the CLO to actively manage the handful of efficiency and effectiveness measures that have been targeted for improvement. Data may not be available for all courses for some of the selected measures, in which case simply let the reader know that data is for selected programs only. Ideally, the selected measures will fit on one page but should certainly not exceed one and one-half pages, since considerable effort is required to drive improvement in just a few measures.

A simple operations report is presented in Table 9.3. Efficiency measures are at the top but the order can be reversed. The columns are standard for TDRp reports: unit of measure, last year's actual, plan for this year, year-to-date results,

TABLE 9.3

Simple Operations Report for L&D

Results Through June

Efficiency Measures	Unit of Measure	2016 Actual	For 2017 Plan	Jun YTD Results	Comparison to Plan	Forecast	Comparison to Plan
Total Participants	Number	19,369	31,905	14,589	46%	31,000	97%
Total Unique Participants	Number	4,552	5,000	3,426	69%	5,000	100%
Course Management							
Total Developed or Revised	Number	34	43	24	56%	40	93%
Number Meeting Deadline	Number	24	43	21	49%	35	81%
% Meeting Deadline	%	71%	100%	88%	12% below	88%	12% below
Total Delivered	Number	212	250	132	53%	235	94%
Number Meeting Deadline	Number	137	250	112	45%	205	82%
% Meeting Deadline	%	65%	100%	85%	15% below	87%	13% below
LMS							
Complaints	Number	214	107	45	42%	80	27 below
Uptime	%	96%	99%	98%	1% below	99%	On Plan
Support ticket resolution time	Hours	32	24	27	3 above	21	3 below
Costs (Budget)	Thousands $	$3,815	$4,537	$2,896	64%	$4,300	95%

Effectiveness Measures	Unit of Measure	2016 Actual	For 2017 Plan	Jun YTD Results	Comparison to Plan	Forecast	Comparison to Plan
Level 1: Participant Reaction (All programs)							
Quality of content	% favorable	76%	80%	79%	1% below	79%	1% below
Quality of instructor	% favorable	80%	85%	86%	1% above	85%	On Plan
Relevance	% favorable	72%	78%	73%	5% below	75%	3% below
Alignment to goals	% favorable	68%	75%	69%	6% below	71%	4% below
Total for Level 1	Average of measures	74%	80%	77%	3% below	78%	2% below
Level 1: Sponsor Feedback (Select programs)	% favorable	76%	90%	81%	9% below	85%	5% below
Level 2: Learning (Select programs)	Score	82%	90%	85%	5% below	88%	2% below
Level 3: Application rate (Select programs)							
Intent to apply (from survey at end of course)	% top two boxes	70%	90%	78%	12% below	84%	6% below
Actual application (after three months)	% who applied it	51%	70%	61%	9% below	67%	3% below

comparison of year-to-date results to plan, forecast, and comparison of forecast to plan. As always, the report will be used to answer two questions: 1) Are we on plan? and 2) Are we going to make plan for the year? Selected measures come from the business plan, particularly the detailed work plan, and measurement and evaluation strategy. In practice, the CLO would meet with her team at the start of the year to select measures for improvement. Advice is to start with just a few, perhaps 3-5 each for efficiency and effectiveness. The team can tackle additional measures the following year. The measures in Table 9.3 come from the sample business plan in Appendix B (the plans can also be found in Figure 9.1).

We will start with the efficiency measures. Total and unique participants come directly from the business case in Table 6 of the sample business plan (Table 6 in Appendix B is identical to Table 5.4). The plan calls for reaching 5000 employees and, given that many programs consist of multiple courses, total participants are planned to be 31,905. These two efficiency measures are obvious choices since they are in the business case. Next are measures focused on course management, including number developed and delivered, number meeting deadline, and percentage meeting deadline. The number to be developed or revised (43) comes from Table 6. The 250 to be delivered cannot be found in Table 6 but would be developed by the learning leadership team. The team has decided to plan on 100% being both developed and delivered on time (an aggressive goal!). Next are measures related to the learning management system (LMS). Since complaints have been high and uptime has been an issue, the CLO has targeted this area for improvement. Plan is to reduce complaints by 50% to 107, and increase uptime by three percentage points to 99%. Plans also call for reducing support ticket resolution time by 25% to 24 hours. Last, the CLO needs to manage costs to not exceed $4.537 million.

Effectiveness measures are found at the bottom of the page, starting with level 1 participant reaction or satisfaction. The learning leadership team has looked at industry benchmarks and believes improvements are possible and worthwhile not just for level 1 but all three levels. They have set a goal to improve level 1 reaction by participants by six percentage points to 80% and level 2 learning by eight points to 90%. Further, they want the all-important level 3 application rate to increase by 20 points to 90% for intent to apply and by 19 points to 70% for actual application. Finally, the team wants to improve its performance in the eyes of the goal owners, which will be reflected in the level 1 sponsor feedback increasing by 14 points to 90%.

The team created action plans to achieve the planned improvements in both the efficiency and effectiveness measures, and the CLO assigned responsibilities to ensure the planned improvements would occur. How are we doing? The report reflects data through June so we would expect to be near the halfway point in accomplishing the plans. Learning has reached 69% of the planned unique participants and 46% of total participants. To evaluate whether we are on plan we really need to know what percentage of participants have been reached by June 30 in past years. If we typically reach about 70% of total-year participants in the first six months, then we are on plan. If we typically reach 80% then we may be in trouble. The forecast would incorporate this knowledge and indicates that we should reach all 5000 by year end, although it does show us falling 3% short on total participants, which is still very close to plan. Courses developed and delivered appear to be on plan year-to-date, and the forecast shows us coming close to plan by year end, falling just 3 courses short of plan for development and 15 courses short for delivery. However, we are considerably below plan year-to-date meeting deadlines for both development and delivery (12% and 15% respectively). Furthermore, the forecast shows that we are not going to improve much in the second half. This indicates that the CLO and learning leaders need to dig deeper into what is preventing us from achieving our plans to meet deadlines. It may still be possible to improve second-half performance if actions are taken now. On the other hand, we are doing better than plan in reducing LMS complaints and resolving support tickets, and we are on plan to improve uptimes. Forecasts show us holding these gains through year end or improving even further. Last, we have spent more than 50% of our budgeted costs but this would be typical with development front-end loaded. The forecast for cost shows ending the year below plan, so no worries there.

The report shows that we are below plan on all of our effectiveness measures and unlikely to make up the difference by year end. Participant level 1 is 3% below plan year-to-date and forecast to end 2% below plan. Likewise, sponsor level 1 is 9% below plan and forecast to end the year 5% below plan. Level 2 learning is 5% below through June and expected to end 2% below. The biggest shortfalls are in level 3 application where intent to apply is 12% below plan and actual application is 9% below. Forecast indicates improvement in the second half, but we still end the year 6% below on intent and 3% below for actual application. In practice, effort would be focused on application and the team needs to determine if there is anything else that can be done. Given the shortfall in the first six months, this may be the best that is possible for the twelve months.

You can see how the operations report focuses your attention on the measures that are underperforming. You can immediately tell where you are not on plan and the forecast tells you whether special actions will be necessary to get back on plan by year end. The report provides all the leadership team needs to isolate issues and begin the discussion of what to do about measures that are coming in below plan.

An expanded operations report is presented in Table 9.4 which contains all the efficiency and effectiveness measures from the sample business plan for learning in Appendix B. The format is the same but cycle time and cost measures have been added in the efficiency portion, and level 4 and 5 measures have been added in the effectiveness portion. Practically speaking, this is probably the upper limit for the number of measures that should be included in an operations report. It would be very difficult to manage any more throughout the year.

Improvement in cycle time measures would be important in meeting deadlines, so measures have been included for performance consulting (or needs analysis), development, and delivery. Improvement is targeted for performance analysis (two days) and development (eight days) for a total improvement of 10 days. Opportunity costs have also been added as an efficiency measure to be managed. On the effectiveness side, significant improvements are planned for level 4 impact and level 5 net benefits and ROI. Plans call for improving initial estimates of impact by 18 percentage points to 70% and for improving the final estimate by 18 points to 50%. This should lead to a significant improvement in net benefits to $3.38 million and an improvement in ROI to 41%.

The report indicates that improvement has been made in performance consulting (one day) and the forecast shows the planned two-day improvement. The cycle time for development has improved by five days but the forecast still shows it falling short of plan by two days. This is a significant improvement over last year but the team may still be able to identify some special action to come closer to plan by year end. Opportunity cost, like budget cost, is forecast to come in under plan and in line with development and delivery, also coming in under plan. Looking at the effectiveness measures, the initial estimate of impact has increased by 10 points to 62% and the final estimate has increased by 14 points, both very significant improvements that the team should celebrate. Forecast shows plans being achieved for both by year end so no need to spend more time on these measures. Likewise, net benefits and ROI are both in good shape year-to-date and the forecasts show both exceeding plan by year end.

TABLE 9.4

Expanded Operations Report for L&D
(Consistent with Table 5.4 and the Sample Business Plan in Appendix B)

Results Through June

			For 2017				
Efficiency Measures	*Unit of Measure*	*2016 Actual*	*Plan*	*Jun YTD Results*	*Comparison to Plan*	*Forecast*	*Comparison to Plan*
Total Participants	Number	19,369	31,905	14,589	46%	31,000	97%
Total Unique Participants	Number	4,552	5,000	3,426	69%	5,000	100%
Course Management							
Total Developed or Revised	Number	34	43	24	56%	40	93%
Number Meeting Deadline	Number	24	43	21	49%	35	81%
% Meeting Deadline	%	71%	100%	88%	12% below	88%	12% below
Total Delivered	Number	212	250	132	53%	235	94%
Number Meeting Deadline	Number	137	250	112	45%	205	82%
% Meeting Deadline	%	65%	100%	85%	15% below	87%	13% below
Cycle time							
Performance consulting (needs analysis)	Days	15	13	14	1 above	13	On Plan
Development	Days	40	32	35	3 above	34	2 above
Delivery	Days	10	10	10	On Plan	10	On Plan
Total	Days	65	55	59	4 above	57	2 above
LMS							
Complaints	Number	214	107	45	42%	80	27 below
Uptime	%	96%	99%	98%	1% below	99%	On Plan
Support ticket resolution time	Hours	32	24	27	3 above	21	3 below
Costs							
Budget	Thousands $	$3,790	$4,537	$2,896	64%	$4,300	95%
Opportunity	Thousands $	$3,025	$3,634	$1,689	46%	$3,500	96%
Total	Thousands $	$6,815	$8,171	$4,585	56%	$7,800	95%

TABLE 9.4 (continued)

Effectiveness Measures	Unit of Measure	2016 Actual	For 2017 Plan	Jun YTD Results	Comparison to Plan	Forecast	Comparison to Plan
Level 1: Participant Reaction (All programs)							
Quality of content	% favorable	76%	80%	79%	1% below	79%	1% below
Quality of instructor	% favorable	80%	85%	86%	1% above	85%	On Plan
Relevance	% favorable	72%	78%	73%	5% below	75%	3% below
Alignment to goals	% favorable	68%	75%	69%	6% below	71%	4% below
Total for Level 1	Average of measures	74%	80%	77%	3% below	78%	2% below
Level 1: Sponsor Feedback (Select programs)	% favorable	76%	90%	81%	9% below	85%	5% below
Level 2: Learning (Select programs)	Score	82%	90%	85%	5% below	88%	2% below
Level 3: Application rate (Select programs)							
Intent to apply (from survey at end of course)	% top two boxes	70%	90%	78%	12% below	84%	6% below
Actual application (after three months)	% who applied it	51%	70%	61%	9% below	67%	3% below
Level 4 (Select programs)							
Initial estimate by participants (end of course)	% contribution to goal	52%	70%	62%	8% below	70%	On Plan
Final estimate (after three months)	% contribution to goal	32%	50%	46%	4% below	50%	On Plan
Level 5 (Select programs)							
Net benefits	Thousands $	$2,658	$3,380	$1,423	42%	$3,500	104%
ROI for completed programs	%	29%	41%	37%	4% below	45%	4% above

Summary Report

The summary report is designed more for demonstrating alignment, impact, and good management than for actually managing programs or departments. The actual management of programs will occur using the program report, and management of improvements in efficiency and effectiveness measures will occur using the operations report. Senior leaders like the CEO and CFO, however, are very interested in how well aligned learning is to their goals and they care deeply about the potential learning may have on those goals. And, while they usually are not interested in a lot of detail, they would also like to know that the L&D department is working hard to improve its efficiency and effectiveness. So, the primary audience for the summary report includes senior leaders like the CEO, CFO, and SVP of HR, and a governing board if you have one. In addition, the summary report is perfect for sharing with L&D employees at monthly team meetings and with other groups when the CLO makes a presentation on the L&D department. Since summary reports are not really used for monthly management of the function, they are typically generated quarterly. The summary report features the organization's goals, learning's impact on those goals (outcome measures), and the most important effectiveness and efficiency measures. Standard TDRp columns are used. Last, since the primary audience is composed of senior leaders, the report should be free of learning jargon and acronyms like "level 3", "cycle times", or "LMS".

> ADVICE: In order to maintain the strategic link between learning and an organization's goals, it is strongly recommended that you include the organizational goal and YTD results as well as the plan and results for the learning program whenever possible. Do this to remind both senior leaders and your own staff why you are investing in learning.

The top part of the summary report features what is most important to senior company leaders: alignment of learning to their goals and its impact on those goals. (See the book by Jack Phillips on what CEOs really want.) The summary report is designed to give them what they want in a format they are used to seeing. After demonstrating that you know their goals and are doing all you can to help achieve those goals, the bottom portion will share a few efficiency and effectiveness measures to assure them that you are also focused on improving your efficiency and effectiveness. A simple summary report is presented in Table 9.5 based on the business case in Table 5.4 (or Appendix B Table 6) and the detailed work plans and measurement strategy in the sample business plan.

Notice first that the organization's top five or six goals are listed in priority order. The goals and their priority come from the CEO before the year begins. If the goals are not rank ordered then list them from High to Low Priority. Underneath each organization goal is the outcome measure which is leaning's impact on the goal. In this example, learning supports all five goals, but in practice it is possible there may be one or two goals not supported by learning. For example, the

TABLE 9.5

Summary Report for L&D

Results through June

				For 2017				
Priority	***Organization Goals and L&D Outcome Measures***	***Unit of Measure***	***2016 Actual***	***Plan***	***Jun YTD Results***	***% of Plan***	***Forecast***	***Forecast as % of Plan***
1	Increase Sales by 10%	%	3%	10%	4%	On plan	10%	On plan
	Corporate Goal or Actual	%	2%	2%	1%	On plan	2%	On plan
	Impact of L&D Initiatives: 20% contribution to goal							
	Consultative Selling Skills, Ten NPI Modules							
2	Reduce Defects by 20%							
	Corporate Goal or Actual	%	11%	20%	12%	Above plan	25%	5% above
	Impact of L&D Initiatives: 70% contribution to goal	%	5%	14%	10%	Above plan	18%	4% above
	Four Design Courses for engineers							
3	Reduce Injuries by 25%							
	Corporate Goal or Actual	%	8%	25%	10%	Below plan	22%	3% below
	Impact of L&D Initiatives: 60% contribution to goal	%	5%	15%		Below plan		Near plan
	Eight Safety Courses for associates and supervisors							
4	Improve Leadership Score by 5 points							
	Corporate Goal or Actual	Points	NA	5 pts	3 pts	On plan	6 pts	1 pt above
	Impact of L&D Initiatives: 40% contribution to goal	Points	NA	2 pts		Above plan		Above plan
	Three leadership orograms for supervisors, managers, dept heads							
5	Increase Retention by 5 points							
	Corporate Goal or Actual	Points	NA	5 pts	2 pts	Below plan	4 pts	1 pt below
	Impact of L&D Initiatives: 30% contribution to goal	Points	NA	1.5 pts		On plan		On plan
	IDPs for all associates and Performance Mgt for all mgt employees							
	Effectiveness Measures							
	Participation Reaction	% favorable	74%	80%	77%	3% below	78%	2% below
	Sponsor Feedback	% favorable	76%	90%	81%	9% below	85%	5% below
	Learning	Score	82%	90%	85%	5% below	88%	2% below
	Application Rate	% who applied it	51%	70%	61%	9% below	67%	3% below
	Efficiency Measures							
	Total Participants	Number	19,369	31,905	14,589	46%	31,000	97%
	Unique Participants	Number	4,552	5,000	3,426	69%	5,000	100%
	% Courses Meeting Deadline for Development	%	71%	100%	88%	12% below	88%	12% below
	% Courses Meeting Deadline for Delivery	%	65%	100%	85%	15% below	87%	13% below
	Learning management system Complaints	Number	214	107	45	42%	80	75%

first goal is to increase sales by 10%. You have met with Ortega, SVP of Sales, and both of you agree that learning has the potential to help achieve the goal this year. Following a needs analysis, you suggest two programs for Ortega's consideration and approval: consultative selling skills to close more deals and get higher price realization, and new product information (NPI) to help reps sell the value in the new products about to be released. List the agreed-upon programs under the goal to show the alignment of learning to the key goals of the organization. After you and Ortega agree on the programs and target audience, you discuss the planned impact from the two programs, properly designed, delivered, and reinforced. The two of you agree that it would be reasonable to plan for a 20% contribution from learning, which would result in 2% higher sales due to learning (10% higher sales x 20% contribution from learning = 2% higher sales due to learning). You both understand that this is a best guess about what is reasonable and achievable – there is no guarantee that sales will go up 10% or that learning will contribute 20% to the rise. In other words, both the 10% and 2% are business plan numbers and you will work together to try to achieve them. This will require clear roles and responsibilities and action plans, and it will require you both to manage results on a monthly basis.

The four other goals follow in priority order. Learning is planned to support each one and you have worked with the goal owners to agree on the planned programs that are summarized for each. You and the goal owner also have discussed and agreed upon outcome measures, which in this case are all quantitative. (You might have agreed to use qualitative instead or use a mix of both.) In practice, you would likely have program reports for each of the five goals so you would simply pull the information you need off each program report. You could also add HR or compliance goals below the CEO's goals. (See Table 4.9 for an example.) At the bottom of the report are 3–5 effectiveness measures and 3–5 efficiency measures. Pull these directly from the operations report, but just be sure to remove any learning jargon. In conclusion, the summary report is the easiest to set up because everything you need comes directly from the business case and the operations report.

Once the year is underway, the year-to-date and forecast numbers will simply come from the program reports for the top part and from the operations report for the bottom part. If you don't have program reports yet for all the key goals you support, then you will get what you need for the top part of the report from company systems and from discussions with the goal owner. Year-to-date results for organization goals often can be obtained directly from a corporate system. If not, ask the goal owners for them each month. Rest assured, they will have them as soon as they are available. Forecasts for the organization goals may also be available in a corporate system, but if not, just ask the goal owner for these as well.

Actual year-to-date results for the outcome measures may be available but more likely you will need to estimate them. If the programs in support of the goal have concluded and you have done an impact study, then you will have actual results to use in the year-to-date column. Or, you may have asked participants (and perhaps their supervisors) to estimate the impact in a post-event survey. In this case you will also have what you need to calculate year-to-date results due to just the learning. The year-to-date measures in Table 9.5 for the first two goals are based on the assumption that you have actual results from one of these methods. For the other three goals it will be assumed that no such "hard data" exists for year-to-date results and consequently the corresponding cells are left blank. However, you will notice that in the adjacent cells under the "% of Plan" column that a qualitative statement has been made comparing year-to-date results to plan. This represents the best thinking by the goal owner, CLO, and program manager on the contribution of learning. As discussed under program reports, measures with data for the year-to-date period are used as leading indicators to characterize the contribution of learning. If level 0-3 measures are all on or near plan, and the goal owner is happy with the learning, then you might conclude that the impact of learning (level 4) is "on plan". If the leading indicators are below plan then you might conclude the level 4 learning impact is "below plan" and conversely if the leading indicators are above plan then you might conclude the level 4 learning impact is "above plan". While this may be somewhat subjective, just remember that your CEO simply wants the best thinking from you and the goal owner. She is not looking for perfection or absolute certainties (which don't exist often in her world anyway).

Combine the year-to-date results with expectations for the rest of the year to determine the forecasts for the outcome measures. If you are on plan year-to-date, and you believe the rest of the year will go according to plan, then forecast "on plan" for the year. If you are behind plan year-to-date but believe you can make up the shortfall by year end, then forecast "on plan" for the year. If you cannot make up the shortfall, then forecast "below plan". There are a lot of combinations but you get the idea. The discussion around the forecast is critically important because it forces you to think about where you are today, why you are where you are today, what you expect to happen in the remainder of the year, and what you can do to change that if you don't like it. This is really the fun part of management: if things are not going according to plan, what can you do and what should you do about it?

With this background we are ready to analyze the top of Table 9.5. (The bottom has already been discussed under the operation report.) Sales are on plan year-to-date and are forecast to end the year on plan (up 10%). Learning is making the planned contribution, contributing to 1% higher sales year-to-date based on both our pilot study and participant estimation. Ortega, the CLO, and program manager all agree that learning will have the planned 20% contribution, resulting in a 2% increase in sales solely due to learning. The reduction in defects is going much better than planned with a 12% reduction registered already, and the goal owner is now projecting a 25% reduction by year end (5% above plan). All agree that learning is partly responsible for this out-performance and is having an above plan impact, which is supported by the impact results from the participants and their supervisors. The forecast indicates that learning will lead to at least an 18% reduction in defects versus the plan of 14%. (Alternatively, you might simply say that learning will be "above plan" in the forecast column.) The company is below plan in its goal to reduce injures by 25%, which is primarily due to low application of the new safety behaviors. Swilthe, with guidance from the learning program manager, is implementing new reinforcement plans that are expected to close much of the gap by year end. The forecast shows injuries falling 22%, just shy of plan, and learning's contribution ending the year near plan due to the focus on reinforcement. Leadership scores are rising and are now expected to end the year one point over plan, due to greater than anticipated success in the leadership development program. Last, while employees are responding well to the additional learning opportunities provide them this year, the retention rate is just slightly below plan year-to-date. Forecast shows the rate at the end at the year still to be one point below plan due to factors other than learning. The above analysis would typically be conveyed in a face-to-face meeting with the CEO, CFO, or governing board, where questions could easily be answered and additional information provided.

Summary for TDRp Reports

Senior organizational leaders will appreciate the format of the summary report and the information in it. Today most CEOs and CFOs only receive results for select efficiency and effectiveness measures – no outcome measures and no mention of organization goals. Moreover, the reports they do receive contain only the results – no plans. So, the leaders conclude that L&D is busy, but they also conclude that the CLO is not running it like a business because there are no plans and no comparison of year-to-date results with plan (because there was never a plan!) and no forecast of how the year is likely to end. Sales, manufacturing, quality, and other departments all have plans and they all have reports comparing year-to-date results to plan. In other words they are running their departments with business discipline. Typically, L&D has not, but we need to start. These three reports provide us the opportunity to manage our programs and departments with the same discipline as our colleagues outside L&D manage theirs.

Common Objections to Running Learning Like a Business

Even at this point there may be some who believe it is not possible to run learning like a business (strategically align learning to goals, develop a business case, create a business plan, and execute with discipline). They might acknowledge that all the planning and processes of chapters four through nine sound good but still believe it is not practical, possible, or perhaps even desirable to run learning like a business. Their main objections are likely to be:

1. It is too difficult.
2. The data simply do not exist.
3. The processes outlined in chapters four through nine require too many estimates and forecasts. They are too subjective.
4. It is too expensive and requires too many resources.

Too Difficult

It can be difficult but no more so than managing other aspects of a business. For example, consider the challenge facing a product manager in a typical company charged with designing, manufacturing, and selling a new product. The product manager must forecast sales and the profit from those sales and then manage throughout the year to deliver those results. What does the manager need to know to make the forecast?

- Growth in the economy (GDP)
- Growth in her particular industry
- Market share for the new product
- Projected inventory levels
- Price of the product
- Cost to manufacture and ship the product
- Cost to sell the product

As you can see, this is a pretty tough assignment. Retail sales will depend on the industry or overall opportunity (which depends on the economy, which in turn depends on interest rates, consumer and business confidence, and so on) multiplied by market share for this particular product (which depends on the features and benefits versus those of competitors, the price, how well it can be sold, and the competitor's actions). Company sales will depend on retail sales and changes in inventory levels. Profitability will depend not just on sales but on the costs to manufacture, ship, and sell the product.

Is putting a business plan together for learning really any harder than this? Think about the data the product manager needs. How much of it is "hard" data or data that is known, precise, and certain? Virtually none! No one knows for certain what the economy will do or how the economy will affect this industry. It is a new product, so no one knows what market share will be. (Even if it were an existing product, share can change from year to year, sometimes significantly.) The manager will have to pick a price and hope it is low enough to be attractive to a buyer and high enough to cover all the costs and generate a profit. The costs are all forecasts. So, is it really harder to forecast the number of participants, level 1 or 2 measures, or even impact and net benefits? No. The fact is that your colleagues in the company are creating business plans in the face of tremendous uncertainty. That is how business is done. Is it difficult? Yes. Is that a reason not to do it? No.

Now consider the challenge of managing through the year. Some learning managers contend that learning cannot be run like a business because learning involves people who by their nature are unpredictable. Again, that may be so, but almost every aspect of business is unpredictable. The product manager cannot control the economy or the size of the industry. He can control the product price but cannot control the competitors' reaction to the new product, including their price or marketing adjustments. The manager may not even be able to control the costs and certainly cannot control the input costs like commodity prices. So the product manager is responsible for delivering the planned results even though he cannot control the majority of factors driving those results. Do you think he would have any sympathy for a learning manager who complains it is too difficult to manage learning through the year to achieve the plan? Not a chance.

In fact, the product manager would say the learning manager has an easier task since more factors are under the learning manager's control. Typically, a CLO or learning manager does have some control over the number of courses developed and participants who take them. Managed properly, there is time to react to low level 1–4 scores and do something about them. The learning manager can work with the sponsor on reinforcement to increase application and impact. Although most of the driving factors are beyond the control of the product manager, the learning manager can influence many, and sometimes most, of the factors in the learning space.

So, learning really is *not more* difficult to plan or manage than other aspects of business. It can be difficult, but so can most other aspects of business. Refusing to recognize this only makes the profession look bad.

Data Do Not Exist

This is often true at the application, impact, and net benefit levels. Data generally do exist, though, at the 0, 1, and 2 levels. Since most of the data is collected at these lower levels, there is usually a lot of data available. Even at the higher levels, post-program data can be collected to derive levels 3–5. You can also easily gather intent-to-apply data and initial estimates of impact from the post-event survey when you get participant reaction.

In our example above the product manager would have had historical data on the economy, industry, and inventory and perhaps on market share and price for similar products. There would have been no data on price, share, or cost for this particular product. In the business world complete information seldom exists. Managers use what they have and estimate or forecast the rest.

Too Many Estimates and Forecasts

Since data often do not exist, estimates and forecasts are employed. Some feel that using these in place of hard data introduces too much subjectivity and invalidates the planning or the analysis. The fact is that planning must be done, and performance must be managed throughout the year. Managers will use the best information available to plan and manage. Where there is hard data, use it. Where there is not, estimates and forecasts are routinely employed. In the example above both industry and market share data require information from competitors. Often, trade associations exist to gather industry data and share it with all the participants. Then all the participants can calculate their market share as their own sales divided by industry sales. Unfortunately, the industry data is usually incomplete, so the size of the industry and market share is not known with certainty. Does this stop companies from using it? No. They use it because it is the best they have and better than nothing at all.

Learning managers need to adopt the same philosophy. Estimates and forecasts will not be perfect, but properly constructed, they will be good enough and certainly better than nothing at all. So, the learning profession needs to embrace their use and stop worrying so much about the lack of hard data. Be humble, conservative, and transparent. Solicit input and feedback. Then move ahead.

Too Expensive and Requires Too Many Resources

Finally, some might agree in principle that learning should and could be run like a business but would say they do not have the resources to do it. Now it is true that all the processes described so far from strategic alignment to disciplined execution do require time and some system support. This challenge, however, can be overcome.

First, a strategic approach, while requiring more time to be invested in the planning process, will save time throughout the rest of the year. With most of the learning planned for the year, little time will be spent in the inefficient reactive mode responding to "training emergencies," which often require last-minute reprioritizations and program stops as resources are shifted to other projects. So, the strategic alignment process and creation of the business plan may not actually require more time or resources in total, although more time will be required in the planning cycle.

Second, if additional resources are required to run learning like a business but are not available, then it becomes a matter of setting priorities with your existing resources. Make running learning like a business a priority and reprioritize staff time to accomplish at least the basics. If this means one or two fewer programs are developed and delivered, then so be it. The learning function, run like a business, will have a much greater impact on the enterprise than one run without a business focus, even if it offers fewer courses. In other words, it is better to focus on fewer strategically aligned and well-executed programs than on many unaligned and poorly executed programs. Remember, the goal is strategic impact, not merely number of participants or courses!

Conclusion

With specific and measurable goals, clear roles and responsibilities, and a disciplined monthly process using reports, you should now be ready to execute your business plan successfully. Do not be overly concerned about the use of estimates and forecasts in the original plan or in place of "hard" measures as you manage throughout the year. This is common in most organizations. You need data to be good enough to make good decisions, and, fortunately, this does not require perfection or certainty.

Chapter 9 to Do List

1. Confirm that your goals are specific and measurable and that someone owns each one. The key goals should be included in the annual performance goals of the CLO and program managers.
2. Ensure the program manager, CLO, and goal owner understand their own roles and responsibilities as well as the roles and responsibilities of the other two. Consider putting them on paper and passing them out.
3. If a data-driven, disciplined process already exists, are there opportunities for improvement? Could the monthly results meeting be improved? Could data collection be further automated? Could the scorecard be improved?
4. If a data-driven, disciplined process does not exist, put one in place:
   a. Decide on the frequency and length of the results meeting (for example, monthly for three hours).
   b. Schedule those times for the next twelve months.
   c. Decide on the agenda. What does the CLO expect of the program managers?
   d. Review your data. What is readily available? What could be automated? What are you missing, and how much would it cost to get it?
   e. Create program reports with the program managers. Use monthly.
   f. Create the operations report. Decide which efficiency and effectiveness measures you want to improve. Use monthly.
   g. Create a summary report. Share it with your CEO and governing body. Incorporate their input. Put it to use. Use at least quarterly.
5. The CLO and program managers should review and discuss the use of plans, estimates and forecasts. Is everyone comfortable with them? Is there an opportunity to improve them? Is it worth the effort and cost?
6. If you are not already doing so, resolve to run learning like a business without apology (not enough hard data) or complaint (too difficult, too expensive, not enough resources). Practice first inside the learning function and then, when you are ready, project your new-found confidence to others outside the group.

Further Reading

Israelite, Larry (editor). *More Lies about Learning: Leading Executives Separate Truth from Fiction*. Alexandria, Virginia: ASTD Press, 2015. See Chapter 4 by Edward Trolley titled "Lies about Managing the Learning Function."

Phillips, Jack and Patti Phillips. *Measuring for Success: What CEOs Really Think about Learning Investments*. Alexandria, Virginia: ASTD Press, 2010. See Appendix D for survey results.

Phillips, Jack and Lynn Schmidt. *Implementing Training Scorecards in Action*. Alexandria, Virginia: ASTD Press, 2003.

PART FOUR

The Economics of Learning: Improving Your Efficiency and Making Better Choices

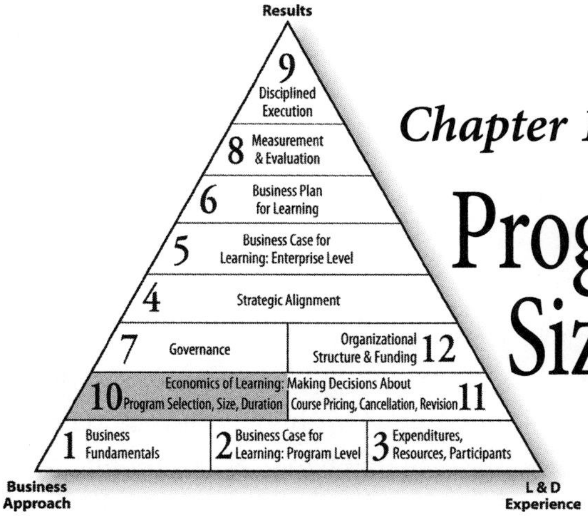

Chapter 10

Program Selection, Size, and Duration

THE FIRST NINE chapters covered the basics from business fundamentals to creation and execution of the business plan for learning. Chapters 10 and 11 go beyond the basics to explore how economic concepts can provide insight into both the theory and practice of managing the learning function. Consider them optional but important in addressing questions of program selection, size, and duration as well as addressing issues of course pricing, class cancellation, and plan revision.

Net benefits can be integrated with economic theory to provide a theoretical foundation for decision making in learning. This foundation, in turn, provides a common language and framework for learning professionals to use in discussing a program's merits, duration, and costs. And this, in turn, will increase the professional judgment of the learning manager, leading to better decisions. Chapter 10 will employ economics to provide additional insight into three questions:

Key Concepts for Chapter 10

10

1. Economic theory can provide a framework for important learning decisions concerning:
    a. Program selection
    b. Program size
    c. Program duration
2. Two key economic concepts are the theory of the firm and marginal analysis.
    a. Both firms and learning functions seek to optimize their impact subject to constraints.
        i. The learning function seeks to optimize net benefits subject to the very important constraints of strategic alignment and organization priorities.
    b. Marginal analysis, investment analysis, and ROI can help managers make better decisions.
3. Economic theory applied to learning can improve the learning manager's professional judgment and increase the impact of the investment in learning.

1. How large should a program be (target audience)?
2. Which programs should be selected?
3. How long should a program be (duration)?

Reader's Guide

Chapters ten and eleven take a deep dive into the application of economic theory to learning. Since this cannot be found elsewhere, the treatment is comprehensive and detailed. Consequently, unlike the rest of the book, these chapters contain theory along with lots of graphs and tables involving lots of numbers. Some readers will not be interested in the theory and will not care for all the graphs and numbers. With these readers in mind, a summary is provided for each chapter containing the essential concepts and their relevance for learning—without all the graphs and numbers. So, start with the summary and perhaps you will be intrigued enough to want to explore the chapter in detail. You can also skip the theory and go straight to the applications, beginning on page 346.

Also, please note that the concepts in these two chapters are not required for other chapters.

Executive Summary

Economic Theory

The economic concepts of marginal analysis and the theory of the firm, combined with the basics of investment analysis, can provide insight on the important questions of program selection, size, and duration.

Marginal Analysis

Marginal analysis focuses on what happens when one more unit of output is produced, or in learning, when one more participant takes a class. It answers the question, "What happens if one more unit (or participant) is added?" or "What happens at the margin (when one more is added)?" The concept sounds incredibly simple but turns out to be very powerful. We will be concerned with the marginal revenue, cost, and profit from one additional unit of production. In other words, what happens to revenue when one more unit is produced? What happens to cost, and what happens to profit? In terms of learning, we will be concerned with marginal gross benefit, marginal cost, and marginal net benefit. What happens to gross benefit when one more participant takes the class? What happens to cost, and what happens to net benefit?

Theory of the Firm

In economics the theory of the firm seeks to explain how firms act and more specifically how much they should produce to maximize profit. The bottom line is this: A firm should keep producing until the marginal cost equals the marginal revenue or, in other words, until the marginal profit is zero. So here is another relatively simple sounding concept (if you can get past all the references to "marginal") that is very powerful. You might have thought the answer would depend on total revenue and/or total cost or the average cost, but it does not. You do not need to know any of those to maximize profit—just keep producing until the marginal profit on the next unit is zero, then stop.

Now, a little background on costs is required to make sense of the above. Marginal costs typically decline at first as operating efficiencies improve and then increase as production is pushed past the efficient range and as the cost of inputs begins to rise. So, imagine a "U"-shaped curve. For many firms marginal revenue is flat. It is just the price they get for their product, which often does not change. So, if the product is priced at $10, then the sale of one more brings in $10, and the sale of the next brings in another $10. The marginal revenue is always $10. Combine rising marginal cost with flat marginal revenue, and you can imagine some level of production where marginal cost has risen to $10. At this point marginal cost equals marginal revenue and marginal profit is zero. The very next unit produced will have a marginal cost greater than $10 (because the curve is sloping up because of inefficiencies). Since marginal revenue will still be $10, marginal cost will exceed marginal revenue, and there will be a marginal loss. Stop production! Profit has been maximized.

Investment Analysis

The theory of the firm explains how much to produce, but what led the company to produce that particular product in the first place? This is a question of project selection or capital allocation, and investment analysis holds the answer. A firm wants to maximize its profit over a multi-year period, perhaps over ten or twenty years. Consequently, it will examine the projected revenue and costs over the entire period and consider only those projects that will be profitable over the long period. Furthermore, since capital for projects is scarce and may be expensive, a firm will fund only the projects with the highest expected rate of return. The rate of return is the expected profit divided by the cost of the initial investment. This is called the return on investment or ROI. A firm will rank its projects by ROI and fund as many as it can afford.

Application to Learning

Theory of the Firm Applied to Learning

The theory of the firm can be applied to learning to create a framework for analysis and to provide a common language for discussion. Just as a firm seeks to maximize profit subject to a number of constraints, a learning function may seek to maximize net benefit subject to a number of constraints. In this framework net benefit is like profit, and gross benefit is like revenue (cost is similar in both). The most important constraints for the learning function are strategic alignment, priorities, and budget. In other words, a learning function should seek to maximize net benefit subject to the results of the strategic alignment and prioritization process and subject to budget and staff constraints. Note that strategic alignment and prioritization take precedence over net benefit maximization.

How Large Should a Program Be?

Now, let us apply these concepts to questions facing the learning manager, starting with how large a program should be (i.e., how many participants there are). Economic theory says to stop adding participants when the marginal cost exceeds the marginal gross benefit—in other words, when marginal net benefit becomes negative. Just as with a typical firm, the marginal cost of a learning program will eventually begin to increase as the number of participants grows. Unlike a typical firm in which marginal revenue is flat (or constant), in learning the marginal gross benefit will begin to decline at some point as the number of participants increases. So, it is easy to imagine that for a large-scale program a point will be reached where marginal gross benefit is falling and marginal cost is increasing. At some point the marginal cost will equal the marginal gross benefit and marginal net benefit will be zero. The program should not be any larger than this level. In other words the goal is to restrict the number of participants to those who really will benefit from the learning and who will have a positive net benefit.

So how is this done in practice? First, determine whether marginal cost is likely to begin rising in the range of participants being considered. If it is, that is a danger signal, and you should let the sponsor know that the program begins to become "really expensive" at this point. Second, get a feel for marginal gross benefit by rank ordering all the groups that might benefit from the learning. At the top are those who really need it, will definitely learn the material, and will definitely apply it. At the bottom are those who may not be motivated even to attend and are highly unlikely to apply it even if they learn it. Discuss this ranking with the sponsor and factor in the marginal cost discussion. Make a subjective determination of where marginal net benefit may be close to zero or where it is about to decline significantly. This is probably a good place to cut it off.

Sponsors often want too many people to take the course. Now you have a way of thinking about how to limit program size to those who really will benefit from it.

Which Programs Should Be Selected?

Applying investment analysis to learning would lead us to select those programs with the highest ROI. Of course, it should go without saying that the strategic alignment and prioritization process have already been completed so that the programs under consideration are those that will contribute the most to achieving the company's highest-priority goals. With that understanding, here are the implications for learning: 1) If there are multiple programs of equal priority and all are strategically aligned, select the program with the highest ROI subject to budget constraints and advice from your governing body. 2) If there are multiple strategically aligned programs of differing priority, select the highest priority programs subject to resource constraints. Do not rank by ROI. 3) If all the strategically aligned and high-priority programs have been funded and resources remain, use ROI and other factors to select unaligned programs.

How Long Should a Program Be (Duration)?

For some programs the needs analysis will indicate exactly how long a program should be to accomplish the learning objective and deliver the planned impact. For other programs like leadership and performance management, however, there often is no definite answer. It could be one day, two days, three days, or as many as five days. When the needs analysis is not specific, we could use a forecast of ROI for each possible duration (such as one day, two days, etc.) to help choose a duration. Unfortunately, it would be very time consuming to forecast all those ROIs and probably not worth the effort.

Instead, use your understanding of the course to determine whether marginal gross benefit is likely to increase, decrease, or remain constant over the five days. In some courses the greatest benefit or return comes in the first day or two. In others it may not come until the end. Some peak in the middle. If a similar course has been offered before, look at the evaluations and talk with some students to see if they exhibit one of these patterns. Talk with the instructional designer and ask about the learning objectives for each day. Ask what would be lost if it were one day shorter or two days shorter. Try to determine what the marginal gross benefit is for each day relative to the day before and day after. In other words, use marginal analysis to find the optimum duration. Here are the implications: 1) If decreasing marginal gross benefits (decreasing returns) seem likely, less is better. Do as little as absolutely required to meet the objective. 2) If increasing marginal gross benefits (increasing returns) seem likely, more is better. In this case, you might approve a three- to five-day ILT. 3) If mixed returns seem likely (increasing then decreasing returns), target the sweet spot where marginal gross benefits peak.

End of Executive Summary

Economic Theory

Economics can be divided broadly into two areas: macroeconomics and microeconomics. Macroeconomics is the big picture, exploring the size, growth, and price levels of entire economies. Microeconomics, on the other hand (and economists really do not say this all the time!), focuses on the consumer and the firm, seeking to understand how prices for individual goods and services are determined and how much will be produced and consumed. A key concept in microeconomics is marginal analysis, used to develop theories of both consumer and firm behavior. It also is a very valuable analytical tool in its own right, which can be applied to the management of learning. We will examine the concept and the theory of the firm and then apply both to learning.

Marginal Analysis

One of the most useful concepts in microeconomics is marginal analysis. In fact, it holds the key to maximizing profit for the firm and satisfaction for the consumer. Marginal analysis focuses on what happens at the margin or right at the point when a decision is made. Applied to the firm, it focuses on the revenue, cost, or profit of producing the next item in order to make a decision about how much to produce. Of course, totals and averages are also important. Let us take a closer look at the three concepts.

We will start with what you already know. For example, suppose a small firm makes one model of a very nice desk and produces 100 desks per year. If the total cost to make all 100 desks is $500,000, then the average cost per desk is $500,000/100 = $5,000. Total cost is important because the owner wants to be profitable, so revenue needs to exceed $500,000. Average cost may help the owner set a price, perhaps average cost plus 10% or $5,500 per desk, which would lead to revenue of 100 x $5,500=$550,000. Profit would then be $50,000.

Unlike average cost, the marginal cost is likely to be different for each desk produced. It is the cost of producing one more unit of output, in this case the next desk. The marginal cost for the 100th desk is simply the total cost for the 100 desks less the total cost for 99 desks. In other words, how much more did it cost to produce the 100th desk? If the cost tally after producing 99 desks was $494,700, then the marginal cost for the 100th desk is $5,300 ($500,000 - $494,700). Suppose, based on a similar calculation, the marginal cost for the 50th desk is $3,000. If the price is always $5,500, the marginal profit on the 50th desk was $2,500 while the marginal profit on the 100th desk was only $200.

You can see that this might be important information to have, especially if there is a trend or some predictability in marginal costs. This brings us to the theory of the firm.

Theory of the Firm

In the economic world a firm strives to maximize its profit or net income. Economic theory has been developed to explain how a typical firm might best accomplish this goal. One of the key questions for the owner or manager is how much to produce. Here is what theory says: keep producing until the marginal profit of the last item is zero. Let us see what this means.

The Theory

Costs: Let's start with the basics. Say we have a company that produces goods (although services work just as well). It costs money to produce the goods. Generally, there will be fixed costs like a factory, lease, or long-term contract, which cannot be changed in the short run and do not depend on the level of production. There will also be variable costs that change (vary) depending on the level of production. Examples of variables costs are labor and materials. Variable costs start at $0 and rise with production. Consequently, total cost (fixed plus variable) will rise with production. These costs are illustrated in Figure 10.1, where variable costs are assumed to rise sharply at first, then more slowly as an efficient scale is achieved, and finally more rapidly as constraints on space and inputs drive costs much higher. Notice that the total cost curve is just the variable cost curve shifted up by the amount of fixed cost (total cost = variable cost + fixed cost).

FIGURE 10.1

Fixed, Variable, and Total Costs for a Representative Firm

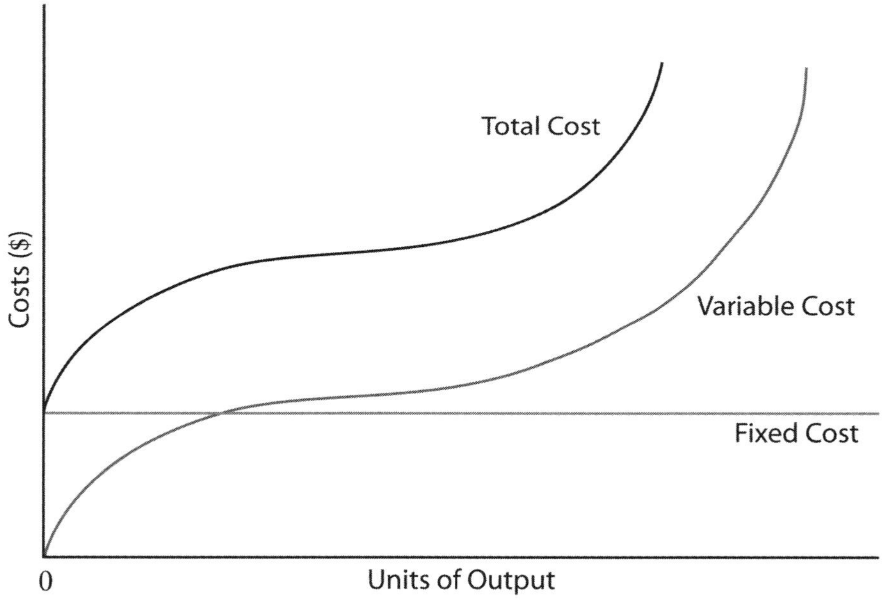

The cost per unit or average cost will simply be cost divided by the number of units produced. Figure 10.2 illustrates the average cost curves for fixed, variable, and total costs along with marginal cost. Start with the bottom panel and notice how rapidly average fixed cost declines as the fixed cost is spread over more and more units.

Now look at Figure 10.2 and notice how marginal cost declines initially up to point M and then increases. Up to point M workplace efficiency is increasing.

FIGURE 10.2

Marginal and Average Cost Curves for a Representative Firm

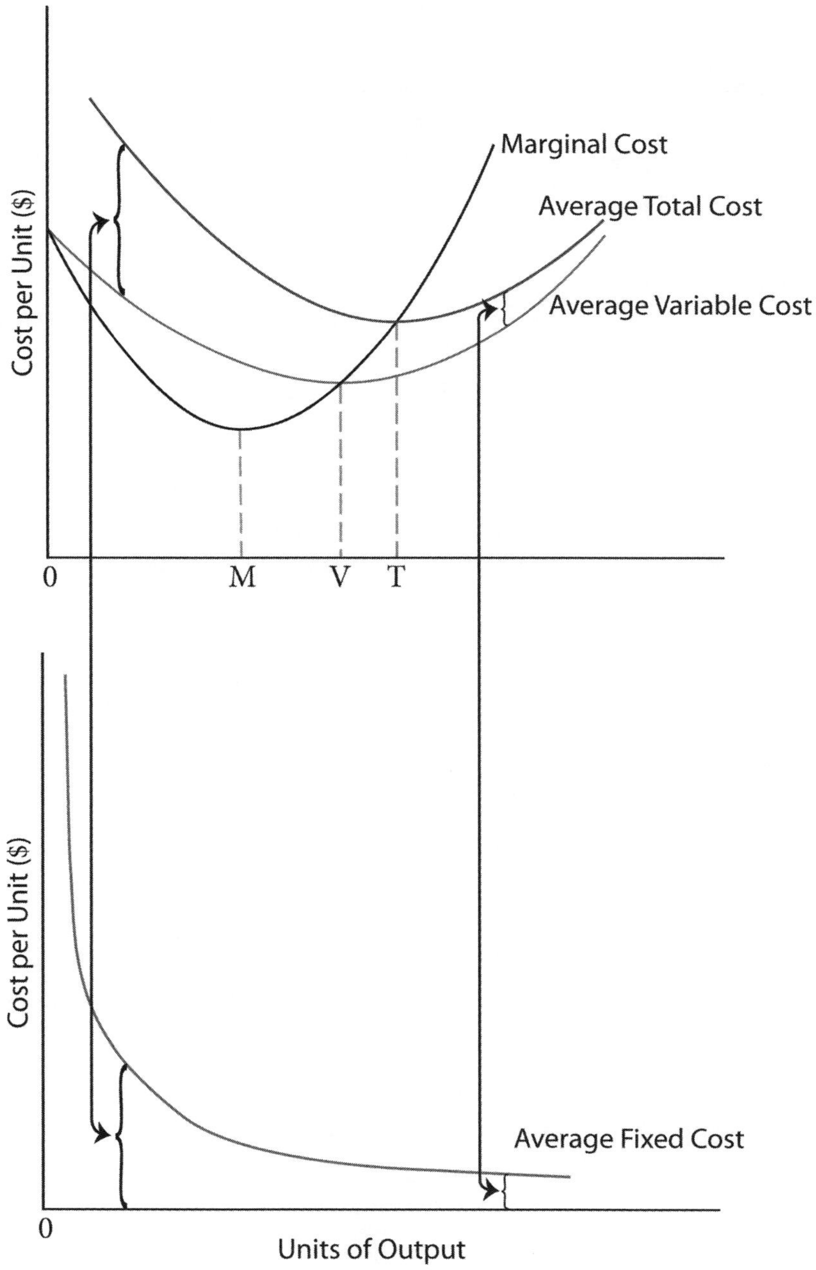

At point M the factory is operating in an optimal range (say 75–90% of capacity), and inputs remain plentiful, so their price per unit is not rising. After M, however, efficiency begins to decline, pushing the marginal cost of each unit higher. Even though marginal cost is rising between points M and V, it is still less than average variable cost, and thus it pulls the average variable cost lower. After point V marginal cost exceeds average variable cost and pushes the average variable cost up. Similarly, after point T, marginal cost exceeds average total cost and pushes it higher as well. Marginal cost is the driving force here, influencing the shape of the variable and total cost curves.

Notice also that the average total cost curve is simply the addition of the average fixed cost and average variable cost curves. In other words, it is just the average variable cost curve shifted higher by the amount of average fixed cost. So, after point T, the average total cost curve begins to rise as higher average variable costs more than offset continually declining average fixed costs.

***Implications for profit*:** When a firm faces decreasing marginal costs, profits are likely to be rising as long as demand for its product continues to be strong. Even if the company cannot raise its price as it sells more, the total profit and the marginal profit (profit on the last desk made) rises with each additional or incremental unit produced. (Assume everything produced is sold so that there is no inventory.) This is a fun range for owners and employees because it just keeps getting better and better. Think of successful startups such as Microsoft and Google, whose salaries, benefits, profit sharing, and stock prices were all rising smartly.

At some point marginal costs will begin to increase. There is still profit on each sale, so total profits are increasing, but the marginal profit on each incremental sale is declining. Unless prices can be increased, marginal cost will eventually increase enough to equal the price, wiping out any profit on that sale (zero marginal profit). Beyond this point, the firm will lose money on every unit sold (marginal profit is negative). Eventually, the profit made on the earlier sales will be totally wiped out by losses on the later sales, and the firm will have an overall loss.

***Profit maximization*:** Now, let us return to the economic theory for maximizing profit. Theory says the firm should produce until marginal profit equals zero, which will occur somewhere in the zone of increasing marginal costs. Up until that point in the range of increasing marginal costs, the firm will still be making a profit on every unit sold, even though the profit on each sale is less and less. So, if this is the only product produced, why not keep producing and selling it as long as each incremental or marginal sale is profitable. When you start to lose money on a sale, stop. This seems like common sense!

Figure 10.3 illustrates the profit-maximizing level of output for a typical firm. At Q, the marginal cost of the last unit produced just equals the price we have assumed is fixed. Thus, marginal profit is zero, and production should stop. Before that point (to the left of Q) there was marginal profit on each unit produced since the price (which is also the marginal revenue) exceeded the marginal cost. Point A is an example of a level of production where there is marginal profit (denoted as "a"). Producing beyond Q will result in a marginal loss on each unit produced since the marginal cost now exceeds the price or marginal revenue. Point B is an example of a level of production in which there is a marginal loss (denoted as "b"). At Point M, where marginal cost is at a minimum, marginal profit would be the greatest, but the firm will still make a profit on every unit sold up until point Q. (Note: The logic works just as well when the price line or marginal revenue curve slopes down to reflect that additional sales require higher discounts.)

FIGURE 10.3

The Profit Maximizing Level of Output for a Representative Firm

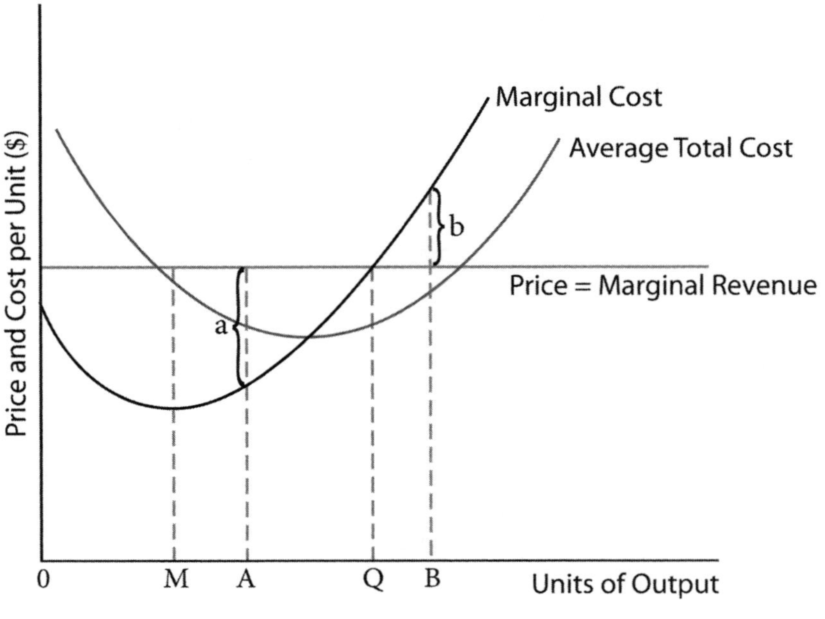

An Example

In the example above of the desk manufacturer, suppose the marginal cost was $6609 for the 86th desk, $6808 for the 87th desk, $7012 for the 88th desk, and $7222 for the 89th desk. Each desk sells for $7000. How many should the firm produce? The answer, compliments of marginal analysis, is 87. The marginal profit was $391 on the 86th desk, $192 on the 87th desk, a loss of $12 on the 88th desk, and a loss of $222 on the 89th desk. Since the marginal profit was still positive for the 87th but negative for the 88th, stop at 87. This level of production maximizes profit at $144,586. Convince yourself by looking at total profit in Table 10.1.

TABLE 10.1

Costs, Revenue, and Profit for a Representative Firm Manufacturing Desks

Desk #	Point in Fig 10.3	Fixed Cost	Variable Cost	Total Cost	Marginal Cost	Average Cost	Price	Total Revenue	Total Profit	Marginal Profit
1		$75,000	$10,000	$85,000		$85,000	$7,000	$7,000	($78,000)	
20		$75,000	$130,994	$205,994	$4,234	$10,300	$7,000	$140,000	($65,994)	$2,766
41	M	$75,000	$199,591	$274,591	$2,796	$6,697	$7,000	$287,000	$12,409	$4,204
60		$75,000	$258,113	$333,113	$3,479	$5,552	$7,000	$420,000	$86,887	$3,521
78		$75,000	$334,819	$409,819	$5,217	$5,254	$7,000	$546,000	$136,181	$1,783
86		$75,000	$382,606	$457,606	$6,609	$5,321	$7,000	$602,000	$144,394	$391
87	Q	$75,000	$389,414	$464,414	$6,808	$5,338	$7,000	$609,000	$144,586	$192
88		$75,000	$396,425	$471,425	$7,012	$5,357	$7,000	$616,000	$144,575	($12)
89		$75,000	$403,647	$478,647	$7,222	$5,378	$7,000	$623,000	$144,353	($222)
100		$75,000	$503,969	$578,969	$11,011	$5,790	$7,000	$700,000	$121,031	($4,011)

This is the answer to the question, "How much should be produced?" It also demonstrates the magic of marginal analysis. Knowledge of total costs and total revenue was not even required to identify the optimum production—just knowledge of the marginal costs and price. Note that the profit optimizing point did not come from looking at average costs, which continued to run below price.

Investment Analysis

There is one more important component before we apply these concepts to learning, which is the issue of project selection or capital allocation. How are projects chosen?

The theory of the firm addressed how much of a single item to produce given that the decision had already been made to produce that particular item. The question remains how the firm decided to produce it in the first place.

Start with the goal of long-term profit maximization. A firm will choose investments that maximize profit over the long term, which may be twenty or more years. Proposals for new investments or projects will include forecasts of revenue, costs (start up and ongoing), and profit over the appropriate period as well as the initial investment required to build the factory or design the new product or service. Capital for such projects, however, is always limited, so all the proposed projects cannot be funded. There is simply not enough capital at a reasonable rate to make the initial investments in all the projects.

The profit maximizing firm, therefore, will fund only the projects with the highest expected rate of return as long as that return exceeds their cost of borrowing or the opportunity cost of internally generated funds. (What else could these funds be used for, and what would be the return?) Basically, the rate of return is the expected profit divided by the initial investment. This is called return on investment or ROI. A firm will maximize its long-term profit by selecting those projects with the highest ROI.

For example, assume a firm has the following investment proposals, a capital budget of $10,000,000, and a threshold of 15%. (No projects with returns below 15% will even be considered.) The proposals are ranked by ROI.

TABLE 10.2

Investment Analysis for Five Proposed Projects

Project	*Investment*	*Rate of Return (ROI)*
A	$2,200,000	35%
B	$3,500,000	29%
C	$4,000,000	21%
D	$1,500,000	19%
E	$1,800,000	14%

In this example, project E is ruled out immediately since it falls below the threshold of 15%. The firm should fund projects A, B, and C, which consume \$9,700,000 of the \$10,000,000 budget. The capital budget is insufficient to fund project D, even though the ROI is above the threshold.

So, investment analysis employs ROI to answer the question of how projects are selected.

Application to Learning

The economic theory discussed above can be used to provide insight into three important questions for the management of learning:

1. How large should a program be (target audience)?
2. Which programs should be selected?
3. How long should a program be (duration)?

We will begin by applying the concept of profit maximization to learning and then proceed to answer the three questions.

Concept of Profit Maximization Applied to Learning

Start by making the analogy to economics. Although the analogy may not be perfect, it is instructive and provides a framework for discussion and further analysis. Learning has a product that it offers to customers, just like a firm. The learning function has costs (total, average, and marginal) for its products, just like a firm. The learning organization is likely to offer many different products (courses, for example) just like most firms offer multiple products. And learning faces numerous real-world constraints of budget, staffing, and organizational priorities, just like a firm.

The Goal

Now, consider net benefit as the analogy to a firm's profit. Just as a for-profit firm desires to maximize profit in pursuit of its goals, a *learning function may strive to maximize net benefit as it supports the organization's goals, subject to important considerations* detailed below. (Remember that net benefit is gross benefit less all the costs associated with it, including opportunity costs.) Where a firm sells products to generate revenue, the learning function offers products to generate gross benefits (the dollar impact of learning). The analogy is shown in Figure 10.4.

FIGURE 10.4

Comparison of the Firm and Learning Function

	Firm	*Learning Function*
Language	Costs	Costs
	Revenue	Gross Benefit
	Profit	Net Benefit
Goals	Achieve Corporate Objectives	Achieve Corporate Objectives
	Maximize Profit	Maximize Net Benefit
Constraints	Budget	Budget
	Employees	Employees
	Capital	Capital (for a new building perhaps)
	Priorities	Priorities
	Guidance	Guidance
	Regulation	Mandatory Training

Some might point out that many learning functions have revenue and ask why the goal is not profit maximization, just like the firm. Although a learning function could be managed in such a way to maximize its own profit, most would say that is not their mission. The mission of most learning functions is to contribute to the success of the overall organization (which may include maximizing the organization's profit), and this can be measured best through the use of the net benefit concept *if* the learning has been strategically aligned to the highest priority goals of an organization.

The Constraints and Considerations

For both the firm and the learning function, there are likely to be goals or priorities that need to be addressed without regard to profit or net benefit. A firm may have a strategic goal to increase market share, which at least for this year requires losing money on each sale for a particular product. Likewise in the learning function, the list of highest priority programs produced by the strategic alignment process may not be the same list in the same order as the list of programs with the highest net benefits or ROI. So, neither profit nor net benefit maximization takes the place of strategic planning. Each must operate within the context of strategy, priorities, and goals. For learning, that means starting with strategic alignment and then using net benefit maximization to answer specific questions subject to all the relevant constraints.

Regulation may also require the firm to offer products that are less profitable. (Think of the auto manufacturers and mileage requirements.) In learning, there may also be some compulsory or mandatory training that must be provided even if its net benefits are lower.

Bottom line, the real world complicates things a bit in both cases. The strategy of the firm is to try to maximize total profit across all products even if some are less profitable (or even losers). Basically, do the best possible given the real-world constraints of resources, regulation, and other considerations that cannot be ignored. Likewise, the strategy of the learning function is to maximize net benefit across an organization, subject to all the real-world constraints of budget, staff, priorities, and requirements. In both cases, "production" should continue as long as constraints permit and as long as the marginal profit or net benefit remains positive. If marginal profit or net benefit turns negative, stop even if budget or staff remains (unless the loss is strategically necessary).

Although never perfect or easy in practice, the theory of the firm provides good guidance for firms and for learning functions. It is a mental model or framework for thinking about how to manage the firm or function, and it provides a common language and approach. It causes the right questions to be asked, even when they cannot be answered with certainty.

The same can be said for learning. A framework of maximizing net benefits subject to constraints can provide a common approach and language for analyzing investments in learning. It can provoke deeper examination and richer dialogue about expected impact, benefits, and costs as well as honest discussion about constraints. The bottom line for learning is this: Look for ways to increase the net benefit while still focusing on the highest priority and strategically-aligned learning and meeting other important constraints and requirements.

How Large Should the Program Be?

Applying the theory of the firm directly to learning would imply the net benefits can be maximized by "producing" learning right up to the point where the marginal net benefit of learning is zero. In other words, increase the number of participants until there is zero net benefit from the last one. At this point marginal cost will be just equal to the marginal gross benefit of the learning. Adding more students beyond this point will only detract from the overall net benefit since the marginal cost will exceed the marginal gross benefit.

Increasing Marginal Costs

What might this mean in practice? In learning, the marginal cost of a program may be relatively stable over a wide range of participants since it is often easy to hire additional instructors and procure more materials at the existing rates. Eventually, though, marginal cost is almost certain to rise. Classroom space may become a limiting factor, forcing you to rent space at a higher cost. Or the cost of instructors may rise as you exhaust your internal instructors and hire from the outside (which becomes even more expensive if you have to fly them in and cover their lodging and meals). Even for online courses, you will eventually use up your contractual allotment of seats in your LMS and have to pay an incremental amount to add seats. So, at some point marginal cost will begin to rise as a program grows.

FIGURE 10.5

Marginal Cost for a Typical Course

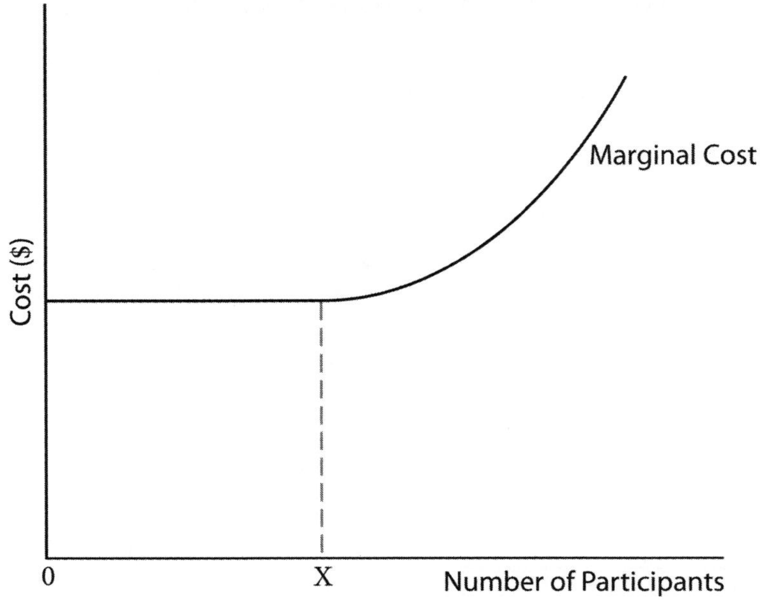

Figure 10.5 illustrates the nature of marginal cost for a typical course. As long as the number of participants remains below X, the marginal cost is constant. Beyond X, however, the marginal cost increases and will likely rise at an increasing rate.

Note: The marginal cost curve above assumes that costs are constant up to X, which would be typical for many learning functions. It is possible, though, that the volume discounts for instructors, rooms, and materials could lead to declining marginal costs up to X, which would result in a marginal cost curve resembling that for a representative firm in Figure 10.2. In either case, the following framework will still apply.

Decreasing Marginal Benefits

Unlike a typical firm, which faces a constant price (and thus constant marginal revenue) for its product, the gross benefit of learning is likely to vary considerably by participant. Some participants will get a lot out of the learning and apply it successfully. In this case the learning will have an impact and create gross and net benefits for the organization. Other participants will be less interested or may

FIGURE 10.6

Marginal Gross Benefit for a Typical Course

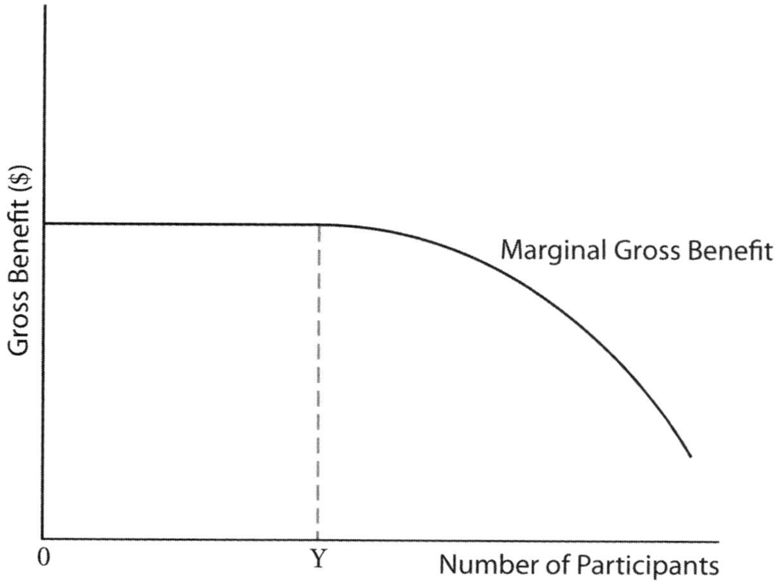

simply not get as much out of it. They may never apply it or not apply it effectively. In this case little or no gross benefit is created. In fact, it is likely for some that the net benefit will be negative, as the marginal cost of learning exceeds the marginal gross benefit. So, the marginal gross benefit will begin to decline at some point as the number of participants increases.

Figure 10.6 illustrates the nature of marginal gross benefit for a typical course. As long as the number of participants remains below Y, the marginal gross benefit remains constant. Beyond Y, however, the marginal gross benefit begins to decline and will likely fall at an increasing rate.

Finding the Optimum Size for a Course

So, the challenge in learning is to select the right participants and the right size for the target audience, such that the net benefit of the last participant is still positive. In other words, the last participants really need the learning *and* will benefit from it *and* will apply it so that their contribution to gross benefit exceeds the marginal cost of their learning. Often, the sponsor for the learning will initially suggest that *all* the employees in a group should take the training. Even if the sponsor is paying for it, it may not make economic (or common) sense. The learning manager needs to question the sponsor enough to determine whether everyone really needs to take it. In a large group there are usually some for whom the training does not make sense, and thanks to the theory of the firm, we can state exactly what we mean by that: the marginal cost will exceed the marginal benefit. When that point is reached, stop production!

Figure 10.7 illustrates the determination of optimum course size graphically by combining the marginal cost and gross benefit curves. Three scenarios are shown. Scenario A shows the marginal gross benefit curve declining when it crosses a still constant marginal cost curve. The number of participants should not exceed ZA, where marginal gross benefit just equals marginal cost. Beyond ZA, marginal cost will exceed marginal gross benefit, resulting in a negative marginal net benefit.

FIGURE 10.7

Three Scenarios for Determining the Optimum Size for a Course

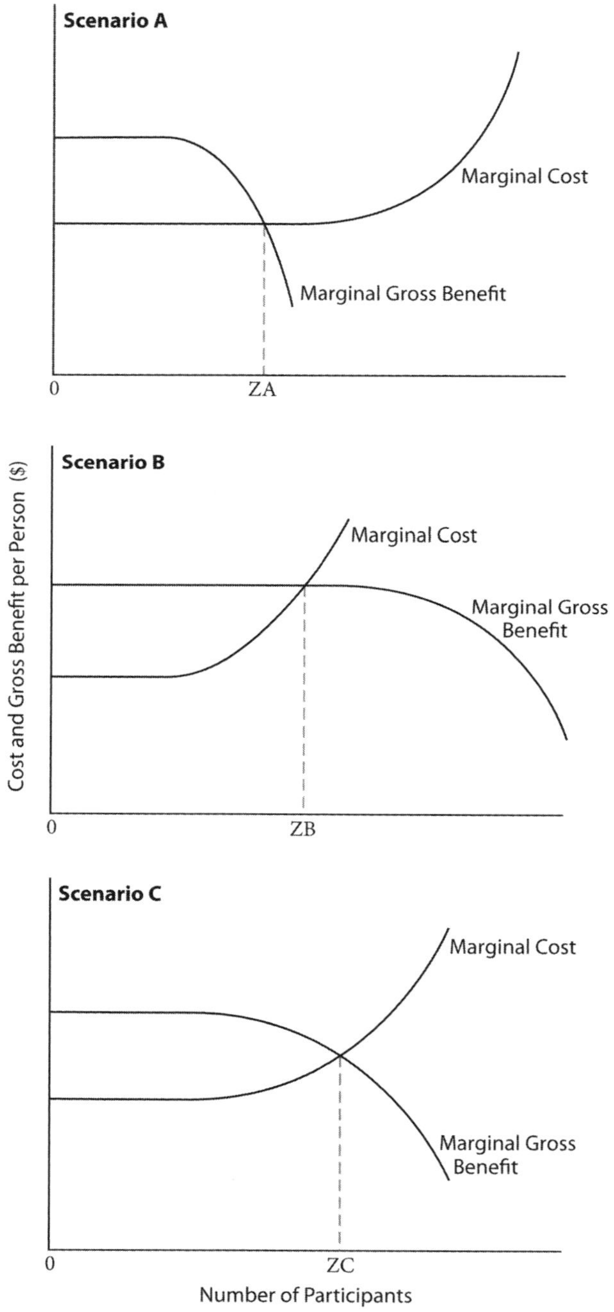

Scenario B shows the opposite situation, where a rising marginal cost curve intersects a still constant marginal benefit curve. The number of participants should not exceed ZB. Finally, scenario C shows intersection occurring when marginal cost is rising and marginal gross benefit is falling. The number of participants should not exceed ZC. All three scenarios are feasible. (Note: Figure 10.7 is not meant to imply that ZC > ZB > ZA.)

In practice, you can try to ensure that net benefit will be positive by identifying the groups in the potential target audience and ranking them by the expected impact of the learning (i.e., marginal gross benefit). For example, consider a course on fraud and insider trading that the sponsor wants to provide to everyone at headquarters. In consultation with the sponsor, identify the groups and rank them in descending order of likely impact (gross benefit). Those at the top of the list are most likely to need, use, and apply the learning, and thus the gross benefit will be the greatest. At some point the gross benefit will begin to decline. It may even become negative for those at the bottom, who are unmotivated to take the learning and are unlikely ever to apply it.

FIGURE 10.8

Ranking of Subgroups by Expected Impact

	Target Audience	
Groups	*Number*	*Cumulative*
Finance managers	10	10
Purchasing managers	12	22
Finance staff	95	117
Purchasing staff	125	242
Public affairs managers	7	249
Public affairs staff	25	274
Treasury managers	6	280
Sales managers	20	300
HR managers	12	312
IT managers	15	327
Treasury staff	35	362
IT staff	115	477
R&D managers	15	492
Medical staff	10	502
R&D staff	95	597
Other HQ staff	200	797

You would know whether marginal cost is expected to be constant through 797 participants or whether it starts to increase before that. If marginal cost is expected to increase, then you would want to share that point with the sponsor and give her an idea of how fast costs will begin to increase. You might say that the "learning becomes really expensive" at this point.

In this example you and the sponsor might agree that it makes sense to target HR managers and above for a total target audience of 312. These groups are the most at risk for fraud and insider trading and are most likely to have opportunities to detect it. For the other 485 employees (797 - 312) the marginal cost is likely to exceed the marginal gross benefit since they are unlikely to have an opportunity to apply it.

Constraints

In the real world, of course, there are budget and staff constraints for both firms and learning functions. So, both firms and learning functions often will run out of resources before they come close to reaching the point of profit (net benefit) maximization. In other words, firms will still be making a marginal profit on the last product sold, and learning functions will still be generating a positive net benefit on the last participant. This may not be profit (net benefit) maximizing behavior, but at least the marginal profit (net benefit) will still be positive. (What we really want to avoid is producing to the point where we have a marginal loss, which would mean we have gone too far.)

Implication for Management

Work with the sponsor to limit the number of participants to those who are likely to benefit enough from the learning to more than offset the costs (including their opportunity costs). Think carefully about the last groups included in the target audience and convince yourself the marginal net benefit of learning is still positive.

Which Programs Should Be Selected?

Applying investment analysis to learning would lead us to select programs with the highest ROI to maximize total net benefits. Of course, and it should go without saying at this point, strategic alignment will already have been completed, so the programs to be evaluated are those that will contribute to the highest priority goals of the organization. We are not starting with a clean slate here and are merely ranking programs by ROI. Maximizing net benefits through the use of ROI is a procedure that can be applied to the selection of an option for a program or of a program itself.

Program Option Selection

The first application of ROI is in the selection of learning options for a single program. Suppose the learning objective is to reduce defects by $400,000. Options might include instructor-led classes, online modules, simulations, performance support, or informal learning, to name a few. Assume the strategic alignment process has been completed and that it has been determined that this is a high-priority need that can and should be addressed by learning. The needs analysis has been completed. The instructional designers believe a variety of options could be used to meet the learning objective. Each option is expected to deliver the $400,000 in reduced defects. The options are provided in Table 10.3.

TABLE 10.3

Summary of Options to Meet the Learning Objectives

Option	*Development Cost*	*Delivery Cost*	*Opportunity Cost*	*Total Cost*	*Gross Benefit*	*Net Benefit*	*ROI*
1) 3 Day ILT	$50,000	$45,000	$180,000	$275,000	$400,000	$125,000	45%
2) 2 Day ILT with 4 WBTs	$40,000	$30,000	$165,000	$235,000	$400,000	$165,000	70%
3) 1.5 Day ILT with mentoring	$45,000	$25,000	$150,000	$220,000	$400,000	$180,000	82%
4) 2 Day Simulation	$75,000	$30,000	$120,000	$225,000	$400,000	$175,000	78%

The cost data in Table 10.3 should be readily available and would be a part of developing the business case. The gross benefits should also be part of the business case and in this example are identical since each option is designed to meet the learning objectives precisely. Options 3 and 4 are both projected to deliver an ROI of about 80% and deliver about $175,000 in net benefit. Either one looks to be superior to option 1 with an ROI of 45%. Investment analysis would suggest choosing option 3 or 4 and would rule out option 1.

Notice that a framework for analysis and discussion is now in place. It is easy to ask questions and challenge assumptions. Does option 3 indeed make sense? Are all the cost forecasts reasonable? Since both options 3 and 4 produce about the same net benefit, are there other factors to favor one over the other? If a learning manager is advocating option 1, this framework provides a basis for reasoned discussion. Does he believe the cost forecasts for option 1 are too high or those for options 3 and 4 too low? Are there some other important factors not captured in the analysis that should be considered?

Notice that the option with the highest ROI has the lowest total cost, and the option with the lowest ROI has the highest total cost. Since each option was designed to deliver the same gross benefit of $400,000, the preferred option can also be found by simply identifying the least cost alternative. This will be the case whenever all the options produce the same gross benefit.

Program Selection

The same theory can be applied to analyzing two or more different programs. Assume there are several programs of equal priority, all strategically aligned to the organization's objectives. These may not be the highest priority programs, and the budget is not large enough to fund them all. Which should be chosen?

Investment analysis provides a framework to answer this question or at least serve as a starting point. Like Table 10.3 above, forecasts should be available for the costs and benefits of each program. Unlike Table 10.3 above, the gross benefits are different for each program as well as the costs. This will be the case when programs are designed to meet different learning objectives or where the learning objectives permit a range of different programs and impacts.

Consider the five programs in Table 10.4, which have been ranked by ROI.

If the budget for this category of programs was $150,000, investment analysis would indicate that the first three should be chosen with ROIs of 61% to 72%. (Add up the budget costs: $65,000 + $25,000 + $60,000 = $150,000, which is the total budget available.) This will produce the highest impact and net benefit for the organization. Likewise, if the budget was $220,000, the first four should be chosen ($65,000 + $25,000 + $60,000 + $65,000 = $215,000, which leaves $5,000 left over).

Note that program A does not have the highest net benefit. Both programs C and E have higher net benefits but cost considerably more, so the ROI is lower than program A. You can convince yourself that selecting programs with the

TABLE 10.4

ROI Ranking for Five Equal Priority, Strategically Aligned Programs

Rank	Program	Development/ Puchase Cost	Delivery Cost	Budget Cost	Opportunity Cost	Total Cost	Gross Benefit	Net Benefit	ROI
1	A	$45,000	$20,000	$65,000	$80,000	$145,000	$250,000	$105,000	72%
2	B	$25,000	$0	$25,000	$105,000	$130,000	$212,000	$82,000	63%
3	C	$30,000	$30,000	$60,000	$120,000	$180,000	$290,000	$110,000	61%
4	D	$50,000	$15,000	$65,000	$60,000	$125,000	$187,000	$62,000	50%
5	E	$205,000	$10,000	$215,000	$40,000	$255,000	$370,000	$115,000	45%

highest ROI produces the highest net benefits by comparing the first four programs (A to D) with program E. The first four programs have a budget cost of $215,000, the same as program E. The total net benefit of the first four programs is $359,000. The net benefit of program E is $115,000, significantly less net benefit for the same investment. (The same reasoning applies, using total costs instead of budget costs.)

Ranking by ROI and Net Benefit

Table 10.4 also illustrates that ranking by net benefit is not necessarily equivalent to ranking by ROI. If the costs of the options or programs are identical, then the ranking will be the same. The closer costs are to being identical, the more likely the ranking will be the same. For example, the first three options in Table 10.3 were similar in costs and even option 4 was not far from the other three. In this case, ranking by net benefit was the same as ranking by ROI.

TABLE 10.5

Ranking by Net Benefit

Options of Table 10.3

Rank	Option	Total Cost	Net Benefit	ROI
1	1.5 Day ILT	$220,000	$180,000	82%
2	2 Day Sim	$225,000	$175,000	78%
3	2 Day ILT	$235,000	$165,000	70%
4	3 Day ILT	$275,000	$125,000	45%

Programs of Table 10.4

Rank	Program	Total Cost	Net Benefit	ROI
1	E	$255,000	$115,000	45%
2	C	$180,000	$110,000	61%
3	A	$145,000	$105,000	72%
4	B	$130,000	$82,000	63%
5	D	$125,000	$57,000	46%

For the programs of Table 10.4, the costs differ significantly, especially for program E. Thus, a ranking by ROI would have produced a very different order.

Implications for Management

If there are multiple options for a single program and all options have roughly the same gross benefit, select the least cost option (unless other factors dictate a more expensive option). The least cost alternative will have the highest ROI and will maximize net benefits, but in this case, neither the gross benefits nor ROI have to be calculated. Just find the least cost option to deliver the results.

If there are multiple programs of equal priority and all are strategically aligned, select the programs with the highest ROI subject to budget constraints and advice from your governing body.

If there are multiple strategically aligned programs of differing priority, select the highest priority programs subject to resource constraints. In this case, do not use ROI to rank the programs. Trust the strategic alignment process, which may result in funding a higher-priority strategically aligned program with a lower ROI than a lower-priority strategically aligned program with a higher ROI. Remember, the goal is to maximize net benefits *subject to strategic alignment*. In other words, strategic alignment and the priorities of the organization take precedence over ROI.

If all the strategically aligned and high-priority programs have been funded and resources remain, use ROI and other factors to select unaligned programs.

How Long Should a Program Be?

Sometimes, the needs analysis does not result in a high-confidence, specific recommendation for duration. This may be particularly true of "softer" programs like leadership, performance management, and business acumen. The need for better leadership, performance management, and business acumen may be well-established and strategically aligned to an organization's goals, but in practice it is often difficult to determine exactly how much learning should be provided. Would two days be better than one in terms of gross benefit for the right target audience? Almost certainly. And would four days be better than two in terms of gross benefit to the participants and the organization? Probably. Where do we stop? What is the optimum program duration? Marginal analysis can provide guidance.

First, consider what gross benefit is likely to be achieved if employees attend class for only one day? Two days? Three days? In many cases this may reflect the rate at which knowledge is transferred or comprehension occurs. In other words, what will they get out of each day that is likely to translate into application and eventual impact?

The answer to this question will be different for different courses and different participants. For this analysis we will assume that there are greater differences among the courses than among the participants in a single course, so we will focus on differences in courses rather than in participants. There are four scenarios to describe what might be called the knowledge transfer rate (acknowledging that the process is more complex than simple knowledge transfer), and each will be explored below over a hypothetical five-day class. These are important because each scenario has a different implication for course duration.

Decreasing Marginal Returns

The first scenario shows decreasing marginal returns. The gross benefit per person is shown below, along with the marginal gross benefit in both table form and graph. In this case gross benefit increases each day for all five days, *but* the marginal increase is less with each day. In the first day of class, each participant receives knowledge (or gains insight or experience or practices a skill) that should eventually lead to a gross benefit of $4,000. In the second day each still learns something of value, which they could apply, but the marginal benefit of day two is only $3,000—not quite as good as day one but still very good. Likewise, the marginal value of day three is $1,800, day four $1,000, and day five $200. Notice that the curve for total gross benefit rises slowly toward the right, reflecting smaller gains each day. Meanwhile, the lower curve for marginal gross benefit starts at $4,000 for the first day but drops quickly toward zero.

FIGURE 10.9

Example of Decreasing Marginal Returns

Gross Benefits per Person

Days	Total	Marginal Increase
1	$4,000	$4,000
2	$7,000	$3,000
3	$8,800	$1,800
4	$9,800	$1,000
5	$10,000	$200

Decision Rule

Less is better

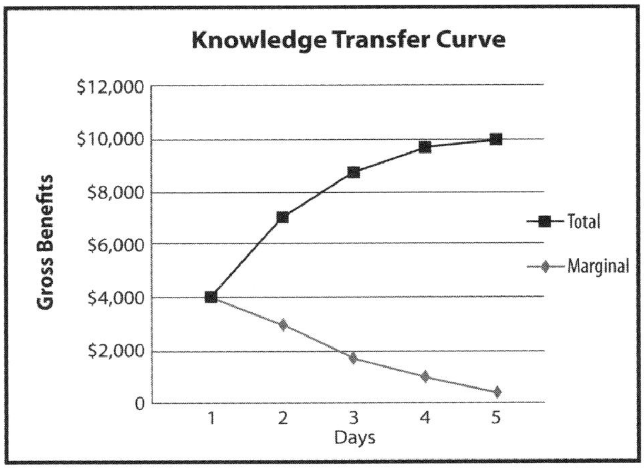

What characterizes a course with decreasing returns? Typically, this kind of course has the biggest payoff in the first day. The essence of the course is conveyed in the first day, and the following days are spent refining or extending the central lesson of the first day.

What are the indications or signs that the course might have decreasing returns?

1. Participants are very excited after the first day and are really looking forward to the second day. Some, though, are less excited or even disappointed with the second day, and more are disappointed with the third, fourth, and fifth days. So, you have decreasing enthusiasm, starting with day two.
2. Attendance the second day is at least as good as the first day as "word" gets around about the first day. The attendance falls off for day three. By day five many have stopped coming.
3. Level 1 feedback is outstanding the first day and declines steadily thereafter.

Implication for management: Do as little as possible. If the needs analysis indicated a range of one to five days, do one day. If the minimum is two days, do two days and no more. Depending on the marginal cost per participant, the marginal net benefit is likely to turn negative quickly. In our example, just the opportunity cost alone easily could be $200 per day, so marginal net benefit would definitely be negative in day five and perhaps sooner, depending on the marginal delivery costs. If the course is designed in this way or previous similar courses have elicited the patterns described above, then make it as short as possible. In the real world, of course, the learning manager will not know the marginal gross benefit or cost by day but should be able to recognize the type of course.

Increasing Marginal Returns

As you would guess, increasing marginal returns is just the opposite of decreasing marginal returns. In this case each day is better than the day before. In the example below day two generates a marginal increase of $1,500, only to be outdone by day three at $2,000 and again by day four at $2,500 and day five at $3,000. The slope of the total gross benefit curve says it all as it rises ever more steeply. The marginal benefit curve rises instead of falling as it did for decreasing returns.

FIGURE 10.10

Example of Increasing Marginal Returns

Gross Benefits per Person

Days	Total	Marginal Increase
1	$1,000	$1,000
2	$2,500	$1,500
3	$4,500	$2,000
4	$7,000	$2,500
5	$10,000	$3,000

Decision Rule

More is better

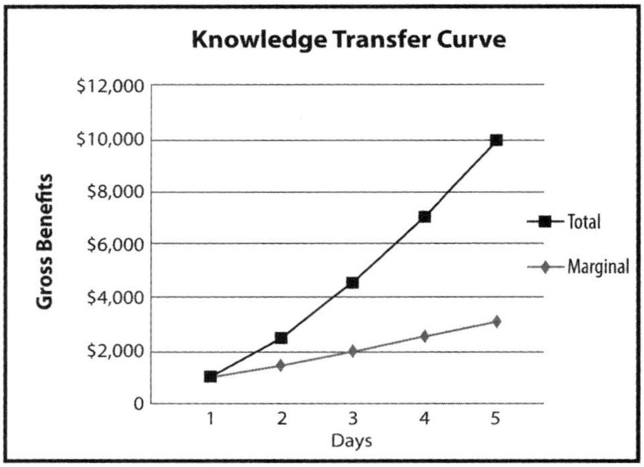

What characterizes a course with increasing returns? Typically, this type of class starts out slowly, building gradually toward the last day, when "it all comes together." It may be a class in which participants take a survey or complete a diagnostic in day one or two and then get the results in day three or four and create an action plan on day five. In this type of class the payoff comes at the end of the course, and anyone who misses the end misses the most important part of class.

What are indications or signs that a course might have increasing returns?

1. Participant excitement and enthusiasm increases each day. The first day's level may not have been high, but the second day was better, and it improves every day.
2. Attendance remains strong throughout the whole class. No one wants to miss class, especially the final class or two. Participants come even when they are sick.
3. Level 1 feedback gets stronger every day. It may not have been very high after day one, but at the end participants are saying this is one of the best classes they have ever taken.

Implication for management: More is better. If the needs analysis indicated three to five days to meet the learning objectives, do five days. If it could be a one or two day course, do two. Assuming the marginal net benefit was positive for day one, there is no need to worry about it going negative since marginal gross benefit is rising each day (unless marginal costs rise even faster, which is usually not the case for a given course).

Note: This is not a suggestion to structure all courses in this way. Remember, the total delivery and opportunity cost will continue to increase every day, so these types of courses are likely to be costly. Reserve them for the situations where they really are necessary and ideally where there are increasing returns.

Constant Marginal Returns

It is possible over short periods that the marginal gross benefits are relatively constant. This means that each day is as good as the day before in terms of knowledge or insights gained. If participants gain $2,000 on day one, then they gain an additional $2,000 on day two and another $2,000 on day three and so on. Graphically, both the total gross benefit and marginal lines are straight. The total line rises steadily to the right while the marginal line is flat at $2,000.

FIGURE 10.11

Example of Constant Marginal Returns

Gross Benefits per Person

Days	Total	Marginal Increase
1	$2,000	$2,000
2	$4,000	$2,000
3	$6,000	$2,000
4	$8,000	$2,000
5	$10,000	$2,000

Decision Rule

Decide on other factors

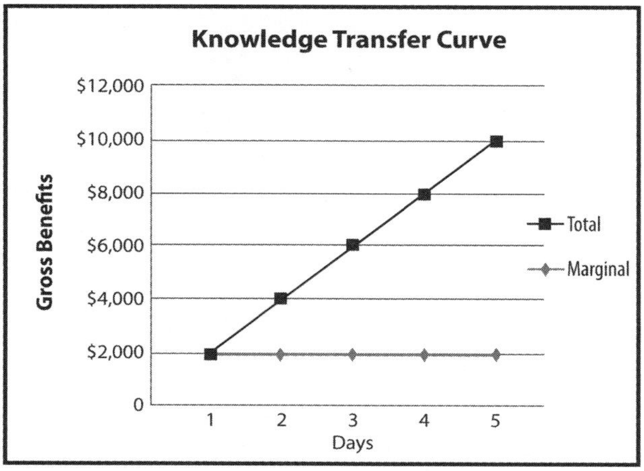

What characterizes constant returns? This type of course unfolds at a steady pace over its entire duration. It neither starts especially strong nor ends especially strong.

What are indications or signs that a course might have constant returns?

1. Participant excitement and enthusiasm are steady throughout the course, neither rising nor falling.
2. Attendance is steady or declines slowly (normal attrition).
3. Level 1 scores are steady with no significant differences from day to day.

Implication for management: None. Make a decision about optimum duration on other factors. Constant returns do not provide a reason for longer or shorter duration.

Mixed Returns to Scale

This is the last scenario and represents a combination of the first three. In practice, a course may exhibit several of the characteristics described above over even a few days. In the example below, the course exhibits increasing returns for the first three days and then decreasing returns for the last two days. The maximum marginal increase occurs on day three at $4,500, after which increasing returns are replaced by decreasing returns. The graph of the marginal gross benefits clearly peaks at day three.

FIGURE 10.12

Example of Mixed Marginal Returns

Gross Benefits per Person

Days	Total	Marginal Increase
1	$1,500	$1,500
2	$3,500	$2,000
3	$8,000	$4,500
4	$9,500	$1,500
5	$10,000	$500

Decision Rule

Target the sweet spot

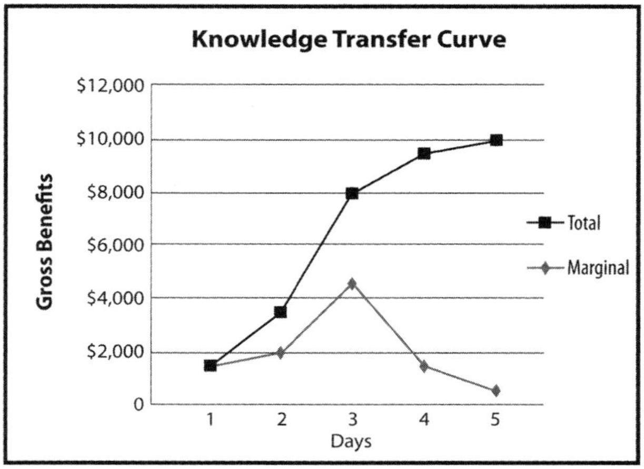

A course with mixed marginal returns will have the characteristics of at least two of the above. The probability of a course with mixed returns increases with duration since it becomes increasingly difficult to manage increasing returns day after day, and a course should not be designed for decreasing returns over a four- or five-day period.

What are indications or signs that a course might have mixed returns?

1. Participant excitement and enthusiasm are mixed, rising one day and falling the next or vice versa.
2. Attendance is irregular since the course appears to be unpredictable to participants. Attendance may rise initially if the course exhibits increasing returns only to fall off as decreasing returns are exhibited. Attendance may also fall for several days and then stabilize as increasing or constant returns take over.
3. Level 1 scores are mixed. They may be up for several days and then down or vice versa.

Implication for management: Target the sweet spot. Since this type of course may be the most common for three-to-five-day durations, target a duration near the maximum marginal gross benefit. In this example, that would be the third day, on which marginal gross benefit is $4,500.This is clearly superior to day two at $2,000 or day four at $1,500. So, if the needs analysis indicates a range of two to five days, target a duration of about three days.

Determining the Returns to Scale in the Real World

Okay, you understand the theory, but you may still be wondering how to apply it. In the real world figures for marginal gross benefits and knowledge transfer graphs do not exist. What can we do? We can use this framework to help make better decisions. Even if those decisions are not perfect, they will be better than if we did not apply this framework.

Use the conceptual framework along with the characteristics and indications provided above to decide what type of course is being designed. Is it likely to have decreasing or increasing returns or mixed or constant returns? Discuss it in detail—day by day—with the instructional designer to find out. Here are some questions to ask:

- What duration are you considering?
- Why?
- Could it be shorter?
- What are your objectives day by day?
- When do participants get the real value in the course?
- What does day two add? What would they miss without day two? How important is it?
- What does day three add? What would they miss without day three? How important is it?
- And so on.

These questions all are aimed at determining the *marginal* gross benefit of each additional day (or hour of online learning). Make them convince you of the need and value of going additional days or hours.

Their first response may be, "It has to be five days. This is the minimum. Anything less, we cannot accomplish the learning objective." Acknowledge that they are dedicated professionals who want to be sure the needs are addressed. But seldom is a five-day course really necessary, and your job as a learning manager is to make the best decision for the company. Not only will delivery costs increase with length but so will opportunity costs and outright resistance (if not by the participants then by their managers and coworkers, who have to cover for them). Some leaders simply will not let their employees take a four- or five-day course. So, long courses are costly and, although they may be necessary from time to time, it is your job to make sure the duration makes sense. You have to think critically about at least the marginal benefit of each additional day (or hour) and convince yourself it is worth it.

ROI Applied to Duration Decisions

In the discussion above we approached duration as a marginal exercise in gross benefits, which is a useful way to think about it in the real world, where marginal net benefit data do not exist. If such data did exist, then each duration option (like two days) could be considered a distinct option, and ROI could be applied to determine (theoretically) the optimum duration, all other considerations aside. Since the marginal analysis above focuses just on gross benefits, it offers a less complete picture than ROI, which brings costs into the equation and will maximize net benefits.

The good news is that both methods provide similar advice and, with some adjustment, the marginal analysis above can approximate the results of the ROI analysis. To see how the two approaches compare, look at the options in Table 10.6. The duration options for ILT A exhibit decreasing returns for marginal gross benefits across all five days (from $3,000 for day one to $500 for day five). So, by just talking with the instructional designer, the learning manager may have concluded the course was likely to exhibit decreasing returns and be looking to make it shorter rather than longer. ROI analysis, if it were available, would point to a two-day course with a maximum ROI of 296%.

Even if these numbers were known, however, in the real world it is impossible to distinguish 296% from 282% from 272%—they all are incredibly high and in the same general range (282% +/- 14%). Practically speaking, ROI says duration of one to three days is optimal. Marginal analysis said less is better and pointed to one or two days. So, everything else being equal and consistent with the needs analysis, choose one or two days.

Next consider the options for ILT B, which exhibits increasing returns and is just the mirror image of ILT A. If the learning manager had concluded that this course was likely to have increasing returns across all five days, then the decision rule is to go for the maximum dictated by the needs analysis. If the needs analysis indicates a range of three to five days, then marginal analysis points to the maximum five-day duration with a marginal gross benefit of $3,000 on day five. ROI analysis, if available, would confirm that the five-day duration maximizes net benefits. Notice that the 211% ROI for five days is clearly superior to the 133% for day four.

Now look at the duration options for WBT. These exhibit constant returns, so the marginal analysis is not helpful. If you knew the ROI, two hours is the best, but in this example all these duration options are terrible. WBT should not be used in this case.

The duration options for simulation exhibit mixed returns with the sweet spot at three days. So, a discussion with the instructional designer (and/or examination of previous courses with similar design) would have led the learning manager to target three days (plus or minus one). If ROI were known, a four-day course would maximize net benefits with an ROI of 432% although a three-day course is close behind at 401%. So, choose three or four days.

TABLE 10.6

Options Available to Improve Customer Support

(Costs and benefits in dollars)

	Total Cost	Cost per Person	Marginal Cost per Person	Gross Benefit per Person	Marginal Gross Benefit per Person	Total Gross Benefit	Total Net Benefit	Net Benefit per Person	Marginal Net Benefit per Person	ROI
ILT A										
Five day	1,029,000	2,573	429	8,000	500	3,200,000	2,171,000	5,428	71	211%
Four day	857,500	2,144	441	7,500	1,000	3,000,000	2,142,500	5,356	559	250%
Three day	681,000	1,703	441	6,500	1,500	2,600,000	1,919,000	4,798	1,059	282%
Two day	504,500	1,261	454	5,000	2,000	2,000,000	1,495,500	3,739	1,546	296%
One Day	323,000	808	808	3,000	3,000	1,200,000	877,000	2,193	2,193	272%
ILT B										
Five day	1,029,000	2,573	429	8,000	3,000	3,200,000	2,171,000	5,428	2,571	211%
Four day	857,500	2,144	441	5,000	2,000	2,000,000	1,142,500	2,856	1,559	133%
Three day	681,000	1,703	441	3,000	1,500	1,200,000	519,000	1,298	1,059	76%
Two day	504,500	1,261	454	1,500	1,000	600,000	95,500	239	546	19%
One Day	323,000	808	808	500	500	200,000	(123,000)	(308)	(308)	-38%
WBT										
Eight hour	343,000	858	303	800	200	320,000	(23,000)	(58)	(103)	-7%
Four hour	222,000	555	198	600	200	240,000	18,000	45	3	8%
Two hour	143,000	358	99	400	200	160,000	17,000	43	101	12%
One hour	103,500	259	259	200	200	80,000	(23,500)	(59)	(59)	-23%
Simulation										
Five day	1,079,000	2,698	441	11,000	(1,000)	4,400,000	3,321,000	8,303	(1,441)	308%
Four day	902,500	2,256	460	12,000	3,000	4,800,000	3,897,500	9,744	2,540	432%
Three day	718,500	1,796	460	9,000	4,000	3,600,000	2,881,500	7,204	3,540	401%
Two day	534,500	1,336	479	5,000	3,000	2,000,000	1,465,500	3,664	2,521	274%
One Day	343,000	858	858	2,000	2,000	800,000	457,000	1,143	1,143	133%

***Conclusion*:** For decreasing returns (ILT A and the last two days of simulation), ROI indicates a slightly longer duration than the marginal analysis (one day in each of these). For increasing returns (ILT B and the first three days of simulation), ROI and marginal analysis identify the same optimum duration.

Implications for Management: Summary

If the needs analysis provides a range of possible durations, conduct an informal analysis of marginal gross benefits by talking with the instructional designer and reviewing previous courses that were similar.

- If decreasing returns seem likely, target a duration near or slightly higher than indicated by the marginal analysis.
- If increasing returns seem likely, target the duration indicated by the marginal analysis. No adjustment is necessary.
- If mixed returns seem likely, target the sweet spot. You might go a little longer if the sweet spot is transitioning from increasing to decreasing returns.

This approach will help you maximize net benefits, increasing your effectiveness.

Conclusion

In this chapter we explored economic theory and its application to learning. Specifically, we applied marginal analysis and the theory of the firm to answer three questions:

1. How large should a program be (target audience)?
2. Which programs should be selected?
3. How long should a program be (duration)?

Economic theory provides guidance in answering all three questions. The analogy was made between the firm and the learning function, with the firm seeking to maximize net profits and the learning function seeking to maximize net benefits, both subject to very important constraints. For learning the most important constraints are strategic alignment and the priorities of the organization. Within this framework, however, tools such as marginal analysis, investment analysis, and ROI can be very helpful in making the best decisions.

The chapter provided both a theoretical framework and practical guidance. Both should help hone the professional judgment of the learning manager and increase the impact of the investment in learning.

Chapter 10 to Do List

1. Reflect on the application of economic theory to learning.
2. Start thinking and talking in terms of marginal benefits and marginal costs.
3. Try to apply the thought process when answering the three questions above in practice.
4. Use the concepts to ask better questions of sponsors and staff.
5. Use the approaches recommended in this chapter to make more disciplined decisions, even when no "hard" data exist.

Further Reading

Case, Karl, Ray Fair, and Sharon Oster. *Principles of Economics*, ninth edition. Upper Saddle River, New Jersey: Pearson Prentice Hall, 2009. (See Chapters 7 and 8: "The Production Process: The Behavior of Profit-Maximizing Firms" and "Short-Run Costs and Output Decisions.")

Chapter 11

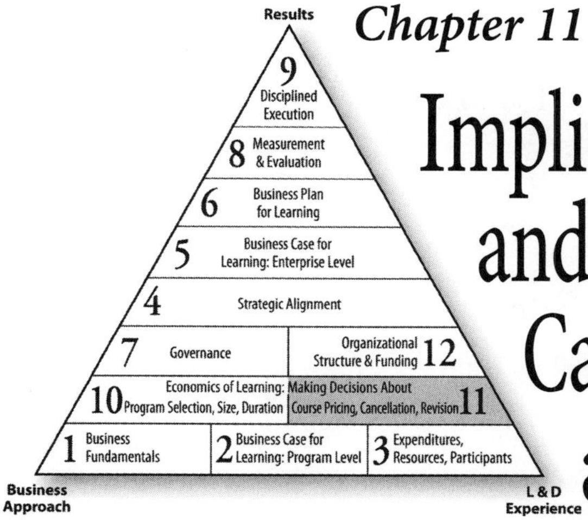

Implications of Scale and Cost for Pricing, Canceling Classes, and Plan Revisions

SCALE IS SIZE. In a learning context it may be the number of participants in a program or a class. Alternatively, it could be the number of unique or total participants served in a time period or the number of courses offered. It could also be the number of classrooms, instructors, or learning locations.

However it is defined, scale makes a difference in terms of the economics of learning. In Chapter 10 we discussed decreasing, constant, and increasing marginal costs and how the concept of marginal analysis could be used to make better decisions about program duration. In this chapter we will explore scale and cost in more depth to understand their implications thoroughly for the pricing and canceling of classes and for plan revisions. The focus will be on the number of participants in a program, which is the most common application of scale in learning.

Key Concepts for Chapter 11

11

1. Scale can have a significant impact on costs and consequently on net benefits and ROI.
2. Fixed cost in particular is a key determinant in many decisions involving pricing or canceling a course or revising the plan.
3. If fixed cost is present, the average total cost curve will slope down, meaning that average cost may be very sensitive to scale.
4. Consequently, it is critical to understand the cost structure of a course.
5. Economic theory can provide a framework for important learning decisions concerning:
   a. Pricing of a class or course
   b. Canceling a class or course
   c. Revising your plan during the year
6. Key economic concepts are average and marginal cost pricing and use of marginal analysis to make decisions regarding cancellations and revisions.
7. Use of these economic tools will improve the decision-making capability of the learning manager, leading to higher efficiency and effectiveness.

Chapter 11 will use the economics of learning to answer the following three questions:

1. How should a class or course be priced?
2. When does it make sense to cancel a class or entire course (program)?
3. How will scale and cost impact revisions to plan?

Reader's Guide

Like Chapter 10, this chapter contains a lot of theory, tables, and graphs and is number intensive. Read the five-page executive summary first and then decide if you want more. The first ten pages are theory, so if theory does not interest you, go straight to the application beginning on page 395. If you decide to go for it, do not get lost in the numbers! Remember, the goal is for you, the learning manager, to develop a deeper understanding of costs and a feel for how scale affects costs. Look for the connections between the different types of costs and for the connections between scale and costs.

Executive Summary

Scale and Cost

Cost is very sensitive to scale. As you would expect, total cost rises with scale or the number of participants. Average cost, though, is especially sensitive to scale, particularly when fixed costs are present. Since average cost is the primary driver for pricing a course, this sensitivity to scale has serious implications for pricing. Average cost and scale also have serious implications for net benefit and need to be clearly understood when creating or revising a business plan. Last, fixed and marginal costs are the key to knowing when to cancel a course or a class, which is really just a decision about scale.

The Basics: Economic Theory of Costs

Total cost is made up of fixed cost (which does not vary with production) and variable cost (which does vary with production). An example of a fixed cost is a building or a long-term lease. These costs will not change during the year, whether production is 100 units or 10,000. Examples of variable costs include inputs to the production process like steel and tires for an auto maker. More steel and tires are required for every car. If a plant is closed for a month, then no steel or tires are required. So, total cost = fixed cost + variable cost.

Average fixed cost (fixed cost / number of units) declines as the number of units produced increases. If fixed cost is \$100, then average fixed cost for 5 units is \$100/5 = \$20, \$10 for 10 units, and \$1 for 100 units. There are two important points here: (1) average fixed cost declines rapidly with scale, and (2) average fixed cost will approach zero at very large scale.

Since average total cost (average cost) equals average fixed cost plus average variable cost, it must reflect the pull of each. Average fixed cost always declines, fast at first and then slower, but always declining. Average variable cost, on the other hand, reflects marginal cost, which falls and then rises with scale for a typical firm ("U"-shaped curve). So, average total cost will decline at first (both average fixed and variable costs are falling). At some point, though, the average variable cost will start to increase. Eventually, the average variable cost will increase faster than the average fixed cost is decreasing, and the average total cost will begin to rise. So, the average total cost for a typical firm will have the same shape as marginal and average cost: a "U" shape.

The Basics: Theory Applied to Learning (Course Development and Delivery)

In learning, course development is typically a fixed cost. Whether done by your own staff or purchased from a vendor, the cost of development does not change once the development is completed. Once completed, it will not vary with class size (scale). In some circumstances, a portion of management time dedicated to managing the deployment may also be fixed and not vary with scale.

Variable costs include instructor costs, room costs, materials, opportunity costs, and, in some circumstances, management time for deploying and reinforcing. Some variable costs like materials and opportunity costs are continuously variable, going up with each additional participant. Other variable costs like instructor and room costs go up in a stair-step fashion each time a new class needs to be set up. These variable costs act like a fixed cost up until the maximum class size is reached, and then they act like a continuously variable cost when the next instructor is hired and the next room rented.

Here is what you should expect for a typical ILT course:

- Total cost increases with scale.
- Average fixed cost declines rapidly with scale and will approach \$0 at large scale.

- Average variable cost is constant at each step.
    - But it does decline between steps as the class fills up.
- Average total cost declines but it does so unevenly.
    - It will decrease steadily up until class capacity is reached.
    - It will increase slightly at each stair step when a new class is added, and then it will resume its decline.
    - It will be lower at each successive stair step.
    - It will decrease the fastest when scale is small.
- Marginal cost is constant.
    - In between steps it equals the materials and opportunity cost for one more participant.
    - At each step it equals the material and opportunity cost for one more participant *plus* the cost of an additional instructor and room.

Here is what you should expect for a typical WBT course:

- Total cost increases with scale.
- Average fixed cost declines rapidly with scale and will approach $0 at large scale.
- There are no steps in the cost functions since the only variable cost (opportunity cost) is truly variable.
- Since the only variable cost is the opportunity cost, average variable cost and the marginal cost are equal and constant.
- Average total cost will approach the average variable cost, which is the marginal cost.

Implications for Pricing

The cost concepts discussed above provide excellent guidance for pricing a course. Note, though, that opportunity cost is *not* used in pricing. Only the budget costs that appear in the income statement are used.

Average Cost Pricing

Price should be set to average cost if the goal is to break even. This is the only price that will result in revenue exactly matching costs. If some courses are priced below average cost, others will need to be priced above in order to break even on all courses. Often, a course will be priced slightly above average cost, in recognition of the possibility that fewer participants than planned may attend or that costs may be greater than expected. This is especially true for small-scale courses, in which average cost will be particularly sensitive to scale.

Marginal and Variable Cost Pricing

Sometimes breakeven has already been achieved and fixed cost has been fully recovered. This would be the case for a course that has already been developed and deployed to the planned number of participants. Typically, the learning function would maintain the original price and simply make a profit on the course. There may be a situation, though, where there is a desire to offer the course at a lower price. In this case, how should it be priced? The price should recover at least the marginal cost of the additional participants. If one more class is being contemplated, then the price has to cover the cost of an instructor and a room and the materials costs for the expected participants. For a full class, this price will be lower than the original price since there are no fixed costs to recover. If only a few people are expected to take the class, the price could turn out to be higher than the original since the instructor and room costs will not be spread over a full class.

Some learning functions employ a funding model (see Chapter 12) in which the sponsor funds all the development costs. In this case the learning function just needs to recover the variable costs, which it can do by setting the price equal to the average variable cost. (Since there are no fixed costs, average variable cost equals average total cost, so this is really a special case of average cost pricing.)

There may be some circumstances in which breakeven is not the goal. Perhaps the learning function wants to maximize profit. In this case, price will be set above average cost. Trial and error will be required to find the profit maximizing price since progressively higher prices will discourage an increasing number of people from taking the course. For example, if a price 10% higher than average cost leads to only a 3% drop in participants, revenue will increase 6.7%. Suppose, however, that a price 30% higher than average cost leads to a 40% drop in participants. Now, revenue will be 22% less than at average cost pricing. In practice, the price typically will be limited by outside competition and internal complaints.

Implications for Canceling Classes and Courses

From time to time, a decision must be made about canceling a class because of low registration. From an economic point of view, the goal is to minimize your loss. So a class should be canceled if doing so results in a smaller loss than proceeding to host it. Fixed, variable, and marginal costs as well as scale all play a role in this decision. Marginal analysis is the tool used to answer the question.

Basically, the procedure is to perform a marginal analysis to determine whether holding the class will result in a marginal profit or loss. At this point fixed costs are considered "sunk costs" and do not enter the analysis. Compare the marginal revenue (participants x price) from holding the class with the marginal cost (which includes all the variable budget costs: instructor, room, materials) of holding the class. If marginal revenue exceeds marginal cost, holding the class will result in a marginal profit, and the class should be held. If marginal cost exceeds marginal revenue, holding the class will result in a marginal loss, and the class should be canceled.

Sometimes the underlying assumptions about the gross benefits or costs of a course change after development is complete or while deployment is underway. Either lower-than-expected benefit or higher-than-expected cost could be a reason to cancel a course. The answer requires a marginal analysis of continuing with the course given the new information about benefit or cost. Recalculate total net benefit and ROI given the new information and then decide whether it's worth continuing.

Implications for Plan Revisions

Implications of scale and cost to keep in mind when creating the business plan include:

- Large fixed costs likely will require a large scale for the course to be viable.
- At a very large scale, average fixed costs approach zero and become almost irrelevant.
- Larger scale often will produce higher total and average net benefit and ROI (assuming constant marginal costs and constant marginal gross benefit).

Implications of scale and cost to keep in mind when revising the business plan include:

- When fixed costs are present, reducing scale will reduce the total net benefit, average net benefit, and ROI.
    - o The percentage reduction in total net benefit will exceed the percentage reduction in scale.
    - o The higher the fixed costs, the greater the percentage reduction in total net benefit, average net benefit, and ROI.
- When fixed costs are present, increasing scale will increase total net benefit, average net benefit, and ROI.
    - o The percentage increase in total net benefit will exceed the percentage increase in scale.
    - o The higher the fixed costs, the greater the percentage increase in total net benefit, average net benefit, and ROI.
- When fixed costs are not present, any percentage change in scale will lead to an equal percentage change in total net benefit.
    - o Average net benefit and ROI will not change.

Note: These conclusions apply when marginal costs and marginal gross benefits are constant, which should hold over a fairly large range.

End of Executive Summary

Scale and Cost

Cost is very sensitive to the scale or size of a program. We saw this in the graphs of Chapter 10. Just as a reminder, Figure 10.2 is repeated below as Figure 11.1, showing the average and marginal cost curves. Notice how rapidly average fixed cost declines with scale. Recall also how marginal cost drove the shapes of the average variable and total cost curves and how the shapes changed with increasing levels of output (scale).

FIGURE 11.1

Marginal and Average Cost Curves for a Representative Firm

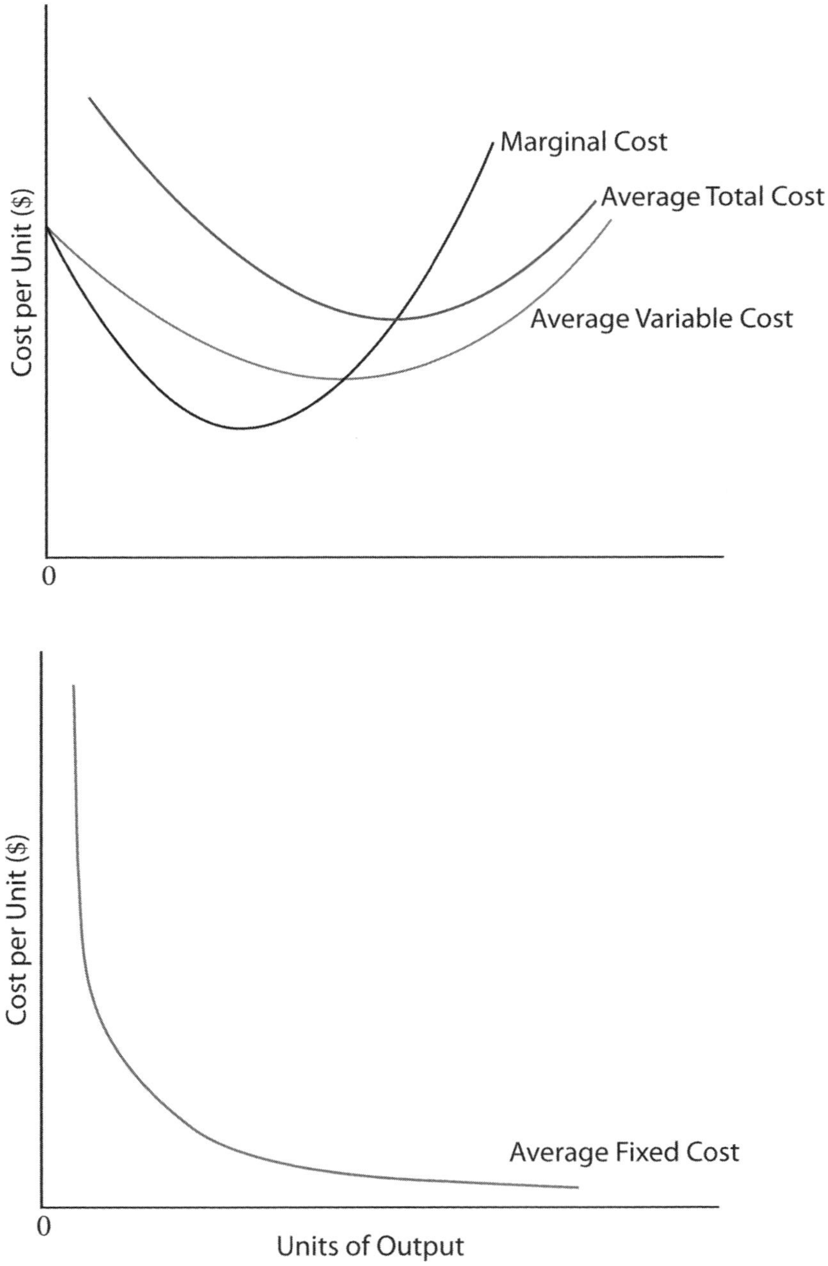

In this chapter we will develop cost curves for courses to help us answer the three questions posed above. We will begin with an example showing costs for a small number of participants and then consider two examples with thousands of participants.

The Basics of Scale and Cost

Small-Scale Instructor-Led Training with Constant Marginal Costs

Our first example is a hypothetical one-day instructor-led program with the following assumptions:

- Development cost of $25,000 for the one-day program, either by a partner or internal staff
- Instructor cost of $2500 per day, including preparation
- Average class size of 20
- Room charge of $250
- Materials charge of $50 per participant
- Opportunity cost of the participants' time valued at their labor and related rate of $400 per day
- Constant marginal costs (The daily cost for additional instructors and rooms does not rise as additional instructors and rooms are added.)

In practice, other costs also may be present, such as participant travel (variable) and management and reinforcement of the program (probably some fixed and some variable).

The development cost is fixed, meaning it does not vary depending on how many participants eventually take the class. Furthermore, the entire $25,000 will be spent before the first participant takes the class. The delivery costs are variable, meaning they increase with the number of participants. Note, though, that the instructor and room charges do not increase with every additional participant like materials charges do. Instead, the instructor and room charges increase in a stair-step fashion with every twenty participants, when a new instructor and room are required. (In other words, the instructor and room charges act like fixed costs until room capacity is reached.) Opportunity cost, like that for materials, is truly (or continuously) variable and increases with every additional participant. The three different cost patterns are illustrated in Figure 11.2.

FIGURE 11.2

Graphs of Development, Instructor, and Materials Costs

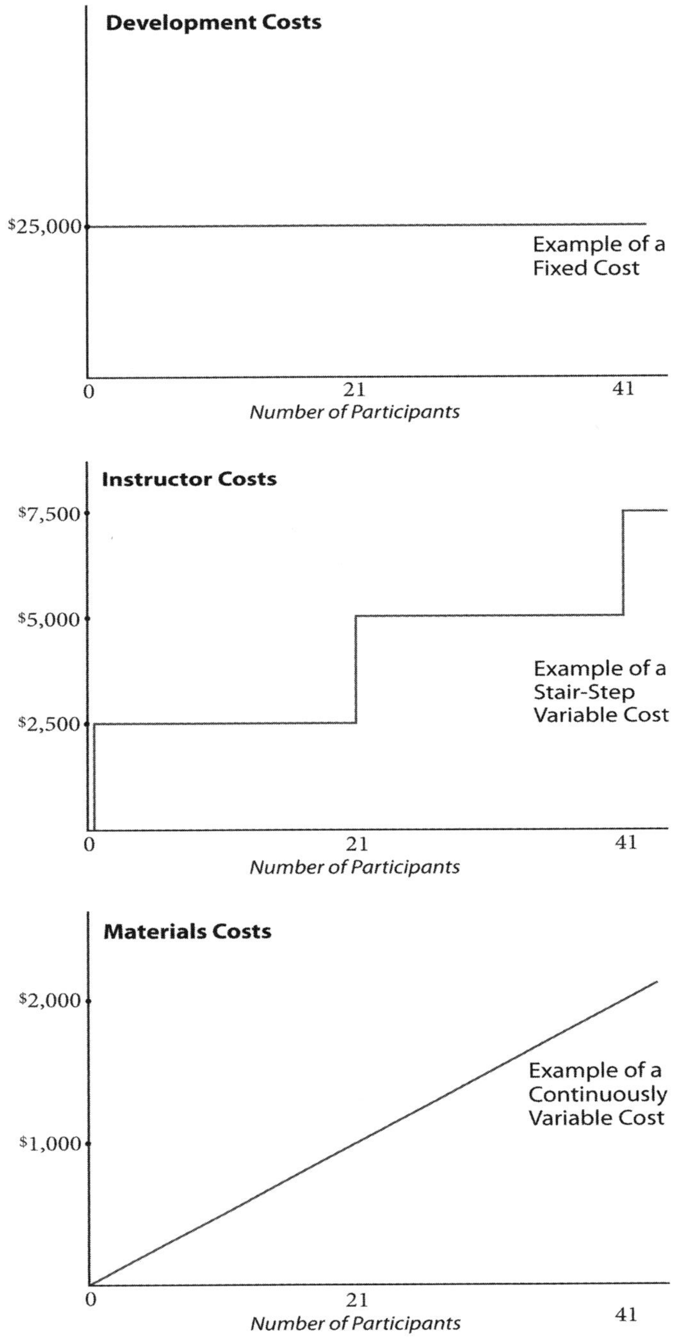

Table 11.1 shows all three types of costs for analysis: total, average, and marginal. Average is simply the total divided by the number of participants. Marginal is the incremental cost of adding one more participant. By definition the fixed development cost of $25,000 is incurred before the class is offered, so it is listed starting with participant 0. Variable cost begins with the first participant.

Notice the following:

- Fixed Costs
    - Average fixed costs decline rapidly with scale. The average fixed cost for development is $25,000 for one participant, $5,000 for five participants, and only $1,000 for 25 participants. By participant 20 average fixed costs have declined 95% from $25,000 to $1,250.
    - The marginal cost of development is $25,000 and then zero. There are no marginal fixed costs for adding participants once it is developed.
- Variable Costs
    - Delivery
        - Average variable costs for delivery within each step also decline with scale although not quite as rapidly as average fixed costs for development. By participant 20 average delivery costs have declined 93% from $2,800 to $188.
        - The decline within each step is driven by the decline in average costs for the instructor and the room, which act like fixed costs until another class is added. In fact, if it were not for material costs, average delivery cost would also have declined 95% by participant 20.
        - The average variable cost for a class of 20 is constant at $188 (see the lines for 20 and 40 participants). The $188 simply represents delivery ($2500/20 = $125) plus room ($250/20 = $12.50) plus materials ($50).
        - Because of the stair-step function when average class size is reached, notice that average cost does rise from $188 to $312 for the 21st participant and again from $188 to $251 for the 41st participant.
        - The marginal cost is $2,800 (instructor + room + materials) for the first participant but then only $50 (materials) after that until the second instructor and room are required. In this example marginal costs are constant between stair steps ($50) and constant in the rise of each step ($2,800).
    - Opportunity
        - Average and marginal opportunity costs are a constant $400.
- Total
    - Total cost rises with scale.

TABLE 11.1

Detailed Costs for 1-41 Participants

	Fixed Costs			Variable Costs												Total Costs		
Participant	Development			Delivery						Opportunity			Total					
Number	Total	Average	Marginal	Instructors	Room	Materials	Total	Average	Marginal	Total	Average	Marginal	Total	Average	Marginal	Total	Average	Marginal
0	$25,000	NA	$25,000	$0	$0	$0	$0	NA	NA	$0	NA	NA	$0	NA	NA	$25,000	NA	NA
1	$25,000	$25,000	$0	$2,500	$250	$50	$2,800	$2,800	$2,800	$400	$400	$400	$3,200	$3,200	$3,200	$28,200	$28,200	$3,200
2	$25,000	$12,500	$0	$2,500	$250	$100	$2,850	$1,425	$50	$800	$400	$400	$3,650	$1,825	$450	$28,650	$14,325	$450
3	$25,000	$8,333	$0	$2,500	$250	$150	$2,900	$967	$50	$1,200	$400	$400	$4,100	$1,367	$450	$29,100	$9,700	$450
4	$25,000	$6,250	$0	$2,500	$250	$200	$2,950	$738	$50	$1,600	$400	$400	$4,550	$1,138	$450	$29,550	$7,388	$450
5	$25,000	$5,000	$0	$2,500	$250	$250	$3,000	$600	$50	$2,000	$400	$400	$5,000	$1,000	$450	$30,000	$6,000	$450
6	$25,000	$4,167	$0	$2,500	$250	$300	$3,050	$508	$50	$2,400	$400	$400	$5,450	$908	$450	$30,450	$5,075	$450
7	$25,000	$3,571	$0	$2,500	$250	$350	$3,100	$443	$50	$2,800	$400	$400	$5,900	$843	$450	$30,900	$4,414	$450
8	$25,000	$3,125	$0	$2,500	$250	$400	$3,150	$394	$50	$3,200	$400	$400	$6,350	$794	$450	$31,350	$3,919	$450
9	$25,000	$2,778	$0	$2,500	$250	$450	$3,200	$356	$50	$3,600	$400	$400	$6,800	$756	$450	$31,800	$3,533	$450
10	$25,000	$2,500	$0	$2,500	$250	$500	$3,250	$325	$50	$4,000	$400	$400	$7,250	$725	$450	$32,250	$3,225	$450
11	$25,000	$2,273	$0	$2,500	$250	$550	$3,300	$300	$50	$4,400	$400	$400	$7,700	$700	$450	$32,700	$2,973	$450
12	$25,000	$2,083	$0	$2,500	$250	$600	$3,350	$279	$50	$4,800	$400	$400	$8,150	$679	$450	$33,150	$2,763	$450
13	$25,000	$1,923	$0	$2,500	$250	$650	$3,400	$262	$50	$5,200	$400	$400	$8,600	$662	$450	$33,600	$2,585	$450
14	$25,000	$1,786	$0	$2,500	$250	$700	$3,450	$246	$50	$5,600	$400	$400	$9,050	$646	$450	$34,050	$2,432	$450
15	$25,000	$1,667	$0	$2,500	$250	$750	$3,500	$233	$50	$6,000	$400	$400	$9,500	$633	$450	$34,500	$2,300	$450
16	$25,000	$1,563	$0	$2,500	$250	$800	$3,550	$222	$50	$6,400	$400	$400	$9,950	$622	$450	$34,950	$2,184	$450
17	$25,000	$1,471	$0	$2,500	$250	$850	$3,600	$212	$50	$6,800	$400	$400	$10,400	$612	$450	$35,400	$2,082	$450
18	$25,000	$1,389	$0	$2,500	$250	$900	$3,650	$203	$50	$7,200	$400	$400	$10,850	$603	$450	$35,850	$1,992	$450
19	$25,000	$1,316	$0	$2,500	$250	$950	$3,700	$195	$50	$7,600	$400	$400	$11,300	$595	$450	$36,300	$1,911	$450
20	$25,000	$1,250	$0	$2,500	$250	$1,000	$3,750	$188	$50	$8,000	$400	$400	$11,750	$588	$450	$36,750	$1,838	$450
21	$25,000	$1,190	$0	$5,000	$500	$1,050	$6,550	$312	$2,800	$8,400	$400	$400	$14,950	$712	$3,200	$39,500	$1,902	$3,200
22	$25,000	$1,136	$0	$5,000	$500	$1,100	$6,600	$300	$50	$8,800	$400	$400	$15,400	$700	$450	$40,400	$1,836	$450
23	$25,000	$1,087	$0	$5,000	$500	$1,150	$6,650	$289	$50	$9,200	$400	$400	$15,850	$689	$450	$40,850	$1,776	$450
24	$25,000	$1,042	$0	$5,000	$500	$1,200	$6,700	$279	$50	$9,600	$400	$400	$16,300	$679	$450	$41,300	$1,721	$450
25	$25,000	$1,000	$0	$5,000	$500	$1,250	$6,750	$270	$50	$10,000	$400	$400	$16,750	$670	$450	$41,750	$1,670	$450
26	$25,000	$962	$0	$5,000	$500	$1,300	$6,800	$262	$50	$10,400	$400	$400	$17,200	$662	$450	$42,200	$1,623	$450
27	$25,000	$926	$0	$5,000	$500	$1,350	$6,850	$254	$50	$10,800	$400	$400	$17,650	$654	$450	$42,650	$1,580	$450
28	$25,000	$893	$0	$5,000	$500	$1,400	$6,900	$246	$50	$11,200	$400	$400	$18,100	$646	$450	$43,100	$1,539	$450
29	$25,000	$862	$0	$5,000	$500	$1,450	$6,950	$240	$50	$11,600	$400	$400	$18,550	$640	$450	$43,550	$1,502	$450
30	$25,000	$833	$0	$5,000	$500	$1,500	$7,000	$233	$50	$12,000	$400	$400	$19,000	$633	$450	$44,000	$1,467	$450
31	$25,000	$806	$0	$5,000	$500	$1,550	$7,050	$227	$50	$12,400	$400	$400	$19,450	$627	$450	$44,450	$1,434	$450
32	$25,000	$781	$0	$5,000	$500	$1,600	$7,100	$222	$50	$12,800	$400	$400	$19,900	$622	$450	$44,900	$1,403	$450
33	$25,000	$758	$0	$5,000	$500	$1,650	$7,150	$217	$50	$13,200	$400	$400	$20,350	$617	$450	$45,350	$1,374	$450
34	$25,000	$735	$0	$5,000	$500	$1,700	$7,200	$212	$50	$13,600	$400	$400	$20,800	$612	$450	$45,800	$1,347	$450
35	$25,000	$714	$0	$5,000	$500	$1,750	$7,250	$207	$50	$14,000	$400	$400	$21,250	$607	$450	$46,250	$1,321	$450
36	$25,000	$694	$0	$5,000	$500	$1,800	$7,300	$203	$50	$14,400	$400	$400	$21,700	$603	$450	$46,700	$1,297	$450
37	$25,000	$676	$0	$5,000	$500	$1,850	$7,350	$199	$50	$14,800	$400	$400	$22,150	$599	$450	$47,150	$1,274	$450
38	$25,000	$658	$0	$5,000	$500	$1,900	$7,400	$195	$50	$15,200	$400	$400	$22,600	$595	$450	$47,600	$1,253	$450
39	$25,000	$641	$0	$5,000	$500	$1,950	$7,450	$191	$50	$15,600	$400	$400	$23,050	$591	$450	$48,050	$1,232	$450
40	$25,000	$625	$0	$5,000	$500	$2,000	$7,500	$188	$50	$16,000	$400	$400	$23,500	$588	$450	$48,500	$1,213	$450
41	$25,000	$610	$0	$7,500	$750	$2,050	$10,300	$251	$2,800	$16,400	$400	$400	$26,700	$651	$3,200	$51,700	$1,261	$3,200

- Since fixed cost is present and average fixed cost declines rapidly with scale, average total cost will also decline with scale.
- If no fixed cost is present, average total cost would just equal average variable cost.
    - o Average total cost declines in stair-step fashion, but not as fast as average fixed cost, which declines continuously.
    - o Marginal cost is constant at $450 per participant in between steps and $3,200 at each step. In other words, it costs $450 to add each new participant unless a new room and instructor are required, in which case the marginal cost becomes $3,200.

TABLE 11.2

Cost Summary for 1-80 Participants

Cost	*Fixed or Variable*	*Number of Participants* 1	20	40	60	80
Development	Fixed	$25,000	$25,000	$25,000	$25,000	$25,000
Delivery						
Instructor	Variable	$2,500	$2,500	$5,000	$7,500	$10,000
Room	Varibale	$250	$250	$500	$750	$1,000
Materials	Variable	$50	$1,000	$2,000	$3,000	$4,000
Total		$2,800	$3,750	$7,500	$11,250	$15,000
Opportunity	Variable	$400	$8,000	$16,000	$24,000	$32,000
Total Costs		$28,200	$36,750	$48,500	$60,250	$72,000
Fixed		$25,000	$25,000	$25,000	$25,000	$25,000
Variable		$3,200	$11,750	$23,500	$35,250	$47,000
Average Costs						
Fixed		$25,000	$1,250	$625	$417	$313
Variable		$3,200	$588	$588	$588	$588
Total		$28,200	$1,838	$1,213	$1,004	$900
Marginal Cost						
Between steps		NA	$450	$450	$450	$450
At steps		$3,200	$3,200	$3,200	$3,200	$3,200

Table 11.2 summarizes the key costs from Table 11.1 and includes results for sixty and eighty participants as well. Notice that average fixed cost declines rapidly, pulling down the average total cost. Marginal cost is constant in between steps and at each step.

Note in particular how quickly average total cost declines when the scale increases from 1 to 20. The average total cost for 20 participants is $1,838, compared to $28,200 for one participant, a decline of 93%. Compare this with the 34% reduction in going from 20 to 40 participants, the 17% reduction in going from 40 participants to 60, or the 10% reduction in going from 60 participants to 80. When fixed cost is present, scale will have the greatest percentage impact on cost when the number of participants is small.

Figure 11.3 illustrates the cost curves from Table 11.2. The first graph shows marginal costs at each step (1, 21, 41, 61, and 81) and in between each step. The second graph shows other costs at the class sizes of 1 to 80. The presence of a fixed cost combined with constant marginal costs produces the downward sloping average variable and total costs curves. The impact of the spike in marginal cost at each step is clearly evident.

Take-aways

The tables and graphs should have convinced you of the following:

1. Scale has a significant influence on total and average cost.
2. Total cost rises with scale.
    a. If fixed costs are present, total cost will rise more slowly than scale. (The percentage increase in total cost will be less than the percentage increase in scale. In other words, a 50% increase in scale will not lead to a 50% increase in total cost.)
3. Average costs decline with scale.
    a. Average fixed cost declines the fastest and never stops declining.
    b. Average variable cost is constant at each step ($588) and declines between steps.
    c. Average total cost declines because of falling average fixed cost but does so unevenly because of the step-like nature of variable costs associated with adding the next instructor and classroom.
    d. Average total cost will be most sensitive to changes in scale when scale is small.

FIGURE 11.3

Marginal and Average Cost Curves for Table 11.2

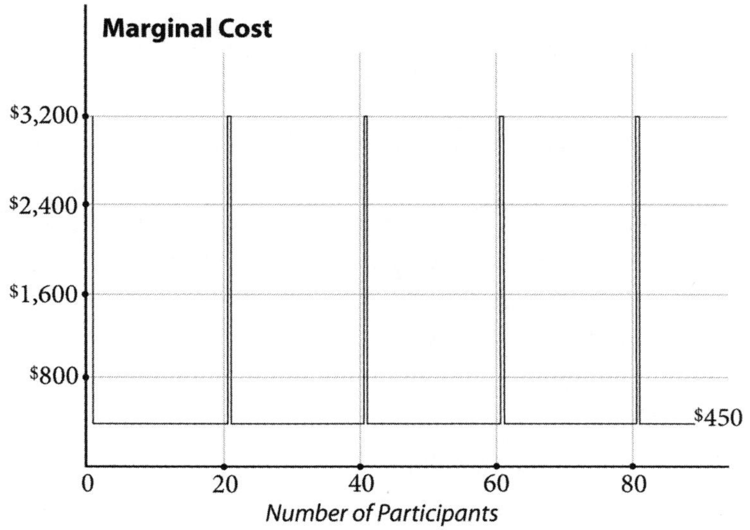

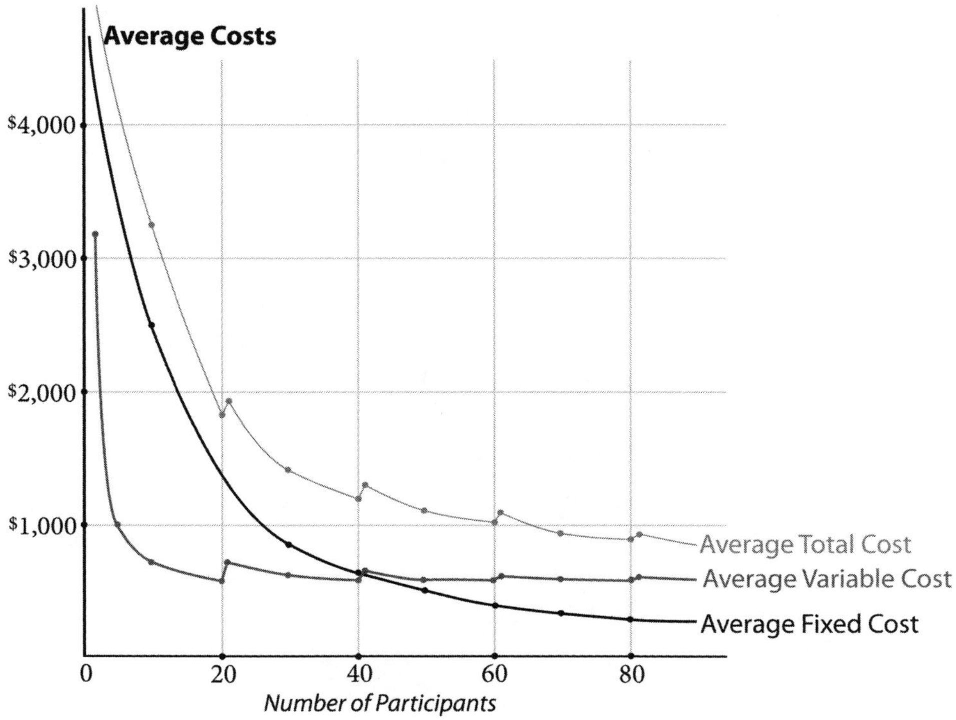

4. Marginal cost between steps is just the materials and opportunity cost, which will be constant.
5. Marginal cost at each step is higher by the amount of the additional instructor and room charge.
   a. It will be the same at each step since constant marginal costs have been assumed.

Note: The declining average costs for delivery in Tables 11.1 and 11.2 are typical of a situation in which marginal costs are constant. As discussed in the last chapter, it is possible to reach a point where marginal costs start to increase. For instance, it may become more and more expensive to hire instructors or procure space. In this case, increasing marginal costs eventually will lead to increasing average costs. An example is provided below.

Large-Scale Programs

Now consider larger scale programs with thousands of participants, which can drive average fixed costs to almost zero.

Instructor-Led Training with Constant Marginal Costs

The example: Assumptions remain unchanged from above with regard to development, delivery, and opportunity costs for a one-day instructor-led program with constant marginal costs. Table 11.3 provides the relevant costs for scale up to 5000 participants.

As you would expect, average fixed costs decline rapidly. In fact, for 5,000 participants the average fixed cost is only $5. So, for very large instructor-led programs average fixed costs can become negligible. Although average variable costs decline within each step, they are constant at $588 when the class average is reached. The $588 simply represents delivery ($2,500/20 = $125) plus room ($250/20 = $12.50) plus materials ($50) plus opportunity costs ($400).

Since average variable costs are constant at each step, average total costs are driven down entirely by the decline in average fixed costs. For 5,000 participants the average total cost declines to $593, about one-third of the $1,838 average for 20 participants. Even if the average fixed cost approaches zero, the average total cost will never decline below $588, which is the constant average variable cost.

TABLE 11.3

Cost Summary for an ILT Course with up to 5,000 Participants and Constant Marginal Costs

		Number of Participants				
Cost	*Fixed or Variable*	*10*	*20*	*100*	*1000*	*5000*
Development	Fixed	$25,000	$25,000	$25,000	$25,000	$25,000
Delivery	Variable	$3,250	$3,750	$18,750	$187,500	$937,500
Opportunity	Variable	$4,000	$8,000	$40,000	$400,000	$2,000,000
Total Cost		$32,250	$36,750	$83,750	$612,500	$2,962,500
Fixed		$25,000	$25,000	$25,000	$25,000	$25,000
Variable		$7,250	$11,750	$58,750	$587,500	$2,937,500
Average Costs						
Fixed		$2,500	$1,250	$250	$25	$5
Variable		$725	$588	$588	$588	$588
Total		$3,225	$1,838	$838	$613	$593
Marginal Costs						
Between steps		$450	$450	$450	$450	$450
At steps		NA	$3,200	$3,200	$3,200	$3,200

FIGURE 11.4

Marginal and Average Cost Curves for Table 11.3

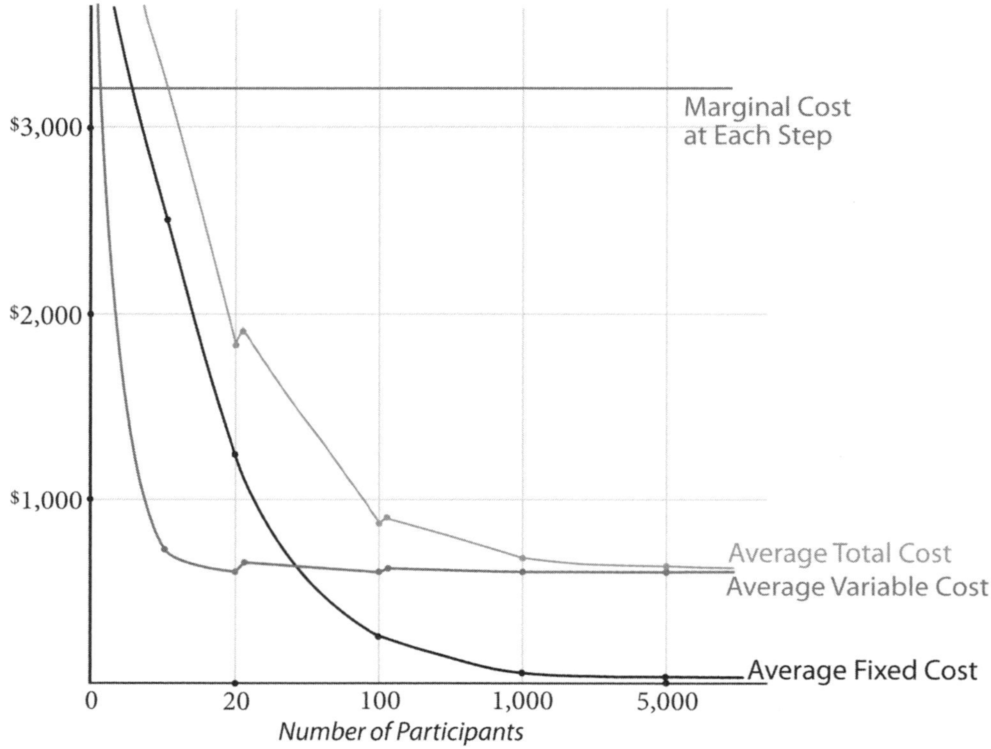

Note: Marginal cost of $450 between steps not shown

Figure 11.4 illustrates the cost curves from Table 11.3. The graph shows marginal costs at each step (1, 21, 101, 1,001, and 5,001) and other costs at the class sizes of 1 to 20, 100, 1,000, and 5,000. As in Figure 11.3, constant marginal costs produce the downward sloping average variable and total costs curves, which become very tightly compressed beyond 1,000 participants.

As in the small-scale example earlier, cost is most sensitive to changes in scale when scale is smaller. In other words, the fewer the participants, the more sensitive average total cost will be. In the large scale example above in Table 11.3, compare the impact on cost of a five-fold increase from 20 to 100 participants with a five-fold increase from 1,000 to 5,000 participants. The average total cost falls 54% ($1,838 to $838) from 20 to 100 participants but only 3% ($613 to $593) from 1,000 to 5,000 participants.

Take-aways when marginal costs are constant:

1. At large scale, average fixed cost approaches zero
2. Average variable cost will be a constant at average class sizes such as 20, 40, and so on, all the way to 5,000 ($588 in the above example).
3. For most programs at large scale, average variable cost will significantly exceed average fixed cost.
   a. Thus, average total cost will approach the average variable cost.
4. The average total cost will be most sensitive to changes in scale when the scale is small.
5. The marginal cost is constant at each step (which is how the example was created).

Instructor-Led Training with Increasing Marginal Costs

The example: In practice marginal costs are likely to start increasing at some point as instructor and venue resources become limited. Higher marginal costs will lead to higher average variable costs and thus higher average total costs.

To show the impact of rising marginal costs, assume the same as above except that the cost of instructors and rooms begins to rise after 10 classes, according to the following schedule:

TABLE 11.4

Schedule of Increasing Marginal Costs for Instructor and Room

Class Number	*Instructor*	*Room*
1-10	$2500	$250
11-25	$3000	$300
26-50	$4000	$400
51-100	$5000	$500
101-250	$6000	$600
251-500	$7000	$700
501-1000	$8000	$800

Under these assumptions variable costs begin to rise after 10 classes or 200 participants (200 participants / an average of 20 per class = 10 classes). The marginal cost schedule shows the marginal cost for instructors rising by $500 to $3,000 for the 11th class as well as the $50 increase for room rental to $300. In the table below, notice the $550 ($500 + $50) increase in marginal cost for the 201st participant from $3,200 to $3,750. Likewise, the marginal cost increases $1,100 for the 501st participant or 26th class as the instructor cost goes up $1,000 and room cost goes up $100.

Once marginal costs begin to increase, variable and average total costs will follow. Table 11.5 shows the average variable costs increasing from $588 for 200 participants to $604 for 500 participants. By 1,000 participants, the average total cost has begun to increase, rising from $654 to $661 as the increase in average variable cost of $32 ($636 - $604) more than offsets the continued decline in average fixed cost of $25 ($50 - $25). (In this example, the minimum average total cost of $649 comes at about 900 participants.)

Figure 11.5 illustrates the cost curves from Table 11.5. The graph shows marginal costs at each step (1, 21, 101, 1001, 5,001 and 10,001) and other costs at the class sizes of 1 to 20, 100, 200, 500, 1,000, 2,000, 5,000, and 10,000. Although the average variable and total cost curves converge in the graph beyond 2,000 participants, notice that neither curve is continually downward sloping as in Figure 11.4 above.

TABLE 11.5

Cost Summary for an ILT Course with up to 10,000 Participants and Increasing Marginal Costs

Cost	*Fixed or Variable*	*Number of Participants* 20	100	200	500	1000	2000	5000	10,000
Development	Fixed	$25,000	$25,000	$25,000	$25,000	$25,000	$25,000	$25,000	$25,000
Delivery	Variable	$3,750	$18,750	$37,500	$102,000	$236,000	$561,000	$1,701,000	$3,876,000
Opportunity	Variable	$8,000	$40,000	$80,000	$200,000	$400,000	$800,000	$2,000,000	$4,000,000
Total Cost		$36,750	$83,750	$142,500	$327,000	$661,000	$1,386,000	$3,726,000	$7,901,000
Fixed		$25,000	$25,000	$25,000	$25,000	$25,000	$25,000	$25,000	$25,000
Variable		$11,750	$58,750	$117,500	$302,000	$636,000	$1,361,000	$3,701,000	$7,876,000
Average Costs									
Fixed		$1,250	$250	$125	$50	$25	$13	$5	$3
Variable		$588	$588	$588	$604	$636	$681	$740	$788
Total		$1,838	$838	$713	$654	$661	$693	$745	
$790									
Marginal Costs									
Between steps		$450	$450	$450	$450	$450	$450	$450	$450
At steps		$3,200	$3,200	$3,750	$4,850	$5,950	$7,050	$8,150	$9,250

FIGURE 11.5

Marginal and Average Cost Curves for Table 11.5

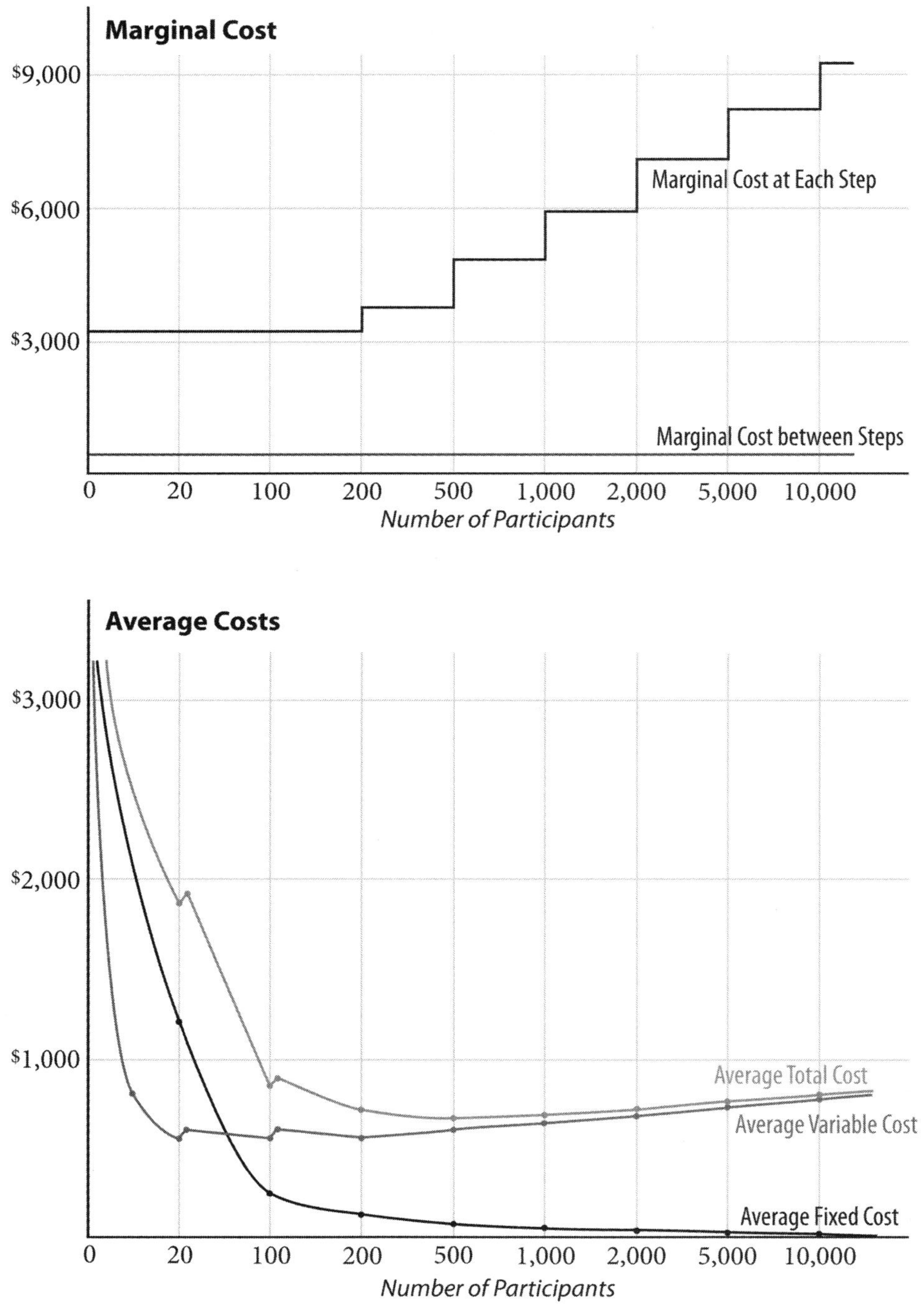

For clarity we can smooth the cost curves from Figure 11.5 to better see the impact of rising marginal cost on average variable and total costs. Figure 11.6 illustrates the key costs that have now been smoothed out. Notice that shortly after marginal cost begins to rise (1), average variable cost will begin to rise (2), which in turn will eventually cause the average total cost to rise (3).

FIGURE 11.6

Smoothed Cost Curves for a Typical Course with Increasing Marginal Costs

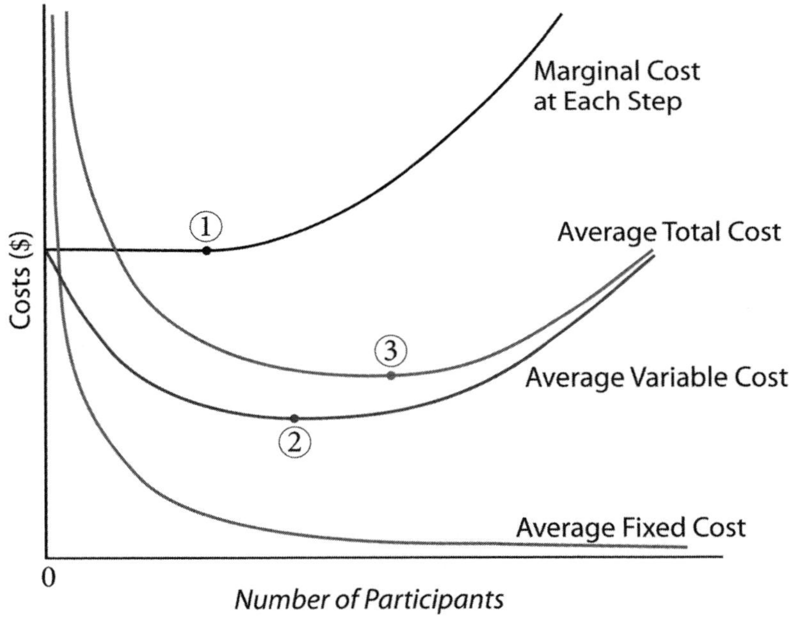

Take-aways when marginal costs are increasing:

1. At large scale, average fixed cost still approaches zero.
2. Average variable cost will decline at first, reflecting constant marginal costs and then an increase following the increase in marginal cost.
3. Average total cost will continue to decline for a while after variable cost begins to increase but will eventually begin to increase as the increasing average variable cost more than offsets the declining average fixed cost.

Web-Based Training with Constant Marginal Cost

The example: Finally, consider a web-based example for a one-hour online offering. Assume development costs of $10,000 and no incremental LMS expense. Opportunity cost will be for one hour or $50 per participant. Table 11.6 illustrates the costs.

TABLE 11.6

Cost Summary for a WBT Course with up to 5,000 Participants

Cost	*Fixed or Variable*	Number of Participants *10*	*20*	*100*	*1000*	*5000*
Development	Fixed	$10,000	$10,000	$10,000	$10,000	$10,000
Delivery	Variable	$0	$0	$0	$0	$0
Opportunity	Variable	$500	$1,000	$5,000	$50,000	$250,000
Total Cost		$10,500	$11,000	$15,000	$60,000	$260,000
Fixed		$10,000	$10,000	$10,000	$10,000	$10,000
Variable		$500	$1,000	$5,000	$50,000	$250,000
Average Costs						
Fixed		$1,000	$500	$100	$10	$2
Variable		$50	$50	$50	$50	$50
Total		$1,050	$550	$150	$60	$52
Marginal Cost		$50	$50	$50	$50	$50

Average fixed cost declines rapidly, dropping to $2 per participant for 5,000 participants. The only remaining cost is the opportunity cost (variable cost), which is constant at $50 per participant. So, at a scale of 5,000 participants, the opportunity cost is *25 times* greater than the development cost and nearly the entire average cost.

Take-aways:

1. At large scale, average fixed cost approaches zero.
2. Since the only variable cost is the constant marginal cost, the average variable cost and the marginal cost are equal and constant.
3. The average total cost will approach the average variable cost, which is the marginal cost.
4. There are no steps in the cost functions since the only variable cost (opportunity cost) is truly variable.

Implications for Pricing

Now we are ready to put these concepts to work to answer three important questions in learning:

1. How should a class or course be priced?
2. When does it make sense to cancel a class or entire course (program)?
3. How will scale and cost impact revisions to plan?

We start with pricing. In many organizations course prices are based on expected scale and costs. Typically, prices will be set at average total cost or marginal cost. Each approach is explored below. In each case the focus will be on budget costs and not on the opportunity costs.

Average Cost Pricing

Average cost pricing is used when the goal is to break even. If the scale is projected accurately and the price is set to average total cost (budget), the revenue will just cover all the budgeted expenses. Since most learning organizations are cost centers (not profit centers), their goal is to recover costs, and this approach will accomplish exactly that.

Example

Suppose a one-day instructor-led program is planned for one hundred participants. The average class size is twenty, so five days of instruction will be required along with five days of room use. The planned costs are the following:

- Development: Fixed cost of $25,000
- Delivery
  - o Instructors: One outside instructor for five days at $2,500 per day = $12,500
  - o Room: One room for five days at $250 per day = $1,250
  - o Materials: $50 per participant = $5,000
- Program management including reinforcement and measurement: 1/6 FTE fully-burdened = $20,050 (Note: FTE is a full-time equivalent, meaning one-sixth of a person's time. If internal staff is used, their cost must reflect their fully-burdened rate. See Chapter 1 for the definition and examples.)
- Opportunity: Not used in pricing

In this example the total budget costs are $63,800 and average total budget costs are $638 ($63,800/100).

FIGURE 11.7

Calculation of Average Cost for a Typical Course

Development	One-time cost	$25,000
Delivery		
Instructor	Five days @ $2500/day	$12,500
Room	Five days @$250/day	$1250
Materials	100 sets @$50/set	$5,000
Total		$18,750
Program management	1/6 FTE	$20,050
Opportunity	not used for pricing	NA
Total		$63,800

Average total cost = total cost / number of participants = $63,800/100 = $638

To break even, set the price at the average total budget cost of $638. (In practice this would probably be rounded to $640 or $650.) If 100 participants take the course and each pays $638, total revenue will be $63,800 (100 x $638), which just equals the total budgeted cost.

Considerations

Remember the lessons from above about impact of scale on cost! Success in using this approach depends on an accurate forecast of participants. If only 80 participants actually take the course and pay the $638, the total revenue will be $51,040 or $12,760 short of breakeven. In this case average total cost will be $798 ($63,800/80, assuming the materials for all 100 participants would be purchased, in any case so total cost did not change). A shortfall of 20 participants (20%) will lead to a 25% ($798/$613) increase in average total cost. Since fixed costs are present and scale is relatively small, average total cost will be very sensitive to scale!

Success also depends on an accurate forecast of costs. If costs were to come in 10% over budget, total budget cost would be $70,180 (110% x $63,800). Even if 100 participants take the course, cost will exceed revenue by $6,380 or 10%. So breakeven is very sensitive to both scale and costs.

In practice, these shortfalls can be avoided by planning conservatively. Since forecasts of scale and cost are likely to be wrong, many practitioners allow a margin of error. For example, if the intended target audience is 100, plan on a smaller number like 80 or 90 to calculate the average total cost. In our example, suppose we had planned on 90 participants to calculate the breakeven price. This would have resulted in an average total cost of $63,800/90 = $709. Alternatively, plan on actual expenses being slightly higher or put in an amount for contingencies. If costs were 10% higher, the average total cost for 100 participants would be $702 ($70,180/100). So, to be conservative, you might set the price at $705 or $710, which provides about a $70 per person or 10% margin of error.

With experience (if you are measuring!) you will learn how much of an error margin is needed. It may be that no error margin is needed, not because your forecasts are always perfect, but because you have offsetting errors. On a single course, perhaps the number of participants is less than expected but costs are also less than expected. With multiple courses, some may fall short on attendance whereas others do better than expected. Likewise, costs may run over on some and under on others, providing a natural offset. Your ability to forecast scale and cost will also improve over time, reducing the need for large error margins.

Success in breaking even also depends on the use of fully-burdened labor rates for internal staff and an accurate forecast of internal staff time required. Use of just their labor and related rate will leave overhead costs unrecovered. (See Chapter 1 for a detailed discussion.)

Marginal and Variable Cost Pricing

Although average cost pricing is the norm, there are situations in which prices will be set at other values. Just remember, though, that if the goal is to break even on a particular course, the price for that course will need to be the average total cost. Likewise, if the goal is to break even on all the courses offered, some might be priced below average cost, but the loss from those courses will need to be offset by a surplus on other courses priced above average cost.

So, what are the circumstances in which prices might not be set to average total cost? There are several:

- Breakeven has already been (or will be) achieved.
- Fixed costs have already been recovered or paid for.
- Breakeven is not the goal.

In these cases marginal or variable costs may provide guidance in setting the price. Be warned, however, that moving away from average cost pricing can be very damaging to your price structure and your integrity as people begin to question this special pricing. Once a lower price is introduced, it may be difficult to reestablish average cost pricing.

Breakeven Has Been Achieved

There may be circumstances in which breakeven has already been achieved (the planned number of participants has taken the course) or where you are confident that the plan will be reached. For example, suppose the average total cost was based on ninety participants, and ninety have already taken and paid for the course. Further suppose that costs came in as expected so you are at breakeven.

Additional class: Now, the sponsor asks for a special price for an additional class (with twenty participants). How much should you charge if you decide to grant a special price? (Granting a special price to some individuals may lead to complaints about fairness and equity, especially from those who paid full price. You will have to decide whether you want to create multiple prices for one course.)

You should charge at least the *marginal cost* if you do not want to lose money. In this case the marginal cost is the incremental cost to offer one more class, so it would include the instructor, the room rental, materials for twenty participants, and any additional internal staff time to manage the class. For example, marginal costs might include the following:

- Instructor: One outside instructor for one day at \$2,750 per day = \$2,750.
- Room: One room for one day at \$300 per day = \$300.
- Materials: \$50 per participant = \$1,000.
- Program management: 20 hours at \$62.50 per hour fully-burdened = \$1,250.

In this example the total marginal cost is \$5,300 or \$265 per participant (\$5,300/20). Compare this price with the average total cost price of \$638 in the last section. The marginal cost price is almost \$400 less than the average cost price, even with slightly higher instructor and room charges (due to last-minute scheduling). Why? The marginal cost price does *not* include any fixed costs (remember that after a course is developed there are no marginal fixed costs), and it includes a much smaller program management cost of only \$62.50 per participant versus \$250 initially since most of the work has already been done.

Pricing the class at \$5,300 will exactly recover the incremental costs and maintain breakeven for the course.

***Additional participant*:** Suppose that instead of asking for an additional class, the sponsor asks for an additional participant to be accommodated and again wants a special price. What should you charge? (As above, the answer depends first on whether you want to offer a special price at all. If this is an open enrollment course instead of a sponsored course, it is probably best to preserve the price structure and not offer any discounted prices.)

The answer again is at least the marginal cost, this time for one more participant. If there are no more scheduled classes, then the marginal cost is the cost of one more class, which is probably not practical for just one participant. In this case the sponsor might want to put more participants through, and the calculation would be the same as above for an additional class.

Suppose, however, the request comes just before the last class begins. Twenty participants are already registered and have paid, so your costs are fully covered. The room can accommodate one more. What do you charge?

Charge at least the marginal cost for one more participant in the existing class, which would be just the materials cost of \$50. The instructor and room cost do not change (unless these costs are tied to the number of participants), and it is unlikely to cost any more to administer one more participant. So, the only variable cost remaining is materials, which will go up by \$50.

Fixed Costs Have Already Been Recovered

There are circumstances in which the fixed costs have already been recovered, allowing for a lower price to be charged.

***Sponsor or corporate funding*:** For example, in some funding models the fixed cost of development is covered by the sponsor or by corporate, so that the learning function only has to recover the variable costs of delivery and management.

In this case, price should be set to the average variable cost if the goal is to break even. Suppose costs are the same as in the example for average cost pricing (a one-day instructor-led course for 100 participants with an average class size of 20):

- Development: Fixed cost of $25,000
- Delivery
  - o Instructors: One outside instructor for five days at $2,500 per day = $12,500
  - o Room: One room for five days at $250 per day = $1,250
  - o Materials: $50 per participant = $5,000
- Program management including reinforcement and measurement: 1/6 FTE fully-burdened = $20,050 (Note: If internal staff is used, their cost must reflect their fully-burdened rate. See Chapter 1 for the definition and examples.)
- Opportunity: Not used in pricing

In this case the $25,000 fixed cost for development has been paid by the sponsor or by corporate, so the price does not need to reflect it. Program management is more complicated. In practice, part of this expense is probably fixed (working with the vendor to develop the course, working with the sponsor on plans for reinforcement) and another part is truly variable, depending on how many participants actually take the course. So, this $20,050 must be split between fixed and variable. Let us say that $10,000 is fixed (will be spent before the first class) and will be covered along with the development costs by the sponsor or corporate. The remaining $10,050 will be treated as a variable expense to be recovered in the price.

So, total variable cost in this example comes to $28,800, representing delivery ($18,750) and a portion of management ($10,050). For the planned 100 participants, the average variable cost is $288 ($28,800/100), considerably less than the average total cost of $638.

This is really just a special case of average total cost pricing, where fixed costs are set to zero. If the funding model had not provided funding for the fixed management expenses, then the price should be set to average total cost, which would include $10,000 of fixed management expense.

Existing course: It may be that the course was developed and deployed in the past and that all the fixed costs have already been recovered. Now there is new demand for the course, which does not need to be updated. What should the price be?

As we have discussed previously, first a decision has to be made about whether to create a second price for the course. If people were happy with the course and its price initially, one option is simply to leave the price unchanged and let the course produce a surplus, perhaps offsetting unexpected costs or low enrollment elsewhere. On the other hand, if there is pressure to offer it at a lower price or if the goal is for each course to break even, then a lower price can be set.

The price can be set at average variable cost to break even. The same considerations apply to program management costs as in the previous example, although in this case the fixed management cost should be lower since the course has already been developed.

Breakeven Is Not the Goal

In some learning functions breakeven is not the goal. Some are run as profit centers and charge a price that may be above or below the average total cost for any particular course but on the whole must be above the average total cost (or else they will be a loss center!). So, if a learning function were to operate as a profit-maximizing business, how would it set prices?

For the majority of courses and participants, the price would be set as high as the internal market would allow and would be above the average total cost. The profit on each course (revenue less total cost) likely would be greatest for those courses in high demand, for which employees are willing to pay a high price. Trial and error will be required to find the profit-maximizing price since progressively higher prices will discourage an increasing number of people from taking the course. For example, if a price 10% higher than average cost leads to only a 3% drop in participants, revenue will increase 6.7%. Suppose, however, that a price 30% higher than average cost leads to a 40% drop in participants. Now, revenue will be 22% less than at average cost pricing. The limiting factor on price would be competition from the outside (can business units and employees bypass the learning function and find lower cost providers?) and internal complaints about high prices.

Occasionally, the learning function might offer a "loss leader" (a price below the average total cost) to attract attention or gain good will, but the loss on it will have to be offset elsewhere. In these cases, price will be set to cover all the variable costs but not all of the fixed costs. Seldom would a profit-maximizing function offer a course with a price below average variable cost or discount individual seats below its marginal cost.

Implications for Canceling Classes and Courses

Learning functions are frequently faced with a decision to cancel a class because of low registration. Occasionally, a decision must be made about canceling an entire course or program (multiple classes) because of changed assumptions about benefits or costs. These decisions are usually made based on scale, cost, and impact. Although other factors such as reputation, consistency, and integrity may also play a role in the decision, economics is generally the decisive factor. In the following discussion we will assume that the decision will be based on economics alone. (Note: There are a host of other reasons to cancel a class or program that are not related to registration. For instance, your measurement and evaluation work may have shown that the class was not achieving its intended result, or the company's strategy may have changed, making the course a much lower priority. In this discussion we will focus just on the decision to cancel based on lower-than-expected registration.)

The Decision to Cancel a Class

From an economic point of view, the goal is to minimize your loss. So a class should be canceled when doing so results in a smaller loss than proceeding to host it. Fixed, variable, and marginal costs as well as scale all play a role in this decision.

Suppose costs are the same as in the last example (a one-day, instructor-led course for 100 participants with an average class size of 20):

- Development: Fixed cost of $25,000
- Delivery
  - o Instructors: One outside instructor for five days at $2,500 per day = $12,500
  - o Room: One room for five days at $250 per day = $1,250
  - o Materials: $50 per participant = $5,000

- Program management including reinforcement and measurement: 1/6 FTE fully-burdened = $20,050. Fixed cost = $10,000 and variable cost = $10,050
- Opportunity: Not used in pricing

Given these costs and a goal to break even, the price would have been set at the average total cost, or $638. Thus, planned revenue would be $63,800 (100 x $638), which is just equal to total costs.

Let us assume the class has been offered three times for a total of thirty participants—only half the expected registration for three classes. Ten are registered for the fourth class and only three are registered for the fifth class. (Assume they cannot be combined into one class because of their work schedules.) Should the fourth and fifth classes be canceled?

The answer is mixed. The fourth class should be held even if no one else registers. The fifth class should be canceled if registration remains below six unless commitments have already been made to the instructor and for the room. These decisions minimize the expected loss and represent the best that can be done in this circumstance.

After three classes here is a summary of the current situation:

- Revenue
  - o 30 participants at $638 each for revenue of $19,140
- Costs
  - o Development: Fixed cost of $25,000 already spent. This is now a "sunk" cost.
  - o Delivery
- ▪ Instructors: $7,500 paid for three classes
- ▪ Room: $750 paid for three days
- ▪ Materials: $1,500 paid for 30 sets
  - o Program management: Fixed cost of $10,000 already incurred with program development and launch. Furthermore, $3,015 of variable cost incurred for the first 30 participants. (30/100 x $10,050 = $3,015. Or $10,050/100 = $100.50 per person x 30 participants = $3,015.)
  - o Total costs
- ▪ Fixed: $25,000 + $10,000 = $35,000
- ▪ Variable: $7,500 + $750 + $1,500 + $3,015 = $12,675

- Total = \$35,000 + \$12,675 = \$47,675
- Profit
  - Profit = \$19,140 - \$47,675 = -\$28,535

There is a loss of \$28, 535 after the first three classes.

Now, use marginal analysis to determine whether it is better to go ahead with the class or cancel. If the fourth class is offered, the 10 participants will bring in an additional \$6,380 (10 x \$638). This is the marginal revenue from the fourth class. The marginal cost of holding the fourth class is an instructor (\$2,500) plus the room (\$250) plus materials (10 x \$50 per participant = \$500) plus program management (10 x \$101 per participant = \$1,010) for a total of \$4,260. So, the marginal profit from holding the fourth class is \$2,120 (\$6,380 - \$4,260). Holding the fourth class will reduce the course loss to \$26,415. Since it will generate a marginal profit and reduce the cumulative loss, the fourth class should be held.

Notice that the \$35,000 of fixed costs (\$25,000 for development and \$10,000 for program management related to the development) did not play a role in this decision. It is what economists call a "sunk cost": once it has been made, there is no "unspending" it. Furthermore, the marginal cost of development is zero, so it has no role in the marginal analysis for the fourth or fifth class.

Apply the same marginal analysis to the fifth class. If the fifth class is offered, the three participants will bring in marginal revenue of \$1,914 (3 x \$638). The marginal cost of holding the fifth class is an instructor (\$2,500) plus the room (\$250) plus materials (\$150) plus program management (3 x \$101 per participant = \$303) for a total of \$3,203. The revenue from the three participants does not even pay for the instructor, let alone the other variable costs. The marginal loss from holding the fifth class for three participants is \$1,289 (\$1,914 - \$3,203). Holding the fifth class will increase the loss by \$1,289 to \$29,824. Since the fifth class will result in a marginal loss, it should not be held.

So, how many registrations are required to hold the class? The answer is six, which is the minimum number to avoid a marginal loss. The class should be held for six or more and canceled for less than six. Marginal revenues and costs for adding one more class are illustrated in Table 11.7.

TABLE 11.7

Scale Required to Avoid a Marginal Loss

Number of Participants	Revenue $638/part.	Costs					Net Income
		Instructor	Room	Materials $50/part.	Program Mgt $101/part.	Total Cost	
1	$638	$2,500	$250	$50	$101	$2,901	-$2,263
2	$1,276	$2,500	$250	$100	$202	$3,052	-$1,776
3	$1,914	$2,500	$250	$150	$303	$3,203	-$1,289
4	$2,552	$2,500	$250	$200	$404	$3,354	-$802
5	$3,190	$2,500	$250	$250	$505	$3,505	-$315
6	**$3,828**	**$2,500**	**$250**	**$300**	**$606**	**$3,656**	**$172**
7	$4,466	$2,500	$250	$350	$707	$3,807	$659
8	$5,104	$2,500	$250	$400	$808	$3,958	$1,146
9	$5,742	$2,500	$250	$450	$909	$4,109	$1,633
10	$6,380	$2,500	$250	$500	$1,010	$4,260	$2,120

The minimum required to avoid a marginal loss may also be calculated by setting the marginal revenue for the class equal to the marginal cost for the class, solving for the number of participants, and then rounding up.

Let N = Number required to cover marginal cost
P = Price for the course
Z = Variable costs, which act like fixed costs for one class (instructor, room)
V = Variable costs, which are truly variable, such as materials

Set marginal revenue for the class equal to marginal cost for the class and solve for N.

Marginal revenue = P*N
Marginal cost = Z + V*N

Marginal revenue for the class = marginal cost for the class
$P * N = Z + V * N$
$P * N - V * N = Z$
$N * (P - V) = Z$
$N = Z/(P - V)$

In our example P = \$638, Z = \$2,500 + \$250 = \$2,750, V = \$50 + \$101 = \$151
Solve for N
N = Z/(P - V) = \$2,750/(\$638 - \$151) = 5.65 (Round it up to 6.)

Test for N = 5 and 6 to confirm result
For N = 5: Marginal revenue = \$638 * 5 = \$3,190
Marginal cost = \$2,750 + \$151 * 5 = \$3,505
Marginal profit = \$3,190 - \$3,505 = (\$315) Marginal Loss of \$315

For N = 6: Marginal revenue = \$638 * 6 = \$3,828
Marginal cost = \$2,750 + \$151 * 6 = \$3,656
Marginal profit = \$3,828 - \$3,656 = \$172 Marginal Profit of \$172

So, six participants will produce a marginal profit of \$172 while five will produce a marginal loss of \$315.

The answer changes if the instructor or room charges are really fixed costs. This would be the case if an irrevocable contract had been signed, guaranteeing five days of instruction and five days of room rental. In this situation the only variable costs are materials (\$50 per person) and program management (\$101 per person). Since the price of \$638 exceeds the marginal or variable costs of \$161 per person, it would make economic sense to hold the class for even one participant!

The Decision to Cancel a Course

You might wonder whether there is ever an economic reason to cancel a course. The question might arise when a course is under development, or after development but before or during deployment. The decision here would be to halt development or cancel all future classes. There are several good reasons, and all involve a reduction in projected net benefits.

Recall from Chapter 5 that a business case was made for each course included in the annual business plan for learning. The business case relied on a projection of dollar impact or gross benefit and on a projection of total cost. Either a reduction in planned gross benefit or an increase in planned cost could lead to a reduction in net benefit to the point where a course is no longer viable.

Projected Gross Benefits Have Decreased

It is possible that during development or deployment one of the assumptions used to calculate the expected gross benefit of the learning might be revised down. It might be the net income impact of achieving the corporate goal or the expected impact of learning on that goal. Either would reduce the dollar impact or gross benefit of learning.

For example, consider the corporate goal from Table 5.4 to increase sales by 10%, which is expected to increase net income by $3 million. Sales learning was expected to contribute 50% to achieving that goal or 5% higher sales with a dollar impact of $1.5 million. Either a reduction in the $3 million or in the 50% impact will reduce the expected gross benefit of $1.5 million.

A reduction in the expected impact of learning may be due to other factors assuming greater importance like the economy or a sales incentive program. A reduction in the impact of learning may also reflect a reduction in the scale of the learning program. In the example above, one hundred marketing employees were expected to take the learning to have a 50% impact on sales. If only twenty employees are now expected to complete the learning, the expected impact of learning will be reduced by 80% to a 1% increase in sales and $300,000 gross benefit. So, gross benefits can be very sensitive to scale.

Projected Costs Have Increased

It is also possible that costs have increased from those used in the business case. This might reflect higher-than-expected development costs as vendors submit their final proposals or higher-than-expected costs for instructors, rooms, materials, or program management. Higher costs may also reflect revised assumptions about class size or duration.

Example: Course Development Not Yet Started

Four scenarios are shown in Table 11.8, where the corporate goal is a 10% increase in sales. In the original business plan the 10% increase in sales was expected to generate $4 million in net income. A five-day, instructor-led course for two hundred marketing professionals was expected to contribute 30% toward the achievement of the goal, leading to a 3% or $1.2 million increase in net income. After budget and opportunity costs, the learning was expected to have a net benefit of $417,000 with an ROI of 53%. Development cost is $100,000.

TABLE 11.8

The Decision to Cancel a Course: Four Scenarios

	Impact of Corp Goal on Net Income [Thousands $]	*Partici-pants*	*Expected Impact on Corp Obj*	*Impact of Learning*	*Dollar Impact of Learning on Net Income*	*Budget Cost*	*Opport. Cost*	*Net Benefit*	*ROI*
Original Plan	$4,000	200	30%	3.0%	$1,200	$383	$400	$417	53%
Scenario A	$2,000	200	30%	3.0%	$600	$383	$400	-$183	-23%
Scenario B	$4,000	200	10%	1.0%	$400	$383	$400	-$383	-49%
Scenario C	$4,000	100	15%	1.5%	$600	$242	$200	$158	36%
Scenario D	$4,000	200	30%	3.0%	$1,200	$767	$400	$33	3%

***Scenario A*:** Suppose new information indicates that a 10% increase in sales will only produce a $2 million increase in net income instead of $4 million. No assumptions about the learning have changed, but the net benefit drops to a negative $183,000 with an ROI of -23%. The program is no longer worth undertaking.

***Scenario B*:** In this case assume that the expected impact of learning falls from 30% to 10%. At this low level of impact the net benefit and ROI turn negative. The program should be halted.

***Scenario C*:** What if only one hundred participants could take the course instead of the expected two hundred? Assuming that impact will be reduced in proportion to scale, the impact of learning will now be only half the original plan. Both net benefit and ROI are decreased, but the program is still viable and should be continued.

***Scenario D*:** In this case suppose new information shows budget costs will be twice the expected level ($766,000 instead of $383,000). The net benefit and ROI will be significantly reduced. The program will no longer be viable.

Example: Development already completed

Given the large opportunity costs in this example, it would make sense to cancel the course in scenarios A and B even if development had already been completed. Perform a marginal analysis to be sure by setting development costs to zero, which will reduce the budget cost for each scenario by $100,000 (Table 11.9).

Since you cannot "unspend" the $100,000, treat it as sunk cost and ask whether the benefits and costs going forward justify offering the course. For scenario A the ROI rises to -12% and is still not viable. For scenario B ROI improves to only -41%, which definitely indicates the course should be canceled.

TABLE 11.9

The Decision to Cancel a Course: Four Scenarios with Development Cost Already Incurred

	Impact of Corp Goal on Net Income [Thousands $]	*Partici-pants*	*Expected Impact on Corp Obj*	*Impact of Learning*	*Dollar Impact of Learning on Net Income*	*Budget Cost*	*Opport. Cost*	*Net Benefit*	*ROI*
Original Plan	$4,000	200	30%	3.0%	$1,200	$383	$400	$417	53%
Scenario A	$2,000	200	30%	3.0%	$600	$283	$400	-$83	-12%
Scenario B	$4,000	200	10%	1.0%	$400	$283	$400	-$283	-41%
Scenario C	$4,000	100	15%	1.5%	$600	$142	$200	$258	76%
Scenario D	$4,000	200	30%	3.0%	$1,200	$567	$400	$233	24%

In Scenario D, however, treating the development cost of $200,000 as a sunk cost results in an ROI of 24%, so the program should be deployed even if all variable costs have doubled.

Example: Deployment underway

If deployment were already underway when the above information became available, it would still make sense to shut the course down in scenarios A and B. Again, a marginal analysis would confirm it. In each scenario assume that the course has been deployed to one hundred participants. The question is whether to deploy it to the remaining one hundred participants in light of the new information about impact. Table 11.10 starts with Table 11.9 and sets participants to one hundred (except scenario C, where there were only one hundred to start). Since all budget costs are now variable, the budget cost for each scenario will be just half that in Table 11.9. Opportunity cost will also be halved.

TABLE 11.10

The Decision to Cancel a Course: Four Scenarios with Development Already Underway

	Impact of Corp Goal on Net Income [Thousands $]	*Remaining Partici-pants*	*Expected Impact on Corp Obj*	*Impact of Learning*	*Dollar Impact of Learning on Net Income*	*Budget Cost*	*Opport. Cost*	*Net Benefit*	*ROI*
Original Plan	$4,000	200	30%	3.0%	$1,200	$383	$400	$417	53%
Scenario A	$2,000	100	15%	1.5%	$300	$142	$200	-$42	-12%
Scenario B	$4,000	100	5%	0.5%	$200	$142	$200	-$142	-41%
Scenario C	$4,000	0	15%	1.5%	$0	$0	$0	$0	NA
Scenario D	$4,000	100	15%	1.5%	$600	$283	$200	$117	24%

Assuming that one hundred participants will deliver only half the impact of two hundred, the ROI results for the last one hundred participants are exactly the same as in Table 11.9: -12% for scenario A, -41% for scenario B, and 24% for scenario D. (When fixed costs are zero, scale will have no impact on the average net benefit or ROI.)

Implications for Plan Revisions

Scale and cost should also play important roles in decisions about revising the business plan through the year. Generally, by midyear if not sooner, it will be apparent that the actual scale for the year is going to be higher or lower than planned. In some circumstances it will be significantly higher or lower. The goal in this section is to explore how sensitive results are to scale so the learning manager can better anticipate the impact of scale revisions on results.

Impact of Fixed Costs and Scale

Results will be most sensitive to scale when fixed costs are large compared to variable costs and when the scale is small. These concepts are most easily demonstrated by example.

ILT Example

Table 11.11 shows net benefit per person and ROI for three different fixed cost scenarios for scale ranging from 10 to 10,000 participants. The following assumptions were used to construct the example:

- The course consists of a two-day instructor-led class.
- The gross benefit per person is a constant $3,000.
- The average class size is twenty.
- The development cost ranges from zero (i.e., the course already exists) to $200,000 (for a high-end simulation).
- Variable costs include the instructor ($2,500 per day), room ($250 per day), materials ($50 per participant), and opportunity ($60 per hour or $960 for the two days).

***Fixed costs are $0*:** Begin with the top scenario, in which fixed costs are zero. Once the average class size is reached at twenty, the average net benefit becomes a constant $1,715 and ROI a constant 133%. In other words, scale has no impact when fixed costs are zero and average class size is reached.

Scale will matter when a class is not at the average or planned size. For ten participants, the average net benefit is only $1,440 with an ROI of 92% since the costs of the instructor and the room are being spread over just ten people as opposed to the planned class size of twenty.

***Fixed costs are $50,000*:** Once fixed costs are introduced, however, scale becomes important, and the average net benefit and ROI are reduced for any given level of scale. The middle scenario contains fixed costs of $50,000. Now, instead of a constant average net benefit and ROI, the average net benefit will range from ($785) for 20 participants to $1,710 for 10,000. Likewise, ROI now ranges from -21% for 20 participants to 133% for 10,000. As you would expect, the addition of $50,000 in cost has depressed returns, but notice that the effect is significant at small scale and completely negligible at large scale. Clearly, the course would be canceled for only 20 participants (ROI of -21%) and may not be viable for 40 (ROI of 18%).

At a scale of 10,000, however, average net benefit is almost identical to the scenario with no fixed cost, and ROI is the same 133%. Why? Because at large scale the average fixed cost approaches zero. Look at the average fixed costs in column three. For only 10 participants, average fixed cost is $5,000, but it declines rapidly

TABLE 11.11

Impact of Fixed Cost and Scale on ILT

Fixed Costs = $0

Number of Participants	Gross Benefit	Cost: Fixed Total	Cost: Fixed Ave.	Cost: Variable Total	Cost: Variable Ave.	Cost: Total Total	Cost: Total Ave.	Net Benefit Total	Net Benefit Ave.	ROI
10	$30,000	$0	$0	$15,600	$1,560	$15,600	$1,560	$14,400	$1,440	92%
20	$60,000	$0	$0	$25,700	$1,285	$25,700	$1,285	$34,300	$1,715	133%
40	$120,000	$0	$0	$51,400	$1,285	$51,400	$1,285	$68,600	$1,715	133%
100	$300,000	$0	$0	$128,500	$1,285	$128,500	$1,285	$171,500	$1,715	133%
200	$600,000	$0	$0	$257,000	$1,285	$257,000	$1,285	$343,000	$1,715	133%
500	$1,500,000	$0	$0	$642,500	$1,285	$642,500	$1,285	$857,500	$1,715	133%
1,000	$3,000,000	$0	$0	$1,285,000	$1,285	$1,285,000	$1,285	$1,715,000	$1,715	133%
10,000	$30,000,000	$0	$0	$12,850,000	$1,285	$12,850,000	$1,285	$17,150,000	$1,715	133%

Fixed Costs = $50,000

Number of Participants	Gross Benefit	Cost: Fixed Total	Cost: Fixed Ave.	Cost: Variable Total	Cost: Variable Ave.	Cost: Total Total	Cost: Total Ave.	Net Benefit Total	Net Benefit Ave.	ROI
10	$30,000	$50,000	$5,000	$15,600	$1,560	$65,600	$6,560	-$35,600	-$3,560	-54%
20	$60,000	$50,000	$2,500	$25,700	$1,285	$75,700	$3,785	-$15,700	-$785	-21%
40	$120,000	$50,000	$1,250	$51,400	$1,285	$101,400	$2,535	$18,600	$465	18%
100	$300,000	$50,000	$500	$128,500	$1,285	$178,500	$1,785	$121,500	$1,215	68%
200	$600,000	$50,000	$250	$257,000	$1,285	$307,000	$1,535	$293,000	$1,465	95%
500	$1,500,000	$50,000	$100	$642,500	$1,285	$692,500	$1,385	$807,500	$1,615	117%
1,000	$3,000,000	$50,000	$50	$1,285,000	$1,285	$1,335,000	$1,335	$1,665,000	$1,665	125%
10,000	$30,000,000	$50,000	$5	$12,850,000	$1,285	$12,900,000	$1,290	$17,100,000	$1,710	133%

Fixed Costs = $200,000

Number of Participants	Gross Benefit	Cost: Fixed Total	Cost: Fixed Ave.	Cost: Variable Total	Cost: Variable Ave.	Cost: Total Total	Cost: Total Ave.	Net Benefit Total	Net Benefit Ave.	ROI
10	$30,000	$200,000	$20,000	$15,600	$1,560	$215,600	$21,560	-$185,600	-$18,560	-86%
20	$60,000	$200,000	$10,000	$25,700	$1,285	$225,700	$11,285	-$165,700	-$8,285	-73%
40	$120,000	$200,000	$5,000	$51,400	$1,285	$251,400	$6,285	-$131,400	-$3,285	-52%
100	$300,000	$200,000	$2,000	$128,500	$1,285	$328,500	$3,285	-$28,500	-$285	-9%
200	$600,000	$200,000	$1,000	$257,000	$1,285	$457,000	$2,285	$143,000	$715	31%
500	$1,500,000	$200,000	$400	$642,500	$1,285	$842,500	$1,685	$657,500	$1,315	78%
1,000	$3,000,000	$200,000	$200	$1,285,000	$1,285	$1,485,000	$1,485	$1,515,000	$1,515	102%
10,000	$30,000,000	$200,000	$20	$12,850,000	$1,285	$13,050,000	$1,305	$16,950,000	$1,695	130%

with scale, reaching only $5 at 10,000 participants. Thus, the total average cost is only $5 more (and average net benefit only $5 less) than in the top scenario with zero fixed costs.

***Fixed costs are $200,000*:** Just to see what happens, let us push fixed costs to $200,000. As expected, average net benefit and ROI deteriorate further, especially at the small scale, remaining negative through 100 participants. Now, the course does not become viable until the scale reaches 200. Notice, however, that for 10,000 participants the average net benefit ($1,695) and ROI (130%) are almost the same as for no fixed costs. The average fixed cost has dropped to $20, which is negligible compared to variable costs of $1,285.

WBT Example

Next, consider a WBT example. Table 11.12 shows the average net benefit per person and ROI for three different fixed-cost scenarios for scale, ranging from 10 to 10,000 participants. The following assumptions were used to construct the example:

- The course consists of a one-hour online class.
- The gross benefit per person is a constant $300.
- The development cost ranges from zero (the course already exists) to $30,000 (high-end with interaction).
- Variable costs include only the opportunity ($60 per hour).

***Fixed costs are $0*:** Like the ILT example, if fixed costs are zero, then all costs are variable and scale has no impact. The average net benefit is constant at $240, and the ROI is constant at 400%.

In this case, though, the variable costs are truly (or continuously) variable, and there are no variable costs like the instructor or room, which increase in stair-step fashion. So, in contrast to the ILT example, the average total cost, average net benefit, and ROI are the same for ten participants as for twenty.

***Fixed costs are $15,000*:** The impact of scale is now clearly seen once fixed costs have been introduced. The average net benefit ranges from -$1,260 for 10 participants to $239 for 10,000. Corresponding ROIs range from -81% to 388%. Once again, this range is explained by the average fixed cost plummeting from $1,500 for 10 participants to $2 for 10,000. At a scale of 10,000, the average total cost of $62 is driven almost entirely by the opportunity cost ($60).

TABLE 11.12

Impact of Fixed Cost and Scale on WBT

Fixed Costs = $0

Number of Participants	Gross Benefit	Cost: Fixed Total	Cost: Fixed Ave.	Cost: Variable Total	Cost: Variable Ave.	Cost: Total Total	Cost: Total Ave.	Net Benefit Total	Net Benefit Ave.	ROI
10	$3,000	$0	$0	$600	$60	$600	$60	$2,400	$240	400%
20	$6,000	$0	$0	$1,200	$60	$1,200	$60	$4,800	$240	400%
40	$12,000	$0	$0	$2,400	$60	$2,400	$60	$9,600	$240	400%
100	$30,000	$0	$0	$6,000	$60	$6,000	$60	$24,000	$240	400%
200	$60,000	$0	$0	$12,000	$60	$12,000	$60	$48,000	$240	400%
500	$150,000	$0	$0	$30,000	$60	$30,000	$60	$120,000	$240	400%
1,000	$300,000	$0	$0	$60,000	$60	$60,000	$60	$240,000	$240	400%
10,000	$3,000,000	$0	$0	$600,000	$60	$600,000	$60	$2,400,000	$240	400%

Fixed Costs = $15,000

Number of Participants	Gross Benefit	Cost: Fixed Total	Cost: Fixed Ave.	Cost: Variable Total	Cost: Variable Ave.	Cost: Total Total	Cost: Total Ave.	Net Benefit Total	Net Benefit Ave.	ROI
10	$3,000	$15,000	$1,500	$600	$60	$15,600	$1,560	-$12,600	-$1,260	-81%
20	$6,000	$15,000	$750	$1,200	$60	$16,200	$810	-$10,200	-$510	-63%
40	$12,000	$15,000	$375	$2,400	$60	$17,400	$435	-$5,400	-$135	-31%
100	$30,000	$15,000	$150	$6,000	$60	$21,000	$210	$9,000	$90	43%
200	$60,000	$15,000	$75	$12,000	$60	$27,000	$135	$33,000	$165	122%
500	$150,000	$15,000	$30	$30,000	$60	$45,000	$90	$105,000	$210	233%
1,000	$300,000	$15,000	$15	$60,000	$60	$75,000	$75	$225,000	$225	300%
10,000	$3,000,000	$15,000	$2	$600,000	$60	$615,000	$62	$2,385,000	$239	388%

Fixed Costs = $30,000

Number of Participants	Gross Benefit	Cost: Fixed Total	Cost: Fixed Ave.	Cost: Variable Total	Cost: Variable Ave.	Cost: Total Total	Cost: Total Ave.	Net Benefit Total	Net Benefit Ave.	ROI
10	$3,000	$30,000	$3,000	$600	$60	$30,600	$3,060	-$27,600	-$2,760	-90%
20	$6,000	$30,000	$1,500	$1,200	$60	$31,200	$1,560	-$25,200	-$1,260	-81%
40	$12,000	$30,000	$750	$2,400	$60	$32,400	$810	-$20,400	-$510	-63%
100	$30,000	$30,000	$300	$6,000	$60	$36,000	$360	-$6,000	-$60	-17%
200	$60,000	$30,000	$150	$12,000	$60	$42,000	$210	$18,000	$90	43%
500	$150,000	$30,000	$60	$30,000	$60	$60,000	$120	$90,000	$180	150%
1,000	$300,000	$30,000	$30	$60,000	$60	$90,000	$90	$210,000	$210	233%
10,000	$3,000,000	$30,000	$3	$600,000	$60	$630,000	$63	$2,370,000	$237	376%

***Fixed costs of $30,000*:** With higher fixed costs, the average net benefit and ROI remain negative through 100 participants. At 10,000 participants, the average fixed cost is only $3 with average net benefit and ROI almost identical to the scenario with no fixed costs.

Lessons from Examples

The examples should have convinced you of the following:

1. Fixed costs and scale can have a significant impact on the net benefit and ROI.
2. Scale can dramatically improve results as average fixed costs approach zero.
3. Fixed costs have a more significant impact on results when the ratio of fixed to variable cost is large.
4. If fixed costs are zero, scale will not have any impact on ILT results as long as classes are full.
5. If fixed costs are zero, scale will not have any impact on WBT results.

Implications

These lessons have important implications for both the original planning process and the revision process.

Creating the Business Case and Plan

Planned scale was discussed in Chapters 5 and 6 ("Creating the Business Case" and "Business Plan") and in the last chapter. Decisions about scale should be made to deliver the agreed-upon impact or benefit to the organization, reflecting a careful (and perhaps marginal) analysis of potential target-audience size on impact. That said, the learning manager needs to be aware that the scale and cost structure will make a tremendous difference on the viability of the program.

Key points for the manager to keep in mind during the planning process:

- Large, fixed costs will likely require a large scale for the course to be viable.
- At very large scale, average fixed costs approach zero and become almost irrelevant.
- A larger scale will often produce a higher total and average net benefit and ROI (assuming constant marginal costs and constant marginal gross benefit).

These points might seem to argue in favor of the largest scale possible, but remember that the marginal gross benefit is likely to decline as the scale increases and the course is increasingly prescribed for those less likely to benefit from it. At some point marginal costs are also likely to begin to increase. In Tables 11.11 and 11.12, a constant marginal gross benefit and a constant marginal cost were assumed all the way up to 10,000 participants. At some point, though, the marginal gross benefit will decline, and the marginal cost may start to rise, limiting the positive benefit of scale on costs.

Revising the Plan

The business plan for learning will include the planned impact and net benefit from the investment in learning. Since revisions to the planned scale will impact costs, net benefits, and ROI, the learning manager needs to be acutely aware of their impact to make an informed decision about the program in question and to make the appropriate tradeoffs between programs when necessary.

Key points for the manager to keep in mind when making revisions:

- When fixed costs are present, reducing the scale will reduce the total net benefit, the average net benefit, and the ROI.
    - The percentage reduction in total net benefit will exceed the percentage reduction in scale.
    - The higher the fixed costs, the greater the percentage reduction in total net benefit, average net benefit, and ROI.
- When fixed costs are present, increasing scale will increase the total net benefit, average net benefit, and ROI.
    - The percentage increase in total net benefit will exceed the percentage increase in scale.
    - The higher the fixed costs, the greater the percentage increase in total net benefit, average net benefit, and ROI.
- When fixed costs are not present, any percentage change in scale will lead to an equal percentage change in total net benefit.
    - Average net benefit and ROI will not change.

Note: These conclusions apply when marginal costs and marginal gross benefits are constant, which should hold over a fairly large range.

Example of revising scale down when fixed costs are present**:** Consider the data from Table 11.11 to analyze a revision in scale. Suppose the plan was for 200 participants in a course with fixed costs of $50,000. In this case the average net benefit was expected to be $1,465, with an ROI of 95%. Now, suppose that 40 people have completed the course through June and a lack of funding, instructors, or time has forced the manager to consider scaling back the deployment for the rest of the year. What are the consequences of revising the scale down?

First, the corporate goal (impact) is unlikely to be achieved if 200 participants do not complete the course in a timely manner. Second, total net benefits will be less than the plan calls for, resulting in lower average net benefit and ROI. Specifically, if only 40 participants go through the course, total net benefits will be $18,600 instead of the planned $293,000, a reduction of $274,400 or 94%! The average net benefit drops from a projected $1,465 to $465 (a reduction of 68%), and ROI drops from 95% to 18% (a reduction of 81%). Even if 60 more people complete the course, for a total of 100, total net benefits are only $121,500, a reduction of $171,500 or 59% from the plan. (Notice that because fixed costs are present, a 50% reduction in participants results in a greater than 50% reduction in net benefits.) The average net benefit for 100 participants is $1,215 as opposed to the plan's figure of $1,465, and ROI is 68% compared to a projected 95%.

TABLE 11.13

Impact of Downward Revision to Scale

Fixed Costs = $50,000

Number of Participants	*Versus Plan*	*Gross Benefit*	*Total Cost*	*Net Benefit*	*Versus Plan*	*Ave. Net Benfit*	*Versus Plan*	*ROI*	*Versus Plan*
200	0%	$600,000	$307,000	$293,000	0%	$1,465	0%	95%	0%
100	-50%	$300,000	$178,500	$121,500	-59%	$1,215	-17%	68%	-29%
40	-80%	$120,000	$101,400	$18,600	-94%	$465	-68%	18%	-81%

Fixed Costs = $200,000

Number of Participants	*Versus Plan*	*Gross Benefit*	*Total Cost*	*Net Benefit*	*Versus Plan*	*Ave. Net Benfit*	*Versus Plan*	*ROI*	*Versus Plan*
200	0%	$600,000	$457,000	$143,000	0%	$715	0%	31%	0%
100	-50%	$300,000	$328,500	-$28,500	-120%	-$285	-140%	-9%	-128%
40	-80%	$120,000	$251,400	-$131,400	-192%	-$3,285	-559%	-52%	-267%

Next, consider the same revisions if the fixed costs were $200,000 instead of $50,000. Now, if only 40 people attend the course, the total net benefit would be -$131,400 as opposed to a projection of $143,000, a reduction of $274,400, or a 192% deviation from the plan. If the revision calls for 100 to attend, there is still a loss of $28,500 because of the higher fixed costs, which result in a net benefit of 120% below plan. So, with higher fixed costs, the 50% reduction in scale leads to a 120% reduction in net benefit, a 140% reduction in average net benefit, and a 128% reduction in ROI. Clearly, higher fixed costs make the downward revision in scale much more painful.

***Example of revising the scale up when fixed costs are present*:** Now use the same data to consider the reverse, namely an increase in scale, which may occur because the size of the original target audience was underestimated or early results demonstrate that the course would be beneficial for a larger audience than anticipated. Start with a plan of 200 participants and fixed costs of $50,000 (see Table 11.14). What are the consequences of revising the scale up?

First, the impact on the corporate goal is likely to be greater than planned. Second, the total net benefit will be greater than the plan, resulting in a higher average net benefit and ROI. If 500 participants complete the course instead of 200, the total net benefit will be $807,500, an increase of $514,500 or 176% above the plan. The average net benefit increases from $1,465 at plan to $1,615 (an increase of 10%), and the ROI increases from 95% to 117% (an increase of 23%). If 1,000 people complete the course, the total net benefit rises to $1,665,000, the average net benefit goes to $1,665, and ROI hits 125%. (Notice that because fixed costs are present, a 150% increase in scale leads to more than a 150% increase in total net benefit.)

TABLE 11.14

Impact of Upward Revision to Scale

Fixed Costs = $50,000

Number of Participants	Versus Plan	Gross Benefit	Total Cost	Net Benefit	Versus Plan	Ave. Net Benfit	Versus Plan	ROI	Versus Plan
200	0%	$600,000	$307,000	$293,000	0%	$1,465	0%	95%	0%
500	150%	$1,500,000	$692,500	$807,500	176%	$1,615	10%	117%	22%
1000	400%	$3,000,000	$1,335,000	$1,665,000	468%	$1,665	14%	125%	31%

Fixed Costs = $200,000

Number of Participants	Versus Plan	Gross Benefit	Total Cost	Net Benefit	Versus Plan	Ave. Net Benfit	Versus Plan	ROI	Versus Plan
200	0%	$600,000	$457,000	$143,000	0%	$715	0%	31%	0%
500	150%	$1,500,000	$842,500	$657,500	360%	$1,315	84%	78%	149%
1000	400%	$3,000,000	$1,485,000	$1,515,000	959%	$1,515	112%	102%	226%

Next, consider the same revisions if the fixed costs were $200,000 instead of $50,000. Now, if 500 participants complete the course, the total net benefit will be $657,500 as opposed to $143,000 in the plan, an increase of $514,000 or 360%. If the scale were revised to 1,000, the total net benefit would be $1,515,000 for an increase of $1,372,000 or 959% greater than the plan. The higher fixed costs serve to magnify the impact of upward revisions.

***Example of revising scale when fixed costs are not present*:** If there are no fixed costs, any percentage change in scale will lead to exactly the same percentage change in total net benefit. Furthermore, there will be no change to the average net benefit or ROI. Consider the data from the first panel of Table 11.11, where the fixed cost is zero, and assume the plan was for 200 participants.

A 50% reduction to 100 will cause the total net benefit to decline 50% from $343,000 to $171,500 (see Table 11.15). The average net benefit will be unchanged at $1,715, and the ROI will remain at 133%. Similarly, an 80% reduction to 40 reduces the total net benefit by 80% but leaves the average net benefit and ROI unchanged.

TABLE 11.15

Impact of Revision to Scale when Fixed Cost = $0

Downward Revision

Number of Participants	*Versus Plan*	*Gross Benefit*	*Total Cost*	*Net Benefit*	*Versus Plan*	*Ave. Net Benfit*	*Versus Plan*	*ROI*	*Versus Plan*
200	0%	$600,000	$257,000	$343,000	0%	$1,715	0%	133%	0%
100	-50%	$300,000	$128,500	$171,500	-50%	$1,715	0%	133%	0%
40	-80%	$120,000	$51,400	$68,600	-80%	$1,715	0%	133%	0%

Upward Revision

Number of Participants	*Versus Plan*	*Gross Benefit*	*Total Cost*	*Net Benefit*	*Versus Plan*	*Ave. Net Benfit*	*Versus Plan*	*ROI*	*Versus Plan*
200	0%	$600,000	$257,000	$343,000	0%	$1,715	0%	133%	0%
500	150%	$1,500,000	$642,500	$857,500	150%	$1,715	0%	133%	0%
1000	400%	$3,000,000	$1,285,000	$1,715,000	400%	$1,715	0%	133%	0%

Likewise, a 150% increase to 500 participants will cause the total net benefit to increase 150% from $343,000 to $857,000. The average net benefit and ROI will remain unchanged.

Conclusion

Scale can have a dramatic effect on cost and, consequently, on pricing decisions, determination of net benefit and ROI, and on decisions to cancel classes and courses. Fixed costs play an especially important role in all of these determinations. Accordingly, a learning manager must understand the cost structure of courses, particularly the fixed and variable costs. The concepts of average and marginal costs, borrowed from economics, can be used to improve decision-making even when all the data are not known.

Chapter 11 to Do List

1. Introduce the concepts of fixed and variable costs in the learning function.
2. Require an analysis of fixed and variable costs for each new course.
3. Introduce the concepts of marginal and average costs.
4. Calculate the expected average cost for each new course.
5. Decide on a pricing philosophy (like the use of average cost).
6. Agree on permissible exceptions to your pricing philosophy.
7. Use the marginal analysis methodology to help make decisions about canceling a class or course. The goal is to minimize your loss.
8. Be aware of the scale effect on impact, net benefit, and ROI when revising the plan.
9. In general, resolve to use the tools of business and economics to help make decisions about pricing and canceling a course and about revising your plan.

Further Reading

Case, Karl, Ray Fair, and Sharon Oster. *Principles of Economics*, ninth edition. Upper Saddle River, New Jersey: Pearson Prentice Hall, 2009. (See Chapters 7 and 8: "The Production Process: The Behavior of Profit-Maximizing Firms" and "Short-Run Costs and Output Decisions.")

PART FIVE

Conclusion

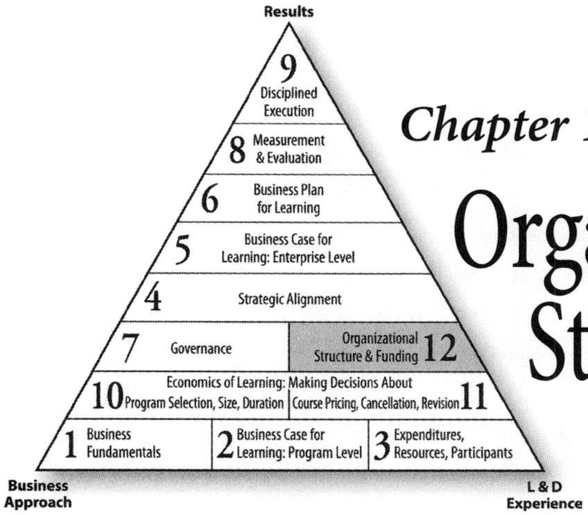

Chapter 12

Organizational Structure and Funding

IN THIS CHAPTER we will explore the implications of running learning like a business on the learning organization's structure and funding. Both are critical to the learning department's success and need to support the goals for the learning organization. Then, with all the elements in place, we will be ready to conclude with a discussion of the journey toward the vision of a world-class learning organization in the final chapter.

Key Concepts for Chapter 12

12

1. There are three common organizational structures for a learning department, each with its advantages and disadvantages.
2. Only two, the centralized and hybrid models, will support a strategic focus.
3. Choose the one that is right for you, based on your particular situation and needs.
4. There are three common funding models for a learning department, each with its advantages and disadvantages.
5. The recommended model is a mix, reflecting your situation and needs.

Structure of the Learning Organization

There are many ways to structure the learning organization; the goal is to find the right one to enable your success. We will start by exploring some of the common structures and then look at the decision criteria for selecting among them.

Three Common Organizational Structures

The three most common are the fully centralized model, the decentralized model, and a hybrid model. Each is examined in turn.

Fully Centralized

In this model the corporate learning function has authority and responsibility for all learning in the enterprise, which includes all the learning in the business units and around the world and may also include learning for dealers, suppliers, and customers. Staff, in this model, does not need to be centrally located, but all learning staff would report to the corporate learning department. The budget for the corporate learning group would be equivalent to the learning budget for the entire enterprise. Figure 12.1 lists characteristics of a centralized model, although all may not be achieved in practice.

FIGURE 12.1

Characteristics of a Centralized Model

- All learning staff in the organization are part of the same learning function, regardless of physical location.
- Programs, policies, and procedures are consistent across all business units and around the world.
- Common platforms and systems are used for learning management, knowledge sharing, and social learning.
- Common processes are used for reporting, planning, budgeting, prioritizing, needs analysis, and course design.

The fully centralized model will support the goals of strategic alignment and the creation of a business plan for learning since the CLO or VP for learning will have the authority to implement these practices. A centralized model can also readily support and interact with a board of governors at the enterprise level since the CLO will have the power to implement decisions that affect the entire enterprise.

Of course, each structure has its drawbacks. The fully centralized model may become so large in staff and budget that it becomes a ready target for cost reduction. Because of its size and common policies, processes, and procedures, it may be perceived as (or may truly be) bureaucratic and slow moving, unresponsive and out of touch with local needs. It almost certainly will be slower to react to individual business unit needs than a decentralized group. Moving to this model from a less centralized one can be very difficult politically, especially if the business units are reluctant to lose direct control over their own learning.

Decentralized

In this model each business unit has its own learning function staffed with its own employees. The budget comes from the business unit, and the head of the business unit has complete authority over the group. Figure 12.2 lists the characteristics of learning in an enterprise with decentralized learning.

FIGURE 12.2

Characteristics of a Decentralized Model

- Each business unit has its own learning function staffed with its own employees.
- Programs, policies, and procedures are consistent only within each business unit (if that). Only by chance would they be consistent across several units or the entire enterprise. Consequently, there will be duplicate programs for leadership, soft skills, etc.
- Since each business unit makes decisions independently, multiple platforms and systems are used across the enterprise for learning management, knowledge sharing, and social learning.
- Different processes are used across the enterprise for reporting, planning, budgeting, prioritizing, needs analysis, and course design. Consequently, there is unlikely to be any enterprise aggregation of learning data, and no enterprise business plan for learning will exist.

Although a fully decentralized model may exist, more typically some corporate learning function will exist, even if it is only one person with a very narrow scope. For example, there may be one person in corporate HR who runs an annual leadership program or manages succession planning for the enterprise. General Electric is an example of a large corporation in which learning is decentralized except for its leadership program at Crotonville, which pulls leaders in from business units worldwide.

Many organizations start with a decentralized model, which evolves naturally from the need to train workers on skills specific to their jobs and business units. Further, if a business is growing by acquisition, it will acquire companies (which become business units) with their own learning staff, programs, policies, and platforms already in place, which reinforces the decentralized model.

For the most part, a decentralized model is not supportive of a strategic approach to learning at the enterprise level. By definition, there are no mechanisms and no authority to establish enterprise-wide priorities and to create an enterprise business plan for learning, although these might be done inside each business unit. With no central responsibility for budget or outcomes, a decentralized model is likely to be less efficient from an enterprise point of view because of duplicate programs, systems, and platforms. On the other hand, a decentralized model will almost certainly be more responsive to the very specific needs of a business unit and may be able to meet those needs more efficiently than a centralized model. And the head of the business unit may set and enforce his own priorities for the internal learning group, which could not be done in a centralized model.

Hybrid or Federated

Most learning functions probably fall in between the fully centralized and decentralized models. They are not completely centralized, but their corporate learning function has more enterprise responsibility than described above in the decentralized model. In this case some learning professionals report to the business units and some to corporate. Each business unit has a learning budget and so does corporate. Business units have some, but perhaps not complete, authority over their own learning staff. Thus, this model is a hybrid of the two models above. Some refer to it as a federated model, in which each party has some authority and responsibility.

> NOTE: This model is characterized by the existence of learning staff in BOTH company headquarters AND in the business units where those in the business units report up through the business unit chain of command. Some organizations will station corporate learning employees in the business units to be closer to their internal customers. If the business unit has no learning staff of its own, then this is a centralized model. On the other hand, if the business unit has learning employees of its own (either working alongside the co-located corporate learning employees or working in the absence of any corporate learning employees), then it is hybrid model. Bottom line, to be a hybrid model there must be some learning employees who report to corporate (headquarters) and some who report to the business units. Stated differently, the reporting relationship, not the geographic location, is the key to determining the organizational model.

As you might imagine, this model comes with many variations, reflecting the particular needs and characteristics of the overall organization. Typically, the model is designed to capture the benefits of the centralized model while remaining responsive to the needs and concerns of the business units. The corporate group will focus on those programs, systems, and processes where it makes sense to have a common, enterprise-wide approach. Business units may contribute to and support corporate efforts while continuing to provide business unit specific learning.

The key to success is clearly defining the roles and responsibilities of all parties and ensuring that the CLO has the authority to make the federation work. Figure 12.3 illustrates how the roles and responsibilities may be divided.

FIGURE 12.3

Roles and Responsibilities in a Hybrid Model

Corporate focuses on developing and managing common, enterprise-wide

- Programs (like leadership, marketing, project management, Six Sigma)
- Systems and platforms (like one LMS)
- Processes for reporting, planning, budgeting, prioritizing, needs analysis, course design

Business units

- Contribute to the identification of enterprise needs and the development of enterprise solutions
- Deploy corporate programs and assist in corporate initiatives
- Supplement with their own learning for business unit specific needs
- Use corporate systems (LMS)
- Follow corporate processes for reporting, planning, budgeting, prioritizing

There are many ways to structure and implement staffing a hybrid model. In some cases, the corporate group will have one of its own employees reside in the business unit learning group or will have a representative dedicated to the business unit group. In other cases there may be dotted line or dual solid line reporting between the head of the business unit learning group and corporate. In place of or in addition to these staffing arrangements, many companies create learning councils in which employees from the business unit and corporate learning groups meet regularly to make joint decisions on programs, systems, processes, and priorities.

Hybrid models generally will support the goals of strategic alignment and the creation of a business plan as well as efficient management of enterprise learning. A hybrid model is also supportive of a board of governors and program-level advisory boards. Because of their federated nature, a CLO likely will have a greater challenge delivering enterprise results than in a completely centralized model, but the tradeoff is often worth it in terms of greater responsiveness to business units and less bureaucracy.

Choosing a Structure

The chosen structure should support your goals and be consistent with your company's culture. It should be right for the present and immediate term, say three to five years. Do not worry about finding the absolute right structure for all time because circumstances will change and may well require modifying the structure anyway. Start by answering some basic questions. The answers should lead to a structure that is right for you.

Some Basic Questions

Focus: The most basic question is about focus. Do you aspire to a strategic focus for your learning function or not? We have made the case in chapters two to six for a strategic focus and would argue this is the only way to maximize the impact of learning on enterprise results. A strategic focus implies strategic alignment to the company's highest priority goals followed by the building of a business case and the creation of a business plan for learning.

A decentralized structure will not support a strategic focus at the enterprise level. In other words, it will be nearly impossible to achieve strategic alignment, prioritize, build the business case, and create the business plan for enterprise learning in a decentralized structure. The corporate learning group, if it exists, will not have the authority to accomplish these tasks or to execute the plan once it is created. It is unlikely that a board of governors would exist in this case, which makes success even less likely. More fundamentally, without common systems and processes, data on existing efforts would not be aggregated across the enterprise. In most cases, companies with decentralized learning do not know how much is being spent on learning, how it is being spent, or how many employees are being trained. And there is certainly no enterprise estimate of past or expected impact or benefit from the learning.

So, a strategic focus demands a centralized or hybrid structure. Of course, there will be companies where a strategic focus does not make sense. At a certain scale, too much bureaucracy is introduced to justify a strategic approach at the enterprise level. This is especially true when the business units have little in common, and thus there is little to gain through the deployment of common, enterprise-wide programs, systems, and processes. Each business unit may be very strategic internally and may take a strategic approach to learning, but it will not be an enterprise approach.

For example, suppose a company has 400,000 employees in forty very different and independent business units. There is no horizontal integration across the enterprise and no movement of employees between units. Each unit (with an average size of ten thousand employees) is really its own company. It would make sense for each unit to take a strategic focus to learning, but it probably does not make sense for the parent company to enforce commonality among all forty units.

***Accountability*:** This is an important question from the viewpoint of the CLO. What has the CLO been asked to do? If the CLO has been asked to make enterprise learning more effective and efficient, eliminate duplication and waste, and deploy common programs across the enterprise, then a centralized or hybrid model must be employed. Under a decentralized model, the CLO would certainly fail since she would not have the authority to accomplish the given goals.

***Culture*:** What is the culture of the company with respect to centralization and central authority? If many other functions are centralized and if this is viewed positively, then it may make sense to opt for full centralization. In fact, if that is viewed as a critical success factor, then it may be the only way to proceed. On the other hand, if few other functions are fully centralized and/or it is viewed negatively, then full centralization must be approached with caution. It may still be the preferred structure in light of focus and accountability, but the change management challenge will be significant, and the CLO risks failure because of overwhelming resistance. In this case, a hybrid structure may be a better way to go, at least for the first several years.

If any degree of central authority is viewed very negatively and other efforts to centralize have failed, then it may simply be impossible to take a strategic focus at this time.

Top Cover: How much support does the CLO have from the CEO? How important are learning and the corporate learning function to the CEO? How strong and how enduring is the CEO's support? What structure does the CEO support? These are all critical questions, especially if change is being considered. There is likely to be significant resistance in moving from a decentralized to a centralized or hybrid structure, and success may very well depend on the CEO's personal involvement in sponsoring the change. Chances are some officers will appeal their loss of control directly to the CEO, who will need to stand firm in his support of the CLO and of the change. So, it is critical that the CEO supports the recommendation for the new structure and is willing to fight for it actively.

The Best Structure

Answers to the above four questions should point to an appropriate structure. Start by deciding on focus. A strategic focus requires a fully centralized or hybrid model. Considerations about accountability, culture, and top cover should provide guidance on hybrid versus full centralization. And recognize that it may be impossible to achieve a fully centralized or hybrid structure without the active support of the CEO, especially if the culture views centralization very negatively.

The appropriateness of the three structures is summarized in Figure 12.4.

FIGURE 12.4

Choosing the Best Structure

	Decentralized	*Hybrid*	*Centralized*
Focus			
Strategic		X	X
Reactive	X	X	X
Accountability of CLO for Results			
High expectations, short time to deliver		X	X
Lower expectations, longer time to deliver	X	X	X

	Decentralized	Hybrid	Centralized
Culture			
Supportive of centralization		X	X
Not supportive of centralization	X	X	
Top Cover (starting from decentralized)			
Strong		X	X
Weak	X		

CATERPILLAR EXAMPLE: The Choice of a Hybrid Model

Cat U was created in 2001 to provide a strategic focus to enterprise learning and to increase the effectiveness and efficiency of enterprise learning significantly. Since the economy was just entering the 2000–2001 recession, expectations were high for some immediate results and savings.

The culture, however, was very much opposed to centralization. In fact, the word itself was not used in polite company. Caterpillar had been centralized in the 1970s and 1980s (corporate marketing, engineering, manufacturing, etc.) and had decentralized almost completely in 1992 to restore a sense of entrepreneurship, to reduce bureaucracy, and to improve responsiveness to customers. Decentralization had been viewed as a tremendous success by all and was still viewed that way in 2000. Twenty-five autonomous business units had virtually complete authority to reach their goals of profitability with very little intervention from headquarters (as long as they were on target to meet their goals). One other initiative, Six Sigma, was launching at the same time as Cat U, and Six Sigma would be centralized.

Support from the CEO for Cat U and our mission was strong and unwavering. Several officers argued for delaying the start of Cat U and later for shutting it down in light of the recession. The CEO stood firm. The CEO suggested I consider full centralization but left the decision to me. My boss, the VP for HR, advised that full centralization would be the worst decision of my career. His boss, the group president who reported to the CEO, agreed it would be a terrible mistake given the decentralized culture.

So, what model to adopt? Clearly, the status quo of decentralized learning would not allow me to achieve the objectives I had been given. The structure had to be changed if we were going to become strategic and if results were to change. I had the support of the CEO for whatever model I chose as long as I delivered results. Full centralization would provide the surest way to deliver results except that resistance would be incredible, and my boss (and his boss) would not support me, meaning that I would always have to rely on the intervention of the CEO.

We searched for another way short of full centralization that would give us the authority and structure required for success. We decided on a hybrid model with clearly defined roles and responsibilities for Cat U and the business units along with dual solid line connection to the learning managers in each business unit.

First, we defined roles and responsibilities as in Figure 12.3 above. Cat U would be responsible for the development of common, global learning that would be used by multiple business units. Leadership, Six Sigma, engineering, marketing, business acumen, change management, and compliance-related learning were examples. Business units could no longer develop learning in these areas on their own or through the use of a consultant. We had 11 LMSs around the company, and we began a migration to one (which took six years). They would have to use the corporate LMS as soon as it could meet their needs. We instituted common reporting, budgeting, and planning systems, which they had to use.

Business units were expected to participate in the development of the new common, global programs and then to help deploy them. They were, however, free to continue to develop and deliver learning specific to their units, where it did not make sense for Cat U to become involved. The business planning process each year would decide which programs Cat U would take on and which would be left for the units.

Second, business unit learning staff would continue to report to their own business unit. (About two hundred of the three hundred full-time learning professionals at Cat worked in the business units.) However, each business unit (some consisted of five to seven thousand employees) would appoint one lead learning manager who would be the head of learning for the unit. This lead learning manager would also report to one of the five deans, who in turn reported to me. Each dean would set three or four goals for the lead learning manager, such as contributing to the development of common, global learning, deploying common, global learning, adhering to corporate processes, and contributing to the global learning community. The dean would review these goals with the lead learning manager's boss, who would also have provided three or four goals. Progress would be reviewed every quarter with the lead learning manager and her boss.

What made this a dual solid line was the fact that 40% of the lead learning managers' performance evaluation (and subsequent merit increase) would depend on the Cat U evaluation. This was enough to get their attention and ensure all twenty-five lead learning managers were aligned with Cat U and working toward common goals.

The model was supplemented by the creation of a global learning community and by monthly teleconferences with the lead learning managers, senior Cat U staff, and me. We also began holding an annual conference in which we would all get together for three days to review programs and plans and share concerns.

The model worked well. The first year, however, was difficult. The lead learning managers and their business units resented the loss of autonomy. I met with the VP of each business unit twice each year, every year. Most were not happy with the creation of Cat U. Several complained directly to the CEO, who always backed me up. The lead learning managers did not want to report to Cat U, but I explained they had only two choices. One, we make the hybrid model work, or two, we go with full centralization, and they all report directly (100%) to Cat U. Grudgingly, they agreed to option one.

The second year was easier, and by the third year most of the resistance was gone. Once all the learning professionals got to know each other on a personal basis, the learning community evolved into a very cohesive group. By the third year, everyone looked forward to the annual in-person conference—a vast improvement from the first year when tension at the conference was off the charts.

Funding

It is equally important to have the right funding model for your learning organization. Like the model for organizational structure, there is no single funding model that is right for all organizations. The goal is to find the right model for the near term, realizing that the model may need to be adjusted in several years. We will begin with a review of the common funding models, examine some decision criteria, and conclude with recommendations on selecting the right model.

The Common Funding Models

There are three common funding models: corporate, business unit allocation, and business unit discretionary. The last two involve charge backs to the business units but differ in how the charge backs are determined and how much discretion the business has in paying them.

Corporate

In the corporate model, all the funding comes from corporate. A budget is provided for the learning organization, and expenditures cannot exceed the corporate budget. The learning group does not bill business units or charge participants for attending courses, so the learning is "free" from their point of view.

This model is very common for startups. Corporate pays for all the expenses, including staff, initial program development, and systems expenses like an LMS. Since a startup does not have a product to "sell," and since it has not yet proven its value, business units are often reluctant to pay for course development or to cover the full price of a class. So, without corporate funding, it could be very difficult to generate revenue at this early stage.

Key advantages and disadvantages of corporate funding on a sustained basis are listed in Figure 12.5.

FIGURE 12.5

Advantages and Disadvantages of the Corporate Funding Model

Advantages

- Funding comes from a single source.
- You only have to sell your budget through a single chain of command (your boss through the CEO) and perhaps a board of governors.
- It's the easiest way to fund a program when it works.

Disadvantages

- Funding comes from a single source.
    - o It may be cut during the budget process or later in the year.
    - o You are totally dependent on corporate funding.
- A corporate university is not tested in the "free market."
- A corporate university may not be responsive to business units.
- Demand may exceed budgeted capacity, resulting in rationing of learning.

Apart from the advantages at startup, the chief advantage is that corporate funding may be easy to obtain since it comes from just one source. This is great if your boss, your boss's boss, and your CEO all are strong supporters and can provide the desired level of funding. In the best case, the CLO makes one budget presentation, and the funds are granted.

Of course, the single source of funding can also be the biggest weakness of this model. Perhaps your boss or others in the chain of command are not such strong supporters and decide to fund the function at a level far below what you believe is appropriate. It is also *very easy* for the learning budget to be cut during the year in this model in response to business conditions. All it takes is one phone call from the CEO and your budget is 20% less.

The other drawbacks of corporate funding reflect the arbitrary nature of setting the budget. There may be no input from the customers (business units), so the corporate university is not subject to the test of the free market, where consumers buy more of the products they like. How would the CEO know whether the corporate university was creating good courses or whether the pricing was correct? With a free market approach, there is high demand for good courses and participants are willing to pay at least the average cost.

If the learning function is responsive to the units and the courses are good, a different problem will develop under this model. Demand will exceed capacity, and the learning function will not be able to offer more classes even if participants would gladly pay for them because this model limits expenditures. One very large corporate university found itself in exactly this situation. It chose to meet the additional demand by running a significant loss for the year, which had repercussions for the following year.

Allocation

This is the first of the two funding models in which the customers (the business units, dealers, suppliers, or external customers) pay for the costs of the learning function. In this model the learning function recovers all of the expenses associated with the learning organization (labor and related, internal, and external overhead) by completely allocating these expenses to its customers. The customers have no choice or discretion. They must pay their allocation.

Typically, the learning function will set its annual budget and then allocate it entirely among its customers, where it becomes part of their annual budgets as well. The most common formula for allocation is headcount, in which each business unit (assume only internal customers) pays in proportion to the number of employees. For example, if total expenses for the learning group were expected to be $1,000,000 and the company had 2,000 employees, then a business unit with 200 employees would pay for 10% (200/2,000) or $100,000 (10% x $1,000,000) of the learning group's total cost. Alternatively, the costs could be allocated by proportion of business unit expense to total corporate expense or by some other formula, providing that the necessary data are readily available.

In this model the learning group could be held to its original budget (like in the corporate model above), or it could be allowed to spend over its initial budget in response to higher demand from its customers. If it is allowed to exceed its budget, it will need to recover the additional costs from its customers, which could be accomplished through a year-end bill to each customer for their share of the overage (using the same formula employed for the original allocation).

Also note that in this model course prices do not play any role. Prices do not need to be established or published since the customers will pay their allocation regardless of the cost of the courses attended by their employees.

Advantages and disadvantages for the allocation model are listed in Figure 12.6.

FIGURE 12.6

Advantages and Disadvantages of the Allocation Funding Model

Advantages

- Guarantees that all corporate university expenses will be reimbursed
- Negotiation not required with each customer
- Easy to calculate allocation and simple to administer
- No course prices required

Disadvantages

- Customers may not like their allocation; after all, they will have had no input
- Allocation does not reflect actual usage, raising issues of fairness and equity
- The corporate university has not been tested on the market
- The corporate university may not be responsive to customers

The chief advantage of this model lies in the simplicity of the approach. The corporate university is guaranteed full reimbursement, so there is no worry about generating enough revenue to cover costs. Further, the cost recovery mechanism is straightforward, easy to explain, and easy to administer. No negotiations are required with the customers, who must pay the allocated amount. Since there are no published course prices, there is no need to calculate them.

Not surprisingly, the simplicity also represents the major drawback. Although easy to understand, some customers will not like the allocation formula, particularly those who underutilize learning. From their point of view they are being required to "subsidize" the cost of other customers, who are using more than their fair share of this corporate resource. On the other hand, those customers who are heavy users of learning will like it since their marginal cost of sending one more participant is $0. For them it is a great deal. Even if there is an additional charge at the end of the year, they still benefit because other customers will have to help pay the cost.

Since customers have no choice, the model suffers some of the same disadvantages as the corporate model with regard to the lack of a market test on quality and price. Customers must pay the same whether quality is high or low, and since there are no prices, there is no way to tell whether customers view the course as appropriately priced.

Discretionary or Charge-back

In this model the corporate university acts like a business. It is expected to set its prices so that it can recover all of its costs on an annual basis. It offers its services and courses to its customers, who are free to take them or not. Customers in this model have complete discretion to take as much or as little as they want. This is a very common model for more mature corporate universities.

There are several ways a corporate university can operate in this model. First, the corporate university may self-fund the development of courses (and the acquisition of systems such as an LMS) and then price the courses and other services to recover the total cost (labor and related, internal, and external overhead). The learning function is free to price some offerings below the average total cost but will need to price others above the average total cost in order to break even at year's end.

Another approach is for the corporate university to charge customers (like a business unit) separately for the development of a course it has requested. In this case the learning function makes a proposal to the business unit to develop the course. If the business unit accepts (at its discretion), then the learning function will develop the course and bill the business unit for the development. The learning function also will determine a price for the course (perhaps as part of the proposal), which allows it to recover all its costs except the direct development cost, which is being billed separately to the business unit. Participants will choose to take the course at the stated price at their discretion. (The business unit may direct certain employees to take the course and monitor to ensure they complete it.) The learning function then bills the business unit each month for the participants who took the course.

Regardless of the arrangement, the central feature of this model is the discretion of the customer. The corporate university bears the risk of poor quality, mispriced courses, and lack of planned demand. The corporate university in this model is often not subject to an expense constraint and can exceed budgeted expense as long as revenue also exceeds plan so that breakeven is maintained.

Advantages and disadvantages of the discretionary model are listed in Figure 12.7.

FIGURE 12.7

Advantages and Disadvantages of the Discretionary Funding Model

Advantages

- It forces the corporate university to be very responsive to customer needs.
- Each offering is tested in the market, thereby providing feedback on quality and price.
- Customers pay only for what they use and want.
- The corporate university can exceed budget to meet high demand.

Disadvantages

- The corporate university may fail to recover costs if prices are set incorrectly or demand is weaker than expected.
- It is very difficult to negotiate with multiple customers (business units) to fund the development of an enterprise program.
- A serious problem arises if one business unit, which had agreed to share funding for an enterprise program, withdraws. Who picks up its share?
- Billing business units for the services used by their employees can be time consuming.

The advantages of this funding model derive from its responsiveness to the market and from its flexibility. In this free enterprise model, there are no guarantees, and a corporate university will fail if it is not responsive to its customers. It must get the pricing right (neither too high nor too low), and it must forecast expected demand accurately enough. Customers like this model because they pay only for what they choose. A unit that is not a heavy user of learning is not required to subsidize other units, and a customer may decide not to participate in any learning.

If it is successful managing these aspects of the business, however, this model provides for tremendous flexibility since in most cases the function is free to exceed budgeted expenses as long as it can break even for the year. Thus, there is no need to ration learning or leave learning needs unmet.

Customer discretion, however, does pose some potentially serious problems. There will be times when business conditions suddenly deteriorate and demand declines significantly. In these cases it will be nearly impossible for the learning function to recover its fixed costs for the year.

Another issue arises from the need to fund enterprise programs. First, it can be time consuming and difficult to negotiate with multiple customers on the funding of a common enterprise program. For example, suppose five business units want a leadership program. The corporate university would like to meet this demand with one program and have the cost shared by all five units. Each unit, however, may want slightly different features and may not agree on the formula for sharing the cost.

Second, there is the very serious issue of a unit or units opting out, creating stranded costs. Suppose the five units agree on the program and further agree to share the development cost of $500,000 equally. So, each agrees it is worth $100,000 and puts that amount in its budget. After budget negotiations are complete (and perhaps even after development is underway), one of the units decides to withdraw its funding because of a drop in sales. The total cost for development is still $500,000. How does the corporate university cover the last $100,000? It could ask the remaining four units to pick up the difference, which means each now has to pay $125,000. Although this may not seem like much, in practice a representative of at least one unit is likely to say, "I agreed to $100,000 and had a hard enough time getting that approved. My unit will not pay any more than the agreed-upon amount." If even one unit refuses to pay, it is highly unlikely the others will pay the $125,000, let alone a higher amount.

This is the beginning of a death spiral for this program. If the corporate university insists that it has to cover its costs and each of the remaining four has to pay $125,000, at least one more is likely to drop out. Now the remaining three would need to pay $166,667 each to cover the cost, and it is likely that at least one cannot afford this latest increase. This spiral will continue until no one is left who is willing to cover the $500,000 in costs.

To prevent the death spiral, the university will likely need to maintain the original agreed-upon price of $100,000 for the four remaining units. This leaves the university with $100,000 in stranded costs. The only alternative is to cancel the program, and a marginal analysis would show whether this minimizes the loss or not. Even if canceling minimizes the loss, it may not be politically feasible, given that the other four units still want the program.

Choosing a Funding Model

Like organizational structure, the funding model needs to fit your particular needs at the present point in time. We have seen that each model has advantages and disadvantages, so there is no perfect funding model. The goal is to find the right one for your organization for the near term. Implement it, learn from it, and be prepared to modify it in a year or two if necessary.

Some Basic Questions

***Culture*:** Which model is most consistent with your culture and budgeting practices? You might still choose a different approach, but you should know what the norm is. Do most service-providing internal functions rely entirely on corporate funding, or do they use allocation or discretionary models to recover their costs? If the former, does this same approach make sense for you? If you think a different model is better, how hard would it be to implement? Would it even be allowed or supported by corporate procedures and by accounting?

***Maturity*:** Is this a startup or a more mature organization? Startups usually need to rely more on corporate funding or on allocation to the business units. A more mature organization will be expected to be self-sustaining, which implies the discretionary model.

***Responsiveness*:** How responsive do you want to be to the customer? The discretionary model will drive a learning organization to be very responsive to its customers. The other two models, at least from a funding viewpoint, do not demand as much responsiveness.

***Cost Structure*:** What is the cost structure for the learning organization? What percentage of total cost is variable? How quickly and easily can fixed costs be cut? The discretionary model works best when variable cost is a high percentage of total cost and when fixed costs can be reduced within a year. A high fixed cost structure argues for a guaranteed revenue stream like that provided in the corporate or allocation models.

***Risk Aversion*:** A high aversion to risk by the CLO or the learning organization in general argues against the discretionary model, under which the corporate university bears most of the risk.

***Demand*:** The discretionary model is best if demand is likely to exceed budgeted capacity since the learning function will be able to accommodate it. On the other hand, if demand is hard to predict and likely to fluctuate widely, then a model with a more guaranteed revenue stream might be more appropriate.

***Number of Programs Funded by Multiple Units*:** The discretionary model is very susceptible to stranded costs arising from business units withdrawing their support for a program under development. These programs are more easily funded with the other two models.

Recommendation: Use a Mixed Model

Answers to the above questions may lead you to just one of the models. It is just as likely, however, that the answers point to different models, depending on the question. Often a mixed model with the attributes of two or all three of the models will work best. This approach tries to capture the advantages of each model while avoiding the disadvantages.

There are many ways to structure a mixed model, but the bottom line guidance is this:

1. Cover fixed costs with a dependable revenue stream.
2. Build variable costs into your cost structure.
    a. Use part-time employees and consultants.
    b. Avoid long-term contracts with suppliers.
    c. Negotiate escape clauses to longer-term contracts in advance.
3. Be prepared to manage all your costs aggressively so you can withstand a sudden decrease in demand from your customers.

One such mixed model is outlined in Figure 12.8.

FIGURE 12.8

A Sample Mixed Model for Funding

- Use corporate funding or business unit allocation for expenses that are not variable and not easily charged out. These might include the following:
    - Support staff, senior leadership
    - System costs like the LMS
    - Process costs like creating the business plan for learning, managing metrics, and conducting evaluations

    - Enterprise programs where the corporate university is the owner, or there is no single business unit sponsor or owner
- Use business unit discretionary funding to recover
    - Delivery costs for instructor-led training
    - Program development costs for which the sponsor or owner is in a business unit and has a budget

This mixed model employs corporate funding or business unit allocation to cover fixed costs, which position the corporate university to withstand a sudden drop in demand from the business units. (Of course, the CEO can still cut funding significantly, so there are no guarantees!) This model also employs corporate funding or business unit allocation to develop those programs for which there are multiple owners in order to avoid the problem of stranded costs.

The mixed model brings in discretionary funding for delivery and for program development where there is a single sponsor (no stranded cost issues here). Thus, prices will be established for each course and published. Each course will be tested in the market for quality, price, and value, providing important feedback to the learning function.

The ratio of corporate or allocated funding to discretionary funds is also likely to change through time. Startups often rely almost exclusively on corporate funding since there are no courses to sell in the beginning and since customers might be reluctant to fund development or pay the published course price. As the corporate university establishes a reputation for quality and value, it will be in a position to charge upfront for development and recover more of its cost through course prices.

CATERPILLAR EXAMPLE: An Evolution

An initial focus of Cat U was to develop high-priority programs that could be used by most of the twenty-five business units. In other words, we would focus on common, global programs for which consistency was important and the investments could be leveraged enterprise wide. Since Cat U was new (deans had to be hired, a predecessor learning group had to be integrated, governing boards had to be established, etc.) and since none of these programs existed at the time, there was going to be very little "new product" created in the first year. Therefore, a discretionary model would not work. Since Cat U had yet to prove itself and since there was considerable resistance to its creation, an allocation model would simply have angered the business units further. Therefore, 80% of the funding in the first two years was corporate, which also reflected the strong support of the CEO. The remainder came from existing programs and was charged on a discretionary basis.

In the second year we began to deploy our newly developed programs, which provided more revenue for us. (Course prices were set to recover delivery costs.) The programs were well received and much (but not all) of the initial resistance to Cat U had dissipated. Consequently, in preparing our budget for year three, we were ready to wean ourselves from the heavy reliance on corporate funding. We proposed a glide path to reduce the proportion of corporate funding from 60% in year three to 20% in year five. The board of governors and the CEO were very supportive of this plan. The remainder would come from business unit charges using the discretionary model. Beginning in year three business units would pay Cat U for the development they requested. Cat U would continue to charge (through the course price structure) for delivery.

After five years we were at the 20% level for corporate funding. The funding model had worked very well for us. Unfortunately, in a large company with numerous business units, this internal charge-back model can prove very burdensome. Negotiations at budget time with each unit were time consuming as were calculations of the monthly charges for services used. Each month a number of units would question their charges, which would require our business manager to take the time to check class rosters and confirm we had charged the unit correctly. A similar effort was required for the hundreds of departments that charged other departments for their services. Even as a service unit, Cat U would be charged by twenty to forty other departments for services they provided us. So, every service unit charged the rest of the units (service and profit) and was in turn charged by all the other service units. One study indicated this business of internal charges consumed the time of two hundred accountants.

Consequently, the company abandoned the discretionary funding model. Internal service providers like corporate HR and Cat U would allocate their expenses by headcount. There would be no more negotiating with units and no more monthly charge backs. Although it did immediately save time for the accountants, the allocation model caused tremendous problems for providers like Cat U, which offered discretionary services. The business units wanted to pay just for what they used. Worse, all internal service charges for corporate HR functions were bundled together and one annual bill presented to each business unit. There was no breakdown by Cat U, succession planning, compensation and benefits, etc., so units had no idea what each cost and how it compared to the previous year.

In my opinion, the combination of discretionary and corporate funding was just right for us. It provided the required transparency for the business units and ensured our responsiveness. The pricing mechanism for development and delivery ensured good discussion between the sponsors, business units, and Cat U. Yes, there is a price to maintain the discretionary funding model in terms of staffing, but I believe it is worth it to support the "free market" approach. Information always comes with a price, and the appropriate question to ask is whether the value of that information exceeds its cost. In the case of learning at Caterpillar, I believe the value of pricing, negotiating, and charging back very definitely exceeded the cost of the accountants required to provide the information. In my opinion, the discretionary funding model should have been maintained.

Conclusion

The right models for both organizational structure and funding are critical to the overall success of the learning function, including the ability to run it like a business. In each case there are several models commonly used, and each model has its own advantages and disadvantages. The goal is to select the best model for the current situation that will enable the function to achieve its goals.

Several recommendations, however, can be made. If the goal is to make all enterprise learning more strategic, then an organization should adopt the centralized or hybrid model for learning. An enterprise-wide strategic focus for all learning is simply not possible in a decentralized model. With regard to funding, a mixed model is generally preferred, combining elements of the corporate or allocation models (to cover fixed costs) with elements of the discretionary model (to ensure responsiveness and to test the quality and pricing of courses).

All the key elements of the business of learning have now been covered. The last chapter will discuss the journey to world class.

Chapter 12 to Do List

1. Consider the advantages and disadvantages of the three organizational models.
2. Which structure is indicated by your answers to the decision questions?
3. If the best structure is different than the status quo, determine whether it is feasible and desirable to adopt the new model.
4. Consider the advantages and disadvantages of the three funding models.
5. Is a single funding model indicated by your answers to the decision questions?
6. Would a mixed model be the best choice? If so, how would it be structured?
7. If the best funding model is different than the status quo, determine whether it is feasible and desirable to adopt the new model.

Further Reading

Allen, Mark, ed. *The Corporate University Handbook: Designing, Managing, and Growing a Successful Program*. New York: Amacom, 2002. (See Chapter 2.)

Meister, Jeanne. *Corporate Universities: Lessons in Building a World-Class Work Force*. Boston: McGraw Hill, 1998. (See Chapter 2.)

Wheeler, Kevin. *The Corporate University Workbook: Launching the 21st Century Learning Organization*. San Francisco: Pfeiffer, 2005. (See Chapters 5 and 7.)

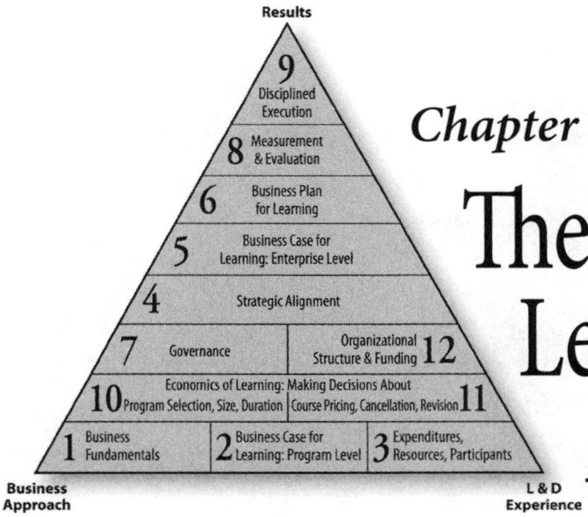

Chapter 13

The Business of Learning: Pulling It All Together

WE ARE NOW ready to pull together all the key elements of running learning like a business. We have explored the key applications of business and economics to learning from strategic alignment and the creation of a business plan for learning to issues of course size, duration, price, and the impact of scale on cost and net benefit. We have explored the key issues of structure and funding as well as the elements of good management, including governance, measurement strategies, and disciplined execution.

All that remains is to explore the role of vision and mission statements for the learning organization. Then we will be ready to combine all these elements to produce a world-class corporate university or learning function that brings bottom-line results to an organization.

Key Concepts for Chapter 13

13

1. A learning organization should have vision and mission statements.
2. Vision and mission statements should be used to manage and guide the learning organization.
3. There are ten key elements to running learning like a business, starting with a strategic focus.
4. All ten elements are important for success.
5. There are fifteen steps to running learning like a business.
6. Successfully communicating the vision, mission, and milestones is imperative. A journey chart can be very helpful to show plans for the next five years to achieve the vision.
7. The results of running learning like a business are numerous and significant for both the overall organization and the learning function.
8. Lessons learned offer advice on how to begin.
9. Enjoy the journey.

Vision and Mission

World-class corporate universities have a compelling vision and a clear mission, which they use to organize their efforts, build shared mental models, and communicate with others. In Chapter 1 we explored the importance of an organization's vision and mission statements. Now we will focus on the vision and mission statements of the corporate university.

Vision

A vision statement should describe what you want to be or become in the future. It is aspirational, implying that you want to progress or evolve from your present state to the desired future state, which is typically five to ten years away.

Creating the Vision Statement

There is tremendous value in the process of creating and building consensus for the vision as well as in the daily use of the finished vision statement. Senior learning leaders may easily spend a day or more crafting an initial vision. These discussions are likely to focus on what the corporate university hopes to achieve and what will be required to get there. Typically, the draft statement will then be shared with the rest of the learning organization to elicit input, suggestions, and support. The senior leadership team will then meet again to discuss proposed changes and to address concerns and objections. After incorporating some of the suggestions, the revised draft may be shared again before being finalized.

Some organizations like to build from the bottom up by first engaging all employees in the discussion. In this model, multiple drafts work their way up the learning organization. Senior leadership starts with these drafts and creates one final draft for review. In either case, the process of engaging everyone in the learning function in a discussion about their future is very powerful in terms of both learning and creating buy-in.

Sample Vision Statements

Following are some examples of vision statements. No one vision statement is right for all organizations. Create one that is right for your organization and that will help you achieve your goals. The vision statement should be just one short- to medium-length sentence. Avoid multiple sentences and long sentences. The goal is to have it be memorable.

- Be (or become) a world-class corporate university, providing highly valued strategic services to your company.
- Be a highly valued, strategic partner, contributing significantly to the success of your company.

- Become an indispensable ally of your business units to realize your company's aggressive five-year goals.

Each statement combines a vision for the learning group itself (world-class, strategic partner, and indispensable ally) with a vision for its impact on the broader organization. These types of vision statements reflect a strategic focus and are more powerful than statements about just the learning group itself. Strategic vision statements help remind everyone inside and outside the corporate university why the learning group exists. Learning exists to help the organization reach its goals.

Mission

A mission statement describes purpose. It is why employees come to work each day. It is not aspirational like the vision statement. It is about the present. What does the learning function do day in and day out?

Creating the Mission Statement

Vision and mission statements are often created at the same time and as part of the same process. Mission statements typically can be created and consensus reached more quickly since they are about the present. The difficulty may come in deciding what to include and what to leave out. Like the vision statement, the mission statement should be short and concise. That means one reasonably short sentence. It should be easy to remember.

Sample Mission Statements

Like vision statements, there is not one mission statement that is right for all organizations. Create one that is right for your organization. There is often confusion in practice between vision and mission statements. If an organization has only one it is probably a mission statement. Remember, a vision statement is about the future while a mission statement is about the present.

Following are some examples of mission statements:

- Improve organizational performance through learning and development
- Help our company achieve its annual goals
- Improve (or achieve) business results through learning
- Ensure that our company has the talent to achieve its goals

Each states the business reason for learning. The mission statement should answer the question, "Why does our company invest in learning?" In short, it is the business case for learning.

The difference between a vision and mission statement should now be clear. Both should make a connection to the organization's goals, but the vision will be about the future while the mission is about the present.

Using Vision and Mission Statements

Vision and mission statements are used many ways.

They can be used to create a shared mental model for the learning function and for its role in the organization. For example, if the learning function aspires to a strategic role, then the vision statement will reflect that. The process of creating these statements will provide an opportunity for leaders to share their visions and for employees to respond, ask questions, and make their own suggestions. It is a time for excellent dialogue, which can bring to the surface misunderstandings and fundamental differences of opinion about the purpose of the function and where the corporate university is going. It may turn out that some employees simply do not agree with the new mission or vision, and the sooner they move on the better for the learning group.

Once in place, the mission and vision statements provide guidance for management of the function. The vision statement provides long-term guidance for multi-year planning. Each year's annual business plan should take the learning group one year closer to achieving the vision. If it does not, then either the business plan or the vision needs to be changed. The mission statement also provides guidance for the annual business plan. Does the plan provide the resources necessary to execute the mission? If not, more resources need to be found or the mission may need to be altered. There is no point in having a mission that cannot be achieved, and it is very demoralizing for employees and leaders alike.

Mission and vision statements should also be used in hiring employees into the learning group and then in their on-boarding. A prospective employee who is uncomfortable with either the mission or vision should not be hired. The same goes for partners and others on whom you will rely. Once in the door, use the statements and the thinking that went into their creation as part of the on-boarding process so that new employees thoroughly understand the mission and vision and can articulate it to others.

The vision and mission cannot be repeated too many times. It is the role of the CLO in particular to look for opportunities to remind employees and partners of the mission and vision. Include them in regular all-employee meetings and in your literature. Include them in your PowerPoint presentations, describing the learning group to internal and external audiences. Expect all employees of the learning function to have them memorized and be able to give an elevator speech to anyone about what they mean.

In summary, the goal is to embed the vision and mission deeply in the culture of the learning organization. Leaders should refer to the vision and mission often in planning, budgeting, setting priorities, and when answering questions. These statements are not meant to sit on a shelf only to be reviewed at the annual planning meeting. They should be used on a daily basis to guide the corporate university.

Running Learning Like a Business

Key Elements

We now have explored all the elements needed to run learning like a business. Each element is necessary for success, and most elements are closely integrated with other elements. In other words, although addressing just a few of the elements may lead to some improvement, significant improvement requires addressing them all.

The key elements are listed in Figure 13.1.

Focus, Vision, and Mission: Not surprisingly, the list begins with a strategic focus for the learning function, which relates directly to the mission and vision of the company or organization. Learning exists to help the company achieve its goals, which should also be expressed in the mission for the learning organization. The learning group also needs its own vision, which will guide it for the next five to ten years.

Structure and Funding: The structure of the group must support its goals and be supportive of its vision. Although there is no single right answer for all organizations, only the centralized or hybrid structures will support a strategic focus. Likewise, no single funding model is right for all groups. A mixed model is recommended, employing corporate or allocated funding to cover the majority

FIGURE 13.1

Key Elements of Managing Learning Like a Business

• Focus	=>	Strategic
• Vision and Mission	=>	Must have
• Structure	=>	Depends, but should be centralized or hybrid for a strategic focus
• Funding Model	=>	Depends, but a Mixed Model is recommended
• Strategic Alignment	=>	Absolutely critical
• Business Plan for Learning	=>	Must have, includes business case
• Governance	=>	Need at least a Board of Governors
• Measurement & Evaluation Strategy	=>	Must have
• Disciplined Execution	=>	Absolutely critical
• Application of Business and Economic Concepts	=>	Some are required, others highly recommended

of fixed and shared expenses, and discretionary funding to cover the majority of variable expenses as well as development for a single internal customer.

Strategic Alignment: Alignment of learning to the company's strategy is essential if the corporate university is to have a strategic focus, aspires to be a strategic business partner, and wants to maximize its impact on bottom-line results. This is a case in which the three elements of focus, vision, and strategic alignment are closely integrated.

Business Case and Business Plan: The development of the business case and the creation of the business plan are also essential if learning is to be run as a business. Without them, there is no case for additional funds, no connection to the corporate goals, and no specific, measurable goals by which to judge success. Why would any well-run organization allocate funding to its learning group without a business case and a business plan in place?

Governance: Strong governance is essential in most organizations with a strategic focus, especially in a hybrid structure where the learning group does not have complete authority over all learning resources. A board of governors will provide crucial counsel for achieving a strategic focus, aligning learning to company goals, setting priorities, building the business case, creating the business plan, and executing with discipline. The board can also remove roadblocks, settle disputes, and help secure funding and staffing.

Measurement, Evaluation, and Disciplined Execution: Running learning like a business also requires the necessary measurement and evaluation tools for the business plan to be executed with discipline. This requires that progress is compared to specific, measurable goals on at least a monthly basis. Significant deviations are highlighted and managed appropriately as soon as they arise. There are no year-end surprises, and the process ensures that planned impact and net benefit are delivered.

Application of Business and Economic Concepts: Lastly, running learning like a business really does require the use of business and economic concepts. Business basics such as understanding monthly operating reports and department financial statements are required. Understanding cost structure (fixed and variable costs), pricing a course, and knowing when to cancel a class are also required basics. More advanced topics like optimum size for a course, optimum duration of a class, and the effect of scale on costs, although not absolutely necessary, are required if the learning manager really wants to make the best decisions possible. Other advanced topics like the analogy to the theory of the firm and constrained net benefit maximization are certainly optional but do provide a framework and common vocabulary for learning professionals to explore these issues further in a rigorous way.

Checklist of Action Items

A checklist for running learning like a business is included in Figure13.2. For some items order is important (for example, strategic alignment must precede the business case and business plan), and for others it is not (for example, the creation of the board of governors could come later). Also, every organization starts at a different point, so some may have already completed most of the items while others are ready to start at #3, #6, or some other point.

FIGURE 13.2

Checklist for Running Learning Like a Business

Step	Task
1.	Appreciate that learning is a business and is expected to produce business results.
2.	Resolve to run learning like a business.
3.	Adopt a strategic focus.
4.	Create a board of governors.
5.	Create a vision and mission statement.
6.	Create a multi-year plan to achieve your vision.
7.	Ensure that your organizational structure will support a strategic focus.
8.	Adopt a workable funding model.
9.	Strategically align learning to your organization's goals.
10.	Build the business case for learning.
11.	Create the business plan for learning.
12.	Plan for monthly, disciplined execution of the plan, using standard measures and reports.
13.	Adopt a measurement and evaluation strategy that ensures planned impact is achieved and provides for continuous improvement.
14.	Use business and economic concepts to make better decisions.
15.	Benchmark with others. Learn. Improve.

Step 1: The starting point is to understand that learning is very much a business and should be an integral part of an organization's success. That means learning has to deliver results that are important to the organization and particularly to the CEO and senior leaders.

Step 2: Once the CLO and senior leaders of the learning function agree that learning is a business, they need to resolve to manage it like one. For those with a business background or P&L experience (responsible for the profit or loss of a business unit), this may come naturally, although they may need to learn how to apply their knowledge of business to the learning field. For others it may represent an entirely new way to view management of the learning function, and they will need to learn the business concepts covered in this book.

***Step 3*:** The adoption of a strategic focus should come early in the process and will influence the completion of most of the remaining steps. This means that learning will be aligned to the highest priority goals of an organization so that it will have the maximum impact on the organization. It may mean reducing or completely eliminating time spent on the lowest priority programs. It also means that most of the learning for the coming year is planned in advance, ideally as part of a business plan for learning. A strategic learning function spends little of its time reacting to unexpected or "surprise" calls for learning.

***Step 4*:** Somewhere early in the process a board of governors should be established. This governing body can be very helpful in the early stages of a startup or a transformation by providing invaluable advice on strategic focus, vision and mission, multi-year plans, organizational structures, funding models, strategic alignment, and the creation of the initial business case and business plan. Once up and running, the board will provide critical input into each year's organizational goals and priorities, priorities for the learning function, and funding. The board will approve the business case and the business plan and then regularly review progress in achieving it.

***Step 5*:** The vision and mission statements should also be created early in the process since they will guide many of the activities in later steps. They will ensure that leaders and employees have a common understanding of the learning group's vision and purpose. These statements should also play an important role in hiring staff for the learning function, selecting partners and vendors, and communicating both internally within the group and externally to the rest of the organization.

***Step 6*:** Typically a multi-year plan is required to reach the vision, which may be set five to ten years in the future. Creation of the plan provides an opportunity for learning leaders to come to a shared understanding or mental model of what the future looks like and how it will be achieved. It is also an opportunity to get input from the CEO and board of governors in order to take advantage of their knowledge and perspective and to ensure their buy-in.

***Step 7*:** Another early step is to ensure that you have the right organizational structure in place to support your focus, mission, vision, and multi-year plan. This is especially critical for a strategic focus that requires a centralized or hybrid structure.

Step 8: Like organizational structure, the right funding model needs to be adopted to ensure the learning group's success. Although a corporate funding model may be appropriate for a startup, most functions adopt a mixed model as they mature.

Step 9: Learning should be strategically aligned to an organization's highest priority goals. This alignment needs to take place every year as part of a disciplined process to identify the organization's goals and priorities. Of course, there may be additional learning, which is conducted every year (new hire, compliance, etc.) and which may not be viewed as strategic but is essential and will be a part of the learning plan.

Step 10: Although all the steps are important to manage learning like a business, building a business case for the investment in learning is certainly the most obvious and yet seldom happens. The CEO, board of governors, and other senior leaders want to see a business case. Even if they are supporters of the learning function, they want to know how learning is going to help them achieve their goals. They want to know where learning will be focused and what impact it is likely to have. And they want to know what it will cost. With this information on impact and cost, they can make a decision on the appropriate funding in a corporate or allocation model and be comfortable with the planned spending in a discretionary model.

Step 11: Creating the business plan for learning is the next logical step. All of the work has been done to identify key company goals and priorities, plan learning programs, set specific, measurable goals for each program, forecast impacts, benefits and costs, and build the business case and prepare a budget. Now capture all this work in a written business plan to share with the board of governors, CEO, and senior leaders for review and approval. This is how a good business operates, and the learning function should as well. Not only is it very professional, but it is also excellent discipline for the learning function to ensure that the best possible plan has been prepared for the next year. It also ensures that everyone knows exactly what that plan is.

Step 12: With a plan in place, the next step is to execute it with discipline to ensure that the planned impact and net benefit are delivered. Learning leaders and managers should be held accountable for delivering the specific, measurable goals in the plan. This requires the use of reports and at least monthly meetings to review progress. The goal is to discover problems early when there is still time to address them.

Step 13: Part of disciplined execution is having and implementing a comprehensive evaluation strategy designed to ensure that planned results are delivered and that opportunities are identified for improvement. The evaluation strategy should specify the level of evaluation and sample size for each program, along with the individual or party responsible for performing the evaluation and any applicable deadlines.

Step 14: Business and economic concepts are already embedded in many of the steps above. This step simply serves as a reminder that these concepts can be used to go beyond the basics in the steps above to make much better decisions about optimum levels of investment, program selection, class duration, course size, cancellation, and plan revision. Understanding cost structure and the effect of scale on cost are two key concepts to manage the function more efficiently.

Step 15: Lastly, benchmarking with others is a great way to learn and improve. Attend conferences, visit other organizations, and read the literature to discover how others have overcome the same challenges you face. Enter the annual competition for corporate university awards and submit your data for annual rankings of learning organizations. You will get ideas for improvement just by completing the applications, and then you will have an opportunity to learn from the others when the results are announced.

The Journey

For most learning organizations, the realization of their vision and the implementation of all the steps described above will require a multi-year journey. For startups or young corporate universities the journey may take five to ten years. It cannot simply be done in one or two years. (For a great description of a very successful journey reinventing learning at Defense Acquisition University, see *Leading a Learning Revolution* by Frank Anderson, Chris Hardy, and Jeffrey Leeson.)

In light of the time required to realize the vision and the challenge of explaining the journey to others, it is imperative to find a way to communicate the mission, vision, and journey effectively, both inside and outside the learning function. Everyone needs to understand the vision and appreciate that it will take years of hard work to achieve it. This will not only help get people on board with the required changes, but it will also serve to manage expectations so no one expects the vision to be achieved overnight.

There are many ways to convey the mission, vision, and journey effectively. Like so much else we have discussed, the key is to find a way that works in your organization. The mission and vision statements can often be conveyed in writing or through PowerPoint slides. The journey, and its connection to the mission and vision, may present a greater challenge. At the same time, you may want to convey that learning will be run like a business and that you have adopted a strategic focus.

Figure 13.3 is an example of an approach that worked well at Caterpillar, a company with a lot of analytical employees (engineers, IT professionals, attorneys, accountants, etc.) who were comfortable with graphs. In this approach, the mission is represented on the Y axis and time on the X axis. The plotted points represent the journey or key milestones toward achieving the vision, which is the final point in the upper right-hand corner. (The mission, vision, and milestones are illustrative and not exactly what we used at Caterpillar.)

We found that this approach accomplished all of our key communication objectives in a single page and was far more effective than a PowerPoint with the same information.

Specifically, the journey chart did the following for us:

- Stated the mission and vision
- Showed that a multi-year journey would be required to achieve the vision
- Showed the key milestones along the journey
- Grouped key milestones by year
- Characterized progress through time from a reactive learning focus to a strategic performance focus
- Demonstrated a disciplined, business-like approach to running learning through the establishment of short and long-term goals

A common reaction was, "Okay. I get it now. I understand how Cat U is different than the old learning function, and I see where you want to go. I like the goals for each year." They could see that we were focused on business results and that we had a detailed plan about how to achieve our vision.

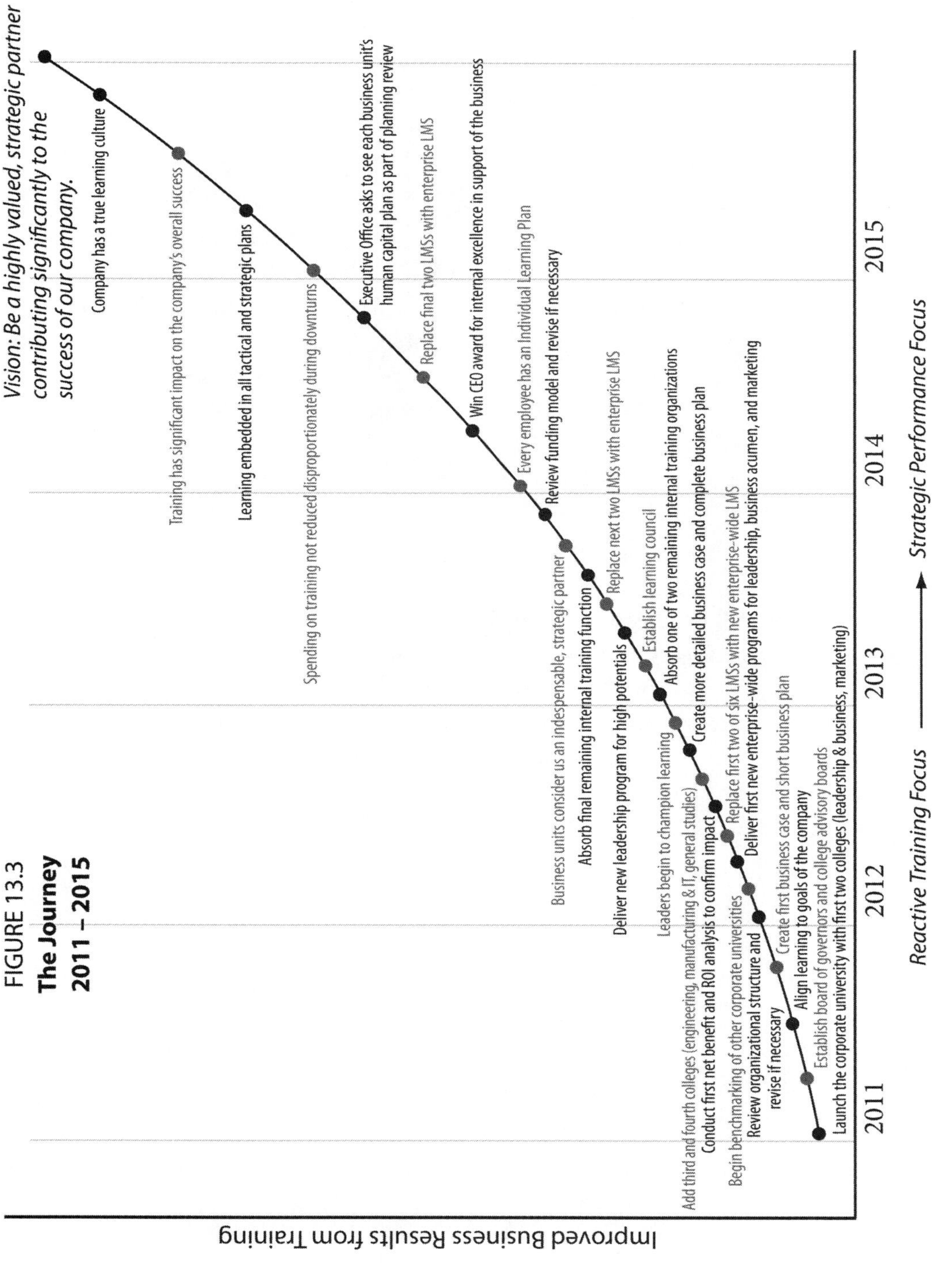

FIGURE 13.3
The Journey
2011 – 2015

This particular approach would not be right for all organizations, but it is imperative that you find one that works. It may require some trial and error. Do not give up until you find a way to communicate that resonates with your audience.

CATERPILLAR EXPERIENCE: We tried a standard ten to twenty slide PowerPoint for the first six months. People were bored, and the message did not get any traction. After the presentation they would say, "I still do not understand what is different about Cat U than what we had before." This, of course, was very frustrating because the twenty slides had just detailed the reasons for launching Cat U, our strategic approach, and the new programs that were planned. It was perfectly clear to us, but the message was lost on others. One day while several of us were bemoaning our inability to convey the message, we conceived the journey chart on the back of a napkin and decided to give it a try. It was an immediate hit! We had found what would work at Caterpillar.

The journey approach, whether done graphically or in text slides, allows for a tremendous amount of flexibility, especially in the type of milestones that are included. Most of the milestones in Figure 13.3 are specific and tangible, like opening a third college or replacing a business unit LMS with the corporate LMS. A journey chart could be constructed with more milestones, which are less tangible and more difficult to measure but very important nonetheless. Examples would include the following:

- Leaders champion learning.
- Leaders are teachers.
- Mistakes are viewed as opportunities to learn.
- Leaders admit mistakes and share lessons learned from mistakes.
- Leaders and employees know and practice Senge's five disciplines.
- Employees share information freely and openly.

These milestones might be found in the journey chart of an organization that has a continual learning element in its vision. (We incorporated most of these in our journey.)

Conclusion

Summary

The reader should now have everything necessary to run learning like a business. We have explored all of the necessary business and economic concepts and have applied them to learning through numerous examples. We focused on the importance of strategic alignment, the development of a business case, and the creation of a business plan. Templates and a sample business plan were provided to make the first time easier. Metrics, evaluation, and disciplined execution were explored and additional templates provided. Important issues of governance, structure, and funding were discussed, including multiple models for each and a recommended approach. Finally, we pulled all the elements together in this last chapter and suggested fifteen specific steps to run learning like a business.

Results

The results of implementing these steps and running learning like a business are the following:

- Learning will be viewed as an indispensable, strategic partner in achieving the goals of the organization.
- Strategic alignment and the development of the business case and business plan will ensure that learning is directed toward the highest priority goals of the organization and delivers the greatest possible value for the investment.
- Learning will play an increasingly important role in achieving the organization's goals.
- The costs of learning as well as the cost structure (fixed and variable costs along with total, average, and marginal costs) will be fully understood and managed accordingly.
- The learning function will be run efficiently with optimum program selection, course duration, and number of participants.
- The learning function will be run with discipline to ensure that planned results are delivered and that performance is continually enhanced.
- The credibility of the learning function will grow.

As senior leaders see the results described above, the budgeting process is likely to become less contentious and may even result in additional funding and staffing as leaders become more confident in the ability of learning to deliver bottom-line results.

> CATERPILLAR EXPERIENCE: As a result of running learning like a business, we had the confidence of the CEO, which was demonstrated vividly at the December 2006 Board of Governors meeting. We were discussing the 2007 business plan for learning, and the CEOs focus was on one program in particular, for which he wanted to see faster results. He asked what it would take to get the results, and we told him $3 million. He told us to put it in the budget. No further discussion was necessary.

These results will also lead to increased recognition and satisfaction for the learning professionals. After several years this may even include internal and external awards for the learning group.

> CATERPILLAR EXPERIENCE: We submitted our first external award applications in 2004, which was our fourth year. In hindsight it probably would have been a good experience for us to submit sooner, but we felt we were not ready. As it turned out, we won the Best Overall Corporate University award in 2004 from both the International Quality & Productivity Center (IQPC) and Corporate University Xchange (CUX). In 2005 we placed first in the ASTD BEST awards. These were tremendous honors for CAT U, for all the learning professionals at Caterpillar, and for the company as a whole. And the awards definitely increased our credibility within the organization. We continued to enter in other categories and won other awards.
>
> We found the experience of filling out the applications was always worthwhile and inevitably made us reflect more deeply on our own practices. The awards ceremonies also provided an excellent opportunity to learn what others were doing and in particular to learn from other award winners.

Lessons Learned on the Journey

For some, the journey may seem overwhelming. This is especially true for those involved in a startup or in the transformation of reactive learning function into a strategic, proactive, performance-oriented function. It may seem like there is so much to be done and so many steps to be taken that it is not worth even embarking on the journey.

There are four lessons learned to help you get started and be successful. First, identify the steps you need to take and create your own journey plan with milestones. It should be a multi-year plan and may very well cover five years. Be realistic about how much you can accomplish each year, especially your first year. It is important to deliver what you promise, so do not over-promise. Aggressive goals are fine as long as they are achievable. Typically, goals prove harder to achieve than anticipated, so allow for surprises and some setbacks.

Second, once you have your steps determined, take the first step. This may seem blatantly obvious, but many become paralyzed by the magnitude of the undertaking and the number of uncertainties. They lack the confidence to push ahead and want more time to study options, benchmark others, and resolve all remaining outstanding issues. Since there always will be new information and unresolved issues, this is a prescription for continual delay and eventual failure. Just take the first step and then the next and then the next. Do not worry about steps in the following year or how you will resolve an issue in year three or four. Focus on the immediate steps in front of you. Trust your journey. Before you know it, you will have accomplished a great deal and be well on your way.

Third, and related to the second lesson, do not wait for perfection or absolute certainty. These conditions do not exist in the real world (sorry to disillusion anyone). They are unhealthy myths. Remember, learning is a business. Businesses never have perfect information or perfect solutions to a problem, and they face incredible uncertainty on a daily basis. Learning may, in fact, have better information than business in general and may face fewer uncertainties, but imperfection and uncertainty will still exist. Learning professionals simply need to accept this fact and get on with it. Use the best information available to make the best decision possible and accept that some mistakes will be made because better information was not available.

Fourth and related to the third lesson, approach your journey from a learning perspective. This should come especially easy for the learning professional. Mistakes will be made. Learn from them. Be open to surprises, to new approaches.

Learn as you go. Create a diverse team in your learning function and encourage risk-taking and innovation. The team will likely plan the journey better, set goals better, and solve problems better than any one individual, including the CLO. Create and nurture a learning organization within the learning group.

These lessons learned should give encouragement and confidence to those at the beginning of a long journey. Rest assured that the journey is worth it from both an organizational and personal viewpoint. For your author, the creation and leadership of Caterpillar University was both the hardest and most satisfying challenge of his career.

Enjoy the journey!

Further Reading

Anderson, Frank, Chris Hardy, and Jeffrey Leeson. *Leading a Learning Revolution: The Story behind Defense Acquisition University's Reinvention of Training.* San Francisco: Pfeiffer, 2008.

Van Adelsberg, David and Edward Trolley. *Running Training Like a Business: Delivering Unmistakable Value.* San Francisco: Berrett-Koehler, 1999. (See Chapter 9.)

Appendix A

Enterprise Learning Data Template

A TEMPLATE IS provided on the following page to assist in the collection of data discussed in Chapter 3. This type of template is useful when the central learning function does not have ready access to information from an enterprise-wide learning management system (used by all units for all employees) where courses are tagged by program and when corporate accounting cannot provide expense statements for all business units that have learning expenditures.

The template gathers the following types of information:

- Employees dedicated to learning (full-time, part-time, and FTE)
- Costs by expense statement category
- Costs by program category
- Vendor expenses
- Participants (unique and total) by category
- Total participants by program

APPENDIX A
Enterprise Training Data Template

Data for calendar year 2017 unless otherwise specified

1 Business Unit Name: ______________________________

2 Location(s): ______________________________

3	**Employees dedicated to training**	***Region A***	***Region B***	***Region C***	***Region D***	***Total***
4	Full time (December 31)	0	0	0	0	0
5	Vacant positions normally occupied (Dec 31)	0	0	0	0	0
6	Part time (anytime during year)	0	0	0	0	0
7	FTE (full time equivalent for year)	0	0	0	0	0
8						
9						
10	**Costs**	***Region A***	***Region B***	***Region C***	***Region D***	***Total***
11	Labor & Related Costs					
12	Full time	0	0	0	0	0
13	Part time	0	0	0	0	0
14	Total	0	0	0	0	0
15						
16	Overhead					
17	Dues, fees, subscriptions	0	0	0	0	0
18	Materials, printing	0	0	0	0	0
19	Equipment leases, rentals	0	0	0	0	0
20	Travel	0	0	0	0	0
21	Vendors, partners, consultants	0	0	0	0	0
22	Occupancy (internal or external for space, utilities)	0	0	0	0	0
23	Internal charges (IT, HR, Accounting,etc)	0	0	0	0	0
24	Miscellaneous	0	0	0	0	0
25	Total	0	0	0	0	0
26						
27	Total Expenses	0	0	0	0	0
28						

29	**Cost Allocation**	*Region A*	*Region B*	*Region C*	*Region D*	*Total*	
30	Administrative	0	0	0	0	0	
31							
32	Costs by Program						
33	Program A	0	0	0	0	0	
34	Program B	0	0	0	0	0	
35	Program C	0	0	0	0	0	
36	Program D	0	0	0	0	0	
37	Program E	0	0	0	0	0	
38	Program F	0	0	0	0	0	
39	Program G	0	0	0	0	0	
40	Total Programs	0	0	0	0	0	
41							
42	Total	0	0	0	0	0	Must equal line 27
43							

44	*Vendors*	*Name*	*Office Location*	*Type (Develop, Deliver, Both)*	*Amount*	
45	Vendor 1				0	
46	Vendor 2				0	
47	Vendor 3				0	
48	Vendor 4				0	
49	Vendor 5				0	
50	Total				0	Must equal line 21
51						

52	**Participants**	*Region A*	*Region B*	*Region C*	*Region D*	*Total*
53	Total					
54	Employees	0	0	0	0	0
55	Dealers	0	0	0	0	0
56	Suppliers	0	0	0	0	0
57	Customers	0	0	0	0	0
58	Total	0	0	0	0	0
59						
60	Unique					
61	Employees	0	0	0	0	0
62	Dealers	0	0	0	0	0
63	Suppliers	0	0	0	0	0
64	Customers	0	0	0	0	0
65	Total	0	0	0	0	0
66						

67	**Total Participants by Program**	***Region A***	***Region B***	***Region C***	***Region D***	***Total***	
68	Program A	0	0	0	0	0	
69	Program B	0	0	0	0	0	
70	Program C	0	0	0	0	0	
71	Program D	0	0	0	0	0	
72	Program E	0	0	0	0	0	
73	Program F	0	0	0	0	0	
74	Program G	0	0	0	0	0	
75	Total Programs	0	0	0	0	0	Must equal line 58
76							
77							
78							

79 Prepared by ____ Date:________________

Appendix B

A Sample Business Plan for Learning

APPENDIX B CONTAINS a forty-page sample business plan for learning, following the outline and recommendations of Chapter 6. The plan is an internally consistent document for a fictitious corporate university called Corporate University, which provides leadership to learning and the majority of learning for a vertically-integrated manufacturing company with five thousand employees.

The goal of this appendix is to provide a sample plan for you to read so you can see how all the elements discussed in chapters one through six come together in a short document. Moreover, you may wish to use this plan as a starting point in the creation of your own plan. (An electronic version is available at the author's website.)

It should go without saying that this sample will not perfectly represent your own situation. So, it is only meant as a starting point to illustrate what is possible and how a plan might be constructed. You will have to modify it accordingly to fit your situation and culture.

With all the facts in hand, a plan like the one in this sample should take about twelve hours to write. Create the figures and tables first and then write "Last Year's Accomplishments" through "History." Save the "Executive Summary" for last.

The 2017 Business Plan for Learning for XYZ Corporation

Corporate University

Approved by the Board of Governors
December 16, 2017

Contents

PAGE

List of Figures

Figure

List of Tables

Table

Executive Summary

Learning continues to be a critical driver of our company's success. In 2016 Corporate University initiatives supported all five top priorities and more than half of the remaining corporate goals (See Table 1). Moreover, learning is believed to have had a significant impact on achieving many of these goals and in some cases is thought to have contributed more than any other single factor. (The learning impact estimates below represent the consensus view of the corporate goal owners and university leadership.)

TABLE 1

Learning's Contribution to 2016 Results

		Plan		Estimated Actual	
Priority	*Corporate Goal*	*Target*	*Expected Impact of Learning*	*Result*	*Expected Impact of Learning*
1	Reduce Injuries	10%	5%	8%	5%
2	Reduce Defects	10%	5%	11%	5%
3	Increase Sales	5%	3%	3%	2%
4	Reduce Mfg Costs	6%	2%	5%	3%
5	Increase Innovation	4%	1%	2%	1%

Learning is conservatively estimated to have produced net benefits of more than $2.6 million in 2016, up $450,000 or 24% from 2015 and just slightly below plan of $2.7 million. The number of unique participants rose 8% to 4,552, reflecting higher company employment and expanded offerings. The number of total participants rose even faster at 10% to 19,769 as the average number of courses taken continued to rise.

Learning is planned to have an even greater impact on results in 2017. (See Table 2 for a summary.) Once again learning will contribute significantly to the five top goals and to the achievement of the remaining goals. Learning initiatives are expected to account for more than half of the planned reduction in defects and injuries and about half of the planned increase in leadership scores. Learning is also expected to contribute about 30% of the planned improvement in employee retention and 20% of the planned increase in sales.

Learning will also contribute to the achievement of other key goals, including reduction in purchase costs, support complaints, and exposure to fraud and insider trading. In each case learning is expected to account for half or more of the planned reduction, making learning the single most critical driver to goal achievement.

Taken together, these learning initiatives are expected to reach all five thousand employees and yield more than $3.3 million in net benefits to the company resulting in a return on investment of more than 40%. Total participation in learning is forecast to rise 65%, reflecting the safety initiative with five courses for each manufacturing employee, the drive for every employee to have an individual development plan (IDP), and the comprehensive compliance campaign for fraud and insider trading.

To achieve these results, enterprise-wide expenditures on learning are forecast to increase by $700,000 or 18% to $4.5 million. All of the increase will occur at the Corporate University, which will constitute 74% of the total enterprise spending on learning. The remaining 24% ($1.6 million) will be managed by the business units and is directed primarily at technical skills and other specialties, which are unique to individual units. Corporate University will continue to focus on learning, which can be leveraged across the enterprise or where consistency across units is required.

Staffing is projected to increase modestly to support the increased workload, although most of the increase in demand will be met through greater use of flexible resources, including our partners and part-time (PT) employees. Only one additional full-time (FT) hire is planned in 2017 for the Corporate University. Six additional part-time employees (three full-time equivalents or FTEs) will bring the totals for the Corporate University to 21 FT, 12 PT, and 27 FTEs. No increases are planned in the business units, which have six FT employees and six PT employees.

Evaluation and measurement will continue to be central to our efforts to manage for results and continuous improvement. Application, impact, and bottom-line results will continue to be measured for critical programs to ensure the planned net benefits are delivered to the company. Continuous improvement plans for 2017 include a system-wide upgrade to the LMS, a new knowledge-sharing platform, and improved synchronous online learning capabilities.

Finally, we plan to build on last year's success and continue to invest in our university and company brand by hosting benchmarking companies, publishing articles, speaking at conferences, and entering awards competitions. We are proud of the internal and external awards we have received over the last two years but know we still have a long way to go to be the best we can be.

TABLE 2

2017 Summary Business Case for Learning

		2016 Estimated Actual					2017 Plan				
2017 Priority	*Corporate Goal*	*Results*	*Estimated Impact of Learning*	*Unique Partici pants*	*Total Partici pants*	*Total Net Benefits (thous.)*	*Target*	*Planned Impact of Learning*	*Unique Partici pants*	*Total Partici pants*	*Total Net Benefits (thous.)*
1	Increase Sales	3%	2%	105	105	$420	10%	2%	100	1,100	$893
2	Reduce Defects	11%	5%	103	276	$412	20%	14%	200	800	$1,018
3	Reduce Injuries	8%	5%	1,167	4,698	$233	25%	15%	3,100	13,600	$415
4	Improve Leadership	-2 pts	NA	50	50	NA	+5 pts	+2 pts	180	180	$316
5	Increase Retention	-4 pts	NA	NA	NA	NA	+5 pts	+1.5 pts	5,000	7,500	$310
	Subtotal Top Five Goals			**1,425**	**5,129**	**$1,065**			**5,000**	**23,180**	**$2,952**
	Subtotal Other Goals			2,421	10,381	$2,193			1,950	4,725	$1,028
	Total All Goals			2,997	15,510	$3,258			5,000	27,905	$3,980
	Unaligned Learning			3,651	3,859	0			4,000	4,000	$0
	Other Costs (not included elsewhere)					-$600					-$600
	Grand Total for All Learning			**4,552**	**19,369**	**$2,658**			**5,000**	**31,905**	**$3,380**

TABLE 3

Impact of Learning on 2016 Results

		2016 Plan					2016 Estimated Actual				
2016 Priority	*Corporate Goal*	*Target*	*Planned Impact of Learning*	*Unique Partici pants*	*Total Partici pants*	*Total Net Benefits (thous.)*	*Result*	*Estimated Impact of Learning*	*Unique Partici pants*	*Total Partici pants*	*Total Net Benefits (thous.)*
1	Reduce Injuries	10%	5%	1,200	4,800	$240	8%	5%	1,167	4,698	$233
2	Reduce Defects	10%	5%	100	300	$400	11%	5%	103	276	$412
3	Increase Sales	5%	3%	120	120	$720	3%	2%	105	105	$420
4	Reduce Mfg Costs	6%	2%	1,400	7,200	$640	5%	3%	1,578	7,256	$900
5	Increase Innovation	4%	1%	200	200	$400	2%	1%	188	188	$383
	Subtotal Top Five Goals			**2,260**	**12,620**	**$2,400**			**2,189**	**12,523**	**$2,348**
	Subtotal Other Goals			1,430	2,996	$912			1,657	2,987	$910
	Total All Goals			2,874	15,616	$3,312			2,997	15,510	$3,258
	Unaligned Learning			3,500	3,500	$0			3,651	3,859	$0
	Other Costs (not included elsewhere)					-$600					-$600
	Grand Total for All Learning			**4,300**	**19,116**	**$2,712**			**4,552**	**19,369**	**$2,658**

Last Year's Accomplishments

Learning contributed significantly to our company's success in 2016. Corporate University initiatives supported all five top priorities and more than half of the remaining corporate goals. Learning's impact on corporate goals ranged from a low of 20% to more than 60%. Overall, more than 4,500 employees participated in Corporate University programs, generating more than $2.6 million in net benefit to the company. (See Table 3 for a summary by goal.)

The majority of participants (12,523) were engaged in learning that directly supported the top five corporate priorities and delivered about $2.3 million in net benefit. About a quarter as many (2,987) participated in programs to support the remaining corporate goals while the remainder (3,859) pursued learning opportunities not directly tied to the 2016 goals.

Highlights

- More than 1,100 manufacturing employees participated in classes and online learning to reduce injuries in the workplace. Learning is estimated to have reduced injuries by 5% or about half of the corporate goal of 10% and more than half of the actual 8% reduction.
- More than one hundred engineers took part in the first courses created to reduce design defects. The design courses are estimated to have reduced defects by 5% or almost half of the estimated actual 11% total reduction.
- Learning programs to increase sales are estimated to have contributed to a 2% increase in sales, slightly less than the planned impact of 3% but still more than half of the actual increase of 3%.
- More than 1,500 employees took an average of five classes each to learn how to reduce manufacturing costs. The learning is believed to have reduced costs by 3%, one percent more than planned, and contributed almost $1 million in net benefits.
- Almost two hundred engineers took the innovation workshop, which contributed to a 1% increase in Tier One workable concepts. Although the corporate target of 4% was not achieved, the workshop contributed half of the actual 2% increase and generated almost $400,000 in net benefits.
- More than 1,600 employees participated in learning to support five of the remaining eight corporate goals. For these five goals learning is believed to have contributed from 20% to 70% of the corporate result, generating almost $1 million in net benefits.

In addition, the Corporate University staff achieved $100,000 in efficiency gains by consolidating vendors, standardizing RFPs, and reducing development time. Another $100,000 in opportunity costs were saved by substituting web-based learning for classroom instruction where appropriate.

The above results were accomplished without exceeding budget for 2016. Expenses came in at $10,000 below budget, partially offsetting the $32,000 short-fall in income. Net income was $22,000.

TABLE 4

Corporate University 2016 Financial Performance

	Thousands of Dollars			*Variance*	
	2015 Actual	*2016 Plan*	*2016 Estimate*	*$*	*%*
Income	$3,485	$3,800	$3,768	($32)	.8%
Expense	$3,460	$3,800	$3,790	($10)	.3%
Net Income	$25	$0	($22)	($22)	

Strategic Alignment for 2017

A business plan for learning starts with the strategic alignment of learning to the company's highest priority goals. This approach ensures that the investment in learning will make the greatest possible contribution to 2017 results.

The process of alignment begins with the 2017 corporate goals and input from the CEO. It ends with specific learning programs aligned to support the company's objectives. Figure 1 contains a brief description of the process, which started in August and concluded with approval by the board of governors in December.

FIGURE 1

Description of the Strategic Alignment Process

- Interviewed CEO, group presidents, and members of the board of governors with regard to goals and priorities
- Discussed goals in detail with each goal owner or sponsor and explored whether learning could contribute to achieving the goals

- Compiled preliminary findings on goals, priorities, and the appropriateness and impact of learning and identified target areas for learning
- Held detailed discussions with targeted goal owners or sponsors on potential learning programs, impact of learning, requirements, and costs
- Refined impact and cost estimates
- Finalized strategic alignment and shared it with the CEO and the board of governors for review; revised as necessary

The results of the strategic alignment process are shown in Figure 2 and Table 5 on the following page.

FIGURE 2

Strategic Alignment of Learning to the Organization's Goals

Summary Matrix

	Learning programs for								
Corporate Objectives	*Sales*	*Design*	*Safety*	*Leadership*	*Perf Mgt*	*Product*	*Purch.*	*Customer Skills*	*Compliance*
High Priority									
Increase sales	X					X		X	
Reduce defects		X							
Reduce injuries			X						
Medium Priority									
Improve leadership				X					
Increase ee retention					X				
Increase innovation									
Reduce purch. costs							X		
Increase bench strength									
Low Priority									
Open Beijing office									
Reduce tech sup complaints						X		X	
Reduce fraud & insider trading exposure									X

NOTE: Objectives in *italics* not addressed by training for next year.

TABLE 5

Strategic Alignment of Learning to Organization Goals

Priority		Corporate Goal	Key Learning Programs	Target Audience	Unique Participants	Planned Contribution from Learning	Planned Impact of Learning	Goal Owner	Include In Plan ?
1	High	Increase sales by 10%	Consultative selling skills (new)	Marketing employees	100			Ortega	Yes
			New product information (revised)	Marketing employees	100				
			Total key programs		100	20%	2% higher sales		
2	High	Reduce defects by 20%	Four Design courses (3 new)	New, other engineers	200	70%	14% reduct. in defects	D'Agoto	Yes
3	High	Reduce Injuries by 25%	Five Safety courses (3 new)	Manufact. associates	2,500			Swilthe	Yes
			One Safety course (revised)	Factory supervisors	100				
			Two Safety courses (1 new)	Office employees	500				
					3,100	60%	15% reduct. in injuries		
4	Medium	Improve leadership score by 5 points on employee survey	Intro to supervision (revised)	New, other supervisors	100			Wang	Yes
			Leadership for managers (new)	Division managers	65				
			Advanced leadership (existing)	Department heads	15				
					180	40%	2 point increase		
5	Medium	Increase employee retention by 10 points	Individual development plans	All employees	5,000			Dreise	Yes
			Performance management(new)	Mgt employees	2,500				
					5,000	30%	3 point increase		
6	Medium	Increase innovation by 20% (patent applications)	Establish communities of practice	Design engineers	100			Chan	No
			Innovation workshop(new)	Design engineers	100				
					100	20%	4% increase in innov.		
7	Medium	Reduce cost of purchased materials by 5%	Five Purchasing courses (5 new)	Purchasing employees and managers	200	60%	3% reduction in costs	Murphy	Yes
8	Medium	Increase internal bench-strength for officers	None				NA	Dreise	No
9	Low	Open office in Beijing	Orientation	New employees	25	Low	Not essential	Li	No
10	Low	Reduce technical support complaints by 30%	Product training (new)	Call center employees	50			Salvatore	Yes
			Customer relations skills (revised)	Call center employees	25				
					50	50%	15% reduct. in complaints		
11	Low	Reduce exposure to fraud and insider trading	One online fraud course (new)	Select employees	1,700			Omwetti	Yes
			One online insider trading (existing)	Select employees	1,500				
					1,700	High	Essential		

Learning has been identified to support all three high-priority corporate goals and three of the five medium priority goals (see Table 5). The planned impact on corporate objectives for this group ranges from a low of 20% for increased sales and innovation to a high of 70% for a reduction in defects. Investment in learning is recommended to support all of these goals except a) innovation, where the planned impact of learning (20%) is simply too low to justify the investment this year for a medium priority, and b) increasing the officer bench strength, which will not require any formal learning next year.

In addition, learning is recommended for two low-priority goals (reduce technical support complaints and compliance) because of its planned high impact (50%+) on achieving those goals. For 2017 learning is not essential to opening the office in Beijing.

Although there will be learning that is not directly in support of the above corporate goals (learning for goals below the corporate level, professional development, and personal growth), the priority for learning will be the learning aligned to the corporate goals.

The 2017 Business Case for Learning

The business case for learning starts with the strategic alignment process and adds the costs and dollar benefits of the recommended learning. Costs are forecast for each program, including all direct external costs (for example, contract vendors and room rental) and the internal costs including fully-burdened internal labor costs to develop, deliver, reinforce, and manage the programs. In addition to these budget costs, opportunity costs are calculated for each program to capture, at a minimum, the value of the participants' time (using their labor and related rate). Total cost equals budget plus opportunity costs.

For the business case, dollar benefits have been forecast (where appropriate) by the goal owner and Corporate University based on the planned impact of the corporate goal on net income and on the planned impact of learning on achieving the corporate goal. For example, the corporate goal of a 10% increase in sales is expected to have a bottom-line impact of $7.5 million. Learning programs, properly conceived, developed, deployed, and reinforced, are expected by the goal owner and by the Corporate University to contribute 20% of the 10% increase in sales. In other words, learning is expected to deliver a 2% increase in sales (10% increase in sales x 20% contribution from learning), which would be worth $1.5

million to the bottom line. Where the impact on net income was not available for a corporate goal, we worked with the goal owner to derive a forecast of the dollar impact of the learning on net income.

The net benefit of learning is simply the gross benefit of learning (like $1.5 million for the sales example) less the total cost of the learning. For sales, the cost of learning is forecast to be $607,000 ($490,000 in budget costs plus $117,000 in opportunity costs), so the net benefit of sales-related learning is $893,000. The budget impact of learning is the dollar impact less just the budget cost. So for the sales-related learning the budget impact is $1.5 million - $490,000 or $1.010 million. The budget impact will always be higher since it does not include the opportunity costs.

The 2017 business case for learning is shown in Table 6. Learning is planned to make a significant contribution to all top five goals for 2017:

- **Sales**: Two learning programs are planned for 100 unique participants to increase sales by 2% resulting in a net benefit of $893,000 and an ROI of 147%.
- **Defects**: One learning program consisting of four design courses is planned for 200 engineers to reduce defects by 14%, which represents a net benefit of $1.02 million and an ROI of 94%.
- **Injuries**: Three safety programs are planned for 3,100 unique participants to reduce injuries by 15%, resulting in a net benefit of $415,000 and an ROI of 53%.
- **Leadership**: Three leadership programs are planned for 180 of our leaders to improve the leadership score on the employee opinion survey by 2 points, which will result in a net benefit of $316,000 and an ROI of 36%.
- **Employee retention**: All 5,000 employees will have an individual development plan in 2017, and 2,500 management employees will receive training in performance management. Together, these two initiatives are planned to increase retention by 1.5 points, resulting in a net benefit of $310,000 and an ROI of 21%.

The gross benefit of learning on net income for the top five corporate goals is forecast to be $7.8 million. Subtracting the budget costs of $2.39 million generates a budget impact of $5.41 million. Subtracting the opportunity costs of $2.46 million leaves a net benefit of $2.95 million for a return on investment (ROI) of 61%.

Learning for the other corporate goals is also expected to have a significant

TABLE 6

2017 Business Case for Learning

Priority	Corporate Goal	Key Learning Programs	Target Audience	Unique Partici-pants	Total Partici-pants	Planned Contribution from Learning	Planned Impact of Learning	Thousands of Dollars: Gross Benefit	Budget Cost	Budget Impact	Opport-unity Cost	Net Benefit	ROI
1	Increase sales by 10%	Consultative selling skills (new)	Marketing employees	100	100								
		Ten NPI modules (10 new)	Marketing employees	100	1,000								
		Total key programs		100	1,100	20%	2% higher sales	$1,500	$490	$1,010	$117	$893	147%
2	Reduce defects by 20%	Four Design courses (3 new)	New, other engineers	200	800	70%	14% reduct. in defects	$2,100	$570	$1,530	$512	$1,018	94%
3	Reduce Injuries by 25%	Five Safety courses (3 new)	Manufact. associates	2,500	12,500								
		One Safety course (revised)	Factory supervisors	100	100								
		Two Safety courses (1 new)	Office employees	500	1,000								
		Total key programs		3,100	13,600	60%	15% reduct. in injuries	$1,200	$410	$790	$376	$415	53%
4	Improve leadership score by 5 points on employee survey	Intro to supervision (revised)	New, other supervisors	100	100								
		Leadership for managers (new)	Division managers	65	65								
		Advanced leadership (existing)	Department heads	15	15								
		Total key programs		180	180	40%	2 point increase	$1,200	$582	$618	$302	$316	36%
5	Increase retention by 5 points	Individual development plans	All employees	5,000	5,000								
		Performance mgt (new)	Mgt employees	2,500	2,500								
		Total key programs		5,000	7,500	30%	1.5 point increase	$1,800	$340	$1,460	$1,150	$310	21%
Total for Top Five Goals		**Learning for Top Five Goals** Courses: 20 New, 2 Revised		**5,000**	**23,180**	**Range = 20%-70%**		**$7,800**	**$2,392**	**$5,408**	**$2,457**	**$2,952**	**61%**
Total for All Other Goals		**Learning for All Other Goals** Courses: 16 New, 2 Revised		**1,950**	**4,725**	**Range = 50%-70%**		**$3,050**	**$1,245**	**$1,805**	**$778**	**$1,028**	**51%**
		Total for All Aligned Learning Courses: 36 New, 4 Revised		**5,000**	**27,905**	**Range = 20%-70%**		**$10,850**	**$3,637**	**$7,213**	**$3,234**	**$3,980**	**58%**
		Unaligned Learning Courses: 2 New, 1 Revised		**4,000**	**4,000**	**Assume Net Ben = 0**		**$700**	**$300**	**$400**	**$400**	**$0**	**0%**
		Other Costs (not included elsewhere)		NA	NA			NA	$600	($600)	$0	($600)	NA
Grand Total		**Grand Total for All Learning** **Courses: 38 New, 5 Revised**		**5,000**	**31,905**	**Range = 20%-70%**		**$11,550**	**$4,537**	**$7,013**	**$3,634**	**$3,380**	**41%**

impact. A learning program to support purchasing is planned to contribute a 3% reduction in costs, and two programs for technical support are planned to reduce complaints by 15%. Compliance-related training is expected to reduce our risk exposure by 70% and is considered essential. In total, learning for these three goals is expected to generate a gross benefit of $3.05 million for a budget impact of $1.81 million. After subtracting opportunity costs, the net benefit of learning is forecast to be $1.03 million for an ROI of 51%.

The business case also includes the cost and expected benefit for the unaligned learning, although the gross benefit has been conservatively forecast to just offset the total costs. All other costs not built into the fully-burdened labor rate (like the office of the CLO and the staff, systems, and vendors for support functions like measurement, planning, and strategy) are included as the last line with no offsetting dollar impacts.

In total, the 2017 business case for learning shows a dollar impact from learning of $11.6 million. This impact can be achieved through the development of thirty-eight new courses and the revision of five existing courses, combined with successful deployment to more than thirty-one thousand participants, reaching all five thousand employees. The budget cost to achieve the $11.6 million dollar impact is $4.5 million, resulting in a planned budget impact of $7 million. Subtracting opportunity costs, the net benefit of learning for 2017 is conservatively estimated to be $3.4 million for an ROI of about 41%.

Note: The business case in Table 6 represents only the Corporate University investment in learning. Accordingly, the budget cost of $4.537 million matches the $4.5 million in Corporate University expenditure in Table 7 (line 1) and in Table 11.

Enterprise Learning Expenditures, Budgets, and Statistics

This section provides a summary of learning expenditures, budgets, and key statistics for both the Corporate University and the enterprise. It answers the following questions:

- How much is being spent on learning?
- What is it being spent on?
- How many resources are dedicated to learning?
- What is the Corporate University budget for 2017?

How Much Is Being Spent on Learning?

Enterprise spending is shown in Table 7. For 2016 the company spent \$5.4 million on learning, not including opportunity costs. That represents a \$325,000 or 6% increase over 2015. The Corporate University spent \$3.8 million or 70% of the total while business units spent the remaining \$1.6 million or 30%. Half of the business unit spending occurred in manufacturing, where most of the technical training takes place. The other half was spread fairly evenly over marketing, IT, R&D, finance and accounting, and purchasing.

TABLE 7

Enterprise Learning Expenditures for 2016 and 2017

(Millions of dollars)

	2015 Actual	*2016 Estimated Actual*	*% of Total*	*2017 Plan*	*% of Total*
Corporate University	\$3.5	\$3.8	70%	\$4.5	74%
Business Units	\$1.7	\$1.6	30%	\$1.6	26%
Total	\$5.1	\$5.4	100%	\$6.1	100%

The business plan for 2017 calls for enterprise spending to increase 13% or \$700,000 to \$6.1 million. All of the increase is forecast for the Corporate University to meet the goals described in the last chapter and deliver an additional \$800,000 in net benefits (after covering the additional \$700,000 in costs). With this increase, Corporate University spending will constitute 74% of the total company spending on learning.

What Is It Being Spent On?

For 2016, more was spent on manufacturing (\$1.4 million or 26% of the total) than any other area, reflecting the high priority given to reducing manufacturing costs. The second largest focus area for 2016 was marketing, where \$540,000 or 10% of the total was invested. Leadership, engineering, and compliance each comprised 6–7% of the total, with safety accounting for about 4%.

Table 8 shows spending for all key focus areas for 2016 and 2017 as well as other, general and administrative. "Other" represents the technical skills not identified specifically elsewhere in the table. "General" refers to learning in support of employees' general skills, such as writing, speaking, language, team building, and personal growth. "Administrative" refers to learning expenses not otherwise allocated, like the office of CLO and LMS and measurement costs.

TABLE 8

Enterprise Expenditures by Area

	2016 Est Actual		*2017 Plan*		*2017 vs 2016*	
	Thous $	*%*	*Thous $*	*%*	*Thous $*	*Change in %*
Leadership	$324	6%	$582	10%	$258	80%
Marketing	$540	10%	$880	14%	$340	63%
Engineering	$324	6%	$570	9%	$246	76%
Safety	$216	4%	$410	7%	$194	90%
Manufacturing	$1,432	26%	$800	13%	-$632	-44%
Compliance	$381	7%	$230	4%	-$151	-40%
Purchasing	$115	2%	$775	13%	$660	574%
Other	$656	12%	$725	12%	$69	11%
General	$846	16%	$515	8%	-$331	-39%
Administrative	$600	11%	$600	10%	$0	0%
Total	$5,434	100%	$6,087	100%	$653	12%

The composition of spending shifts noticeably for 2017, reflecting the year's goals and different priorities. The share spent on manufacturing declines to 13% while the share for purchasing increases substantially by 11%. Shares for leadership, marketing, engineering, and safety all increase by 3–4 percentage points. Spending on general or unaligned learning declines significantly from 16% to 8% as resources are redirected to higher-priority goals. The administrative share declines slightly as the dollar amount remains unchanged.

How Many Resources Are Dedicated to Learning?

In 2016 twenty-six full-time employees, twelve part-time employees, and twelve vendors were employed across the enterprise to develop, deliver, reinforce, and manage the learning to over 4,500 employees and 19,000 participants (Table 9). For 2017 the number of employees and vendors is forecast to increase to meet the additional demand for learning. The plan calls for one more full-time employee, six more part-time employees, and two additional vendors to deliver the additional $700,000 of learning.

TABLE 9

Enterprise Learning Resources for 2016 and 2017

	2016 Est Actual		*2017 Plan*		*2017 vs 2016*	
	Number	***Thous $***	***Number***	***Thous $***	***Number***	***Thous $***
Employees						
Full time	26	$1,622	27	$1,685	1	$62
Part time	12	$250	18	$374	6	$125
Total	38	$1,872	45	$2,059	7	$187
External Resources	12	$1,978	14	$2,444	2	$466
Total	50	$3,850	59	$4,503	9	$653

Table 10 provides detail by the Corporate University and the business unit. All of the increase in headcount is planned for by Corporate University, where the additional six part-time employees will help meet the increased demand for 2017 but not add to the permanent headcount. Corporate University will also manage the increase in vendors.

TABLE 10

Corporate University and Business Unit Learning Resources for 2016 and 2017

	2016 Estimated Actual			*2017 Plan*		
	Corp Univ	*Bus Units*	*Total*	*Corp Univ*	*Bus Units*	*Total*
Employees						
Full time	20	6	26	21	6	27
Part time	6	6	12	12	6	18
Total	26	12	38	33	12	45
External Resources	6	6	12	8	6	14
Total	32	18	50	41	18	59

What Is the Corporate University Budget for 2017?

The Corporate University budget for 2017 is presented in Table 11. Both income and expense are expected to be $4.54 million since the university is expected to break even. Income is projected to increase $769,000 or 20% as significantly higher income from the business units more than offsets a planned decrease in corporate support. External sales (primarily learning for dealers and joint venture partners) also are forecast to increase, doubling to $200,000.

TABLE 11

2017 Corporate University Budget

	2015 Actual	*2016 Estimate*	*% Change*	*2017 Plan*	*2017 vs 2016 $*	*%*
Income						
Corporate	$1,400	$1,200	-14%	$1,000	-$200	-17%
Business Unit	$2,031	$2,465	21%	$3,337	$872	35%
External	$54	$103	91%	$200	$97	94%
Total	$3,485	$3,768	8%	$4,537	$769	20%
Expense						
Labor & Related	$1,235	$1,354	10%	$1,560	$206	15%
IM&E						
Vendors	$1,287	$1,376	7%	$1,842	$466	34%
Other	$615	$704	14%	$685	-$19	-3%
Total	$1,902	$2,080	9%	$2,477	$397	19%
Internal Charges	$323	$356	10%	$450	$94	26%
Total	$3,460	$3,790	10%	$4,537	$747	20%
Net Income	$25	-$22		$0	$22	

Expenses are budgeted to increase $747,000 or 20%, primarily due to a 34% or $466,000 increase in spending with vendors. This reflects the corporate university philosophy to outsource development and delivery whenever feasible, which allows university staff to focus on reinforcement and management of the learning. Nonetheless, some additional staff are needed to meet the higher demand and ensure that the planned impact of learning on the corporate goals is realized. Consequently, labor and related spending is projected to increase by 15% or $206,000 to fund one additional full-time and six part-time positions as well as to provide for a 4% merit pool. The staffing plan is shown in Table 12 and reflects four additional full-time equivalents for 2017.

TABLE 12

2017 Corporate University Staffing Plan

	2016 Plan	*2016 31-Dec*	*2017 Plan*
Full-time Associates	20	20	21
Part-time Associates	8	6	12
[Full-time equivalents]	[4]	[3]	[6]
Total	28	26	33
[Full-time equivalents]	[24]	[23]	[27]

Detailed Work Plan for 2017

Learning Aligned to Corporate Goals

Sales

The plan is to deploy one consultative selling skills class (ILT) and ten NPI modules (WBT) to a total of one hundred unique participants in support of the corporate goal to increase sales by 10%. VP Ortega, the corporate owner, and the corporate university agree that this learning, properly developed, deployed, and reinforced, should have a considerable impact (20%) on achieving the 10% goal. In other words, the sales-related training has the potential to increase sales by 2%. Participant reaction for each course should be at least 80% favorable and the actual application rate for each course should be at least 85% to achieve the planned outcome. Furthermore, Corporate University should receive a rating of at least 90% from Ortega for the partnership in designing, developing, delivering, and reinforcing the learning in pursuit of the goal to increase sales 2% due just to learning.

Consultative Selling Skills

Working with a vendor, develop a two-day instructor-led course to significantly improve the consultative selling skill competencies of the primary sales force to enable higher closure rates, higher price realization, a better sales experience for the customer, and increased customer loyalty. This will be a new offering and will use the competencies and proficiency levels already in place for marketing.

The target audience will be the one hundred primary sales associates selected by VP Ortega. Development will be completed by March 31. Input, review, and approval are required from VP Ortega and senior sales leaders. Deployment will be done in four classes with about twenty-five in each at headquarters in April. VP Ortega will develop a reinforcement plan, including incentives to use consultative selling skills.

New Product Introduction (NPI)

Working with a vendor and relying heavily on subject matter experts in marketing and manufacturing, develop ten one-hour online modules to increase the knowledge of the primary sales force about the features, benefits, and competitive advantages of the ten new products introduced over the last year or coming this next year. These will be new offerings. (A one-day, instructor-led course was developed three years ago with the same purpose, but the material and delivery mode are both outdated.)

Target audience will be the same one hundred primary sales associates. Development will be completed by April 30 *if* subject matter experts make their time and expertise available to the development team. Review and approval are required from VP Ortega and senior sales leaders. The ten modules will be available on the corporate university learning management system (LMS), and progress will be tracked and reported to VP Ortega on a weekly basis, beginning in May. Completion of all ten modules is expected by May 31. Each module will contain an online test, and a score of 85% is required for successful completion.

Quality

The plan calls for the deployment of four design courses for two hundred design engineers to reduce defects in the design and drawings for new products and components. This should make a significant contribution to the corporate goal of reducing defects by 20%. In fact, VP D'Agoto and the corporate university believe that this learning, properly delivered and reinforced, has the potential to reduce defects by 14% (in other words, a 70% impact on the corporate goal).

Participant reaction for each course should be at least 80% favorable and the actual application rate for each course should be at least 85% to achieve the planned outcome. Furthermore, Corporate University should receive a rating of at least 90% from D'Agoto for the partnership in designing, developing, delivering, and reinforcing the learning in pursuit of the goal to reduce defects by 14% due just to learning.

Design Courses

Four design courses are planned. One currently exists and is in use. The other three will be developed working with a vendor and senior design engineers. Each will be a two-day instructor-led course designed to teach and reinforce best-in-class design methods to prevent design defects and support defect-free manufacturing. Each course will incorporate examples of actual design defects and visits to the factory floor. The target audience of two hundred consists of newly hired engineers and junior engineers as well as others chosen by VP D'Agoto. Each engineer will take all four courses. Development of the three new courses will be completed by April 30. Completion of all four courses is expected by July 31. A test will be administered at the end of each course, and a passing score of 90% will be required. Biweekly progress reports will be provided to VP D'Agoto.

Safety

The plan calls for deploying eight safety courses reaching 3,100 unique participants in support of the corporate goal to reduce workplace injuries by 25%. The corporate goal owner, VP Swilthe, and the corporate university agree that the planned learning coupled with strong reinforcement should reduce injuries by 15% this year. In other words, safety training by itself should account for 60% of the reduction in injuries. Participant reaction for each course should be at least 80% favorable and the actual application rate for each course should be at least 95% to achieve the planned outcome. Furthermore, Corporate University should receive a rating of at least 90% from Swilthe for the partnership in designing, developing, delivering, and reinforcing the learning in pursuit of the goal to reduce injuries by 15% due just to learning.

Courses for Manufacturing Associates

Five one-hour online modules are planned for all 2,500 manufacturing associates. With the assistance of a vendor, plant supervisors, and subject matter experts, the three new modules should be developed by February 28. Two modules are already live. The five modules will cover injuries to the hand, foot, back, and head, as well as whole body injuries. Time will be made available at work to take all five modules by April 30 and will involve some overtime. Modules may also be taken from home by accessing the corporate leaning management system. The successful completion of each module requires a score of 90%.

Course for Factory Supervisors

An existing course will be revised for the one hundred factory supervisors to improve their competency in managing for safety, including identifying safety risks, providing reinforcement, and being an effective sponsor and change agent. The one-day instructor-led course with role playing will be available on February 1 and will be offered seven times in February. VP Swilthe has required all supervisors to complete it by the end of February. Weekly progress reports will be provided.

Courses for Office Employees

Two new one-hour online safety courses will be purchased for office employees. The goal is to increase awareness of safety issues and to teach employees to avoid accidents and injuries. The two courses will be available on February 15 with completion expected by April 15. Successful completion requires a passing grade of 90% on the test at the end of each module. The target audience consists of five hundred office employees identified by VP Swilthe who have not taken office safety in the last two years or who work in areas with high injury rates. VP Swilthe will send a memo to employees and their bosses. Progress will be tracked biweekly.

Leadership

The 2017 plan includes a focus on all levels of leadership in support of the corporate goal to improve overall leadership and specifically to increase the leadership score on the semi-annual employee opinion survey by five points. The three leadership programs are expected by HR VP Wang and the corporate university to contribute 40% or two points of the five-point increase. Participant reaction for each course should be at least 85% favorable and the actual application rate for each course should be at least 80% to achieve the planned outcome. Furthermore, Corporate University should receive a rating of at least 90% from Wang for the partnership in designing, developing, delivering, and reinforcing the learning in pursuit of the goal to increase the leadership score by 2 points due just to learning.

Course for Supervisors

The existing five-day instructor-led course will be deployed to one hundred new and existing supervisors to share the corporate leadership philosophy, framework, and competencies and to explore practical issues of leadership. Since this is the first time many participants will have had leadership responsibilities, the course will include a significant amount of role-playing and group discussion. More senior leaders also will serve as teachers. Since this course was not offered last year, all new supervisors over the last year and the coming year are required to take the course. In addition, forty other supervisors with fewer than five years of experience are expected to take it voluntarily or at the request of their manager. The course is offered at headquarters every month. Existing supervisors are expected to take it by March 31 and new supervisors within sixty days. Corporate university staff will provide reinforcement ideas.

Course for Division Managers

A new two-day course is planned for division managers to increase their proficiency in leading and managing leaders. The course will be developed in conjunction with a vendor and will explore the leadership framework in much greater detail, including a 360-degree assessment and follow-up action plan for continuous improvement. All sixty-five division managers are expected to take the course, which will be available in May. The course will be offered each month through November. Corporate university staff will work with the division managers and their bosses on reinforcement.

Course for Department Heads

A new two-day instructor-led course is planned for all fifteen department heads to provide advanced leadership education with an emphasis on strategic planning, leading large-scale change, and increasing effectiveness of your department. Company officers will do much of the teaching, and there will be a significant use of simulation and role-playing. The course will be developed in conjunction with a university partner and with significant input from the executive office. It will be offered once in July at a corporate retreat.

Employee Retention

Two important initiatives are planned in response to the corporate goal to increase employee retention by five points and in response to the results of the employee opinion survey last year on employee engagement and learning and development. These two initiatives are expected by the goal owner, VP Dreise, and by the corporate university to increase retention by 1.5 points or 30% of the 5.0-point goal. Corporate University hopes to receive a rating of at least 90% from Driese for the partnership in deploying the IDPs and for designing, developing, delivering, and reinforcing the performance management learning.

Individual Development Plans

The first initiative is not formal learning. Since few employees currently have an individual development plan (IDP) and since the employee opinion survey shows the importance of development and specifically having a plan for development, the 2017 plan calls for the creation of an IDP for each employee by the end of the year. The IDP will include formal and informal learning as well as developmental assignments, reading, serving on committees, and professional association involvement. The IDP will include development for higher proficiency on the current job as well as preparation for possible next positions. The corporate university will create the template for the IDP on the learning management system and pre-populate all relevant sections. VP Dreise and corporate university staff will create a change management plan and work closely with all levels of leadership to provide guidelines and facilitate the discussion between employee and supervisor. Progress will be tracked monthly. By December 31 all employees (expected to be five thousand) should have a plan in place and at least one development discussion with their bosses.

Performance Management

The second initiative to increase employee engagement and retention is to focus on performance management. The target audience for 2017 is all 2,500 management employees, including associates and leaders. A new one-day, instructor-led course is planned, which will include group discussion and role-playing. Each class is expected to include associates and leaders. Topics to be covered include goal-setting, performance reviews, the evaluation process, feedback, listening, and conflict resolution. The course will be developed in conjunction with corporate HR and a vendor and will be ready by May 31. Pilot classes will be conducted in June, with the final class ready in July. Classes will be offered every month in multiple locations through October. Monthly progress reports will be prepared for all leaders. VP Dreise and corporate university staff will share the change management plan in February and will follow-up with reinforcement tools and suggestions. Participant reaction for each course should be at least 75% favorable and the actual application rate for each course should be at least 80% to achieve the planned outcome.

Purchasing

Five new purchasing classes are planned in support of the corporate goal to reduce purchase costs by 5%. Corporate goal owner, VP Murphy, and the corporate university agree that these five new courses, properly developed, deployed, and reinforced should reduce purchase costs by 3%. In other words, learning has the potential to contribute 60% of the planned reduction in purchase costs. Participant reaction for each course should be at least 80% favorable and the actual application rate for each course should be at least 80% to achieve the planned outcome. Furthermore, Corporate University should receive a rating of at least 90% from Murphy for the partnership in designing, developing, delivering, and reinforcing the learning in pursuit of the goal to reduce purchase costs by 3% due just to learning.

Courses for Purchasing

Since most of the experienced purchasing professionals retired years ago, the plan calls for development of five two-day, instructor-led courses for the two hundred purchasing professionals to increase their proficiency in all aspects of purchasing. The courses will be developed in conjunction with a vendor, senior purchasing managers, and in-house subject matter experts. The five courses will be sequential, beginning with basics that apply across the industry and finishing with advanced topics for our company. The first course will be ready in February, the second in March, the third in April, the fourth in June, and the fifth in September. A passing score of 85% will be required for successful completion. Each class will be offered ten times over the three months following rollout, and employees are expected to complete the class by that time. Progress will be tracked monthly. There will be one set of make-up classes at year's end for employees hired during the year. VP Murphy will work closely with his leaders to ensure timely completion by all participants.

Technical Support

Two courses are planned in support of the corporate goal to reduce technical support complaints by 30%. Needs analysis reveals that the current high level of complaints is due to a lack of product knowledge and customer relationship skills on the part of the call center employees. The corporate goal owner, VP Salvatore, and the corporate university believe that effective learning to address these two issues combined with effective and meaningful reinforcement can reduce complaints by 15% or half of the corporate goal of 30%. Participant reaction for each course should be at least 80% favorable and the actual application rate for each course should be at least 90% to achieve the planned outcome. Furthermore, Corporate University should receive a rating of at least 90% from Salvatore for the partnership in designing, developing, delivering, and reinforcing the learning in pursuit of the goal to reduce complaints by 15% due just to learning.

Product Training

Ten new one-hour online modules are planned to provide call center employees the product knowledge they need to address technical support issues and complaints more effectively. The ten modules will be developed in conjunction with a vendor, senior call center managers, and subject matter experts. The first two modules will be online by February 28, the next four by March 31, and the final four by April 30. The target audience is all fifty call center employees, who are expected to complete the modules in the month they come online. A score of 85% on the integrated online test will be required for successful completion. Monthly progress reports will be provided.

Customer Relationship Skills

An existing customer relationship skills course will be updated and revised for the twenty-five call center employees less than two years on the job who have not completed this type of training previously. The two-day, instructor-led course will contain a significant amount of role-playing and simulation. The course will be ready for deployment in March and will be offered off shift (paid) in three classes (one in March and two in April). All twenty-five participants are expected to complete the course by the end of April.

Compliance Learning

Two courses are planned to address the corporate objective of reducing exposure to fraud and insider trading. Although difficult to measure, the goal owner, Director Omwetti, believes that learning will be the most important factor in meeting this goal and will contribute at least 70% of the reduction in exposure. Participant reaction for each course should be at least 80% favorable and the actual application rate for each course should be at least 95% to achieve the planned outcome. Furthermore, Corporate University should receive a rating of at least 90% from Omwetti for the partnership in designing, developing, delivering, and reinforcing the learning to reduce corporate exposure to fraud.

Course on Fraud

One new one-hour online course is planned for select management employees to increase their understanding and awareness of fraud and its potential impact on the company. The course will also teach employees how to recognize potential fraudulent activity and what actions to take. The course will be developed in conjunction with a vendor, internal subject matter experts, internal security, and members of the ethics committee. It will be available in June. The target audience is 1,700 management employees in departments and positions selected by Director Omwetti as being most at risk. Director Omwetti will provide initial and ongoing communication. Completion is expected by September 30 and requires a score of 90% on the integrated test. Monthly progress reports will be provided to the director and all affected department heads.

Course on Insider Trading

One existing one-hour online course will be deployed for select management employees to increase their understanding of insider trading. The course also will cover the potential criminal and civil penalties that may accrue to them and to the company for engaging in insider trading. The course is already online, and Director Omwetti will launch the 2017 compliance campaign with this course in February. The target audience is 1,500 management employees in select departments and positions. Completion is expected by April 30. A score of 90% on the integrated test is required for successful completion. Monthly progress reports will be provided to the director and all affected department heads.

Unaligned Learning

The plan also includes the development of two new instructor-led courses, revision of one existing instructor-led course, and the annual review of usage, feedback, and effectiveness for all other courses. The two new courses are Communication in the Web 2.0 Age and Managing Your Career. Both courses will be available March 1. The project management course will be revised and reduced in length from five days to three days. The revised course will be available October 1.

The annual review includes both instructor-led and web-based courses. Particular attention will be paid to the library of two hundred online courses provided by our vendor. Since 20% of the courses may be changed every quarter, frequent reviews are necessary to ensure all the courses represent the best value for our investment.

Measurement Strategy

Measurement is a key component of our strategy to run learning like a business. Our measurement and evaluation strategy is designed to manage the function for results and to identify opportunities for continuous improvement. Only a rigorous and disciplined strategy will ensure that we deliver the promised results and the maximum return on the corporate investment in learning.

Following is our measurement strategy for 2017. It represents the next step along our path to become a world-class corporate university by fully integrating our LMS with the capabilities of our measurement partners to automate the collection and analysis of data. This will allow us to gather and analyze more data much more efficiently and effectively with no additional staff.

The discussion is organized by the Talent Development Reporting Principles framework for efficiency and effectiveness measures and by the six levels of measurement commonly employed in the learning field, progressing from the most straightforward to the most complex.

Efficiency Measures

Level 0: Volume or Activity Measures

Data on the number of unique and total participants are collected for every course. Completions are also tracked. For informal learning, we track participation in our communities of practice, the mentoring programs, and our virtual books program.

All costs of development and delivery are tracked and compared to industry benchmarks. The duration of the development is also tracked and compared to benchmarks. Actual completion dates for development and delivery are also tracked and compared to planned dates. LMS uptime, the number of complaints, and the speed of complaint resolution are tracked. Key efficiency measures to be managed are reported monthly and compared to plan.

Effectiveness Measures

Level 1: Satisfaction or Initial Reaction

Level 1 measures the initial satisfaction or reaction of the participants to the learning. Level 1 measures are collected for every course to answer the following types of questions:

- Was the learning relevant to your work?
- Would you recommend this course to others?
- How would you rate the instructor?
- Were the materials helpful?
- Was the length of the class appropriate?
- How would you rate your overall satisfaction with the course?

This is accomplished electronically via a survey at the conclusion of an online course and within two days for an instructor-led course. We employ the Metrics That Matter program from our partner CEB to gather, compile, and parse the data. Random samples are used in many cases for established courses to lessen the survey burden on participants. Surveys are designed to be completed in less than three minutes and are managed internally and in an ongoing basis throughout the year, with real-time reporting. Results are used to identify course content that needs to be reworked and instructors who need to be coached or replaced. Summary results are captured in monthly reports, with details available online. We will also send a short survey to each sponsor or goal owner to solicit their feedback on working with us.

Level 2: Knowledge or Skill Acquisition

Level 2 measures the knowledge or skills gained by the participants from the learning program. A test of knowledge is appropriate for about 50% of our courses. Many times, the sponsor or goal owner wants to ensure that the participants have a firm grasp of the subject matter and have established a minimum passing score. This is especially true for online courses and compliance-related courses for which a permanent record of successful completion is important. The sponsor and subject matter expert assist in developing the test, approve the final version, set the minimum passing score, and determine the number of unsuccessful attempts allowed.

Level 2 knowledge checks are planned for the following courses: New Product Introduction, Design, Safety, Purchasing, Product Training, and Fraud and Insider Trading. The checks are managed internally and on an ongoing basis throughout the year, with real-time reporting. Summary results are captured in monthly scorecards, with details available online.

Level 3: Application

Level 3 measures the application of the new knowledge, skills, or behaviors by the participants when they return to their job. Application of the new knowledge and skills is critical if learning is going to achieve the intended impact on corporate results. Learning professionals design learning to maximize its application, but the sponsor or goal owner is ultimately responsible for the required change management, incentives, and reinforcement to ensure its application.

The survey at the conclusion of the online course or the post-event survey at the conclusion of an instructor-led course will be designed to provide data on the *intent* to apply the learning. Best practice is to follow up with participants three to six months later to determine whether they have, in fact, applied it. This is done through a survey, phone conversation, or focus group with a random sample of participants. Since it is time consuming and more expensive than levels 0–2, it is not conducted every year for every course. Through time, though, level 3 will be done on all key programs.

Intent to apply data will be collected for all programs. Actual application will be measured the second half of 2017 by a specialized consultant for the following courses: Consultative Selling Skills, Design, Leadership (Division Managers and Department Heads), and Purchasing. Results will be used to make changes to the course content, delivery, change management, incentives, or reinforcement.

Levels 4 and 5: Impact and ROI

Level 4 measures the actual impact of the learning on the company's goals. For example, the business plan calls for sales to increase by 10% in 2017 and learning is planned to contribute 20% of the 10% increase, resulting in a 2% increase in sales due just to the training. Level 4 measures the actual impact of training on sales. Doing so, however, requires the impact of training to be isolated from all other possible contributors to higher sales such as growth in the economy, introduction of new products, adoption of a new salesperson incentive plan, and a failed competitor. We will use the industry-standard practice of collecting estimates of isolated impact from participants and their supervisors and then adjusting for their confidence in those estimates.

Level 5 begins with the level 4 isolated impact of learning and assigns a dollar value to that impact. We will work closely with the goal owners and accounting to calculate this dollar impact of gross benefit of the training. Next we will subtract the total cost of the learning to find the net benefit. Return on investment (ROI) in learning is simply the net benefit divided by the total cost expressed as a percentage.

Since the process for obtaining level 4 and 5 measures is resource intensive and specialized, a consultant will be employed to conduct a level 4 and 5 evaluation on two high-priority programs (Consultative Selling Skills and Design for engineers), using randomly selected samples and/or control groups. The study is to be conducted in the third quarter, with results available by October 31 to be incorporated in next year's business planning. Results also may indicate that changes need to be made to the course content or delivery, change management, incentives, or reinforcement. Disappointing results may also indicate a misdiagnosis of the underlying issues, leading to a thorough reexamination of the performance issue and needs analysis. An initial estimate of impact will be obtained for both of these programs plus Purchasing, Product Training and Customer Relations Skills.

Summary

Table 13 provides a summary of the measurement strategy for each program.

TABLE 13

Measurement Strategy Matrix for Course-Specific Measures

	Effectiveness Measures				Efficiency Measures					
Corporate Goal	*Level 1*	*Level 2*	*Level 3*	*Levels 4 & 5*	*Number of Participants*	*Costs*	*Completions*	*Cycle Time*	*Development Completed on Time*	*Delivery Completed on Time*
Consultative Selling Skills	P,S		I,A	IE,AI,R	U	X	X		X	X
NPI	P,S	X	I,A		U,T	X	X	X	X	X
Design for Manufacturing	P,S	X	I	IE,AI,R	U,T	X	X	X	X	X
Safety	P,S	X	I,A		U,T	X	X	X	X	X
Introduction to Supervision	P,S		I		U	X	X	X	X	X
Leadership for Managers	P,S		I,A		U	X	X	X	X	
Advanced Leadership	P,S		I,A		U	X	X			X
Performance Management	P,S		I		U	X	X	X	X	X
Purchasing	P,S	X	I,A	IE	U,T	X	X	X	X	X
Product Training	P,S	X	I	IE	U,T	X	X	X	X	X
Customer Relations Skills	P,S		I	IE	U	X	X	X	X	X
Fraud Detection	P,S	X	I		U	X	X	X	X	X
Insider Trading	P,S	X	I		U	X	X			X
General (unaligned)					U	X				

Legend:
P = Participant
I = Intent to apply
A = Actual application
IE = Initial estimate of impact
AI = Actual impact
R = ROI
U = Unique participants
T = Total participants (used when there is more than one course in the program)

Communication Strategy

Good communication is critical to our success. The communication strategy describes how we plan to interact with the Board of Governors, sponsors, officers, employees, the learning community, and our partners.

Board of Governors

Corporate University senior leadership will meet with the Board of Governors quarterly to share progress, review the scorecard, solicit feedback and counsel, and secure board approval for key items. An in-depth presentation on one topic will also be made at each board meeting. We will provide advance materials to the board. Each governor will receive a copy of the annual business plan for learning.

Goal Owners or Sponsors

Corporate University leaders meet with goal owners or sponsors several times during the business planning process to secure agreement on programs, target audiences, timelines, expected impact, reinforcement, and roles and responsibilities. The program manager will continue to meet with the sponsor throughout the year. The CLO will meet with the sponsor for a midyear review and a wrap-up review. The sponsor will be asked for formal feedback twice a year through a short survey.

Officers

The CLO will visit all officers who are not sponsors semi-annually to update them on progress and issues and to understand their issues and concerns better. Each officer will receive a copy of the annual business plan for learning.

Employees in the Corporate University

The CLO and senior leadership will communicate with university employees formally on a monthly basis through town hall meetings, which will include progress updates, scorecard reviews, upcoming special events, topics of general interest, and question-and-answer sessions. Each leader will also hold weekly or monthly staff meetings with their direct reports. In addition, all university leaders will meet monthly for lunch to discuss leadership issues. An internal Facebook is also planned for 2017.

Informal communication and performance feedback are encouraged on a real-time basis. Formal performance reviews are conducted quarterly.

The Corporate University website provides another avenue for communication. The calendar of events will be updated in real time, and new articles will be published monthly. The annual business plan for learning will be provided to all leaders and will be available to any employee who requests it.

Employees Outside the University

The CLO and senior university leadership will communicate with all employees through periodic postings and articles on the corporate website and real time through the corporate Facebook. The corporate LMS also provides a medium for short messages to employees. The CLO and senior university leaders will also make numerous presentations to employee groups throughout the year.

The Learning Community

The CLO and senior university leadership will meet with the leaders in the enterprise learning community, including those not directly reporting to the Corporate University, via teleconference on a monthly basis. This affords an opportunity to update the entire community on learning initiatives, issues, budgets, and challenges. It also provides an opportunity to hear directly from others in the enterprise involved in learning and to share successful practices. The CLO will meet individually at least semi-annually with learning leaders who are not part of the Corporate University. The Corporate University website also serves as a resource for the enterprise learning community. Each leader outside the university will receive the annual business plan for learning.

Partners

Since the Corporate University relies on many partners for development, delivery, and measurement, it is important to keep them informed as well. The CLO or other senior university leaders will meet at least twice per year with all key partners to discuss the relationship and look for ways to improve it. Strategic partners will be invited to the Partner Symposium in the fall, where the emerging needs for the next year will be discussed along with the overall business and planning climate. Partners will be asked to provide formal feedback twice per year with the goal of improving the partnership.

Outside the Company

There is also value in communicating outside the company to build the brand and make the company more attractive for prospective employees and partners. Toward this end, leaders and employees are encouraged to participate in professional learning organizations like ATD, to attend and participate in industry conferences like ATD's International Conference & Exposition, CLO Symposiums, Bersin & Associates Impact Conferences, and others, and to write articles for learning publications. In order to learn more about best practices and to improve continuously, it is our goal in 2017 to compete in two award competitions in the learning field.

Continuous Improvement Strategy

Our vision to be a world-class corporate university can only be achieved through continuous improvement. We have been working on a number of initiatives to move us closer to that goal.

For 2016 we focused on the systems and change management that would be required for each employee to have an Individual Development Plan (IDP) in the LMS in 2017. This required various system enhancements and a tremendous amount of integration to allow for automated inputs to that plan from corporate (requirements to take compliance-related courses, for example), from discipline leaders (accounting requirements from the CFO), from business unit leaders, and from the supervisor. The system is now ready to be launched on January 1st, although a tremendous amount of change management will still be required to ensure all employees are using the system and meeting frequently with their supervisors.

In the second half of 2017, another LMS system upgrade is planned to take advantage of the latest version offered by our vendor. The release of V12.4 is expected in January, but we have chosen to wait until the second half of the year to be sure the new version is stable and to avoid a conflict with the IDP rollout. This new version will support two more languages and will meet the upcoming European Union privacy requirements as well as offer greater speed for integrated platforms such as ours. With these improvements to our LMS, the goal is to reduce the number of complaints by 50%, increase uptime to 99%, and reduce the support ticket resolution time by 25%.

In 2017 we will introduce a new platform for knowledge sharing that will support more communities of practice with greater search functionality by area of interest and expertise. The platform also supports much more robust report generation. A new synchronous learning platform is also planned for the fourth quarter to support our fastest growing medium. This will allow each participant to see all other participants and will support virtual breakouts.

Cycle time is another area targeted for improvement in 2017. The adoption of a common performance analysis process and better design/develop training for our staff should reduce the average time for performance analysis by two days and the time for development by eight days, for a total cycle time reduction of 10 days.

Lastly, based on feedback and focus groups last year, we plan to modify our sponsor and partner surveys to elicit their actionable feedback more readily so that we can do our part in improving these relationships.

History

Significant progress has been made since the Corporate University was founded five years ago. A brief history highlights the most important developments and milestones.

Corporate University founded January 1, 2012

- CEO Stratham establishes the Corporate University to provide enterprise leadership to learning, to ensure that learning is aligned with the company's highest priorities, to increase the impact of learning and its return on investment, and to capture synergies through centralized leadership.
- The university absorbs predecessor organization and two other learning functions.
- The Board of Governors is established with the CEO as a member.
- The first three colleges are established: business, engineering, and leadership.
- The first enterprise-wide learning leaders' conference is held.
- The Corporate University bench marks best in class corporate universities.
- At year's end, staff size was thirteen, and annual expenditures were $1.8 million.
- Unique participants total 3,589 and total participants 12,369.

2013: Second Year

- Corporate LMS is upgraded and extended to 70% of the enterprise.
- The College of Marketing is added.
- The first business plan for learning is completed.
- The Board of Governors approves the long-term strategy.
- Two more learning organizations are integrated.
- The implementation of best practices from benchmarking begins.

- At year's end, staff size was seventeen (nineteen FTE), and annual expenditures totaled $2.6 million.
- Unique participants stand at 3,974, with total participants at 15,897.

2014: Third Year

- Corporate University does its part to reduce expenses in response to the global recession. Spending is cut by 15%, three positions are left unfilled, and the use of partners is scaled back.
- The first special meeting of the Board of Governors to reprioritize and approve spending cuts is held.
- The remaining business unit learning organizations are integrated into the Corporate University.
- Online learning grows rapidly as instructor-led offerings are curtailed because of the recession.
- Corporate University provides leadership for knowledge sharing, using communities of practice.
- The Learning Council is established.
- The first entries in national and international award competitions for learning are submitted.
- Corporate LMS reaches 80% of the enterprise.
- At year's end, staff size was seventeen FT (also seventeen FTE) and annual expenditures were $2.3 million.
- Unique participants stand at 3,789, with total participants at 14,985.

2015: Fourth Year

- Corporate University is well positioned to respond to the economic upturn by scaling up the use of partners, rehired retirees, and part-time employees.
- All colleges are growing.
- The first benchmarking of our university by others occurs.
- Corporate University receives internal recognition from the CEO for being a well-run, strategic partner in the company's success.
- Corporate University receives recognition from ATD, IQPC, and *Chief Learning Officer* magazine for strategic alignment, measurement, and specific programs. The university is named one of the one hundred best corporate universities by ATD and *Training* magazine.
- The Board of Governors approves a strategy for the university to become a continual learning organization.
- Corporate LMS reaches 90% of the enterprise.

- At year's end, staff size was eighteen FT (twenty-one FTE), and annual expenditures were $3 million.
- Unique participants stand at 4,233, with total participants at 17,895.

2016: Fifth Year

- The College of Manufacturing (technical skills and safety) is split from the College of Engineering (design, engineering skills, quality) for a total of five colleges.
- Growth accelerates across all colleges in response to significant increases in sales, new hires, and expansions into new lines of business.
- Board of Governor meetings are extended to three hours.
- Corporate University wins first and second place awards from Corporate University Xchange and *CLO* magazine.
- Corporate LMS reaches 97% of the enterprise.
- At year's end, staff size was twenty FT (23 FTE), and annual expenditures were $3.8 million.
- Unique participants stand at 4,552, with total participants at 19,369.

Contact Information and List of Learning Groups and Staff

Contacts for questions or additional information:

Barb Smith, Editor at xxxxxxxxxx@yyy

Donna Jones, VP for Learning at xxxxxxxx@yyyy

Corporate University	Name	Email	Phone
Administration			
VP for Learning	Donna Jones	xxxxxxxx@yyyy	541.235.8759
Administrative assistant			
College of Marketing and Purchasing			
Dean			
Senior Program Manager			
Program Manager			
Performance Consultant			
Performance Consultant			
College of Leadership and Business			
Dean			
Senior Program Manager			
Program Manager			
Performance Consultant			
Performance Consultant			

College of Manufacturing and Engineering
- Dean
- Senior Program Manager
- Program Manager
- Performance Consultant
- Performance Consultant

College of General Studies
- Dean
- Manager
- Performance Consultant
- Performance Consultant

Business Support (financial, LMS, measurement and evaluation, business planning, communication)
- Manager
- Business Manager
- Planning Manager
- Measurement Analyst
- Systems Manager
- Systems Analyst
- Communication Manager

Other Learning Groups	Name	Email	Phone
Manufacturing			
Director of Learning			
Learning Manager for U.S. Plants			
Learning Manager for European Plants			
Learning Manager for Asian Plants			
Performance Consultant			
Learning Analyst			
Purchasing			
Learning Manager			
IT			
Learning Manager			
Marketing			
Learning Manager			
Engineering			
Learning Manager			
Accounting			
Learning Manager			
Corporate HR			
Learning Manager			

Appendix C

Introduction to Talent Development Reporting Principles (TDRp)

THE WORLD IS changing and the field of Human Resources (including learning and development) has not kept pace. Human capital is now the primary driver of value in most organizations, and yet the profession has had no standard principles, measures or reports to manage its contribution.

An initiative was launched in 2010 to meet this need. Kent Barnett, at the time CEO of Knowledge Advisors, and Tamar Elkeles, VP of Learning and Communication at Qualcomm, pulled together a group of industry thought leaders and preeminent practitioners to create standards for learning and development (L&D). Over a two-year period this group of 31 leaders developed a set of standards not just for L&D but for all of HR. (See appendix A for a list of all contributors.) The standards include principles to be followed in planning, measuring, reporting, and executing HR initiatives. The standards also included a classification of HR measures into three types (effectiveness, efficiency, and outcome) and the creation of three reports to be used in the monthly management of HR initiatives and functions. In late 2012 the nonprofit Center for Talent Reporting (CTR) was created to be the permanent home for TDRp. Since then, hundreds of organizations around the world have adopted TDRp, and CTR has further refined the principles, measures and reports based on feedback from the early adopters.

As a result of this initiative and the success of TDRp, HR now has a set of standards to manage the contribution of human capital. As a profession, we also now have a classification scheme for the hundreds of HR measures and we have three standard reports – just as accountants do. Furthermore, building on the work of pioneering individuals like Jac Fitzenz and Jeff Higgins, and pioneering organizations like the Association for Talent Development (ATD, formerly ASTD), we have a measures library with over 600 measures that practitioners can use as a resource and which, hopefully, in time will contribute to the standardization of names and definitions. (See Appendix B for references.)

At this point, you might acknowledge that TDRp is needed and should benefit the profession but still ask how it would benefit your organization and you individually.

> *The primary benefit to an organization from adopting TDRp will be significantly greater impact on the organization's goals from its HR initiatives – with no increase in HR's budget. Implementing TDRp will result in better strategic alignment to the organization's goals, a stronger partnership with the goals' owners, and much better planning and execution of HR initiatives – all leading to a higher bottom line impact at no additional cost. At the individual level, adopting TDRp will lead to a significant increase in business acumen; increased knowledge and skill about planning, measuring, reporting and executing; and an enhanced ability to work successfully with senior leaders—all of which will improve your current job performance and make you a more attractive candidate for promotion.*

To be clear: The focus of TDRp is on improving the management of human capital in order to deliver greater bottom line value to all organizations. The HR function in most organizations is not having the impact it should on the organization's success. While standardizing the names and definitions of HR measures is important for the profession (and will save practitioners considerable time in the future), the benefits to the organization and individual are much more direct and down to earth. Implementing TDRp will increase the bottom line in for-profit companies, increase the surplus for nonprofits and help all types of organizations (profits, nonprofits, educational, government) better achieve their goals. While this may sound overly optimistic, remember that human capital is now the greatest organizational asset and most organizations today are not managing it with any discipline. The potential for improvement is tremendous.

To achieve this dramatic improvement in HR's impact requires new knowledge and skills on the part of HR leaders, which TDRp can help provide. It also requires their willingness to set specific, measurable goals, and then be held accountable for achieving those goals – just like their colleagues in other parts of the organization.

TDRp was originally developed just for L&D, but it quickly became apparent that the work would have to be extended to other HR processes as well so that organizations could implement across their entire HR function. After a thorough review of the literature and in recognition of the need to provide clarity on processes versus outcomes, the group of industry leaders decided to develop measures and reports for the following six key primary human capital processes:

- Learning & Development
- Leadership Development
- Performance Management
- Talent Acquisition
- Capability Management
- Total Rewards

(It is understood that organizations may define the scope of these processes differently and may call them by different names, but these six will be used to organize the measures and reports for the purpose of describing TDRp.)

In the TDRp framework these processes are the primary drivers of organizational outcomes which may be financial & operational as well as talent related. Eight supporting processes also were identified. Figure 1 below illustrates the relationship among sample outcomes (each organization will have its own desired outcomes), the six key talent processes, and the eight supporting processes.

FIGURE 1

HR Outcomes and Processes

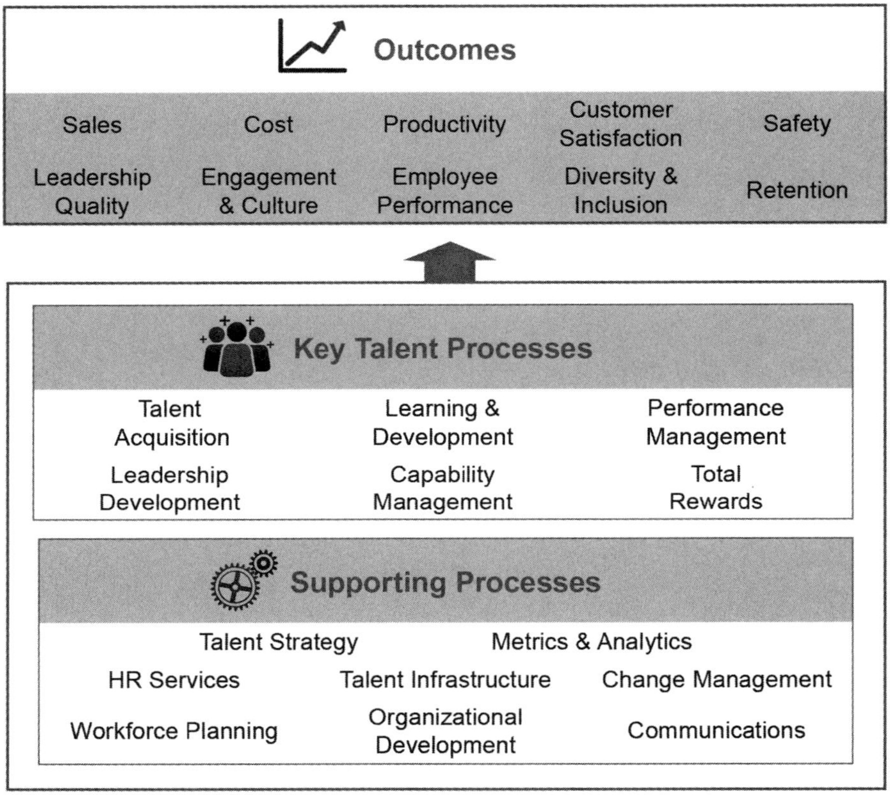

Leadership, engagement, employee performance, diversity, retention (talent acquisition could also be added) are treated as outcomes rather than processes implying that organizations with goals for these outcomes would plan programs and initiatives involving the six key talent processes to achieve the desired outcome.

The audience for this TDRp includes leaders and decision makers at all levels:

- Senior Executives (CEO, CFO, COO, line of business executives, SVP or HR)
- Talent Executives (HR Department Heads and Directors)
- Program Managers who lead major talent initiatives

TDRp is designed on the premise that department heads must have reports to manage results with direct reports and staff on a monthly basis, and that program managers must have reports on at least a monthly basis to manage ongoing initiatives.

Analysts are another important audience for TDRp. These professionals are the ones who manage the data, create the statements and reports, and perform all the required internal analyses. TDRp is designed to provide all the definitions and guidance required as well as the underlying principles. Two other important audiences are consultants and vendors who will assist organizations implementing TDRp and who will develop software to generate TDRp compliant statements and reports.

Running HR with Business Discipline

Running HR with business discipline is the key to understanding both the TDRp approach and the dramatic impact this initiative can have on an organization's success. The TDRp framework and reports which follow will not make sense without it.

By business discipline we simply mean applying standard management principles to HR. These principles are

1. Set specific, measurable goals (plans)
2. Manage throughout the year to deliver what you promised. If you are not on plan, or if it appears you may not end the year on plan
   i. Understand why
   ii. Identify corrective action
   iii. Decide if the corrective action is worth taking
   iv. Implement corrective action if justified and feasible

So, managers need to set goals and then come as close as they can to achieving them. Managers will need regular reports (at least monthly) to know how they are doing.

These reports will have to show the plan for the year, year-to-date (YTD) results, and ideally a forecast of how the year is likely to end if special action is not taken. A manager will start by comparing YTD results with plan. If the year is progressing according to or better than plan, great! If the year is not progressing according to plan, then the manager will need to understand why, what can be done, and how much will it cost to get back on plan. The manager must then decide to take corrective action or not. Even if the year-to-date progress is on plan, it is possible that something is now expected to happen during the rest of the year that will prevent plan from being achieved. So, next the manager will compare forecast to plan and YTD results. If the forecast shows plan is not likely to be achieved, then the manager will want to know why, what can be done and what it will cost to do it. The manager must then decide to whether to take corrective action.

Establishing good plans and managing to achieve them is what managers get paid to do. It may sound simple on paper but in practice both parts can be challenging. The good news is that it gets easier with practice. The bad news is that many HR managers have never been asked to either create a plan with specific, measurable goals or manage to it. And they are not used to being held accountable to deliver a plan.

Now let's apply these management principles to HR. First, we need to appreciate why HR exists and the contribution it can make to an organization's success. Traditionally, HR performed transactional functions like payroll and compliance and also provided guidance to the rest of the organization to keep it out of trouble. Today, however, in most organizations HR also plays a very exciting strategic role in helping the organization achieve its goals. Since human capital is now often an organization's most important asset, HR can devise initiatives and programs to help increase sales and reduce operating costs, improve quality, improve employee retention and engagement, and improve leadership. All of these initiatives, either directly (through efforts to increase sales, quality or reduce costs) or indirectly (through better leaders or more engaged employees who in turn help achieve the other goals), will contribute to the organization's success.

Consequently, HR first needs to align its strategic initiatives to organization goals. This process starts by talking to the CEO to learn next year's goals and priorities. Then HR leaders need to talk with the owners (sponsors) of these goals and determine if some HR initiative (s) can help achieve their goal. If they can, then the parties need to work out the details of the initiative, including some measure of success for the initiative that both will commit to try to achieve. So, in this case, HR leaders don't set the organization goals - they align their initiatives to the goals of the organization. But they do set a plan or target for the measure of success that they (HR) and the goal owner believe can be achieved by the HR initiative.

In addition to helping the organization achieve its goals, each department head (the head of HR in a smaller organization or the heads of separate departments like L&D in larger organizations) should set specific, measurable goals. Examples might be to improve the quality of new hires by 4 points, provide training to 90% of the organization's employees, improve the participant satisfaction with training by 3 points, or reduce the ratio of classroom training to e-learning by 10%. These goals will reflect what the department believes is most important to accomplish in the coming year.

At this point, HR leaders would have identified measures of importance for the coming year and established plans for each important measure. Once the year is underway HR leaders will need regular reports to know how they are doing. Each report will need to include the plan, YTD results and forecast for each measure to be managed – just as in our discussion above. TDRp is designed to facilitate the plan setting and produce the reports needed to manage throughout the year.

TDRp Framework

Overview

With the above background on running HR with business discipline, let's turn our attention to the TDRp framework.

The TDRp framework contains four elements:

1. Assumptions
2. Guiding Principles
3. Three Types of Measures
4. Three Reports

Figure 2 illustrates the interplay between these four components which will be explored further below. The focus here is on executive or high-level reporting, meaning the reports which will be used by talent executives (department heads and directors) and program managers to actively manage their initiatives on a monthly basis. The measures in these executive reports must all have a plan and once the year is underway the reports will also show YTD results and forecast for each measure. In contrast, detailed reports may also be generated which contain less important measures. These reports typically include just the actual results for measures (no plan or forecast) and much more granularity or greater reporting frequency (weekly or monthly versus year to date or annual) than executive reports. Detailed reports are meant to supplement executive reports are especially helpful in discerning trends and answering questions.

FIGURE 2

TDRp Framework

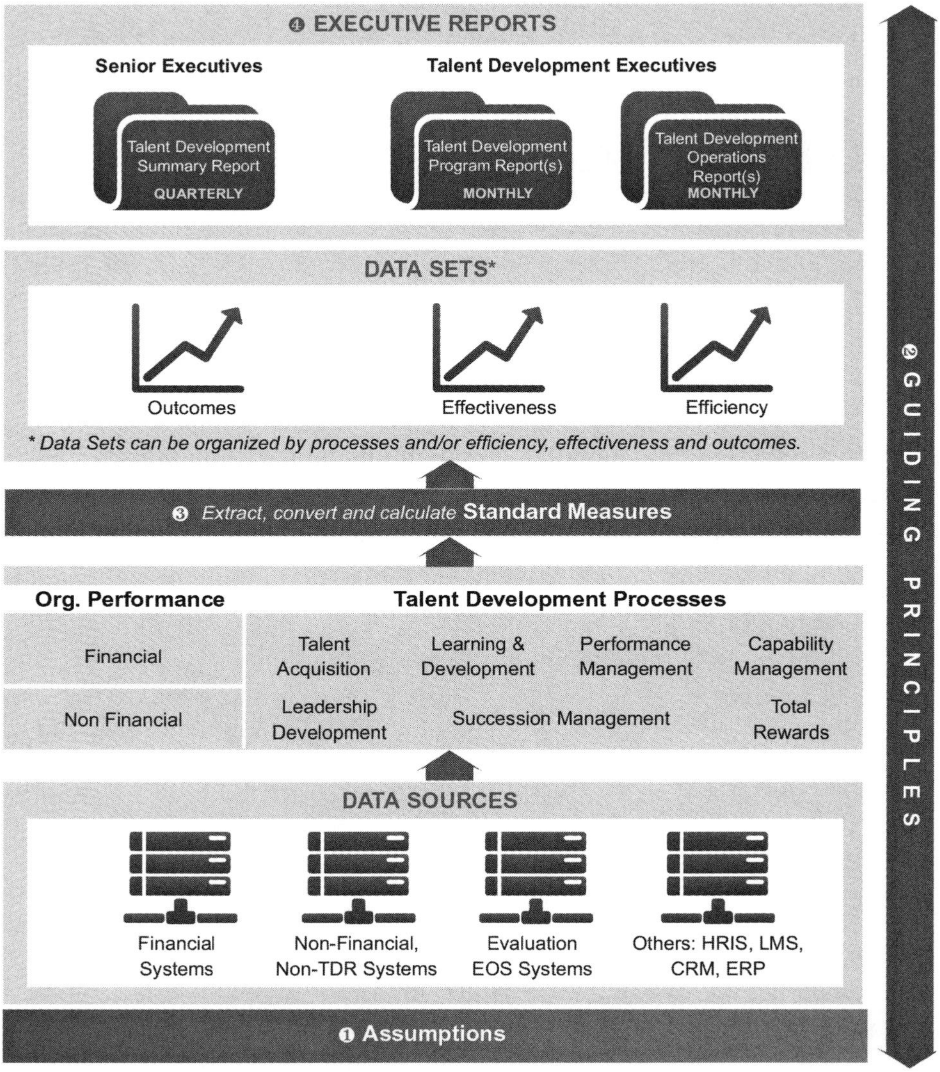

In brief, TDRp classifies human capital measures into three types: outcomes, effectiveness, and efficiency. These measures are then organized into three standard reports (Summary, Operations, Program) that enable active management of human capital initiatives. TDRp also provides names and definitions for more than 700 measures.

The Summary Report contains key measures (all three types) and is designed for overall management of a department and for sharing with senior organization leaders. The Program Report enables department heads and program manager to ensure the planned results are delivered for a specific program or initiative. Finally, the Operations Report focuses on the management of the key effectiveness and efficiency measures at the department level.

TDRp provides a simple, yet comprehensive framework with three types of measures organized into three reports with a focus on actively managing the investment in human capital to produce results

Assumptions

Four important assumptions underlie the TDRp framework and reflect the application of management principles to HR. Understanding these assumptions up front should reduce potential misunderstandings and provide context for the other elements. The first assumption clearly states the strategic role of HR while the second addresses the need for strategic alignment. The third addresses planning in an uncertain world while the fourth acknowledges the role of competent managers.

1. The primary purpose of human capital initiatives and processes is to build organizational capability that enables the organization to achieve its goals or achieve its goals more quickly or at lower cost.
2. Whenever possible, human capital initiatives and processes should be aligned strategically to the goals of the organization. HR leaders will meet proactively with stakeholders to discuss and agree on the role of initiatives and processes in meeting the organization's goals and will set appropriate goals for the initiative or process. It is understood that goal setting will involve uncertainty and will entail the use of estimates and forecasts.
3. It is understood that the business environment is characterized by significant uncertainty and yet plans must be made with the best information available. Waiting for absolute certainty and perfection is not an option.
4. The recommended reports and the underlying data will be used appropriately by competent, experienced leaders to manage the function to meet agreed-upon goals and to continuously improve.

Guiding Principles

These principles provide direction for the standards, reports and analysis just as GAAP (Generally Accepted Accounting Principles) and IFRS (International Financial Reporting Standards) provide direction for accounting concepts, statements, analysis and reports.

There are eight guiding and generally accepted reporting principles for executive-level reporting.

1. Executive reporting should employ concise and balanced measures that are reported in a consistent and clearly defined format
    a. Key effectiveness, efficiency, and outcome measures should be reported and tracked on a regular basis.
    b. Plans should be set for key outcome, effectiveness, and efficiency measures. Performance to plan should be tracked and reported.
    c. Executive reports should include, at a minimum, results for last year, current year plan, current year-to-date (YTD) results, and a forecast for the current year. Detailed reports typically include just the results which may be daily, weekly, monthly, quarterly or yearly.
2. Executive reports should be produced and communicated with a frequency and thoroughness to enable appropriate management of the function
3. Executive reporting should include actionable recommendations
4. Data integrity and completeness should be maintained
5. Appropriate analytical methods should be employed
6. The impact and value or benefit of initiatives and processes should be identified whenever appropriate, preferably by the stakeholder at the outset of the initiative
7. The full costs of human capital initiatives and processes should be capture and reported whenever possible
8. Executive reporting and the underlying data bases should support continuous improvement of talent processes and programs

This guidance not only influences the format of the reports but, in combination with the assumptions of strategic alignment and proactive sponsor discussion, it offers critical management guidance for all HR leaders to follow in terms of setting plans, tracking YTD progress, and forecasting how the year is expected to end.

These eight principles, combined with the four assumptions above, provide the foundation for TDRp.

Three Types of Measures

The third element of TDRp is the use of standard measures which provide consistency in use and calculation. TDRp defines three types of measures: outcomes, effectiveness, and efficiency. Every organization should collect and report all three types of measures although the choice of specific measures will depend on the goals of the organization and the department.

- **Outcomes measures** identify an organization's desired results and the impact of human capital initiatives and processes on those results. Examples of outcome measures include revenue, market share, quality and cost reduction as well as talent-oriented outcomes like engagement, leadership, retention, and talent attraction.
- **Effectiveness measures** provide indicators of quality or how well human capital contributes to organizational outcomes. Examples of effectiveness measures include quality of content and delivery, application to job, impact, and value for L&D; quality of hire index and first-year separation rate for Talent Acquisition; percentage of defined positions with an identified successor for Leadership Development; and employee bench strength for Capability Management
- **Efficiency measures** provide indicators of an organization's level of activity and investment in human capital. Examples of efficiency measures include the number of participants, courses and hours for L&D; recruitment rate and cost-per-hire for Talent Acquisition; span of control and management tenure for Leadership Development; and average number of months to promotion for Capability Management.

The measures will be extracted and/or calculated from various data sources within an organization and then housed in a data set or warehouse.

It is important to have a balanced set of measures to obtain a holistic view of performance and to reduce the probability of unintended consequences. For example, if a department were to focus just on efficiency measures (like number of participants or activity levels) this may incent employees to forego quality in an effort to achieve the efficiency goal. So, outcome measures are necessary to ensure focus on the right organizational goals; effectiveness measures are necessary to ensure attention to quality; and efficiency measures are necessary to ensure the required level of activity, participation, reach or investment occurs.

It is recommended that organizations create a list for each type of measure. This will make it easier to see how many of each type they have and to ensure that there is a balance. Organizations also need to decide which measures will be managed versus monitored. The measures to be managed will be those that are most important to the organization and to the HR department. These are the measures that the department head and program managers will need to review every month to determine they are on plan. Consequently, each measure to be managed must have a plan, and once the year is underway, will need year-to- date results and a forecast. Measures to be monitored do not need a plan or forecast – just actual results. Typically there will be just 5-10 outcome measures and these will be aligned to the goals of the organization. Due to their importance all outcome measures will normally be managed. Many organizations have hundreds of effectiveness and efficiency measures – far too many to manage.

In these cases, the department head and senior leadership team need to decide which of the hundreds of measures are the most important for the coming year and will need to be actively managed. There should not be more than 5-10 effectiveness measures and 5-10 efficiency measures selected for management at the department level. The rest of the measures will be monitored. (Note: Each program manager is likely to have about five effectiveness and five efficiency measures related just to his or her specific initiatives. These may be contained in the list of measures to be managed at the department level or they may be different. For example, in L&D a program manager will typically manage the number of participants in the program and the department may well have a goal for the number of participants in ALL programs. Same measure, but applied at two different levels in the organization.)

Three Reports

The fourth element of TDRp is the creation and use of three executive reports for the active management of human capital initiatives to deliver planned results. These reports are constructed from the three lists of measures to be managed.
The three executive reports include one targeted for use with senior executives (CEO, SVP, etc.) and two targeted for use with talent executives (department heads and directors) and program managers (those with specific responsibility for programs, budget and people). Each report, its purpose, target audience and frequency, is depicted in the table below.

Report	Purpose	Target Audience Frequency
Summary Report	Convey progress against high-level organizational goals	• Senior executives and talent executives • Quarterly
Program Report	Manage programs and initiatives to deliver planned results	• Talent executives and program managers • Monthly
Operations Report	Manage operations effectively and efficiently	• Talent executives and program managers • Monthly

The Summary Report serves as a stand-alone report for the senior executives while the talent executive is expected to use all three reports to manage the function. Program managers will use the Program Report to manage a specific program, initiative or process.

These three executive or high-level reports focus on the most important measures at an aggregate level. Where greater detail is required to answer questions that are triggered by the reports, detailed reports or underlying data bases will provide the data to answer those questions. The three executive reports combined with the detailed reports and underlying data sets should provide comprehensive reporting on the effectiveness, efficiency and organizational impact of the human capital programs. All three executive reports should include the following for each measure:

- Last year's results (when available)
- Current year plan
- Year-to-date results
- Forecast for the current year
- Comparison of current YTD results to plan, and forecast to plan.

This constitutes the minimum recommended for executive reporting with the understanding that organizations will add measures of relevance to them where applicable. Detailed reports may focus just on actual results (no plan, forecasts or comparison to plan) and provide higher frequency data. In addition, some may choose to display data visually in a dashboard and provide analytical commentary. It is recommended that a quarterly Summary Report be generated with data, visuals, and analysis to enforce a discipline similar to financial reporting.

Of course, the key to successful management of the HR function lies not just in the reports themselves but in the analysis and actionable recommendations which flow from the reports. Consequently, the guiding principles include recommendations on reporting, and further guidance is available on using the reports as well as constructing them.

Summary Report

The Summary Report should contain the outcome measures from the outcome list, four to five effectiveness measures to be managed from the effectiveness measures list, and four to five efficiency measures to be managed from the efficiency measures list. The report should be concise and limited to one (or one and a half pages) with supporting materials available as appropriate. No HR jargon should be used since the primary target audience is senior executives. The report should be interpreted for the audience either in a face-to-face presentation or in writing with a focus on summary conclusions and actionable recommendations.

Because the Summary Report contains all three types of measures, it must be read holistically to obtain an accurate picture of progress against plans. In practice, it will often be impossible to achieve all the stated plans as the year progresses requiring that tradeoffs be made among goals. Moreover, changes in the external environment (economy, market, competition) or internal environment (company goals and priorities, or human capital resources) may impact the achievement of plan.

A best practice is to share a draft of the Summary Report with the CEO and other senior leaders at the beginning of the year to solicit their input on the chosen measures. They are the primary target audience for this report so it is important to ensure the report meets their needs. Typically, they will ask for additional measures to be added or indicate that some may be removed. In either case, the report now becomes "their" report and will facilitate much better discussion when used to review quarterly progress against plan.

A sample Summary Report for L&D is provided in Figure 3 for L&D. This particular report is organized into three sections (Impact, Effectiveness, and Efficiency), but each organization is free to organize and label the measures in accordance with their own needs and vocabulary. (Note: Sample reports for other HR processes like talent acquisition are available at the CTR website.)

Notice first that the Summary Report is a "business-centric" report meaning that it shows information as a senior business executive would like to see it. Reading from left to right, the report begins with the goals of the organization in

FIGURE 3

Sample Summary Report for L&D

Results through June

Priority	Organization Goals and L&D Outcome Measures	Unit of Measure	2015 Actual	For 2016 Plan	Jun YTD	YTD Compared to Plan	Forecast	Forecast Compared to Plan
1	Revenue: Increase Sales by 20%							
	Corporate Goal or Actual	%	10%	20%	20%	100%	25%	125%
	Impact of L&D Initiatives: 25% contribution to goal	%	1%	5%		On plan		Above plan
2	Engagement: Increase Engagement Score by 3 Points to 69.4%							
	Corporate Goal or Actual	Points	1 pt	3 pts	1.9 pts	63%	3 pts	100%
	Impact of L&D Initiatives: Low Impact on goal	H/M/L	Low	Low		On plan		On plan
3	Safety: Reduce Injuries by 20%							
	Corporate Goal or Actual	%	10%	20%	15%	75%	20%	100%
	Impact of L&D Initiatives: High Impact on goal	%	Medium	High		Below plan		On plan
4	Costs: Reduce Operating Expenses by 15%							
	Corporate Goal or Actual	%	5%	15%	2%	13%	10%	67%
	Impact of L&D Initiatives: Medium Impact on goal	H/M/L	Low	Medium		Below plan		Below plan
5	Retention: Improve Retention of Top Performers by 5 Points to 90%							
	Corporate Goal or Actual	Points	-3 pts	5 pts	2 pts	67%	5 pts	100%
	Impact of L&D Initiatives: None Planned	NA						
6	Quality: Improve Quality Score by 4 Points to 80%							
	Corporate Goal or Actual	Points	1.6 pts	4 pts	2.9 pts	73%	3.5 pts	100%
	Proxy for impact: Application of Key Behaviors	% who applied them	84%	95%	80%	15% below	90%	5% below

Effectiveness Measures	Unit of Measure	2015 Actual	For 2016 Plan	Jun YTD	YTD Compared to Plan	Forecast	Forecast Compared to Plan
Participant Feedback	% favorable	74%	80%	77%	3% below	78%	2% below
Sponsor Feedback	% favorable	66%	80%	68%	12% below	75%	5% below
Learning	Score	78%	85%	83%	2% below	85%	on plan
Application rate	% who applied it	51%	65%	55%	10% below	63%	2% below
Efficiency Measures							
Percentage of employees reached by L&D	%	85%	88%	72%	16% below	88%	on plan
Percentage of ee's with development plan	%	82%	85%	84%	1% below	90%	5% above
Percentage of courses developed on time	%	73%	92%	67%	15% below	78%	14% below
Participants in All Programs							
Total Participants	Number	109,618	147,500	67,357	46%	145,000	98%
Unique Participants	Number	40,729	45,300	36,998	82%	44,000	97%

priority order. The goals and the priority come from the CEO or most senior leader for the organization HR is supporting. The priority may be designated as high, medium, or low instead of rank ordered, but goals are seldom of equal priority. Continuing from left to right the next columns shows the unit of measure, last year's actual results, plan for this year, year-to-date (YTD) results, YTD results as a percentage of plan, the current forecast for how the year is expected to end if no special action is taken, and last the forecast as a percentage of plan. These columns are typical of a standard internal report used in any organization. (Actually, many organizations would have additional columns showing plan and results by month and/or quarter as well.)

Reading from top to bottom, the report focuses first on the outcome measures (organization goals and HR's impact on them) and then on select effectiveness and efficiency measures at the bottom. Outcome measures come first because this is what senior leaders care most about. Following the discipline of running HR like a business discussed above, talent executives will have met with the CEO to learn the goals and priority for the new year and then will have met with the owners of those goals to discuss whether and how HR can help them achieve their goals. If both the goal owner and the talent executive agreed that HR could help achieve the goal, then they worked out the details of the initiative. They also reached agreement on a measure of success and a reasonable plan for that measure. (Remember, there are no guarantees in the real world. A plan is just that, a plan, which may or may not be achieved.) These measures and the plans for each are shown underneath each corporate goal in the Summary Report.

For example, in Figure 3 the first goal is to increase sales by 20% (came from the CEO and SVP of Sales). Since this is an example for L&D, the VP of L&D along with the program manger would have met with the SVP of Sales. They would have agreed that training could help achieve the goal and agreed on specifics like offering consultative selling skills and product features training to the 200 person sales force over the first two months of the year. Then they would have discussed how success could be measured. In this example, they agreed to use the direct impact of the training on sales as the outcome measure and they further agreed that it would be reasonable to plan on a 25% contribution from training towards the goal of increasing sales by 20%. (A webinar is dedicated to reaching agreement with the owner on a percentage or some other measure of success.) In other words, the two training programs, properly designed, delivered and reinforced, are expected to lead to a 5% increase in sales (25% x 20% = 5% increase in sales due just to the training). Now, is there any guarantee that sales will increase 5% due just to the training? Of course not. There is also no guarantee that the company will achieve any of its goals including the 20% increase in sales. Both the 5% and the 20% are simply plans which are believed to be reasonable and achievable if all goes well.

The next goal in Figure 3 is to increase the employee engagement score by 3 points. This is an example of a "softer" goal (which is also an HR goal), but many organizations have goals for improving engagement, leadership, diversity or retention. In this case the owner of the goal is likely to be the SVP of HR so the head of L&D would meet with the SVP of HR to discuss the impact of L&D initiatives on increasing employee engagement. In this example, they agreed to use impact on the goal as the outcome measure but felt more comfortable using high, medium, or low rather than assigning a percentage contribution. Further, they agreed that while the L&D initiatives would have some impact on the goal, it would not be much and consequently agreed on a plan of Low impact.

This Summary Report is typical in that many organizations use a mix of quantitative (using a number) or qualitative (using adjectives) outcome measures for impact. In some cases, the agreed-upon measure of success is not impact on the goal, but a proxy for impact or some other measure all together. In this example, a proxy is used for Goal 6: Improve the Quality Score by 4 Points. The head of quality and the head of L&D agreed to use the application rate of the training (easier to measure) as a proxy for the actual impact of the training (harder to measure). Next they agreed on a plan to get 95% of those who take the training to apply the three key behaviors within the first 90 days.

At the bottom of the Summary Report, four effectiveness and four efficiency measures are reported to let the senior executives know that L&D is interested not only in doing the right learning but doing it effectively and efficiently. Typically, the values for these measures will be aggregated at the enterprise level. In practice, a draft Summary Report should be shared with the senior executives at the beginning of the year to reach agreement on the effectiveness and efficiency measures of most interest to them.

To recap, the Summary Report is a business centric report that focuses first on the organization's goals and HR's impact on those goals (outcome measures), and then on the most important effectiveness and efficiency measures. The goals and priorities come from the CEO. Plans for those goals come from the CEO or the owners of the goals. Owners of the goals and talent executives agree on measures of success, plans for those measures, and roles and responsibilities to achieve those plans. The Summary Report lets senior executives know that.

1. HR knows the organization's goals and priorities for the year
2. HR leaders have met with the goals' owners and the two have agreed on whether HR can help achieve the goal
3. If HR does have a role to play, the two have agreed on a measure of success and a plan or target for that measure. Moreover, the two have agreed on the roles, responsibilities, and action items required to achieve the agreed-upon plan.
4. HR leaders will manage the initiatives just like managers in other functions reporting regularly on progress against plan
5. HR leaders are willing to be held accountable for results

For senior executives, the Summary Report is the most important of the three and really the only one most will care to see. The talent executive can use the Summary Report in monthly meetings with the senior leadership team, in all employee meetings, and in presentations to other departments. And you are free to add additional information. For example, many organizations like to list their key programs or initiatives under each goal. Others choose to list the key effectiveness or efficiency measures related to each goal below the Impact line.

Operations Report

The Operations Report includes all the effectiveness and efficiency measures selected for management (versus monitoring) throughout the year. These will be the most important effectiveness and efficiency measures, reflecting the goals of the department head and senior leadership team. Typically the report will contain 5-10 effectiveness measures and 5-10 efficiency measures. Some may contain up to 20 in total but any higher number will prove very difficult to manage. The selected measures will be managed on a monthly basis to achieve plan. Measures in the Operations Report will cover the total enterprise or as much of it as the HR group supports. (In other words, the data in the report will represent totals or averages across the reach of the HR group.) Unlike the Summary Report, HR jargon may be used in the Operations Report since the audience is purely HR.

A sample Operations Report for L&D is shown in Figure 4. (Note: Sample reports for other HR processes like talent acquisition are available at the CTR website.)

FIGURE 4

Sample Operations Report for L&D

Results through June

Effectiveness Measures	*Unit of Measure*	*2015 Actual*	For 2016 *Plan*	*Jun YTD*	*Comparison to Plan*	*Forecast*	*Comparison to Plan*
Level 1: Participant Feedback (All programs)							
Quality of content	% favorable	76%	80%	79%	1% below	79%	1% below
Quality of instructor	% favorable	80%	85%	86%	1% above	85%	on plan
Relevance	% favorable	72%	78%	73%	5% below	75%	3% below
Alignment to goals	% favorable	68%	75%	69%	6% below	71%	4% below
Total for Level 1	Average of measures	74%	80%	77%	3% below	78%	2% below
Level 1: Sponsor Feedback (Select programs)	% favorable	66%	80%	68%	12% below	75%	5% below
Level 2: Learning (Select programs)	Score	78%	85%	83%	2% below	85%	on plan
Level 3: Application rate (Select programs)							
Intent to apply (from survey at end of course)	% top two boxes	70%	75%	70%	5% below	72%	3% below
Actual application (after three months)	% who applied it	51%	65%	55%	10% below	63%	2% below

Efficiency Measures	*Unit of Measure*	*2015 Actual*	For 2016 *Plan*	*Jun YTD*	*Comparison to Plan*	*Forecast*	*Comparison to Plan*
Total Participants	Number	"109,618"	"147,500"	"67,357"	46%	"145,000"	98%
Total Unique Participants	Number	"40,729"	"45,313"	"36,998"	82%	"44,000"	97%
Courses Taken by Type of Learning							
ILT only	% of total	56%	25%	40%	15% below	33%	8% below
vILT only	% of total	3%	12%	9%	3% below	10%	2% below
E-learning only	% of total	35%	48%	39%	9% below	42%	6% below
Blended only	% of total	6%	15%	12%	3% below	15%	on plan
Total courses	% of total	100%	100%	100%		100%	
Utilization of E-learning Courses							
Available	Number	60	74	65	88%	70	95%
Taken by more than 20	Number	50	70	19	27%	55	79%
% taken by more than 20	%	83%	95%	29%	66% below	79%	16% below
Reach							
% of employee reached by L&D	%	85%	88%	72%	16% below	88%	on plan
% of employees with development plans	%	82%	85%	84%	1% below	90%	5% above
Course Management							
Total Developed	Number	22	36	18	50%	36	100%
Number Meeting Deadline	Number	16	33	12	36%	28	85%
% Meeting Deadline	%	73%	92%	67%	25% below	78%	14% below
Total Delivered	Number	143	178	99	56%	180	101%
Investment							
L&D Expenditure	Million $	$15.8	$20.2	$12.0	59%	$20.2	100%
Cost Reduction (internal to L&D)	Thousand $	$63	$295	$115	39%	$230	78%

In this example, the VP of L&D and senior L&D leaders have chosen to focus on four effectiveness measures: participant feedback, sponsor feedback, learning score, and the application rate for the learning. The first and fourth have subcategories of measures which provide more detail (in the case of the first measure) or show different methods of measurement (in the case of the third measure). After reviewing last year's results and monthly trends, comparing their company's results to others, and considering the opportunities and resources for improvement, the L&D leadership team agreed on plans to improve each measure. The team believes that the overall level 1 score for participants can be improved from 74% favorable last year to 80% favorable this year while the leadership team would like to increase the sponsor satisfaction from 66% to 80%. Likewise the team believes the learning score can be improved from 78% to 85% and the actual application rate from 51% to 65%. The team has identified action items to achieve these improvements and assigned responsibilities.

Similarly, the team has chosen seven broad efficiency measures with most having subcategories resulting in about 20 unique measures in total. Given the relatively small number of effectiveness measures the combined number of measures is still manageable. After reviewing the history, benchmarking, opportunities and resources, the team agreed to the plans in the report. The team plans on more unique participants but significantly more total participants, implying a large increase in the average number of courses taken by each employee. The team is also focused on increasing the amount of e-learning and decreasing the amount of classroom learning. Related to these first two measures, the team is looking to increase the utilization rate for e-learning and reach a higher percentage of employees. They have also identified opportunities for better course management (perhaps due to complaints last year about missing deadlines). Just as with the effectiveness measures, the team would have action plans in place to achieve these plans.

The Operations Report will be used by the talent executive each month in a meeting with his or her direct reports to review progress against plan and decide on corrective action if it appears plan may not be achieved.

Program Report

The Program or Initiative Report pulls together all the key measures related to the programs or initiatives in support of achieving an organizational goal. Unlike the Summary and Operations Reports which focus on enterprise-wide data, the Program Report focuses just on data for the programs(s) in support of a single goal.

The Program Report will include the goal supported by the programs, the outcome measure agreed upon by the goal's owner and the talent executives, and the effectiveness and efficiency measures related achieving the goal. The goal and the outcome measure will be the same as in the Summary Report if the goal is important enough to be included in the Summary Report. The effectiveness and efficiency measures and their plans will typically be chosen by the program manager and approved by the department head, although the goal owner or staff in the goal owner's function may also help select the measures and set the plans. The Program Report should be one page in a font that is easily legible. A Program Report would typically be created for programs in support of each of the CEO's high-priority goals.

A sample Program Report for L&D is shown in Figure 5. (Note: Sample reports for other HR processes like talent acquisition are available at the CTR website.)

In this example, the company's goal is to reduce injuries by 20%. L&D leaders have met with the VP of Manufacturing, and agreed that L&D can very definitely help achieve this aggressive goal. In fact, the two have agreed that is reasonable to plan on learning to drive most of the planned reduction in injuries, contributing to most of the overall reduction. In other words, learning alone will have a high impact on reducing injuries by 20%.

What will be required to have this kind of impact on the company's goal? The Program Report lays it out in terms of the effectiveness and efficiency measures. First, Phase 1 courses have to be of the highest quality (effectiveness measures) with a 80% favorable response by participants and a 90% rating from the sponsor, 90% score on the learning, and a 95% application rate – all very high numbers and not easy to achieve. And two Phase 1 courses need to be deployed to 3000 employees for a total of 6000 participants by March 31st (efficiency measures). Second, three Phase 2 courses need to be developed by March 31 and meet the expectations of the VP of Manufacturing. Third, the three Phase 2 courses must be of high quality (95% application rate) and must be successfully deployed to 1000 employees in by July 31st. Furthermore, the goal owner's reinforcement plans have been discussed and documented. If all of these plans are achieved for the effectiveness and efficiency measures, then both the VP of Manufacturing and the L&D leadership team believe that learning can reduce injuries by a large amount. If these plans are not achieved, then the company goal of a 20% reduction in injuries is in jeopardy.

Notice how the Program Report pulls all the relevant measures together on one page. It keeps the program manager focused on the company goal (20%

FIGURE 5

Sample Program Report for L&D

Results through June

	Metric	2015 Actual	2016 Plan	YTD	YTD Compared to Plan	Forecast	Forecast Compared to Plan	Notes
Goal Owner: Swilthe, VP of manufacturing								
Enterprise Goal: Reduce Injuries	%	12%	20%	15%	75%	20%	100%	
Impact of Learning: High contribution	%	NA	High		Below Plan		On Plan	YTD and FC contribution based on level 1 and 3 results and ongoing discussions with sponsor

Programs to Reduce Injuries	Metric	2014 Actual	2015 Plan	YTD	YTD Compared to Plan	Forecast	Forecast Compared to Plan	Notes
1 Deliver Phase 1 Courses								
Effectiveness measures								
Level 1: Participants	%	70%	80%	85%	5% above	82%	2% above	YTD sample size = 1872
Sponsor	%	75%	90%	88%	2% below	88%	2% below	
Level 2: Test score	%	86%	90%	95%	5% above	92%	2% above	YTD sample size = 3848
Level 3: Application rate	%	53%	95%	75%	20% below	95%	On plan	YTD sample size = 270. Reinforcement plan in place
Efficiency measures								
Unique Participants	Number	452	3,000	2,800	93%	3,200	107%	Manufacturing leaders responsible for attendance
Total Participants	Number	858	6,000	5,542	92%	6,300	105%	
Percentage complete by 3/31	%	NA	95%	92%	97%	92%	97%	
2 Develop Phase 2 Courses								
Efficiency measure: Complete by 3/31	Number	NA	3	3	100%	3	100%	
Effectiveness measure: Sponsor Satisfaction	%	NA	90%	90%	100%	90%	100%	
3 Deliver Phase 2 Courses								
Effectiveness measures								
Level 1: Participants	%	NA	80%	80%	On plan	82%	2% above	YTD sample size = 39
Sponsor	%	NA	90%	90%	On plan	88%	2% below	
Level 2: Test score	%	NA	90%	92%	2% above	90%	On plan	YTD sample size = 98
Level 3: Application rate	%	NA	95%	71%	14% below	95%	On plan	YTD sample size = 215. Reinforcement plan in place
Efficiency measures								
Unique Participants	Number	NA	1,000	892	89%	1,100	110%	Manufacturing leaders responsible for attendance
Total Participants	Number	NA	3,000	2,651	88%	3,200	107%	
Percentage complete by 7/31	%	NA	90%	88%	98%	92%	102%	
Summary								
Total								
Courses Developed	Number	1	3	3	100%	3	100%	
Unique Participants	Number	452	4,000	3,692	92%	4,300	108%	
Total Participants	Number	858	9,000	8,193	91%	9,500	106%	
Cost (not including opportunity cost)	Thousand $	$37	$250	$178	71%	$255	102%	

reduction in injuries), the impact of the program on the goal (outcome measure), and the effectiveness and efficiency measures which will are critical to delivering the agreed-upon impact. The effectiveness and efficiency measures are really leading indicators of the outcome measure, and they are all under the control of the L&D department and the goal owner. L&D may exercise more control over the design of the learning but the goal owner will have more control over actual deployment and application. After all, the participants report to the goal owner, not to L&D, so the L&D team cannot make the participants attend or apply the learning. Clearly, training will only have the planned impact if both parties work diligently together. This requires monthly management to know if the program is on plan and if not, to undertake immediate corrective action to get back on plan. The Program Report is designed to provide just information and is indispensable if the program is going to be managed with business-like discipline.

Using the Reports

The three reports are intended to be used in a dedicated monthly staff meeting with the department head and his or her direct reports. This meeting would typically be 60-120 minutes, scheduled for the same day and time each month. The meeting should occur as early in the month as possible after the reports have been updated for last month's results and leaders have had time to analyze the results.

A typical agenda would cover all three reports:

1. Start with the Summary Report for the big picture and focus on the outcome measures. How we are doing overall? Identify any goals where outcome measures are not on plan. (5 minutes)
2. Move on to the Operations Report. How are we doing on our selected effectiveness and efficiency measures at an enterprise level? If it appears we are not going to make plan, discuss further and decide on corrective action. (15-30 minutes)
3. Move on to the Program Reports. Start with those where the outcome measures are not on plan. Each program manager walks the team through their own Program Report. Special attention is focused on measures not meeting plan, where the program manager explains the issue and steps to address it or asks the team for help. Discussion follows resulting in identification of action steps to be taken prior to next month's meeting. (30-90 minutes depending on the number of Program Reports and the discussion)

The reports will provide all the data needed to identify where action may be required to end the year on plan.

The Summary Report is also meant to be shared with the CEO, governing board, and other senior leaders at least quarterly. The HR department head would brief them in person or write a memo to accompany the report, highlighting the most important measures with particular attention to those which are behind plan. The report would never be sent by itself without commentary. The Summary Re- port is also excellent to share at all-employee meetings and when sharing your department's activities with others.

Conclusion

By now it should be evident that TDRp provides a very powerful and robust framework for managing the most important HR initiatives. It employs management principles to bring business discipline to HR and offers a framework for measurement and reporting—all new to the profession. Adoption of these principles has the potential to significantly increase the impact of HR on an organization's success, especially in light of the dominant role human capital now plays. By starting with an organization's goals, aligning HR initiatives to them, reaching agreement with the goal owners on planned impact and mutual roles and responsibilities, and actively managing the initiatives, HR can deliver much greater impact for any given budget or staffing level. Similarly, by starting with department goals, choosing the right effectiveness and efficiency measures, reaching agreement on a plan for each, and actively managing them, HR can deliver much higher levels of effectiveness and efficiency.

Conceptually, this is not difficult. Actually implementing it, however, is more difficult given the amount of change required and the relatively low level of business acumen. So, work will be required but the potential payoff is tremendous in terms of impact on our organizations, professional growth, and personal satisfaction.

Much more information is available at the CenterforTalentReporting.org website, including:

- Library of TDRp measures
- Sample reports
- White papers and implementation guidance
- Presentations
- Information about webinars, workshops, and the CTR Conference

Appendix D

Roles and Responsibilities

THIS IS A sample Description of Roles and Responsibilities for a Learning & Development Department and a Sponsor (Goal Owner)

Purpose: This document provides an example of roles and responsibilities that an L&D department can share with a sponsor during the initial planning discussions. These role descriptions enable the L&D department head and the business sponsor to gain clarity and agreement on the roles and accountabilities of each party to deliver the agreed-upon impact from the L&D initiative. Some organizations ask each party to sign their agreement at the bottom.

L&D Introductory Script: "We have found that an understanding and acceptance of the following roles and responsibilities is critical to the success of our learning initiatives. Each party has a very important role to play. If either party believes they may be unable to fulfill their responsibilities, serious consideration should be given to postponing the initiative until a more appropriate time.

Roles and Responsibilities for the Learning & Development Department and the Sponsor (Goal Owner)

Learning and Development (L&D) Department Roles & Responsibilities

- Work with you (the sponsor) to determine if learning can help achieve your goal and, if it can, recommend an appropriate program or initiative.
- Collaboratively agree on the appropriate target audience, approach, and timing of the training.
- Discuss your role as sponsor and change manager. Recommend steps you can take to ensure successful deployment. Discuss your plans to reinforce the learning.
- Reach agreement with you on the planned impact of the initiative. Reach agreement on key effectiveness and efficiency measures required to achieve the planned impact. These will constitute our joint success measures for this initiative.
- Design, develop (or procure), and deliver the learning, including performance support tools, according to the agreed-upon timetable. Create any agreed-upon communities of practice or facilitate other informal learning opportunities.
- Meet with you regularly during development and implementation to share progress and discuss issues. Provide reports with agreed-upon measures. Provide a list of those who completed (or did not complete) the learning by the required dates.
- Conduct a project close-out review upon completion to review results, identify opportunities for improvement and lessons learned.

Business Sponsor (of the business goal, initiative, or program) Roles & Responsibilities

- Be available for discussions about your goal, how you plan to achieve it, and whether learning has a role to play. If you agree it does, then make resources available in your organization to work with the learning and development (L&D) department on an appropriate program and target audience.

- Meet with the L&D department to review and approve the recommended program, target audience and timing. Discuss and agree on the planned impact of this initiative on your goal. Agree on other key measures of success. Discuss what will be required to achieve these goals. Discuss and agree on your role as sponsor and change leader. In particular, agree on steps you will perform to kick off this initiative, how you will manage it through your direct reports, how you and your leaders will reinforce it, and what positive and negative consequences are planned to ensure completion and application. (These first two cannot be delegated to others in your organization.)
- Ensure subject matter experts (SMEs) and others in your organization are available to the L&D department. Communicate the importance of providing the required assistance per the agreed-upon timetable. Follow up with them if necessary.
- Meet with the L&D department regularly through development and deployment to review progress and resolve issues. Eliminate road blocks. Let the L&D department know what else you need from them.
- Take required action with your leaders to ensure the target audience has completed the learning by the agreed-upon dates. The L&D department will provide lists of those who have (or have not) completed the training.
- Establish accountability (and consequences) for employees in your organization to achieve the desired application and impact. (Note: The L&D department can provide suggestions and guidance for creating accountability but only you and those in your organization ensure that your employees apply the learned behaviors and knowledge.)
- Meet with the L&D department at the completion of the program to review results and identify opportunities for improvement and lessons learned.

Agreed to on ______________________________

Regarding the program or initiative to ______________________________

By:

______________________________	______________________________
Printed Name of L&D Representative	Signature of L&D Representative
______________________________	______________________________
Printed Name of Sponsor or Goal Owner	Signature of Sponsor or Goal Owner

To order additional copies of

THE BUSINESS OF LEARNING

go to

www.PoudreRiverGroup.com

Index

About the Author

David Vance

Executive Director, Center for Talent Reporting
President, Manage Learning LLC
Founding and Former President, Caterpillar University

DAVID VANCE is the Executive Director of the Center for Talent Reporting, which is a nonprofit organization dedicated to the creation and implementation of best practices and standards for human capital measurement, reporting and management. He is the former President of Caterpillar University, which he founded in 2001. Until his retirement in January 2007, he was responsible for ensuring that the right education, training, and leadership were provided to achieve corporate goals and efficiently meet the learning needs of Caterpillar and dealer employees. Prior to this position, Dave was Chief Economist and Head of the Business Intelligence Group at Caterpillar Inc. with responsibility for economic outlooks, sales forecasts, market research, competitive analysis, and business information systems.

Dave received his bachelor of science degree in political science from M.I.T. in 1974, a master of science degree in business administration from Indiana University (South Bend) in 1983, and a Ph.D. in economics from the University of Notre Dame in 1988. After pursuing various "personal growth" experiences, such as being a house builder, a traveler, and a YMCA camp director, he joined a medium-sized consulting firm in 1980, where he was an economist and financial manager until 1984. He was also an economics and statistics instructor at Indiana University from 1983–1987. Dave joined Caterpillar in 1987 as an economist.

He is a member and former director and treasurer of ATD (Association for Talent Development). He is also a trustee and lead independent director for State